235 W773 v.3 1992
Wink, Walter
Engaging the powers. vol. 3 :
discernment and resistance ...

DISCARDED

1993 Academy of Parish Clergy
1993 Midwest Book Achievement A<

CRITICAL ACCL
ENGAGING THE

D0020542

DATE DUE

FEB 2 7 2007
APR 1 3 2007
NOV 2 0 2007
NOV 1 2 2009
DEC 0 1 2009
DEC 1 0 2009
DEC 0 6 2018

"**In his remarkable trilogy on the principaliti**s and powers, Walter Wink has biblically verified what more and more of us intuitively; namely, that underneath and within the social, al crisis we face, there are profoundly spiritual realities which this newest and final volume Wink offers keen insight into not only be exposed but actually engaged and resisted. His re g of prayer, both in our lives and in our world, are some of tl n. Building on the work of earlier pioneers like William Str nts us with the sobering and illuminating truth that moveme will simply never succeed unless they come to terms with the ve presence of the structural and spiritual forces the Bible refe nd powers. And there is no better treatment of the biblical a ning of the powers than Walter Wink's."

—JIM W

"**Sheer grace, that** *Engaging the Powers* **shoul**d come at a **time** when world leaders have captured the language of 'new nsolidating the power to enforce a dominating vision of geop h confronts these worldly schemes and what conscientious (ear faithful and effective witness to a higher order is the prop nd in these pages."

—JAMES r,
Rivers City

"*Engaging the Powers* **is a courageous, scholarly, and yet intensely personal attempt** to help us better understand the problem of evil. In this third volume of his encyclopedic work on the forces he calls 'the powers,' Wink provides an incisive analysis that repeatedly shows the centrality of gender equity to a world of partnership and peace. And he powerfully challenges us to change the social institutions that throughout recorded history, all too often in the name of God and good, have abetted so much demonic energy, and to reconceptualize theology so it may serve as a tool for personal and social transformation."

—RIANE EISLER, author,
The Chalice and the Blade

COLUMBIA BIBLE COLLEGE

3 4444 00035 2898

"**The Quaker, Elton Trueblood, once commented to the effect,** 'You can accept Jesus; you can reject Jesus; but you cannot reasonably ignore him.' To agree with everything in this book might be to betray your own power of discernment. To deliberately ignore it would be to betray your very humanity."

—M. Scott Peck, author,
The Road Less Traveled and
People of the Lie

"*Engaging the Powers* **forcefully drives home one of the impelling truths of our era:** the real battle against the evil in today's world is a spiritual battle. Walter Wink, with exceptional moral and intellectual force, convinces us that the weapons for this battle are not carnal, such as our habitual employment of domination and violence, but rather they are spiritual, among the most effective being prayer. I could not agree more that 'History belongs to the intercessors.' "

—C. Peter Wagner,
Professor of Church Growth,
Fuller Theological Seminary

"**In the third volume of his trilogy on the powers** Walter Wink prompts us to reconsider the impoverished character of so much of our theology. In a wide-ranging study with a plethora of insights on familiar biblical texts he reminds us of Christianity's counter-cultural message and the practice it demands. It is a salutary message for any who would capitulate to the spirit of the age and find that they are in thrall to the Powers."

—Professor Christopher Rowland,
Oxford University

"**Delivering more than he promised in his first two volumes,** this proves to be the most profound in Wink's trek towards the cultural and personal interior. This book does for the last generation of this century what Barth's *Commentary on Romans* did for the first. This is a major contribution, not just to scholarship, but to the planet."

—Arthur J. Dewey, Xavier University

"**In this extraordinary and seminal book,** Walter Wink applies trenchant New Testament scholarship to the growing phenomenon of 'people power' uprisings and nonviolent movements across the planet. The result is a challenging examination of just war theories and violent liberation struggles from which the revolutionary power of Jesus' 'third way' is demonstrated in a fresh and bold way."

—Richard Deats,
Fellowship of Reconciliation

"**A masterwork.** Combines skillful biblical exegesis with prodigious knowledge of our modern world to produce a radically new understanding of Christianity as victory over the Powers that dominate and enslave."
—ROBERT T. FORTNA, Vassar College

"**God has blessed the writing of this book.** It has been a turning point in my understanding."
—BISHOP STEPHEN VERNEY,
The Abbey, Sutton Courtenay, England

"**This is the most important and exciting theological work to emerge in a generation.** It will have a profound effect on Christian thinking well into the next century. Whether the institutional churches will be able to take it fully on board is an open question. If they cannot, we are in for a new Dark Age."
—CHARLES ELLIOTT, Cambridge University

"**A stirring and important work!** This is Wink at his best—provocative, insightful, always challenging and prodding with good exegesis, argument, and analysis. You're not among the living if you have no arguments of your own with the author, but you'll be much the poorer if you fail to join him where he excels in this volume: engaging the Powers, and ourselves in the process."
—LARRY L. RASMUSSEN,
Union Theological Seminary,
New York City

"**No one else has produced such a far-reaching, comprehensive, and incisive understanding of 'the powers'** as they are disclosed in biblical literature, and no one else has articulated their significance for today through such relevant interpretation. Wink's book should be read by all Christians and especially by pastors and divinity students as they lead congregants into a more penetrating understanding of the contemporary world. It is ideally suited for adult Bible study."
—HERMAN J. WAETJEN,
The Christian Century

"**For years now Wink has been relentlessly Naming, Unmasking, and now Engaging those artful spiritual dodgers, the principalities and powers.** . . . One grows lighthearted amid the riches. His social and political analysis of the braggadacio, the sheer, horrid 'normalizing' of domination and death in America in the '90s, is devastating. The exegesis of Revelation 13 is masterfully to the point of our social and political derangement. But there is more, and better: a solid hope of liberation. . . . Extraordinary work."
—DAN BERRIGAN,
Pax Christi

OTHER FORTRESS PRESS BOOKS
BY WALTER WINK

The Bible in Human Transformation:
Toward a New Paradigm for
Biblical Study
(1973)

THE POWERS SERIES

Naming the Powers:
The Language of Power in
the New Testament
(1984)

Unmasking the Powers:
The Invisible Forces That
Determine Human Existence
(1986)

WALTER WINK

ENGAGING THE POWERS

Discernment and Resistance in a World of Domination

FORTRESS PRESS   MINNEAPOLIS

ENGAGING THE POWERS
Discernment and Resistance in a World of Domination

Copyright © 1992 Augsburg Fortress. All rights reserved. Except for brief quotations in critical articles or reviews, no part of this book may be reproduced in any manner without prior written permission from the publisher. Write to: Permissions, Augsburg Fortress, 426 S. Fifth St., Box 1209, Minneapolis, MN 55440.

Scripture quotations, unless otherwise noted, are from the New Revised Standard Version Bible, copyright © 1989 by the Division of Christian Education of the National Council of Churches in the USA and used by permission.

Other credits may be found on p. 424.

Cover design: Terry Bentley
Cover art: Pomona Hallenbeck

Library of Congress Cataloging-in-Publication Data

Wink, Walter.
    Engaging the powers : discernment and resistance in a world of
domination / Walter Wink.
       p.   cm. — (The Powers ; v. 3)
    Includes bibliographical references and index.
    ISBN 0-8006-2646-X (alk. paper)
    1. Powers (Christian theology)—Biblical teaching.   2. Good and
evil—Biblical teaching.   3. Violence—Biblical teaching.
4. Nonviolence—Biblical teaching.   5. Bible.   N.T.—Criticism,
interpretation, etc.   I. Title.   II. Series: Wink, Walter.   Powers;
v. 3.
BS2545.P66W56   1984 vol. 3
235 s—dc20
[235]   92-20578
                                                   CIP

The paper used in this publication meets the minimum requirements of American National Standard for Information Sciences—Permanence of Paper for Printed Library Materials, ANSI Z329.48-1984. ∞™

Manufactured in the U.S.A.   AF 1-2646

96   95   94   93   3   4   5   6   7   8   9   10

With June—
"Costing not less than everything"
T. S. Eliot, *Four Quartets*

Contents

Preface

Awkward as it is to express mathematically, there are really four books that belong to this trilogy. In addition to *Naming the Powers*, *Unmasking the Powers*, and this volume, there is also *Violence and Nonviolence in South Africa: Jesus' Third Way*.[1] The book on South Africa provides what this one lacks: a practical case study of the relevance of nonviolent direct action applied to a concrete situation. Some of the abstractness of this study can be mitigated by a reading of that volume.

The completion of this project causes me a bit of grief. It has absorbed, off and on, almost three decades of my life, has led me into fascinating areas of study that I would not otherwise have explored, and has been the source of tremendous excitement. I hope some of the intellectual and spiritual adventure rubs off on the reader.

This volume was brought to completion during 1989–90, when I was honored to be selected as a Peace Fellow at the United States Institute of Peace in Washington, D.C. The views expressed do not reflect those of the Institute, nor has the Institute attempted in any way to censor anything in this book. It is important for an organization like USIP to be able to support, among other things, serious religious scholarship in a number of traditions that bears on peacemaking. I am grateful for the stimulation of colleagues there and at Oxford University, where part of the year was spent. Parts of this book were presented in workshops on nonviolence in Chile, South Africa, Northern Ireland, East Germany, and South Korea.

This book is immeasurably strengthened by the many friends who were kind enough to read it. Special thanks are due to John Pairman Brown and Robert T. Fortna, who doubled as theological critics and volunteer copy editors—a task they performed splendidly on all three volumes of this series. Others critiqued all of the manuscript or parts of it: Anne Barstow, Brewster Beach, Gil Bailie, Andrew Canale, Richard Deats, Arthur Dewey, James W. Douglass, Tom Faw Driver, Riane Eisler, Charles Elliott, James Forbes, Jane Garrett, Maria Harris, John Helgeland, William R. Herzog II, Robert L. Holmes, Robert Jewett, June

Keener-Wink, Bill Wylie Kellermann, Madeleine L'Engle, David Little, Thomas Moore, Larry Rasmussen, Robert Reber, Stephen Verney, Barbara Wheeler, Rebecca Wink, and John Howard Yoder. Pomona Hallenbeck patiently and prolifically painted a whole series of covers from which to choose. I am grateful to Auburn Theological Seminary for its collegial spirit and continuing support. Thanks also to Marshall Johnson, David Lott, and the staff of Fortress Press, who saw the book through publication.

Questions for a Bible study on the Powers can be found in my *Transforming Bible Study,* 2nd ed. (Nashville: Abingdon Press, 1990).

Abbreviations and Symbols

ANF	*The Ante-Nicene Fathers*, ed. A. Roberts and J. Donaldson (Grand Rapids: Wm. B. Eerdmans, 1951)
ANRW	*Aufstieg und Niedergang der römischen Welt*, ed. H. Temporina and W. Haase (New York and Berlin: Walter de Gruyter)
CW	Carl G. Jung, Collected Works, Bollingen Series XX (Princeton: Princeton Univ. Press, 1954–78)
IDB(S)	*Interpreter's Dictionary of the Bible*, ed. G. A. Buttrick, 4 vols. (Nashville: Abingdon Press, 1962); *Supplement*, ed. K. Crim (1976)
JB	Jerusalem Bible
KJV	King James Version of the Bible
LXX	The Septuagint (a Greek translation of the Hebrew Scriptures)
NEB	New English Bible
NHL	*The Nag Hammadi Library*, ed. James M. Robinson, rev. ed. (San Francisco: Harper & Row, 1988)
NIV	New International Version
NPNF	*Nicene and Post-Nicene Fathers*, ed. Philip Schaff (Grand Rapids: Wm. B. Eerdmans, 1956)
NRSV	New Revised Standard Version of the Bible
NT Apoc.	*New Testament Apocrypha*, ed. Edgar Hennecke and Wilhelm Schneemelcher, 2 vols. (Philadelphia: Westminster Press, 1965)
OT Ps.	*The Old Testament Pseudepigrapha*, ed. James H. Charlesworth, 2 vols. (Garden City, N.Y.: Doubleday, 1983–85)
Phillips	*The New Testament in Modern English*, trans. J. B. Phillips, rev. ed.
REB	Revised English Bible
RSV	Revised Standard Version of the Bible
SNTSMS	Society for New Testament Studies Monograph Series

TDNT   *Theological Dictionary of the New Testament*, ed. G. Kittel and G. Friedrich, trans. and ed. G. W. Bromiley, 10 vols. (Grand Rapids: Wm. B. Eerdmans, 1964–74)

TEV   Today's English Version of the Bible (The Good News Bible)

*   An asterisk indicates that the translation of the preceding passage of Scripture is my own.

ENGAGING THE POWERS

FUGITIVE.	The beast is in the king.
JOURNEYER.	The beast is in the king?
FUGITIVE.	But the king doesn't see it. In the palace only the slaves see the beast.
JOURNEYER.	But the king sent me to kill the beast, To bring back its claws!
FUGITIVE.	The king was a liar. He told you to "get claws" So you would believe there were claws. He told you to "kill it" So you would believe it could be killed. But the beast has no claws. It can't be killed. In the palace we killed the king.
JOURNEYER.	You killed the king!
FUGITIVE.	But there was still the beast. We put a doll on the throne *But* there was still the beast. We destroyed the doll *But* there was still the beast.
JOURNEYER.	In my village we need help. In my village they are forgetting.
FUGITIVE.	But if the beast has no claws, If the beast can't be killed—
JOURNEYER.	Still, I have to find the beast Whatever it is, Or isn't.

Jean Claude von Itallie, *A Fable*[1]

Introduction

One of the most pressing questions facing the world today is, How can we oppose evil without creating new evils and being made evil ourselves?

It is my conviction that any attempt to face the problem of evil in society from a New Testament perspective must be bound up with an understanding of what the Bible calls the "Principalities and Powers." I am also convinced that no social ethic can be constructed on New Testament grounds without recognition of the role of these Powers in sustaining and subverting human life.[2]

The Powers, unfortunately, have long since been identified as an order of angelic beings in heaven, or as demons flapping about in the sky. Most people have simply consigned them to the dustbin of superstition. Others, sensing the tremendous potential in the concept of the Powers for interpreting social reality, have identified them without remainder as institutions, structures, and systems. The Powers certainly are the latter, but they are more, and it is that "more" that holds the clue to their profundity. In the biblical view they are both visible *and* invisible, earthly *and* heavenly, spiritual *and* institutional. The Powers possess an outer, physical manifestation (buildings, portfolios, personnel, trucks, fax machines) and an inner spirituality, or corporate culture, or collective personality. The Powers are the simultaneity of an outer, visible structure and an inner, spiritual reality. The Powers, properly speaking, are not just the spirituality of institutions, but their outer manifestations as well. The New Testament uses the language of power to refer now to the outer aspect, now to the inner aspect, now to both together, as I have shown in *Naming the Powers*. It is the spiritual aspect, however, that is so hard for people inured to materialism to grasp.

Perhaps this understanding of the Powers can be clarified by a comparison of worldviews, since our perception of the Powers is colored to a great extent by the way we view the world.

1. The Ancient Worldview. This is the worldview reflected in the Bible (see fig. 1). In this conception, everything earthly has its heavenly counterpart, and everything heavenly has its earthly counterpart. Every event is thus a simultaneity of both dimensions of reality. If war begins on earth, then there must be, at the same time, war in heaven between the angels of the nations involved on earth. Likewise, events initiated in heaven would be mirrored on earth. There is nothing uniquely biblical about this imagery. It was shared not only by the writers of the Bible, but also by Greeks, Romans, Egyptians, Babylonians, Assyrians, Sumerians—indeed, by everyone in the ancient world— and it is still held by large numbers of people in Africa, Asia, and Latin America. It is a profoundly true picture of reality.[3]

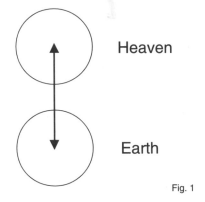

Heaven

Earth

Fig. 1

2. The Spiritualistic Worldview. What distinguishes this worldview (see fig. 2) from all other types is that it divides human beings into "soul" and "body"; one understands oneself as the *same* as one's "soul" and *other* than one's "body." In this account, the created order is evil, false, corrupted. Creation was itself the fall. Matter is either indifferent or downright evil. Earthly life is presided over by imperfect and evil Powers. When the soul leaves its heavenly bliss and is entrapped in a body, as a result of sexual intercourse, it forgets its divine origins and falls into lust, ignorance, and heaviness. The body is a place of exile and punishment, but also of temptation and contamination. Salvation comes through knowledge of one's lost heavenly origins and the secret of the way back. This worldview is usually associated with Gnosticism, Manichaeism, some forms of Neoplatonism, and, in regard to sexuality, Puritanism. (Something of the same picture would fit some forms of Eastern religions, except that they would see the world not as evil but as illusion.)

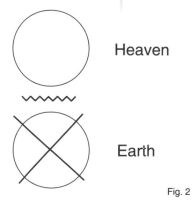

Heaven

Earth

Fig. 2

3. The Materialistic Worldview.

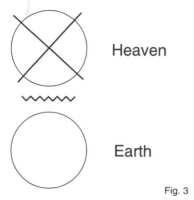

Heaven

Earth

Fig. 3

This view (see fig. 3) became prominent in the Enlightenment, but is as old as Democritus (ca. 460–ca. 370 B.C.E.), and is in many ways the antithesis of the world-rejection of spiritualism. In this view, there is no heaven, no spiritual world, no God, no soul—nothing but material existence and what can be known through the five senses and reason. The spiritual world is an illusion. There is no higher self; we are mere complexities of matter, and when we die we cease to exist except as the chemicals and atoms that once constituted us. This materialistic worldview has penetrated deeply even into many Christians, causing them to ignore the spiritual dimensions of systems or the spiritual resources of faith.

4. The "Theological" Worldview.

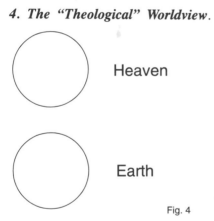

Heaven

Earth

Fig. 4

In reaction to materialism, Christian theologians invented the supernatural realm (see fig. 4). Acknowledging that this supersensible realm could not be known by the senses, they conceded earthly reality to modern science and preserved a privileged "spiritual" realm immune to confirmation or refutation—at the cost of an integral view of reality and the simultaneity of heavenly and earthly aspects of existence. This view of the religious realm as hermetically sealed and immune to challenge from the sciences has been held not only by the Christian center and right, but by most of theological liberalism and neoorthodoxy.

5. An Integral Worldview.

This new worldview (see fig. 5) is emerging from a confluence of sources: the reflections of Carl Jung, Teilhard de Chardin, Morton Kelsey, Thomas Berry, Matthew Fox, process philosophy, and the new physics. It sees everything as having an outer and an inner aspect. It attempts to take seriously the spiritual insights of the ancient or biblical worldview by affirming a withinness or interiority in all things, but sees this inner spiritual reality as inextricably related to an outer concretion or physical manifestation. It is no more intrinsically "Christian" than the ancient worldview, but I believe it makes the biblical data more intelligible for people today than any other available worldview, including the ancient.

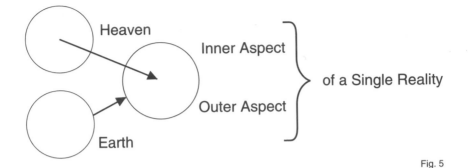

Fig. 5

   The integral worldview that is emerging in our time takes seriously all the
aspects of the ancient worldview, but combines them in a different way. Both
images are spatial. The idea of heaven as "up" is a natural, almost unavoidable
way of indicating transcendence. But in the West, which has been irremediably
touched by modern science, few of us can any longer actually think that God,
the angels, and departed spirits are somewhere in the sky, as most ancients
literally did. (And some people today who disbelieve still do—including atheists.
Remember the glee of the Soviet cosmonauts in announcing to the world that
they had encountered no supernatural beings in space?)

   The image of the spiritual as "withinness" is not, however, a flat, limited,
dimensionless point. It is a within coterminous with the universe—an inner realm
every bit as rich and extensive as the outer realm. The psychologist Carl Jung
spoke of this rich inner dimension as the collective unconscious, meaning by
that a realm of largely unexplored spiritual reality linking everyone to everything.
The amazement of mystics at the discovery of this realm within is matched only
by the amazement of physicists upon discovering that the "final" building block
of matter, the atom, has an interiority also, and that the electrons and protons
they had once thought so substantial are not best described as matter but as
energy-events: what we might call, from the perspective of this book, spirit-
matter. It appears that everything, from photons to subatomic particles to corporations to empires, has both an outer and an inner aspect.[4]

   My thesis is that what people in the world of the Bible experienced and called
"Principalities and Powers" was in fact real. They were discerning the actual
spirituality at the center of the political, economic, and cultural institutions of
their day. The spiritual aspect of the Powers is not simply a "personification"
of institutional qualities that would exist whether they were personified or not.
On the contrary, the spirituality of an institution exists as a real aspect of the
institution even when it is not perceived as such. Institutions have an actual
spiritual ethos, and we neglect this aspect of institutional life to our peril.[5]

   When people speak to me about their experiences of evil in the world, they
often use the language of the ancient worldview, treating demons and angels as

separate beings residing in the sky somewhere, rather than as the spirituality of institutions and systems. When I suggest restating the same thought using the new integral worldview, they often respond, "Oh, yes, that's what I meant." But it is not at all what they have said. In fact, they have just said something utterly different. I can only explain this anomalous behavior, not as woolly thinking (these are generally exceptionally perceptive people, or they would not have discerned these spiritual realities), but as an indication that this new integral worldview has only just come of age, and that the old conceptuality is repeated merely for lack of a better one. When a more adequate language is suggested, it is instantly recognized, not as a *new* idea to which they capitulate, but as *what they wanted to say all along*, and simply lacked the vocabulary for saying. People are groping for a more adequate language to talk about spiritual realities than the tradition provides. I conclude that a very rapid and fundamental sea change has been taking place in our worldview that has passed largely unrecognized but is everywhere felt. A new conceptual worldview is *already* in place, latently, and can be triggered by its mere articulation.

The less-known aspect of the Powers is the *spiritual* or *invisible* dimension. It is generally only indirectly perceptible, by means of projection. In New Testament times, people did not read the spirituality of an institution straight off from its outer manifestations. Instead, they projected its *felt* or *intuited* spiritual qualities onto the screen of the universe, and perceived them as cosmic forces reigning from the sky.

There were, in the first century, both Jews and Christians who perceived in the Roman Empire a demonic spirituality that they called Sammael or Satan.[6] But they encountered this spirit in the actual institutional forms of Roman life: legions, governors, crucifixions, payment of tribute, Roman sacred emblems and standards, and so forth. The spirit that they perceived existed right at the heart of the empire, but their worldview equipped them to discern that spirit only by intuiting it and then projecting it out, in visionary form, as a spiritual *being* residing in heaven and representing Rome in the heavenly council.

In the ancient worldview, where earthly and heavenly reality were inextricably united, this view of the Powers worked effectively. But modern Westerners are, on the whole, incapable of maintaining that worldview. What we usually encounter instead is either fundamentalist treatments of the Powers as demons in the air, wholly divorced from their concretions in the physical or political world (the theological worldview), or denials that this spiritual dimension even exists (the materialistic worldview).

What is necessary is to complete the projection process by *withdrawing* the projections and recognizing that the real spiritual force that we are experiencing is emanating from an actual institution. In the ancient worldview, a seer or prophet was able to sense the diseased spirituality of an institution or state, and then bring that spirituality to awareness by projecting it in visionary form onto the heavenly realm and depicting it (even *seeing* it) as a demon on high. Our task today, working with a unitary worldview, is to withdraw that projection from on high and locate it in the institution in which it actually resides.

Projection is not a falsification of reality. It is sometimes the only way we have of knowing certain internal things. The demons projected onto the screen of the cosmos really are demonic, and play havoc with humanity; only they are not *up there* but *over there*, in the socio-spiritual entities that make up the one-and-only real world.[7] Thus the New Testament insists that demons can have no effect unless they are able to embody themselves in people (Mark 1:21-28 par.; Matt. 12:43-45//Luke 11:24-26), or pigs (Mark 5:1-20 par.), or political systems (Revelation 12–13).

Visitors to Nazi Germany in the late 1930s spoke of the palpable evil in the "air," of a pervading "atmosphere" that hung over the entire land, full of foreboding and menace. Those who leave South Africa remark on the sense of an enormous weight of anxiety and tension that drops off their shoulders as the plane leaves South African airspace. People who remember the assassination of President John F. Kennedy will still recall a feeling of darkness over the face of the nation that lasted for days. These "spirits" are real, but they are not independent operatives from on high; they are the actual spirituality of the nations involved, and the sheer intensity of evil renders them, for a brief time, almost visible.

It is merely a habit of thought that makes people think of the Powers as personal beings. In fact, many of the spiritual powers and gods of the ancient world were not conceived of as personal at all (the Lares, the Penates, Virtue, Victory, Providence, and so forth). Even the angels in Judaism were impersonal agents of God. For a long time the Jews resisted naming the angels for fear they would detract from the sole sovereignty of God. The entire interest of early Judaism was in the angels' function, not in their personal characteristics, which we see emerging only in late apocalyptic literature.

I prefer to think of the Powers as impersonal entities, though I know of no way to settle the question except dogmatically.[8] It is a natural human tendency to personalize anything that seems to act intentionally. But we are now discovering from computer viruses that certain systemic processes are self-replicating and "contagious," behaving almost willfully even though they are quite impersonal. Generally, I have bracketed the question of the metaphysical status of the Powers, and have instead treated them phenomenologically—that is, I have attempted to describe the *experiences* that got called "Satan," "demons," "powers," "angels," and the like. Thus I speak of "demons" as the actual spirituality of systems and structures that have betrayed their divine vocations. I use the expression "the Domination System" to indicate what happens when an entire network of Powers becomes integrated around idolatrous values. And I refer to "Satan" as the world-encompassing spirit of the Domination System.[9] Do these entities possess actual metaphysical *being*, or are they the "corporate personality" or ethos or gestalt of a group, having no independent existence apart from the group? I leave that for the reader to decide.[10] My main objection to personalizing demons is that they then are regarded as having a "body" or form separate from the physical and historical institutions of which, on my theory, they are the actual interiority.[11] Therefore I prefer to regard them as the impersonal spiritual realities at the center of institutional life.[12]

Think, for example, of a riot at a soccer game, in which, for a few frenzied minutes, people who in their ordinary lives behave quite decently on the whole suddenly find themselves bludgeoning and even killing opponents whose only sin was rooting for the other team. Afterwards people often act bewildered, and wonder what could have possessed them. Was it a Riot Demon that leaped upon them from the sky, or was it something intrinsic to the social situation: a "spirituality" that crystallized suddenly, precipitated by the conjunction of an outer permissiveness, heavy drinking, a violent ethos, a triggering incident, and the inner violence of the fans? And when the riot subsides, does the Riot Demon rocket back to heaven, or does the spirituality of the rioters simply dissipate as they are scattered, subdued, or arrested?

Frank Peretti's best-selling novel, *This Present Darkness*,[13] grandly illustrates the hopelessness of trying to repristinate the ancient worldview today. While I appreciate his treatment of the interconnection of heavenly and earthly reality, the role of human freedom, the centrality of prayer, the angels of cities and nations, and the subtle coincidence of demonic promptings and people's words or thoughts, what we are served up is a consistently paranoid view of reality. With such a worldview one cannot help seeing demons everywhere, even among the saints. Rather than learning from our enemies, this view causes one to dismiss them as possessed by Satan. The author is welcome to his politics; but it is one thing to regard the United Nations as a dangerous idea, and another to portray it as a conspiracy of the Devil. We have here a case of the total projection of evil out on others. The view of evil is scary but finally trivial; his demons are simply imaginary bad people with wings, and the really mammoth and crushing evils of our day—racism, sexism, political oppression, ecological degradation, militarism, patriarchy, homelessness, economic greed—are not even mentioned. It is simply Pentecostal political naïveté writ large on the universe.

But equally naive is the blind refusal to recognize the reality of the demonic in this most demonic of centuries.

The relevance of the Powers for an understanding of structural evil should by now begin to be clear. Any attempt to transform a social system without addressing both its spirituality and its outer forms is doomed to failure. Only by confronting the spirituality of an institution *and* its concretions can the total entity be transformed, and that requires a kind of spiritual discernment and praxis that the materialistic ethos in which we live knows nothing about.

To put the thesis of these three volumes in its simplest form:

> The Powers are good.
> The Powers are fallen.
> The Powers must be redeemed.

These three statements must be held together, for each, by itself, is not only untrue but downright mischievous. We cannot affirm governments or universities or businesses to be good unless at the same time we recognize that they are fallen. We cannot face their malignant intractability and oppressiveness unless we remember that they are simultaneously a part of God's good creation. And reflection on their creation and fall will appear only to legitimate these Powers and blast hope for change unless we assert at the same time that these Powers can and must be redeemed.

Hobbes got it wrong when he argued that governments are necessary because people are evil and need to be defended from each other. For governments are also necessary because people are good and need to be organized to assist each other to meet each other's needs. Rousseau got it wrong when he argued that people are born good and that institutions make them evil. For institutions also socialize them to prevent them from doing harm to one another and to think of the common good. Marx got it wrong when he argued that people are basically good and are alienated by capitalist means of production. For communist means of production have alienated them every bit as much and failed to make good on the promise to produce new, nonalienated human beings.

Perhaps these comments shed light on the title of this volume. I could not name it "Confronting the Powers," or "Combating the Powers," or "Overcoming the Powers," because they are not simply evil. They can be not only benign but quite positive. (One of the friendliest, most helpful people in my community is a bureaucrat—the postmaster.) Thus the title, *Engaging the Powers*. It is precisely because the Powers have been created in, through, and for the humanizing purposes of God in Christ that they must be honored, criticized, resisted, and redeemed. Let us then engage these Powers, not just to understand them, but to see them changed.

Part 1

THE DOMINATION SYSTEM

© 1936, King Features Syndicate, Inc.

Great Britain rights reserved.

E. C. Segar,
Popeye the Sailor[1]

1. The Myth of the Domination System

Violence is the ethos of our times. It is the spirituality of the modern world. It has been accorded the status of a religion, demanding from its devotees an absolute obedience to death. Its followers are not aware, however, that the devotion they pay to violence is a form of religious piety. Violence is so successful as a myth precisely because it does not seem to be mythic in the least. Violence simply appears to be the nature of things. It is what works. It is inevitable, the last and, often, the first resort in conflicts. It is embraced with equal alacrity by people on the left and on the right, by religious liberals as well as religious conservatives. The threat of violence, it is believed, is alone able to deter aggressors. It secured us forty-five years of a balance of terror. We learned to trust the Bomb to grant us peace.

The roots of this devotion to violence are deep, and we will be well rewarded if we trace them to their source. When we do, we will discover that the religion of Babylon—one of the world's oldest, continuously surviving religions—is thriving as never before in every sector of contemporary American life, even in our synagogues and churches. It, and not Christianity, is the real religion of America. I will suggest that this myth of redemptive violence undergirds American popular culture, civil religion, nationalism, and foreign policy, and that it lies coiled like an ancient serpent at the root of the system of domination that has characterized human existence since well before Babylon ruled supreme. In order to get our bearings, however, we have to go back to the mythic source.

The Myth of Redemptive Violence

Jesus taught the love of enemies, but Babylonian religion taught their extermination. Violence was for the religion of ancient Mesopotamia what love

13

was for Jesus: the central dynamic of existence. For this early civilization, life was as cruel as the floods and droughts and storms that swept the Fertile Crescent. Recurrent warfare between the various city-states in the region exhausted resources. Chaos threatened every achievement of humanity. The myth that enshrined that culture's sense of life was the *Enuma Elish*, dated to around 1250 B.C.E. in the versions that have survived, but based on traditions considerably older.

In the beginning, according to this myth, Apsu and Tiamat (the sweet- and saltwater oceans) bear Mummu (the mist). From them also issue the younger gods, whose frolicking makes so much noise that the elder gods cannot sleep and so resolve to kill them. This plot of the elder gods is discovered, Ea kills Apsu, and his wife Tiamat pledges revenge. Ea and the younger gods in terror turn for salvation to their youngest, Marduk. He exacts a steep price: if he succeeds, he must be given chief and undisputed power in the assembly of the gods. Having extorted this promise, he catches Tiamat in a net, drives an evil wind down her throat, shoots an arrow that bursts her distended belly and pierces her heart; he then splits her skull with a club, and scatters her blood in out-of-the-way places. He stretches out her corpse full length, and from it creates the cosmos.[2]

We are indebted to Paul Ricoeur for his profound commentary on this myth.[3] He points out that in the Babylonian myth, creation is an act of violence: Tiamat, "mother of them all," is murdered and dismembered; from her cadaver the world is formed.[4] Order is established by means of disorder. Creation is a violent victory over an enemy older than creation. The origin of evil precedes the origin of things. Chaos (symbolized by Tiamat) is prior to order (represented by Marduk, god of Babylon). Evil is prior to good. Violence inheres in the godhead. Evil is an ineradicable constituent of ultimate reality, and possesses ontological priority over good.

The biblical myth is diametrically opposed to all this. There, a good God creates a good creation. Chaos does not resist order. Good is ontologically prior to evil. Neither evil nor violence is a part of the creation, but both enter as a result of the first couple's sin and the machinations of the serpent. A basically good reality is thus corrupted by free decisions reached by creatures. In this far more complex and subtle explanation of the origins of things, evil for the first time emerges as a problem requiring solution.

In the Babylonian myth, however, there is no "problem of evil." Evil is simply a primordial fact. The simplicity of its picture of reality commended it widely, and its basic mythic structure spread as far as Syria, Phoenicia, Egypt,

Greece, Rome, Germany, Ireland, and India. Typically, a male war god residing in the sky—Wotan, Zeus, or Indra, for example—fights a decisive battle with a female divine being, usually depicted as a monster or dragon, residing in the sea or abyss.[5] Having vanquished the original Enemy by war and murder, the victor fashions a cosmos from the monster's corpse. Cosmic order equals the violent suppression of the feminine, and is mirrored in the social order by the subjection of women to men. Male supremacy and contempt for the womanly is explicit in the *Enuma Elish*: "What male is this who has pressed his fight against thee? It is but Tiamat, a woman, that flies at thee with weapons!"[6]

At the same time, Marduk's accession to supremacy over the gods means the ascendancy of Babylon over earlier city-states like Nippur and Eridu. Heavenly events are mirrored by earthly events, and what happens above happens below.[7]

After the world has been created, the story continues, the gods imprisoned by Marduk for siding with Tiamat complain of the poor meal service in their jail. Marduk and Ea therefore execute one of the captive gods, and from his blood, Ea creates human beings to be servants to the gods.[8]

The implications are clear: humanity is created from the blood of a murdered god. Our very origin is violence. Killing is in our blood. Humanity is not the originator of evil, but merely finds evil already present and perpetuates it. Our origins are divine, to be sure, since we are made from a god, but from the blood of an assassinated god.[9] We are the consequence of deicide. Human beings are thus naturally incapable of peaceful coexistence; order must continually be imposed upon us from on high. Nor are we created to subdue the earth and have dominion over it as God's regents; we exist but to serve as slaves of the gods and of their earthly regents. The tasks of humanity are to till the soil, to produce foods for sacrifice to the gods (represented by the king and the priestly caste), to build the sacred city Babylon, and to fight and, if necessary, to die in the king's wars. Such a myth reflects a highly centralized state in which the king rules as Marduk's representative on earth. Resistance to the king is treason against the gods. Unquestioning obedience is the highest virtue, and order the highest religious value. "The king's word is right; his utterance, like that of a god, cannot be changed!"[10]

In their ritual the Babylonians reenacted the original battle by which world order was won and chaos subdued. This victory was celebrated liturgically in the New Year's Festival, when the king ceremonially played the part of Marduk, reasserting that victory and staving off for another year the dreaded reversion of all things into formlessness and disorder.

This ritual is not only cultic, therefore, but military. As Marduk's representative on earth, the king's task is to subdue all those enemies who threaten the tranquility that he has established on behalf of the god. The whole cosmos is a state, and the god rules through the king. Politics arises within the divine sphere itself. Salvation *is* politics: identifying with the god of order against the god of chaos, and offering oneself up for the holy war required to impose order and rule on the peoples round about. And because chaos threatens repeatedly, in the form of barbarian attacks, an ever-expanding imperial policy is the automatic correlate of Marduk's ascendancy over all the gods.

Do you begin to sense where all this is leading?

An added dimension of depth was given the myth when Marduk (represented by the king) was pictured as undergoing ritual humiliation at the New Year's Festival. The priest strikes the king's face and pulls his ears. This action may have been associated with death and lamentation as the god descends into the underworld. The people, thrown into confusion, weep for him as for a suffering and dying god. Creation reverts to chaos (winter). With the aid of the ritual the god is revived, liberated, and released (spring). His enthronement is reenacted and the people celebrate the victory over chaos in a magnificent feast. Finally, a sacred marriage revives all the life-giving forces in nature and humanity.[11] This motif of the "suffering of the hero" is central to our own contemporary depictions of the myth, as we shall see.

The ultimate outcome of this type of myth, remarks Ricoeur, is a theology of war founded on the identification of the enemy with the powers that the god has vanquished and continues to vanquish in the drama of creation. Every coherent theology of holy war ultimately reverts to this basic mythological type.[12] The relation of King versus Enemy becomes the political relation par excellence. According to this theology, the Enemy is evil and war is her punishment. Unlike the biblical myth, which sees evil as an intrusion into a good creation and war as a consequence of the Fall, this myth regards war as present from the beginning.

This ancient mythic structure has been variously called the Babylonian creation story, the combat myth, the ideology of zealous nationalism, and the myth of redemptive violence. The distinctive feature of the myth is the victory of order over chaos by means of violence. This myth is the original religion of the status quo, the first articulation of "might makes right." It is the basic ideology of the Domination System. The gods favor those who conquer. Conversely, whoever conquers must have the favor of the gods. The mass of people exists to perpetuate that power and privilege which the gods have conferred upon the king, the aristocracy, and the priesthood.[13] Religion exists to legitimate power and privilege. Life is combat. Any form of order is preferable to chaos, according to this myth. Ours is neither a perfect nor a perfectible world; it is a theater of perpetual conflict in which the prize goes to the strong. Peace through war, security through strength: these are the core convictions that arise from this ancient historical religion.

This myth also inadvertently reveals the price men have paid for the power they acquired over women: complete servitude to their earthly rulers and heavenly gods. Women for their part were identified with inertia, chaos, and anarchy. Now "Woman is to man as nature is to culture"—the ideology that rationalizes the subordination of women in patriarchal societies by presenting their subordination as if it were a natural fate.[14]

This primordial myth is far from defunct. It is as universally present and earnestly believed today as at any time in its long and bloody history. I will now suggest that it is the dominant myth in contemporary America (more influential by far than Judaism or Christianity), that it enshrines a cult of violence at the very heart of public life, and that even those who seek to oppose its oppressive violence often do so using the very same means.

The Myth of Redemptive Violence in Popular Culture Today

The myth of redemptive violence inundates us on every side. We are awash in it yet seldom perceive it. We will look presently at its impact on foreign policy, nationalism, the Cold War, militarism, the media, and televangelism, but first we must identify its simplest, most pervasive, and most influential form, where it captures the imaginations of each new generation: children's comics and cartoon shows.

Here is how the myth of redemptive violence structures the standard comic strip or television cartoon sequence. An indestructible good guy is unalterably opposed to an irreformable and equally indestructible bad guy. Nothing can kill the good guy, though for the first three-quarters of the strip or show he (rarely she) suffers grievously, appearing hopelessly trapped, until somehow the hero breaks free, vanquishes the villain, and restores order until the next installment. Nothing finally destroys the bad guy or prevents his reappearance, whether he is soundly trounced, jailed, drowned, or shot into outer space.

I am not referring to programs that do not feature violence, but to what I would call the "classic" type of cartoon, where the mythic pattern of redemptive violence is straightforward.[15] Examples would include Teenage Mutant Ninja Turtles, Superman, Superwoman, Mighty Mouse, Captain Marvel, Captain America, Green Hornet, Lone Ranger, Superfriends, Courageous Cat, Submariner, Batman and Robin, Roadrunner and Wile E. Coyote, Darkwing Duck, and Tom and Jerry. A variation on the classic theme is provided by humorous antiheroes, whose bumbling incompetence guarantees their victory despite themselves (Underdog, Super Chicken, the Banana Splits, Super Six, GoGo Gophers, Wackey Racers). Then there is a more recent twist, where an evil or failed individual undergoes a transformation into a monstrous creature who—amazingly—does good (Spider Man, The Hulk, Iron Man, the Herculoids). It is almost as if people believe that heroes of sterling character can no longer arise in our society, and that goodness can be produced only by a freak of technology (such as electrocution or chemicals). All these cartoons, however, adhere rigidly to the mythic structure, no matter how cleverly or originally it is re-presented.

Few cartoon shows have run longer or been more influential than Popeye and Bluto. In a typical segment, Bluto abducts a screaming and kicking Olive Oyl, Popeye's girlfriend. When Popeye attempts to rescue her, the massive Bluto beats his diminutive opponent to a pulp, while Olive Oyl helplessly wrings her hands. At the last moment, as our hero oozes to the floor, and Bluto is trying, in effect, to rape Olive Oyl, a can of spinach pops from Popeye's pocket and spills into his mouth. Transformed by this gracious infusion of power, he easily demolishes the villain and rescues his beloved. The format never varies. Neither party ever gains any insight or learns from these encounters. Violence does not teach Bluto to honor Olive Oyl's humanity, and repeated pummelings do not teach Popeye to swallow his spinach *before* the fight.

Only the names have changed. Marduk subdues Tiamat through violence, and though he defeats Tiamat, chaos incessantly reasserts itself, and is kept at bay only by repeated battles and by the repetition of the New Year's Festival, where the heavenly combat myth is ritually reenacted. The structure of the combat myth is thus faithfully repeated on television week after week: a superior force representing chaos attacks aggressively; the champion fights back, defensively, only to be humiliated in apparent defeat; the evil power satisfies its lusts while the hero is incapacitated; the hero escapes, defeats the evil power decisively, and reaffirms order over chaos.[16] Willis Elliott's observation underscores the seriousness of this entertainment: "Cosmogony [the birth of the cosmos] is egogony [the birth of the individual person]: you are being birthed through how you see 'all things' as being birthed." Therefore, *"Whoever controls the cosmogony controls the children."*[17]

The psychodynamics of the television cartoon or comic book are marvelously simple: children identify with the good guy so that they can think of themselves as good. This enables them to project onto the bad guy their own repressed anger, violence, rebelliousness, or lust, and then vicariously to enjoy their own evil by watching the bad guy initially prevail. (This segment of the show actually consumes all but the closing minutes, and thus allows ample time for indulging the dark side of the self.) When the good guy finally wins, viewers are then able to reassert control over their own inner tendencies, repress them, and reestablish a sense of goodness. Salvation is guaranteed through identification with the hero.

This structure cannot be altered. Bluto does not simply lose more often—he must *always* lose. Otherwise this entire view of reality would collapse. The good guys must always win. In order to suppress the fear of erupting chaos the same mythic pattern must be endlessly repeated in a myriad of variations that *never in any way alter the basic structure*.[18]

Cartoon strips like Superman and Dick Tracy have been enormously successful in resolving the guilt feelings of the reader or viewer by providing totally evil, often deformed and inhuman scapegoats on whom one can externalize the evil side of one's own personality and disown it without coming to any insight or awareness of its presence within oneself. The villain's punishment provides catharsis; one forswears the villain's ways and heaps condemnation on him in a guilt-free orgy of aggression.[19] No premium is put on reasoning, persuasion, negotiation, or diplomacy. There can be no compromise with an absolute evil. Evil must be totally annihilated or totally converted. As Dick Tracy said on the day following Robert Kennedy's assassination (quite by coincidence; the strip had already been drawn earlier), "Violence is golden when it's used to put evil down."[20]

Cartoon and comic heroes cast no shadows. They are immortals; they cannot be killed. They are not beset by the ordinary temptations, never take advantage of damsels in distress, accept no bribes, usually receive no remuneration, and generally live above the realm of sin. Repentance and confession are as alien to them as the love of enemies and nonviolence. As Ariel Dorfman puts it, "The Lone Ranger himself contains not a single internal contradiction."[21]

Superman, for his part, intervenes in the lives of the people he encounters without ever challenging them to evaluate their beliefs and values or expose themselves to the anguish of transformation. He merely manipulates the environment. Villains are relegated to outer darkness but not redeemed from their bondage to evil or restored to true humanity.[22]

Batman, who lacks the godlike qualities of Superman, compensates with commitment. To avenge the murder of his parents he swears to spend "the rest of my life warring on all criminals." He will, in short, be a vigilante. He communicates well with the police commissioner, to be sure, but "the Caped Crusader" is answerable to no one in his role as a self-appointed crime-stopper.

His is a sacred vow, binding him to holy war on all the vermin of evil. His motives are not generous at all. He wants revenge.[23]

In this respect Batman parallels the classic gunfighters of the "western," who settle old scores by shoot-outs, never by due process of law. The law, in fact, is suspect, too weak to prevail in the conditions of near-anarchy that fiction has misrepresented as the wild West. The gunfighter must take matters into his own hands, just as, in the anarchic situation of the big city, a beleaguered citizen finally rises up against the crooks and muggers and creates justice out of the barrel of a gun (the movie *Dirty Harry* and, in real life, Bernard Goetz).

As Robert Jewett points out, this vigilantism betrays a profound distrust of democratic institutions, and of the reliance on human intelligence and civic responsibility that are basic to the democratic hope. It regards the general public as passive and unwise, incapable of discerning evil and making a rational response (as in the film *High Noon*). Public resources are inadequate, so the message goes; we need a messiah, an armed redeemer, someone who has the strength of character and conviction to transcend the legal restraints of democratic institutions and save us from an evil easily identifiable in villainous persons.

These vigilantes who deliver us by taking the law into their own hands will somehow do so without encouraging lawlessness. They will kill and leave town, thus ridding us of guilt. They will show selfless and surpassing concern for the health of our communities, but they will never have to practice citizenship, or deal with the ambiguity of political decisions. They neither run for office nor vote. They will reignite in us a consuming love for impartial justice, but they will do so by means of a mission of personal vengeance that eliminates due process of law.[24]

The possibility that an innocent person is being executed by our violent redeemers is removed by having the outlaw draw first, or shoot from ambush. The villain dresses in dark clothing, is swarthy, unshaven, and filthy, and his personality is stereotyped so as to eliminate any possibility of audience sympathy. The death of such evil beings is necessary in order to cleanse society of a stain. The viewer, far from feeling remorse at another human being's death, is actually made euphoric.[25] Such villains cannot be handled by democratic means; they are far too powerful, for they are archetypally endowed with the transcendent qualities of Tiamat. So great a threat requires a Marduk, an avenger, a man on a white horse.

Rather than shoring up democracy, the strongman methods of the superheroes of popular culture reflect a nostalgia for simpler solutions. They bypass constitutional guarantees of legal procedure in arrest, or the tenet that a person is to be regarded as innocent until proven guilty. What we see instead is a mounting impatience with the laborious processes of civilized life and a restless eagerness to embrace violent solutions. Better to mete out instant, summary justice than risk the red tape and delays and bumbling of the courts.[26] The yearning for a messianic redeemer who will set things right is thus, in its essence, a totalitarian fantasy.

The myth literally replays itself, without any awareness on the part of those who repeat it, under the guise of completely secular stories. Take the movie *Jaws*, for example. Recall that in the Babylonian myth, Marduk spread a net over Tiamat, and when she opened her jaws to devour him, "he drove in the evil wind so she could not close her lips. . . . He let fly an arrow, it pierced her belly." With her destruction, order is restored. The community is saved by an act of redemptive violence.

In the movie *Jaws*, Police Chief Brody encounters a shark larger by one-third than any known shark, of which a preview says, "It is as if nature had concentrated all its forces of evil in a single being." Brody kicks an oxygen tank into the attacking shark's throat, then fires a bullet that explodes the tank, thus forcing into the shark's body a wind that bursts it open. Brody is transformed into a superhero, chaos is subdued, and the island is restored to a tourist's paradise.[27]

Or take the spy thriller. In the service of one's country, the spy is permitted to murder, seduce, lie, steal, commit illegal entry, tap phones without a court order, and otherwise do anything necessary to protect the values of Christian civilization (the James Bond movies, "Mission: Impossible," etc.). This genre was literally enacted under the Reagan administration by Lt. Col. Oliver North and his colleagues in the Iran-Contra scandals. These men lied to Congress and the American people, possibly withheld vital information and decisions from their own president, appropriated funds for their own private use, and condoned drug running to finance their adventures—all in the name of a rabid patriotism that scorned democratic restraints or public accountability.

The basic attitude is summed up in an episode of that ultimate spoof on the spy thriller, "Get Smart." As I recall the scene decades after viewing it, the show ends with the villain being tricked by a loaded cigarette and blown off a cliff to his death on the rocks below. Agent 99 watches in horror, then comments, "You know, Max, sometimes I think we're no better than they are, the way we murder and kill and destroy people." To which Smart retorts, "Why, 99, you know we have to murder and kill and destroy in order to preserve everything that's good in the world."

And who are 99 and Smart fighting, week after week? An international conspiracy of evil intent called KAOS. And for whom do they work? CONTROL.

The archetype is able to reproduce itself, not only in the public media, but in actual history. In the mid-1970s, Congressman Les Aspin uncovered a secret CIA operation intended to disrupt domestic dissident groups in the 1960s. Though its work was expressly forbidden by law, this surveillance operation infiltrated fully legal antiwar groups and organizations that were attempting to rectify injustices, and sought to undermine them, often by trying to provoke violence. The name of the program: OPERATION CHAOS.[28] History itself becomes mythic.

How is it possible that this ancient archetypal structure still possesses such power in a modern, secular, scientific culture? Thanks to the American penchant for letting viewer interest determine programming, the story lines of cartoons, television shows, comics, and movies tend to gravitate to the lowest common denominator of mythic simplicity. The head of programming at a major network was asked to describe the thinking process that led to the network's selection of programs. He answered: There was no thinking process whatsoever. Television and film producers provide whatever fare the ratings and box offices tell them will generate the most immediate profit.[29] With important exceptions (Mr. Rogers, Captain Kangaroo, Sesame Street, and a few of the more benign cartoons listed in n. 15), the entertainment industry does not create materials that will be good for children to watch—material that will inculcate high values, ethical standards, honesty, truthfulness, mutual care and consideration, responsibility, and nobility of character. Instead, what children themselves prefer determines what is produced. The myth of redemptive violence is the simplest, laziest, most exciting, uncomplicated, irrational, and primitive depiction of evil the world has ever known. Furthermore, its orientation toward evil is one into which virtually all modern children (boys especially) are socialized in the process of maturation. The myth that lay like a threshold across the path of burgeoning empires also lies across the path of each individual bred in such societies. Children select this mythic structure because they have already been led, by culturally reinforced cues and role models, to resonate with its simplistic view of reality. Its ubiquity is not the result of a conspiracy of Babylonian priests secretly buying up the mass media with Iraqi oil money, but a function of inculcated values endlessly reinforced by the Domination System.[30]

Once children have been indoctrinated into the expectations of a dominator society, they may never outgrow the need to locate all evil outside themselves. Even as adults they tend to scapegoat others (the Commies, the Americans, the gays, the straights, the blacks, the whites) for all that is wrong in the world.

They continue to depend on group identification and the upholding of social norms for a sense of well-being. There is a cultic dimension to our television violence, involving the public in a reaffirmation of group values through the ritualization of collective ideas.[31] It is tragic that the mass media, which could be so effectively used (and occasionally are) to help people mature beyond the infantilisms of scapegoating behavior, have been made the chief exponent of the myth of redemptive violence.[32]

In a period when Christian Sunday schools are dwindling, the myth of redemptive violence has won children's voluntary acquiescence to a regimen of religious indoctrination more exhaustive and effective than any in the history of religions. Estimates vary widely, but the average child is reported to log roughly thirty-six thousand hours of television by age eighteen, including some fifteen thousand murders.[33] In prime-time evening shows, our children are served up about sixteen entertaining acts of violence (two of them lethal) every night; on the weekend the number of violent acts almost doubles (thirty). By age sixteen, the average child spends as much time watching television as in school.[34] What church or synagogue can even remotely match the myth of redemptive violence in hours spent with children or quality of presentation? (Think of the typical "children's sermon"—how bland by comparison!)

No other religious system has ever remotely rivaled the myth of redemptive violence in its ability to catechize its young so totally. From the earliest age children are awash in depictions of violence as the ultimate solution in human conflicts. Nor does saturation in the myth end with the close of adolescence. There is no rite of passage from adolescent to adult status in the national cult of violence, but rather a years-long acclimatization to adult television and movie fare. Not all shows for children or adults are based on violence, of course. Reality is far more complex than the simplicities of this myth, and maturer minds will demand more subtle, nuanced, complex presentations. But the basic structure of the combat myth underlies the pap to which a great many adults turn in order to escape the harsher realities of their everyday lives: spy thrillers, westerns, cop shows, and combat programs. It is as if we must watch so much "redemptive" violence to reassure ourselves, against the deluge of facts to the contrary in our day-to-day lives, that reality really is that simple.

With the right kinds of support, children might outgrow the simplicities of the myth of redemptive violence. Our modern tragedy is that just when boys ought to be transcending it, they are hit by an even more sophisticated barrage of unmitigated violence—violence so explicit and sexually sadistic that it cannot even be shown on television. I refer to a new wave of ever more brutal comic books, video games, and home videos. Recently I spent an hour browsing through a mall comic shop, examining such fare as The Uncanny X-Men, Swamp Thing, War of the Worlds, The Warlock Five, The Avengers, The Spectre, Shattered Earth, Scout: War Shaman, The Punisher, Gun Fury, The Huntress, Dr. Fate, The Blood Sword, and so on: an entire store devoted to the promulgation of a paranoid view of reality, where the initiation of violence is the only protection against those plotting our doom. And boys are almost the exclusive readership. "Over the last decade, comics have forsaken campy repartee and outlandishly byzantine plots for a steady diet of remorseless violence."[35]

Likewise, the "video nasties," such as The Texas Chain Saw Massacre, The Evil Dead, or Zombie Flesh-Eaters, have reached new levels of inventiveness in brutality. "Adult only" home videos such as these have been viewed by one-quarter of British children aged seven to eight; by age ten, half have seen them, if not at home, then at a friend's. Many have their first introduction to explicit sex in these films, in the form of rape, followed by decapitation, dismemberment, and cannibalism. With alarming frequency, crimes are being committed that are modeled after video violence.[36]

If such shows only provided a needed catharsis of violence, they might be defensible. But virtually all of the seven hundred studies done by 1984, along with those since, conclude that video violence increases substantially the degree to which adolescent boys engage in serious violence themselves.[37] In the past, villains tended to be depicted as undesirable models; the less human the model, the weaker the tendency to copy the model's behavior. Marduk is humanoid; Tiamat is a monster with seven heads. Marduk therefore attracts the greater identification. But realistic human figures portrayed as wholly evil on videos invite the very identification that earlier myths and fairy tales tried to deflect.

To the degree that programs present violence in the context of close personal relationships, show violence being done by "good" guys in the maintenance of law and order, or feature gratuitous violence, they appear to incite actual violent behavior. Violence is largely learned behavior.[38] Unlike imaginative tales, these brutalities are not enacted in the manner of playful pretense in some remote fantasyland. They are carried out in familiar environments: in homes, bedrooms, railway trains, and back streets.[39] There is a quantum leap from a child's singing, "They all ran after the farmer's wife, she cut off their tails with a carving knife," seated securely on mother's lap, to a child's watching an adult woman be decapitated in utter realism, from the killer's angle of vision, in the solitude of one's home while one's parents are away at work.

Perhaps most disturbing, many of these video films do not portray the age-old confrontation of good versus evil, with the "bad guys" eventually being overcome by the good. What we find is far more crude: simply the assault of pure evil. It is the Babylonian religion without Marduk, myth without redemption. Redemptive violence gives way to violence as an end in itself—not a religion that uses violence in the pursuit of order and salvation, but a religion in which violence has become the ultimate concern, an elixir, sheer titillation, an addictive high, a substitute for relationships. Violence is no longer the means to a higher good, namely order; violence itself becomes the goal.

Teachers report increased violence in children: rejection of fair play, greater cruelty, far more frequent and previously unthinkable verbal and physical attacks on teachers, fistfights between two boys replaced by a whole circle of children kicking one child on the ground, games that imitate video violence with the stronger playing the heroes and the weaker forced to play the villains.[40] "We are beginning to create a generation of children with a different set of values from previous ones," the authors of Video Violence and Children conclude.[41]

Perhaps we are just witnessing one of many oscillations in the intensity of violence throughout history. Violence in earlier times was chronic and highly public. Whole cities came out to be entertained by executions. Perhaps for some people violence has always been an end in itself. It would be naive to expect a gradual reduction in violence even if more egalitarian values were to take hold. Such values will instead incite a ruthless reaction. The Gospels anticipate an escalation of violence, not its decline, as the Epoch of Domination enters its final countdown to supersession.

But there is an even more significant aspect of the myth of redemptive violence that we have not developed: its contribution to the maintenance of international conflict.

Redemptive Violence and the National Security State

In every age, the myth of redemptive violence reappears in one form or another as a religion dedicated to the support of the powerful and privileged through violence. In the original Babylonian story, the price Marduk exacts for killing Tiamat is rulership over the pantheon of the gods. In that myth the council of the gods, and their mode of governing the universe, exactly reproduces the structure of Hammurabi's kingdom.

An older way of evaluating this correspondence between heavenly and earthly powers was to regard the gods as merely cosmic personifications that disguise the power arrangements of the state. The myth was thus seen as a mystification of actual power relations that provided divine legitimacy for oppressive earthly institutions.

In the first volume of this series I suggested that this reductionistic reading misses the mark.[42] The gods are not a fictive masking of the power of the human state—*they are its actual spirituality*. The *Enuma Elish* depicts the ascendancy of Marduk, the youngest god, to supreme authority over the other gods in the heavenly council, simultaneous with the ascendancy of the king of Babylon over the surrounding region. That myth, far from mystifying power relations, shows by the precise correspondence between heavenly and earthly events that it has faithfully and accurately brought to expression the actual power relations at work. As above, so below: Babylon is explicitly said to be "a likeness on earth of what he [Marduk] has wrought in heaven" (*Enuma Elish* VI.113; so also VI.104: "Let his command be supreme above and below"). This masks nothing. The myth plainly shows, for everyone to see, that Babylon has acquired hegemony over the other city-states in Mesopotamia. It states clearly that the king acts on behalf of Marduk to suppress chaos and impose order. The state is a mirror of cosmic order; therefore, resistance or rebellion is a crime against heaven.

We saw earlier that in the myth of redemptive violence, the survival and welfare of the nation are elevated as the highest earthly and heavenly good. There can be no other gods before the nation. This myth not only establishes a patriotic religion at the heart of the state, but also gives that nation's imperialistic imperative divine sanction. As Georges Khodr notes, all war is metaphysical; one can only go to war religiously.[43] The myth of redemptive violence is thus the spirituality of militarism.[44] By divine right the state has the power to order its citizens to sacrifice their lives to maintain the privileges enjoyed by the few. By divine decree it utilizes violence to cleanse the world of evil opponents who resist the nation's sway. Wealth and prosperity are the right of those who rule in such a state. And the name of God—any god, the Christian God included— can be invoked as having specially blessed and favored the supremacy of the chosen nation and its ruling caste.[45]

The unique contemporary form of Western redemptive violence (the Soviet Union had already shaped its own version under Lenin and Stalin) was sired by the Cold War. In 1947, the United States created new political institutions that would drastically alter the character and even the future prospects of democracy: the National Security Council and the Central Intelligence Agency. To propagate national security doctrine, the National War College was established in Washington in 1948. Through its doors have passed thousands of military and police officers from Latin America and other "Third World" nations. These institutions were but the outer form of a new Power being spawned: the national security system. Every Power, as we have seen in *Naming the Powers*, has an inner spirituality as well as outer institutional forms. The spirituality of the national security system is the ideology of the national security state.

José Comblin has trenchantly analyzed this relatively new development within the history of nationalism in *The Church and the National Security State*.[46] According to this doctrine, "the survival of the nation is the absolute goal. National strategy intends to incorporate the whole nation into the national survival plan, to make it the total and unconditional object of each citizen's life." On this view, all times are times of war. Peace is nothing more than the conventional name given to the continuation of war by other means. All politics is a politics of war. In Chile or South Africa or El Salvador, what this means in actual practice is that the army and its weapons are not used against outer geopolitical threats so much as against *their own people*.

The national security ideology is thus nationalism raised to ultimacy. Origen long ago warned Christians that the greatest temptation was participation in the national cults, which were nothing less than idolatrous worship paid to the angels of the nations as if they were God.[47] Though our contemporary idolaters never tire of speaking about the democracy and Christianity that they are defending with dictatorship and war (and the war never ends), the real faith of these National Securocrats is redemptive violence. As Brazilian General Golbery do Couto e Silva, one of the most influential geopolitical thinkers, put it,

> To be nationalist is to be always ready to give up any doctrine, any theory, any ideology, feelings, passions, ideals, and values, as soon as they appear as incompatible with the supreme loyalty which is due to the Nation above everything else. Nationalism is, must be, and cannot possibly be other than an Absolute One in itself, and its purpose is as well an Absolute End—at least as long as the Nation continues as such. There is no place, nor should there be, nor could there be place for nationalism as a simple instrument to another purpose that transcends it.[48]

Since such a nationalism cannot accept the existence of a higher power, it must destroy any forms of Christian faith that go beyond mere cultural inheritance. Nevertheless, national security ideologues saturate their language with religious platitudes. Their documents are drenched with phrases cribbed from the Bible and from papal encyclicals, and they may even be active attenders of church. But it is clear that what they mean by Christianity is merely the perpetuation of the privileges of a tiny capitalistic minority by whatever means necessary. It is new-old redemptive violence, the Domination System pure and simple.

Here is a cool and reflective rendition of the creed of regenerative violence from a contemporary spokesman from the American religious right:

That it is a privilege to engage in God's wars is clearly seen in the Psalms, perhaps nowhere better than in Ps. 149:5-7, where the saints sing for joy on their beds while they contemplate warring against God's enemies, or Ps. 58:10, "The righteous will rejoice when he sees the vengeance; he will wash his feet in the blood of the wicked." Those who cannot say "Amen" to such sentiments have not yet learned to think God's thoughts after him. . . . We have no problem rejoicing in His judgments, or in seeing it a privilege to be called to execute them. . . . The righteous . . . are called by God's law to exercise a holy "violence" against certain of the wicked, thereby manifesting God's wrath.[49]

Zealous nationalism of this stripe cannot simply be dismissed as aberrant, however; it is, indeed, "biblical." The Bible is full of bloodthirsty deeds of Yahweh, and those who wish to "think God's thoughts after him" can easily multiply references: the "ban" requiring the total destruction of every living being at Ai and Jericho; the atrocities committed by Jehu in the name of the prophet Elisha; Phinehas's zeal in murdering a couple whose sin was racial intermarriage; the picture of sinners being tortured in fire and brimstone for all eternity that Matthew has added to his sources; the lust for vengeance in the Book of Revelation—all these and many, many more examples attest to the success of the myth of redemptive violence in penetrating the Bible itself.[50]

The Rev. Gerald Derstine, defending U.S. government aid to the Contras fighting in Nicaragua, commented, "God uses war to cleanse the earth from wickedness. When it's time for a war, God allows certain evils to be exterminated."[51] The same orientation recently led the Rev. R. L. Hymers to pray with his congregation for the death of Supreme Court justices who support legalized abortion, and for God to remove ailing justice Harry Blackmun "in any way that God sees fit."[52] Televangelists like Pat Robertson and Jerry Falwell are only a little less crude in their support for apartheid, their opposition to disarmament, and their advocacy of militarism. The national security church thus becomes the kept court chaplain of the national security state.[53]

The myth of redemptive violence thus uses the traditions, rites, customs, and symbols of Christianity in order to enhance the power of a wealthy elite and the goals of the nation narrowly defined. It has no interest in compassion for the poor, or for more equitable economic arrangements, or for the love of enemies. It merely uses the shell of religion—a shell that can be filled with the blasphemous doctrine of the national security state. Emptied of their prophetic vitality, these outer forms are then manipulated to legitimate a power system intent on the preservation of privilege at all costs.[54]

Why then do large masses of the nonprivileged submit to such a myth? Why, for example, do blue-collar workers, who are among those most victimized by the ruling elite, continue not only to support their oppressors but to be among their most vociferous fans? The answer is quite simple: the promise of salvation. The myth of redemptive violence offers salvation through identification with Marduk and his earthly regents.

The modern individual, stripped of the values, rites, and customs that give a sense of belonging to traditional cultures, is the easy victim of the fads of style, opinion, and prejudice fostered by the communications media. At once isolated and yet absorbed into the masses, people live under the illusion that the views and feelings they have acquired by attending to the media are their own.[55] Overwhelmed by the giantism of corporations, bureaucracies, universities, the military, and celebrities, individuals sense that the only escape from utter insignificance lies in identifying with these giants and idolizing them as the true bearers of their own human identity.

Salvation through identification: whether it be in cartoon shows or westerns or confrontation with a foreign power, one's personal well-being is tied inextricably with the fortunes of the hero-leader. Right and wrong scarcely enter the picture. Everything depends on victory, success, the thrill of belonging to a nation capable of imposing its will in the heavenly council and among the nations. For the alternative—ownership of one's own evil and acknowledgment of God in the enemy—is for many simply too high a price to pay.

This longing to identify with a winner was glaringly evident during the Persian Gulf War. The orgy of patriotism unleashed in the United States revealed how strongly people wanted to be able to think well of their nation again. Here at last was what seemed to many a truly "just" war, and its incomparably successful military prosecution led to a flood of self-congratulatory euphoria. But for many people patriotism was merely a mask for a shame that they wanted to bury: our defeat in Vietnam; our failure domestically to provide adequate jobs, housing, education, and safety; and, perhaps most important, our failure to live by our own professed ideals. All that ambivalence could be submerged under a tide of national pride. Salvation comes, not by insight, repentance, and truth, but by identification with American military might: the Marduk solution. And the tragedy is that violence proved so incredibly "successful" for the Allies. Why consider nonviolent sanctions when our smart bombs are wiser than our diplomats?

The structure of the ancient combat myth is not then just the basis of comics and cartoons; it is the framework of much that passes as foreign policy. Subdue Tiamat, the argument runs, and a new world order will prevail. It is so simple, so unarguable, so irresistible. Before such a prospect, who would think of negotiating a peace that requires all parties involved to concede their own culpability for the crisis and to surrender advantages they have gained unjustly?

When the Viet Cong overran Ben Tre, a city of 35,000, American bombers were ordered to level the entire city on the grounds that "it became necessary to destroy the town to save it." As absurdly contradictory as such statements may appear to us today, they fit precisely the structure of the mystique of violence.[56] As Richard Slotkin put it, the myth of regenerative violence is the structuring metaphor of the American experience.[57]

Is there no escape from this myth of redemptive violence? Yes, there is, but it is difficult. To face the fear of enemies would finally require us to acknowledge our own inner evil, and that would cost us all our hard-earned self-esteem. *We* would have to change, laboriously, struggling daily to transform or redeem our shadow side. We would have to see ourselves as no different in kind from our enemy (however different we may be in degree). It would mean seeing God in the enemy as we learn to see God in ourselves—a God who loves and forgives and can transform even the most evil person or society in the world. Such insight would require conversion from the myth of redemptive violence to the God proclaimed by the prophets and by Jesus. We would have to abandon our preferential option for violence and replace it with a preferential option for the oppressed. We could no longer rely on absolute weapons for the utter annihilation of an absolute enemy. We could no longer justify unchristian means to preserve at all costs the hollow shell of a "Christian civilization" that has, in effect, been filled with the creed of redemptive violence.

The myth of redemptive violence is nationalism become absolute. This myth speaks *for* God; it does not listen for God to speak. It invokes the sovereignty of God as its own; it does not entertain the prophetic possibility of radical denunciation and negation by God. It misappropriates the language, symbols and scriptures of Christianity. It does not seek God in order to change; it claims God in order to prevent change. Its God is not the impartial ruler of all nations but a biased and partial tribal god worshiped as an idol. Its metaphor is not the journey but a fortress. Its symbol is not the cross but a rod of iron. Its offer is not forgiveness but victory. Its good news is not the unconditional love of enemies but their final liquidation. Its salvation is not a new heart but a successful foreign policy. It usurps the revelation of God's purposes for humanity in Jesus. It is blasphemous. It is idolatrous.

And it is immensely popular.

I love my country passionately; that is why I want to see it do right. There is a valid place for a sensible patriotism. But from a Christian point of view, true patriotism acknowledges God's sovereignty over all the nations, and holds a healthy respect for God's judgments on the pretensions of any power that seeks to impose its will on others. There is a place for a sense of destiny as a nation.[58] But it can be authentically embraced and pursued only if we separate ourselves from the legacy of the combat myth and "enter a long twilight struggle against what is dark within ourselves."[59] There is a divine vocation for the United States (and every other nation) to perform in human affairs. But it can perform that task, paradoxically, only by abandoning its messianic zeal and accepting a more limited role within the family of nations.

"What are you women doing out alone?"
"We're not alone; we're with each other."

Lily Tomlin,
"Saturday Night Live"[1]

2. The Origin of the Domination System

How did the Domination System get started? The myth of redemptive violence gives this answer: war, conquest, plunder, rape, and enslavement are all ordained in the very constitution of the universe, which itself is formed from the corpse of a murdered goddess. "Civilization" is a condition of periodic or perpetual warfare, "peace" the achievement of warfare, "prosperity" the fruit of warfare successfully accomplished. If human beings are created from the blood of a slaughtered god, how can one expect from them anything but violence?

Are Human Beings Violent by Nature?

Is violence then our fate? Is there no alternative to the Domination System? Students of animal violence such as Konrad Lorenz, Niko Tinbergen, Robert Ardrey, and Desmond Morris have argued that violence, domination, and hierarchical ranking do not originate with Homo sapiens but are already observable in some species of birds, insects, and primates.[2] And René Girard argues that only those human societies were able to survive that were able to contain the violence of escalating retaliation by means of the scapegoat mechanism. Society itself is the outcome of successfully managed violence.[3]

If violence is that deep in our bones, is there then any hope for its alleviation or restraint? Is the human species simply a maladapted mutant destined for self-extinction?

Girard's theory of the scapegoat mechanism is not necessarily pessimistic, as we shall see (chap. 7). If the scapegoating mechanism is exposed for what it is, and if human beings acknowledge their proclivity to project their own inner violence onto others, there is some ground for hope that violence might at least be reduced in human affairs.

As for the comparisons drawn from animal behavior, Lorenz popularized the belief that there is an "aggressive instinct" that requires constant discharge or release and drives human beings to war.[4] But there is convincing evidence that, though the capacity for aggression is inherited, the acting out of aggression has to be learned. It is not an instinct. We are not "prewired" for aggression. Human

33

beings are potentially aggressive, and aggression is a natural and indispensable element in full human life, but people are not inherently warriors. Otherwise the existence of peaceable peoples would be inexplicable. A wolf raised in a kennel will, on being released in the wild, stare lackadaisically at caribou nearby even though it is starving. It must be taught to hunt.[5]

Nor is there, as it is alleged, any human need to discharge aggression periodically through warfare.[6] War historian Sue Mansfield points out that, though a majority of cultures in historic times have engaged in war, the majority of human beings have not been participants. In peasant societies it was very rare for more than 1 or 2 percent of the male population to be actually engaged in soldiering. In World War I and II, only about 10 to 15 percent of the population of the warring states were under arms. The vast majority of males have never participated in battle, to say nothing of women (of whom nothing is normally said in these discussions), and neither men nor women exhibit physiological symptoms indicating that their aggressive instinct has been frustrated. No one complains about deferment from military service; instead, people do all in their power to avoid induction into the army, except in very popular wars.[7] Brigadier Gen. S. L. A. Marshall discovered that even in veteran units with good morale, it was rare for more than 25 percent of frontline soldiers to fire their weapons *once* during a battle in World War II, and 15 percent was the more common figure.[8]

Nor is aggression a necessary ingredient in battle. Often it clouds judgment and leads to rash or inappropriate action. Especially today, when a bomber pilot coolly flies tens of thousands of feet above his target or a naval gunner pounds shells into an indistinct land mass fifteen miles away, aggression is not a key motivation at all, but rather professional pride and a sense of camaraderie with one's buddies.[9]

Violence is not, in fact, a constant in human societies. There are primitive peoples surviving even today among whom violence is almost nonexistent. In the Philippines, Africa, New Guinea, and Malaysia there are tribes that are still preliterate, relatively lacking in gender role specialization, nonhierarchical, and remarkably free of violence. They do not deal with conflict by scapegoating or sacrifice, but by early socialization into cooperation and nonviolence.

Observation of the Batek Negrito of the Malay Peninsula by Karen Lampell Endicott can serve as a representative example. Although the Batek have fled ever deeper into the forest to escape the encroachment of "civilization," they have contacts with the dominant culture through trade in rattan. Their basic subsistence, however, is through hunting and gathering. Numbering only about 350 persons, they live a nomadic existence in camps of five to eight nuclear families. Hunters share all the meat they obtain, but there is no status or social reward for being a successful hunter, nor shame at being unsuccessful or blind or too lame to hunt. There are loosely defined gender roles, but they are not stereotyped or ranked. There are no words for "boy" or "girl," only "children," until puberty. Women can hunt whenever they want, but usually do so only for small game and near the camp. Women usually dig for tubers, but men often join them.

Both men and women collect and trade rattan. All share the earnings, since some have had to gather extra food to support those collecting rattan. Women specialize in building lean-tos when setting up a new camp, while the men leave to hunt before the game is frightened away. Both sexes collect firewood and water. Men seldom weave or plait rattan. Men specialize in hunting because, the Batek said, they have stronger breath for the blowguns. They are also more expendable in case of tiger attack (the camps have a fairly constant ratio of 11 men to 8 women). Hunting is one of the few really skilled tasks, and takes years to learn. Nursing mothers with babies and the younger children are, of course, unable to hunt.

The Batek have no sense of property or ownership. The area they forage is not "theirs," nor do they prohibit others from camping or foraging in it. They have no domination hierarchies. There are leaders that emerge naturally, through age, wisdom, and strength; sometimes (as in the camp studied) the leader is a woman. Leaders have no power to impose their will on anyone. Disputes are settled only by reasoning. An aggrieved or offending party may decide to leave the camp for another, but there are no punishments, not even exile. Each evening the whole camp plans its moves or activities for the next day.

Children's games are noncompetitive and nonaggressive. Small children are not punished, but simply diverted or ignored. Aggression toward others is discouraged. Children are taught not to be possessive by the general devaluing of private ownership. If people are angry, they will sit in a shelter and speak loudly of what is bothering them, without addressing anyone in particular. Others may join in. They thus model for children the use of communication to resolve aggression. Because they discourage overt aggression and have found ways to dissipate it, the Batek men are no more violent than the women.

By devaluing violence in anyone, male or female, the Batek have created a social environment in which women and men can interact as equals. The observation of Michelle Zimbalist Rosaldo and Louise Lamphere that "all contemporary societies are to some extent male-dominated" may be true of domination societies, but it is manifestly untrue of the Batek and other primitive peoples like them.[10] Despite exposure to the modern world, the Batek maintain a remarkably egalitarian society in every respect, including most gender roles. Batek men do not own their wives, children, or sisters, nor do they have control over women's work, sexuality, offspring, or any decision-making power over them. Men do not dominate women in Batek society. Independence is valued equally by men and women, yet theirs is a society of unusual closeness, physical touching, and interdependence, without any social need for prestige and status from wealth, political power, or social position.[11] And this state of affairs has been documented in other such societies that have had no apparent contact with each other for thousands of years.[12]

What we do not know is whether such societies are similar to prehistoric societies, or whether a modern society fully exposed to urban civilization could survive if it embraced comparable values. Every such primitive society that has thus far come up hard against modern civilization has been destroyed. But what these survivors of a simpler time show—even stronger, prove—is that human beings *are* capable of living without violence.[13]

A Time before the Domination System?

At least some archaeological remains from Neolithic cultures tend to confirm the picture provided by surviving primitive societies like the peaceful Batek. Most strikingly, there is very little evidence of warfare between 9000 and 4000 B.C.E., and not a great deal until around 3000, after which it proliferates dramatically. Even in the region that would later spawn the myth of redemptive violence, Mesopotamia, there are no indications of the resort to overt hostility between groups in that earlier period, even after population density increased and agriculture and animal domestication were invented. Stone tools were used at first for scraping vegetable matter or the hunt; they were not fashioned for warfare.[14] Earliest Sumer apparently practiced democracy.[15] Thorkild Jacobsen cautiously concludes, "As far as we can judge, the fourth millennium and the ages before it had been moderately peaceful. Wars and raids were not unknown; but they were not constant and they did not dominate existence."[16] Such domination as existed was not systemic and institutionalized, and so was unable as yet to assert in full its life-negating character.

Excavations at Çatal Hüyük and Hacilar in Turkey and at numerous sites in Minoan Crete, Old Europe, and early pre-Columbian America reveal societies in which there was not a glaring inequality in the size of houses or the apparent status of persons. Religion was characterized by domestic, household cults rather than organized societal cults or state religions. Earlier theories traced the origin of warfare to the rise of agriculture and the capacity to store surplus goods that marauding tribes might covet. We now know, from carbon-dating techniques and dendrochronology, that the domestication of wild plants and animals goes back as far as 9000 to 8000 B.C.E. Civilization began four to five thousand years before the first evidences of war.[17]

What is most startling is what archaeologists have found missing. As Riane Eisler notes in *The Chalice and the Blade*, some cities existed for hundreds of years, undisturbed, unplundered, not razed to the ground, and *unwalled*, located in choice valleys rather than on fortifiable crags. Equally astonishing, there are no evidences in Neolithic paintings of "noble warriors," heroic conquerors, captives, or slaves, nor are there any indications of thrusting weapons, battle-axes, or swords (though mace heads have been found). Burial grounds show no trace of lavish chieftain burials, or of mighty rulers who take with them into the afterlife less powerful human beings sacrificed at their death (wives, concubines, children, slaves). And in Neolithic art, neither the Goddess nor her son-consort carries the emblems we have learned to associate with might—spears, swords, or thunderbolts, the symbols of an earthly sovereign or deity who exacts obedience by maiming or killing.[18]

The evidence is not unambiguous. A few cities were fortified.[19] If warfare was infrequent and tended to cease with the first letting of blood or the first killing,[20] hunting weapons or maces (normally used to finish off wounded game) would have sufficed. Some societies were probably more warlike than others, but insularity would have at first prevented much contact. Clashing warriors were probably completely unorganized militarily, and suffered more from hoarseness caused by shouting threats than from wounding. But most of the time these early peoples seem to have dwelt in peace. Egypt flourished without a standing army for the first 1,500 years of its history.[21]

In short, the evidence suggests that at least some early societies were unstratified and basically egalitarian. For the purpose of this study, it is not necessary to establish that *all* Neolithic societies were peaceful (they clearly were not), but only that *some* were peaceful, in order to refute the notion that human beings are genetically wired for warfare. It appears that these relatively tranquil communities existed, not to conquer, pillage, and loot, but to cultivate the earth and provide the material and spiritual means for a satisfying life. Nor were such societies limited to Old Europe and the Near East. Some Native American peoples apparently lived in relative peace over a span of more than nine thousand years without any sign of cataclysm or replacement of local inhabitants through annihilation—five hundred generations unmarred by violent calamity.[22] Prior to the blood-soaked conquest-state of the Aztecs, formative Mesoamerican cultures (2000 B.C.E.–300 C.E.) in the valley of Mexico were egalitarian and peaceful, with only modest differences in status or wealth, and no sign of deaths by war or sacrifice.[23]

Many of these early societies appear to have been matrilineal (with descent through the mother) and matrilocal (where the husband comes to live with the wife's family, a situation still reflected in Gen. 2:24), but they were *not* matriarchal (ruled by women).[24] So far as we know, matriarchy has never existed anywhere. No doubt men fear that women liberated from patriarchy would revenge themselves by treating men the way men have treated women. But the archaeological evidence, and the sexual equality evident in contemporary primitive groups, indicate rather that at least some prehistoric societies were partnership societies characterized, not by "power over," but by "power with"; by cooperation more than by competition; and by actualization hierarchies (where leaders serve the community) rather than domination hierarchies (where communities must serve the leaders).[25]

In a society in which a surplus is nonexistent or only temporary, observes Gerhard Lenski, no one, however greedy, can rise to a position of economic dominance. People in such societies will, of necessity, tend to be relatively equal, at least with respect to the distribution of goods and services. In such societies, rule must be by persuasion. One strong person is no match for three others. As a result, democratic councils seem to have been virtually universal in primitive societies.[26]

It is, of course, hazardous to build an interpretation of world history in its entirety on the sandy foundations of archaeological guesswork and speculation. Some experts on the Neolithic period would no doubt reject elements of the above reconstruction as fanciful. Eisler and other feminists have found it important to identify an era when equality prevailed, just as Marx and Freud felt compelled to postulate a primitive socialism or a primal parricide in order to ground their theories in the very nature of things. But there may be a kind of genetic fallacy involved in the idea that our efforts to transform the present world system depend on there having once been a "golden age" in which current evils were nonexistent. One could even turn the genetic argument on its head (though I do not wish to do so) and say that, since the conditions that made egalitarian societies once possible have everywhere disappeared with the ascendancy of the Domination System and increased density of populations, egalitarian societies are no longer possible.[27] It has always proved hazardous to import the myth of a Fall into history, or to exempt some group or period from the effects of the Fall, and that may be no less the case here. The moral and theological case against the Domination System is solid without an appeal to origins. So why try?

Because there is something powerfully attractive in the description of partnership societies, with their lack of extreme class differences, their relative gender equality, and the apparent absence of war. Perhaps that is our clue: it is the *picture* that we find so helpful. We need a way to visualize what a domination-free society would be like. Whether a truly egalitarian society ever existed or not, it should. Such a society is one to which all humanity should aspire, whether or not it has ever existed before on the face of the earth. It would indeed strengthen hope and give it empirical grounding if such a dream was once reality. But we need not argue that something has to have existed in the past to be a real possibility in the future. It is not the protology but the eschatology that people find appealing in such hypotheses.

Indeed, some such story of a golden age seems to be preserved in the folk memories of hundreds of societies. Western anthropologists have generally dismissed these tales as lacking any basis in fact. After all, Western civilization is the apex of evolutionary progress, so how could primitives have achieved what has eluded us? But even the Israelites preserve the memory of an ecological paradise. Despite flagrantly patriarchal motifs in the Yahwist creation accounts (creation of the male first, and creation of the female from the male), Genesis 2–3 depicts a society in which the woman took the initiative in making decisions. The woman is the product of a special creative act in the Yahwist version, filling a gap in creation and a need in the male without which the original creation would have been incomplete. The first couple are depicted as agriculturalists, not hunters or herders—and women played a more central role in agricultural societies. The Fall was the loss of female freedom and submission to males in a patriarchal society: in short, the rise of androcracy, or rule by men. Genesis 1, by contrast, is explicitly egalitarian. The image of God is male and female, and the first couple are created together as a reflection of the divine nature.[28]

The idea that humanity once experienced more just social arrangements is also helpful because people are already mired in a counter-narrative that they endow with indubitable historicity: the belief that domination by males, by the powerful, and by the rich is given in the nature of things, from time immemorial, from the very mind of God. Male supremacy is uncritically assumed to be normative, natural, inevitable, as are white supremacy and rule by elites. The very idea of supremacy as the prerogative of a few is challenged by our new account of prehistory. It is possible that broad sectors of humanity once existed in greater tranquility together than today. But even if this cannot be proved, neither can anyone assert with confidence that human societies have been autocratic from the beginning. And if the Domination System is a relatively late social invention that only achieved hegemony five thousand years ago, perhaps it is not ineradicable.

I am *not* saying that evil first entered the world through the Domination System. Sin, mortality, idolatry, alienation from God, oneself, and the world are existential realities intrinsic to being human. But Satan, demons, and the Powers are rather late arrivals. Humanity was slow to perceive the spirituality of complex institutions and forces. These spiritual realities are the peculiar distillate of domination, and they only became discernible after human societies had reached a certain threshold of density, complexity, and conflict.

The Rise of the Domination System

It is difficult to date the rise of systemic domination and its legitimations. By the time of the massive city-states of Sumer and Babylon around 3000 B.C.E., autocracy was already the accepted order of things.[29] Warfare flourished. Soldiers in standing armies fought with new bronze weapons, and sometimes from horseback. Their social system had become rigidly hierarchical, authoritarian, and patriarchal. Some of these warrior peoples worshiped their weapons.[30] Others revered divinities of war, whose will decreed the massacre of their male victims and the sexual subjugation of their female victims.[31] Women were beginning to be deprived of the right both to speak their minds and to control their bodies, though repression fluctuated widely at different times and places.[32] The earliest known law code, Urukagina's edict (ca. 2300 B.C.E., Mesopotamia), declares, "The women of former days used to take two husbands (but) the women of today (if they attempt this) are stoned with stones (upon which is inscribed their evil) intent." "If a woman speaks . . . disrespectfully to a man, that woman's mouth is crushed with a fired brick."[33]

No matter how high in the patriarchal social order a woman might now rise, she was always controlled by men sexually and reproductively. Every class had two tiers, one for men, and a lower one (in the same class) for women. Power lost by men through submission to a ruling elite was compensated by power gained over women, children, hired workers, slaves, and the land. In the increased violence and brutality of the new order, it was in the interest of women to seek out a male protector and economic supporter. But the price they paid was sexual servitude, unsalaried domestic labor, and subordination to their husbands in all matters, often those once theirs by gender specialization. As a fringe benefit, women were permitted to exploit men and women in races or classes lower than their own.[34]

Human destiny was being driven in a direction that people did not intend and most would not have consciously chosen. The new capacity for expansion and enrichment through conquest created a situation of anarchy in which no one could choose that the struggle for dominance should cease. According to Andrew Bard Schmookler, as violence between groups increased, humanity inadvertently stumbled into a chaos that had never before existed. "The relations among societies were uncontrolled and virtually uncontrollable. Such an ungoverned system imposes unchosen necessities: civilized people were compelled to enter a struggle for power."[35]

The irony is that successful defense against a power-maximizing aggressor requires a society to become more like the society that threatens it. Thus domination is a contaminant, a disease that, once introduced, will inexorably spread throughout the system of societies. It is, says Schmookler, as if the process of natural selection had come to favor behavior characterized by those who dominated over others.

> The selection for power can discard those who revere nature in favor of those willing and able to exploit it. The warlike may eliminate the pacifistic; the ambitious, the content. Civilized societies will displace the remaining primitives, modern industrial powers will sweep away archaic cultures. The iron makers will be favored over those with copper or no metallurgy at all, and the horsemen will have sway over the unmounted. Societies that are coherently organized and have strong leadership will make inviable others with more casual power structures and more local autonomy . . . what looked like open-ended cultural possibilities are channeled in a particular, unchosen direction.[36]

The struggle for domination meant that many humane cultural options that people might have preferred were closed off. The self-interests of individuals were subordinated, often even sacrificed, to the interests of the larger systems in which they were imbedded. This does not imply that striving for domination is intrinsic to human social existence. It is not. Nor does it imply that everything that emerges with dominator societies is evil; much is good and beautiful. A great deal of effort was devoted to formulating laws that would limit violence and secure justice for the weak—though always in a context that preserved advantage for the strong.[37] Women found ways to assert power, through or around existing conventions, and occasionally a woman would achieve genuine power, like Urukagina's queen or, much later, Cleopatra. But they were able to wield power only on terms already laid down by the power system itself. The Domination System has constrained the profound transformations in the evolution of human civilization in such a manner that human destiny is no longer governed by free human choice. *"No one is free to choose peace, but anyone can impose upon all the necessity for power."*[38]

China had a long tradition of opposition to war. It developed no tradition of the holy war, and war itself was sharply criticized. It had no emphasis on competitive values or sports. Yet it suffered almost three millennia of virtually uninterrupted warfare. The source of war is not physiological (aggression) nor philosophical (ideas) nor psychological (competition), but structural—the contest for domination means that everyone is forced to become involved.[39] Likewise, men in Tanzania relate to the earth and have both feminine and masculine gods, yet they routinely brutalize women. In India, where goddesses are widely worshiped, the oppression of women is widespread. And both women and children are abused by some Christian men, despite the emphasis on love in the teaching of Jesus. The problem is once again structural—males *must* dominate women (even if some do so rather gently) if they wish to preserve male ownership of property, the family name, and political control.

There is some correlation, however, between patrilineality and sexual inequality, and matrilineality and sexual equality. Fifty-two percent of matrilineal societies are sexually equal; only 19 percent of patrilineal are. Fifty percent of matrilocal societies are sexually equal; only 21 percent of patrilocal ones are. Warfare is absent, periodic, or occasional in 50 percent of societies where sexes are equal. Where males dominate, warfare is endemic or chronic in 82 percent of societies. Fathers spend more time with infants in societies having feminine creation symbolism. In 63 percent of these societies, fathers are in frequent contact with infants. But where societies have masculine origin symbolism, fathers are, at best, only occasionally involved with infants. In 72 percent of societies with mixed masculine and feminine origin symbolism, the father is in occasional to frequent contact with infants.[40]

It is characteristic of the Powers that, though they are established, staffed, and perpetuated by people, they are beyond merely human control. It was the *experience* of a total system operating (as it seemed) autonomously and even, at times, malevolently, that gave rise to a perception of the role played by the Powers in human destiny. "For our struggle is not against enemies of blood and flesh, but against the rulers, against the authorities, against the cosmic powers of this present darkness, against the spiritual forces of evil in the heavenly places" (Eph. 6:12). The Powers are the structures and institutions, in both their outer and inner manifestations, that embody the Domination System in any historical moment.

No one person or group of people imposed the Domination System on us; it came wholly unbidden. People inadvertently stumbled into a struggle for power beyond their ability to avoid it or to stop. This struggle, says Schmookler, generated a selective process, beyond human control, which molded change inevitably toward power maximization in human societies. Not only does power tend to corrupt, but often it is the most ruthless and corrupt who tend to gain power. Leaders seem to be chosen by "impersonal and ungoverned forces," "an unchosen selective process";[41] and they are not usually those whom humanity would prefer to guide its destiny.

Nor are these leaders free. They appear to choose, but the selective process generated by the ungoverned system confers upon them that role. "The powerful get to speak because the unchosen structure of the system determines which messages will be heard. . . . *That which chooses the chooser determines the choice*."[42] Decisions are determined not by what would enhance the quality of human life but by what will increase competitive power.[43]

People have thus become the slaves of their evolving systems, rather than civilized society being the servant of its members. Not that the selection for domination systematically selects what is injurious to people. The process is not hostile to human welfare; it is simply indifferent. Many things that serve domination serve people as well, such as a degree of social order or art or adequate nutrition.[44]

Those of us who now enjoy affluence and freedom as well as power are predisposed to believe that benign forces shape our destiny. But to the extent that our blessings are incidental by-products of our citizenship in nations that currently enjoy domination status over others, our well-being may be more a result of flagrant injustice than divine providence.[45]

The pain of living a life so alienated from what is natural and pleasurable exacts a psychic cost, says Schmookler: numbing. Most of us, winners and losers alike, are profoundly unable to grasp the severity of our loss. Numbness in turn produces amnesia about what a fully human life would be like, and even a fear of remembering. We internalize the ethic of productivity, the constraints of patriarchy, the imperative of success, the drivenness of modern life, the obligations of machismo, the laws that prevent our achieving for ourselves what the powerful achieve at our expense. We become complicit. And so we leave unopposed the world that injures us, restructuring ourselves to appease the

Powers we depend upon. To achieve peace with the world, we declare war upon ourselves.[46]

No social system, to be sure, has ever been purely totalitarian. There is always a mix of egalitarianism, dominance, and altruism; no one mode ever prevails exclusively. Even in the most oppressively patriarchal structures, women and men continue to protest and to dream of a more equitable way.[47] But once states arose, male supremacy always prevailed. New myths (among them, the *Enuma Elish*) were created to socialize women, the poor, and captives into their now inferior status. Priesthoods (usually male), backed up by armies, courts of law, and executioners, inculcated in people's minds the fear of terrible, remote, and inscrutable deities. Earlier songs, tales, myths, and rituals from a more equalitarian time were suppressed. Wife beating and child beating began to be seen as not only normal but right. Evil was blamed on women (Tiamat, Eve).[48]

Fleeing refugees and fast-pursuing predators spread this culturally regressive new society widely. Few peoples were remote or isolated enough to escape the new pattern of conquest, sack, and domination. At the same time, new, androcratic myths depicted the Goddess as being killed (Tiamat), or raped (Ninlil), or reduced to a mere consort or wife of male deities (Astarte), or eroticized to meet male desires (Aphrodite), or militarized (Athena).[49] Medusa, whose glance turned men to stone, was originally a fertility goddess; the snakes that coil around her head symbolized regeneration but became an image of death, terror, and ugliness.[50] In songs, lore, and mores, men were depicted as masters, women as slaves; men as superior, women as subordinate; men as active, women as objects; men as owners, women as property; men as virile, women as seducers. Male supremacy became the cultural context of *all* relationships between human beings.[51] At the same time, masculinity was rendered problematical. All females are women, but not all males are men. One must learn to be a man, be made a man of, earn the right to the name "man" by showing control, developing muscles, killing a lion, or undergoing arduous initiation rites.[52]

The biblical myth in Genesis 2 reverses universal human experience and has the woman taken out of the man. So, too, Athena was born from the brow of Zeus, and (in another strategy for discounting the contribution of women) the Egyptian god Ptah created all the other gods by masturbating.[53] In the close-knit societies that may have preceded the Domination Era there would have been little cause to feel awe toward fellow humans; now, with so much power concentrated in the hands of the king, reverence before might became not only a political requirement but a religious *feeling*, as the gods increasingly took on characteristics of domination.[54]

The Emergent Biblical Alternative

Neither Judaism nor Christianity escaped this violent ethos. The early Hebrews all too often behaved in a manner indistinguishable from the predators of an earlier time. Though many of the teachings of Isaiah and other prophets call for a partnership society rather than a dominator one, much of Hebrew Scripture, as Riane Eisler sees it, is "a network of myths and laws designed to impose, maintain, and perpetuate a dominator system of social and economic organization."[55] Yahweh is depicted as ordering the Israelites to destroy, plunder, and kill all but the virgin daughters of their enemies, and to take these as sexual slaves, concubines, and involuntary wives.

Eisler, who with her family barely escaped Austria after the Nazi takeover, assesses her own heritage severely. She sees in ancient Israel a rigidly male-dominated system in which God willed that women be subjugated to men and treated as property or chattel. Daughters were sold to prospective husbands, or into slavery, and were stoned if their commercial value was destroyed by losing their virginity (Deut. 22:13-29; Exod. 21:1-11; Num. 31:18). They could be given up to murderous crowds to be gang raped until they perished, in order to protect the lives of male visitors or a husband (Genesis 19; Judges 19). New wives for the defeated Benjamites could be had by simply seizing them in Shiloh vineyards (Judges 21). In all this, no law was violated; the law actually protected these male prerogatives. Yet, comments Eisler, millions of people still today can read these passages without a twinge of horror at the moral bankruptcy of an androcratic system that could countenance such treatment.[56]

Religious people have long been accustomed to passing such criticisms off by a theory of progressive revelation: these poor, benighted primitives knew no better, and ascribed to God attitudes that later generations would sharply condemn. If these were not "primitives," but the brutal successors of a more egalitarian society, however, the picture has to be reversed. This is not so much "progressive revelation" as a cultural *regression* that in many ways only worsened over the thousand years of Israel's history. The freedom of a Rachel to move among men and speak to them in the second millennium B.C.E. (Gen. 29:9-12) had been sharply circumscribed a thousand years later, so that by the time of Jesus, respectable women were being sequestered in their homes and could speak to no man but their husbands and kin, and then not in public.[57] Women were not full members of the covenant, but were saved through their fathers and husbands and through childbearing.

Killing in war is divinely sanctioned in Scripture, but even the mildest sexual indiscretion is punishable by death (Leviticus 18; 20:13; Deut. 22:22-29). Reproduction, the act of giving life, is now tainted and unclean. And this is true, not just in the Hebrew Scriptures, but in all androcratic societies. Except for those regions isolated from the spread of its virus, the Domination System ruled the world.[58]

This negative judgment on the Hebrew Bible is not the whole story, however. There are also powerful prophetic denunciations of domination, and the longing for a different dispensation where peace, justice, and equality would reign, most notably the servant song of Isaiah 53. Abraham J. Heschel remarks that the Prophets were the first people in history to regard a nation's reliance on force as evil.[59] Daniel represents the attitude of a wing of Judaism that rejected the militarism of the Maccabees and trusted in divine intervention and governance in public life (167 B.C.E.). By Jesus' day, many Jews, especially those of the Pharisaic party, were, practically speaking, nonviolent.

But it was Jesus who revealed to the world, for the first time since the rise of conquest-states, God's domination-free order of nonviolent love. His message was not wholly new; much of it was already contained or foreshadowed in those portions of the Hebrew Bible congruent with a partnership society. But, says Eisler, that new order "was obviously most forcefully—indeed, in the eyes of the religious elites of his time, heretically—articulated by this young carpenter from Galilee." For although the liberation of women was not his central focus, if we look at what Jesus preached from the perspective of a critique of domination, we see a single, unifying theme: a vision of the liberation of *all* humanity through the replacement of androcratic with partnership values.[60]

> Even more striking—and all-pervasive—are Jesus' teachings that we must elevate "feminine virtues" from a secondary or supportive to a primary and central position. We must not be violent but instead turn the other cheek; we must do unto others as we would have them do unto us; we must love our neighbors and even our enemies. Instead of the "masculine virtues" of toughness, aggressiveness, and dominance, what we must value above all else are mutual responsibility, compassion, gentleness, and love. . . . What he was preaching was the gospel of a partnership society.[61]

In his beatitudes, in his extraordinary concern for the outcasts and marginalized, in his wholly unconventional treatment of women (speaking to them in public, touching them, eating with them, even with harlots, above all, teaching them), in the seriousness with which he took children, in his rejection of the dogma that high-ranking men are the favorites of God, in his subversive proclamation of a new order in which domination would give way to compassion and communion, Jesus overturned the most rigidly upheld mores of his time.

But the Domination System proved too strong. Soon sinners were being excluded from the church, women were being squeezed out of leadership, and the wealthier, educated males were taking over authority from the poor and unschooled. The Roman Empire joined the Jewish leadership in attempting to crush this nonviolent movement of compassion and equality. From within and without, enormous pressures forced the church ineluctably toward precisely the kind of hierarchical and violence-based system that Jesus had rejected. The rest is all too painfully evident: heretics and "witches" hunted down and burned, inquisitions, crusades, emperors and kings settling doctrinal disputes with armies, wars of Christians against Christians, pogroms against Jews. The dream of the New Reality of Jesus has long since turned into the nightmare, first of

Christendom, then of our more recent secular totalitarianisms. In all this, the conquest of women went hand in hand with the exploitation of the poor, the conquest of weaker nations, and the rape of the environment.

Throughout the Era of Domination, egalitarian resurgences have appeared—the troubadours, St. Francis, the abolitionist movement, women's suffrage, the civil rights movement, the feminist movement. Rebellions by burghers, workers, peasants, black slaves, colonials, and women—all were and are against a system in which ranking is the primary principle of social organization. But none of them has been able to overturn belief in the fundamental right of some to dominate others.

The Future of God's Reign

The distinction between a partnership society and a domination society, between the reign of God and the Domination System, between the story of Jesus and the myth of redemptive violence, provides just the sharp contrast we need for distinguishing between what the Bible calls the way of God and the way of the world. And it supplies a framework for comprehending dozens of lesser struggles as parts of a single overarching conflict between two fundamentally incompatible human systems. Here at last we are able to see the links between efforts toward nuclear disarmament and feminism, struggles of campesinos for land and attempts to save whales, campaigns to counter fundamentalist book censorship and nonviolent efforts to topple dictatorships of the right and of the left.

The chart below may help to clarify the differences between the Domination System and God's domination-free order.

Societal Mode	The Domination System	God's Domination-free Order
Gender differences	Patriarchal; difference implies superiority/ inferiority	Equality of sexes; differences may lead to specialization but not to ranking
Power	Power over; power to take life, control, destroy	Power with; power to give, support, nurture life
	Win–lose	Win–win
	Domination	Partnership
	Competition	Competition/cooperation
Politics	Conquest	Diplomacy
	Autocracy	Democracy
	Authoritarian	Enabling
	Bureaucratic	Decentralized

Societal Mode	The Domination System	God's Domination-free Order
Economics	Exploitation, greed, privilege, inequality	Sharing, sufficiency, responsibility, equality
Religion	Male God—jealous, wrathful, punishing, lawgiving	Inclusive God-images—Mother/Father, loving/judging, compassionate/severe, merciful/demanding
Relationships	Ranking Domination hierarchies Slavery, classism, racism We/they Rigidity	Linking Actualization hierarchies Equality of opportunity We/we Flexibility
Transformative mode	Violence, force, war Suppression of conflict	Nonviolent confrontation, negotiation, inclusiveness Nonviolent conflict resolution
Ecological stance	Exploitation, control, contempt	Harmony, cooperation, respect
Logic	Either/or, analytic	Both/and, analytic/synthetic
Role of ego	Self-centered	Affiliation-oriented
Education	Indoctrinating	Enabling
Sexual responsibility	Subordination of women's reproductive capacities and sexual expression to male control	Control of sexuality by individuals in the light of community values
Eschatology	Status quo, holding and keeping power; "this world," "this evil aeon" Eternity in the future, injustice in the present	Cultural transformation, the reign of God, the coming aeon Eternity in the present, justice in the future[62]

God's reign does not represent the polar opposite of the Domination System. Otherwise it would need the latter to supply the tension of the opposites. The opposites are contained *within* God's reign. "Masculine" would not be androcratic, and "feminine" normative; rather, they would coexist and complement each other in an egalitarian order.

Eisler has agreed (in conversation) that the Goddess is not wholly adequate to human needs. God as Mother needs to be supplemented with the positive qualities of God as Father. Negative father qualities must be expunged from our God-image, and perhaps negative mother qualities as well. What we need are images that encompass the positive aspects of both. The issue of sexist language in our God-talk goes far deeper, then, than matters of simple justice and fairness to women. What is at stake is a veritable revolution in our God-images. Nothing could be more crucial, because *our images of God create us.* We will be better served, not by an androgynous view of deity (since we have no human models for that), but by a variety of God-images, each with its strengths and liabilities fully acknowledged: God as Mother, God as Father, God as Lover, God as Wisdom/Sophia/Shekinah, God as Friend, God as Judge, God as the Human, and so on.[63]

Without a clear idea of the contrast between God's domination-free order and the Domination System, the gospel is proclaimed in a sociopolitical vacuum, a timeless, placeless, noncontextual, eternal nowhere. Gospel truths are handled like everlasting principles entirely unrelated to the specificity of any real world. And the Powers are consequently reduced to general structural constants ostensibly prevailing ineluctably everywhere and in every time.

In fact, the gospel has a very specific context, even if it has been essentially the same context for five thousand years: the Domination System. And the gospel has a specific response to that system: the liberating message of Jesus. *The gospel is a context-specific remedy for the evils of the Domination System.* This means that the overthrow of any particular manifestation of oppression can never satisfy the demands of the gospel if what replaces one form of domination is simply another. The gospel is thus permanently critical of every political program, reform, and revolution.

This does not mean that improvements are not possible, though we tend to fight for them piecemeal. Every act that weakens the Domination System strengthens the new order of God. The gospel message is not an ideal beyond realization. It is rather a continual lure toward the fullest conceivable life for all—the life intended for us by our loving Mother/Father God.

The gospel is not *just* a remedy for domination. It also deals with sickness and death, finitude and faithlessness, tragedy and meaninglessness. But failure to acknowledge the centrality of its emancipatory message has often rendered the gospel politically reactionary and spiritually repressive. In the face of the collapse of communism in the East and secular optimism in the West, perhaps we can now see the gospel for what it has always been: the most powerful antidote for domination the world has ever known.

Only against a backdrop so vast do we see the world-historic significance of the liberation struggles that have come to fruition especially these past two hundred years:

- the rise and spread of democracy as a check on centralized power wielded only by a few;
- the abolition of slavery;
- attempts to develop alternative economic systems;
- the women's movement;
- the nonviolence movement;
- the civil rights movement;
- the human rights movement;
- the ecology movement;
- liberation theology;
- the gay rights movement (rejecting yet another way sexuality is used to disempower people and deprive them of choice).

The sheer density of these efforts in the past two centuries suggests that our conflict-ridden times are in fact part of a larger groundswell of protest against domination. We must not let the intensity of conflict blind us to the significance of these struggles; indeed, the desire for a more just order increases rather than decreases societal conflict. Rather than feel discouraged at the immensity of the task, we should take heart at the tremendous changes made in so short a time.

In Parts Two through Four I focus on the content of Jesus' liberating message to a world under the Domination System. But first we need to understand more fully the nature of the present scheme of things. The Powers are not that system; they are merely the individual institutions and structures deployed under the overall aegis of the Domination System. The Domination System is what obtains when an entire network of Powers becomes hell-bent on control. The Domination System is, so to speak, the system of the Powers, in a satanic parody of God, who might be called the System of the systems. The Domination System is thus equivalent to what the Bible so often means by the terms "world," "aeon," and "flesh." The Bible's insight into this system is essential if we are to oppose the Powers and the system that perpetuates them. How then does the Bible name the Domination System?

The owners of the land came onto the land, or more often a spokesman for the owners came. . . . Some of the owner men were kind because they hated what they had to do, and some of them were angry because they hated to be cruel, and some of them were cold because they had long ago found that one could not be an owner unless one were cold. And all of them were caught in something larger than themselves. . . . If a bank or a finance company owned the land, the owner man said, The Bank—or the Company—needs—wants—insists—must have—as though the Bank or the Company were a monster, with thought and feeling, which had ensnared them. These last would take no responsibility for the banks or the companies because they were men and slaves, while the banks were machines and masters all at the same time. . . . The owner men sat in the cars and explained. You know the land is poor. You've scrabbled at it long enough, God knows.

The squatting tenant men nodded and wondered and drew figures in the dust, and yes, they knew, God knows. If the dust only wouldn't fly. If the top would only stay on the soil, it might not be so bad. . . .

Well, it's too late. And the owner men explained the workings and the thinkings of the monster that was stronger than they were. . . . You see, a bank or a company . . . those creatures don't breathe air, don't eat side-meat. They breathe profits; they eat the interest on money. If they don't get it, they die the way you die without air, without side-meat. It is a sad thing, but it is so. It is just so. . . . The bank—the monster has to have profits all the time. It can't wait. It'll die. No, taxes go on. When the monster stops growing, it dies. It can't stay one size. . . .

We have to do it. We don't like to do it. But the monster's sick. Something's happened to the monster. . . .

Sure, cried the tenant men, but it's our land. We measured it and broke it up. We were born on it, and we got killed on it, died on it. Even if it's no good, it's still ours. . . .

We're sorry. It's not us. It's the monster. The bank isn't like a man.

Yes, but the bank is only made of men.

No, you're wrong there—quite wrong there. The bank is something else than men. It happens that every man in a bank hates what the bank does, and yet the bank does it. The bank is something more than men, I tell you. It's the monster. Men made it, but they can't control it.

John Steinbeck,
The Grapes of Wrath[1]

3. Naming the Domination System ·

The New Testament is thoroughly familiar with the Domination System, and has specific terms for describing it. In this chapter we examine three terms whose real meaning has sadly been obscured for many readers of the Bible. They are the Greek words *kosmos* (world), *aiōn* (age), and *sarx* (flesh). With these terms the biblical writers named the Domination System and thus stripped it, for those who understood, of its invisibility and legitimacy.

Kosmos: The Domination System

The Greek word *kosmos* means, variously, world, universe, the creation, humanity, the planet earth, the theater of history.[2] These conventional usages of *kosmos*/"world" are roughly similar in Greek and English. But alongside them, there is in the New Testament another usage that is quite unique in that period. It refers to *the human sociological realm that exists in estrangement from God*.[3] "World" in the New Testament has this apparently contradictory range of meanings because it refers to the totality of human social existence. It is the good creation of a good Creator (John 1:10ab), it is estranged or fallen existence (John 1:10c and the vast majority of other references), and it is capable of redemption (John 12:47).

In John's Gospel, where the term is given the status of a central theological category,[4] Jesus is depicted as retorting to the high priest at his arraignment, "I have spoken openly to the world (*kosmos*), I have always taught in synagogue and in the Temple" (John 18:20).[5] The parallelism in this sentence indicates that here *kosmos* includes at least the central religious institutions of Judaism, where Jesus has declared his message. The term thus has a structural sense. It refers, in this instance, to a religious system that, as the author portrays it, is unaware of its alienation from God.

51

Because the range of meanings assigned to the term "world" is so wide, I suggest that the special New Testament sense of world as an alienating and alienated ethos may be translated more meaningfully as "system."[6]

For example, in South Africa, many blacks are fully aware that they are fighting the apartheid system, not merely white people. They know that they cannot gain freedom simply by changing the color of the people at the top and leaving the system intact. When police are at the door, people inside will warn, "The System is here." When they see propaganda on television, they quip, "The System is lying again." Of a strike: "We're struggling against the System." According to Albert Nolan, the most effective way to get a black to stop behaving in collusion with the government is to say, "You are supporting the System."[7]

In the light of our understanding of the Domination System, the translation of *kosmos* as "system" opens a new dimension of meaning. "The System (*kosmos*) cannot hate you," Jesus is shown as telling his own brothers, who refuse to believe in him; "but it hates me because I testify against it that its works are evil" (John 7:7). Whenever Christians have understood this as meaning that the *physical world* is evil, they have tended to reject the created order, sexuality, and even their own bodies, and to manifest open contempt for efforts at political change. "System" yields an entirely different meaning, however, one far closer to John's intent, which cannot have been to despise the creation that this gospel itself affirms was created by God through the word (1:1-5). But the Domination System does hate Jesus, regards him as a mortal threat, and sees to his brutal execution: it hates him because he testified against it that its works were evil.

Thus when the Pharisees challenge Jesus' authority to attack their religious order, he responds, "You are of this System, I am not of this System" (John 8:23). Again, as long as *kosmos* in this statement was translated as "world," the impression was given that Jesus was otherworldly, nonhuman, a "docetic" (only "seeming") person: "I am not of this *world*." With the meaning "system," however, his statement is literally true. He belonged to God's system. He was not "of" the Domination System. Rejection of the *kosmos*, as John H. Elliott remarks, is not antiworldly but antiestablishment.[8]

Those who belong to the Domination System cannot comprehend the values displayed by Jesus, or understand why he is turning their world upside down. Theirs is a hermetically sealed language-system: "They belong to the Domination System (*kosmos*); therefore what they say is determined by that System, and that System listens to them" (1 John 4:5). Thus the writer of Ephesians can speak of existence in the System as a living death: You "were spiritually dead all the time that you drifted along on the stream of this world's ideas of living (*kosmos*)" (Eph. 2:2, Phillips, 1st ed.). Literally, the concluding phrase runs,

"You walked according to the *aiōn* of this *kosmos*." This *kosmos* is the prevailing world-atmosphere that we breathe in like toxic air, often without realizing it.

Nazi Germany provides a striking example. As early as 1923, D. H. Lawrence, with his astonishing capacity to discern developments at their inception, accurately described the new spiritual atmosphere that was possessing Germany:

> It is as if life had retreated eastwards. As if the Germanic life were slowly ebbing away from contact with western Europe, ebbing to the deserts of the east. . . . Returning again to the fascination of the destructive east, that produced Attila. . . . at night you feel strange things stirring in the darkness, strange feelings stirring out of this still unconquered Black Forest. You stiffen your backbone and you listen to the night. There is a sense of danger. It is not the people. They don't seem dangerous. Out of the very air comes a sense of danger, a queer, *bristling* feeling of uncanny danger.
>
> Something has happened. Something has happened which has not yet eventuated. The old spell of the old world has broken, and the old, bristling, savage spirit has set in. . . . Something has happened to the human soul, beyond all help. . . . It is a fate; nobody now can alter it. . . . At the same time, we have brought it about ourselves—by a Ruhr occupation, by an English nullity, and by a German false will. We have done it ourselves. But apparently it was not to be helped.[9]

The "atmosphere" that Lawrence so clairvoyantly discerned in Germany can be detected in any setting within the Domination System, even when it is less portentous. This spirit-killing atmosphere penetrates everything, teaching us not only what to believe, but what we can value and even what we can see.

It teaches us what to *believe*: it offers us the acceptable beliefs that society at any given time declares to be credible. The current world-atmosphere has decreed that spirits are not real, nor God, nor miracles, nor spiritual healing. Therefore no respectable intellectual discourse is permitted on these themes. Oddly enough, acceptable beliefs keep changing, even from decade to decade, so that the arbitrary character of these pontifications soon becomes embarrassingly apparent.

A case in point would be the attitude of historians toward spiritual healing. In the early part of this century, biblical scholars of a critical bent argued that the healing stories in the Gospels could not have happened, since they would have violated the "laws" of the Newtonian universe. After the development of psychosomatic medicine (spurred by the study of shell-shock victims in World War I), scholars changed their tune a bit; now Jesus could have healed people having psychosomatic illnesses, but the rest of the miracle tradition were legends invented to exalt Jesus. Today, in the light of new studies on the placebo effect, scientific research on paranormal psychology and meditation, and the development of a new worldview based on the new physics (in which laws have been replaced by probabilities), the idea of what is acceptable to believe is shifting again. The point is that these changes were not based on new data from the first century; they were totally the result of what the prevailing worldview countenanced as "believable."

The world-atmosphere teaches us what we can *value*. In the Domination System generally, it teaches us to value power. In any particular society, however, power is given specific shape by the peculiar conditions of the time. What characterizes our society is the unique value ascribed to money.[10] People in every age have coveted wealth, but few societies have lionized the entrepreneur as ours does. Aristocratic societies—and most societies have been aristocratic— have tended to look down on acquisitiveness and to despise merchants. Modern capitalism, by contrast, has made wealth the highest value. Our entire social system has become an "economy"; no earlier society would have characterized itself thus. Profit is the highest social good. Consumerism has become the only universally available mode of participation in modern society. The work ethic has been replaced by the consumption ethic, the cathedral by the skyscraper, the hero by the billionaire, the saint by the executive, religion by ideology. The Kingdom of Mammon exercises constraint by invisible chains and drives its slaves with invisible prods. (How rare it is for rich people to say, "I have enough.") But Mammon is wiser in its way than the dictator, for money enslaves not by force but by love.

The world-atmosphere also teaches us what to *see*. "One can say not only that as individuals we live within a sociocultural organism but also that the sociocultural organism lives within us. Not only are we individual units within an organized society, but organized society is represented and incarnated within our brains."[11] Whatever the System tells our brains is real is what we are allowed to notice; everything else must be ignored. *"We give the system the power to make the known unknown."*[12] Thus we are taught to mistrust our own experiences.

Every observation is a *directed* observation, that is, an observation for or against a point of view. Every mind is a "contaminated mind," a mind constructed of a network of suppositions and assumptions. All descriptions are paradigm-conditioned and value-laden. A Skinnerian and a Freudian will not only describe the same behavior in incompatible ways, but their conceptual frameworks actually cause them to *see* different behaviors. The *observed* behavior is different in each case.[13] The result of this limitation on what we are allowed to see is a miniaturization of our living world.

These limitations of sight are to a degree merely a consequence of finitude. But to some extent they are also the result of a system that is deliberately blinding us to God's true intent for humanity: "For judgment I came into this System, that those who do not see may see, and that those who see"—here the religious authorities, who believe themselves to be God's spokesmen, but who have reduced religion to a male club that excludes all but the morally upright and the financially privileged—"may become blind" (John 9:39). "And this is the judgment"—the last judgment, moved right up to the present moment of encounter with this truth—"that the light has come into the System, and people loved darkness rather than light" (John 3:19).

As Rome's representative, Pilate does not—cannot—understand that there is another order of reality breaking in on the hegemony of violence that, under the temporary guise of Rome, now straddles the world. Jesus answers him: "The New Reality (*basileia*) of which I speak is not of this old System of Domination (*kosmos*); if it were, my aides would fight, that I not be delivered to the Jewish authorities. But the New Reality of which I speak does not take its rise from the Domination System (*kosmos*)" (John 18:36).[14] How different that sounds from the usual translation, "My kingdom is not of this world"! The values of the Domination System and those of Jesus are incommensurable. Violence cannot cure violence. The New Reality eschews violence, but it has its own, quite amazing forms of power, which those inured to violence cannot comprehend.

Jesus discovered that there were many, both women and men, ready to be delivered from the Domination System, who longed for the equalitarian, non-hierarchical sufficiency of the reign of God. To these Jesus declares: "What does it profit people, to gain the whole System (*kosmos*) and forfeit their lives?" (Mark 8:36).[15] "Those who hate their life in this System will keep it for *aionic* life" (John 12:25)—not an injunction to self-loathing, but a very down-to-earth observation: only those who find their lives detestable under the Powers That Be will have the courage to reject the latter's overblown authority.

> Consider your own call, brothers and sisters: not many of you were wise by human standards (*kata sarka*), not many were powerful, not many were of noble birth. But God chose what appears foolish to the System in order to shame the wise; God chose what appears weak to the System in order to shame the strong, God chose what appears low and despicable to the System, mere nothings, to reduce to nothing things that are.
>
> (1 Cor. 1:26-28)

So also the Epistle of James: "Has not God chosen those who are poor in the Domination System to be rich in faith and heirs of the New Reality (*basileia*) that he has promised to those who love God?" (2:5). "Do you not know that friendship with the Domination System is enmity with God?" (4:4).

Those who once had no hope and "were without God in the System" (Eph. 2:12), and who have now had their eyes opened, must jettison the socialization that held them complicit in their own oppression and that of others.

Do not love the Domination System or the things pertaining to it. If anyone loves that System, the love of the Abba [loving divine parent] is not in that person. For everything in that System—the desire engendered by an alienated body and a wandering eye and the arrogant pretensions of those who are full of themselves— is not of the Abba but is begotten by the Domination System itself. That System is passing away with all its perverse desires, but the person who does what God wants done remains "into the *aiōn*" that is coming.

(1 John 2:15-17)[16]

Those liberated from the tyranny of the old order receive a new, holy spirit— "not the spirit of the Domination System (*kosmos*), but the Spirit that is from God" (1 Cor. 2:12); "the Spirit of truth, which the Domination System is not able to receive, because it can neither recognize it nor comprehend it. You know it, because it is already in your midst, and will be inside your very beings" (John 14:17). This new Spirit resocializes believers into the New Reality.

Not only do those liberated from the old System receive a new Spirit, they receive a new world. "What is real," asserts Jürgen Habermas, "is that which can be experienced according to the interpretations of a prevailing symbolic system."[17] Most symbolic systems have served to shore up the power and privileges of those at the top. In the New Testament, by contrast, the insights of the exodus were expanded by the revelation of the cross and resurrection; the particularity of a slave revolt by an oppressed people, the Israelites, was universalized by the recognition of the nature of the Domination System. Consequently, those whose eyes had been opened by the exodus and the cross now saw a *different* reality, a new "world." What had been invisible—the all-pervasive exploitation of the many by the few—was rendered visible, judged, and found wanting. And those with this new sight needed no longer to subject themselves to the delusions that formerly shaped their alienated picture of the "world."

In that Spirit, Paul can exult, "May I never boast of anything except the cross of our Lord Jesus Christ, by which the Domination System (*kosmos*)"— which crucified Jesus—"has been crucified to me, and I to that System" (Gal. 6:14). The Johannine community also celebrates the great reversal of the cross: "In the old System you face persecution. But take courage," Jesus says; "I have vanquished the Domination System!" (John 16:33). The disciples are still "in" the System (John 17:11), but not of it: "If the System hates you, be aware that it hated me before it hated you. If you would collaborate with the System, the System would love you for it; but because you have turned your backs on it (because I have extricated you from the System!), it hates you" (John 15:18-19). "Do not be astonished, brothers and sisters, that the System hates you" (1 John 3:13). For "the one who is in you is greater than the one who is in the

System" (1 John 4:4). "For whatever is born of God conquers the Domination System. And this is the victory that overcomes that System: our faith" (1 John 5:4).

Not surprisingly, Satan is the presiding spirit of the Domination System. "I will no longer talk much with you, for the ruler (*archōn*) of this System (*kosmos*) is coming. He has no power over me; but I do as the Abba has commanded me, so that the System may know that I love the Abba" (John 14:30-31). To love openly the all-embracing divine Parent is to undermine in the most fundamental way the mind-set of domination, with its satanic lust for control over others and the world. Hence Satan's most insidious temptations include offering Jesus all the power of the Domination System itself, if only he will surrender his soul to its presiding spirit: "Then the devil led him up and showed him in an instant all the kingdoms of the Domination System. And the devil said to him, 'To you I will give their glory and all this authority; for it has been given over to me, and I give it to anyone I please" (Luke 4:5-6).[18]

When 1 John 5:19 says then that "the whole *kosmos* lies under the power of the Evil One," this obviously does not refer to the world as God's good creation. It can only mean that the Domination System is inspired, sustained, and presided over by Satan. The psychologist David Bakan characterizes the satanic as self-assertion, self-protection, and self-expansion; the formation of separations, isolation, alienation; the repression of thought, feeling, and impulse.[19] Jesus has come, the Gospel of John declares, in order to identify and judge this everyday spirituality as satanic: "the ruler (*archōn*) of this System of Domination has been condemned" (John 16:11).

Perhaps the human race needed to "fall" upward, as it were, into autonomy and consciousness, bought at the terrible cost of losing our native fusion with phenomena. But human beings cannot indefinitely live alienated from their groundedness in nature, their communion with others, or their relatedness with the divine. Therefore humanity needed a revealer and a savior: "Christ Jesus came into the System (*kosmos*) to save those who have missed the point of living" (1 Tim. 1:15).[20]

When it is referring to the alienated and alienating system of oppression, the Gospel of John treats *kosmos* as a wholly negative category. But as I mentioned earlier, *kosmos* can also refer to the created universe, or to humanity as the object of God's love and concern, or to the human social order as capable of divine redemption.[21] As the Domination System is transformed into the New Reality of God, it loses its malevolent character and becomes a neutral concept, virtually synonymous with "humanity" or "human society." This ambiguity in the use of *kosmos* is not caused by confusion on the Fourth Evangelist's part, but is a consequence of the complexity of the perception of the world as being simultaneously God's good creation, fallen, and capable of redemption. "I did not come in order to condemn the System, but to heal the System" (John 12:47). "This [Jesus] is indeed the savior of the System" (4:42). "Behold, the Lamb of God, who takes away the sins of the System" (1:29).

As chaos theory teaches us, initially small fluctuations can lead to large-scale transformations of whole systems. When systems reach states of disequilibrium, says Eisler, chaotic or strange attractors may sometimes with relative rapidity and unpredictability become the nuclei for building a wholly new system. Consider the attractive power of democracy in Eastern Europe, the Soviet Union, and China and the unprecedented transformations it evoked in 1989, for example. Or there may be a more gradual or subtle transformation, as former attractors (those ideas, myths, and institutions that act like magnets to provide cohesiveness to a system) lose some of their attractiveness and new attractors become progressively more desirable.[22]

However it comes, then, God's system will replace the Domination System, not by violent confrontation, but as increasing numbers of people find themselves drawn toward its values: "You see, you can do nothing. Look, the *kosmos* has gone after him" (John 12:19). The old order begins to lose its intelligibility: "Has not God made foolish the wisdom of the Domination System (*kosmos*)? For since, in the wisdom of God, the System did not know God through wisdom, God decided, through the foolishness of our proclamation, to save those who believe" (1 Cor. 1:20-21).

Only God can bring about a new system in its entirety; a new kind of earthly existence will be given us by the selective process itself. And yet, though it cannot be built, it is our task to try to create the conditions that would make that selection possible. Prayer, persuasion, and social struggle thus occupy the community that lives "as if" God's reign has already begun.

Until the new order of God arrives, believers are "to deal with the old System as though they had no dealings with it. For the basic structure (*schēma*) of the dominant System (*kosmos*) is passing away" (1 Cor. 7:31).[23] "I do not pray that you should take them out of the System," for that is the theater in which God's sovereignty must be established, "but that you keep them from the Evil One," that is, from succumbing to the System's spirituality (John 17:15). The Domination System will attempt to crush every vestige of authentic living. "The System has hated them, because they have disavowed allegiance to the System" (John 17:14). "If you belonged to the System, the System would love you as its own. Because you do not belong to the System, but I have chosen you out of the System—therefore the System hates you" (John 15:19).[24] Ignatius of Antioch, martyred for his faith about 107 C.E., perceptively observed that "the greatness of Christianity lies in its being hated by the world [read 'Domination

System'], not in its being convincing to it" (Rom. 3:3). "You will weep and mourn," says John, "but the System will rejoice"; like a woman in travail, "you will have pain, but your pain will turn into joy" (John 16:20), as you help midwife the birth of a new and happier system.

Aiōn: The Domination Epoch

The second biblical term, often interchangeable with *kosmos* and translated "world" in the English versions,[25] is the mysterious word *aiōn*. Just as the imagery of *kosmos* is spatial or systemic, that of *aiōn* is temporal. It conjures up a vision, not of the structure of reality, but of the flow of time from its inception: "time like an ever-flowing stream." Hence it could be used for the created order in its temporal ongoingness: God "created the aions" or world-periods (Heb. 1:2; the NRSV conveys the temporal sense by translating "worlds," indicating a succession of epochs). Time began: "the aions were created by the word of God" (Heb. 11:3). Time past is time "from of old"—literally, "from the *aiōn*" (Luke 1:70). When a blind man is cured people cry, "Never since the world began [lit., 'not out of the *aiōn*'] has it been heard that anyone opened the eyes of a person born blind" (John 9:32).[26] Any major time period in the total temporal flow can be categorized as an *aiōn*, used here in the same way as our English derivative "aeon," a long time.[27]

The present world-period, however, is under the power of evil. Here again, as with *kosmos*, the term *aiōn* takes on a unique sense in some New Testament passages. Thus the *kosmos* can be called "the present evil epoch (*aiōn*)" (Gal. 1:4), organized under Satan, "the god of this world-period (*aiōn*)" who "has blinded the minds of the unbelievers, to keep them from seeing the light of the gospel of the glory of Christ" (2 Cor. 4:4).[28] Satan's subordinates can even be characterized by their relationship to this period: they are "the *archōns* (rulers) of this *aiōn*, who are doomed to perish" (1 Cor. 2:6; see also 2:8).

Where John uses *kosmos* to unmask the Domination System from a structural point of view, Paul prefers *aiōn* for demarcating what we might call the Domination Epoch. This period is not just fallen time, time characterized by the loss of presence, clock time, time ticking down toward death, time as a commodity not to be wasted, an enemy that must be "fought," a precious fluid that we cannot hold in our hands. All these point to natural human limitations. But time under the sway of the Domination System becomes more sinister. It marks the intolerable extension of oppression from generation to generation and century to century, presided over by Satan, the god of the Domination Epoch.[29]

Liberation thus must involve the healing of our relationship to time. We must "redeem the time," as Col. 4:5 puts it. Evil in history was not always present; it had an origin in time. Likewise, evil will not always exist; it has an end in time, when "this *aiōn*" is superseded by "the *aiōn* to come" (Matt. 12:32). Thus, like "world," "time" is good, fallen, and must itself be redeemed.

Lest we overstress the simultaneity of creation, fall, and redemption, we must also acknowledge that they appear in temporal sequence in the Christian story: once, now, and then. And "now" is the era of the Fall, when the created goodness of the social order may only flicker dimly, or be repressed, and the redeemed future of these orders is only glimpsed momentarily, if at all.

The era of the Fall is characterized by "the cares of the *aiōn*," which choke the liberating message that might set its victims free (Mark 4:19 par.). People grow up regarding its sexual stereotypes, class attitudes, and racial prejudices as normal: we "walked according to the *aiōn* of this *kosmos*" (Eph. 2:2)—a remarkable phrase that combines both the structural and the temporal elements of the alienating system into a single God-hostile front.

Those who are "in love with this present *aiōn*" (2 Tim. 4:10), the "children of this *aiōn*," are "more shrewd in dealing with their own generation than the children of light" (Luke 16:8). Here "generation" (*genea*) further limits *aiōn* to the present or currently living representatives of the Domination Epoch.

Jesus gave himself "to set us free from the present evil *aiōn*" (Gal. 1:4). Paul enjoins his readers, "Do not be conformed to this Domination Epoch (*aiōn*), but be transformed by the renewing of your minds" (Rom. 12:2). "If you think that you are wise in the ways of this Domination Epoch (*aiōn*), you should become fools so that you may become wise. For the wisdom of this System (*kosmos*) is foolishness to God" (1 Cor. 3:18).

> Where is the intellectual? Where is the scholar? Where is the debater of this Domination Epoch (*aiōn*)? Has not God rendered ridiculous the wisdom of the Domination System (*kosmos*)? For since, in the craftiness of God, the Domination System did not know God through wisdom, God decided, through the nonsense that we declare, to save those who believe.
>
> (1 Cor. 1:20-21)

The Powers attempted to silence the revealer of God's "nonsense":

> Yet among the mature we do speak wisdom, though it is not the received wisdom of the Domination Epoch (*aiōn*) or its rulers (*archontōn*), who are already in process of being superseded. But we impart a mysterious wisdom from God that has been, till now, suppressed (*tēn apokekrymmenēn*)—a wisdom that God established as true from the very beginning ["before the aions"] for our transformation into beings of light. None of the rulers (*archontōn*) of this Domination Epoch (*aiōn*) understood what God was doing; for if they had, they would not have crucified the one who dispenses that light.
>
> (1 Cor. 2:6-8)[30]

While the New Testament speaks of the coming *aiōn* or age when the divine plan will be realized, it says nothing about another *world* (*kosmos*) coming in the future.[31] God's triumph over the Domination System will take place in the created order as a transformation of fallen reality into the reality it was intended to be. The Bible knows of successive aions, but only one world, the good creation of God, which will be redeemed from "its bondage to decay" (Rom. 8:21) when a new social order of sharing, partnership, compassion, and equality will replace the politics of ranking, oppression, and violence.

The days of the Domination Epoch are numbered. It will be supplanted by an "aion that is coming" at "the end of the aions" (Mark 10:30//Luke 18:30; 1 Cor. 10:11)—"that in the aions to come God might show the immeasurable riches of the divine grace in kindness toward us in Christ Jesus" (Eph. 2:7). Christ will "set us free from the present evil aion, according to the will of our God and Abba; to whom be glory into the aions of the aions [for ever and ever, for all eternity, time infinitely extended]" (Gal. 1:4-5).

It is a testimony to the wisdom of the early Christians that they were able to perceive the fundamental incompatibility of the new order Jesus preached with the dominant order of their day, and that they were able to arm themselves against losing hope by the vision of a transformed future. The expectation of a return of Jesus functioned mythologically to keep alive the conviction that the values he incarnated would be vindicated in humanity's future. How ironic, and utterly predictable, that his return became weighed down with androcratic fantasies of revenge, violence, and autocratic rule, so that at his second coming Jesus would do everything he so resolutely refused to do at his first.

The *aiōn* to come is properly that mode of human existence in which domination is no more, where God's will for liberated human life is given institutional and structural forms (for there can be no human life without institutions and structures, not even in the Reign of God), where the "reign of this *kosmos*," that old Domination System, has become "the reign of our Lord and of his Christ, and God shall reign into the aions of the aions" (Rev. 11:15).

Sarx: Dominated Existence

Perhaps the most unfortunate mistranslation in English Bibles has been the use of "flesh" for the Pauline phrase, *kata sarka. Sarx* can refer to the physical substance we are made of or to the physical body; it can be used for the self or one's being, or for human beings or humanity in general. Less frequently it denotes physical genetic descent or ethnicity, or earthly existence, or, rarely, sexual desire.[32] But its most striking and theologically weighty use, found especially in Paul, is in reference to the self in its alienated mode.[33] Life lived "according to the flesh" (*kata sarka*) denotes the self externalized and subjugated to the opinions of others. It is the self socialized into a world of inauthentic values, values that lead it away from its own centeredness in God. It is the beachhead that the Domination System establishes in our beings. *Sarx* means more than "the pursuit of the merely human, the earthly-transitory";[34] it is pursuit of the values of the Domination System.

"Fleshly" or "carnal" refers to a life that has abandoned the transcendent and become fixated on personal satisfactions. But these are not, as popular piety thinks, merely lustful desires, for Paul lists as "fleshly" even asceticism and self-denial when they are practiced as a way of trying to secure one's life by one's own power (Col. 2:20-23). Everything an alienated person does is infected by alienation, even the quest for God. Therefore God has taken the initiative and come searching for us.

The best paraphrase I can render for *kata sarka* is "dominated existence"— a life lived according to the dictates of the Domination System. The term as it is used in the New Testament in no way denotes rejection of the body. It refers to existence robbed of its authenticity by the imposition of domination. Like *kosmos* and *aiōn*, *sarx* also partakes of the simultaneity of creation, fall, and needed redemption.

Nor does salvation entail deliverance from the body. On the contrary, what we await is precisely "the redemption of our *body* (*sōma*)" (Rom. 8:23). Paul, writing Greek, is perhaps thinking of the Hebrew term *nephesh*, which means the breathing person, the total self, the animated body, the total human being, body and soul together. Acts 2:26 reflects the same view: "my flesh (*sarx*) will live in hope" (Acts 2:26, citing Ps. 16:9). We will not cease to have bodies in the new age to come, but they will be transformed; Paul speaks of them paradoxically as "spiritual bodies" (1 Cor. 15:35-57). In the meantime, our bodies are the locus of conflict in which God and the Powers struggle to become embodied.

> For though we are living in the Domination System (*en sarki*), we are not fighting it by means dictated by the Domination System (*kata sarka*); for the weapons of our warfare are not the System's (*sarkika*), but have divine power to tear down defenses. We overthrow rational calculations and everything that exalts itself against the knowledge of God, taking captive every thought into the obedience exemplified by Christ.
>
> (2 Cor. 10:3-5)

Those who enter the new reality of God receive, not just a new heart and a new spirit, but a transformed relationship to the world, to time, and even to their bodies. That is the pledge of the One who says, "See, I am making all things new" (Rev. 21:5).

• • •

The Domination System, having suppressed the egalitarian order that may have preexisted it, or that at very least coexisted brokenly alongside it, has become the object of God's wrath and redemptive activity. That System, named in the New Testament chiefly by the terms "world," "aeon," and "flesh," has woven around itself the magical ideological armor of the myth of redemptive violence, by which it shelters, for the very few, fantastic privileges denied the many. Yet the exploited many are nevertheless beguiled into supporting the system that oppresses them, even to the point of voluntarily offering up their own lives. They have been "taken captive through that type of philosophy and rationalistic sophistry which has its origins in human tradition, in the fundamental assumptions of the Domination System (*stoicheia tou kosmou*) and not in Christ" (Col. 2:8*). Such an irrational state of affairs cannot be resolved by pure rationality. It requires a greater wonder, a divine mystery, seemingly impossible yet true—a redemptive act of God that exposes the Powers and their system and works toward their subjugation, transformation, and healing.

Many will find it foreign to speak of the redemption of the Powers. Their Christianity is one of escape from the Powers to a life in the "world" beyond. But that entire conception is based on the mistranslation of the terms *kosmos*, *aiōn*, and *sarx*. What does it mean to speak, not only of our salvation, but of the salvation of the socio-spiritual orders themselves?

The greatness of Christianity lies in its being hated by the Domination System (*kosmos*), not in its being convincing to it.

Ignatius of Antioch,
To the Romans 3:3

4. The Nature of the Domination System

The good news is that God not only liberates us from the Powers, but liberates the Powers as well. The gospel is not a dualistic myth of good and evil forces vying for ascendancy, as in the myth of redemptive violence. It is a sublimely subtle drama about the intertwining of good and evil in all of historical reality. The Powers are not simply evil. They are a bulwark against anarchy, and a patron, repository, and inspirer of art. They inculcate values that encourage interdependency, mutual care, and social cohesiveness. They encourage submission of personal desires to the general good of everyone. Their evil is not intrinsic, but rather the result of idolatry. Therefore they can be redeemed. The New Testament presents this insight as a drama in three simultaneous acts:

> The Powers are good,
> the Powers are fallen,
> the Powers will be redeemed.

The Powers Are Good

In the hymn of the cosmic Christ in Col. 1:16-17, the Powers are described as having been created in, through, and for Christ. "For in him all things in heaven and on earth were created, things visible and invisible, whether thrones or dominions or rulers or powers—all things have been created through him and for him. He himself is before all things, and in him all things hold together."[1]

The Colossians hymn is the brash assertion, against the grain of human suffering, that the Principalities and Powers that visit the world with so much

65

evil are not autonomous, not independent, not eternal, not utterly depraved. The social structures of reality are creations of God. Because they are creatures, they are mortal, limited, responsible to God, and made to serve the humanizing purposes of God in the world.

In the verses that precede the hymn of Colossians these Powers are referred to collectively as "the dominion of darkness" from which believers have been delivered (Col. 1:13). Ernst Käsemann has argued that this hymn was sung at the liturgy of baptism, and that it marks a change of spheres of influence, from the sphere of darkness (Col. 1:12-14 being added to give the hymn a "liturgical introduction") to the sphere of light. Believers are delivered from the Domination System and freed from the enslaving power of the old aeon. "In baptism the Christian changes from one jurisdiction to another. Henceforth he belongs not to the cosmos, but to the Cosmocrator."[2]

Following the hymn, likewise, Paul reminds his readers that they were "once estranged and hostile in mind, doing evil deeds" (1:21). The context therefore makes clear, whereas the hymn itself does so only by allusion (v. 20), that these Powers are or have become hostile to the purposes of God in their creation.[3] Nevertheless, the hymn itself celebrates their creation in, through, and for Christ. They are not demonized as utterly evil; they are the good creations of a good God, and God, in the Genesis story of creation, creates no demons. But their rationale for existence is to serve the human needs and values revealed as ultimate by the identification of Jesus with Wisdom and Christ.

These Powers are the necessary social structures of human life, and it is not a matter of indifference to God that they exist.[4] God *made* them. And all this is asserted—chanted, intoned, sung—into the teeth of the everyday experience of institutional and structural evil.

Without institutionalization, ideas never materialize into action. Institutions are indispensable for human existence, and they have a right to be concerned about their own survival. But they must keep this concern penultimate, not ultimate. For this reason, von Rad reminds us, the account of creation in Genesis does not end in chapter 2, with the creation of the world, but in chapter 10, with the creation of the nations. The meaning is clear: humanity is not possible apart from its social institutions.[5] Subsystems, like people, continually need to weigh their needs against the needs of the system as a whole. "Order is not sufficient," wrote Whitehead. "What is required, is something much more complex. It is order entering upon novelty; so that the massiveness of order does not degenerate into mere repetition; and so that the novelty is always reflected upon a background of system."[6]

Even in their apostasy and dereliction from their created vocation, the Powers are incapable of separating themselves from the principle of coherence. When subsystems idolatrously violate the harmony of the whole by elevating their own purposes to ultimacy, they are still no more able to achieve autonomy than a cancer can live apart from its host. Like a cancer, again, they are able to do evil only by means of processes imbedded in them as a result of their good creation.

We must be careful here. To assert that God created the Powers does not imply that God endorses any particular Power at any given time. God did not create capitalism or socialism, but there must be some kind of economic system. The simultaneity of creation, fall, and redemption means that God at one and the same time *upholds* a given political or economic system, since some such system is required to support human life; *condemns* that system insofar as it is destructive of full human actualization; and *presses for its transformation* into a more humane order. Conservatives stress the first, revolutionaries the second, reformers the third. The Christian is expected to hold together all three.

This is the point, and perhaps only this, of Rom. 13:1-7 ("Be subject to the governing authorities").[7] It does not legitimate blind obedience to an oppressive system. It says, rather, that governments are indispensable for the preservation of social order and protection against criminals and invaders. They are supposed to be a terror not to good conduct, but to bad (vv. 3-4). Oppressive regimes, however, are just the reverse: they reward bad conduct and are a terror to those who do good.[8]

To say that the Powers are created in, through, and for the cosmic Christ, then, does not imply endorsement of any particular economic or political system. What the hymn sings is recognition that it is God's plan for us to live in interrelationship with each other, and to this end God has determined that there will be subsystems whose sole purpose is to serve the human needs of the One who exemplifies and encompasses humanity.

An institution may place its own good above the general welfare. A corporation may cut corners on costs by producing defective products that endanger lives. Union leadership may become more preoccupied with extending its personal advantages than fighting for better working conditions for the rank and file. The point of the Colossians hymn is not that anything goes, but that no matter how greedy or idolatrous an institution becomes, it cannot escape the encompassing care and judgment of the One in and through and for whom it was created. In that One "all things hold together" (Col. 1:17—lit., "receive their systemic place"—*synistēmi*, the source of our word "system"). The Powers are inextricably locked into God's system, whose human face is revealed in Christ. They are answerable to God. And that means that every subsystem in the world is, in principle, redeemable.

We may pollute our water supply and the air we breathe with no regard for the future; but we are systemically inseparable from the ecosystem, and the judgment of the system rebounds on us in escalating carcinogenic illnesses. A nation can behave as if it did not belong to the world-system of nations, as did Nazi Germany, and can attempt to subordinate the system to itself; but its very attempt to do so mobilizes the wrath of the nations against it and brings about its own collapse. No subsystem that aspires to the status of God's system itself can long remain viable. The myth of Satan's rebellion and expulsion from heaven symbolically depicts the fate of any creature that lusts after ultimate power and authority.

The bound-togetherness celebrated by this hymn thus serves as the foundation of the ethic of nonviolence and the love of enemies. Nothing is outside the redemptive care and transforming love of God. The Powers are not intrinsically evil; they are only fallen. What sinks can be made to rise again. We are freed, then, from the temptation to satanize the perpetrators of evil. We can love our nation or church or school, not blindly, but critically, recalling it to its own highest self-professed ideals and identities. We can challenge these institutions to live up to the vocation that is theirs by virtue of their sheer createdness. We can oppose their actions while honoring their necessity.

For example, a factory is polluting the water and air of our city, and we want it cleaned up. We can engage in that struggle knowing that its employees need jobs, and that their families also are at risk from the pollution, just as ours are. We can talk without hatred to the hard-nosed representatives of the plant, because we know that they, and we, and this factory, are encompassed by the love of God, and exist to serve the One in and through and for whom we were all created. We do not have to struggle to bring this plant into the orbit of God's system. It is already there. We have only to remind its managers that it exists to serve values beyond itself (though this "reminding" may require a protracted boycott or strike).

Adam Smith himself acknowledged this when he wrote that the ultimate goal of a business is not to make a profit. Profit is just the means. The goal is the general welfare.[9] It is part of the church's task to remind corporations and businesses that profit is *not* the "bottom line," that as "creatures" of God they have as their divine vocation the achievement of human benefaction (Eph. 3:10). They do not exist for themselves. They were bought with a price (Col. 1:20). They belong to the God who ordains sufficiency for all.

The Powers Are Fallen

Talk of the Fall is not popular in a period when certain New Age and Eastern gurus are proclaiming our divinity; when secularism, by virtue of denying the spiritual realm, is incapable of conceiving of radical evil; when in legitimate reaction to the morbid Christian overemphasis on sin and guilt, many are emphasizing the goodness of creation and the open-endedness of our potentials (an emphasis I endorse).[10]

Nevertheless, the doctrine of the Fall is essential for understanding both ourselves and the Powers. And, curiously enough, it is part of the good news, a source of immense relief, and a sentinel against seduction. I submit (1) that the doctrine of the Fall provides an account of evil that acknowledges its brute reality while preserving the sovereignty and goodness of God and the creation; (2) that it is not just a temporal myth and thus did not simply happen "once upon a time," but is also a structural aspect of all personal and social existence; (3) that the doctrine of the Fall frees us from delusions about the perfectibility of ourselves and our institutions; and (4) that it reminds us that we cannot be saved from the Powers by anything within the Power System, but only by something that transcends it.

In the first place, the doctrine of the Fall affirms the radicality of evil. Frankly, most of us, myself included, simply do not *want* to believe in radical evil. The implications are too terrible. It violates the reasonable, middle-class paradigm to learn that children are kidnapped for prostitution rings, satan cults, and pornographic "snuff" movies (where actual murders are filmed).[11] And like most people when their paradigm is challenged, we question the data rather than our presuppositions. (I am thinking of those who deny that the Holocaust ever happened.) Thus when a friend of ours went to his colleagues in the peace community for support in dealing with a victim of satanic abuse, they responded by regarding him as deranged. Evil of such magnitude could not exist—this from people opposing the most insane evil of all, nuclear weapons!

Evil is within us (in Jungian terms, the personal "shadow") and among us (as collective "shadow"), but much of that can be raised to consciousness and transformed. We are speaking now of a deeper evil—a layer of sludge beneath the murky waters that can be characterized only as a hellish hatred of the light, of truth, of kindness and compassion, a brute lust for annihilation. It is the sedimentation of thousands of years of human choices for evil (not *wrong* choices merely, but actual choices *for* evil) that has precipitated Satan as the spirituality of evil. Call it what you will, it is real. The doctrine of the Fall is merely a mute pointer to that sludge, lest we deny its reality and foolishly attempt to erect a society on this base.[12]

Second, talk about a Fall is mythical language.[13] It is true that the myth is presented sequentially, as if it can be segmented into three chronological phases: once the Powers were good, then they fell, and in the future (tomorrow, next year, at the end of time) they will be redeemed. But the biblical myth is both temporal and timeless. A given Power can and, at one time or another, probably does manifest all three aspects simultaneously: it performs a necessary function and is created in, through, and for Christ; it is fallen; and it may experience moments when it becomes transparent to the purposes for which it was created. It is possible, right in the midst of the old reality, for both people and Powers to live in relative emancipation from the power of death.[14]

Past, present, and future are temporal realities, yet they are also gathered into the eternal now of today. The Creation, Fall, and Final Judgment are now, as the flat perspective of history opens out into the depth of eternity. The final subjugation of the Powers under Christ's feet will happen (1 Cor. 15:24-25), but it is already, in anticipation, experienced now (Eph. 1:19-23), in the new reality of resurrection existence. "Now is the judgment of the Domination System (*kosmos*), now shall the ruler of that System (*kosmos*) be cast out" (John 12:31*). The "heavenly" becomes efficacious now; we have already been raised up with Christ and made to sit "with him in the heavenly places" (Eph. 2:6). The final restoration of all things in harmonious unity is tasted now, fragmentarily, de-liciously—and gone. The reign of God is not "built," but sampled. We have a foretaste, an appetizer, an aperitif, a down payment (Rom. 8:23; 2 Cor. 1:22; 5:5; Eph. 1:14). We "have tasted the goodness of the word of God and the powers of the age to come" (Heb. 6:5). There may be no measurable progress (yes, some things do get better over time, but others get worse). There are just these blinding (or feeble) flashes of the beyond in our midst; just these moments of lucidity, when a subsystem offers itself to the whole; just these acts of sacrificial love, costly reminders of the cross at the heart of reality.

It is precisely this simultaneity of Creation, Fall, and Redemption, freed from literalistic temporalizing, that delivers us from naïveté regarding our personal or social powers for transformation. It liberates us from the illusion that at least some institutions are "good" and viable and within human direction, or can be rendered so by discipline or reform or revolution or displacement.[15] The Powers are at one and the same time ordained by God and in the power of Satan. They can, to some degree, be humanized, but they are still fallen. They can be open to transcendence, but they will still do evil. They may be benign, but within a Domination System of general malignancy. As Reinhold Niebuhr once remarked, no society ever achieved peace without incorporating a degree of injustice into its harmony,[16] and that will prove to be as true in the immediate future as in all previous periods.

The Powers are good, fallen, and redeemable all at once; and they were good, they fell, and they will be redeemed in God's domination-free order that is coming. This tension between the timeless and the temporal enables us to eye each successive sincerity, each new utopian solution or structural arrangement, with dispassionate realism. It can prevent our being swept away by new visions of transformation that as yet have no history of failures (as they surely will). It leads us to expect each new intervention for good to bring in its wake unintended consequences, some of them evil. We can join in struggles for social justice without being suckered by slogans promising what cannot be delivered and without crumbling under the inevitable setbacks and reverses. We can work for a society which will not make people good, but in which it will be easier for them to be good.

Third, the doctrine of the Fall frees us from delusions about the perfectibility of ourselves and our institutions, and from the diabolical belief that we are responsible for everything that happens. The very success of a reform effort helps to produce its decline, since the improved situation reduces the public outrage necessary to sustain opinion and activity on behalf of change. Social progress is thus self-limiting; every movement forward is usually followed by at least some movement back. Furthermore, we are usually able to understand only the system that is crumbling, not the one emerging. This means that our perception of reality generally arrives too late to save a society, but just in time to explain its demise.

Dreams of perfection are fatal to social change movements. As Michael Lerner points out, despite their vision of a better society, such movements are made up of idealists who are far from perfect. They are attempting to change a society that has already profoundly conditioned them to believe themselves unworthy of love, and the system to be incapable of change. Consequently, they tend to act in ways that engender despair, causing them to choose tactics that alienate the very people they need to affect. Driven by their ideals, they denigrate their own accomplishments as inadequate, as if they should have been able to do more. Or they change the goal just as they are close to realizing it so that they never get to celebrate victories along the way. They burn themselves out trying to live in utopian fashion with all their old socialization intact. They believe they should be able to overcome their racist and sexist attitudes by a mere act of will. Then, when they experience the persistence of these attitudes, they turn on each other with demands for movement purity. Rather than recognizing that we are all racist or sexist or undemocratic as a result of our social upbringing, and developing ways to assist people gently in the needed transformation, the movement declares that anyone with these attitudes is a traitor or a deviant. When they can no longer stand their own hypocrisy or that of others, many drop out to enter psychotherapy, meditate, or earn money. The Powers once again, acting from concealment, entice courageous and dedicated people to blame their own personal inadequacies for what are in fact systemically induced delusions. Here the traditional religions can come to our aid, Lerner insists, since they, almost alone in our society, are able to mount a consistent counter-cultural critique of domination.[17]

The nonperfectibility of the world does not make us passive. We still act by the best lights we have. It only makes us modest, so that we can be expectant toward God. And modesty is an enormous relief. It is the infallible sign that one has been awakened from dreams of perfection. The Powers can be redeemed, but not made flawless. And when we no longer have to believe that we must make everything happen ourselves, we are well-positioned to live in anticipation of miracles.

Finally, the doctrine of the Fall reminds us that we cannot be saved from the Powers by anything within the Power System, but only by something that transcends it. The notion of the Fall is good news. No doubt the doctrine of the Fall has been perverted to justify the worst kinds of oppression, on the grounds that our inherent sinfulness must be kept under check by government, and that any order is better than the risk of chaos that every attempt at change harbors.[18] If the gospel is understood to teach that people are basically rotten, one is unlikely to look to it for resources to reconcile them or to create more equitable social structures. Worst of all, the doctrine of the Fall has occasionally been debased to the bizarre idea of total depravity: the notion that there is nothing good in us, that we are incapable of any good whatever.[19]

All that is perversity. The gladsome doctrine of the Fall does not say that people and the social order are utterly sinful or basically wicked or incapable of good. It teaches quite the opposite: people and the Powers are *not* evil by nature; evil is, on the contrary, unnatural, a disorder, a perversion. We, and the Powers, are the good creations of a good God. By contrast, there is in Scripture no account of the creation of the demons. Unlike the Powers, the demonic is not a constituent part of the universe. Its emergence is always an event in time, the consequence of wrong choices. An institution becomes demonic when it abandons its divine vocation for the pursuit of its own idolatrous goals. But what has become perverted in time can be redeemed in time.

Evil is not our essence. God intended us for better things. "Fallenness" does not touch our essence, but it characterizes our existence. No one can escape it. "Good" and "bad" people alike are fallen. The tax collectors and harlots are fallen, but so are the scribes and Pharisees and Jesus' disciples. Saints are fallen, together with sinners. The church is fallen along with the empire. "Fallen" simply means that we all live under the conditions of the Domination System.

The Fall does not revoke the gift of life, or the vocation to live humanly in the midst of a fallen creation. The Fall does not mean that everything we do is evil, vain, or hopeless, but merely that it is all ambiguous, tainted with ego-centricity, subject to deflection from its divine goal, or capable of being co-opted toward other ends. All that distinguishes Christians is the confidence that we have been reconciled with God in the very midst of a fallen world.

Paradoxically, those in the grip of the cultural trance woven over us by the Domination System are usually unaware of the full depth of their soul-sickness. It is only after we experience liberation from primary socialization to the world-system that we realize how terribly we have violated our authentic personhood—and how violated we have been. For we are not just sinners, but the sinned against. We not only have defected from higher values, but we have been trained, schooled, cajoled, and bullied into defecting from them by the combined on-slaught of much that goes to make up our world. In part, our sin is that we acquiesced in this socialization.

Like addicts who cannot tell how distorted their perceptions have become until they get off drugs, we too cannot recognize the depth of our alienation from life until we are well on the way toward healing. Like addicts, we are not completely "redeemed," with all our former cravings gone and the damage we have done to ourselves and others all undone. We continue to live redemptively as fallen people in a fallen world, as God's good creations. Like addicts, again, we cannot redeem ourselves from a system whose malignancy we scarcely recognize and whose blandishments we have come to crave. We need revelation, to see our state, and liberation, to be freed from it. We, too, like other addicts, must turn over our lives to a higher power, not just another of the Powers but the God who transcends the Powers.[20] For no Power, in the act of freeing us from another Power, can deliver us from itself.

The simultaneity persists: we and the Powers are good, fallen, and redeemed, all at the same time. We do not escape into utopia. The doctrine of the Fall keeps our feet anchored firmly in the harsh reality of the one and only real world, known in both its inner and outer aspects, even as God continues to work in us transformations we were not even aware, in our estranged state, that were needed or were possible.

The Powers Will Be Redeemed

A devout Roman Catholic charismatic in Chile attempted to persuade me that Christians have no business trying to change structures, that we are simply called to change individuals, and that as a consequence of changed individuals, the structures will automatically change. Jesus himself, she asserted, did not try to reform the structures of first-century society. He was not a revolutionary, nor did he propose alternative institutions. Political science is a field of great complexity requiring specialist knowledge. Christians have no business telling politicians what to do or how to do it. The church's task is to nurture persons who feel called to politics and are steeped in Christian values.[21]

The Irreducibility of the Personal to the Social

Comments like these contain an element of truth. There is sometimes a leavening process in institutions as individuals change. People *can* make a difference in the way an office or factory or nation is run. Gorbachev has had an immense impact on the history of our time. One person's integrity can have a marked effect in checking a dozen employees' dishonesty. We must never deny the incredible power of a few dedicated people. Almost every major reform can be traced back to a single person or a small group of people who were outraged by wrong. It is true that Christians often have no grasp of the complexity of issues, even when they have made their best efforts to be informed, and that many "Christian" solutions have given rise to new and sometimes even greater evils. One thinks of the Latin American "Christian Democratic" parties, which so often have been neither. The church *can* have a salutary effect on society by nurturing people with special callings in the secular world, and must forswear the grandiosity of thinking that it has a solution for every problem.

Nor may the individual ever be treated as of lesser value than the social system. Changed people, reconciled with God and in process of transformation, are at the very core of the gospel message. The harmony of the whole is not worth the involuntary sacrifice of a single life. The problem of society lies far too deep to be settled through mere systemic changes, as Václav Havel insisted when his was one of the few voices of dissent in Czechoslovakia before the collapse of communism there. He deplored the willingness of those who, for the sake of fundamental social change, were always ready to sacrifice things less fundamental—like human beings. "A better system will not automatically ensure a better life. In fact the opposite is true: only by creating a better life can a better system be developed."[22] The main rationale for changing structures is precisely in order to liberate people from whatever deprives them of the opportunity to realize as fully as possible their own God-given potential. Our freedom under God means that, in the final analysis, each person is responsible for choosing life, regardless of the structure.

Grant this much to my Chilean friend: we must not reduce the personal to the social. No structural change will, *of necessity*, produce good or transformed people. I have considerable sympathy with conservative groups in the mainline

American denominations who fault church leadership for ignoring evangelism altogether or redefining it as struggles for social justice. Ultimately, as liberation theologian Domingos Barbé comments, the sickness of our world is a spiritual illness that comes from a lack of a living relationship with God.[23] Without reestablishing that relationship, there can be no deep and lasting social change. Many people do need to undergo a change of heart. God must supplant the upstart ego. People do need to be "reborn" from their primary socialization in an alienated and alienating system—though conservatives are generally too acculturated themselves to go that far—and take on the radical values of God's nonviolent commonwealth.

Our times have produced tragic illusions about the power of new systems to create new people. The abolition of slavery in the American South did not produce transformed people, however much it may have improved the former slaves' lot and theoretically enhanced their capacity to achieve their true potentials. Soviet communism did not lead to the much-vaunted "New Man" (sic), but to an actual decline in human happiness and fulfillment. No doubt private property prompts greed, but greed is also observable where private property has been abolished. In intentional communes, fathers still molest their daughters sexually, treasurers abscond with community funds, and envy over the fairness of the distribution of power and goods persists. Social arrangements can perhaps help reduce the profitability and attraction of sin, but they cannot make it disappear.

Human misery is caused by institutions, but these institutions are maintained by human beings. We are made evil by our institutions, yes; but our institutions are also made evil by us. Not all sin can be projected outside the self; it is within us as well, far deeper than mere socialization. *It is, in part, what makes socialization necessary.*

Marx had rightly stressed that the self is "the ensemble of social relations." But that is not all it is. The self is that ensemble of social relations which also knows itself to be primordially grounded in being-itself, to have a name uttered over it, or within it, from all eternity. No state, or family, or employer can reach all the way to the core of our beings; and it is this residual irreducibility of the self to the social that makes it possible to resist society, to oppose the Powers, to transcend our own socialization. Much as we might like to lay the blame for all evil on the rise of the Domination System, we cannot do so without at the same time sacrificing responsibility and freedom. We are not merely socialized in sin, or sinned against; we also *choose* to sin, and it is this ontological capacity to sin that, paradoxically, insures our human freedom.[24]

Marx, Rousseau, Ernest Becker, Eisler, Schmookler, and a host of others want to bring humanity the good news that evil is not our fault, that it is all a confidence trick played on us by the structures we innocently and unwittingly created to dike ourselves against the rising flood of civilized anarchy. But anyone who has looked deeply within knows that not all evil has been introjected into us by the means of production or the government or patriarchy or the structures of society. Some evil would remain in our souls regardless of the social system. Otherwise, how can we account for the creation of these alienating structures in the first place? No arrangement of social cooperation, in which power controls power and anarchy is tamed, will produce human beings free from the lust for power.

Humanity longs for a world where the travail of personal transformation will not be necessary, where the arduous effort to develop a virtuous character can be avoided, where our neighbors will be judged by the standards we idealize but have exempted ourselves from achieving. Behind all such dreams of a perfected social structure lies the nightmare of totalitarianism. At what cost in personal freedoms must the dream of an anarchy-free society be bought? Unless people as well as their systems are changed, the crystal utopias of our fantasies will continue to dawn blood-drenched and inhospitable.

For once our dreams of paradise start to turn into reality, comments Milan Kundera, reflecting on his experience under Polish communism, people start to crop up here and there who stand in its way.

> So the rulers of paradise have to build a little gulag on the side of Eden. In the course of time this gulag grows ever bigger and more perfect, while the adjoining paradise gets ever smaller and poorer. . . . Hell is already contained in the dream of paradise and if we wish to understand the essence of hell we must examine the essence of the paradise from which it originated. It is extremely easy to condemn gulags, but to reject the totalitarian poesy which leads to the gulag by way of paradise is as difficult as ever.[25]

We must not, then, confuse any coming epoch (the Age of Aquarius, a harmonic convergence, a world federation of states, or whatever) with the reign of God. While history lasts, God's New Creation remains the transcendent criterion by which every system is judged. And any new social order instituted by human beings, whatever its form, will inevitably be a new, possibly better, but still pervasively fallen society. Such attempts may be able to ameliorate evil; that is the proper function of politics. But they will also recast evil into other forms.

The Fall is not a temporal event, the reach of whose effects we might someday, by sheer perseverance, outrun. It is mythic, which means it is always present. Whatever redemption, social change, improvement of working conditions, or restructuring of government that takes place within history will take place under the conditions of the Fall.

Evil finally can be dealt with only through myth. And here the biblical myth repeatedly reveals its capacity to unveil the *not-said* and the *not-yet-thought*. The objection above, that evil cannot be wholly ascribed to our social or political or economic or religious systems, or all of them in concert, is not just an inference from the experience of the evil within ourselves. It is also a deduction from the narratives of the Fall in Genesis. The first fall is that of the man and the woman: human sin is ontologically prior to all social systems and structures. Therefore, it cannot be reduced to social determinism, but is an act of willful rebellion against God (Genesis 3).

The second fall is that of the angels: there is a rupture in the very spirituality of the universe (Gen. 6:1-4). Human sin cannot therefore account for all evil. There is a "withinness" or spirituality in things that is capable of covetousness and insatiable greed.

The third fall is that of the nations: the systems and structures that exist to protect human life become idolatrous and unjust, and subordinate the people they exist to serve to ends not ordained by God (Genesis 11).

Together, these three mythical tableaux from Genesis provide a vast panorama for contemplation. They prevent us from reducing people to society or society to people, the spiritual to the structural or the structural to the spiritual. They negate every attempt to blame evil solely on humanity (as most theology still insists on doing), solely on spiritual powers (as pentecostalism sometimes does), or solely on institutions and systems (as materialism does). Together these stories tell how evil came into a good world created by a good God, and they offer inexhaustible resources for discernment in the complex flux of everyday life.

The Irreducibility of the Social to the Personal

The problem with my Chilean friend's approach is not so much with what it affirms as what it leaves out. It ignores altogether the implications of Eph. 6:12 and all the companion references to the Powers: "For our struggle is not against human foes, but against cosmic powers, against the authorities and potentates of this dark age, against the superhuman forces of evil in the heavenly realms" (REB). As long as these Powers were thought of personalistically—that is, as long as they were themselves reduced to the categories of individualism and imagined as demonic beings assaulting us from the sky—their institutional and systemic dimension was mystified, and belief in the demonic had no political consequences. But once we recognize that these spiritual forces are *the interiority of earthly institutions or structures or systems*, then the social dimension of the

gospel becomes immediately evident. These Powers with which we contend—
and the biblical writer assumes we are all engaged in that struggle—are the
inner *and* outer manifestations of political, economic, religious, and cultural
institutions. Despite any excellences these institutions may individually possess,
they are collectively caught up in a world-system blind to its Creator and drunk
on self-aggrandizement. They are at one and the same time divinely ordained,
and acolytes of the kingdom of death.

The principle of the irreducibility of persons to systems must therefore be
matched by its opposite: the irreducibility of systems to persons. Structures have
their own laws, their own trends and tendencies, quite independent of the human
agents involved in them. The laws relevant to collectivities cannot be reduced
to those of individuals, just as the laws of engineering that regulate the functioning
of a tractor cannot be reduced to the laws of physics and chemistry that determine
the behavior of the individual molecules and atoms that make up its parts. There
are hierarchies of laws. People are the atoms and molecules of social systems.
Every person is subject to the "laws" of personal development. But their interactions in a transnational corporation may have very little to do with the way
their personal development is progressing. (I am told that over half of the
managers of the Fortune 500 companies have had sensitivity training. Has the
world noticed a difference?) The host of junior and senior managers surely vary
in skill, maturity, and ethical integrity, but they are to a very high degree
interchangeable and replaceable.

And what *motivates* them is almost irrelevant. They need not be greedy for
profit at all; *the system is greedy on their behalf.*

Berdyaev once remarked that social changes cannot wait until people are
made morally perfect. "The putting of an end to torture of the weak by the
strong cannot await the moral perfection of the strong. . . . The weak must be
supported by actions which change the structure of society."[26]

Even the moral concern of a few is usually insufficient to change an oppressive
system. The owner of a business, for example, may undergo an experience of
spiritual rebirth, and genuinely desire to humanize the conditions under which
her employees work. But she encounters immediately a fixed constraint: cost.
If she deviates too much from the general norm for wages and benefits, the cost
of the product will price her out of business. So she must be extremely cautious
in introducing fundamental change, because her business is dependent on a
world economic system that is utterly indifferent to her ethical concerns.

This is not to dismiss the value of that one business person's attempt to be
more humane. That attempt, within the narrow range of her freedom, may be
the thin margin between making work pleasant for her workers or miserable.

Her free choices can have a limited effect on her employees' satisfaction in life. And that is by no means negligible. New management styles have helped to humanize existence in some workplaces. But she cannot raise salaries sharply and still remain competitive when a factory owner in Taiwan or South Korea is making the same product with teenage girl laborers paid one-tenth of the salary and working twelve or fourteen hours a day six days a week. The system is greedy on her behalf, and if she rejects the system's values she may be ejected by the system. It is not just that people are making choices about how they will behave in the economic system: the system is also making choices about who will remain viable in the system. We do not contend against flesh and blood, but against the world rulers of this present darkness.

That example is rather simple. Consider now the more complex case of an agricultural researcher at a state agricultural experiment station. He typically hails from a farm or at least a small-town agricultural service community. The researcher has a genuine desire to serve the farmer by making farming easier and more profitable. Let us even imagine that the researcher feels this as a genuine vocation from God, as my Chilean friend would put it.

But now watch how the Powers strip from his hands the very capacity to fulfill his vocation. The researcher responds directly to the needs of the farmers. But these needs are *imposed* on the farmer by the system of production and marketing for farm products. That means he virtually has to use a tractor instead of a horse to plow and cultivate. He must till more acres to insure profitability and justify the cost of the tractor. He must buy commercial fertilizer because he no longer can produce enough manure locally, and he must buy a harvesting machine because he is farming more acreage, and an adequate labor force is costly and undependable.

So the farmer calls on the researcher to develop seeds with higher yields, and herbicides to kill the weeds. The researcher responds with a will, determined to serve the farmer. But all these demands are dictated, not by the farmer, but by the technological innovations that must be used in order to maintain profitability in a market in which competitors are taking advantage of these technological innovations also.

And our researcher? With the best will in the world, he perseveres in producing a hybrid corn seed that will increase yields for the farmer. But this backs the farmer into even greater dependency on the four seed companies that supply most of the U.S. corn belt. Since hybrids do not breed true, the farmer must now buy new seed each year instead of harvesting his own seed from the choice stock of his own crop. All this takes money; in the past seventy-eight years the average farmer's indebtedness increased eightyfold.[27] The agricultural researcher does not intend to drive his clients into debt, yet this is the unintended result of his endeavors on the farmer's behalf. And since all such highly mechanized farmers can now produce tremendous yields, the price of corn drops, they cannot pay off their debts, and the bank forecloses.[28]

The tragedy is that many farmers blame themselves entirely for what is in large part a systemic catastrophe. They feel shame for a failure that has all the inevitability of an avalanche. Our individualistic blinders cause us to seek private causes for public malfunctions. It is easier, for them and us, to blame bankrupted farmers for their own personal incompetence than to unmask the system that is doing them in. (And we have not even considered the role of agribusiness and the U.S. Congress in the farm debacle!)

We in the West have a tendency to think of people as primary and social institutions as secondary, as if the latter were an arbitrary and inessential framework invented by human beings. Studies of birds, dolphins, whales, and primates have shown, however, that social organization is by no means a human invention. We emerged as humans already graced with a broad repertoire of social institutions. Ervin Laszlo goes so far as to call these institutions "natural systems," because they are apparently as intrinsically and indispensably human as the need for food, drink, and sexual expression.[29]

As long as human societies were small, minimal organization was required. Even with the emergence of the great empires of the Near East, Egypt, and China in the Bronze and Early Iron ages, where the king was identified with the high god, we find little awareness of the intermediate Powers that so profoundly determine human existence. Polytheism, to be sure, reflected a keen awareness of the multiplicity of Powers that shape the human psyche, but these primary intuitions were not given sociopolitical expression until the time of Alexander the Great, at least in the region in which the biblical religions took their rise.

With the sudden collapse of the city-states and the emergence of the Hellenistic cosmopolis, people were simultaneously stripped of the religious cosmologies that had sustained them and plunged into a world of vast and imponderable forces vying for supremacy. For the first time, the language of Principalities and Powers emerged as a way of identifying the *experiences* people were having of new spiritual forces embodied in the social and political institutions of Alexander's successors. If these spiritual Powers had been there all along, how can we account for their being identified so late? If they had eternal metaphysical status, why were they stored up so long and released only in the Hellenistic age? But if they were *new* spirits, the interiority of new social forces identified as the result of new perceptions, then their emergence precisely at that moment in history makes perfect sense.

These forces were not altogether new. The Hebrew Bible was already familiar with angels of the nations, for example (Deut. 32:8-9, a very ancient text; see also 2 Sam. 5:24; Ps. 82:1-8). But the range and ubiquity of these forces for the first time came to awareness in the post-Alexandrine era.[30] And what those capable of discernment testified is that these Powers were beyond simple human control.

This sense that affairs have passed out of human hands into those of supra-human Powers increased in the Roman period. A change of emperor might affect the ordinary Roman incidentally for good or evil, comments Harold Mattingly, but it was really the system that mattered, and the system changed very little, whatever particular occupant might be enthroned in the seat of the Caesars.[31] The office of the emperor seemed to possess a power independent of its incumbent: "It was inevitable that the system should come to tyrannize over each Emperor of the moment, that caprice, never to be completely excluded, mattered less and less, that the Emperor should end by being as much a prisoner of his office as the meanest serf among his subjects."[32] A highly placed officer at the Pentagon expressed to me the same sentiments: "Sometimes it feels like it's just a massive system that got going and no one knows how it happened or how to stop it."

For we are not contending against mere human beings, but against suprahuman systems and forces, against "the *spirituality* (*pneumatika*) of the evil Powers in the invisible order."[33]

The modern sociologist Peter Blau concurs that institutions seem to be beyond human control: "Once firmly organized, an organization tends to assume an identity of its own which makes it independent of the people who have founded it or of those who constitute its membership."[34]

People establish institutions, but they are in turn themselves molded by the institutions they have established. We come into a world already institutionally organized, often for injustice. "I suppose that at first, it was people who invented borders," writes the Russian poet Yevgeny Yevtushenko, "and then borders started to invent people."[35]

"Fate" means literally "what is spoken"—not what we speak, but what is spoken over us to predetermine our future by blocking our free access to the reality we would choose.[36] It refers to the fact that not only individuals, but whole groups, classes, and races can find themselves in a state of physical or psychic detention. We are each defined in part by the sum total of possibilities that are denied to us, that is, by a future more or less blocked off.[37] The final triumph of the Powers, then, is to cause us to will to be where we have been detained.

To be created by God means that no system can totally determine us. But there is such a thing as "natal alienation," as someone has called it: the experience of being born into a world in which one is condemned in advance, by virtue of one's skin color, or gender, or disability, or malnutrition, or a mother's addiction, or AIDS, to a future more or less blocked off. We are talking here about not just an occasional aberration but about hundreds of millions of people. If South African "Bantu education" has been intentionally geared to teach just enough to train blacks for work in the mines but not enough for them to achieve competitive parity with whites, how free are they to "be all that they can be" under God?

Jesus denounced the Domination System of his day and proclaimed the advent of the reign of God, *which would transform every aspect of reality, even the social framework of existence*. To this end he founded an anti-structure[38] that provided a haven for those whose encounter with Jesus left them nowhere else to go (prostitutes, toll collectors, "sinners," the landless). It bodied forth a new existence under God, freed from legalism and the purity code. It also liberated people from the alienating spirituality of the Hellenistic ethos.[39] And it set in motion a permanent revolution against the Power System whose consequences we are still only beginning to grasp to this day.

Our charismatic friend in Chile regarded Jesus as only the savior of souls, not the savior of the world. Her Jesus was not the bringer of the New Order into this time and space, but a redeemer who saves people from this time and space into an afterlife. The proclaimer of God's reign on earth had become, for her, the divine broker who negotiates our forgiveness for personal infractions of the moral code. Christianity was, in her eyes, a fairly private affair, a matter of "spiritual life" only, which left uncriticized and unopposed a System exemplified in Chile, at the very moment we were speaking, by the iron-fisted dictator, Gen. Augusto Pinochet. The General had nothing to fear from her.

The Jesus who died at the hands of the Powers died every bit as much for the Powers as he died for people. The statement in Col. 1:20 that God was pleased to reconcile to himself all things, whether on earth or in heaven, by making peace through the blood of the cross, cannot apply just to people, since we are not in "heaven." It must mean the Powers referred to in v. 16, in both their visible and invisible aspects, as the reiteration of the phrase "on earth or in heaven" (1:16, 20) makes clear. It is these Powers that Christ reconciles to God through his death on the cross. That death is not, then, merely an unmasking and exposure of the Powers for what they are (Col. 2:15), but an effort to transform the Powers into what they are meant to be.

Philippians 3:21 further specifies: Christ will transform the world "by the power that also enables him to make all things subject to himself." The paradox of the cross, however, prevents this from being just another dream by the powerless of a reversal of power. The one who subjects all things to himself is precisely the same one who abandoned all mimetic rivalry with God—"who, though he was in the form of God, did not regard equality with God as something to be exploited"—and emptied himself of all desire to dominate, taking the form of the oppressed, identifying himself with the enslaved, and suffering a criminal's death (Phil. 2:6-8*). Subjection to such a ruler means the end of all subjugation. The rulership thus constituted is not a domination hierarchy but an enabling or actualizing hierarchy.[40] It is not pyramidal but organic, not imposed but restorative. It is presided over by naked, defenseless truth—the Crucified—not by a divine dictator. Christ makes all things subject to himself, not by coercion, but by healing diseased reality and restoring its balance and integrity.

Reinhold Niebuhr taught that organizations reflect the lowest common denominator of morality of their members, and are therefore less moral than most of the people that make them up.[41] This is depressingly true of a great many groups; if it is the whole story, however, hopes for transforming institutions are incredibly slim. But in fact we all know of groups that lift people to a *higher* level than the individuals who compose them: Alcoholics Anonymous and groups for addicts of other kinds; or certain intentional Christian communities like the Latin American base communities, or Ground Zero, Church of the Savior, Sojourners, Koinonia Farm, and the Iona Community. Many clergy feel they have been able to help improve the churches they have served, as do many business executives their companies. Even this side of the reign of God, institutions can be impacted for the better.

The gospel is not a message of personal salvation *from* the world, but a message of *a world transfigured, right down to its basic structures*. Redemption means actually being liberated from the oppression of the Powers, being forgiven for one's own sin and for complicity with the Powers, and being engaged in liberating the Powers themselves from their bondage to idolatry. The good news is nothing less than a cosmic salvation, a restitution of all things (Acts 3:21), when God will "gather up all things in him [Christ], things in heaven and things on earth" (Eph. 1:10). This universal rectification will entail both a healing and a subordination of rebellious structures, systems, and institutions to their rightful places, in service to the One in and through and for whom they exist.[42]

Redemption of the Powers requires neutralizing[43] their proclivity to evil and bringing them into subjection to Christ ("under his feet," 1 Cor. 15:24-27; Eph. 1:22; Heb. 10:12-13).[44] The Powers will enter the heavenly city, redeemed, transformed (Rev. 22:2), bearing as their "glory" all the artistic, cultural, political, scientific, and spiritual contributions whereby they have enriched the world (Rev. 21:24). On this side of the New Jerusalem they will remain relatively good and evil, none perfect, none totally depraved. But some will become so destructively demonic in their self-idolization that they must be resisted with all our might.

The understanding that the Powers are created, fallen, and redeemable helps negotiate a truce between two camps long at odds. The one argues that all governmental, economic, educational, and cultural systems are intrinsically evil, though capable of some limited good. This position is held by some Amish, Mennonites, and others from the Anabaptist tradition. The other insists that governments and other public institutions are not just post-Fall phenomena but intrinsic elements of God's creation, and therefore capable not only of reform but even of being "christianized." This position is associated with the Calvinist tradition, but is also characteristic of Catholicism and most mainline Protestants.[45] Without such a truce, the invidious "either/or" of the debate leaves us either abandoning the Powers to secularity or installing an establishment Christianity: either withdrawal or theocracy.

Instead of these two extremes, the New Testament view of the Powers gives us a broad continuum of possible emphases, adaptable to every situation. There are no prepackaged answers that tell us how Christians should engage the Powers. One person may be called to try to reorganize the office where she works in a more humane fashion; another may have to walk out to protest sexual harassment. One may run for political office; another may despair of the electoral system and work to overthrow it. But all live in the paradox of "as if not," as being in but not of the Domination System. "Come out of her, my people" (Rev. 18:4) may be our marching orders, but so may be the call to assume secular office (as with Joseph and Daniel). Spiritual discernment takes the place of fixed rules. As Jacques Ellul argues, there really is no such thing as a "Christian ethic," only the ethical inventiveness of Christians.[46]

Social entities *can* be changed, but they can only be fundamentally changed by strategies that address the socio-spiritual nature of institutions. Since we are not out to destroy people but to change the systems that hold even their beneficiaries in thrall, we must take as our spiritual weapons the "whole armor of God," the nonviolent armament of which Ephesians so eloquently speaks: truth, justice, peace, faith, salvation, the word of God, and above all, prayer (Eph. 6:10-20). That is, the church's peculiar calling is to discern and engage both the structure and the spirituality of oppressive institutions.

Have I ended by agreeing with my Chilean charismatic friend? We are certainly of one mind that the church's unique task is spiritual. We differ only in the recognition that part of the church's evangelistic task is proclaiming to the

Principalities and Powers in the heavenly places the manifold wisdom of God (Eph. 3:10). And that means addressing the spirituality of actual institutions that have rebelled against their divine vocations and have made themselves gods.

We are slowly beginning to read the events of our time in ways that honor both the social and the personal. The irreducibility of the personal to the social, and the irreducibility of the social to the personal: these two principles form an indissoluble and necessary duality that must be maintained against all simplistic attempts at individualistic *or* sociological reductionism. God's will is the transformation of people *and* society. Individuals will enter the New Jerusalem, but so also their nations, redeemed and healed by the leaves of the tree of life (Rev. 21:24-26; 22:2). Evangelism and social struggle are the twin pincers of a single movement for world transformation.

The Powers are good, the Powers are fallen, but the Powers will be redeemed. That is a hope worthy of the One in and through and for whom all things exist, and whose praises we hymn in anticipation of the final restitution of all things in the embrace of divine love.

No, they are all a delusion;
their works are nothing;
their images are empty wind.

Isaiah 41:29

5. Unmasking the Domination System

If the Domination System is so insufferable, why do people tolerate it? Why do they not rise up against a way of life that provides advantages to so few and misery to so many? How is it possible that literally billions of people permit themselves to be hoodwinked and fleeced by tiny circles of elites propped up by armies far from adequate to subdue the population of the world? Surely this is the greatest political mystery ever: the regular failure of the masses to use their overwhelming numerical superiority to throw off their oppressors.

One of the first to identify this political confidence trick was the French political philosopher Étienne de la Boetie. Writing around 1552, he asked how it came about that so many people, so many villages, so many cities and nations, suffer under a single tyrant who has no other power than the power his subjects freely bestow upon him? How can such a ruler maintain power when all that is required is for the people, not to rise up in arms, but simply to refuse to consent to their own enslavement? "It is not necessary to deprive him of anything, but simply to give him nothing," he wrote. You let this one man dominate you, plunder you, take your property and sons, yet

> he who dominates over you has only two eyes, only two hands, only one body, no more than is possessed by the least . . . among the infinite numbers dwelling in your cities; he has indeed nothing more than the power that you confer on him to destroy you. How has he acquired enough eyes to spy upon you, if you do not provide them yourselves? How can he have so many arms to beat you with, if he does not borrow them from you? The feet that trample down your cities, where does he get them if they are not your own? How does he have any power over you, except through you? What could he do to you if you yourselves did not connive with the thief who plunders you? If you were not accomplices of the murderer who kills you? If you were not traitors to yourselves?

Then, in words that not only anticipate the nonviolent struggles of our time but also offer an agenda for a whole new politics, de la Boetie says, "I do not ask that you place hands upon the tyrant to topple him over, but simply that you support him no longer; then you will behold him, like a great colossus whose pedestal has been pulled away, fall of his own weight and break into pieces."[1]

Why have women allowed themselves to be despoiled of their rights, generation after generation, despite often being a majority? Why did so many women oppose the Equal Rights Amendment? How can six million whites subjugate the twenty-nine million other South Africans? Why did the lower and middle classes sit supinely by and watch the Reagan administration scuttle the graduated income tax, providing massive tax relief to a tiny fraction of wealthy people while the real incomes of everyone else were in sharp decline? Why do the poor and homeless not unite to form a powerful political bloc to win their universal human right to adequate food and housing?

A popular saying of the 1960s ran, "The hardest battle isn't with Mr. Charlie. It's with what Mr. Charlie has done to your mind." When Jesus laid out his devastating critique of wealth, and asserted that it is practically impossible for a rich person to enter the reign of God, the disciples responded, "Then who can be saved?" So deeply had they internalized the values of the Domination System, and the apostate theology that identifies wealth with blessedness, that they were incredulous that the wealthy might be excluded from the kingdom of heaven. They apparently regarded economic stratification as ordained by God. As Ched Myers notes, they actually *believed* the rich man's claim to have kept the whole law—to which Jesus had added pointedly, "Do not defraud" (Mark 10:19).[2]

People would not be so acquiescent in their own oppression unless they were caught in a powerful delusion. "Delude" is from the Latin *deludere*, "to play," specifically, "to play with anyone to his injury or frustration, to mock, to defraud; to befool the mind or judgment so as to cause what is false to be accepted as true."[3]

Exposing the delusional system is the central ascetical task in our discernment of the Powers. For the Powers are never more powerful than when they can act from concealment. To drop out of sight and awareness into the general surroundings, to masquerade as the permanent furniture of the universe, to make the highly contingent structures of current oppression appear to be of divine construction—such is the genius of their deceptive art. They have armed might at their fingertips, to be sure, but they know, far better than the oppressed, how fragile and potentially impotent it is. Of what use were Philippine army tanks in 1986 when their commanders refused to carry out orders to roll over unarmed civilians? What power was left to Philippine dictator Marcos when his own pilots refused to bomb nonviolent demonstrators and instead defected to a nearby American air base? The mighty prefer, therefore, to rule by means of invisible constraints: unseen filaments tied to the public's arms and legs, and imperceptible spiritual brain-implants causing the masses to will to be what has been made of them.

The delusional system is a game being played on us by the Powers That Be. That game is nowhere more trenchantly exposed than in the surrealistic images of Revelation 12–13.[4]

The Delusional Apparatus according to Revelation 12–13

Of first significance is the fact that the insights in these chapters are given as revelations. John *sees* what for others is invisible (13:1, 2, 11); what has previously been unseen "appears" to him (12:1, 3). Discernment does not entail esoteric knowledge, but rather the gift of seeing reality as it really is. Nothing is more rare, or more truly revolutionary, than an accurate description of reality. The struggle for a precise "naming" of the Powers that assail us is itself an essential part of social struggle.

The seer does not, however, simply read off the spirituality of the empire or an institution from its observed behavior. The situation is more complex. The demonic spirit of the outer structure has already been internalized by the seer, along with everyone else. That is how the empire wins compliance. The seer's gift is not to be immune to invasion by the empire's spirituality, but to be able to discern that internalized spirituality, name it, and externalize it. This drives the demonic out of concealment. What was hidden is now revealed. The seer is enabled to hear her or his own voice chanting the slogans of the Powers, is shown that they are a lie, and is empowered to expel them. The seer locates the source of the chanting outside, and is set free from it.

What is so striking about the New Testament understanding of the Powers, especially in the light of the esoteric use made of them by later Gnostics,[5] is that it is so exoteric, so lacking in mystifications, secret passwords, occult forces. There are spirits, to be sure, but they are actual spirits of real institutions, laid bare by the discerning power of the gospel.

The Roman Empire had brought peace to a fratricidal world. It presided over a period of unparalleled prosperity (for the prosperous). Its might was so legendary that a single emissary could prompt surrender. But this facade of magnificence was bought at a horrible price. The revelation that comes to John strips off the mask of benevolence and reveals, beneath it, the true spirit of Rome. It is not at all like beautiful Roma, seated (as the altar of the Gens Augusta in Carthage depicts her) on a pile of surrendered arms with a cornucopia of blessings pouring out on all flesh.[6] (The cynicism is boundless: Roma's beneficence, depicted in a city that Rome's armies had earlier razed to the ground!) He sees, instead, a grotesque and monstrous deformity bent on supplanting God (Revelation 13), or a harlot seated on Rome's seven hills, inviting promiscuous intercourse with the client-kings she has intoxicated with the aphrodisiac of power (17:1-18).

It is a signal achievement to have discerned Rome's monstrous spirit, though certain Cynic philosophers may have done as much. What gives John's vision added depth is its awareness that *the Domination System transcends its current embodiments*. No regnant Power is ever identical with the Domination System. There are too many survivals of partnership, too many outbreaks of human decency, too many compassionate, fair-minded people and strong women and equitable laws and humane officials, to achieve pure domination. But beyond each regime (symbolized in Revelation by the Beasts from land and sea) stands the ancient System of Domination, whose spirit is Satan (symbolized by the Dragon).[7]

"And there appeared another sign in heaven: behold, a great fiery red Dragon, having seven heads and ten horns and on its heads seven crowns" (Rev. 12:3). Remarkable: this is none other than ancient Tiamat, the seven-headed hydra, the monster of chaos, the mother of the gods in Babylonian mythology! Murdered by Marduk, the god of order, it was from her corpse that the universe was made. This ancient mythological figure was still known to the first-century Roman world as Python in Greece,[8] Typhon in Egypt, Lotan in Syria,[9] and as Leviathan in the Old Testament (Job 3:8; 41; Ps. 74:13-14—"the head*s* of Leviathan"[10]). Its fiery red color still faithfully depicts the "raging" or "red gleaming" serpent set up in the temple of Marduk at Esagil in Babylon.[11]

There is a fundamental difference in John's vision, however. In Babylonian myth, Tiamat had originally represented chaos, the ultimate threat to the security of the state. Now "she" has become "he"; Tiamat no longer symbolizes the male fear of a reversion to matrilineal and partnership society that would deprive men of their monopoly on power. Men had long since won that battle. What John now sees, for the first time, is that this primordial Dragon has come to represent the spiritual principle behind *empire*. Her chaotic functions have coalesced with those of the ruler and orderer, Marduk. Tiamat and Marduk are one. *Now evil is represented, not as the threat of anarchy, but as the system of order that institutionalizes violence as the foundation of international relations*. The new insight here is that order is not the opposite of chaos, but rather the means by which a system of chaos among the nations is maintained. What this vision reveals is that Marduk has not defeated Tiamat after all, for the order won by violent means is a Tiamatic order. The peace gained by violence is anarchic. In the language of René Girard, through mimesis the opposites have become doubles.[12] Violence tends to turn something into the very thing it opposes. Empire is not, then, the bulwark against disorder, but disorder's quintessence.[13]

John the seer also glimpses a figure even older than Tiamat: "And there appeared a great sign in heaven: a woman clothed with the sun, the moon under her feet, and on her head a crown of twelve stars; she was pregnant, and she cried out from the birth pangs and the torment of bearing her child" (Rev. 12:1-2).

Who is this woman? We may as well abandon all attempts at a narrow definition. She is Mary, the mother of the Messiah (12:5), but she is also Israel, the mother of the messianic hope.[14] From the allusions in 12:14 to the Jerusalem church's flight to Pella during the Jewish War, she is also clearly the Christian church under persecution. Judging from the heavenly symbolism, one could conclude that she also probably evokes Wisdom or the Shekinah (Wis. 7:29).

But this woman is not simply described in the usual Judaic symbols. She encompasses not only the history of Judaism but of all humanity as well; she is the transfigured Eve, in everlasting enmity with the serpent (Gen. 3:15; Rev. 12:9). And she embodies not only the hopes of Israel but the myths of the pagans. Artemis, too, appears with a crescent moon and stars, Leto wears a veil of stars, and Damkina, the mother of Marduk, is called "the lady of the heavenly tiara."[15] So also features of Isis and the constellation Virgo are represented here. Nor do the "twelve" stars represent just the twelve apostles and twelve tribes of Israel; they are also the twelve constellations in the Zodiac. This is an archetypal woman, the Great Mother herself, whose Son will end the Domination System. Is she also a flashback to our origins, before the appearance of the Dragon's rule, when at least some human communities lived in relative peace, in egalitarian social orders ruled by neither men nor women, but in partnership together, when God was a woman? Could it be that she is an image of domination-free existence itself, forced by the androcratic Dragon to flee "into the wilderness, where she has a place prepared by God, so that there she can be nourished for one thousand two hundred sixty days" (Rev. 12:6)— that is, three and a half years, the symbolic half-life of the old order in its countdown to oblivion?

There is nothing ambiguous about the Dragon, however. It represents the spirit of the Domination System in its scorched-earth advance through time. This Dragon has embodied itself in one empire after another (Daniel 7–8; 11–12), always ready to cast one off for another, always ready to ride the winner, because it is assured that the very means necessary for one empire to defeat another will make the victor every bit as much a child of the Dragon as its predecessor (Rev. 17:15-17). This vision thus puts the lie to the vain belief that the violent overthrow of empire will solve the problem created by empire.

Violence can liquidate the current regime, but not this nimble Dragon, who leaps upon its exorcists and possesses them each in turn. Thus John warns: "If you are to be taken captive, into captivity you go; if you kill with the sword, with the sword you must be killed. This is a call for the relentless persistence (*hypomonē*) and fidelity of the saints" (Rev. 13:10).

At the time John writes, the Dragon's current embodiment is Rome, described as a Beast almost identical to the Dragon, arising from the sea. "And the Dragon gave to the Beast his power (*dynamis*) and his throne (*thronos*) and great authority (*exousia*)" (13:2). But these are all prerogatives of *God*! It is God who exercises power over the world (Rev. 4:11; 7:12; 11:17; 12:10; 15:8; 19:1), God who is enthroned over the universe (32 times in Revelation), God or the Messiah who has authority (16:9; 12:10).

Where has the Dragon gotten these powers? No doubt God permits this self-aggrandizement. What else can God do, given God's well-known libertarian tendencies? But God's is mere passive permission. The active handing over has been done by a humanity derelict from responsibility. "In a power-dependence relationship," says Elizabeth Janeway, "what the weak bring to the bargain is the validation of the power of the powerful: its legitimacy," that is, widespread acceptance. What the weak have seldom realized is how much power they have placed in their masters' hands.[16]

Hence the refrain all through Revelation 13—the Beast "was allowed" to exercise authority (v. 5), "was allowed" to make war on the saints and to conquer them (v. 7), "was given" authority over every tribe and people and language and nation (v. 7). The Second Beast, likewise, "is allowed" to perform miracles (v. 14), and it "was allowed" to make the image of the First Beast speak (v. 15). I am not aware of such a concatenation of permissions stated so repetitively anywhere else in Scripture. Luke's temptation narrative, however, reflects the same concept. Satan boasts (accurately, I believe) that all the kingdoms of the world have "been delivered" to him (Luke 4:6).

The human race "allowed" these things—all of them associated here with the centralization of state power under a satanic Domination System. God is not to blame. Humanity has done it to itself. When people suppressed the truth about God and worshiped created things, "God gave them up" to darkened minds and folly (Rom. 1:18-32). Once the dynamic of conquest through force was out of its bottle, however, no one could put it back, and no one can choose to opt out of the game. Unless, that is, one is unafraid to die; unless, as John prefers to put it, their names "have been written from the foundation of the world in the book of life of the Lamb that was slain" (Rev. 13:8).

In a legitimate society, people freely give their consent even to rulers they despise, because they approve of the political framework by which those rulers come to power and exercise it. In such a system the citizen is an active, creative, and critical participant who becomes more and more identified with the social system as the social system becomes more acceptable to the participant.[17] The rules by which society functions are backed by sanctions, to be sure (embarrassment, public censure, fines, arrest, incarceration, execution), but their real power depends on trust.[18] When a government or institution must resort to threat or the use of force, its power has already eroded, and the system is in crisis.

An empire is, by its very nature, a system in a permanent crisis of legitimation. It is not a natural system, but an artificial amalgam held together by force. That is why propaganda is so essential to it. People must be made to believe that they benefit from a system that is in fact harmful to them, that no other system is feasible, that God has placed the divine imprimatur on this system and no other.

The Manufacture of Idolatry
according to Revelation 13

In order thus to delude humanity, to achieve a maximal level of stupefaction, the Dragon creates "another Beast that rose out of the earth; it had two horns like a lamb, but it spoke like the Dragon" (13:11). This is not a natural, earthly, chthonic creature. It is not a deep archetype bursting from the unconscious. It is a wholly artificial creation. It will later be identified as the "false prophet" (16:13; 19:20; 20:10), whose task it is to persuade people that their salvation lies in the political order. "It works great miracles . . . and by these miracles . . . it deceives the inhabitants of the earth" (13:13-14).[19]

In appearance this Second Beast is as meek as a lamb—imitating the Lamb who is to rule the nations—but it speaks with the Dragon's voice. It is a Dragon in sheep's clothing. The Second Beast is the priestly propaganda machine of empire. "It exercises all the authority of the First Beast on its behalf, and *compels* the earth and its inhabitants to worship the First Beast" (13:12). This goes beyond the realm of religious preference and into the domain of religio-political terrorism.

In historical terms, John is alluding to the civic cultus that grew up around the worship of the emperors, which by John's time had become the litmus test to expose the acids eating at the fabric of empire.[20] Anyone suspected of revolutionary designs or subversive thoughts could be required to burn a pinch of incense before the emperor's image, and refusal was punishable by death.

The Second Beast, therefore, proselytizes by means of a civil religion that declares the state and its leaders divine. This element of power-worship is stressed over and over by John: people "worshiped the Dragon, for he had given his authority to the Beast, and they worshiped the Beast, saying, 'Who is like the

Beast, and who can fight against it?' " (13:4); "it was given authority over every tribe and people and language and nation, and all the inhabitants of the earth will worship it, everyone whose name has not been written in the book of life of the Lamb that was slaughtered from the foundation of the world" (vv. 7-8); the Second Beast "makes the earth and its inhabitants worship the First Beast" (v. 12); and it can "cause those who would not worship the image of the [First] Beast to be killed" (v. 15). Why does the Beast demand worship? Why is it not content merely with obedience?

Because the Beast knows that the public is fickle; that opinion swings wildly in response to the slightest shifts on the world scene. What is needed is something that can lash loyalty to the mast where it can ride out the waves of social unrest. Ethnic feeling is not enough. Patriotism is not enough. What is needed is worship of the state. That is what nationalism is and has always been. Nationalism is not, in its essence, a political phenomenon; it is a religious one. Only a transcendent cause can induce young men to risk their lives voluntarily in the absence of any conceivable self-interest.

Propaganda is not merely deception, then. It is the manufacture of idolatry. It is not enough that people be misinformed about the nature of the System, for powerful disconfirming truths could easily slip in to shatter such illusions. But *if you can cause people to worship the Beast, you have created a public immune to truth.* As studies of cognitive dissonance show,[21] worshipers do not surrender their beliefs in the presence of disconfirming facts. They simply adjust their beliefs to neutralize the facts.

We are all too familiar with the trappings of propaganda: the big lie, or the daily small ones; doctored news dispatches and photographs, planted stories, falsified scientific reports, gossip, innuendo, slander. Even more insidious are the misrepresentations of facts carried by the mass media, which avoid stories that contradict the "elite consensus," even when the data are highly visible, verifiable, and important.[22] Powerful newspapers like the *New York Times* often simply parrot national policy, even when their reporters are feeding them information sharply at variance with the official picture, as during the Vietnam War.

But propaganda is extremely weak, as is shown by its failure after forty-four years to convert people in the Eastern bloc to communism. Illusion requires incessant repetition in order to mimic the appearance of reality. Propaganda works only through constant reiteration. It is only in quantity that corrupt values, false perceptions, and bogus facts can be sold. Truth, by contrast, though its lot is never easy, makes its way with but a few friends, or even a single utterance. It does not need the apparatus of salesmanship, because reality itself is waiting to confirm it. Hence the power of the beleaguered prophet, or the mothers of the "disappeared" demonstrating daily in Argentina or El Salvador, or the witnesses by the tracks where the White Train carried nuclear explosives to Trident submarine bases: normal people with no economic stake never choose to suffer this much *just to lie.*

The Delusional Assumptions

Propaganda is only the tip of the delusional iceberg, however. Other nations or disaffected internal critics can easily spot and expose it. Propaganda is ad hoc; it responds to short-term needs; it changes to fit every situation. But the basic delusional system has altered little since the ascendancy of the Domination System some five thousand years ago. It has successfully held the vast majority of humanity in its thrall by means of a series of largely unexamined *assumptions* that go far deeper than propaganda. These delusional assumptions are what Col. 2:8 and 20 call the *stoicheia tou kosmou*: the fundamental assumptions of the Domination System. Not all of these hold true for all countries in all times, and some would be held by only a minority of people in a given country. But over the five millennia that the delusional game has been playing, these assumptions have continually reasserted themselves. Here are some of them:

- The need to control society and prevent chaos requires some to dominate others.
- Those who dominate may use other people as a means to achieve their goals.
- Men are better equipped by nature to be dominant than women, and some races are naturally suited to dominate others.
- A valued end justifies the use of any means.
- Violence is redemptive, the only language enemies understand.
- Ruling or managing is the most important of all social functions.
- Therefore rulers and managers should be rewarded by extra privileges and greater wealth of all kinds.
- Those who have military strength, who control the most advanced technology, the greatest wealth, or the largest markets, are the ones who will and should survive.
- Money is the most important value.[23]
- The possession of money is a sign and proof of political and social worth.
- The production of material goods is more important than the production of healthy and normal people and of sound human relationships (or the former automatically produces the latter).
- Property is sacred, and property ownership an absolute right.

- In an organization or nation, great size is proof of its power and value.
- Institutions are more important than people.
- There is no higher value or being or power than the state. If there is a God, God is the protector and patron of the state.
- God, if there is one, is not revealed to all, but only to select individuals or nations and their rulers and priesthood.[24]

These assumptions hold for parties on both sides of a conflict. They would have been as true for the Parthians as for the Romans, as binding for the Soviets as for Americans. Propaganda divides nations; the delusional assumptions unite them in the mutual but antagonistic quest for domination. The Beast from the land is busy in its propaganda office churning out press releases and desirable images for the powerful; but transcendent to the nations stands the Dragon, holding together the total chaotic system in its Tiamatic order. From the propaganda point of view, the United States and the Soviet Union were enemies during the Cold War. From the prophetic point of view they were pathetically similar, sharing most of the same fundamental delusional assumptions.

Socialization is not the problem; rather, the problem is that into which one is socialized. Some elements of socialization are universal, shared by all societies and persons: concepts of space, time, number, measurement, causality, classification. Likewise, people are not merely passive recipients of tradition. They not only take in their socialization, but take it over, leaving out what they dislike.[25] But that freedom is exercised within a highly circumscribed space, and as long as the delusional assumptions remain unconscious, they are seldom effectively transcended.

Christians have docilely sided with their governments, and justified the slaughter of millions of other Christians who, for their part, supported the other side, without any recognition that *both* sides were serving the values of the kingdom of death. Political elections are not a contest to see which party is capable of the greater compassion, but to see which will be truer to the delusional assumptions (increased military budgets, more prisons, stiffer sentencing for criminals). *The church has no more important task than to expose these delusionary assumptions as the Dragon's game.*

Liberation from the
Delusional System

The perception that the delusional system runs deeper than propaganda leads to a further important insight: those who are victims of the delusional system are nevertheless responsible for how they have been shaped. And if they are responsible, then they can choose to be liberated from it.

People are socialized into their roles by means of the delusional assumptions from the earliest age—and this includes oppressors as well as the oppressed. They will further have learned to deny to themselves and others the fact that this misinformation causes them pain. We can hold out hope for the transformation of oppressors because to some degree they too are victims of the system and at some level have felt conflicted, as in the case of white boys in South Africa when they discover that they must kill the love they had for the black maids that have cared for them since birth. (Some of those who have refused conscription have actually given this as the reason: they could not go into black townships and shoot at those who had nursed them.)

Both oppressors and oppressed have often attempted to resist the system that malformed them into their roles and assumptions, and have only given in because of the material rewards offered by the system and the terrible penalties attached to resistance. Society continually reinforces and justifies the mistreatment of the oppressed group, so that the oppressed tend to "misbelieve" the same misinformation about itself that the social system as a whole teaches.[26]

The rulers of the earth do not know that they too are held in thrall by the Domination System. They do not know whom they serve. They probably believe that the delusional assumptions are true. They are being "played with" (*delusi*) every bit as much as their victims, though they are, of course, highly rewarded for playing. They may even be good fathers and mothers, contributors to charities, attenders of churches, and upholders of "traditional morality."

And yet, for almost fifty years now these rulers of East and West have kept the Damoclean sword of nuclear omnicide poised over the heads of all humanity, rationalized under the theory of Mutually Assured Destruction (MAD—though what the United States really had was a policy of first strike). That they were quite prepared to destroy virtually all sentient life on the planet, possibly forever, is an index of the degree to which humanity has been irrationally captive to the delusional system. And both sides were *agreed* on these values. Neither side had sufficient confidence in its own people's commitment to their national identity and ideology to consider nonviolent national defense as an option. Folly on such a colossal scale is almost supranatural. Credit it to the Dragon.

It was fine men who tortured the woman we spoke to in Argentina. One insisted to her, "But I go to Mass every morning too." Another proposed marriage (they had tortured her husband to death two years before). These men were not sadists. They had merely surrendered themselves to the idol of the state. Once they had crossed that line, any evil was good if it served the idol. So their position was coldly rational and logical on their own premises. There is a form of madness, Chesterton remarked, that comes upon those who have lost everything else but reason. The Beast creates an atmosphere that blinds people to higher human values and turns perfectly nice people into beasts. These men were in thrall to the Dragon, to serve the Beast. *But they gave themselves to be captured.*

This is the paradox of moral maturity: we are responsible for what we do with what has been done to us. We are answerable for what we make of what has been made of us. Our capitulation to the delusional system may have been involuntary, but in some deep recess of the self we knew it was wrong. We are so fashioned that no Power on earth can finally drum out of us the capacity to recognize truth. However long it must lie buried, or however severely it has been betrayed, truth will out.

The Czech playwright (and later state president) Václav Havel wrote, while the communist regime was still in power:

> Because the regime is captive to its own lies, it must falsify everything. It falsifies the past. It falsifies the present, and it falsifies the future. It falsifies statistics. It pretends not to possess an omnipotent and unprincipled police apparatus. It pretends to respect human rights. It pretends to persecute no one. It pretends to fear nothing. It pretends to pretend nothing.
>
> Individuals need not believe all these mystifications, but they must behave as though they did, or they must at least tolerate them in silence, or get along well with those who work with them. For this reason, however, they must *live within a lie*. They need not accept the lie. It is enough for them to have accepted their life with it and in it. For by this very fact, individuals confirm the system, fulfil the system, make the system, *are* the system.

When anyone steps out of the system and tells the truth, lives the truth, that person enables *everyone else* to peer behind the curtain too. That person has shown everyone that it is possible to live within the truth, despite the repercussions. "Living within the lie can constitute the system only if it is universal." Anyone who steps out of line therefore "*denies it in principle and threatens it in its entirety.* . . . If the main pillar of the system is living a lie, then it is not surprising that the fundamental threat to it is living the truth." That is why it must be suppressed more severely than anything else.

> For the crust presented by the life of lies is made of strange stuff. As long as it seals off hermetically the entire society, it appears to be made of stone. But the moment someone breaks through in one place—a Solzhenitsyn—when a single person cries out, "The emperor is naked"—when a single person breaks the rules of the game, thus exposing it as a game [*delusio!*]—then the whole crust is exposed as a tissue on the point of tearing and disintegrating uncontrollably.[27]

The delusory web spun around us can be broken. Everyone is capable of liberation. Most people are not deliberately unjust. Even our current enemies are in some sense victims. Jesus can command us to pray for our enemies, not because it is pious to do so, but because they are potentially capable of recognizing the wrongness of the present system. We must love our enemies because they too have been deceived by the Dragon's delusional game.

Often, even the liberator is locked into oppressive conditioning and behavior. The Book of Revelation is a case in point. Never has a more withering political and economic criticism of empire been penned. The author sees with clairvoyant exactitude the bestiality of Rome, and behind it to the satanic spirit undergirding it. But he fails to relate this revelation to other aspects of androcracy. As Tina Pippin notes, he sees powerful, autonomous women as evil (Jezebel, the Whore); the good woman clothed with the sun is valued solely for giving birth to a male messiah, and then dismissed. Women are seductive; their bodies are capable of defiling men. Hence the 144,000 "virgins" who are the firstfruits of the redeemed are men "who have not defiled themselves with women" (14:4). All three of the female figures in Revelation are dealt with violently. The Great Mother is pursued by the Dragon; the Whore is brutally murdered; and Jezebel will be stricken with disease and her "children" killed.[28]

The Book of Revelation contemplates a transformation of power relations in which everyone will be able to enjoy the beauty of gold and gems that the rich had hoarded for themselves (21:18-21). The revolution begun by Jesus is continued and even extended politically and economically by John, but abandoned in reference to Jesus' teaching on love of enemies and the liberation of women. Hence male domination of women remains intact, and it is not even clear that women will be permitted in the New Jerusalem—so deep is this author's misogyny. Concern for justice is never enough; each social struggle must be seen in its relationship to the larger perspective of the inbreaking of God's domination-free order.

The Dragon's strategy is to eviscerate opposition by a sense of *induced powerlessness*. To accept its delusional assumptions is, in effect, to worship the Dragon, to hold its values as ultimate, to stake one's life on the permanence of its sway. "The whole earth followed the [First] Beast, spellbound. They worshiped the Dragon, for he had given his authority to the Beast, and they worshiped the Beast, saying, 'Who is like the Beast, and who can fight against it?' " (Rev. 13:3-4). Obeisance to the Beast requires as its gesture a continuous shrug. "Who is like the Beast, and who can fight against it?" (shrug). "I just carried out my orders. If I hadn't done so, someone else would have" (shrug). "I don't enjoy the violence depicted in my company's films, but this is what the public wants" (shrug). "I didn't want to get on drugs, but I was afraid the other kids would say I was square" (shrug). As R. D. Laing put it, "Each person claims his own inessentiality. . . . In this collection of reciprocal indifference, of reciprocal inessentiality and solitude, there appears to exist no freedom. There is conformity to a *presence* that is everywhere elsewhere. . . . Mind and body are torn, ripped, shredded, ravaged, exhausted by these Powers and Principalities in their cosmic conflict."[29]

"Who is like the Beast, and who can fight against it?" is the mantra whose chanting by the masses guarantees compliance. That melancholy refrain echoes in the minds of citizens in totalitarian societies. The state apparatus is ubiquitous: Who is like the Beast? Anyone could be an informant: Who can fight against it? Soon one begins acting as censor to one's own mind, in terror of the single slip of tongue that could reveal one's thoughts, afraid even of night for fear of babbling sedition in one's sleep.[30]

It is significant that the Satan we see in Job who wanders up and down the earth and to and fro upon it, spying out people's faults, was probably inspired by the model of the Persian secret intelligence agency.[31] Like Freud's superego, Satan represents the harsh internalized voice of one's socialization, not yet lifted to consciousness and therefore to the possibility of being contradicted. Satan "tempts" us, not just with moral indiscretions, but with obedience to oppressive values that the society itself declares to be holy and right. Satan provides mind surveillance for the internalized system, and tattles to God, who is actually betting on people's capacity to be authentic (Job 1–2).

In Chile, during the rule of the military dictator Pinochet, I asked a churchman about repression there. Public censorship of the press and media is not nearly so severe, he replied, as the self-censorship people exercise, out of fear. "In our country," mused an Eastern European, "people are rarely imprisoned for their ideas . . . because we're already imprisoned *by* our ideas."[32] A government does not itself have this power; people must voluntarily surrender this power to the state.[33]

Those in power *want* us to be awed by their power, to act deferentially toward them. The European conquest of the colonies was made possible by vastly superior technology for warfare and communication, but by themselves these advantages could not have secured continued domination once the indigenous peoples had mastered these technologies (running them, indeed, for the masters). Lewis Mumford remarks on the sense of superiority, the arrogant swagger and easy assumption of being better, that characterized colonial administrators and unnerved any opposition. The subjects became convinced of their inferiority in the presence of such men. Britain ruled by teatimes, dress codes, and the flag; only occasionally were weapons needed. *It is not overt force but the symbols of power that rule the hearts of people.*[34] When hundreds of Indians nonviolently submitted themselves to the blows of police in Bombay on June 21, 1930, the men who clubbed them to the ground hour after hour were not British, but several hundred of their fellow Indian countrymen, under the command of only six British sergeants.[35]

Domination is always more than a power relation, notes Joel Kovel. It is a *spiritual state of being*. The dominator exerts power by extracting being from the dominated. Capitalists often get more than the labor power and surplus value of their workers; they also degrade the workers' being and puff up their own being. Thus the unmistakable narcissism of class superiority. White racists do more than materially exploit blacks; they make themselves members of a superior race and regard blacks as less than human, even animalistic. Sexually exploitative males do more than control the labor and bodies of women; they make themselves into the bearers of rationality and history, while the woman is made into dumb nature.[36] Thus domination always entails more than injustice. It wounds—and it intends to wound—the very soul itself.

Domination is all the more potent when it is not perceived at all. In his book *Authority*, Richard Sennett comments on the way many doctors treat their clients as bodies rather than persons, or how bureaucrats can ignore the difficulty their welfare clients have in filling out complicated forms: these very acts of indifference serve to maintain dominance. When one is needed by others more than one needs them, one can afford to be indifferent to them. "Someone who is indifferent arouses our desire to be recognized," Sennett writes; "we want this person to feel we matter enough to be noticed." Afraid of the indifference of persons in authority, not understanding what it is that keeps them aloof, we come to be emotionally dependent. This indifference to ordinary people carries as its coercion a shaming effect: it makes them feel insignificant.[37] For life is not just an encounter between human beings, but a struggle to the death for recognition. One does not merely desire the other, but desires to be desired by the other.[38] And it is this desire to be desired that leaves us so vulnerable to the Powers.

Poor people feel nonexistent, valueless, humiliated. No one takes notice of them, unless their votes are needed by the rich—in which case, likely as not, they even vote against their own self-interest. They often have little confidence in themselves, and actually believe that the rich know what they need better than they themselves. When Jack Nelson-Pallmeyer interviewed Honduran campesinos, their answers would often be prefaced with degrading phrases such as "We are stupid, ignorant people who know nothing," or "We are like oxen who know nothing."[39]

People not only choose to be where they have been detained, but they conclude that because of God, the fates, or their own inadequacies, they deserve it. As a Bolivian Indian woman put it after her eyes had been opened by Bible study in a Christian base community, "Do you mean that *nowhere* in that Book does it say we have to *starve*?"[40]

So deep is this internalized oppression that Gustavo Gutiérrez has based a wholly new task for theology upon it: not helping the bourgeois discover the "meaning of life," but assisting the dehumanized to recover their humanity.[41]

Powerlessness is not simply a problem of attitude, however. There are structures—economic, political, religious, and only *then* psychological—that oppress people and resist all attempts to end their oppression. Psychotherapy has often taken the dominator personality and dominator family as normative, and has tried to adjust the client to the Domination Society. As the family systems therapist Thelma Jean Goodrich puts it, "We need to stop trying to fix up people so that the system works better, and start fixing up the system so that people work better."[42]

Systemic injustice is to a high degree invisible to its perpetrators. The man who uses sexist language is generally unaware of the pain of exclusion experienced by conscientized women. A person may be remarkably free of racial prejudice, having as friends people of disadvantaged races, and yet still support structures that perpetuate the systematic control of one racial group by another. "Racism acts as a spiritual force within our social structure even when the people causing it have no intention of acting from prejudice and are unaware of doing so."[43]

This deeply internalized oppression is the reason that *unmasking* the Powers is seldom enough by itself. As Reinhold Niebuhr observed, people in power generally do not capitulate simply because the ideologies by which they justify their policies have been discredited. "When power is robbed of the shining armor of political, moral and philosophical theories, by which it defends itself, it will fight on without armor; but it will be more vulnerable, and the strength of its enemies increased."[44] Indeed, it fights all the more desperately, because it knows that its time is short (Rev. 12:12).

So besides an unmasking of the oppressors, there must also be a *healing of the servile will* in their victims. Along with revolutionary analysis and praxis, there must be therapies.[45] The task of exposing the delusional system requires the development of a social psychology of domination. Simply criticizing the illegitimacy of the masters can lead to two results, both of them negative. The oppressed may decide to beat the oppressors at their own game, rather than changing the game (hence the espousal of redemptive violence by some early liberation theologians). Or the oppressed may be driven to even deeper alienation. For now, as Richard Sennett points out, the oppressed can no longer respect themselves for having allowed themselves to be pillaged, and yet they are still not free from their masters. Rather than strengthening them to revolt, the recognition of their weakness may foster self-doubt: if I have been so cowardly and stupid as to put up with such treatment, I *deserve* what I get. It is my own fault that I am weak.

Furthermore, Sennett continues, if all are created equal, if we all leave from the same starting gate of life, and you are way ahead and I am far behind, then I have no one to blame but myself for not having made more of my life. Thus workers are entangled in a dragnet that systematically prevents their perceiving the faults of the system (not everyone does start from the same gate; some are far ahead at birth due to family wealth, education, race, gender, and station in life; the gospel does not teach that we are born equally, but born incomparably, each utterly unique, utterly beloved by God).[46] The victims blame themselves, and the system gets off unscathed.[47]

Powerlessness is never an empirical fact, however. It is not the outcome of a realistic analysis. *A sense of powerlessness is always a spiritual disease deliberately induced by the Powers to keep us complicit.* Any time we feel powerless, we need to step back and ask, What Principality or Power has me in its spell? *No one is ever completely powerless.* Even if it is only a matter of choosing the attitude with which we die, we are never fully in the control of the Powers unless we grant them that power. "Christ has left the devil only whatever power unbelief allows him," asserts Heinrich Schlier.[48] The victory of faith over the Powers lies, not in immunity to their wrath, but in emancipation from their delusions. And as to their wrath, even there we do not know the limits of God's redeeming grace. So it is always appropriate to pray for miracles. What seems to us impossible is usually another's limited vision or faithlessness in which we have let ourselves become trapped. Faith is the confidence that possibility transcends compulsion; freedom, necessity; life, death; eternity, time.

> The Impossible is standing in front of me
> and looking me in the face.
> The Incredible is credible.[49]

Those who have internalized their oppression, who are awed by the Beast and its powers into passive obedience, and who worship its show of might, provide it all the permission it needs continually to extend its power. What is so exhilarating about the revelations that came to John is their capacity to disenthrall, to awaken, to unlock what William Blake called "the mind-forg'd manacles"[50] and set people free.

Vision heals. Mere awareness of the state from which we are fallen is not enough to effect systemic change, but it is its indispensable precondition. Apocalyptic (unveiling) is always a protest against domination. Liberation from negative socialization and internalized oppression is a never-completed task in the discernment of spirits. To exercise this discernment, we need eyes that see the invisible. To break the spell of delusion, we need a vision of God's domination-free order, and a way to implement it. For that, we look to God's new charter for reality, as declared by Jesus.

●　　●　　●

In Part One we have attempted to discern the workings of the Powers and their System of Domination. The New Testament provides clues for that process of discernment, but its central focus is what God has done to overcome the Powers. What we learn there about the Powers and "this world" is solely in the context of a description of God's "universal restoration" (Acts 3:21) of the creation to its intended order. The rest of this book will attempt to detail that divine alternative to the Domination System. For if the gospel is true, if its description of "this world" is accurate and its solution correct, then it is the most revolutionary message ever heard, and, far from exhausted in its potential, is just coming into its own today.

Part 2

GOD'S NEW CHARTER
OF REALITY

Concern for the redress of a particular injustice needs to be seen as part of a larger struggle against the Domination System in its entirety. Social justice campaigns have been hampered by the shortsighted inability to see that larger context. Consequently, the means they use often involve domination. Or class or racial divisions are preserved within the social-change movement. Or male supremacy is imposed by its leadership. Piecemeal efforts for social betterment are often unrelated to each other. There is no larger vision that fuses all such striving into a greater whole.

The gospel holds such a vision: the reign of God. But that vision has been clouded and at times totally eclipsed by transferring God's reign to a heavenly afterlife of individual restitution—"pie in the sky when you die bye and bye." For many people "kingdom" or "reign" of God is altogether lacking in any gripping content, and its monarchical language is perceived as both sexist and androcratic ("rule by males"). Consequently, Jesus' vision of a new world in process of coming has been lost, even for most Christians.

In the light of Part One, we can speak of God's reign as a domination-free order characterized by partnership, interdependence, equality of opportunity, and mutual respect between men and women that cuts across all distinctions between people. This egalitarian realm repudiates violence, domination hierarchies, patriarchy, racism, and authoritarianism: a total system detrimental to full human life. For all that we do have an adequate term: the Domination System.

The Domination System is the outcome of the systematic repudiation by institutions of their divine vocations in order to pursue self-aggrandizement and greed. But these fallen Powers and their vicious system are not the last word. God has acted to redeem us from the Powers—and to redeem the Powers as well. It is, however, a redemption filled with paradox. Its greatest strengths appear weak to those who define power as manipulation. Its wisdom seems foolish to those who grow rich at the expense of others.

God's domination-free alternative had first to be revealed, then implemented, then appropriated. The next three chapters trace those steps: revelation ("God's Domination-Free Order: Jesus and God's Reign," chap. 6), implementation ("Breaking the Spiral of Violence: The Power of the Cross," chap. 7), and appropriation ("To Wash Off the Not Human: Becoming Expendable," chap. 8). Here is a vision, not of a hopeless utopia too perfect to be realized, but of a grass-roots, practical, daily world waiting for us to begin living it. It holds, I believe, the only future worth having.

There are a few who, during spans
of historied man's harvest,
have risked a fuller fruit, have
plunged to blind ground
and left behind the rasping years. . .

What is this
they do? What breach in our walls
comes with their coming, to let
into our prison the smell of sun
and grass? Their existence tells
itself to ours through the crack.
One such was Jesus the Jew, bearing
his hours on his back—pedlar
of choices and fisher for God.
Let him pass.

Sheila Moon,
Joseph's Son[1]

6. God's Domination-Free Order: Jesus and God's Reign

The irreducible fact about Jesus is that he was executed. Yet he did not represent an armed threat to the existing order. He broke no civil or criminal laws. He violated religious laws and customs regarding the Sabbath, handwashing, and holiness, but in every case the issue hung on interpretation, and no doubt some rabbis would have supported him; at least they would not have condemned him to death. He mainly taught, healed, and exorcised. Why then was he such a threat that he had to be killed?

Scholars have suggested a variety of reasons, none of them alone adequate to account for his death. None of the charges raised against him by his enemies—that he threatened to destroy the Temple, perverted the nation, forbade the giving of tribute to Caesar, and claimed to be a king—are true as stated.[2]

Even the community of his followers was at a loss to explain his death. After the Jewish authorities have lodged all their charges, Mark can still depict Pilate asking, "Why, what evil has he done?" In the Gospel of John, when Pilate asks the Jewish authorities for the charges against Jesus, they answer, "If this man were not a criminal, we would not have handed him over" (18:30)—in short, "Trust us." The Book of Acts states, "Even though they [the authorities] found no cause for a sentence of death, they asked Pilate to have him killed" (13:28). The whole event was so puzzling that some in the church ascribed it to "the definite plan and foreknowledge of God"; but it was still clear that the actual execution was the work of the authorities, both Jewish and Roman. These were not mere pawns in a divine plan of salvation, but had reasons of their own of sufficient cogency and urgency to act as they did: "You killed him, using heathen men to crucify him" (Acts 2:23, REB).

I have remarked repeatedly concerning the Powers that they act from concealment. Their compulsive might is never more determinative than when it constrains us invisibly. The Powers that executed Jesus did so under a necessity dictated by the Domination System itself. *It was essential that Jesus be killed*

*without the real reasons becoming known, because such knowledge would un-
mask the true nature of the Domination System.* If people actually realized, then
or now, why Jesus was killed, they would rise up and overthrow the delusionary
system that keeps them pacified.

God surely anticipated that a person like Jesus would be killed by an order
established on violence, but God did not kill Jesus, or require his death, or
manipulate others into sacrificing him. God may have found a way to triumph
over this crime, but God did not cause it. Jesus was killed by the definite plan
and malice aforethought of the Powers, as the New Testament writers clearly
state.[3]

They had to kill him, for Jesus represented the most intolerable threat ever
placed against the spirituality, values, and arrangements of the Domination
System. Perhaps we have had our eyes too close to the texts and the period to
sense just how radical his assault was. As Eisler notes, only Socrates and possibly
Pythagoras begin to approach Jesus' vision.[4] Perhaps we have been too concerned
to document or to undermine the claims of divinity made for Jesus to see what
he actually achieved. If we hold up his words and life against the backdrop of
the Domination System, we can see them in a more comprehensive perspective,
and appreciate why the Powers had little choice but to destroy him.

Not only did he and his followers repudiate the autocratic values of power
and wealth, but the institutions and systems that authorized and supported these
values: the family, the Law, the sacrificial system, the Temple, kosher food
regulations, the distinction between clean and unclean, patriarchy, role expectations for women and children, the class system, the use of violence, racial
and ethnic divisions, the distinction between insider and outsider—indeed, every
conceivable prop of domination, division, and supremacy. The gospel, as I
remarked before, is a context-specific remedy for the evils of the Domination
System.

In the analysis of Jesus' teaching that follows I have not attempted to maintain
a careful distinction between statements and deeds that are authentic to Jesus
and those ascribed to him by the church, so long as they both reflect the values
of partnership and reject the System of Domination. At points I differentiate
Jesus' views from those of the church, especially when it failed to maintain his
liberating spirit. It may even be the case that Jesus himself was not entirely free
of ethnocentric attitudes. If we take the story of the Syrophoenician woman
literally, she exposed in him a certain prejudice against Gentiles (whom he calls
"dogs"—or "puppies," if you prefer); but she brings him around by clever
repartee and an indomitable spirit (Mark 7:24-30//Matt. 15:21-28).

Using Jesus' critique of the Domination System as a perceptual lens enables
us to recover emphases lost as the gospel was domesticated to androcratic

attitudes in the early church. Although occasionally Jesus' teachings were further radicalized (as in Stephen's attack on the Temple in Acts 7 or the extension of the mission to include Gentiles), the main tendency of the tradition (as in the Pastoral Epistles) was to accommodate the gospel in significant ways to structures of domination. Using the critique of domination as a standard does not replace the historical criteria worked out with such care by New Testament scholars;[5] it confirms and supplements them.

I am *not* attempting to present a definitive picture of the historical Jesus. I am focusing instead on an originating impulse that issued from him and was continued by his disciples. The words and deeds of Jesus are like holograms, that marvelous laser photography in which the entire photographic image is preserved in any fragment of the negative. Just so, the dramatically new reality proclaimed by Jesus is reproduced in even a single act or saying. Despite the complexity of the tradition, his spirit shines through.

We begin with Jesus' rejection of domination.

Domination

Mimetic rivalry[6] arose among them [the disciples] as to which of them was to be regarded as the greatest. Jesus said to them, "The kings of the nations lord it over their subjects, and those in authority over them are called benefactors. But not so with you; rather let the oldest among you become as the youngest, and the leader as one who serves. For which is the more important, one who sits at table, or one who serves? Is it not the one who sits at table? But I am among you as one who serves."

(Luke 22:24-27*)

Jesus does not condemn ambition or aspiration; he merely changes the values to which they are attached: "Whoever wants to be first must be last of all and servant of all."[7] He does not reject power, but only its use to dominate others. He does not reject greatness, but finds it in identification and solidarity with the needy at the bottom of society (Matt. 5:3-12//Luke 6:20-23). He does not renounce heroism, but expresses it by repudiating the powers of death and by confronting unarmed the entrenched might of the authorities.

His rejection of domination hierarchies could scarcely be more complete than when he taught, astonishingly, "Happy are those servants whom the master finds awake when he comes. Truly I tell you: he will hitch up his robe, seat them [lit., "have them recline," as at a formal banquet or feast] at table, and come and wait on them" himself (Luke 12:37*)!

When you give a banquet, Jesus suggests to the wealthy with a straight face, do not invite your friends, because they will just reciprocate, but invite instead the poor, the maimed, the lame, and the blind.[8] If another invites you to a feast, do not sit down in a place of honor, but in the last place (Luke 14:7-11). Do not be like the religious leaders, who make their prayer shawls ornate and their robes fashionable, and covet salutations in the marketplace and the best seats in the synagogues, and places of honor at feasts, and make long, pretentious prayers.[9] Such status-driven behavior simply humiliates those who lack special privileges and standing in society (1 Cor. 11:22).

These are the words and deeds, not of a minor reformer, but of an egalitarian prophet who repudiates the very premises on which domination is based: the right of some to lord it over others by means of power, wealth, shaming, or titles.

In his beatitudes, his healings, and his table fellowship with outcasts and sinners, Jesus declares God's special concern for the oppressed. God sides with the poor, not because of their virtue, but because of their suffering; not because of their goodness, but because they have been sinned against.[10] And he proclaims them blessed, not because poverty is holy, but because their poverty gives them a perspective to understand Jesus' condemnations of wealth. He declares those who weep fortunate, not because their suffering produces character, but because it opens their eyes, as in the consciousness-raising funerals of black South Africans and Palestinians. Indeed, what are the Beatitudes if not a systematic and explicit repudiation of the Domination System?

Jesus himself seems to have rejected the titles people tried to pin on him. Most scholars agree that he did not claim for himself the status of God, Son of God, or Messiah; these were ascribed to him after the resurrection by his followers, who reinterpreted them in the light of the cross. Jesus refused the roles of Mosaic prophet, priestly Messiah, and Davidic ruler;[11] he would not allow his admirers to make him king (John 6:15). "If you are the son of God," the Devil insinuates, "behave like a messiah: be like the great heroes of Israel." Jesus refuses (Matt. 4:1-11//Luke 4:1-13).

Nor are his followers to take titles: "But you are not to be called rabbi, for you have one teacher, and you are all students. And call no one your father on earth, for you have one Father—the one in heaven. Nor are you to be called instructors, for you have one instructor" (Matt. 23:8-10). His followers are to maintain domination-free relationships in a discipleship of equals that includes women.[12] The hierarchical relationship of master and slave, teacher and student, is not to persist. "I do not call you servants any longer, because the servant does not know what the master is doing; but I have called you friends" (John 15:15).[13] Jesus wants students who can become true peers: "A disciple is not above the teacher, but everyone who is fully qualified will be like the teacher."

Jesus' actions embody his words. According to the Fourth Gospel, Jesus washes the disciples' feet, a duty considered so degrading that a master could not order a Jewish slave to perform it (John 13:1-20).[14] He also prearranges for the Last Supper by having his disciples meet a man carrying a water pitcher, a task strictly confined to women (Mark 14:13; Luke 22:10; Matthew apparently finds this intolerable and omits it).

Consistent with all that he has said and done, Jesus enters Jerusalem farcically, on a donkey. The church later read portentous meaning into this act on the strength of Zech. 9:9 (Matt. 21:5; John 12:15). But Mark and Luke make no reference to Zechariah, and may reflect something closer to Jesus' intent: lampooning the Davidic kingship by paradoxical reversal (Mark 11:1-10//Luke 19:28-38). The human being who has no place to lay his head (Luke 9:57-58//Matt. 8:19-20) is the same "king" who owns nothing and must borrow—not even a horse—an ass! It is conceivable that Zech. 9:9 is already farcical, and that Jesus took his inspiration from it. If he entered Jerusalem by the Horse Gate (Neh. 3:28; Jer. 31:40)—it was on the east side, the direction from which Jesus was coming—the irony would be all the greater.

The church later developed this reversal of values in the magnificent infancy narratives, where, according to the account in Luke 2, the child of the Creator of the universe must be born in a stable because no one would make room for his family in the inn; where shepherds, regarded by the righteous as dishonest, unclean, and no better than gentile slaves, and who were thus banned from being witnesses,[15] are the sole witnesses of Jesus' birth. Thus the witnesses of Jesus' birth (shepherds) and of his resurrection (women) were both largely disallowed in Judaism. The same theme is present in Matthew's account of the homage of the Wise Men (2:1-12); in the Magnificat (Luke 1:46-55); in the claim in Matt. 28:18 that "all authority in heaven and on earth has been given" to this lowly and crucified artisan; and in Paul's rhapsody over the self-abnegation of the Christ in becoming a slave (Phil. 2:5-11).

We must reckon with the possibility that one impulse in the development of Christology was the attempt to insert Jesus back into the hierarchical world of domination by attaching to him honorific titles refulgent with power—the whole operation concealed behind a veil of obsequious devotion (itself a telltale sign of dominator values).

Equality

The gospel of Jesus champions economic equality, because economic inequities are the basis of domination. Ranking, domination hierarchies, and classism are all built on accumulated power provided by excess wealth. In a peasant society, those in power see to it, by taxation, expropriation, debt, and monopolistic control of prices, that the poor are never able to rise above their station. In the modern economic system, the poor are kept compliant by the promise of economic and social upward mobility, whereby individuals are able to rise above their class without subjecting to criticism a system built on class inequality. In either arrangement, brute economic control is given mythological and ideological sanction to guarantee that those who have most to lose from obedience to the ruling class become its staunchest supporters.

Breaking with domination means ending the economic exploitation of the many by the few. Since the powerful are not likely to abdicate their wealth, the poor must find ways of transcending the Domination Epoch while still in it.

John the Baptist set the tone for everything that was to follow: "Whoever has two coats must share with anyone who has none; and whoever has food must do likewise" (Luke 3:11).[16] Jesus, for his part, pours scorn on those who are clothed in soft raiment and dwell in king's houses (Matt. 11:8//Luke 7:25). He challenges creditors, not only to forgo interest, but to ask no repayment whatever.[17] To those who wish to follow him, he counsels selling everything, and warns the rich that they have no access whatever to the new society coming.[18] Those who hoard luxuries and neglect the poor at their doors are presented with the prospect of their own death and divine judgment (Luke 12:13-21; 16:19-31). To the religionist's dream of being able to be "spiritual" and still amass wealth within an unjust system, Jesus pronounces an unconditional no: "You cannot serve God and wealth" (Matt. 6:24//Luke 16:13).

The earth, he insists, is so constituted that it will provide all our needs if, and only if, we share equitably: "Seek first the reign of God and God's justice, and all these things [necessities of life] will be given to you as well" (Matt. 6:33//Luke 12:31*). His followers were to begin living now "as if" the new order had already come. Jesus and his disciples lived from a common purse (Luke 8:1-3; John 12:6; 13:29). He sent them out preaching the new order without food or money or extra clothes, relying on God's providence through the generosity of hearers (Mark 6:7-11 par.; 10:29-30 par.). They "had all things in common, and they sold their possessions and goods and distributed them to all, as any had need" (Acts 2:44-45; 4:32—5:11).[19] They were not to give special status to the rich among them (1 Cor. 11:20-22; James 1:9-11; 2:1-7).

Those who exploit the poor are condemned:

> Come now, you rich people, weep and wail for the miseries that are coming to you. Your riches have rotted, and your clothes are moth-eaten. Your gold and silver have rusted [from lack of circulation], and their rust will be evidence against you, and it will eat your flesh like fire. You have laid up treasure for the last days. Listen! The wages of the laborers who mowed your fields, which you kept back by fraud, cry out, and the cries of the harvesters have reached the ears of the Lord of hosts. You have lived on the earth in luxury and in pleasure; you have fattened your hearts in a day of slaughter. You have condemned and murdered the righteous one, who does not resist you.
>
> (James 5:1-6)

It is rather the poor whom God elects and blesses, the meek and brokenhearted and despised who will inherit God's coming reign on earth. It is the merciful not the mighty, the peacemakers not the warriors, the persecuted not the aristocrats, who will enter into the joy of God (Matt. 5:3-12//Luke 6:20-26). James 2:5 states God's preferential option for the poor: "Has not God chosen the poor in the world to be rich in faith and to be heirs of the kingdom?"

In parable after parable, Jesus speaks of the "reigning of God,"[20] using images drawn from farming and women's work. It is not described as coming from on high down to earth; it rises quietly and imperceptibly out of the land. It is established, not by armies and military might, but by an ineluctable process of growth from below, among the common people. Its colors are not gold and scarlet and purple, but earth tones: brown, yellow, and green. Its symbolism is not masculine (kings, swords, chargers, shields, spears) but feminine (water, soil, dough, women, a home).[21]

While others look heavenward for divine intervention, Jesus reports that God's reigning has already begun, in the very midst of them (Luke 17:20-21). While others ask when the promised time would come, Jesus heals the sick and casts out demons ("But if it is by the finger of God that I cast out the demons, then the kingdom of God has come to you"—Luke 11:20//Matt. 12:28). While others long for Israel to become like a mighty cedar of Lebanon, dominating the gentile nations round about (Ezek. 17:22-24), Jesus sardonically compares the reigning of God to a tiny mustard seed that grows rank and wild in hedgerow and garden, "and becomes the greatest of all . . . shrubs"! (Mark 4:30-32 par. = *Gos. Thom.* 20). He is, in sum, not looking for a kingdom for himself or anyone else where power can be wielded in order to *impose* God's will on the world. He is inaugurating a domination-free society.

Purity and Holiness

Table fellowship with sinners was perhaps the central feature of Jesus' ministry, according to Norman Perrin.[22] In first-century Palestine "sinners" referred not to people suffering a subjective state of guilt (as in later Christianity), but to an identifiable group of social outcasts: people in one of the despised trades (which included tax collectors); those guilty of flagrant immorality (adulterers, prostitutes, extortioners, murderers, idolaters); all who failed to keep the Law according to the standards of the religious authorities; and Samaritans and Gentiles. All these, notes Marcus Borg, had been placed, or had placed themselves, outside the holiness code of Israel as it was being interpreted by certain circles in first-century Palestine. To include outcasts such as these in the kingdom of God was to reject the postexilic self-interpretation of Judaism as separation from the uncleanness of the world. Jesus distinguishes between those falsely called sinners—who are in fact the victims of an oppressive system of exclusion—and true sinners, whose evil is not ascribed to them by others, but who have sinned from the heart (Mark 7:21-23).

Jesus' table fellowship with social outcasts was an acted parable of the dawning of the age of forgiveness. According to Borg, Jesus deliberately contravened the entire program of holiness of the Pharisees and other groups in Judaism. He denied the equation of holiness with separation. He rejected the notion that external things defile or pollute a person's essential being (Mark 7:15//Matt. 15:11).[23] He scandalized his hearers by his positive attitude toward Samaritans.[24] Now it is no longer tombs that render people unclean, but the religious authorities themselves: "Woe to you! For you are like unmarked graves, and people walk over them without realizing it" (Luke 11:44).

Instead of holiness as separation, continues Borg, Jesus offered an economy of mercy that extends to all, especially the outsiders, including Israel's enemies. The command to love enemies—which would have indicated Romans above all—points beyond the exclusiveness of the holiness code to a kindness and compassion which is all-encompassing and unlimited.[25] Like the father watching for the prodigal's return, so God receives with joy even the most hardened sinner (Luke 15:11-32). God searches for those who have lost their way as a woman does for a misplaced coin (Luke 15:8-10). This strange God loves enemies, the ungrateful and the selfish, the good and the evil, the just and the unjust, in an all-inclusive embrace (Matt. 5:43-48//Luke 6:27-28, 32-36).

The laws of clean and unclean were premised on the holiness of God: "Be holy, for I am holy" (Lev. 11:44). Consequently, Jesus, by abrogating the laws of purity, was announcing a new image of God: a God not concerned with cleanliness, who loves precisely the marginalized and rejected, whose tender womb aches for the uninvited and the unloved: a compassionate parent, transcending gender, the Mother and Father of us all.[26]

Rules of ritual purity are what keep the various people and parts of society in their "proper" place.[27] Without purity regulations, there would be a crisis of distinctions in which everyone, and everything, was the same: women equal to men, outsiders equal to insiders, the sacred no different from the profane. There would be no holy place or holy priests or holy people. Gentile would be no different from Jew. "Clean" people would sit at table with "unclean"; no one would be better in God's sight. Socially imposed shame about the body keeps people submissive to societal authority by weakening in them the immediacy of their own sense of what is right. Without such shame, what becomes of societal authority? Domination depends on ranking. Without such distinctions, how can one know whom to dominate?

In contrast to the traditional view that uncleanness was contagious, Jesus regarded holiness/wholeness as contagious. The physician is not overcome by those who are ill, but rather overcomes their illness. Thus Jesus touches the leper, the unclean, women, the sick, without fear of contamination. Jesus is not rendered unclean by the contact; rather, those whom society regarded as defiled are made clean. Holiness, he saw, was not something to be protected; rather, it was God's numinous transforming power. God's holiness cannot be sullied; it can only prevail.[28]

For the early church, then, physical purity was separated from morality and ceased to be a determinative element in one's relationship with God. Those who wished to continue observing rules of physical purity were free to do so, but the gospel message itself dismisses purity regulations across the board. That is the point of the story of the wedding feast at Cana: the waters reserved for the Jewish rites of purification have been changed into the wine of the new order (John 2:1-11). God looks, not on outer cleanness, but on the heart.[29]

Racism/Ethnocentrism

A logical correlate of Jesus' new attitude toward purity is the breaking down of ethnic and racial divisions. It is difficult to determine to what degree Jesus was aware of this implication of his gospel. He healed a centurion's servant (or son), but the soldiers in Galilee were Herod Antipas's militia, not Romans, and the man could well have been a Jew, as in the Gospel of John (Matt. 8:5-13// Luke 7:1-10; John 4:46-53). He healed the daughter of a Syrian woman from Phoenicia (Mark 7:24-30//Matt. 15:21-28) and a demoniac in the Decapolis who was probably a Gentile (Mark 5:1-20 par.); and he is remembered as predicting that many would come from east and west and sit at table with Abraham, Isaac, and Jacob when God's reign is realized, while heirs of the kingdom would be excluded.[30] However, Jesus nowhere flings the doors open to Gentiles. This was a step taken by his disciples under the irresistible logic of his teaching about God as Abba, his preferential love for the marginalized and excluded, and his repudiation of the laws about holiness and defilement.

The church seems to have grasped the universalizing implications of his message early on. Paul, the apostle to the Gentiles, saw the breaking down of the wall of hostility between Jew and Gentile as one of the great watersheds in history. Now Yahweh had become accessible to everyone, through the image of God as Abba.[31] God, the church realized, shows no partiality and is no respecter of persons; God sends sun and rain on good and bad alike.[32] What is often overlooked is that the universalizing of Judaism through the mission to the Gentiles was also one of the most remarkable enactments of Jesus' teaching on nonviolence and love of enemies in the early Christian era. The healing of the ancient enmity, the breaking down of the wall of partition that divided Jew from Gentile, holy people from barbarians, chosen people from the rejected, was Paul's great contribution (though not his innovation) to the gospel of reconciliation.

The follower of Paul who penned Ephesians faithfully developed the implications of the opening to the Gentiles (Ephesians 2–3). Christ's blood has superseded the sacrificial cultus and the Law, thus making "one new humanity in place of the two," Gentile and Jew (2:15). Together, in Christ, they have put away their former way of life, the old self, and have clothed themselves with "the new self, created according to the likeness of God" (4:22-24). This reconciliation of races and peoples in God is the precursor of true human partnership among all the nations of the world.[33]

Family

The family is the most basic instrument of nurture, social control, enculturation, and training in society. It is deeply imbedded in patriarchy, and served as the citadel of male dominance, the chief inculcator of gender roles, and a major inhibitor of change. "It is exactly in the family that women's oppression and men's power are enacted most plainly and personally."[34] It is in families where most women and children are battered, and where the majority of murders take place. In a great many cultures, men are regarded as endowed with the inalienable right to beat, rape, and verbally abuse their wives. The larger structures of patriarchal dominance grow out of the cell of the patriarchal family, notes Gerda Lerner. The archaic state is merely the patriarchal family blown large. "Fathers, empowered to treat the virginity of their daughters as a family property asset, represent an authority as absolute as that of the king. Children reared and socialized within such authority will grow into the kinds of citizens needed in an absolutist kingship."[35]

Obedience to parents was mandated by Moses in the Ten Commandments. Yet Jesus proclaims, "Whoever comes to me and does not hate father and mother, wife and children, brothers and sisters, yes, and even life itself, cannot be my disciple" (Luke 14:26; see Matt. 10:37). "Do you think that I have come to bring peace to the earth? No, I tell you, but rather division! From now on five in one household will be divided, three against two and two against three; they will be divided: father against son and son against father, mother against daughter and daughter against mother, mother-in-law against her daughter-in-law and daughter-in-law against mother-in-law" (Luke 12:51-53//Matt. 10:34-36). In violation of a religious duty known to every culture, Jesus tells a man to leave his dying father's side, to ignore the filial obligation to see to his burial, and to follow him peremptorily (Luke 9:59-60//Matt. 8:21-22).

The first person to attempt to squelch any act of courage, defiance, or revolt is often a family member. So deeply is the family enmeshed in the values of the Domination System that people's own flesh and blood may even betray them rather than see society's values jeopardized: "Brother will betray brother to death, and a father his child, and children will rise against parents and have them put to death" (Mark 13:12 par.)—a trauma the church was in fact undergoing at the time the evangelists wrote.

Jesus may well have been of Davidic descent (Matt. 1:1-17; Luke 3:23-38), but if so, he never appeals to it. In Mark 2:23-28 par., where one would have expected him to argue along bloodlines from the authority of David to that of the son of David, he shifts abruptly to the son of man; and in Mark 12:35-37 he explicitly rejects the concept of the son of David as messiah. He renounces the family as constituted by patrilineal bloodlines. When his own mother and brothers, thinking him mad, come to take him home, Jesus refuses to go out to them, repudiating the blood-tie between them: " 'Who are my mother and my brothers?' And looking at those who sat around him, he said, 'Here are my mother and my brothers! Whoever does the will of God is my brother and sister and mother' " (Mark 3:21, 31-35 par.). He offers an alternative: a new family, made up of those whose delusions have been shattered, who are linked, not by that tightest of all bonds, the blood-tie, but by the doing of God's will. These are "my brother and sister and mother" (Mark 3:31-35 par.).[36] Note the deliberate omission of the father. So also Mark 10:29-30 (RSV)—"There is no one who has left house or brothers or sisters or mother or father or children or lands . . . who will not receive a hundredfold now in this time—houses and brothers and sisters and mothers and children and lands"—but no fathers.

In the new family of Jesus there are only children, no patriarchs: "call no one your father on earth, *for you have one Father*—the one in heaven" (Matt. 23:9). Elisabeth Schüssler Fiorenza remarks,

> The saying of Jesus uses the "father" name of God not as a legitimation for existing patriarchal power structures in society or church but as a critical subversion of all structures of domination. The "father" God of Jesus makes possible the "sisterhood of men" (in the phrase of Mary Daly) by denying any father, and all patriarchy, its right to existence. Neither the "brothers" nor the "sisters" in the Christian community can claim the "authority of the father" because that would involve claiming authority and power reserved to God alone.[37]

Human beings will of course continue to be born to biological families.[38] The family is not intrinsically evil. Like every Power it is created by God, and is thus holy and just and good; it is fallen; and it is capable of redemption. The family is therefore to be protected: radical discipleship must not be allowed to issue in callous disregard for parents (Mark 7:9-13), or spouses (Mark 10:1-12), or children (Mark 10:13-16 par.; 9:37 par.). But families are also to be critiqued and challenged, a function performed by the new family established by Jesus. We never transcend the need for kinship; in fact, comments Eli Sagan, most societies today suffer from the failure to treat one another caringly, as kin. But the failure to transcend the patriarchal kinship system is making democracy impossible in many parts of the world, because as families are structured, so is the state.[39] The goal is not the eradication of the kinship ties, but their transformation into a nonpatriarchal community of mutuality and love. As such, families can become exemplary of the new family of Jesus.

Paul's surprisingly antifamily attitude in 1 Corinthians 7 becomes more intelligible in the light of Jesus' teaching. Paul is not simply anticipating an immediate end to history; he is trying to disentangle believers from the most profoundly soul-shaping institution in human society. Some women may have found welcome relief in being freed from having to marry, bear an unlimited number of children, and live a life restricted to the household.[40] Paul may have been closer to the mind of Jesus here than he has been credited with being.[41]

In respect to the holiness code, the Law, relations with the Gentiles, the Temple, sacrifice, and other issues, the church developed the implications of Jesus' teachings further. In the case of the family and the role of women, however, and all other matters dealing with male supremacy, the church generally softened, compromised, and finally abandoned his position altogether.[42]

Law

The family, even more than the synagogue, was where Jewish boys were taught the Law. (Girls were officially taught only the negative commandments, pertaining mainly to uncleanness, though many no doubt listened in on their brothers' lessons.) The Jewish Law promoted justice, love of neighbor, concern for widows and orphans, periodic cancellation of debts, and the manumission of slaves. Scholars have gone to heroic lengths to scotch the crass Christian caricature of the Law as outmoded, cruel, and callous to human needs. Yet many members of the early church soon abandoned observance of the Law, and barely held on to the Old Testament by means of fantastical allegorizing, arbitrary picking and choosing, and regarding it as prophetic of the coming of Christ. How did a Jewish sect so quickly jettison the Law, unless Jesus had already sown the seeds of that rejection?[43]

Not only did Jesus reject the current interpretation of holiness and purity laws, but he healed on the Sabbath repeatedly.[44] Violation of the Sabbath was punishable by death (Exod. 31:15). But there was much discussion among the rabbis as to what constituted such a violation. It is highly unlikely that the death penalty for Sabbath violation was ever imposed in first-century Palestine. The religious authorities were probably simply fighting a rear-guard action to slow the erosion of Sabbath observance in Galilee.

Why then did Jesus apparently go out of his way to flout current standards, already weakened by the indifference of the common peasants? Clearly there is more here than simply his insistence that acts of compassion and healing are appropriate on the Sabbath (e.g., Mark 3:1-6 par.; Luke 13:10-17). For he also defends his disciples' quite unambiguous infraction of the law against harvesting on the Sabbath (Mark 2:23-28 par.). They simply failed to plan ahead—or else, in following Jesus, they had no place to prepare the Sabbath meals beforehand. On that occasion he articulates a principle: "The Sabbath was made for humanity, not humanity for the Sabbath; so the human being [son of man] is sovereign even over the Sabbath" (Mark 2:27-28*).

As long as "son of man" here is taken as a christological title, the passage appears to elevate Jesus over the Law. Taken simply as a Hebrew idiom meaning "person," "son of man" here may mean just what it says: human beings, who recognize their creation in the divine image, are judges of what constitutes "keeping the Sabbath holy."[45]

On the fringe of Christian tradition there are sayings indicating that the church was concerned to preserve the meaning and intent of the Sabbath, even as it moved to replace it with the day of Jesus' resurrection (Sunday). *Gos. Thom.* 27b states, "If you do not keep the Sabbath as Sabbath, you will not see the Father." And, more interesting yet, Codex Bezae reads, at Luke 6:4, "On the same day, seeing some one working on the Sabbath, he said to him, 'Man [= son of man], if indeed you know what you are doing, you are blessed; but if you do not know, you are cursed and a transgressor of the Law.' " Paul, only twenty or so years after Jesus' death, had already formulated the most brilliant dialectical argument about law ever penned (Romans), and the Fourth Evangelist was to substitute the love command for the whole of Torah.

What had Jesus set loose? Law had been one of the few successful dikes against the flood of violence let loose by the rise of domination societies. By means of law, the violence of the powerful could be regulated. Excessive brutality could be checked. The rights of the less powerful could be championed, if not always enforced. To this day, major transformations in societies are marked by the passage of new laws: the Magna Carta, the Bill of Rights, the Civil Rights Act of 1964. Law at its best is the way ideals become operational and institutionalized.

But law—even Jewish Law (the Torah)—can be expropriated by greed and domination and become captive to violence for its enforcement. The Torah enshrined regulations that diminished women, dehumanized Gentiles, advocated in the name of Yahweh unmitigated violence and even genocidal destruction, mandated the sacrifice of countless animals, and institutionalized patriarchy.

As Paul saw with such dialectical clarity, law is good, fallen, and must be redeemed. It is "holy and just and good" (Rom. 7:12), because it is able to contain, control, or mitigate some forms of violence, and it expresses fundamental values necessary for the survival of human communities. Yet law has been co-opted by sin and domination (Rom. 7:7-13) and has become captive to violence for its enforcement. Law is sucked into the vortex of the contest for power; thus it becomes an instrument of violence and a generator of violence, limiting significantly its utility as a means of reducing or eliminating violence.[46] In the coming reign of God, law will be freed from its bondage to violence and be enforced by nonviolent sanctions—teaching that the early church was already trying to embody in its life (Romans 12; Matt. 5–7//Luke 6).

More concretely, as William R. Herzog II notes, Jesus set himself against those interpretations of the Torah that proved oppressive to the small peasant farmers, artisans, and assorted rural poor among whom he moved. Jesus did not reject the Torah, but only the way it was construed by religious authorities whose power base was in Jerusalem and who produced the readings of the Torah that perpetuated domination by Jerusalem elites and the foreign overlords with whom they collaborated at the expense of the "people of the land." These religious authorities were often power brokers whose scribal retainers served economic ends disguised as religious piety. Consequently, Jesus did not attack Torah observance as such, but the social edifice that had been legitimated by appeal to Torah against the Torah's own emancipatory thrust. Specifically, Jesus was arguing for a reading of the Torah that restored the honor of the marginalized and common people and removed the shame that stigmatized them in the scribal renderings of its meaning.[47] Behind the facade of legality and the demand for obedience to Torah, prophetic critique discerned once more the mask of the Dragon.

Not just Judaism, but all religions of the book degenerate periodically into legalism. And when spiritual degeneracy is coupled with an institution of great economic and political power like the Jerusalem Temple or the Vatican or any other concentration of sacred power, it is utterly predictable that the religious authorities will react decisively and, if necessary, murderously, to maintain their wealth and power. This is a statement about the nature of power, not about any particular religious tradition. It is as true of Christian or Muslim institutions as it is of Jewish.

It is not just the leaders of Judaism, but religious leaders generally, who become preoccupied with ritual minutiae while neglecting the weightier matters of the Law: justice, mercy, and love (Luke 11:42//Matt. 23:23); or who burden people with regulations that they do nothing to lighten (Luke 11:46//Matt. 23:4); or who take away the key of knowledge, neither entering themselves nor allowing others to enter (Luke 11:52//Matt. 23:13). It is well known that the office of the chief priest was sold by the Romans to the highest bidder, who was thus required to come from a wealthy priestly family; and that rural priests were impoverished by the inequities created by the greed of the priestly aristocracy. Religious leaders in every age have far too often blocked access to God rather than enabled it.

It is damningly true that Christians, already in the New Testament, called down everlasting guilt on Jews for their part in the execution of Jesus,[48] and that Roman culpability was downplayed, even in Scripture.[49] But truth is not served by denying the obvious: that Jewish religion in first-century Palestine was corrupt at the top, sometimes legalistic in its observance, and often narrow-minded in its relations with the rest of the world. Jesus attacked it, in the tradition of the prophets, and called it to a fresh relationship with the God of their fathers and mothers that he called Abba. *In their attack on the Law, Jesus and Paul were not attacking Judaism as such, but the entire System of Domination that had subverted even the Law to its own purposes.*

That Jesus abandoned kosher food regulations is doubtful, since otherwise the vision that Peter received canceling them would have been superfluous (Acts 10:1—11:18; 15:7-11). But the issue is moot, since Jesus violated the *principle* behind such regulations by eating with the unclean.[50] He did not require his disciples to wash their hands before eating (Mark 7:1-23//Matt. 15:1-20), and he articulated a principle that, in a single sentence, wiped out the basis for the entire system of purification and defilement: "There is nothing outside a person that by going in can defile, but the things that come out are what defile" (Mark 7:15//Matt. 15:11).

Is it because he had reached this insight that he could lay his hands on a leper (Mark 1:40-45 par.), or allow himself to be touched by a harlot (Luke 7:36-50)? Or was it because he had seen their plight and had compassion that he was led to formulate the principle?

On the strength of Jesus' breakout from the laws of defilement, Paul could declare, against the grain of his entire socialization and training as a Pharisee, "I know and am persuaded in the Lord Jesus that nothing is unclean in itself; but it is unclean for anyone who thinks it unclean" (Rom. 14:14).

In a little-known statement, Jesus asks, "Why do you not judge for yourselves what is right?" (Luke 12:57). Such a challenge requires a maturity in human beings not easily achieved. As Abba, God does not want slavish obedience, but a mutual relationship of love. The Domination System cannot tolerate people who think for themselves. Such sovereign freedom strikes terror in the hearts of the authorities, both religious and secular, both Jewish and Christian. Jesus and his followers checked the wild chaos this freedom might lead to by a tight community that exercised joint discernment about people's perceptions of the divine will. We see the difficulty of maintaining decency and order in Paul's struggles with the fractious Corinthians. Later on, Montanism and Gnosticism would spawn so many Godlings that the church overreacted with a tyrannous hierarchy: its own Scripture, canon law, and an orthodoxy as rigidly and violently defended as anything Judaism had ever known under Moses or Ezra or the Maccabees.

Sacrifice

Not only the Law and the purity system, but even the Temple and the sacrificial system came under the uncompromising scalpel of this surgeon. But here we encounter a genuine riddle. Luke's reconstruction of Stephen's speech includes the charge that Israel's first sacrifice was not to God but to the golden calf, and that God's punishment was to give them over to offering sacrifices to the gods Moloch and Rephan and the host of heaven. But God, he reminds them, does not dwell in houses made by hands—a point Paul later makes to the Athenians.[51] That constitutes a fundamental rejection of the validity of sacrifice from its inception. Where did the impetus for such a sweeping indictment take its rise?

Furthermore, Paul is, in very short order, speaking of the body of Christ as a new temple of which believers are individually members.[52] But if our own personal or corporate bodies can be thought of as temples of the Holy Spirit (1 Cor. 6:19-20), or if we can present our bodies as living sacrifices to God (Rom. 12:1), what further use is the Temple? If Jesus has died, once for all, to free us from sin, then the Temple is superfluous, superseded.[53] Jesus' death is the end of ritual sacrifice. When he dies, the curtain before the Holy of Holies is torn from top to bottom (Mark 15:38 par.), a symbolic statement of the exhaustion of the Temple's holy powers.[54] Spiritual sacrifice has taken the place of animal slaughter (1 Pet. 2:5). God desires mercy, not sacrifice (Matt. 9:13; 12:7 = Hos. 6:6).

Jesus cleanses a leper and sends him to show himself to the priests and offer a sacrifice in the Temple, but the man instead begins to proclaim what Jesus did for him and ignores both priest and Temple.[55] When a woman touches his garment and is healed, he completely ignores the requirement of Lev. 15:25-30 that she offer in the Temple two turtledoves, "one for a sin offering [as if her sins caused her illness] and the other for a burnt offering" (Mark 5:24b-34 par.). Jesus declares sins forgiven (Mark 2:1-12 par.; Luke 7:48), thereby rendering the Temple superfluous—a fact that the scribes are quick to note and label blasphemy.

In the New Jerusalem, according to Revelation 21–22, there will be no temple, no altar, no sacrifice (21:22), even though the imagery of those chapters draws directly on Isaiah 60, where the wealth of the nations flows to Jerusalem specifically to beautify the sanctuary. The offering of sacrifice was a universal rite in the religions of the ancient world—so much so that the church's refusal to perform sacrifices brought down upon it the curious charge of "atheism."[56] One wing of Jewish Christianity even reports Jesus to have said, "I have come to do away with sacrifices, and if you do not cease from sacrificing, the wrath of God will not cease from you" (*Gospel of the Ebionites*, fragment 6).[57]

Jesus' own attitudes toward Temple and sacrifice are an enigma. He predicts the fall of the Temple, but anticipates its disassembly stone by stone rather than, as actually happened, by fire. This suggests that this prediction was not placed in his mouth by the church after the fall of Jerusalem in 70 C.E. (Mark 13:1-2 par.).[58] Was he just anticipating the outcome of violent resistance, or making a judgment on the Temple and the entire cultic system? At his trial, we are told, he was charged with saying *he* would destroy the Temple, but the testimony, significantly, did not agree and, to the high priest's credit, it was not accepted. What had he said? John's Gospel reinterprets Jesus' statement metaphorically: " 'Destroy this temple, and in three days I will raise it up.' . . . But he was speaking of the temple of his body" (John 2:19, 21). Jesus regards the Temple affirmatively in Matt. 5:23-24 and 23:16-22, and tradition still depicts him honoring it as "my Father's house" (Luke 2:49; John 2:16) or God's house (Mark 11:17 par.). If his last supper was a Passover meal (which is hotly debated), then he would have had a paschal lamb slaughtered. Acts 6:7 states that "a great many of the priests" became Christians; ostensibly they continued to offer sacrifices in the Temple. And the early church continued to pray, preach, and heal there.[59] So how did the church move to the eventual outright rejection of the Temple?[60]

No doubt the destruction of the Temple in 70 C.E. was the single most decisive factor in the rethinking of sacrifice. But the seeds of the church's rejection had already been sown much earlier. Perhaps a clue lies in John 2:22—the disciples, John says, did not understand the meaning of Jesus' demonstration in the Temple until he was raised from the dead. They had not comprehended it at the time. What Jesus himself intended by it was certainly not made clear to his followers.

We cannot enter the mind of Jesus to retrace his motives. Whatever he may have intended by his act, the church gradually discerned that his life and teaching had undermined the entire theology of holiness on which the Temple cult was based. Jesus' death, they also came to believe, had exposed and annulled the whole system of sacrificial victimage, and thus terminated Temple slaughter—in short, sacred violence.

His action was understood symbolically. It was not a "cleansing" or reform of the Temple, to restore it to pure sacrifices or to eliminate business activity from the Temple precincts. The Temple could scarcely function at all without these sellers and money changers. Rather, the Gospels depict Jesus as enflamed by the separatism and exclusivity of the Temple ("my house shall be called a house of prayer for all the nations," Mark 11:17a). He is shown attempting to shut it down entirely by preventing payment of the Temple tax, the obtaining of sacrificial victims, and even its use as a shortcut.

The Temple was the embodiment, institutionally, of holiness understood as separation—a holiness that prevented direct access to God by all but "undefiled" Jewish men. Jesus abolishes the pollution system maintained by the Temple through its inherent separation of the sacred and the secular. This separation worked greatly to the financial advantage of the priestly ruling elite ("but you have made it a den of robbers," Mark 11:17b).[61]

At the same time, Jesus' crucifixion laid bare the true nature of the sacrificial system, which projected the need for substitutionary slaughter into the very Godhead. The violence that countless animal sacrifices were supposed to quench was never satisfied. The System required human lives as well. But *this* man was more than just one more innocent victim. This one gave his life voluntarily, freely, *deliberately*.

The church understood his act as a sacrifice to end all sacrifices that exposed the scapegoating mechanism for all the world to see. In giving his body and blood he sealed a new covenant, irrevocable and everlasting. Into that covenant others could enter by undergoing a symbolic, spiritual death to the old order and rebirth to the new (Mark 14:22-25 par.; Rom. 6:1-11).

What was clear to them was that the Powers had used their final sanction against Jesus and had failed to silence him. Not even their last resort, death, could hold him. But if a mere Galilean artisan has withstood the entire Domination System and has *prevailed*, then the power of the Powers is not, after all, ultimate. There is another power at work in the universe that, like water, cuts stone. It is the power of sacrificial love: active nonviolence.

Nonviolence

Jesus repudiates violence. When his disciples request permission to call down fire from heaven on inhospitable Samaritans, Jesus rebukes them (Luke 9:51-56). A fairly widespread addition to the text, which correctly elaborates Jesus' attitude, reads, "You do not know of what Spirit you are. For the Human Being did not come to destroy the lives of people but to save them."*[62] He warns against using repressive means to fight repressive Powers (Luke 13:1-3). When

a disciple cuts off the ear of the high priest's slave in an attempt to save Jesus
from arrest, Jesus is portrayed as commanding, "No more of this!" (Luke
22:51)—an injunction the church took literally for the next three centuries.
Matthew has Jesus say, "Put your sword back into its place; for all who take
the sword will perish by the sword" (Matt. 26:52).[63] Second Cor. 10:4 sum-
marizes the apparently universal view in the early community: "The weapons
we use in our fight are not the weapons of the Domination System (*kosmos*)
but God's powerful weapons to destroy strongholds."* On their missionary
journeys they are not to take staffs for self-defense.[64] When reviled, Jesus'
followers are to bless; when cursed, they are to pray for those who abuse them.
They are to conform their lives to the life of Abba by loving even their enemies,
just as God does, doing good to those that hate them.[65]

Far from being a counsel of perfection or an incitement to cowardice, Jesus'
nonviolent orientation is premised on a power seldom recognized by oppressor
and oppressed alike—a power so integral to the new reality of God's reign that
Part Three of this book will be devoted to it. Its heart is the refusal to mirror
evil, to let one's responses be determined by what one deplores. Turning the
cheek, stripping naked, carrying a soldier's pack the second mile (Matt. 5:39-
41//Luke 6:29) do not at all mean acquiescing passively to evil, as we see in
chapter 9, but are a studied and deliberate way of seizing the initiative and
overthrowing evil by the force of its own momentum.[66]

The Eucharist celebrates Jesus' nonviolent breaking of the spiral of violence
by absorbing its momentum with his own body. Jesus' way means living a life
of forgiveness and doing acts of reconciliation. It involves working with anger
and its projection out on others so as to maintain healthy communal relationships.[67] Perhaps the most fundamental statement of nonviolence is the Golden
Rule: "Do to others as you would have them do to you" (Matt. 7:12//Luke
6:31).

Whatever his attitude toward the messianic role, Jesus clearly rejected military
redress of Jewish grievances. He refused to lead troops in a messianic war, or
defend his own cause by violent means. He endured the cross rather than prove
false to his own nonviolent way. "Christ also suffered for you, *leaving you an
example, so that you should follow in his steps* . . . . When he was abused, he
did not return abuse; when he suffered, he did not threaten" (1 Pet. 2:21, 23).

What Jesus distilled from the long experience of his people in violent and
nonviolent resistance was a way of opposing evil without becoming evil in the
process. He advocated means consistent with the desired end: a society of justice,
peace, and equality free of authoritarianism, oppression, and ranking. His method
and his goal were domination-free. Here at last is a full-blown alternative to
the politics of "redemptive" violence.

Excursus on Jesus' "Violence"

That Jesus taught nonviolence is indisputable. But did he live it? Two passages force on us that question: the "two swords" saying, and the misnamed "cleansing" of the Temple.

The first is Luke 22:35-38. Luke has intruded into his passion narrative a piece of mission discourse: " 'When I sent you out without a purse, bag, or sandals [Luke 10:4], did you lack anything?' They said, 'No, not a thing.' He said to them, 'But now, the one who has a purse must take it, and likewise a bag. And the one who has no sword must sell his cloak and buy one.' " This material is wholly out of place in the passion setting. The saying contemplates a journey ("take"), not the arrest. Surely a purse and a bag are of no use in defending Jesus!

The disciples' response, "Lord, look, here are two swords" (v. 38), is clearly Lukan redaction, most likely prompted by the anomaly of 22:49-50—how did disciples of Jesus come to have swords in their possession? Since Luke has also added the proof from prophecy (Isa. 53:12), Jesus' rebuke for their using the sword, and the healing of the slave's ear, there can be no doubt that Luke, at least, understands Jesus as censuring armed resistance. That the two swords are extraneous to the story is shown by the fact that only "one of them" wields the sword, just as in Mark, Matthew, and John. *Luke has added the "two swords" to the account specifically to provide an occasion for Jesus to condemn their use.* This is consistent with his rejection of violence in 6:27-29.[68]

Jesus' dramatic civil disturbance in the Temple is less complex but more problematic. What constitutes violence? Is it violent to overturn the tables of money changers and pigeon sellers? How did he "drive out" those who sold and those who bought in the Temple (Mark 11:15 par.)? John's Gospel provides an answer of sorts: he made a whip of cords (or possibly rushes)[69] and drove out the oxen and sheep (2:15). The merchants probably retreated as he advanced,[70] and the oxen and sheep not only were normally driven this way with little pain, but owed their lives to Jesus for rescuing them (temporarily at least) from sacrificial slaughter![71]

So the issue is really one of degree: how much aggression constitutes violence? The issue is real: is stone throwing by South African or Palestinian youth violent, especially when their casualties, given the use of rubber or steel bullets by their oppressors, are infinitely higher? Was it violence when the Berrigans poured napalm on draft records to prevent young men from being drafted and possibly killing and being killed in the undeclared Vietnam War?

In simplest terms, violence is injurious or murderous harm. Nonlethal force and some forms of coercion are not the same as violence.[72] Driving cattle or burning draft files are noninjurious. Throwing rocks is borderline: violent, but generally nonlethal.

Each person must struggle with these questions. There is no "normative" answer. At the very least the Temple demonstration indicates that nonviolence may be a good deal more aggressive than certain idealists might like.

Women and Children

Until the rise of feminist exegesis, Jesus' treatment of women had been considered something of an anomaly. Only a few scholars sensed how unique it was.[73] Through the lens of feminist exegesis, however, we can see that in every single encounter with women in the four Gospels, Jesus violated the mores of his time. If we disencumber him from images of Godhead and perfection, his behavior toward women, while not fully "modern" or feminist or all it might have been, is nevertheless astonishing, and, was without parallel in "civilized" societies since the rise of patriarchy roughly three thousand years before his birth.

Respectable Jewish women were not to speak to men in public; Jesus conversed freely with women.[74] A woman was to touch no man but her spouse; Jesus was touched by women, and touched them.[75] When a prostitute[76] bursts into an all-male banquet, kneels at Jesus' outstretched feet and begins to kiss them, washing them with tears of remorse and relief, wiping them with her hair, and anointing them with oil, Jesus, despite the stern censure of the other men, accepts her gift and its meaning, and takes her side, even though she has technically rendered him unclean and has scandalized the guests. Whether or not the concluding lines are original to the story, she was clearly behaving like one who knew her sins had been forgiven, whose faith had saved her. If Jesus did indeed say, "Your sins are forgiven," it was blasphemy, punishable by stoning (Luke 7:36-50).

Jesus calls a woman bent with a spinal disease for eighteen years out into the middle of the synagogue, lays his hands on her, and heals her from her "spirit of weakness." In the ensuing controversy (he had healed her on a Sabbath), Jesus refers to her as a "daughter of Abraham," an expression I have been unable to find in all of ancient Jewish literature. Women were saved through their men; to call her a "daughter of Abraham" was to make her a full-fledged member of the covenant and of equal standing before God with men (Luke 13:10-17). To heal her on a Sabbath was to liberate the Sabbath to be a jubilee of release and restoration. To touch her was to revoke the holiness code with its male scruples about menstrual uncleanness and sexual advances. To speak to her in public was to jettison male restraints on women's freedoms, restraints born of sexual possessiveness and the caricature of women as seducers. To place her in the midst of the synagogue was to challenge the male monopoly on the means of grace and access to God. To assert that her illness was not divine punishment for sin, but satanic oppression, was to declare war on the entire Domination System, whose driving spirit is Satan.

This tiny drama thus assumes world-historic proportions. In freeing this woman from Satan's power, Jesus simultaneously releases her from the encompassing network of patriarchy, male religious elitism, and the taboos fashioned to disadvantage some in order to preserve the advantage of others. The Domination System is precarious. To succeed in shattering its hold at any single point threatens its stability all along the line.

In one of the most beautiful stories in Scripture, though its textual lineage is uncertain, Jesus saves the life of an adulteress. Though her accusers caught her in the act, they did not arrest the man, in clear violation of Deut. 22:22. Intending to entrap Jesus, they ask if she should be stoned, as the Law stipulates. The Domination System treats adultery as the ultimate sexual sin because it is the most egregious violation of male property rights over the woman. Perhaps to divert their attention from her bared breasts (adulteresses were thus shamed, M. *Sota* 1:5), Jesus writes on the ground, then invites whoever is without sin to cast the first stone. Writing again in the dirt so that her accusers can melt away without drawing attention to themselves, he then asks her: "Woman, where are they? Has no one condemned you?" She says, "No one, sir." "Neither do I condemn you; go your way, and from now on do not sin again" (John 7:53—8:11).

The Fourth Gospel also portrays Jesus not only speaking to a Samaritan woman, but taking a drink from her unclean hand. The disciples, when they see it, are "astonished that he was speaking with a woman" (John 4:27). Or again, when a woman who has had a hemorrhage for twelve years touches him in a crowd, rendering unclean, not only Jesus, but everyone else she touched while elbowing her way through the crowd to reach him, he includes her in the new family he is forming, calling her "Daughter," and asserts that her faith, not his power, has healed her (Mark 5:24b-34 par.).

The contagion of holiness overcomes the contagion of uncleanness. And that new family, he makes clear elsewhere, includes not only men but women: "Whoever does the will of God is my brother and *sister* and *mother*" (Mark 3:35 par.—no fathers; so also Mark 10:29-30 and Matt. 23:9).

Even children have a share in this new family, and exemplify the way to enter it (Mark 10:13-16 par.; 9:36-37 par.). This constituted a radically new view of children, says Jeremias, in a world where children, like women, were counted as having little value.[77] "The saying is not an invitation to childlike innocence and naiveté but a challenge to relinquish all claims of power and domination over others."[78]

Some passages in the New Testament are an acute embarrassment and source of outrage for their attitudes toward women; none of them is based on the teaching of Jesus.[79] Jewish texts from the period reflect similar patriarchal attitudes. One such is the following: "If any man gives his daughter a knowledge of the Law it is as though he taught her lechery."[80] The logic is impeccable: to teach her lechery is to cause her alone to sin; to teach her Torah is to break down the division between male superiority and female inferiority, and to threaten the whole apparatus of male dominance, in which the male prerogative of interpreting the Law is central. (This issue very much survives today, in both Christianity and Judaism, in the question of the ordination of women.)

Women were subject to all the negative commandments of the Law, and to the whole force of civil and penal law, but "observance of all the positive ordinances that depend on the time of year is incumbent on men but not on women."[81] Only boys could go to schools. Rabbinical texts reveal, in a period later than Jesus', that some women persisted, nevertheless, in trying to learn the Law.[82] One such in the Gospels is Mary, whose sister Martha complains to Jesus that Mary refuses to help serve the dinner, but is instead seated at Jesus' feet—the prerogative of a *male disciple* of a teacher. However much we might wish that Jesus had gotten up and helped to serve the meal and to clean up afterward—a role to which he seems not to have been averse (Luke 12:37; in John 21:9-14 the risen Jesus confirms his identity by cooking breakfast for the disciples, a task normally reserved for women and servants)—the fact remains that Jesus and Mary were transgressing a deep-seated prohibition from which even Martha could not free herself.[83]

Keep women in their place! "Blessed is the womb that bore you," cries a woman in the crowd, "and the breasts that nursed you!" Why not give his mother credit in the only way the culture allowed it? Jesus refuses: "Blessed rather are those who hear the word of God and obey it!" (Luke 11:27-28). This woman persists in believing that her value, like his mother Mary's, lies in bearing a male child and living out her ambitions through him. But Jesus retorts: You do not have to be "saved" any longer through bearing sons. You yourself, a woman, can hear the word of God and keep it. Indeed, if patriarchy is ever to be overturned, women will have to stop consenting to its expectations. (By the second century, women were again to be silent in worship and saved through childbearing—1 Tim. 2:11-15.)

Jesus institutionalizes the new domination-free order. His loose band of followers is scandalously mixed, including prostitutes like the one who washed his feet with her tears (what else could she do, if she had lost her livelihood, but join his band?), women freed from demons like Mary Magdalene, and aristocratic women like Joanna, wife of Herod's chamberlain, "and many other women, who provided for them out of their means" (Luke 8:1-3*). It was without known precedent for women to travel as disciples with a teacher, and some of them, like Joanna, left home, family, and husband to do so. When the rich young man asked to follow him, Jesus told him to sell all, give it to the poor—not to Jesus' group of followers—and follow him, destitute (Mark 10:17-22 par.). The women, however, he puts in the role of patrons and benefactors.

The first shall be last, and the last first, as a necessary compensatory rectification on the path to full partnership in God.

Jesus also attempts to change a major structural cause of prostitution: the ease with which a man could divorce a woman. The severity of his pronouncement—he allows *no* cause for divorce, not even adultery[84]—is intended to prevent the wholesale dumping of ex-wives onto the streets. Divorce is essential to male supremacist marriage; note the androcratic form of the question the Pharisees put to Jesus: "Is it lawful for a *man* to divorce his wife?" (Mark 10:2). Jesus responds that God did not create or intend patriarchy but created male and female to become one flesh in a *matrilocal* marriage. Is Jesus suggesting that a man is to abandon his own patriarchal family and go live with his wife and her family (Mark 10:7)?[85]

At the same time Jesus completely redefines adultery. A Jewish male could not commit adultery against his own wife, but only against the sexual property of other men. In that setting, lust did not refer to sexual desire or excitement, as we use the term today, but specifically to the *envy of another man's sexual property*. Jesus radicalizes the meaning of lust and adultery to include even the mental act of dehumanizing women. He does so, not in order to shower guilt on people, as the church has used this saying, but to counter the self-righteousness of men who are technically free of adultery under the Law but who continue to treat women as sexual objects.

There may be sex-role stereotyping in Mark 1:29-31 par., where Jesus heals Peter's mother-in-law's fever, almost, it appears, so she can get up and cook supper! But gender specialization may not always be humanly restrictive.[86] Less ambiguously, Jesus features women in his parables as exemplary of the nature of the coming age.[87] In that age to come, women will no longer be the property of men, to be "given in marriage," but equals (Mark 12:18-27 par.).

The passion narrative shows the men weak, vacillating, denying, betraying, hiding. It is a woman who anoints him beforehand for burial, a kindness that he asks to be remembered of her wherever the gospel is preached (Mark 14:3-9//Matt. 26:6-13). It is women who view his death,[88] women who visit the tomb and find it empty,[89] and women to whom he first appears.[90]

I have documented elsewhere the struggle in the early church over who were the valid witnesses to the resurrection, and hence the authentic leaders of the church.[91] Women in that world had little veracity as witnesses.[92] How odd of God, then, to choose women as witnesses of the resurrection! Paul, in his list of witnesses, mentions not a single woman, and gives the impression that the risen Jesus appeared first to Peter (1 Cor. 15:3-8); whereas three of the Gospels (counting Mark's longer ending), and many of the noncanonical Gospels as well, concur that the first witnesses of the resurrected Jesus were Mary Magdalene and the other women with her.[93]

Women received the Holy Spirit at the founding event of the church (Acts 1:14; 2:1) and were coequal with men in receiving prophetic gifts.[94] They headed house churches,[95] opened new fields for evangelism (Phil. 4:2-3), and were Paul's coworkers.[96] They were persecuted and jailed just like the men,[97] were named apostles,[98] disciples,[99] deacons,[100] led churches (Philem. 1-2), and even, in one case, had authority over Paul himself (Rom. 16:1-2—"for she [Phoebe] has been a ruler over many, indeed over me").[101]

The right of women to equality in church leadership and witness continued to be fought out through elaborations of the resurrection story. Thus in the *Epistula Apostolorum* (early second century), the women are still depicted as the first to see Jesus, with additional stress laid on their being sent to witness to the male disciples. So reluctant were the men that the risen Jesus had to send a second woman, and finally, when the men still did not believe, Jesus went along with all the women to convince the men himself.[102]

In the *Gospel of Mani* (second or third century), Magdalene is commanded by the risen Christ to "do this service: be a messenger for me to these wandering orphans. Make haste rejoicing, and go unto the Eleven." Here again their unbelief is anticipated. Mary is even made a "pastor" of Christ to the Eleven, sent to bring "the sheep to the shepherd."[103]

Hippolytus of Rome (second or third century) echoed the theme of Mary Magdalene and the other women as apostles and evangelists, a note carried over in Gnostic literature as well. The apocryphal *Gospel of Mary Magdalene* reverses the usual gender roles of the culture and depicts the men crying and helpless, and Mary as confident, strong, and encouraging. Her very success in consoling the disciples causes them to turn on her in jealousy—particularly Andrew and Peter, who attack her for thinking that she, a woman, might have better access to the truth of Christ than they did. Peter is made to admit, "We know that the Saviour loved you above all other women," but this also leads him to ask irritably, "Has he preferred her over against us?" But Levi chastises him: "But if the Saviour hath made her worthy, who then art thou, that thou reject her? Certainly the Saviour knows her surely enough. Therefore did he love her more than us." Thus persuaded, they all went off to preach the gospel.[104]

The tide, however, had already turned. The vast majority of churches were soon dominated by male hierarchies, and women had been reduced to the roles of deaconesses and enrolled widows. Women who exercised authority were marginalized, accused of heresy, or silenced.

Paul, often criticized for his attitudes toward women, is not responsible for silencing women in the churches (1 Cor. 14:33b-36). This editorial insertion interrupts the flow of Paul's discussion of spiritual gifts, which resumes after the interpolation. It has no relation to the context, and is utterly contradictory to 1 Cor. 11:5, which asserts that women *do* prophesy in church.[105] Whatever his defects, it is Paul who articulates the Christian charter of freedom in Gal. 3:28—"there is . . . no longer male and female; for all of you are one in Christ Jesus." It is Paul who calls for reciprocal rights in marriage, an attitude far in advance of his time (1 Cor. 7:3-5). But old habits die hard; in 1 Cor. 11:2-3 Paul defends hierarchical patriarchy, and 1 Cor. 11:4-16 shows him fumbling to find reasons for a custom (head covering) that he should have rather abandoned, as he himself seems to sense (1 Cor. 11:11-12).

Paul did not write Eph. 5:21-33; 1 Tim. 2:8-15; 5:3-16; or Titus 2:3-5, though they are ascribed to him. But someone in the early church did. With 1 Pet. 3:1-7 and Rev. 14:4, these and other passages document the church's inability to sustain Jesus' radical antipatriarchal perspective. Over time, men gained a monopoly on leadership in the church, and patriarchy demonstrated once more its resiliency under attack.

The church's apostasy from the new order inaugurated for women must not blind us to the significance of what Jesus accomplished. Humanity has scarcely begun to take the measure of his message. Biblical feminism is not only an authentic extension of Jesus' concerns, but has made it possible for us to understand significant aspects of his message for the first time. Now it becomes clear that Jesus treated women as he did, not because he was "gallant" or "nice," but because the restoration of women to their full humanity in partnership with men is integral to the coming of God's egalitarian order.

Healing and Exorcism

Compassion is the hallmark of Jesus' God. Consequently, Jesus' healings and exorcisms, which play such a major role in his ministry, are not simply patches on a body destined for death regardless; they are manifestations of God's Reign on earth now, an inbreaking of eternity into time, a revelation of God's merciful nature, a promise of the restitution of all things in the heart of the loving Author of the universe. "But if it is by the finger of God that I cast out the demons, then the kingdom of God has come to you" (Luke 11:20//Matt. 12:28). God's nonviolent reign is the overcoming of demonic powers through nonviolent means.[106]

Exorcism especially preoccupied the early church. Baptism itself was an entry-exorcism, freeing the initiates from the delusional system that had previously held them in bondage. Exorcism was not, then, a rare and extreme intervention. It was the indispensable prerequisite for getting a "new mind" (*metanoia*). Jesus' teaching itself is a kind of exorcism, a cleansing of the mind of the misinformation that enslaves people to the Powers (Mark 1:21-28). And faith is a healing of blindness, humanity's trained inability to perceive God's presence and deeds even when they are happening before our very eyes (Mark 6:30—10:52).[107]

•   •   •

Space does not permit discussion of all other manifestations of God's domination-free order (the "Kingdom of God") in Jesus' ministry and message: new values, new assumptions, new strategies for social and personal transformation. What makes Jesus' message so powerful, however, is that he did not articulate it as an ideal, unattainable in this world and to be passively awaited in the distant future. He lived it. He acted on it. He brought it to reality by actually freeing people from bondage.

I have already alluded as we went along to some of the ways the church was unable to maintain Jesus' liberating vision; we must now look at others. But first, it is worth noting the areas in which the church was faithful to its founder. Nowhere in the New Testament or in the pre-Constantinian tradition is violence advocated—not even by appeal to the so-called "just war" theory. Likewise, the church was able to maintain openness to outsiders and a genuine universalism, with one exception: after gaining secular power in the fourth century, the churches avenged themselves on the synagogues that had, several centuries before, expelled them. But while the church did not return to animal sacrifice, kosher regulations, or defilement codes, it did develop a new legalism as pernicious as any the Jews had known, and an obedience to dogma that Judaism had never required. Men suppressed women. Domination hierarchies were restored and "manned" by men. The ideal of equality survived, but not much of the practice. Christologies developed that imputed to Jesus all the qualities of androcratic kings. God was portrayed as an oriental monarch.

Perhaps the most frequent deviation in the New Testament itself from Jesus' standard is the lust for punishment of the wicked. This represents an early retrogression to mimetic rivalry, where the church seeks revenge on its persecutors. The overwhelming number of these passages appear in Matthew, and have no parallel in the other Gospels. Matthew clearly has added them out of some need the gospel had not satisfied. All the "weeping and gnashing of teeth" passages are his (8:12; 13:42, 50; 22:13; 24:51; 25:30) except one, which, however, is not set in hell (Luke 13:28). Matthew adds threats of hellfire, eternal torture, and everlasting punishment that he does not find in his sources, as their absence in the Markan and Lukan parallels attests (Matt. 5:22; 7:19; 12:36-37; 13:40, 42; 16:27; 18:34-35; 22:7; 25:41, 46). Occasionally one finds elements of this vindictiveness in Mark (9:43-48 par.; 12:1-12 par.) or Luke (12:46 [Q], 47-48a; 16:23; 19:27), but they are not made central, and in most cases do not appear to go back to Jesus either. Matthew speaks of "tax collectors and Gentiles" in a derogatory way that flatly contradicts Jesus' attitude (Matt. 5:46-47; 18:17). Matthew also vents spleen at the scribes and Pharisees, all of whom are now regarded as hypocrites; John the Baptist's saying about vipers (3:7) is now directed against them (23:33).

Judgment is a necessary aspect of moral existence. It is integral to the demand for justice. God is not just Abba but also Judge, and Jesus no doubt is the source of some of what was elaborated by the evangelists. Likewise, there are some fairly grim statements about accountability before God in Paul, but almost no mention of punishment (1 Cor. 16:22; 2 Thess. 1:6-9). The Book of Revelation, however, despite its penetrating insights about the Domination System, is filled with a craving, not for redemptive violence, but something even worse: punitive violence, to be carried out by God, of course, so that John himself keeps his own hands clean. We are a long, long way from Jesus here.

Conclusion

Looking back over Jesus' ministry, what emerges with bracing clarity is the *comprehensive* nature of his vision. He was not intent on putting a new patch on an old garment, or new wine in old skins (Mark 2:21-22 par.). He was not a reformer, bringing alternative, better readings of the Law. Nor was he a revolutionary, attempting to replace one oppressive power with another (Mark 12:13-17 par.). He went beyond revolution. His assault was against the basic presuppositions and structures of oppression itself. Violent revolution fails because it is not revolutionary enough. It changes the rulers but not the rules, the ends but not the means. Most of the old androcratic values and delusional assumptions remain intact. The world, and even the church, had no categories for such fundamental change. It is no wonder that the radicality of Jesus was soon dampered by the church. But his has proved to be an inextinguishable truth.[108] Whatever we call the coming new order of God, we know that however long it takes to become reality on earth, the values Jesus articulated will be the values it exemplifies.

If Jesus had never lived, we would not have been able to invent him. There is, in the integrity of his teaching and living, an exposé and repudiation of the Domination System that no one trapped within that system could possibly have achieved. No wonder he was regarded as God's Son, descended from heaven. And it is quite true; his being is not "of this world" (the Domination System). I leave it to the reader to account for his unprecedented powers of personal and social transcendence.

With his death, Jesus quickly entered his own myth. He became larger than life. Worship of Jesus as God soon eclipsed the arduous task of continuing his work and living his way. The egalitarian shards of light he let loose upon the earth were systematically tracked down and quenched, or bottled, or enshrined, by the guardians of androcracy. The church itself has been a locus of the struggle between these two forces ever since, while the world at large has done all in its power to snuff out his influence.

But out there in the world, also, are others, not "children of this world," who have seen some of the same lights. They have taken other routes than that of the Wise Men. They have gone the way of renunciation, or of loss, or of outrage, or of unbelief. They too have suffered for their truth at the hands of the reality police. They too have seen revelations of an alternative. They have called it different names. They have embraced different faiths, or none at all. But the truth they serve is one with the truth Jesus served.

If the Domination System is ever actually ended, these prophets will have also played their part. Let us honor them, for they too have overcome the world.

Above the shouts and the shots,
The roaring flames and the siren's blare,
Listen for the stilled voice of the man
Who is no longer there.

Above the tramping of the endless line
Of marchers along the street,
Listen for the silent step
Of the dead man's invisible feet.

Lock doors, put troops at the gate,
Guard the legislative halls,
But tremble when the dead man comes,
Whose spirit walks through walls.

Edith Lovejoy Pierce,
"Drum Major for a Dream"[1]

7. Breaking the Spiral of Violence: The Power of the Cross

The Victory of the Cross

When the Domination System catches the merest whiff of God's new order, by an automatic reflex it mobilizes all its might to suppress that order. Even before Jesus experienced its full fury against himself, he apparently predicted the outcome.[2] The Powers are so immense, the opposition so weak, that every attempt at fundamental change seems doomed to failure. The Powers are seldom content merely to win; they must win overwhelmingly, in order to demoralize opposition before it can gain momentum. Always there is the gratuitous violence, the mocking derision, the intimidating brutality of the means of execution.[3] All of this is standard, unexceptional. Jesus died just like all the others who challenged the Powers that dominate the world.

Something went awry with Jesus, however. They scourged him with whips, but with each stroke of the lash their own illegitimacy was laid open. They mocked him with a robe and a crown of thorns, spit on him, struck him on the head with a reed, and ridiculed him with the ironic ovation, "Hail, King of the Jews!"—not knowing that their acclamation would echo down the centuries. They stripped him naked and crucified him in humiliation, all unaware that this very act had stripped them of the last covering that disguised the towering wrongness of the whole way of living that their violence defended. They nailed him to the cross, not realizing that with each hammer's blow they were nailing up, for the whole world to see, the MENE, MENE, TEKEL, and PARSIN by which the Domination System would be numbered, weighed in the balances, found wanting, and finally terminated (Dan. 5:25-28).

What killed Jesus was not irreligion, but religion itself; not lawlessness, but precisely the law; not anarchy, but the upholders of order. It was not the bestial but those considered best who crucified the one in whom the divine Wisdom

139

was visibly incarnate. And because he was not only innocent, but the very embodiment of true religion, true law, and true order, this victim exposed their violence for what it was: not the defense of society, but an attack against God.[4]

Paul asserts that it was not through the resurrection that the Powers were unmasked, but precisely through the cross:

> And you, who were dead in trespasses and the uncircumcision of your flesh, God made alive together with him, having forgiven us all our trespasses, having canceled the charge that stood against us with its legal demands; this he set aside, nailing it to the cross. Unmasking the Principalities and Powers, God publicly shamed them, exposing them in Christ's triumphal procession by means of the cross.
> (Col. 2:13-15*)[5]

The Law by which he was judged is itself judged, set aside, and nailed to the cross. The authorities that publicly shamed him, stripping him naked, have been stripped of their protective covering and exposed as agents of death. The very Powers that led him out to Golgotha are now led in God's triumphal procession, vanquished by the cross. When they tried to destroy him they in fact stepped into a divinely set trap. "The devil saw Jesus as his prize, snapped at the bait, and was pulled out of the water for all to see" (Luther). As a result, it is the Powers themselves who are now paraded, captive, in God's victory celebration. The cross marks the failure, not of God, but of violence.

How could this defeat issue in such a victory? The Powers were as powerful the day after the crucifixion as the day before. Nothing had visibly changed. And yet everything had changed. For now the Powers were forced to "listen for the silent step of the dead man's invisible feet," and to contend with a spirit that "walks through walls."

Let me illustrate. After Benigno Aquino had decided to renounce violence and commit himself to a nonviolent struggle against the Philippine dictator Ferdinand Marcos, he deliberately chose to return from exile to almost certain death. He was shot by the military before he had even descended from the plane. His death changed nothing. Marcos was more powerful than ever, having disposed of his only viable rival. Yet his death changed everything. Two and a half years later, Marcos was nonviolently removed from power. But for those with eyes to see, Marcos fell when Aquino toppled to the tarmac.

Jesus' death was like that, only he took on more than a single ruler. In his death he challenged the entire System of Domination.

For millennia the delusional system had taught that domination was given in the nature of things. Now the cross revealed evil where one had always looked for good: in the guardians of the faith of the people. The religious elites rejected him and delivered him to the Romans for execution, observes Herman Waetjen, precisely because the rule of God that he was establishing would eventually abolish the moral order that they attributed to divine origin and that they safeguarded through Roman violence.[6]

The cross exposed as well humanity's complicity with the Powers, our willingness to trade away increments of freedom for installments of advantage. It shows us that we are now free to resist the claim of any finite thing as absolute, or of any subsystem to be the whole.

The cross also exposes the Powers as unable to make Jesus become what they wanted him to be, or to stop being who he was. Here was a person able to live out to the fullest what he felt was God's will. He chose to die rather than compromise with violence. The Powers threw at him every weapon in their arsenal. But they could not deflect him from the trail that he and God were blazing. Because he lived thus, we too can find our own path.

Because they could not kill what was alive in him, the cross also revealed the impotence of death. Death is the Powers' final sanction. Jesus at his crucifixion neither fights the darkness nor flees under cover of it, but goes with it, goes into it. He enters the darkness, freely, voluntarily. The darkness is not dispelled or illuminated. It remains vast, untamed, void. But he somehow encompasses it. It becomes the darkness of God. It is now possible to enter any darkness and trust God to wrest from it meaning, coherence, resurrection.

Jesus' truth could not be killed. The massive forces arrayed in opposition to the truth are revealed to be puny over against the force of a free human being. The Chinese student who stood alone before a column of tanks for an eternity of minutes in Tiananmen Square graphically displayed this power. The collapse of Soviet and Eastern-bloc communism is a breathtaking reminder that no evil can hold dominion indefinitely. As Martin Luther King, Jr. could see with a prophet's eyes, the universe bends toward justice.

Those who are freed from the fear of death are, as a consequence, able to break the spiral of violence. On the cross, Jesus voluntarily took upon himself the violence of the entire system. "When he was abused, he did not return abuse; when he suffered, he did not threaten; but he trusted himself to the one who judges justly" (1 Pet. 2:23). The cross is the ultimate paradigm of nonviolence. Through the cross, God is revealing a new way, tried many times before, but now shown to be capable of consistent, programmatic embodiment.

Chai Ling was the Chinese student leader in Tiananmen Square when only five to ten thousand demonstrators were left, surrounded by the Red Army. She discovered that some students had machine guns. Calling them together, she told this story: a billion ants lived on a high mountain. A fire began at the base. It appeared that all billion of them would die. They made a ball, and rolled down the mountain and through the fire to safety. But those on the surface died.

We are the ones on the surface, she said; we must die for the people. So the students destroyed their weapons and sat down peacefully to wait for what seemed certain death. Perhaps as many as three thousand of them were killed.[7] By refusing to use violence, they robbed the communist regime of its "mandate from heaven," guaranteeing its eventual collapse—or transformation. "The June 4 [1989] massacre was no more the end of democracy in China than was the Amritsar massacre by Britain the end of India's freedom struggle," predicts Richard Deats. "Rather than the end, it may some day be remembered as the beginning."[8]

Jesus' nonviolent response mirrored the very nature of God, who reaches out to a rebellious humanity through the cross in the only way that would not abridge our freedom. Had God not manifested divine love toward us in an act of abject weakness, one which we experience as totally noncoercive and nonmanipulative, the truth of our own being would have been forced on us rather than being something we freely choose. By this act of self-emptying, Jesus meets us, not at the apex of the pyramid of power, but at its base: "despised and rejected by others," a common criminal, the offscouring of all things.

As the Crucified, Jesus thus identifies with every victim of torture, incest, or rape; with every peasant caught in the cross fire of enemy patrols; with every single one of the forty thousand children who die each day of starvation. In his cry from the cross, "My God, my God, why have you forsaken me?", he is one with all doubters whose sense of justice overwhelms their capacity to believe in God; with every mother or father who cradles the lifeless body of a courageous son or daughter; with every Alzheimer's patient slowly losing the capacity of recognition. In Jesus we see the suffering of God with and in suffering people.

The cross is God's victory in another, unexpected way: in the act of exposing the Powers for what they are, Jesus nevertheless submitted to their authority as instituted by God. Jesus' way of nonviolence preserves respect for the rule of law even in the act of resisting oppressive laws. By submitting to the authority of the Powers, Jesus acknowledged their necessity but rejected the legitimacy of their pretentious claims. He submitted to their power to execute him, but in so doing relativized, de-absolutized, de-idolized them, showing them to be themselves subordinate to the one who subordinated himself to them.

Therefore, according to the Epistle to the Ephesians, God has enthroned Jesus at God's right hand in the heavenly realms, "far above all government and authority, all power and dominion, and any title of sovereignty that commands allegiance, not only in this age but also in the age to come. God has put everything in subjection beneath his feet."[9] In our struggles with the Powers, consequently, we do not have to make the cosmic Christ their Lord; that is what the cosmic Christ already *is*. We do not have to install Christ as the principle of systemicity

(Col. 1:17—*synestēken*). We simply have the privilege of calling attention to the fact that the world already possesses coherence through him. The Powers, despite their constant effort to deny it, are indissolubly linked to the whole and cannot exist for a single moment, even in their idolatry, apart from the whole. And it was in the event of the cross that this truth became manifest.

In the effort to recall the Powers to their divine vocation, the good usually seems to lose. "Take up your cross and follow" means expecting the wrath of the Powers to break over our bodies. We take up the cross of our tragic impotence and offer it to God, praying for light on the other side of the grave of hope. That is all that black slaves could do for more than a hundred years, and somehow lifting it all up to God was an act of transcendence even in the midst of suffering.[10] We want desperately for the world to have meaning, for things to work, for problems to have solutions. And if not? The cross also encompasses the meaninglessness, the sheer God-forsakenness we experience when we are crushed by the Powers.

Further, the cross is God's victory over the Powers because, in this event, the Christ-principle, which was incarnated and humanized in Jesus, was made universal, liberated to become the archetype of humanness for all who are drawn to him. Jesus not only fulfilled the Law and the Prophets of the Jews; he also fulfilled the myths of the pagans. He not only lived out the inner meaning of the old covenant, lifting it to a new plane; he also lived out, in the daily pattern of his life and teaching, and in an exemplary way, in his death and resurrection, the pattern of dying and rising known to myths around the globe. What these myths depicted as the necessary course of personal and social development, Jesus demonstrated as an actual human possibility. In so doing, his own history became mythic, universal. By historicizing these myths he mythicized his history. At the same time, he demystified these myths by exposing the actual sociopolitical agents of this dying. The timeless pattern of dying and rising is thus historicized as the struggle to humanize existence in the face of Powers that will kill to silence opposition.

Jesus' death on the cross was like a black hole in space that sucked into its collapsing vortex the very meaning of the universe, until in the intensity of its compaction there was an explosive reversal, and the stuff of which galaxies are made was blown out into the universe. So Jesus as the cosmic Christ became universal, the truly Human One, and as such, the bearer of our own utmost possibilities for living.

Killing Jesus was like trying to destroy a dandelion seed-head by blowing on it. It was like shattering a sun into a million fragments of light.

Breaking the Spiral of Violence:
Girard's Hypothesis

But why must there be crosses? Why is the human race so violent? It is clear *that* the Domination System is founded on violence, but not *why*. The cross displays violence directed at the very heart of God, but it does not explain its source. There is, however, a hypothesis, still being tested, but possessed of such remarkable heuristic power that it deserves serious consideration. It is René Girard's theory of the scapegoat.

In a series of brilliant studies, Girard proposes that the roots of violence can be traced back to the mechanism of mimetic conflict.[11] I will present his theory in this section, and offer a few criticisms (though I largely agree with him) in the next.

The problem of violence does not first appear with the rise of agricultural civilization, according to Girard, but is endemic to human society from its earliest beginnings. Human beings, lacking the instinctual braking mechanisms that cause a wolf to spare its defeated rival, fell headlong into endless spirals of ever-escalating retaliation.

Those societies that survived did so, he believes, because they discovered a mechanism by which all parties could perform a "final" killing of a surrogate victim. This "scapegoat," usually randomly chosen, disabled, odd, or marginal, has to be someone whose death or expulsion no one will seek to avenge, and who everyone can agree is to blame for the conflict. The scapegoat is regarded as odious, monstrous, an object of hatred and contempt. Yet, because his or her death brings reconciliation to the quarreling parties, he or she is often regarded as a savior, a god, a cult figure. Herein lies the origin, Girard argues, of the gods, of religion, of sacrifice, of ritual, of myth.

Traditionally, the victim was taken to the edge of a cliff. The entire community formed a half-circle and began to hurl stones. Thus everyone—and no one— was guilty of the victim's death. Having removed this threat, and having celebrated the reconciliation that the scapegoat made possible, the community was restored to peace.

Myth arises to obscure the murderous nature of scapegoating by providing a fictional account of the event, says Girard. The arbitrariness of the victim's murder is covered by declaring it a divine necessity. The gods thus created by humanity demand the death of victims. But the hunger for blood projected onto the gods is in fact a metaphysical howling instituted by the murderers to drown out the cry rising from innocent blood spilled upon the ground.

So powerful is the collective trance, so mesmerizing the dancing, costuming, pageantry, and drumbeats of the ritual, that the victims may even offer themselves to immolation willingly, like the Aztec maidens, or the victims of Stalin's purges. The group thus splits off its violence from consciousness and transfers it not to the unconscious, but to religious or quasi-religious political institutions.[12]

The scapegoat mechanism is characterized by the following elements:

1. *Mimetic Desire*. We become human, in large part, by learning from others what to desire and then copying them. We imitate them (mimesis) by desiring what they desire. Such desire is in itself good. We learn by mimicry what is a good worth striving for. Value is defined for us as that which someone we admire wants.

2. *Mimetic Rivalry*. But in a world of scarcity, mimetic desire issues in a double bind: the one imitated says, "Be like me: value this object." But when the imitator reaches out to take it, rivalry occurs, and the one imitated says, "Do *not* be like me. It's mine."[13] Conflict inevitably ensues from mimetic desire, because both parties now competitively desire the same thing. Oedipal conflict is more simply explained on this model than on Freud's, Girard believes, and all other rivalries can be explained on this theory as well. The rival, who once modeled behavior, becomes the object of hostility and possibly violence.

3. *The Crisis of Distinctions*. When the differences that formerly separated potential rivals are dissolved as a result of their both desiring the same thing, the social distinctions by which order was preserved collapse. Girard calls this a "crisis of distinctions." Students seize the administration building, demanding a share in decision-making power that has previously been the sole prerogative of the administrators. Mill workers shut down the plant, insisting on a voice in shaping their new contract. The hierarchical barriers that society has so carefully erected, unjust as they may be, dike society against the flood of anarchy. When these distinctions collapse (as when soldiers in Vietnam refused to obey orders from their officers), that social system faces the possibility of collapse. Collapse can be averted, however, if society can find a scapegoat.

4. *The Necessary Victim*. The scapegoat can be a foreigner, an eccentric, a communist (or someone labeled "communist"), a witch, a carrier of the plague, a homosexual, a purveyor of new ideas, a prophet—in any case, his or her murder resolves the crisis. The fiction of the scapegoat's guilt must be maintained regardless of the real truth of the matter. The fact that hostilities cease following the scapegoat's death seems to confirm that he or she indeed was their cause and that therefore the execution was justified.[14] The key is the doctrine of Caiaphas: it is expedient that one person die and that the whole nation not perish (John 11:50). The group discharges its violence on the scapegoat and can now redirect its energies into mutual cooperation, even reconciliation.

5. *Sacralizing the Victim*. The necessary victim is rendered sacred by being regarded simultaneously as accursed and life bringing. As compensation for his or her sacrificial death, the victim is endowed with special honors and sometimes even elevated to divinity. Not only can violence now be survived, but it has also provided the impetus for the development of religious ritual and myth, and, through their generative influence, legislation and human culture.

6. *Sacrificial Repetition*. Subsequent sacrifices repeat in strictly controlled ritual the primordial structure of the scapegoat mechanism. Internal aggressions are thus diverted and expended ritually, and the social fabric is preserved.[15]

Religion is therefore, according to Girard, organized violence in the service of social tranquility. Religion covers up the sacrificial mechanism by means of myth, ritual, and prohibition. It institutionalizes amnesia regarding the origins of violence, and endows violence with an aura of necessity and divine ordination that disguises its cost to the victims. Religious systems cannot permit their violence to be known, even to themselves. Søren Kierkegaard identified this obfuscation with characteristic clarity: "The ethical expression for what Abraham did is, that he would murder Isaac; the religious expression is, that he would sacrifice Isaac."[16] By means of ritual, religion substitutes an animal for the original victim. By means of myth, it conceals the original violent murder while still maintaining an invisible connection to its life-giving power. And by elevating the victim to the status of a god, it erases remorse for his or her slaughter.

There is in the universe, however, a counterforce to the power of myth, ritual, and religion, says Girard, one "that tends toward the revelation of the immortal lie," and that is the Christian gospel.[17] Girard understands the Hebrew Bible as a long and laborious exodus out of the world of violence and sacred projections, an exodus plagued by many reversals and falling short of its goal. The mechanics of violence and projection remain partly hidden. The old sacred notions are never quite exposed in their true meaning, despite the process of revelation.[18] Nevertheless, here, and only here, is that process begun.

The violence of the Old Testament has always been a scandal to Christianity. The church has usually ducked the issue, by avoidance, allegorizing, Marcionism, or special pleading.[19] Raymund Schwager points out that there are six hundred passages of explicit violence in the Hebrew Bible, one thousand verses where God's own violent actions of punishment are described, a hundred passages where Yahweh expressly commands others to kill people, and several stories where God kills or tries to kill for no apparent reason (e.g., Exod. 4:24-26). Violence, Schwager concludes, is easily the most often mentioned activity and central theme of the Hebrew Bible.[20]

This violence is in part the residue of false ideas about God carried over from the general human past. It is also, however, the beginning of a process of raising the scapegoating mechanism to consciousness, so that these projections on God can be withdrawn. Now, for the first time in all of human history, God begins to be seen as identified with the *victims* of violence (the Exodus tradition; Isaiah 53; Mic. 4:2-4; Isa. 19:19-25; and Psalm 51, among others). All other myths, Girard says, have been written from the point of view of the victimizers. But these occasional critiques of domination in the Hebrew Bible continue to coexist with texts that call on Israel to exterminate its enemies now or in the last days (Mic. 4:13; Joel 3:1-21).[21]

In the Hebrew Bible, with only a few exceptions that are all legendary, whenever God acts to punish, God does so through human beings attacking each other. This indicates, says Schwager, that the actual initiative for killing does not originate in God, but is projected onto God by those who desire revenge. Yahweh's followers projected their own jealousy on God, and made God as jealous as they were. But something new emerges nonetheless: Yahweh openly insists on this jealousy, which begins to reveal Yahweh's singular relationship to Israel as one of love.[22]

The violence of the Bible is the necessary precondition for the gradual perception of its meaning. The scapegoat mechanism could have come to consciousness only in a violent society. The problem of violence could only emerge at the very heart of violence, in the most war-ravaged corridor on the globe, by a repeatedly subjugated people unable to seize and wield power for any length of time. The violence of Scripture, so embarrassing to us today, became the means by which sacred violence was revealed for what it is: a lie perpetrated against victims in the name of a God who, through violence, was working to expose violence for what it is and to reveal the divine nature as nonviolent.

It is not until the New Testament that the scapegoat mechanism is fully exposed and revoked. Here at last, Girard asserts, is an entire collection of books written from the point of view of the victims. Scripture rehabilitates persecuted sufferers. God is revealed, not as demanding sacrifice, but as taking the part of the sacrificed. From Genesis to Revelation, the victims cry for justice and deliverance from the world of myth where they are made scapegoats. In the cross these cries find vindication.

There is nothing unique about the death of Jesus—his sufferings, his persecution, his being scapegoated. Nor is there anything unique about the coalition of all the worldly powers, intent that one man should die for the people so that the nation should not be destroyed (John 11:50). What is astonishing, says Girard, is that, contrary to other mythological, political, and philosophical texts, the gospel denounces the verdict passed by these Powers as a total miscarriage of justice, a perfect example of untruth, a crime against God. The Gospels are at great pains to show that the charges against Jesus do not hold water, not in order to avoid suspicion of subversion, but precisely to reveal the scapegoating mechanism. The enemy of the state and of religion is, in fact, an innocent victim.

In John's Gospel, Satan is called the "father of lies." "He [Satan] was a murderer from the beginning and does not stand in the truth" (8:44). That lie, says Dominique Barbé, consists precisely in dissembling the violence at the base of society. Murder calls forth murder, and the whole chain of slaughter is the consequence of a lie. Redemptive violence, so celebrated and haloed by memorials, rhetoric, and parades, is the lie spawned by Satan that keeps the world bound by this concatenation of murder and lie.[23] And, painfully, the Johannine church's hatred and rejection of Jews who had rejected it was the poisonous deposit that would later lead—when the church had become powerful—to the slaughter of Jews by Christians.

Jesus never succumbed to the perspective of the persecutors—neither in a positive way, by openly agreeing with his executioners, nor in a negative way, by yielding to vengeance in mimetic repetition of the executioners' crime. In Jesus there is a total absence of positive or negative complicity in violence. In his arraignment, trial, crucifixion, and death, the scapegoating mechanism is at last, categorically, revealed for all the world to see. Insofar as other deaths reflect the truth revealed in his dying, they share its integrity and continue its revelation.[24]

The earliest Christians were not able to sustain the intensity of this revelation, and dimmed it by confusing God's intention to reveal the scapegoating mechanism for what it was with the notion that God intended Jesus to die. This in turn led to their reinserting the new revelation into the scapegoat theology: Jesus was sent by God to be the *last* scapegoat and to reconcile us, once and for all, to God (the Epistle to the Hebrews).

This took the Powers off the hook, however. The earliest Epistles and all the Gospels had attested that Jesus was executed by the Powers.[25] Jesus' own view of his inevitable death at the hands of the Powers seems to have been that God's nonviolent reign could only come in the teeth of desperate opposition and the violent recoil of the Domination System: "from the days of John the Baptist until now, the reign of God has suffered violence."*[26] Now, however, Christian theology argued that *God* is the one who provides Jesus as a Lamb sacrificed in our stead; that God is the angry and aggrieved party who must be placated by blood sacrifice; that God is, finally, both sacrificer and sacrificed. Jesus must therefore cease to be a man executed for his integrity, and becomes a "Godman who can offer to God adequate expiation for us all" (Basil).[27] Rather than God triumphing over the Powers through Jesus' nonviolent self-sacrifice on the cross, the Powers disappear from discussion, and God is involved in a transaction wholly within God's own self. But what is wrong with this God, that the legal ledgers can be balanced only by means of the death of an innocent victim? Jesus simply declared people forgiven, confident that he spoke the mind of God. Why then is a sacrificial victim necessary to make forgiveness possible? Does not the death of Jesus reveal that all such sacrifices are unnecessary?

The God whom Jesus revealed as no longer our rival, no longer threatening and vengeful, but unconditionally loving and forgiving, who needed no satisfaction by blood—this God of infinite mercy was metamorphosed by the church into the image of a wrathful God whose demand for blood atonement leads to God's requiring of his own Son a death on behalf of us all. The nonviolent God of Jesus comes to be depicted as a God of unequaled violence, since God not only allegedly demands the blood of the victim who is closest and most precious to him, but also holds the whole of humanity accountable for a death that God both anticipated and required.[28] Against such an image of God the revolt of atheism is an act of pure religion.

By contrast, the God whom Jesus reveals refrains from all forms of reprisal and demands no victims. God does not endorse holy wars or just wars or religions of violence. Only by being driven out by violence could God signal to humanity that the divine is nonviolent and is antithetical to the Kingdom of Violence.[29] As Simone Weil put it, the false God changes suffering into violence; the true God changes violence into suffering.[30] Jesus' message reveals that those who believe in divine violence are still mired in Satan's universe.[31] To be this God's offspring requires the unconditional and unilateral renunciation of violence. The reign of God means the complete and definitive elimination of every form of violence between individuals and nations. This is a realm and a possibility of which those imprisoned by their own espousal of violence cannot even conceive.[32] "Let the same mind be in you that was in Christ Jesus, who, though he was in the form of God, did not regard equality with God as something to be seized by violence, but emptied himself of the mimetic spirit" (Phil. 2:5-6*).

In its early centuries, the church lived in conflict with the Roman Empire, and used the imagery of conflict to explain the efficacy of the cross. God and Satan were engaged in cosmic struggle. The Son of God became man, wrote Justin Martyr, "for the destruction of the demons."[33] Two irreconcilable systems strove for the allegiance of humanity. The Christus Victor or social theory of the atonement (more a set of images than a systematic doctrine) proclaimed release of the captives to those who had formerly been deluded and enslaved by the Domination System, and it set itself against that system with all its might.

With the conversion of Constantine, however, the empire assumed from the church the role of God's providential agent in history. Once Christianity became the religion of the empire, notes J. Denny Weaver, its success was linked to the success of the empire, and *preservation of the empire became the decisive criterion for ethical behavior*. The Christus Victor theology fell out of favor, not because of intrinsic inadequacies, but because it was subversive to the church's role as state religion. The church no longer saw the demonic as lodged in the empire, but in the empire's enemies. Atonement became a highly individual transaction between the believer and God; society was assumed to be Christian, so the idea that the work of Christ entails the radical critique of society was largely abandoned.[34]

The theory of atonement by blood has usually correlated throughout Christian history with support for a reactionary status quo.[35] It stresses the idea that Jesus died for the forgiveness of our sins, without acknowledging the degree to which the laws that we have broken (human and allegedly "divine") are often themselves sinful, oppressive, and evil (the Southern "Jim Crow" laws, for example, or Islamic rules regarding women). Laws, too, are Powers, are relative, and change from culture to culture and age to age. Like all Powers, they are necessary for human life; they are good, fallen, and need continual correction. Genuine immorality is a symptom that one is in bondage to Powers greater than oneself, or that one is in rebellion against the fundamental requirements of authentic existence in the world. But when God is modeled as an authoritarian lawgiver, then the highest virtue becomes obedience, an obedience required *even when the laws that we obey deprive us of our essential being*.

The Christus Victor or social theory of the atonement, by contrast, states that what Christ has overcome is precisely the Powers themselves. The forgiveness of which Col. 2:13-14 speaks is forgiveness for complicity in our own oppression and in that of others. Our alienation is not solely the result of our rebellion against God. It is also the result of our being socialized by alienating rules and requirements. We do not freely surrender our authenticity; it is stolen from us by the Powers. Before we reach the age of choice, our choices have already been to a high degree chosen for us by a system indifferent to our uniqueness. The Law itself is one of the Powers that separates us from the love of God; it is the "letter" that "kills" (2 Cor. 3:6).[36] Therefore, Jesus "gave himself for our sins to set us free from this Domination Epoch" (*aiōn*—Gal. 1:4*).

Christianity has, on the whole, succeeded no more than Judaism in unmasking the violence at the core of humanity's religions. Its accommodation to power politics through the infinitely malleable ideology of the just war, its abandonment of the Christus Victor or social theory of the atonement for the blood theory, its projection of the reign of God into an afterlife or the remote future—all this gutted the church's message of its most radical elements. Jesus was divinized, as are many surrogate victims; the Mass (in the theology of the Council of Trent) became a perpetual sacrifice, rather than the end of all need for sacrifice; and Jews were scapegoated for the death of Jesus, so that the cycle of mimesis was set loose to run its violent course all over again.[37]

Nevertheless, the story was there for all to read in the Gospels, and it continues to work, like a time-release capsule, as an antidote to the scapegoating that still finds official sanction but diminished credibility in the world. The present cultural order cannot survive the revelation of the scapegoating mechanism, says Girard. The Domination System is premised on the belief that violence must be used to overcome violence. Wherever the gospel is truly heard, the scapegoat mechanism is rendered impotent, the persecutors' reports of their authorized actions are no longer believed, and the complicity of the Powers in officially endorsed executions of innocent victims is exposed as judicial murder. (Herein lies the world-historic significance of the exposure, by groups like Amnesty International and Human Rights Watch, of official torture and disappearances.)

Paul writes, "We speak God's wisdom, secret and hidden, which God decreed before the ages for our glory. None of the Powers (*archontōn*) of this age understood this; for if they had, they would not have crucified the Lord of glory" (1 Cor. 2:7-8*). This secret hidden since the foundation of the world is the scapegoat mechanism, and the rulers would never have crucified Jesus if they had realized that doing so would blow their cover.

Raymund Schwager presses Girard's theory one step further. Jesus "himself bore our sins in his body on the cross" (1 Pet. 2:24), not to reconcile God to us, as the blood-atonement theory has it, but to reconcile us to God (2 Cor. 5:18). God has renounced any accounting of sins; no repayment is required or even possible. God is not a stern and inflexible magistrate but a loving Abba. Why then was a redemptive act necessary? Because our resentment toward God and our will to kill leave us unable to turn to God. "God needs no reparation, but human beings must be extracted from their own prison if they are to be capable of accepting the pure gift of freely offered love. . . . It is not God who must be appeased, but humans who must be delivered from their hatred" of God.[38]

For Paul especially, the essence of sin is the desire to be God, which is in effect to enter into mimetic rivalry with God. Desire, seeing that God had forbidden it the fruit of the tree of the knowledge of good and evil, corrupted itself to envy by persuading itself that God was envious first. We are meant to imitate God, says Robert G. Hamerton-Kelly, but sin enters when imitation turns to envy and God becomes the ultimate rival. Desire thus transforms God into an idol on whom human beings not only project their own violence and hatred, but whom they also depict to themselves as the sanctifier of the violence at the heart of all religious systems.[39] To desire to usurp the place of God inevitably leads a person to create God after the image of a jealous rival, and fosters an unconscious death wish against God.[40]

The human desire to be God is countered by the divine desire to become human. God reveals the divine weakness on the cross, leaving the soul no omnipotent rival to envy, and thus cutting the nerve of mimetic desire. "He had no form or majesty that we should look at him, nothing in his appearance that we should desire him" (Isa. 53:2). Jesus absorbed all the violence directed at him by people and by the Powers and still loved them. But if humanity killed the one who fully embodied God's intention for our lives, and God still loves us, then there is no need to try to earn God's love. And if God loves us unconditionally, there is no need to seek conditional love from the various Powers who promise us rewards in return for devotion.

When the early Christians proclaimed that "there is salvation in no one else" (Acts 4:12), this should be taken as literally true: only through Jesus is the scapegoat mechanism exposed and the spiral of violence broken. "Salvation" here is an anthropological, not a theological, term. It simply states a fact about human survival in the face of human violence. Nothing is hidden except to be revealed (Mark 4:22): even "disappeared" and tortured people serve to reveal the violence of the Domination System, and the ideological justifications that the Powers advance (anticommunism, anticapitalism, national security) become less and less convincing. The problem is that, once the gospel has deprived a society of the scapegoating mechanism, that society is defenseless against the very violence in which it trusts. For us today, the only alternative to love and nonviolence is apocalypse. And it is not a vengeful God who ushers in apocalypse, but ourselves. The "wrath" or judgment of God is precisely God's "giving us up" to the consequences of our own violence (Rom. 1:18-32; Acts 7:42). It is now, in Gil Bailie's words, a race between the gospel and the effects of the gospel: either we learn to stop mimetic violence and scapegoating, or, having been stripped of the scapegoating mechanism as an outlet for our violence, we will consume ourselves in an apocalypse of fire.[41] In a world of nuclear weapons, even more urgently than in that of the Roman Empire, scapegoating must be exposed and eradicated, or we will destroy ourselves.

Evaluating Girard's Hypothesis

A theory of such global perspectives as Girard's cannot be casually assessed. It will require the work of a generation of scholars from a variety of fields to take the measure of his mind. I regard his treatment of violence as fundamentally correct. At the same time there are some matters of dispute.

1. I do not agree with Girard that all myths are lies masking events of generative violence. I believe that they often tell the truth, and that they are, like the Babylonian myth of redemptive violence, rather straightforward depictions of the actual power relations in a given society.

2. I regard the scapegoat motif as merely a subset or variation on the theme of violence (one that does involve attempts to disguise the real injustice of victimage), and see the combat myth of redemptive violence as more generic and common. Squaring off and slugging it out is the norm, and no third-party scapegoat is usually involved (see, e.g., the standard cartoon-show format). Scapegoating occurs more often in intragroup rivalry rather than among nations. In wars, by contrast, the more powerful combatant simply wins, and makes the loser subordinate.

Explicit scapegoating behavior has been documented among long-tailed macaques. What Girard leaves out of his theory, however, is *reconciliatory* behavior, already present among primates perhaps some thirty million years ago. Conflicts are averted or resolved by grooming, submitting, third-party mediation, embracing, and kissing, according to Frans de Waal. Among Homo sapiens children this list extends to include apologizing, gift-giving, pledges to cooperate, and sharing of food or toys.[42] It is not scapegoating alone, but an entire repertoire of behaviors and cultural institutions (law, police, courts, public opinion, mores, etc.) that helps to prevent bloody conflict. Scapegoating is an extreme and violent solution, marking the failure of the more normal means for preventing violence.

3. The idea of the sacrificial, expiatory death of Jesus is far more pervasive in the New Testament than Girard acknowledges (Mark 14:24 par.//1 Cor. 11:24-25; John 1:29, 36; Rom. 3:25; 4:25; 5:6-9; 8:3; 14:15; 1 Cor. 5:7; 10:16-21; 15:3; 2 Cor. 5:14; Gal. 1:4; 2:20; 3:13; Eph. 5:2; Col. 1:20; 1 Thess. 5:10; Hebrews; 1 Pet. 1:2, 19; 3:18; 1 John 1:7; 2:2; Rev. 1:5; 5:9, among others).[43] And it is not Hebrews and the later writings that proved most influential in the reassertion of the sacrificial hermeneutic, but Paul himself.

Paul betrays a certain ambivalence toward the sacrifice of Christ. Girard has stressed one side of that ambivalence, his critics the other. For Paul, Christ is the *end* of sacrificing and the revelation of the scapegoat mechanism, as Girard correctly perceives. But by depicting him as sacrifice, Paul also gives credence to the notion that God caused Jesus to be a *final* "sacrifice of atonement by his blood" (Rom. 3:25). If Christ's death saves us from the wrath of God (Rom. 5:9); if Jesus was sent by God as a sin offering (1 Cor. 15:3; Rom. 8:3, NRSV margin); if Christ is a paschal lamb sacrificed on our behalf (1 Cor. 5:7), it would appear that God's wrath must indeed be appeased. Paul has apparently been unable fully to distinguish the insight that Christ is the *end* of sacrificing from the idea that Christ is the *final* sacrifice whose death is an atonement to God. And Christianity has suffered from this confusion ever since.

4. I doubt that the scapegoat motif is foundational for all the world's myths, or that the Judeo-Christian Scriptures have a monopoly on the criticism of violence. There are myths that are nonviolent (the Hopi emergence myth, to name only one)[44] and as true as anything ever articulated by Christianity, and Girard's Christian triumphalism does them grave injustice. There are branches of major world religions that are nonviolent in many respects (Jainism, Buddhism, Hinduism), and numerous surviving "primitive" societies that are remarkably nonviolent in their actual practice.[45] But (in fairness to Girard) while these traditions do reduce violence by ritual, asceticism, injunction, and example, they do not raise the scapegoating mechanism to consciousness. They do not reveal the secret hidden from the foundation of the world—or whenever scapegoating got started.

5. How early was human sacrifice? There is a smattering of evidence for animal or human sacrifices performed by hunter-gatherers. Gimbutas cites a find of forty-five deer carcasses at Stellmoor near Hamburg, apparently sacrificed by weighting them with stones and throwing them into water (ca. 20,000–12,000 B.C.E.). Bear sacrifice apparently goes back to the Upper Paleolithic, and rams and bulls were sacrificed to the Bird and Snake Goddess in the East Balkan and Vinca civilizations from early times.[46] But animal sacrifice appears on a large scale only after animal domestication by agrarian or pastoral societies.

There seems to be little evidence of human sacrifice prior to the beginning of the androcratic period, however (around 3000 B.C.E.).[47] So whether the scapegoat goes back to the origins of humanity is far from certain. Here again, as with Marx and Freud and Eisler, there is an impulse to ground a mythic motif in historical fact. In Girard's case this is especially ironic, since he regards all myth as untrue.

Both Girard and Eisler may be correct. The scapegoat mechanism may have been precisely the means by which greater violence was averted; hence the relatively pacific societies that antedated the rise of the great civilizations. One could, in fact, modify Eisler's somewhat idyllic picture of early societies by arguing that they were as pacific as they were precisely because they had discovered the scapegoat mechanism. Unfortunately, scapegoating is not likely to have left much archaeological evidence, since it required no altar, but merely stoning;[48] and primitive societies today show no sign of scapegoating rituals.

6. It is risky to build an analytical theory on speculations about prehistorical culture when the evidence is so thin. Universal claims for a single-cause solution to the problem of violence have always proved inflated in the past, and there is no reason to expect anything different here. But the real value of Girard's

hypothesis lies not in its theory of origins, but in its analytical power to unmask the nature of human violence today. Even if aspects of Girard's overall thesis fail to convince, his understanding of mimetic rivalry and conflict and of the scapegoat are among the most profound intellectual discoveries of our time, and will remain permanent contributions to our understanding of the meaning of Jesus' crucifixion.

All that can be annihilated must be annihilated
That the Children of Jerusalem may be saved from slavery.
. . . .
To cleanse the Face of my Spirit by Self-examination,
To bathe in the Waters of Life, to wash off the Not Human,
I come in Self-annihilation & the grandeur of Inspiration.

William Blake,
"Milton"[1]

8. To Wash Off the Not Human: Becoming Expendable

One does not become free from the Powers by defeating them in a frontal attack. Rather, one dies to their control. Here also the cross is the model: we are liberated, not by striking back at what enslaves us—for even striking back reveals that we are still determined by its violent ethos—but by dying out from under its jurisdiction and command. As one founder of New Forum, which orchestrated the collapse of the communist regime in East Germany in 1989, put it, "You don't need courage to speak out against a regime. You just need not to care anymore—not to care about being punished or beaten."[2]

Dying to the Powers

"If with Christ you died to the fundamental assumptions of the Domination System (*stoicheia tou kosmou*)"—here, the customary rules and regulations by which society is regimented[3]—"why do you let yourselves be dictated to as if your lives were still controlled by that System (*kosmos*)?" (Col. 2:20*).

What strange palliative is this, that offers release from the power of death by the power of dying? We have been killed by the Powers, Ephesians says: "You were *dead* through the trespasses and sins in which you once walked, following the course of the Domination System (*kosmos*)" (2:1-2*). How then can dying raise the dead?

We are dead insofar as we have been socialized into patterns of injustice. We died, bit by bit, as expectations foreign to our essence were forced upon us. We died as we began to become complicit in our own alienation and that of others. We died as we grew to love our bondage, to rationalize, justify, and even champion it. And by a kind of heavenly homeopathy, we must swallow what killed us in order to come to life.

Each of us has already lost what would have been our way, had we only known how to find it (Rom. 3:9-20). There is no helping it; children must be socialized. Rules, customs, habits must all be learned, and learned under the supervision of the Domination System. And there is no helping it; at some point we must begin to become ourselves. To do that, we who are dead must die.

Why does the New Testament use this imagery of death for the process of fighting free from the Powers? Because, says Jung, the unconscious still operates on the archaic law that a psychic state cannot be changed without first being annihilated. And the annihilation must be total; "the gift must be given as if it were being destroyed."[4] This is what was symbolized by the nonutility and waste of the whole burnt offering in Israelite sacrifice: the entire victim was consumed by fire so that no benefit might be had of the remains. In the sacrificial system the need to sacrifice the ego was projected upon an animal. When the projection is withdrawn, one faces the task of dying to the socially formed ego in order to become the self one is meant to be.

But rebirth is not a private, inward event only. For it also includes the necessity of dying to whatever in our social surroundings has shaped us inauthentically. We must also die to the Domination System in order to live authentically.

Those born to privilege and wealth may miss life by having been installed at the center of a universe revolving around their own desires. Others, born to merciless poverty and the contempt of the ruling class, may miss life by never feeling really human at all. If the advantaged must die to their egocentricity, the underprivileged must die to their hopelessness, fatalism, and acquiescence in their own despoiling.

Rationalists may need to die to idolatry of the mind; dominating personalities to their power; proud achievers to their accomplishments. Traditionally, these have tended to be men, however, and theologies written by men to counter their own arrogance and pride are oppressive to women struggling under the burden of low self-esteem, prohibitions against achievement, and opportunities denied.[5] Such women need to die to the expectations and prohibitions of androcratic society. Even those whose lives have been stolen from them must lose their lives to find them. They must die to what killed them.

This, it seems to me, accounts for the greater success of evangelistic fundamentalism among the poorer classes. Unlike more liberal groups, who tend to treat "conversion" as a word unfit for polite company, and identify a change of life with changed ideas (and who thus stress education), evangelicals rightly perceive the more radical surgery required. They go for the heart—the whole gestalt of the ego, ideas, emotions, beliefs, and myths. Their chief failing is ignoring the dimension of the Powers. As a consequence, the genuinely converted person is reinserted into the old, unchanged world with little understanding of the social dimensions of sin, which are kept mystified by blaming everything on "Satan," who is conceived as a bugaboo rather than the spirit of the Domination System.

Jesus articulated this process of dying to the Powers as the central paradox of his ministry: "Those who try to make their life secure will lose it, but those who lose their life will keep it."[6] The imagery is fertile: to "make life secure" is literally "to make around" (*peripoiein*), referring to the setting out of boundary markers or property lines. Those who attempt to bound or hem their life in, to delimit or protect it, will lose or destroy (*apolesei*) it, because the conscious or developed fraction of their emergent selfhood (the ego) *has no idea* what the true contours of the self might be. Every line, boundary, or wall is arbitrary, drawn by parental expectations, social norms, or neurotic compensatory stratagems.

Depth psychology and Eastern mysticism alike have spoken profoundly of the death of the ego. Jung identified egocentricity as a mode of being possessed, an "autonomous complex" blind to the larger dimensions of the self.[7] What these approaches have not made clear is the degree to which the ego is also a web of internalized *social* conventions, a tale spun by the Domination System that we take in as self-definition. We are possessed not only by the ego as an autonomous *inner* complex, but also by a heteronomous *outer* network of beliefs that we have internalized. The unquestionably authentic religious experience of "rebirth" often fails to issue in fundamentally changed lives because this social dimension of egocentricity is not addressed. Many Chilean charismatics died to their privatized egos, but not to the dictator Pinochet. Many South African evangelicals died to their privatized egos, but not to apartheid. Many North Americans die to their privatized egos, but not to the hybris of American imperialism. Thus, dying to one's ego can be just another delusional spirituality unless it involves dying to the Powers.

We can no more free ourselves from the ego by means of the ego than we can liberate ourselves from the Powers by means of the Powers. The ego must be totally reoriented with God at the center, but this is impossible for the ego to do. What is required is the crucifixion of the ego, wherein it dies to its illusion that it is the center of the psyche and the world, and is confronted by the greater self and the universe of God.

The ego, to its surprise, discovers itself alive on the other side of annihilation, organized around a new center that is coextensive with the universe. To give oneself proves that one possesses a self that can be given. Paul describes the experience thus:

> I [lit., *egō*] have been crucified with Christ; and it is no longer I [the ego] who live, but it is Christ who lives in me [the true self]. And the life I [the ego] now

live in the flesh I live by faith in the Son of God, who loved me and gave himself for me.

(Gal. 2:19-20)

Far be it from me to glory except in the cross of our Lord Jesus Christ, by which the Domination System (*kosmos*) has been crucified to me, and I to it.

(Gal. 6:14*)

Once the ego is disidentified from the self, and no longer confuses itself with the infinitely more vast self (which is indistinguishable from the activity of God within a person), the ego is free to play its necessary but subordinate role as the organizing factor of consciousness, designated to lift the contents of the unconscious into the light of day.

The ego, as it were, tears up the false deed by which it had claimed possession of the house, and acknowledges that the whole property belongs to God. And lo! God allows the ego to go on living there. The ego now knows Whose the house is, beyond a shadow of doubt, though by force of habit it inevitably slips back into acting as if it owned the house. But now it does not take such a wrenching to let go of the pretense. Usually a simple reminder will do. This is one reason we worship. To worship means to remember Who owns the house.

Confession of sin has traditionally played a central role in Jewish and Christian worship, but it too can be corrupted by the Powers. We *should* be confessing our complicity with the Powers, the ways we benefit from the injustices they structure to our advantage, and the racist and sexual stereotyping that we thoughtlessly perpetuate in our encounters with others. Instead, we tend to confess infractions of the rules the Powers themselves have established. Forgiveness of sins often functions, not as an act of liberation from the delusional system, but as a rite of reinsertion into it. It has always struck scholars as curious that Paul tended to avoid the language of repentance and forgiveness, preferring instead the language of justification. Perhaps his instinct was right, even if he failed to articulate it in systemic terms: what we need is not to be cleaned up and sent right back into a corrupt society, but to be lifted out of it altogether, by a sovereign act of God, who wipes the slate clean and offers us a new reality, the reality intended for us from the foundation of the world.

Prayer is another reminder of Who owns the house. In prayer we rehearse our dying, undergo our disabling fears and come to terms with them in advance, so that we can offer our beings as living sacrifices to God (Rom. 12:1). It is by fear that the Powers keep us docile. "I tell you, my friends," urges Jesus, "do not be controlled by your fear of those who kill the body, and after that can do nothing more" (Luke 12:4*; cf. Matt. 10:28). We cannot, of course, overcome fear as an emotion. It is unavoidable and natural. But instead of letting it stand before us, blocking our way, we can put it behind us. Then we can walk the way that God opens to us, unable to escape fear, perhaps, but not letting it control us either. It may be that it will even diminish for a period, or actually disappear. If so, that will be a special gift of the Holy Spirit, and not the result of repression.[8]

Suffering is not the only or even the best teacher. To *have* to suffer is different from *choosing* to suffer. The latter can be powerfully redemptive for some people. Such martyrdom comes out of abundance. This suffering is not necessary but chosen. "No one takes [my life] from me, but I lay it down of my own accord" (John 10:18). Martyrs are not victims, overtaken by evil, but hunters who stalk evil into the open by offering as bait their own bodies. "Those who are willing to sacrifice nothing or very little, offer nothing or very little to history. It must also be said that they offer little or nothing to their own soul."[9]

This process of dying and rising is menacing to those caught in the myth of redemptive violence because it means facing the evil in themselves, and they see that as equivalent to damnation. For in that myth, salvation consists in identifying oneself as good by virtue of belonging to the right side. Psychologically, this means defining oneself as good in order to achieve a sense of well-being. The intolerable pressure of one's own inner shadow (unacknowledged hatred, anger, violence, lust, greed) can be released then only through projection onto others, against whom it can be exploded in a self-righteous fury. The myth of redemptive violence is mortally threatened by even the smallest amounts of self-knowledge.

Jesus' saying about losing one's life to find it is paired with another: "If any want to become my followers, let them deny themselves and take up their cross and follow me" (Mark 8:34). Jesus does not ask for more self-denial; the word here, *aparneomai,* is the intensive of "to deny" (*arneomai*), and means "to deny utterly, to disown." It is not a question of denying certain things to oneself, like ice cream during Lent, but of *disowning* the ego's claim to possess this life. The task is not ego-conquest by means of the ego (a persistent delusion of many of the "new spiritualities" today), but ego-surrender to the redemptive initiatives of God in God's struggle against the antidivine powers of the world. That means our abandoning egocentricity not only as individuals, but as cultures, as nations, even as a species, and voluntarily subordinating our desires to the needs of the total life system. And because the ego has been entangled with thousands of tendrils from the alienating System of Domination, the process of dying to one's conditioning is never fully over.

A monk asked Lung-ya, "What did old masters attain when they entered the ultimate stage?" "They were like burglars sneaking into a vacant house," came the reply. To which the commentary is given by Nyogen: "This monk probably thought masters have something others do not have, whereas they have nothing others have."[10]

Some "New Age" spiritualities, as well as certain aberrations of Christian spirituality, speak of the deification of human beings in a way that confuses the ego with the self. This can lead to a towering inflation, and is an invitation to psychic collapse whenever the shadow reasserts itself, as it inevitably must. The very desire to claim divinity for oneself may betray just how little of the ego has in fact been annihilated! Why would we want to be gods when we have scarcely begun to discover the wonders of becoming human?

The notion of dying to the ego and being reborn to a fuller life is not unique to Christianity. What is unique is the way Jesus enacted this almost universal myth of death and rebirth in his own life. The process, as he showed, is both inner and outer: a total reorientation within, whereby God becomes "the unconditioned value, the consideration which, if it conflicts with any other, whatsoever it be, will be given preference";[11] and a total reorientation without, whereby the social will of God becomes one's consuming passion.[12]

Because the process of dying to the Powers is both inner and outer, it can be approached from either end. Contrary to much theological prejudice, mystics have been among our most effective activists (St. Francis, Mother Theresa, Frank Laubach, E. Stanley Jones, Dorothy Day, Dag Hammarskjöld, Muriel Lester, Richard Deats), and former contemplative nuns are often among the most intractable foes of injustice.

One can also begin the process of dying to the Powers from the outside. Jeanne M. Paradise documents the effects on a small group of activists who each week worshiped together and then demonstrated at the Draper Laboratories, a weapons-research center in Boston. One participant commented, "Prior to acting, I had always imagined that antinuclear activists had their faith all wrapped up in a neat package and knew what they believed and where they stood and then went out and acted on it. And what I discovered was quite the opposite. I discovered what I believed through getting myself into an action that I felt compelled to take."

Another, whose conventional religious life had not been deep, spoke of undergoing an "essential conversion experience" when she first participated in a nonviolent public action. "I went in as me and came out as another person . . . I had this tremendous feeling life had changed . . . that nothing would be the same again." Of going to jail, a woman said, "It is so freeing. It's funny, going to jail to be free, but it's very freeing to live without concern for the consequences."[13]

Participation in nonviolent movements for change has had a transformative effect on millions of people. In Beijing in May–June 1989, people organized themselves spontaneously throughout the city in support of the prodemocracy demonstrators, throwing off for the brief interval, until repression was reimposed, the mutual suspicion, fear, and alienation that had characterized life under communist tyranny.[14] The same phenomenon was reported in the Philippines and in the American civil rights movement; indeed, it is a nearly universal experience in nonviolent struggles. When people engage in nonviolent resistance, they experience something of their higher selves; for nonviolence is a characteristic of the coming reign of God, and a foretaste of its transcendent reality.

Taking up one's cross refers specifically to Rome's instrument of intimidation and execution. It reminds us again that following Jesus' liberating way puts us on a collision course with oppressive regimes and institutions, which will resort to any means necessary to crush resistance. By voluntarily and deliberately facing the prospect of death, one is freed from its power as a deterrent. "Just as one must learn the art of killing in the training for violence," taught Gandhi, "so one must learn the art of dying in the training for non-violence."[15]

When Richard Steele was about to be jailed for refusing to serve in the South African Defense Force, he had to consider the possibility that he might be killed in prison. "Was I prepared to die for what I believed?" he asked himself.

> I realized finally that I was, and this freed me of a tremendous anxiety. . . . The *power* of fearlessness is astonishing. I think of those who were giving me orders. They were under a real tyranny and far more the victim of it than I was. When they were yelling their orders at me, I had a vivid image of these tiny creatures assaulting my feet, wanting to demolish me with orders, while I was way above, not on their level at all. They could threaten me with anything at all and not get me, because I wasn't afraid. This was immensely liberating to me. I could be the person I was without fearing them. They had no power over me.[16]

This attitude of sovereign transcendence through spiritually "dying" to the power of death is pungently expressed in the line from a John Ylvisaker song: "You can't kill me, I've already died; it's out of your power my fate to decide." It was this inner freedom that enabled Paul Schneider, the first pastor executed by the Nazis, to chant Bible verses during the prison roll call and, despite torture and imposed starvation, to shout at those who beat prisoners, "I have seen you and I will accuse you before God!"[17]

Only those who have died to the Powers can make themselves expendable. What we are talking about is simply the meaning of baptism, with its renunciation of Satan and all his works. Significantly, Jesus is never cited as speaking of baptism except as a dying (Mark 10:38-39; Luke 12:50). Paul also associates baptism with dying: we are buried with Christ "by baptism into death," and our "old self (*anthrōpos*) was crucified with him so that . . . we might no longer be enslaved to sin" (Rom. 6:4, 6). Baptism marks the entry to a community committed to the transformative values articulated and incarnated by Jesus. The church has repeatedly betrayed these values. Yet its sole purpose for being is to begin living now the way the whole world is called to live ultimately, and to represent the promise of another reality that holds the human future.[18]

Dying to the Powers is only the downside of rebirth, however. Rebirth is coming home to the universe, the rediscovery of beauty and of delight in the creation, the recovery of the capacity to love. It is the joy of belonging, of being a child of the Eternal. It is entry into the values of the society of partnership that is coming. And it is struggling with and against an institution the glory of whose task is matched only by the magnitude of its defections: the church.

The Church and the Powers

The church has many functions, not all related to the Powers. With reference to the Powers, however, its task, as we have seen, is to unmask their idolatrous pretensions, to identify their dehumanizing values, to strip from them the mantle of respectability, and to disenthrall their victims. It is uniquely equipped to help people unmask and die to the Powers.

The charter of the church in its struggle with the Powers is published in Eph. 3:10—"that through the church the wisdom of God in its rich variety might now be made known to the rulers and powers in the heavenly places." This was the very passage that so defied conventional explanation, as we saw in *Naming the Powers*: how is the church, an earthly institution, supposed to carry out a revelatory task in reference to the Powers if they are in *heaven*?[19] What we discovered is that "the heavenlies" (*ta epourania*) are not off at the edge of space somewhere, but are in our very midst as the *interiority* of earthly institutions, systems, and structures. The task of the church, then, is to practice a ministry of disclosing the spirituality of these Powers.[20]

In the immediate context of Ephesians, the mystery that has been revealed to the world through the cross of Jesus is that the basis of racial or ethnic enmity has now been dissolved. Jew and Gentile are now one in Christ. The church's task is to make this new fact known to the ruling Powers "in the heavenlies," that invisible sphere where racism is so deeply imbedded.

To root out racism required new outer arrangements, and the church provided that: a fellowship of equals growing together into a "holy temple" (Eph. 2:21). But even more crucial was the eradication of the *spirit* of racism, and that could only be countered by the leveling impulse of the gospel.

The church cannot discharge its divine calling, however, by cozying up to the Powers and trying to win a hearing. What makes such attempts at accommodation to the Domination System so pathetic is that the System already recognizes those elements in the gospel which displeases it, and is contemptuous of those who betray by such adjustments their own embarrassment with the gospel. Ignatius of Antioch sought to scoff such waffling when he said, "The greatness of Christianity lies in its being hated by the Domination System (*kosmos*), not in its being convincing to it."[21]

Those who have devoted their lives to the political side of social struggle may be mystified and even a bit uneasy about talk of changing the spirituality of the Powers as an integral part of resistance. They have seen all too many Christians limit their efforts to perfunctory prayers for the general betterment of humanity. Their fears are well-founded. A recent study of mainline denominations in the United States reveals that 78 percent of adult church members never spend *any* time promoting social justice.[22] It is important to stress that the issue is not either/or but both/and: The effort to change structural arrangements must also include changing the spiritual gestalt that may survive our structural changes and undermine their efficacy.

No social struggle can hope to be effective if it only changes structural arrangements without altering their spirituality. All our letter writing, petitioning, political and community organizing, demonstrating, civil disobedience, prayers and fasting move to this end: to recall the Powers to the humanizing purposes of God revealed in Jesus. We are not commissioned to create a new society; indeed, we are scarcely competent to do so. What the church can do best, though it does so all too seldom, is to delegitimate an unjust system and to create a spiritual counterclimate. We may lack the wisdom to determine how homelessness can be solved; and our attempts as churches to feed, clothe, and house the homeless may only obscure the true causes of homelessness and fill us with false righteousness. But what we can do is create an insistent demand that homelessness be eradicated.

We are not "building the Kingdom," as an earlier generation liked to put it. We simply lack the power to force the Powers to change. We faithfully do what we can with no illusions about our prospects for direct impact. We merely prepare the ground and sow; the seed grows of itself, night and day, until the harvest (Mark 4:26-29). And God will—this is our most profound conviction—bring the harvest.

This does not mean that our opposition to the Powers, pitiful as it may be, is irrelevant. Far from it. The church is to be like a bulldog that sinks its teeth into an elephant's leg. It cannot bring the elephant down, but it can so distract the elephant's attention that it fails to notice the elephant trap and plunges in.

Every oppressive regime regularly digs an elephant trap for itself. Hybris is the very essence of their lust for power. The dictators Marcos and Pinochet themselves called the elections that proved their downfall. The failed coup in the Soviet Union (1991) brought about the very reforms it sought to prevent.

But unless there is a group of people prepared to capitalize on these blunders, nothing comes of them. When people are ready, however, these acts of hybris become what peace activist Bill Moyer calls "trigger events": the coincidence of a prepared opposition and a public outrage that creates general awareness and indignation.[23]

Rosa Parks, whose arrest for refusing to sit in the back of the bus sparked the civil rights movement, was not just "tired"; she was an officer in the NAACP and had attended training sessions in nonviolent resistance. And her arrest could act as the spark to ignite the civil rights movement because Jo Ann Gibson Robinson, an English professor at Alabama State College, had already, a year and a half earlier, threatened the mayor of Montgomery with a boycott if conditions on buses for black people were not improved. Months earlier the black Women's Political Council, of which she was president, had drawn up plans for the distribution of fifty thousand notices calling people to boycott the buses; only the specifics of time and place had to be added. When she heard of Rosa Parks's arrest, she worked through the night with the help of two students mimeographing tens of thousands of leaflets announcing the boycott. Thanks to the distribution system already set up by the women, practically every black man, woman, and child in Montgomery knew of the bus boycott within a few hours.[24] Parks and Robinson were virtually lying in ambush for the trigger event that could launch their movement.

The movement against nuclear energy faithfully built up a constituency, and exercised all available forms of democratic intervention, referenda, and injunctions. But it could not by itself stop the increase of nuclear reactors. Already 260 were operating, ordered, or under contract by 1974. It was the disaster at Three Mile Island in 1979 that galvanized public resistance and halted ground breaking for any additional nuclear reactors.

But a similar disaster occurred at the Fermi reactor in Alabama in 1966, and the fact was withheld from public knowledge. There was no sizable movement of protest to which information about that disaster might be leaked, and the public attitude was still one of trust. Trigger events are wasted when the people are not prepared to capitalize on them.[25] Wisdom's unexpected opportunities must be met by Wisdom's children, ready to press into the opened breach.

Others may be far more competent in actually effecting structural change, but the church is, of all institutions in society, best equipped to expose the idolatrous spirituality of human systems. The slavery which communism imposed on a third of humanity was the outcome of a spirit, not of economics. Nazism's capacity to mobilize emotions was the consequence of a spirit, not of politics. Idolatries so powerful cannot be countered with mere hatred. What is needed is something that recalls these rebellious Powers to the One in and through and for whom they exist. What exposes and confounds them, what drives them into a frenzy of rage that blinds them to the elephant trap of God's historical ironies, is being called upon to praise God. Ps. 29:1-2* shows how this is to be done:

> Ascribe to Yahweh, O heavenly beings [lit., sons of gods],
> ascribe to Yahweh glory and strength.
> Ascribe to Yahweh the glory of God's name;
>   worship Yahweh in the sacred court.

Here the Principalities and Powers in their spiritual manifestation—that is, as the interiority of earthly institutions—are being called upon to abdicate all pretensions to absoluteness, and to offer praise and worship to the true God. Praise is the homeostatic principle of the universe. It preserves the harmony of the whole by preventing usurpation of the whole by its parts. Praise is the ecological principle of divinity whereby every creature is subordinated to its organic relationship with the Creator. *Praise is the cure for the apostasy of the Powers.*

The command expressed in the psalm is not issued by God, however, but by us! In all simplicity, this is finally the task of the church over against the Powers: to remind the Powers to whom they belong. "Ascribe to Yahweh, O heavenly beings, ascribe to Yahweh glory and strength." It is all so clear. We are simply to proclaim to IBM and Gulf + Western and the current political administration and the pettifogging bureaucrat that they do not exist as ends in themselves, but for the humanizing purposes of God as revealed in Jesus. We do not have to relate them to God. They are already, by virtue of their creation, related to God. We simply have to remind them that they exist in and through and for God.

It is a curious fact that people already sense their belonging to that greater whole. Regardless of their ethical barbarity, they want to be *treated by others* according to humane values. People know in their bones that kindness is right and that domination is wrong. Governments and businesses spend billions trying to convince themselves and persuade others that they abide by moral values, even when they are in flagrant violation of them. The church merely has to remind them of what they already, at some deep level, know.

The church, however, is but one among many groups that struggles to humanize the Powers. God, fortunately, is not solely dependent on the church! In Matt. 25:31-46, those who are declared "blessed" of the Abba are not necessarily Christians, but people who actually behave lovingly toward the hungry, homeless, refugees, and prisoners. They do not act this way because they have been taught that in so doing they do it to Christ. Indeed, they are surprised to learn that their acts of compassion were in fact done to him. Nor do they do it out of duty, or to earn a reward. We do not, in fact, know why they do it, or who they are. They may be atheists, Jews, Muslims; they may be addicts, convicts, whores. The tax collectors and the prostitutes will go into the kingdom of God ahead of some religious people, asserts Jesus (Matt. 21:31). Apparently Jesus' God is interested in one thing only: whether we behave in a way consistent with the divine order that is coming. Our religious preferences, practices, and affiliations are, next to that, a matter of indifference.

How then can the church carry on the struggle with the Powers more effectively? How can it shake off the suffocating weight of institutional self-preservation and make a difference in the world? How can it engage the Powers with the redemptive power of the cross? What kinds of action and spirituality must it cultivate to be able to serve God in the redemption of the Powers? We address these questions in the remainder of the book.

Part 3
ENGAGING THE POWERS NONVIOLENTLY

The Powers are not incorrigible. What fell in time can be redeemed in time. Even in their fallenness, institutions are able to some degree to preserve freedoms and secure justice. The flight of the communist bloc from totalitarianism shows how deep is the longing of the human spirit for the liberty to speak, travel, work, and pursue creative initiatives.

Ideally, democracy is nonviolence institutionalized. It is the only political order that rejects domination in principle and grounds itself in equality before the law. Despite its susceptibility to manipulation by the rich and powerful, democracy is the best system yet devised for preserving the rights of individuals while seeking the welfare of all. I am not thinking of democracy American style or Swedish style or Indian style, but democracy generically—a system for the nonviolent resolution of conflict and disputes through representative forms of government and civil life. In practice, of course, most democracies fail in varying degrees to provide equal access to basic needs and human rights. Most functioning democracies are run by oligarchies that maintain power whichever party is elected, and they make common cause with bureaucrats intent on preserving their own fiefdoms. Even at the local level, democratic governance is inefficient, contentious, shortsighted, and miserly. As Churchill put it, "Democracy is the worst form of government, except for all those other forms that have been tried from time to time." But there is no intrinsic reason why institutions cannot become more humane. Some nations, cities, offices, and homes are clearly more just and peaceful than others. Some systems are better than others at allowing input from their members.

When democracies work, nonviolence is simply the modus operandi of the entire system. Nonviolence is expressed through voting, legislative debates, community organization, and voluntary associations for changing public policy or meeting social needs. It happens quietly behind the scenes in informal mediation, committee decisions, investigative reports, news exposés. Nonviolence is implemented by the extension of the mechanisms of law for the settlement of national and international conflicts. It would be well served by the strengthening of the United Nations. To some it may come as a surprise, like the man who discovered that he had been speaking prose all his life, to realize that nonviolence has been what they have been doing as citizens all along.

Democracy continues to draw people to it, despite its evident failings, because no other system comes as close to establishing rule by law rooted in a commitment to the dignity and worth of every human being, without the resort to mass violence or dictatorial control. Democratic nations tend not to wage war with one another.[1] But the best of democracies resist needed change. Elected politicians are often either unresponsive to public opinion, or faithfully fulfil public expectations of abysmal morality. At such times, extra-institutional means must be resorted to: strikes, boycotts, demonstrations, civil disobedience. In authoritarian or totalitarian societies, however, nonviolent direct action may be the only means available for bringing about change, and at a very high cost in human suffering and sacrifice.

James W. Douglass also cautions that the power of Jesus' upside-down kingdom is not fully realized by the replacement of dictatorships by democratic governments. That kingdom "is rather a power expressed momentarily by such transforming movements—a power coming from within and below, a power to overcome domination, not change its forms. This nonviolent power may in fact be repudiated by the same movements that once drew upon it, as they begin in turn their own cycle of consolidating a very different kind of power in themselves."[2]

In the chapters that follow, I use "nonviolence" both in the broadest possible sense, as a nonlethal orientation to life, and also concretely to refer to the variety of strategies and tactics for implementing change without resorting to violence. I also call the latter "nonviolent direct action." The context will, I hope, make clear whether the broader or the narrower meaning is intended. I am acutely aware of the negative tone of the term "nonviolence." I have tried alternatives ("unarmed resistance," "relentless persistence," "satyagraha," "nondestructive aggression," "Jesus' third way"), but none is completely satisfactory. Since the term "nonviolence" already has a noble history, I have made my peace with it. I do wish to make clear from the outset that I do not equate nonviolence with pacifism. What I propose, rather, is nonviolence for the violent—for people like myself who are opposed to war yet unsure of our capacity to respond with love in every situation. Perhaps many pacifists and just-war advocates will see themselves in that definition as well. Perhaps we can move beyond pacifism and just war to a new synthesis, one that embraces nonviolence and at the same time is able to address the thorny issues of armed aggression, terrorism, and civil strife.

In Part Three we examine the basis of nonviolence in the teaching of Jesus (chap. 9), the dangers of mimetic violence (chap. 10), a way of transcending the debate between pacifism and just war theory (chap. 11), the art of imagining nonviolent alternatives (chap. 12), and the future of nonviolence in the light of its remarkable recent successes (chap. 13). Chapter 9 demonstrates that nonviolence is indeed the way of Jesus, 10 that it is responsible, 11 that it is reasonable, 12 that it is in fact feasible, and 13 that it is actually happening.

Nonviolence is no longer a concern limited to pacifists, but has moved into the forefront of human events as perhaps the only viable means to a desirable future. Nonviolence recognizes that the most basic of human rights is the right not to be killed. On one thing, at least, virtually all Christians agree: though the coming reign of God will precipitate the frantic opposition of a violent system, God's reign itself will be nonviolent. The argument of these chapters is that our nonviolent future has already begun.

We have assumed the name of peacemakers, but we have been, by and large, unwilling to pay any significant price. And because we want the peace with half a heart and half a life and will, the war, of course, continues, because the waging of war, by its very nature, is total—but the waging of peace, by our own cowardice, is partial. So a whole will and a whole heart and a whole national life bent toward war prevail over the velleities of peace. . . . "Of course, let us have the peace," we cry, "but at the same time let us have normalcy, let us lose nothing, let our lives stand intact, let us know neither prison nor ill repute nor disruption of ties. . . ." There is no peace because there are no peacemakers. There are no makers of peace because the making of peace is at least as costly as the making of war—at least as exigent, at least as disruptive, at least as liable to bring disgrace and prison and death in its wake.

Daniel Berrigan,
No Bars to Manhood[1]

9. Jesus' Third Way: Nonviolent Engagement

Human evolution has provided the species with two deeply instinctual responses to violence: flight or fight. Jesus offers a third way: nonviolent direct action.[2] The classic text is Matt. 5:38-42:

> [38]You have heard that it was said, "An eye for an eye and a tooth for a tooth." [39]But I say to you, Do not resist an evildoer. But if anyone strikes you on the right cheek, turn the other also; [40]and if anyone wants to sue you and take your coat, give your cloak as well; [41]and if anyone forces you to go one mile, go also the second mile. [42]Give to everyone who begs from you, and do not refuse anyone who wants to borrow from you.[3] (See also Luke 6:29-30.)

Christians have, on the whole, simply ignored this teaching. It has seemed impractical, masochistic, suicidal—an invitation to bullies and spouse-batterers to wipe up the floor with their supine Christian victims. Some who have tried to follow Jesus' words have understood it to mean nonresistance: let the oppressor perpetrate evil unopposed. Even scholars have swallowed the eat-humble-pie reading of this text: "It is better to surrender everything and go through life naked than to insist on one's legal rights," to cite only one of scores of these commentators from Augustine right up to the present.[4] Interpreted thus, the passage has become the basis for systematic training in cowardice, as Christians are taught to acquiesce to evil.

Cowardice is scarcely a term one associates with Jesus. Either he failed to make himself clear, or we have misunderstood him. There is plenty of cause to believe the latter. Let us set aside for the moment the thesis statement (vv. 38-39a), and focus on the three practical examples he gives.

Jesus on Nonviolent Engagement

1. *Turn the Other Cheek.* "If anyone strikes you on the right cheek, turn the other also." Why the *right* cheek? A blow by the right fist in that right-handed

world would land on the *left* cheek of the opponent. An open-handed slap would also strike the left cheek. To hit the right cheek with a fist would require using the left hand, but in that society the left hand was used only for unclean tasks. Even to gesture with the left hand at Qumran carried the penalty of ten days' penance.[5] The only way one could naturally strike the right cheek with the right hand would be with the back of the hand. We are dealing here with insult, not a fistfight. The intention is clearly not to injure but to humiliate, to put someone in his or her place. One normally did not strike a peer thus, and if one did the fine was exorbitant. The mishnaic tractate *Baba Kamma* specifies the various fines for striking an equal: for slugging with a fist, 4 *zuz* (a *zuz* was a day's wage); for slapping, 200 *zuz*; but "if [he struck him] with the back of his hand he must pay him 400 *zuz*." But damages for indignity were not paid to slaves who were struck (8:1-7).[6]

A backhand slap was the usual way of admonishing inferiors. Masters back-handed slaves; husbands, wives; parents, children; men, women; Romans, Jews. *We have here a set of unequal relations, in each of which retaliation would invite retribution.* The only normal response would be cowering submission.

Part of the confusion surrounding these sayings arises from the failure to ask who Jesus' audience was. In all three of the examples in Matt. 5:39b-41, Jesus' listeners are not those who strike, initiate lawsuits, or impose forced labor, but their victims ("If anyone strikes *you* . . . wants to sue *you* . . . forces *you* to go one mile . . ."). There are among his hearers people who were subjected to these very indignities, forced to stifle outrage at their dehumanizing treatment by the hierarchical system of class, race, gender, age, and status, and as a result of imperial occupation.

Why then does he counsel these already humiliated people to turn the other cheek? Because this action robs the oppressor of the power to humiliate. The person who turns the other cheek is saying, in effect, "Try again. Your first blow failed to achieve its intended effect. I deny you the power to humiliate me. I am a human being just like you. Your status does not alter that fact. You cannot demean me."

Such a response would create enormous difficulties for the striker. Purely logistically, how would he hit the other cheek now turned to him? He cannot backhand it with his right hand (one only need try this to see the problem).[7] If he hits with a fist, he makes the other his equal, acknowledging him as a peer. But the point of the back of the hand is to reinforce institutionalized inequality. Even if the superior orders the person flogged for such "cheeky" behavior (this is certainly no way to *avoid* conflict!), the point has been irrevocably made. He has been given notice that this underling is in fact a human being. In that world of honor and shaming, he has been rendered impotent to instill shame in a subordinate.[8] He has been stripped of his power to dehumanize the other. As Gandhi taught, "The first principle of nonviolent action is that of noncooperation with everything humiliating."[9]

This very type of action had already been performed by Jesus' own contemporaries. Shortly after Pilate was appointed procurator in Judea (26 C.E.), he introduced into Jerusalem by night "the busts of the emperor that were attached to the military standards,"[10] which Jews regarded as idols and thus a desecration of the holy city. Crowds of Jews rushed to Pilate's headquarters in Caesarea to implore him to remove the standards. When he refused, they fell prostrate and remained there for five days and nights. On the sixth day, Pilate summoned the multitude to the stadium on the pretext of giving them an answer. Instead, they found themselves surrounded by soldiers, three deep.

> Pilate, after threatening to cut them down, if they refused to admit Caesar's images, signalled to the soldiers to draw their swords. Thereupon the Jews, as by concerted action, flung themselves in a body on the ground, extended their necks, and exclaimed that they were ready rather to die then to transgress the law. Overcome with astonishment at such intense religious zeal, Pilate gave orders for the immediate removal of the standards from Jerusalem.[11]

Jesus was not, then, articulating a notion alien to his people, but elevating it from occasional and spontaneous use to a central element in the coming of God's Reign.

2. *Give the Undergarment.* The second example Jesus gives is set in a court of law. Someone is being sued for his outer garment. Who would do that, and under what circumstances? The Hebrew Scriptures provide the clues.

> If you lend money to my people, *to the poor* among you, you shall not deal with them as a creditor; you shall not exact interest from them. If ever you take your neighbor's cloak (LXX, *himation*) in pawn, you shall restore it before the sun goes down; for it may be your neighbor's only clothing (*himation*) to use as cover; in what else shall that person sleep? And if your neighbor cries out to me, I will listen, for I am compassionate.
>
> (Exod. 22:25-27; LXX 22:24-26)

> When you make your neighbor a loan of any kind, you shall not go into the house to take the pledge. You shall wait outside, while the person to whom you are making the loan brings the pledge out to you. *If the person is poor*, you shall not sleep in the garment given you as the pledge. You shall give the pledge back by sunset, so that your neighbor may sleep in the cloak and bless you. . . . You shall not . . . take a widow's garment (*himation*) in pledge.
>
> (Deut. 24:10-13, 17)

> They who trample the head of the poor into the dust of the earth . . . lay themselves
> down beside every altar upon garments (*himatia*) taken in pledge.
>   (Amos 2:7-8; see also Ezek. 18:5-9)

Only the poorest of the poor would have nothing but a garment to give as collateral for a loan. Jewish law strictly required its return every evening at sunset.[12]

Matthew and Luke disagree whether it is the outer garment (Luke) or the undergarment (Matthew) that is being seized. But the Jewish practice of giving the outer garment as a pledge (it alone would be useful as a blanket for sleeping) makes it clear that Luke's order is correct, even though he does not preserve the legal setting. In all Greek usage, according to Liddell-Scott, *himation* is "always an outer garment . . . worn above the *chitōn*," whereas the *chitōn* is a "garment worn next to the skin."[13] S. Safrai and M. Stern describe normal Jewish dress: an outer garment or cloak of wool and an undergarment or tunic of linen.[14] To avoid confusion I will simply refer to the "outer garment" and the "undergarment."

The situation Jesus speaks to is all too familiar to his hearers: the debtor has sunk ever deeper into poverty, the debt cannot be repaid, and his creditor has summoned him to court (*krithēnai*) to exact repayment by legal means.

Indebtedness was endemic in first-century Palestine. Jesus' parables are full of debtors struggling to salvage their lives. Heavy debt was not, however, a natural calamity that had overtaken the incompetent. It was the direct consequence of Roman imperial policy. Emperors had taxed the wealthy so stringently to fund their wars that the rich began seeking nonliquid investments to secure their wealth. Land was best, but it was ancestrally owned and passed down over generations, and no peasant would voluntarily relinquish it. Exorbitant interest, however, could be used to drive landowners ever deeper into debt. And debt, coupled with the high taxation required by Herod Antipas to pay Rome tribute, created the economic leverage to pry Galilean peasants loose from their land. By the time of Jesus we see this process already far advanced: large estates owned by absentee landlords, managed by stewards, and worked by tenant farmers, day laborers, and slaves. It is no accident that the first act of the Jewish revolutionaries in 66 C.E. was to burn the Temple treasury, where the record of debts was kept.[15]

It is to this situation that Jesus speaks. His hearers are the poor ("if any one would sue *you*"). They share a rankling hatred for a system that subjects them to humiliation by stripping them of their lands, their goods, finally even their outer garments.

Why then does Jesus counsel them to give over their undergarments as well? This would mean stripping off all their clothing and marching out of court stark naked! Imagine the guffaws this saying must have evoked. There stands the creditor, covered with shame, the poor debtor's outer garment in the one hand, his undergarment in the other. The tables have suddenly been turned on the creditor. The debtor had no hope of winning the case; the law was entirely in the creditor's favor. But the poor man has transcended this attempt to humiliate him. He has risen above shame. At the same time he has registered a stunning protest against the system that created his debt. He has said in effect, "You want my robe? Here, take everything! Now you've got all I have except my body. Is that what you'll take next?"

Nakedness was taboo in Judaism, and shame fell less on the naked party than on the person viewing or causing the nakedness (Gen. 9:20-27).[16] By stripping, the debtor has brought the creditor under the same prohibition that led to the curse of Canaan. And much as Isaiah had "walked naked and barefoot for three years" as a prophetic sign (Isa. 20:1-6), so the debtor parades his nakedness in prophetic protest against a system that has deliberately rendered him destitute. Imagine him leaving the court, naked. His friends and neighbors, aghast, inquire what happened. He explains. They join his growing procession, which now resembles a victory parade. The entire system by which debtors are oppressed has been publicly unmasked. The creditor is revealed to be not a legitimate moneylender but a party to the reduction of an entire social class to landlessness, destitution, and abasement. This unmasking is not simply punitive, therefore; it offers the creditor a chance to see, perhaps for the first time in his life, what his practices cause, and to repent.

The Powers That Be literally stand on their dignity. Nothing depotentiates them faster than deft lampooning. By refusing to be awed by their power, the powerless are emboldened to seize the initiative, even where structural change is not immediately possible. This message, far from being a counsel to perfection unattainable in this life, is a practical, strategic measure for empowering the oppressed, and it is being lived out all over the world today by powerless people ready to take their history into their own hands.

Jesus provides here a hint of how to take on the entire system by unmasking its essential cruelty and burlesquing its pretensions to justice. Here is a poor man who will no longer be treated as a sponge to be squeezed dry by the rich. He accepts the laws as they stand, pushes them to absurdity, and reveals them for what they have become. He strips naked, walks out before his fellows, and leaves this creditor, and the whole economic edifice that he represents, stark naked.

3. *Go the Second Mile*. "If one of the occupation troops forces (*angareusei*) you to carry his pack one mile, carry it two miles" (Matt. 5:41, TEV). Jesus'

third example is drawn from the relatively enlightened practice of limiting the amount of forced or impressed labor (*angareia*) that Roman soldiers could levy on subject peoples to a single mile.[17] The term *angareia* is probably Persian, and became a loanword in Aramaic, Greek, and Latin. Josephus mentions it in reference to the Seleucid ruler Demetrius, who, in order to enlist Jewish support for his bid to be king, promised, among other things, that "the Jews' beasts of burden shall not be requisitioned (*angareuesthai*) for our army" (*Ant.* 13.52). More familiar is the passion narrative, where the soldiers "compel" (*angareuousin*) Simon of Cyrene to carry Jesus' cross (Mark 15:21//Matt. 27:32). Such forced service was a constant feature in Palestine from Persian to late Roman times, and whoever was found on the street could be compelled into service.[18] Most cases of impressment involved the need of the postal service for animals and the need of soldiers for civilians to help carry their packs. The situation in Matthew is clearly the latter. It is not a matter of requisitioning animals but people.

This forced labor was a cause of bitter resentment for all Roman subjects. "*Angareia* is like death," complains one source.[19] The sheer frequency, even into the late empire, of legislation proscribing the misuse of the *angareia* shows how regularly the practice was used and its regulations violated. An inscription of 49 C.E. from Egypt orders that Roman "soldiers of any degree when passing through the several districts are not to make any requisitions or to employ forced transport (*angareia*) unless they have the prefect's written authority"[20]—a rescript clearly made necessary by soldiers abusing their privileges. Another decree from Egypt in 133–137 C.E. documents this abuse: "Many soldiers without written requisition are travelling about in the country, demanding ships, beasts of burden, and men, beyond anything authorized, sometimes seizing things by force. . . to the point of *showing abuse and threats to private citizens*, the result is that the military is associated with arrogance and injustice."[21] In order to minimize resentment in the conquered lands, Rome made at least some effort to punish violators of the laws regarding impressment.

The Theodosian Code devotes an entire section to *angareia*.[22] Among its ordinances are these:

> If any person while making a journey should consider that he may abstract an ox that is not assigned to the public post but dedicated to the plow, he shall be *arrested with due force* by the rural police . . . and he shall be haled before the judge [normally the governor]. (8.5.1, 315 C.E.)

> By this interdict We forbid that any person should deem that they may request packanimals and supplementary posthorses. But if any person should rashly act so presumptuously, *he shall be punished very severely*. (8.5.6, 354 C.E.)

> When any *legion* is proceeding to its destination, it shall not hereafter attempt to appropriate more than two posthorses (*angariae*), and only for the sake of any who are sick. (8.5.11, 360 C.E., my emphasis throughout)

Late as these regulations are, they reflect a situation that had changed little since the time of the Persians. Armies had to move through countries with dispatch. Some legionnaires bought their own slaves to help carry their packs of sixty to eighty-five pounds (not including weapons).[23] The majority of the rank and file, however, had to depend on impressed civilians. There are vivid accounts of whole villages fleeing to avoid being forced to carry soldiers' baggage, and of richer towns prepared to pay large sums to escape having Roman soldiers billeted on them for winter.[24]

With few exceptions, the commanding general of a legion personally administered justice in serious cases, and all other cases were left to the disciplinary control of his subordinates. Centurions (commanders of 100 men) had almost limitless authority in dealing with routine cases of discipline. This accounts for the curious fact that there is very little codified military law, and that which exists is late. Roman military historians are agreed, however, that military law changed very little in its essential character throughout the imperial period.[25] No account survives to us today of the penalties to be meted out to a soldier for forcing a civilian to carry his pack more than the permitted mile, but there are at least hints. "If in winter quarters, in camp, *or on the march*, either an officer or a soldier does injury to a civilian, and does not fully repair the same, he shall pay the damage twofold."[26] This is about as mild a penalty, however, as one can find. Josephus's comment is surely exaggerated, even if it states the popular impression: Roman military forces "have laws which punish with death not merely desertion of the ranks, but even a slight neglect of duty" (*War* 3.102–8). Between these extremes there was deprivation of pay, a ration of barley instead of wheat, reduction in rank, dishonorable discharge, being forced to camp outside the fortifications, or to stand all day before the general's tent holding a clod in one's hands, or to stand barefoot in public places. But the most frequent punishment by far was flogging.[27]

The frequency with which decrees were issued to curb misuse of the *angareia* indicates how lax discipline on this point was. Perhaps the soldier might receive only a rebuke. But the point is that the soldier *does not know what will happen.*

It is in this context of Roman military occupation that Jesus speaks.[28] He does not counsel revolt. One does not "befriend" the soldier, draw him aside, and drive a knife into his ribs. Jesus was surely aware of the futility of armed insurrection against Roman imperial might; he certainly did nothing to encourage those whose hatred of Rome was near to flaming into violence.

But why carry his pack a second mile? Is this not to rebound to the opposite extreme of aiding and abetting the enemy?[29] Not at all. The question here, as in the two previous instances, is how the oppressed can recover the initiative and assert their human dignity in a situation that cannot for the time being be changed. The rules are Caesar's, but how one responds to the rules is God's, and Caesar has no power over that.

Imagine then the soldier's surprise when, at the next mile marker, he reluctantly reaches to assume his pack, and the civilian says, "Oh no, let me carry it another mile." Why would he want to do that? What is he up to? Normally, soldiers have to coerce people to carry their packs, but this Jew does so cheerfully, and will not stop! Is this a provocation? Is he insulting the legionnaire's strength? Being kind? Trying to get him disciplined for seeming to violate the rules of impressment? Will this civilian file a complaint? Create trouble?

From a situation of servile impressment, the oppressed have suddenly seized the initiative. They have taken back the power of choice. The soldier is thrown off balance by being deprived of the predictability of his victim's response. He has never dealt with such a problem before. Now he has been forced into making a decision for which nothing in his previous experience has prepared him. If he has enjoyed feeling superior to the vanquished, he will not enjoy it today. Imagine the situation of a Roman infantryman pleading with a Jew to give back his pack! The humor of this scene may have escaped us, but it could scarcely have been lost on Jesus' hearers, who must have been regaled at the prospect of thus discomfiting their oppressors.

Jesus does not encourage Jews to walk a second mile in order to build up merit in heaven, or to exercise a supererogatory piety, or to kill the soldier with kindness. He is helping an oppressed people find a way to protest and neutralize an onerous practice despised throughout the empire. He is not giving a nonpolitical message of spiritual world-transcendence. He is formulating a worldly spirituality in which the people at the bottom of society or under the thumb of imperial power learn to recover their humanity.

One could easily misuse Jesus' advice vindictively; that is why it must not be separated from the command to love enemies, which is integrally connected with it in both Matthew and Luke. But love is not averse to taking the law and using its oppressive momentum to throw the soldier into a region of uncertainty and anxiety where he has never been before.

Such tactics can seldom be repeated. One can imagine that within days after the incidents that Jesus sought to provoke, the Powers That Be would pass new laws: penalties for nakedness in court, flogging for carrying a pack more than a mile! One must be creative, improvising new tactics to keep the opponent off balance.

To those whose lifelong pattern has been to cringe before their masters, Jesus offers a way to liberate themselves from servile actions and a servile mentality. And he asserts that they can do this *before* there is a revolution. There is no need to wait until Rome has been defeated, or peasants are landed and slaves freed. They can begin to behave with dignity and recovered humanity *now*, even under the unchanged conditions of the old order. Jesus' sense of divine immediacy has social implications. The reign of God is already breaking into the world, and it comes, not as an imposition from on high, but as the leaven slowly causing the dough to rise (Matt. 13:33//Luke 13:20-21). Jesus' teaching on nonviolence is thus of a piece with his proclamation of the dawning of the reign of God.

In the conditions of first-century Palestine, a political revolution against the Romans could only be catastrophic, as the events of 66–70 C.E. would prove. Jesus does not propose armed revolution. But he does lay the foundations for a social revolution, as Richard A. Horsley has pointed out. And a social revolution becomes political when it reaches a critical threshold of acceptance; this in fact did happen to the Roman Empire as the Christian church overcame it from below.[30]

Nor were peasants and slaves in a position to transform the economic system by frontal assault. But they could begin to act from an already recovered dignity and freedom, and the ultimate consequences of such acts could only be revolutionary. To that end, Jesus spoke repeatedly of a voluntary remission of debts.[31]

It is entirely appropriate, then, that the saying on debts in Matt. 5:42//Luke 6:30//*Gos. Thom.* 95 has been added to this block of sayings. Jesus counsels his hearers not just to practice alms and to lend money, even to bad risks, but to lend without expecting interest or even the return of the principal.[32] Such radical egalitarian sharing would be necessary to rescue impoverished Palestinian peasants from their plight; one need not posit an imminent end of history as the cause for such astonishing generosity. And yet none of this is new; Jesus is merely issuing a prophetic summons to Israel to observe the commandments pertaining to the sabbatical year enshrined in Torah, adapted to a new situation.[33]

Such radical sharing would be necessary in order to restore true community. For the risky defiance of the Powers that Jesus advocates would inevitably issue in punitive economic sanctions and physical punishment against individuals. They would need economic support; Matthew's "Give to everyone who *asks* [*aitounti*—not necessarily *begs*] of you" may simply refer to this need for mutual sustenance. Staggering interest and taxes isolated peasants, who went under one by one. This was a standard tactic of imperial "divide and rule" strategy.[34]

Jesus' solution was neither utopian nor apocalyptic. It was simple realism. Nothing less could halt or reverse the economic decline of Jewish peasants than a complete suspension of usury and debt and a restoration of economic equality through outright grants, a pattern actually implemented in the earliest Christian community, according to the Book of Acts.[35]

Just on the grounds of sheer originality, the examples of unarmed direct action in Matt. 5:39b-41 would appear to have originated with Jesus. No one, not only in the first century but in all of human history, ever advocated defiance of oppressors by turning the cheek, stripping oneself naked in court, or jeopardizing a soldier by carrying his pack a second mile. For three centuries, the early church observed Jesus' command to nonviolence. But nowhere in the early church, to say nothing of the early fathers, do we find statements similar to these in their humor and originality. These sayings are, in fact, so radical, so unprecedented, and so threatening, that it has taken all these centuries just to begin to grasp their implications.

The Thesis Statement:
Do Not Mirror Evil

A more difficult problem is the meaning of *antistēnai* in Matt. 5:39a. It is translated "resist" in almost all versions (NRSV: "Do not resist an evildoer"). That meaning of the word is certainly well-attested, but its use in this passage is insupportable. Purely on logical grounds, "resist not" does not fit the aggressive nonviolent actions described in the three following examples. Since in these three instances Jesus provides strategies for resisting oppression, it is altogether inconsistent for him to counsel people in almost the same breath not to resist it. Has Matthew added the term, or has it been mistranslated?

Matthew 5:39a also seems to suggest false alternatives: one either resists evil, or resists not. Fight or flight. No other possibilities appear to exist; if Jesus commands us not to resist, then the only other choice would appear to be passivity, complicity in our own oppression, surrender. Submission to evil appears to be the will of God. *And this is precisely the way most Christians have interpreted this passage.* "Turn the other cheek" is understood as enjoining supine acquiescence when someone behaves violently toward us. "Give your undergarment as well" has encouraged people to go limp in the face of injustice and hand over the last thing they own. "Going the second mile" has been turned into a platitude meaning nothing more than "extend yourself." Rather than encouraging the oppressed to resist their oppressors, these revolutionary statements have been heard as injunctions to collude in one's own despoiling.

What the translators have not noted, however, is how frequently *anthistēmi* is used as a military term. Resistance implies "counteractive aggression," a response to hostilities initiated by someone else. Liddell-Scott defines *anthistēmi* as to "*set against* esp. in battle, *withstand*." Ephesians 6:13 is exemplary of its military usage: "Therefore take up the whole armor of God, so that you may be able to withstand [*antistēnai*, lit., to draw up battle ranks against the enemy] on that evil day, and having done everything, to stand firm [*stēnai*, lit., to close ranks and continue to fight]." The term is used in the LXX primarily for armed resistance in military encounters (44 out of 71 times). Josephus uses *anthistēmi* for violent struggle 15 out of 17 times, Philo 4 out of 10. As James W. Douglass notes, Jesus' answer is set against the backdrop of the burning question of forcible resistance to Rome. In that context, "resistance" could have only one meaning: lethal violence.[36]

In short, *antistēnai* means more in Matt. 5:39a than simply to "stand against" or "resist."[37] It means to resist *violently*, to revolt or rebel, to engage in an insurrection. The logic of the text requires such a meaning: on the one hand, do not continue to be supine and complicit in your oppression; but on the other hand, do not react violently to it either. Rather, find a third way, a way that is neither submission nor assault, neither flight nor fight, a way that can secure your human dignity and begin to change the power equation, even now, before the revolution. Turn your cheek, thus indicating to the one who backhands you that his attempts to shame you into servility have failed. Strip naked and parade out of court, thus taking the momentum of the law and the whole debt economy and flipping them, jujitsu-like, in a burlesque of legality. Walk a second mile, surprising the occupation troops with a sudden challenge to their control. These are, of course, not rules to be followed legalistically, but examples to spark an infinite variety of creative responses in new and changed circumstances. They break the cycle of humiliation with humor and even ridicule, exposing the injustice of the System. They recover for the poor a modicum of initiative that can force the oppressor to see them in a new light.

There is good reason to suspect that the original form of this saying about resistance is best preserved in the New Testament epistles. In Romans 12 we find more allusions to Jesus' teaching than anywhere else in all Paul's letters. Among them are:

12:14—"Bless those who persecute you; bless and do not curse them"; cf. Matt. 5:44//Luke 6:28.

12:15—"Rejoice with those who rejoice, weep with those who weep"; cf. Matt. 5:4, 12//Luke 6:21, 23.

12:17—"Do not repay anyone evil for evil" and 12:21—"Do not be overcome by evil, but overcome evil with good"; cf. Matt. 5:39a.

Both 1 Thess. 5:15 ("See that none of you repays evil for evil") and 1 Pet. 3:9 ("Do not repay evil for evil or abuse for abuse; but, on the contrary, repay with a blessing") preserve the same saying as Rom. 12:17. We appear to have here an extremely early fixed catechetical tradition, predating even the earliest preserved epistle.[38] The teaching on nonviolence thus clearly antedates the Jewish War and was not a reaction to it.

The expression "Repay no one evil for evil" conveys precisely the sense we were driven to for Matt. 5:39a: Do not mirror evil. The examples that follow in 5:39b-41 in fact presuppose some such sense. Could this ancient catechetical tradition have originally stood, then, in Matthew's tradition? If "Do not repay evil for evil" and "Do not forcibly resist evil" have equivalent meanings, could they simply be different versions of the same tradition?

We can now, for the first time, answer a cautious yes to that question. George Howard has recently discovered what he regards as an early Hebrew text of the Gospel of Matthew, which reads at 5:39a, "But I say to you, *do not repay evil for evil*."[39] If this remarkable find is indeed as ancient as Howard argues, it reinforces our suspicion that Matt. 5:39a and the catechetical saying in Rom. 12:17; 1 Thess. 5:15; and 1 Pet. 3:9 are indeed derived from the same tradition.[40] And even if this text is not as early as Howard thinks, its very existence, from *any* period, proves that at least one Hebrew version regarded "Do not repay evil for evil" as the proper way to read Matt. 5:39a.[41]

If this line of argument is correct, then the original version of v. 39a was something closer to "Do not repay evil for evil." This is the sense that vv. 39b-42 require. The logic of Jesus' examples in Matt. 5:39b-42 goes beyond both inaction and overreaction, capitulation and murderous counterviolence, to a new response, fired in the crucible of love, that promises to liberate the oppressed from evil even as it frees the oppressor from sin. "Do not react violently to evil, do not counter evil in kind, do not let evil dictate the terms of your opposition, do not let violence draw you into mimetic rivalry"—this is the revolutionary principle, recognized from earliest times,[42] that Jesus articulates as the basis for nonviolently engaging the Powers.

Perhaps the alternatives we are discussing can be more graphically presented by a chart:

Jesus' Third Way

- Seize the moral initiative
- Find a creative alternative to violence
- Assert your own humanity and dignity as a person
- Meet force with ridicule or humor
- Break the cycle of humiliation

- Refuse to submit to or to accept the inferior position
- Expose the injustice of the system
- Take control of the power dynamic
- Shame the oppressor into repentance
- Stand your ground
- Make the Powers make decisions for which they are not prepared
- Recognize your own power
- Be willing to suffer rather than retaliate
- Force the oppressor to see you in a new light
- Deprive the oppressor of a situation where a show of force is effective
- Be willing to undergo the penalty of breaking unjust laws
- Die to fear of the old order and its rules
- Seek the oppressor's transformation

Flight	Fight
Submission	Armed revolt
Passivity	Violent rebellion
Withdrawal	Direct retaliation
Surrender	Revenge

Gandhi insisted that no one join him who was not willing to take up arms to fight for independence. They could not freely renounce what they had not entertained. One cannot pass directly from "Flight" to "Jesus' Third Way." One needs to pass through the "Fight" stage, if only to discover one's own inner strength and capacity for violence (see fig. 1). One need not actually become violent, but one does need to own one's fury at injustice and care enough to be willing to fight and, if necessary, die for its eradication. Only then can such a person freely renounce violence and embrace active nonviolence.

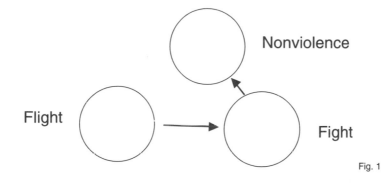

Fig. 1

It is dangerous to be engaged in nonviolent struggle beside people who have not yet learned about their inner violence.[43]

Jesus' third way did not arise out of a vacuum. It was a logical development of Israel's idealized concept of the holy war. One line of Israel's development can be seen as the movement from (1) submission, to (2) holy war, to (3) prophetic peacemaking. As Paul Valliere observes, the Genesis creation narratives are extraordinary, compared with other creation accounts from that time and area, precisely because of their refusal to count war as part of the nature of things. War is not the means used to subdue the cosmos, as in Hesiod's *Theogony* or the Babylonian *Enuma Elish*. Peace is the norm of the cosmos from the beginning. "Holy war" enters the narrative as God's sovereign act of liberating the Hebrew slaves from Egypt without their striking a blow. God, and God alone, fought on their behalf. God would drive out the inhabitants of Canaan by means of hornets, terror, panic, or pestilence, not the sword (Exod. 23:28; Deut. 7:20; Josh. 24:12). Jericho's walls collapsed after ritual, not military, action (though the mopping-up operation was carried out by Hebrew warriors— Joshua 6), and God overcame the Midianites by means of three hundred men armed only with torches and trumpets (Judges 7). Even the "ban," the practice of "devoting" booty to God by destroying it, can be seen as the imposition of extremely ascetical limits on the enjoyment of the fruits of war. (It also reveals the depth to which the myth of redemptive violence had penetrated Israel's theology and politics.) At least one strand of Israelite reflection regarded holy war, not as a war fought for or in the name of God, but as *a war that God alone fights*.

With its defection to monarchy, however, Israel began waging political wars that the false prophets tried to legitimate as holy. Israel came to trust in military might rather than God (Hos. 10:13); yet God continued to offer to save the people, but not "by bow, or by sword, or by war, or by horses, or by horsemen" (Hos. 1:7; see also Zech. 4:6). The unique contribution of the true prophets was their refusal to turn holy war into political war. This led them at times to declare that God was waging holy war *against* faithless Israel.[44] They recognized the impossibility of maintaining a standing army and concluding treaties with foreign powers while still preserving Israel's utter reliance on God alone to fight for them. The prophets turned to a kind of "prophetic pacifism." Holy war came to be seen as a contest fought not with the sword but with the divine word: truth against power. In a new twist on the warrior asceticism of old, the Hebrew prophets waged solitary moral combat against virtually an entire people who were convinced that wars of national defense, liberation, or conquest were their only hope of salvation. Israel had succumbed to the myth of redemptive violence, but the prophets had discovered that the word of God was a mighty sword that cut both ways, for and against God's people (cf. Heb. 4:12).[45]

Out of the heart of that prophetic tradition, Jesus engaged the Domination System in both its outer and spiritual manifestations. His teaching on nonviolence forms the charter for a way of being in the world that breaks the spiral of violence. Jesus here reveals a way to fight evil with all our power without being transformed into the very evil we fight. It is a way—the only way possible—of not becoming what we hate. "Do not counter evil in kind"—this insight is the distilled essence, stated with sublime simplicity, of the experience of those Jews who had, in Jesus' very lifetime, so courageously and effectively practiced nonviolent direct action against Rome.[46]

Jesus, in short, abhors both passivity and violence. He articulates, out of the history of his own people's struggles, a way by which evil can be opposed without being mirrored, the oppressor resisted without being emulated, and the enemy neutralized without being destroyed. Those who have lived by Jesus' words—Leo Tolstoy, Mohandas K. Gandhi, Martin Luther King, Jr., Dorothy Day, César Chavez, Adolpho Pérez Esquivel—point us to a new way of confronting evil whose potential for personal and social transformation we are only beginning to grasp today.[47]

Making Jesus' Teaching Operational

Nothing is deadlier to the spirit of Jesus' teaching on nonviolence than regarding it legalistically. Women beaten by their husbands are told to "turn the other cheek" and let the man continue to brutalize them, with no reference to Jesus' actual intention. If we reenter the freedom Jesus sought to establish in these sayings, we would rather counsel the battered to seize the initiative, force her husband to recognize her rights, expose his behavior publicly, and break the vicious cycle of humiliation, guilt, and bruising.

In the American legal context, according to the social workers I have consulted, the most loving thing a battered wife could do might be to have her husband arrested. This would bring the issue out into the open, put him under a court injunction that would mean jail if the violence continues, position him so that his self-interest is served by joining a therapy group for batterers, and thus potentially begin a process that would not only deliver the woman from being battered, but free the man from battering as well. I cite this suggestion because it is at the antipodes to our sentimental notions of what love entails. Perhaps there are better ways; but they will certainly involve tough love, not the limp collusion that so often masquerades as Christian.

To require a boy who is being bullied at school literally to "turn the other cheek" can simply encourage cowardice. Of course, a nonviolent solution would be preferable, and one can usually be found.[48] But it is a fundamental rule of the life of the spirit that people cannot sacrifice something they do not have. Jesus did not invite slaves to abandon their sense of dignity as a way of mortifying the ego; their egos had been mortified a thousand times, so much so that the vast majority had internalized a sense of their inferiority. They could not give up their self-esteem for the sake of God; they had been robbed of it long since by the very structure of servitude. It was precisely to restore that dignity and self-esteem that Jesus counseled nonviolent assertiveness.

If, then, a boy is willing and able to fight, even at the cost of great pain, then one might have a right to encourage him to renounce violence and seek a third way. But to duck violence under cover of the gospel, without having found the inner strength to fight for one's own rights, is both dishonest and craven.

Gandhi was adamant that nothing could be done with a coward, but that from a violent person one could make a nonviolent one. "I do believe that, where there is only a choice between cowardice and violence, I would advise violence. . . . But I believe that nonviolence is infinitely superior to violence."[49] "At every meeting I repeated the warning that unless they felt that in nonviolence they had come into possession of a force infinitely superior to the one they had and in the use of which they were adept, they should have nothing to do with non-violence and resume the arms they possessed before."[50]

Early on, before he had become fully committed to satyagraha, Gandhi so despaired of teaching his people the art of courageous nonviolence that he even proposed that they enlist in the army, reasoning that men who had risked their lives on the battlefield would be better prepared to risk their lives in a nonviolent struggle.[51] Something of the same militancy can be seen in Jesus' call to a potential disciple in Luke 9:60, where discipleship is comparable to the conscripting of recruits for a holy war. In normal circumstances, no grounds exist that justify flouting the filial obligation to bury one's father; but if the issue is war or something even more urgent (the reign of God), there is no time for normal obligations.

What looks to all the world like passivity may in fact be the third way. When Jackie Robinson became the first black player in major league baseball, Branch Rickey of the Brooklyn Dodgers pressed this intensely competitive athlete to agree that for three years he would take whatever abuse was heaped on him without a word. Robinson finally said, "Mr. Rickey, are you looking for a negro who is afraid to fight back?" Rickey replied, "I'm looking for a ballplayer with guts enough not to fight back."[52]

Humor and wit can help preserve the humanity of all parties in a conflict. Once, a squatter community in South Africa found its shelter infested with lice. When the authorities refused to fumigate it, the leadership committee took bags full of lice-infested blankets to the administrator's office and dumped them on his floor. They got immediate action.[53]

A black woman was walking on a South African street with her children, when a white man, passing, spat in her face. She stopped and said, "Thank you, and now for the children." He was so nonplused he was unable to respond.

Sometimes the wit can have a barb, as when Bishop Desmond Tutu was walking by a construction site on a temporary sidewalk the width of one person. A white man appeared at the other end, recognized Tutu, and said, "I don't give way to gorillas." At which Tutu stepped aside, made a deep sweeping gesture, and said, "Ah yes, but I do."

Ridicule even has a role in shocking people awake to the meaning of their acts. One of the world's most peaceful peoples, the Mbuti, hunter-gatherers of northeast Zaïre, defuse anger through laughter. If a group of children making noise wake a man from his nap, who then shouts at or slaps a child, all the children come rushing together and play the adult role, shouting and slapping each other. The adult, seeing himself ridiculed this way, must either retreat or join the laughter in his own self-ridicule.[54]

Similarly, Chinese students, forbidden to demonstrate against government policy, donned masks of the communist leadership and carried signs: "Support Martial Law," "Support Dictatorship," "Support Inflation."

During the struggle of Solidarity in Poland, one group dressed in Santa Claus outfits distributed scarce sanitary napkins to women as a way of dramatizing the difficulty of obtaining essentials. When these Santas were arrested, other Santas showed up at jail insisting that the others were frauds, that they were the *real* Santas.

Gandhi spoke of entering jail as a bridegroom enters his bride's chamber, as a way of stressing the importance of being fearless of the government's punishment. So when he was arrested during the civil disobedience campaign of 1930, a mass meeting was organized to *congratulate* the government for arresting him. It is difficult for a government to arrest well-wishers![55]

Jesus does not proclaim a nonviolence for the perfect, but for the violent. His is a practical, achievable nonviolence that can be performed by ordinary people. The beatitude about the meek can be translated as "Blessed are the *nonviolent*, for they shall inherit the earth" (Matt. 5:5).[56] Jesus' way is not individualistic, but collective; it usually involves the actions of organizations, communities, social classes, or racial groups. Not just young men of war-making age, but all sectors of the population can participate, from babies to the elderly. "Tradition here is for the men to keep the women in their houses," said Murabak Awad during the Palestinian *Intifada*. "But now husbands are allowing their wives out, to engage in political activity. The women are pouring all their energy into it. Nonviolent action can draw all of the population together and create a powerful unity."[57]

Nor is Jesus' third way averse to using coercion. His way aims at converting the opponent; failing that, it hopes for accommodation, where the opponent is willing to make some changes simply to get the protesters off his back. But if that too fails, nonviolence entails coercion: the opponent is forced to make a change rather than suffer the loss of power, even though he remains hostile.[58] But Jesus' way does not employ *violent* coercion.

As Barbara Deming puts it, in nonviolence one "exerts force upon the other, not tearing him away from himself but tearing from him only that which is not properly his own, the strength which has been loaned to him by all those who have been giving him obedience."[59] The civil rights marchers who crossed the bridge in Selma, Alabama, without a parade permit forced the authorities to decide between two courses, either of which would damage their position: either they allowed the blacks to march, thus recognizing the legitimacy of their protest; or they forcibly stopped it, thus exposing their own endemic violence for all the world to see. The choice of violence proved to be catastrophic for white supremacy and a major victory for the marchers, despite the injuries incurred.

Finally, nonviolence must not be misconstrued as a way of avoiding conflict. The "peace" that the gospel brings is never the absence of conflict, but an ineffable divine reassurance within the heart of conflict: a peace that passes understanding. Christians have all too often called for "nonviolence" when they really meant tranquility. Nonviolence, in fact, seeks out conflict, elicits conflict, exacerbates conflict, in order to bring it out into the open and lance its poisonous sores. It is not idealistic or sentimental about evil; it does not coddle or cajole aggressors, but moves against perceived injustice proactively, with the same alacrity as the most hawkish militarist.

As Eisler reminds us, a partnership society is not a society devoid of conflict. It values conflict as the inevitable price of freedom. But it handles conflict nonviolently. The Domination System, by contrast, deals with conflict by suppressing it.[60] Democracy is a state of perpetual low-level conflict—severe enough to agitate citizens into action, and mild enough to prevent that action from boiling over into violence.

The programmatic task of what we might call the "Jesus project" in the decades ahead will require moving from largely reactive, episodic, and occasional nonviolent actions to an aggressive, sustained movement. Our goal must be the training of millions of nonviolent activists who are ready, at a moment's notice, to swing into action on behalf of the humanizing purposes of God.

That struggle is not the sole preserve of Christians, of course; some of the greatest exponents of nonviolence have been non-Christian: the Hindu Gandhi, the Muslim Abdul Ghaffar Khan, the Buddhist Thich Nhat Hanh. These exponents of nonviolence have helped awaken us to its centrality in our own tradition.

And the world, and the church, are waking up! What an exciting prospect! What an auspicious opportunity! What a time to be alive!

For we knew only too well:
Even hatred of squalor
Makes the brow grow stern.
Even anger against injustice
Makes the voice grow harsh. Alas, we
Who wished to lay the foundations of kindness
Could not ourselves be kind.

Bertolt Brecht[1]

10. On Not Becoming What We Hate

In the previous chapter I suggested that "Resist not evil" is better rendered "Do not return evil for evil," "Do not mirror evil," "Do not respond to evil in kind." This refusal of reactive opposition is one of the most profound and difficult truths in Scripture. We become what we hate. The very act of hating something draws it to us. Since our hate is usually a direct response to an evil done to us, our hate almost invariably causes us to respond in the terms already laid down by the enemy. Unaware of what is happening, we turn into the very thing we oppose.

We Become What We Hate

The arms race was the supreme example of this process. We felt threatened by the Soviets, so we increased our weapons. This in turn threatened them; they escalated production, which in turn led to cries of our being "behind" the Soviets, and so we each took a new loop on the spiral to doomsday. Yet every weapon we added left us feeling more insecure. No matter how much more powerful our resistance to evil became, Soviet resistance grew at the same pace. A. J. Muste deduced an axiom from this behavior: "If you arm yourself, you arm your enemy."[2]

This imitative resistance undermined the economies of both nations. Vice-President Richard Nixon in 1954 articulated the U.S. view of Soviet objectives: "Their [the Soviet] plan, apparently, was to force the United States to stay armed to the teeth, to be prepared to fight—anywhere in the world—that they, the men of the Kremlin, chose. Why? Because they knew that this would force us into bankruptcy; that we would destroy our freedom in attempting to defend it."[3] The Soviets had precisely the mirror perception of our intentions. Despite Nixon's clear understanding of Soviet strategy, the United States played right into their hands—and they into ours. President Ronald Reagan, the supreme Soviet hater, was rendered, by his hatred, especially susceptible to this mimesis.

195

Under his watch, U.S. debt soared by two trillion dollars—the very amount spent on the massive military buildup of the 1980s. As William Blake put it, "They looked at one-another & became what they beheld."[4]

Each nation's strategy worked. The Soviet economy has been destroyed, perhaps for decades into the future. The United States has become the world's largest debtor nation and is losing economic ground daily to Japan and Germany, which devoted funds to research and capital improvements while we were consigning them to weaponry.

In this mimetic rivalry, we took on some of the very qualities in the Soviets that we claimed to be resisting. "We would destroy our freedom in attempting to defend it," Nixon prophesied. To keep communism from spreading in Africa, Asia, or Latin America, we felt we had to move in with our troops, or manipulate elections, or unseat legitimately elected regimes, or assassinate leftist leaders. To fend off revolution in client states, we beefed up and trained local police and soldiers, only to watch the military itself become the gravest threat to democracy in one country that we supported after another. To counter Soviet espionage, we created a spy network; to make sure that no one cooperated with the enemy, we spied on our own citizens. "You always become the thing you fight the most," wrote Jung somewhere, and we have done everything in our power to prove him right.[5]

This is not merely an occasional aberration. It is a fixed rule of human behavior, from intrapsychic conflict to international relations. The alcoholic who tries to "resist evil" quickly discovers that the very attempt to conquer the compulsion by main force is futile. The harder people try to quit drinking, the more they fail, and the more they fail, the less self-esteem and confidence they have to try again. A standard response of recovered alcoholics to those who are still trying to will themselves to stop is, "Sure, you can stop anytime you want. I once quit thirty-seven times in one week!" The experience of Alcoholics Anonymous members is that "resisting evil" seldom works. A person must acknowledge powerlessness over the disease and turn to a higher power and a supportive community for help. As long as we hate something, we only draw it to ourselves.

Prohibition was a grand failure at resisting evil. It called so much attention to alcoholic beverages and engendered so much rebellion against legal constraints that when it was repealed, far more alcohol was being consumed than before prohibition went into effect. Now we are repeating the same folly by our "war" on narcotics, which simply makes it the "forbidden fruit," drives up the market price, turns it into a business far more lucrative than any alternative form of employment, leads to the recruitment of children as sellers, lookouts, and deliverers, prompts gang wars over turf and mindless murders and robberies to obtain cash to buy the coveted drugs. Crack itself is the creation of drug prohibition. "The iron law . . . is that the more intense the law enforcement, the more potent the drugs will become," because more concentrated doses are easier to smuggle.[6]

A frontal attack energizes its opposite; it calls attention to it, creates a conscious or unconscious fascination with it, and lends it enormous quantities of energy. "Whoever fights monsters," warned Nietzsche, "should see to it that in the process he does not become a monster."[7]

The Allies fought Hitler to stop the spread of tyranny in Europe, only to see half of Europe slip under the tyranny of Stalin. England went to war, Churchill told Stalin at Yalta, so that "Poland should be free and sovereign."[8] That war did not save Poland for democracy nor did it save the lives of the Jews. Fascism, crushed in Germany, arose phoenixlike in the soul of the victors, because we chose the same means and fought the Devil with the Devil's own weapons.[9]

Hitler may have been the first to employ terror bombing of civilians (Warsaw, Rotterdam, 1939–40), but after the Luftwaffe bombed British air force ground-support stations in London, Britain reciprocated in kind. Precision bombing was not yet possible. Even the wrong *cities* were being hit. Since the Royal Air Force could not consistently strike military targets, it attempted to destroy the morale of the German people by terrorization from the air. From 1942 until 1944, British flight crews were actually forbidden to aim at factories or military installations. The Allies commenced to destroy systematically Germany's forty-three major cities. Churchill justified this step as a "supreme emergency" necessary to stop an immeasurable evil.[10]

This policy culminated in the firebombing of Hamburg, while nearby factories and shipyards went untouched. Those factories and shipyards had been suffering an acute labor shortage, which was now filled by former waiters, shopkeepers, and office workers who were bombed out of their civilian employment. War production was back to normal in a few weeks. The U. S. Strategic Bombing Survey concluded: "In reducing, as nothing else could, the consumption of non-essentials and the employment [of people] in their supply, there is a distinct possibility that the attacks on Hamburg increased Germany's output of war materiel and thus her military effectiveness."[11]

The precedent set by the incendiary bombing of German and Japanese cities made it easier in turn for the United States to use the atomic bomb on Hiroshima and Nagasaki, when an offshore demonstration of the bomb might have sufficed. Japan was already negotiating surrender, and the terms of surrender we accepted after the bombing were exactly those proposed before it took place. It is not at all clear that an invasion would have been necessary to force capitulation.[12] When the United States dropped the atomic bomb on Japan, one of the largest single casualties was our own moral integrity as a people.

We did not by that act suddenly become violent, of course. The European settlers had been violent from the beginning. But the atomic bomb marked a threshold of unprecedented destructive power that threatened the very survival of life on this planet. When we stepped across that threshold, we found ourselves captive to the very power we had unleashed.

The gradual extension of bombing civilians that culminated in the use of the atomic bomb on Hiroshima and Nagasaki paved the way for the strategy of Mutually Assured Destruction and the policy of "first strike." The nations that gasped at Hitler's genocide of the Jews were now poised to commit ecocide: the genocide of virtually all living species on earth. The very spirit we had gone to war to drive out leaped upon its unwary exorcists and drove us to conceive of crimes against our own consciences and against the planet that beggar the evils we set out to oppose. Such is the power of violence that even its use to destroy a flagrant evil can recoil against the users and make them over into the likeness of the enemy.

> The iron hand crushed the Tyrant's head
> And became a Tyrant in his stead.[13]

"The more a tragic conflict is prolonged, the more likely it is to culminate in a violent mimesis," writes René Girard; "the resemblance between the combatants grows ever stronger until each presents a mirror image of the other."[14] With what visage, then, did the United States emerge "victorious" from forcible resistance to Hitler's evil? We have adopted a permanent war economy and a militarized conception of national security. We see it as our duty to police the "free" world, and we fund a huge army staffed, if necessary, through involuntary conscription. We have created an invisible apparatus of surveillance and espionage that seems incapable of distinguishing patriotic protest from sedition, is unaccountable to public authorities, and inaugurates wars without consent of the Congress.[15] We have increasingly come to rely on military intervention instead of diplomacy, force rather than negotiations. We are one of the major purveyors of armaments to nations all over the globe, many of whom purchase weapons at the cost of the welfare of their own people and the destabilization of their own regions.

We have, in short, granted Hitler a degree of victory by adopting elements of the ethos and mentality of Nazism. H. G. Baynes wrote as early as 1941 that the psychic assimilation of the vanquished by the victors is inevitable. Like the warrior who eats the heart of his slain enemy to assimilate his strength, so we would, in a psychic sense, eat Hitlerism, he warned. And the problem will be that in overcoming the enemy, one tends to swallow not only his better qualities, but also the worst, and to become like the vanquished through victory.

"The very angels must surely hold their breath when it is being decided what part or aspect of Hitler shall be assimilated."[16]

"By intensity of hatred," wrote George William Russell, "nations create in themselves the characteristics they imagine in their enemies. Hence it is that all passionate conflicts result in the interchange of characteristics." The very act of entering into conflict with an antagonist establishes relations where none may have existed before. William Irwin Thompson comments on this "interchange of characteristics" following World War II: "Japan is now Los Angeles and Detroit, and Big Sur, California, is a Zen Mountain Center. Germany is now a consumer society, and we are the largest militarist state in the history of the world. We have become our enemy."[17]

Conquerors have all through history been conquered by those they conquer. Joseph Goebbels, Hitler's propaganda minister, proved either a shrewd student of history or a prophet when he reputedly said, "Even if we lose, we shall win, for our ideals will have penetrated the hearts of our enemies."[18]

We want desperately to believe that our forcible retaliation to evil is like a projectile fired from a gun that will drop evil in its tracks. In fact, it is more like a ball thrown by a pitcher that will, as likely as not, carom back at us, or over the fence.

In *The Devil's Share*, Denis de Rougemont articulated a penetrating warning even before the Nazis had been defeated. We Americans want to believe, he wrote, that the Nazis are animals of an altogether different race from ourselves. We run the risk of discovering someday that, after all, they are people just like us. And it is quite true, he says; they are like us in the sense that their sin is also secretly in us.

> This is why we say today to the worthy democrats: "Look at the Devil who is among us! Stop believing that he can only resemble Hitler or his emulators, for *it is yourselves whom he resembles most*! It is in yourselves only that you will catch him in the act. And then only will you be in a position to unmask him in others, and to fight him successfully. For then only you will be cured of your unbelievable naivete in the presence of the totalitarian danger and be able to withstand the hypnosis."
> We lacked a modern representation of the Demon. We had therefore ceased to believe in him. Then we imagined that the Devil was Hitler. And the Devil rubbed his hands. (And so did Hitler.)[19]

Violent Mimesis

It would make a fascinating study to write a history of the world from the perspective of the principle of forcible resistance changing into what it opposes. Indeed, a full evaluation of René Girard's theory of mimesis would require just that. One can find instances from virtually every period. The Maccabees fought to prevent the forced Hellenization of Jews in Palestine. When they finally secured independence from their Hellenistic overlords (143 B.C.E.), they adopted the model of the Hellenistic kingdom and bureaucracy for their own use. Simon became virtually a military and spiritual dictator (1 Macc. 14:41-48). Hyrcanus paid mercenaries out of funds robbed from the tombs of Israelite kings. Alexander Janneus not only sided with the Hellenizing Sadducees, but seized lands that had been redistributed to Jewish peasants by the earlier Maccabees and converted them back to royal land in order to support his military campaigns.[20]

Later, Rome subjugated the Jews, prompting the Roman philosopher Seneca to complain that Jewish customs had begun to penetrate Roman life: "The conquered have given laws to the conquerors."[21] The last pagan poet, Rutilius Namatianus, concurred: "Would to the gods Judea had never been conquered!"[22] Rome attempted to destroy the Christian church—only to become its Holy See. The church in turn found itself locked in a life-and-death struggle with Gnosticism, and in the process of combatting it, took on not only its exegetical methods, but also its hatred of the body.

In the Middle Ages, the Catholic church fought the successors of the Gnostics, the Cathari and Albigensians. The church declared heretical their Manichaean conception of the eternal warfare of light against dark, good against evil, spirit against matter, God against Lucifer. But in attempting to exterminate heresy by violent means, the church itself became Manichaean. It demonized all Cathari and Albigensians, attacked them with military force, burned them alive, slaughtered whole cities, and ultimately butchered a million people in France alone. During the sack of Béziers, France, on July 21, 1209, the entire population of twenty thousand people was massacred, heretics and Catholics alike, with the papal legate crying all the while, "Kill them all, God will recognize his own!"[23]

Again, in trying to suppress witchcraft, the inquisitors did far more evil than all the witches ever did, and drew so much attention to witchcraft that they actually spread belief in it and fostered the practices they were trying so hard to repress.[24]

Jews emerged from the nightmare of Hitlerism and the Holocaust crying "Never again!" and are now treating Palestinians brutally. Torture and massive overreaction to legitimate protests (which to a surprising degree were nonviolent, once the leadership of the *Intifada* passed from the Palestine Liberation Organization to Gaza and West Bank indigenous leaders) grow in their inhumanity. As the Jewish writer Marc H. Ellis puts it,

> It is not too much to say that the uprising poses the future of Judaism in stark and unremitting terms. The tragedy of the Holocaust is indelibly ingrained in our consciousness. Contemporary Jewish theology helps us come to grips with our suffering; it hardly recognizes that today we are powerful. It holds in tension

Holocaust and the need for our empowerment. Consequently it speaks eloquently
for the victims of Treblinka and Auschwitz yet can ignore Sabra and Shatila [the
sites of massacres in Lebanon at least consented to by the Israeli armed forces].
It pays tribute to the Warsaw Ghetto uprising but has no place for the uprising of
ghetto dwellers on the other side of Israeli power. Jewish theologians insist that
the torture and murder of Jewish children be lamented and commemorated in
Jewish ritual and belief. They have yet to imagine the possibility that Jews have
in turn tortured and murdered Palestinian children. Holocaust theology relates the
story of the Jewish people in its beauty and suffering. It fails to understand the
contemporary history of the Palestinian people as integral to our own. Thus, this
theology articulated who we were but no longer helps us understand who we have
become.[25]

With what convoluted logic is the Israeli taxi driver thinking when he says,
"We should beat [the Palestinians] on the heads, we should beat them and beat
them and beat them until they stop hating us"?[26]

Or, returning to World War II, we fought Japan ostensibly to prevent it from
turning the Pacific basin into its own economic lake. Yet after the war, fueled
by our fears of communism, we helped rebuild Japan as an economic giant in
order to create a capitalist, anticommunist buffer against the Soviet Union and
China. Now the Pacific is a Japanese lake, and even our domestic economy can
scarcely brook the competition.

My point is not simply that war is bad. The issue is far deeper. It is that war
draws intelligent, rational, decent people ineluctably into mimetic violence.
Before they realize it, they are themselves doing or condoning acts of utter
barbarity and feel unable to act otherwise.

Forcible resistance transforms itself into what it opposes. As long as we
continue to justify violence as "Christian," we will remain blind to our own
captivity to the hypnosis of mimetic rivalry. We really do have to choose whether
to continue to support the Domination System, driven as it is by the myth of
redemptive violence. This is the great divide that separates the gospel from all
the apparently compelling justifications provided by the ideological counterfeit
of the gospel. Any religious message that promises that we can win in the terms
laid down by the Domination System is apostate. Any theology that promises
success, national supremacy, or victory through redemptive violence is apostate.
Any piety that equates the gospel with getting ahead, being number one, or
salvation through patriotism is apostate.

When Jesus said, "Those who try to make their life secure will lose it, but
those who lose their life will keep it" (Luke 17:33), he drew a line in the dirt
and asked if we would step across—step out of one entire world, where violence
is always the ultimate solution, into another world, where the spiral of violence
is finally broken by those willing to absorb its impact with their own bodies.

World War II, many still feel, was a just, or at least a necessary, war. Nonviolence as a means for settling international disputes is so recent—an international nonviolent movement (apart from the "peace churches") dates only from 1914—that the means were simply not in place inside and outside Germany to mount an effective nonviolent alternative. (Yet nonviolent direct action proved effective in virtually every case where it was used against the Nazis. See chap. 13.) It may well be that in ten or fifteen years we will be more prepared to respond to conflicts with an international outpouring of nonviolent resistance. So perhaps there was, tragically, no alternative at that time to war.

The point I am making is that even if a war does appear to be just, or at least tragically necessary and unavoidable, it will inevitably require the relatively more just opponent (if there be such) to become increasingly molded into the likeness of its adversary. The greatest evils are usually perpetrated by people determined to eradicate an evil by whatever means necessary. War is not, then, a mere continuation of diplomacy by other means, as Clausewitz claimed. It marks the abject failure of diplomacy, and the adoption of means that have very little likelihood of achieving desirable ends.[27]

"The ultimate weakness of violence," observed Martin Luther King, Jr., "is that it is a descending spiral, begetting the very thing it seeks to destroy."[28] We wish to stop murder from being committed, so we execute murderers—and become murderers ourselves. We try to stop our children from fighting—by hitting them. We had to destroy the city in order to save it—so that the communists could save Vietnam in order to destroy it.[29]

Why do prisons fail to rehabilitate criminals? Because, says Mark Mason, who has been there, the criminal justice system does everything possible to socialize prisoners into the ethos of penitentiary life. The prisoner is taught, by the guards, administration, and other inmates, how a criminal walks, talks, breathes, looks, reacts. Prison strips a person of a sense of self and conditions one to act like a criminal in order to fit into the group. Consequently, as high as eighty percent of released convicts return to prison. Having developed a "criminal self," having identified with the criminal life and criminal population, most find that they cannot live a life apart. The criminal justice system not only is a school for crime; it actually molds people's souls into the very identity prisons are supposed to make them renounce. Having become alienated from their true selves, they can live nowhere else than in this hellish circle of the damned who have nothing left but a collective negative identity.[30]

"The whole Domination System (*kosmos*) lies under the power of the Evil One" (1 John 5:19*). The ancient pattern of violent resistance being transformed into its opposite governs collective life from the nation to the family. We are addicted to violence, and the irony is that this addiction is as prevalent on the left as on the right.

The radical left fringe of the anti-Vietnam War movement, for example, correctly identified the evil our government was doing in Asia and adopted the same violent means to oppose it. Nor was that all; they became the actual image of what they hated. Like the Powers they opposed, they became secretive (as terrorists must). This forced them to abandon all attempts to build a popular political base, so they became increasingly elitist, an oligarchy that "knew what was best for the rest of us." To counter messianic American imperialism they became messianists in turn who would impose their good on the others. Here, as so often, the thesis lived on in the antithesis. Having adopted the same violent means as the government they opposed, members of the Weather Underground became mimetically transformed into the very epitome of irrational violence. In the process, they provided the administration with a pretext to infiltrate, wiretap, harass, and gather information on the far more effective nonviolent groups opposed to the Vietnam War. These so-called radicals could scarcely have served the war effort better had they been members of the CIA (as no doubt some of them were!).[31]

We have played out the principle of mimetic counterresistance even in our relationship with nature. By 1950 many scientists recognized that DDT was toxic to a wide number of species, but we were already "hooked" into its use. For while malarial mosquitoes were becoming increasingly immune to DDT, discontinuing its application was not an easy matter because the DDT had virtually exterminated the other species that fed on the mosquitoes. By 1980, forty-three types of malaria-bearing mosquitoes had become resistant to the leading insecticides. As a consequence, the incidence of malaria in some countries has increased a hundredfold during the past fifteen years. One response has been simply to increase the toxicity level of pesticides being sprayed, in a bizarre parody of Cold War politics.[32] Violent reaction has become a reflexive twitch that threatens the very ecosystem itself.

Western allopathic medicine plays out the same total-war scenario. Prevention through diet, meditation, stress reduction, and exercise has until very recently been almost totally ignored by doctors in favor of "fighting" disease by ingesting highly poisonous chemicals that are deadly not only to harmful agents but to helpful ones as well. Instead of nurturing healthy bodies capable of a high degree of self-healing, our medical profession has been like a bacteriological Pentagon engaged in an endless spiral of escalating warfare against microbes and viruses that generally can coexist without damage in a normal, healthy body.

Just so, like an awkward, stumbling giant we have thrown our might at country after country—Iran, Guatemala, Cuba, Zaïre, Vietnam, Chile, El Salvador, Nicaragua—in order to prevent the expansion of Soviet imperialism. Yet virtually everywhere the CIA or the U.S. military has intervened to enforce order and resist communism, intervention has proved counterproductive.[33] The doctrine that limited wars and interventions were inevitable led military planners to make preparations for their coming. Yet each step in preparation—encircling bases, offshore fleets, aid to national military and police forces, propaganda attacks—served as actual provocations and were already a form of military intervention.

The military theory became a self-fulfilling prophecy. Our leaders were incapable of comprehending that other nations are not keen to be saved from one imperialism merely in order to be engulfed by another. So our foreign policy obsessively tried to prevent the one thing it was driving other nations toward with the full momentum of its awesome might. We squandered billions trying to prevent native insurgencies and guerrilla warfare from spreading in the Third World. There is now no money left to attack the decay, homelessness, and crack wars that besiege us here at home. As a result, we have created native insurgencies and guerrilla warfare in American cities.[34]

The cost of such forcible interventions is not tallied on the battlefield alone. We are still undergoing the shock of Vietnam in manifold and sickening ways. An estimated 700,000 out of the three million veterans of Vietnam suffer from Post Traumatic Stress Syndrome. Nearly a quarter of the total prison population in the U.S. is made up of Vietnam veterans, and three to five times that number have been in jail or prison over the past fifteen years. Eighty thousand Vietnam vets have died by suicide, and untold others by drug and alcohol overdose, single-car accidents and other forms of self-destructive behavior. Perhaps fifty percent of all homeless men are veterans, mainly of the Vietnam War.[35]

The medical writer Lewis Thomas argues that the gravest damage in most diseases is caused by a panicked overreaction by the body's own defenses.[36] This has certainly been the case for the body politic of the United States. Our overreactions to communist imperialism—McCarthyism, the Cold War, the arms race, the pervasive projection of all evil out upon communism, our ill-advised wars of containment against it—unquestionably did more harm to our nation than anything the communists ever did to us. In the process we ineluctably and unwittingly became metamorphosed into the very thing we feared.[37]

Every Soviet act of belligerence, every increase in its influence in other countries, every new weapon it added to its arsenal, provoked alarmed reactions of reflexive militarism or repressive surveillance in the United States. The elements of our immune system—the police, the military services, the courts, the FBI and CIA, the penal system—are perceived by many people no longer as protectors, but as adversaries. The cure has too often been worse than the disease, and we have become a nation suffering chronic stress. And the Soviets, in their resistance to us, were subjected to the identical process, as we came more and more to resemble one another.

I do not wish to suggest that there were no shades of difference between the United States and the Soviet Union. No mimesis is total. Americans enjoyed vastly greater degrees of freedom, economic prosperity, and political power than the Soviets. This is precisely what makes mimesis so diabolical: it causes parties to abandon their most treasured and distinctive values in the competitive race to imitate the opponent.

The Contagion of Evil

Evil is a contagion. No one grapples with it without contamination. In 1982 my wife, June, and I spent four months in Latin America, observing military dictatorships, talking with the tortured, visiting slums. Without realizing what was happening, I began to slip into spiritual darkness, until I was physically emaciated and spiritually wasted. I did not understand what had happened until much later, when I dreamed I was attempting to escape from a Somoza concentration camp in prerevolutionary Nicaragua. The dream faithfully mirrored my state: I was in psychic detention. I had, over a decade, a series of such dreams; always I was trying to escape a ruthless dictator. The stories and scenes of torture and detention had, unknown to me, seeped into my own depths and activated an old wound, and I was quite literally brought down into captivity.[38]

The suffering of those who had been victims of detention had resonated with my own memory of a traumatic experience of punishment and incarceration. When I was a child, I lied quite often out of fear of my father's wrath. One day when he came home from work he asked me if I had put my bike in the garage. I answered yes, and ran out to the front yard to put it away. It was gone. I ran into the house shouting that my bike had been stolen. "Where was it?" Dad asked. "In the front yard," I naively replied. "I thought you said it was in the garage," he said. It was entrapment; he had himself hidden it. After dinner that night, he and my mother convened a trial at the kitchen table while I stood before the bar of justice, being judged. They found me guilty of being a liar, and gave me two choices: to leave home for good, or to spend the night in the "brig" (a garage storeroom). Sensing that my life in my family was over, I opted to leave. I was nine years old. They asked me to whom I planned to go. Every time I suggested someone they said, "Oh, no, they wouldn't want a liar living with them." There appeared to be no alternative to the brig. That night in a very profound sense I "died," emotionally. And now, decades later, amidst the general hopelessness of the situation of the oppressed in Latin America, I found myself sinking back into that old despair I had myself first known as a detainee in my own home.

A woman in one of our workshops shared a similar story. She told how it had broken her heart to see firsthand, with a Witness for Peace delegation, the suffering of Nicaraguans at the hands of U.S.-funded Contras. She returned determined to do everything she could to change U.S. policy. She spoke frequently and well. But every time she sat down to write, all she could do was weep. On being pressed to identify what wound or trauma had been triggered by the trip, she recalled the way her father had brutalized her brother, and to a lesser extent herself. She had wanted to help her brother, and could not. Now, given this chance to help others similarly brutalized, that old sense of powerlessness welled up within her and paralyzed her.

In some way or another, I suspect, every injustice that moves us deeply reenacts our own personal wound. There is a dual action of projection and introjection: we project the evil within us onto the world, and we introject the evil we see out in the world into our own psyches. Resistance to evil thus constellates in our own depths whatever is similar to the outer evil we oppose. Our very resistance *feeds* the inner shadow. The very shrillness of our opposition may indicate that a part of us secretly desires to emulate what we oppose.[39] (How often I have heard people say that the greatest violence they have ever personally encountered was from colleagues in the peace movement!)

Are we not often unconsciously attracted to the very evils we most stridently denounce? Is not our very intensity against evil a dangerous sign that it fascinates us? The very sight of evil kindles evil in the soul, wrote Jung. "Even a saint would have to pray unceasingly for the souls of Hitler and Himmler, the Gestapo and the SS, in order to repair without delay the damage done to his own soul" by viewing their atrocities. We are unavoidably drawn into the uncleanness of evil, whatever our conscious attitude.[40]

Have you never caught yourself secretly pleased to hear that someone higher up the professional ladder you are climbing has had a crippling stroke? Perhaps now you can move up a notch. Or, thank God it was she and not I. Is there not something more than fascination in watching a house burn? There is horror, but there is also a kind of joy—as long as it is not our own! As the Duc de la Rochefoucauld put it, in the misfortune of our friends we find something that does not displease us. And is not one of war's deepest satisfactions the sense of personal exemption from the fate of others—"the joy of being alive when so many around you are not"?[41]

Some of us engaged in struggles for social justice have been incredibly naive about what has been happening in our own psyches. Our very identities are often defined by our resistance to evil. It is our way of feeling good about ourselves: If we are against evil, we must be good. The impatience of some activists with prayer, meditation, and inner healing may itself represent an inchoate knowledge of what they might find if they looked within. *For the struggle against evil can make us evil*, and no amount of good intentions automatically prevents its happening. The whole armor of God that Eph. 6:10-20 counsels us to put on is crafted specifically to protect us against that contagion of evil within our own souls, and its metals are all annealed in prayer.

The struggle against outer evils unleashes evils within our own souls. That is no reason to avoid such struggles; they may be the only way we can discover the spiritual work that our destiny requires of us. Either we face the fearful shadow in ourselves, withdrawing the projections we have placed on our outer enemies, or we will mimetically act it out against some feared opponent and pull down the pillars of the world on our own heads. Either we develop our own inner spiritual fire, or we will be incinerated in a ball of fire. Either we learn to be one world together, without fear of other races and nations and economic systems, or we will die as one world together without distinction of race, nation, or economic system.

Jesus' third way both arrests the outer spiral of retaliation and equips us to face the inner infection that it excites. His is a way of engaging evil that involves neither acquiescing to it nor hurling ourselves against it blindly, on its own terms.

More deeply still, nonviolence is a spiritual challenge of epic proportions. It calls upon the soul's authentic longing for heroism, for risking one's life for an infinite stake, for self-transcendence in giving oneself to others.

In the East, whole systems of martial arts and spirituality have been built around the awareness of the futility of counterresisting evil: jujitsu, aikido, t'ai chi. Though differing in detail, the basic orientation in all of them is using the opponent's own momentum and energy to disarm him, with as little injury as possible. The intention is to use force, but not violence. Women in childbirth have long known the same thing: to tighten against the pain merely increases it. To be able to surrender to the pain, to enter its core by breathing deeply and slowly, reduces the pain of the contractions. Others have applied the same insight to life generally: instead of trying to fight off cancer or loneliness or the shadow that scares us, to accept it, breathe with it, turn toward it, openhanded, and give it love, acceptance, and the possibility of gracious transformation.[42]

Reality appears to be so constructed, whether physically or spiritually, that every action creates an equal and opposite reaction. Thus every attempt to fight the Domination System by dominating means is destined to result in domination. When we resist evil with evil, when we mirror it, when we lash out at it in kind, we simply guarantee its perpetuation. The way of nonviolence, the way Jesus chose, is the only way that is able to overcome domination. To those trapped in the assumptions of domination, nonviolence must appear suicidal—a crucifixion. But to those who have looked unflinchingly at the record of violence in the everyday world, nonviolence appears to be the only way left. And not just for Christians; for the world.

No wonder so many people, gentle and kind people, quiet and unaggressive people, find themselves saying at long last: "There's only one way to deal with the Marcoses and Enriles. There's only one way to deal with the Khmer Rouge. There's only one language these people understand—we say it not joyfully, but reluctantly and sadly—the only thing they understand is the gun."

To such people I say: Welcome home, welcome to the largest consensus the world has ever known: a consensus between east and west, between capitalist and communist, between mosque, church and synagogue. All agree that there comes a time when it is just to kill each other. Welcome home to the consensus on which our world is built.

Ultimately we are faced with two choices: to accept the "myth" of the just war, that as a last resort killing is moral, or to accept the "myth" of nonviolence: we have no last resort; killing is never right. In the first case, sooner or later we will come to the moment when the conditions for using violence are verified, when we reach the "last resort." In the second case, believing in our "myth," that violence is never justified, having no "last resort," human beings come up with alternatives from the depths of their creativeness. . . . We can and we will learn to live together, but only when we have closed off that escape route known as the last resort.

Niall O'Brien,
"Making the Myth Real"[1]

11. Beyond Just War and Pacifism

Early Christian Nonviolence

The new reality Jesus proclaimed was nonviolent. That much is clear, not just from the Sermon on the Mount, but from his entire life and teaching and, above all, the way he faced his death. His was not merely a tactical or pragmatic nonviolence seized upon because nothing else would have "worked" against the Roman Empire's near monopoly on violence. Rather, he saw nonviolence as a direct corollary of the nature of God and of the new reality emerging in the world from God. In a verse quoted more than any other from the New Testament during the church's first four centuries, Jesus taught that God loves everyone, and values all, even those who make themselves God's enemies. We are therefore to do likewise (Matt. 5:45; cf. Luke 6:35). The reign of God, the peaceable kingdom, is (despite the monarchical terms) an order in which the inequity, violence, and domination characteristic of androcratic societies are superseded. Thus nonviolence is not just a means to the kingdom of God; it is a quality of the kingdom itself. Those who live nonviolently are already manifesting the transformed reality of the divine order now, even under the conditions of the Domination System.

The idea of nonviolent resistance was not new. The Hebrew midwives, the Greek tragedians, Jainism, Buddhism, Hinduism, Lao-tzu, and Judaism were all to various degrees conversant with nonviolence as a way of life and, in some cases, even as a tactic of social change. What was new was the early church's inference from Jesus' teaching that nonviolence is the *only* way, that war itself must be renounced. The idea of peace and the more general rejection of violence can be found before Christianity and in other cultures, says Peter Brock, but nowhere else do we find practical antimilitarism leading to the refusal of military service.[2]

Early Christian statements against war are ubiquitous.[3] Justin Martyr is representative when he declares, "We who once killed each other not only do not make war on each other, but in order not to lie or deceive our inquisitors we gladly die for the confession of Christ."[4] "For we no longer take up 'sword against nation,' " wrote Origen, "nor do we 'learn war any more,' having become children of peace, for the sake of Jesus."[5] Tertullian was, if anything, more adamant: Christ, "in disarming Peter, unbelted every soldier." "But how will *a Christian man* war," he asks, "nay, how will he serve [as a soldier] even in peace, without a sword, which the Lord has taken away."[6] The pagan Celsus attacked Christians for disloyalty to the empire, since they refused to serve in the army. If everyone behaved as Christians did, he charged, the empire would be ruined—unmistakable evidence that the teaching of the early theologians was representative of actual practice.[7]

No one disagrees that the early church denounced war. For three centuries, Christians were virtually unanimous in denouncing Christian participation in battle.[8] Such data as we have indicate that involvement in the army even in peacetime was problematic. Tertullian's advice to soldiers who converted was pithy: Quit the army, or be martyred.[9]

What has been hotly debated for over a hundred years now is whether Christians opposed involvement in the army because they were against killing in principle, or only because army life was so saturated with idolatrous practices that it was impossible to avoid taking part in pagan rites. Pacifists have tended to the former position, just war theorists to the latter. As with most inconclusive discussions, both sides are able to assemble considerable evidence for their case. There can be no doubt that in some passages the early theologians object to killing, in others to the idolatry involved in military service, and in others to both, though it is hard to find scholars willing to present both sides dispassionately.[10]

The tempting solution is to compromise. No doubt the early theologians opposed killing in war, though clearly the church had no absolute prohibition on military service. By 170 or so we begin hearing of soldiers who have been converted and remained in the army. The church's leading thinkers tried to stem this tide by condemning both killing and idolatry, but the general laxity of which Origen complained and the increasing absorption of Christians into Roman culture was an irresistible force. Their loyalty to the empire, though nonviolent by nature, made Christians an easy target for co-optation by Constantine. The lack of any uproar in the church over military service in the following century indicates that the church found the transition to full support of the empire, including military service, rather simple, though some parts of the church gave in only with an uneasy conscience.

Such a picture would at least seem to fit the facts and harmonize the various scholarly positions, and it is, I believe, true so far as it goes. What it overlooks, however, is the profound *identity* of the rejection of killing in war and the refusal of idolatry in Roman military service. If the church's sole objection to military service was idolatry, why do some of the fathers categorically forbid soldiers to kill? And if killing was the chief obstacle to military service, why do some (even the same!) church fathers raise the question of military idolatry? Here categories like pacifism and just war, or "hawks" and "doves," merely confuse the issue. Every aspect of Roman military life was sacred. The camp itself was sacred space, its borders sacred demarcations. The standards, banners, and camp flags were worshiped as the legionary gods. Even the uniform and weapons were sanctified to the gods.[11] This sacralized military existence was wholly at the service of Roman imperialism. For those who worshiped Rome and its power, this was a natural extension of the spirituality of the empire—indeed, it was the means by which the empire had been extended.[12]

The implications for Christians were far-reaching, and Tertullian, in *On Idolatry*, perceived them best. Worship of the war machine of androcracy's current representative, Rome, was the acute manifestation of the religion of violence. The issue for the church was not merely squeamishness over blood-letting, or fellow feeling for sufferers and victims, or a pragmatic weighing of the costs, or even regard for the slaughtered lives of people created in the image of God, though these all counted. What these concerns exposed, finally, was the confrontation between the reign of God and the Domination System. The Roman war cult was redemptive violence elevated to absolute value. No Christian could worship the gods of the legions that had given Rome dominion over the world.

The scholarly debate is thus bogus; the issue was not opposition to war versus opposition to Roman army idolatry. They were the same issue. To oppose war was to oppose the very instrument by which Rome had won its empire and become an object of self-worship. To oppose Roman self-worship was to oppose the divinization of war, by which Roman hegemony was gained and maintained. Opposition to war, and opposition to military idolatry, were one. That is why the modern distinction between killing and idolatry never occurred to the early theologians.[13]

When Constantine forbade sacrificing by the army in 321, most Christians apparently read this as removing a major objection to military service. The other objection—killing—was easily rationalized since the empire no longer waged wars of expansion and had to fight only occasionally, in that relatively peaceful period, to protect its borders. Soldiers functioned mostly as police, protecting the mail service and searching for bandits. When the Christian church began receiving preferential treatment by the empire that it had once so steadfastly opposed, war, which had once seemed so evil, now appeared to many to be a necessity for preserving and propagating the gospel.

Christianity's weaponless victory over the Roman Empire eventuated in the weaponless victory of the empire over the gospel. No defeat is so well-disguised as victory! In the year 303, Diocletian forbade any member of the Roman army to be a Christian.[14] By the year 416, no one could be a member of the Roman army *unless* he was a Christian.[15]

No doubt elements of the church's assimilation into Roman society can be found as early as Paul, Luke, the Pastoral Epistles, and *1 Clement*. Equally certain, authentic aspects of Christianity survived the Constantinian compromise. But to deny that a fundamental transformation occurred as the church ceased being persecuted and weak and became instead a persecutor and strong is to ignore the repeatedly documented fact that once a religion attains sufficient power to legitimate the state, it must also, of necessity, engage in repression. For a religion like Zoroastrianism or Islam, such a transition could be made with scarcely a ripple. For a faith that lived from its critique of domination and its vision of a nonviolent social order, the shift was catastrophic, for it could only mean embracing and rationalizing oppression.

Just War Theory

It fell to Augustine (d. 430) to make the accommodation of Christianity to its new status as a privileged religion in support of the state. Augustine believed that Christians had no right to defend themselves from violence. But he identified a problem that no earlier theologian had faced: what Augustine regarded as the loving obligation to use violence if necessary to defend the innocent against evil. Drawing on Stoic just war principles, he articulated the position that was to dominate church teaching from that time right up to the present.

Though most Christians, Catholic or Protestant, will, if questioned, claim that they support the use of violence in certain cases on the basis of just war thinking, they do nothing of the sort.[16] Just war theory is a very rigorous and complex ethical discipline. It has never been taught to the average church member or even to most clergy. The vast majority of professional theologians would be at a loss to list the seven or more criteria used in just war decisions. What most people call "just war" is really something else. Some mean by it the entirely different idea of the *holy war* or *crusade*, which knows no limits and admits no ethical quandaries. From the Hebrew conquest of Canaan to the medieval Crusades to World War I (the war to "make the world safe for democracy"), holy wars have been total wars aimed at the utter subjugation or extermination of an enemy.[17]

Others who believe they are advocates of just war are in reality supporting a *political war*, or a *war of national interests*.[18] Examples would include Iraq's invasion of Iran in 1980 and Kuwait in 1990, the U.S. involvement in Vietnam, Grenada, and Panama, the Soviet war in Afghanistan, the Vietnamese occupation of Cambodia, and a host of other military interventions made by nations into the affairs of other nations for purely pragmatic political and economic reasons. These wars are not justified by ethical reflection but merely by the presumed necessities of power politics. Here might simply makes right.

A third category of war is that pursued for the sake of *machismo* or *egocentricity*. In this case a nation or its leader's pride or honor is so involved in not backing down, or in standing up to an opponent, or in proving his or her courage, that all other considerations—including the loss of human life—are dwarfed by comparison. One thinks of Prime Minister Thatcher and the Falklands/Malvinas war; or Saddam Hussein's suicidal refusal to withdraw from Kuwait; or President Bush's personalizing the war against Saddam Hussein as if it were a face-off between just the two of them.

Just war theory is quite distinct from these three types of war, though it is endlessly confused with them. Every war that Christians of the world's nations have engaged in has been either a holy war crusade, a war of national interests, or an affair of machismo. No authoritative Christian body has ever, prior to the commencement of fighting, decreed that one side or the other is justified in warfare on the basis of just war criteria. Instead, the sorry record reveals that Christian churches have usually simply endorsed the side on which they happened to find themselves. Significant parts of the population may even oppose a war, as in the case of the Mexican-American War, the U.S. Civil War, and the Vietnam War. But I know of no national church body (and very few significant Christian leaders) that, at the inception of hostilities, has ever denounced a war of national interest fought by its own nation. (For the first time, in advance of a war, many prominent Christian leaders, the Pope included, declared that the Persian Gulf War did *not* meet just war criteria.)

My wife, June, and I were in Buenos Aires in 1982 at the height of the Falkland/Malvinas war. All of the theologians we spoke with felt that Argentina's claim on the islands was just. Nobel peace laureate Adolfo Pérez Esquivel was the only critic we found of the Argentinean invasion; but even he considered the Argentinean claim just.

Later, in England, the same pattern repeated itself. All the theologians we spoke with believed England's military response to Argentina was just. Quite apart from the question of who was right and who was wrong, what is striking here is the utter predictability of these responses. Christian moral discrimination tends to follow the flag, and few there are who, like Amos or Isaiah or Thoreau, can entertain the notion that God might not be on their nation's side.

World War II has been almost universally regarded by the victors as a "just war." But no church body, before or at any time during that war, examined it in the light of just war criteria.[19] John Courtney Murray, the leading Roman Catholic interpreter of just war theory at the time, admitted that no sustained criticism of World War II was made before or during that war by Catholic ethicists. "The traditional doctrine was irrelevant during World War II."[20]

Excusing themselves from both the rigors of nonviolence and the demands of just war theory, Christians have, since Constantine, fallen upon each other and others with a ferocity utterly at odds with their origins. Bernard of Clairvaux set the tone when he addressed the Knights Templars: "The soldier of Christ is certain when he kills. . . . He kills with Christ, for he does not carry the sword without reason. He is the servant of God for the punishment of evil men and the praise of good men. When he kills an evil-doer, he is no murderer, but rather, I should say, a killer of evil and an avenger of Christ against those who do evil."[21] Prayers for victory, regimental colors and national flags in churches, stained-glass windows depicting armed fighters, chaplains paid by the military and assigned to uphold morale and salve consciences, all express the mentality either of holy war, or war for national security, or war fought as a matter of pride.[22]

Most Christians assume that any war that they *feel* is just, or merely necessary and unavoidable, *is* just. The just war criteria, however, are extraordinarily demanding. They presuppose that no Christian should be involved in a war unless it meets all or at least most of the criteria.[23] The burden of proof is *always* on those who resort to violence.

Just war theory assumes that initiating war is generally a crime, and that only one party, usually not the aggressor, can be just.[24] Just war theory is not so much a discipline as a tradition. Its intent is not to declare the actors just, but only their acts relatively justified. Just war theory never assumes that survival is an overriding consideration for either the individual or the state. It anticipates situations where victory cannot be gained without using indefensible means, and renounces them, accepting defeat as an honorable outcome.[25]

Various writers present slightly different lists, but the essential conditions that must be met before a decision to go to war is considered justified (*jus ad bellum*) are these:

1. The war must have a *just cause*.
2. It must be waged by a *legitimate authority*.
3. It must be *formally declared*.
4. It must be fought with a *peaceful intention*.
5. It must be a *last resort*.
6. There must be reasonable *hope of success*.
7. The means used must possess *proportionality* to the end sought.

Three additional conditions must be met regarding the conditions for the permissible conduct of war (*jus in bello*):

1. *Noncombatants* must be given immunity.
2. *Prisoners* must be treated humanely.
3. *International treaties and conventions* must be honored.[26]

These general rules can be extremely difficult to apply in concrete situations.[27] What constitutes a legitimate authority in a guerrilla insurgency aimed at overthrowing a dictator? How do we distinguish between an "offensive" and "defensive" war or determine who really started it? Who are noncombatants in the age of democracies and total war? What happens when *both* sides believe they can construct a valid case for a just war? Do some criteria outweigh others? Must they all be met?[28] Are they still applicable in the nuclear age, or in the face of the unparalleled firepower now available to assailants? And why should these criteria be regarded as authoritative?

Despite the casuistic cast of these criteria and the difficulty in applying them, I believe they are indispensable in the struggle to mitigate the violence of war. *It is not the criteria themselves that are problematic, but the fact that they have been subordinated to the myth of redemptive violence.* In that mythic context, the just war criteria have normally been used simply to legitimate wars that are indefensible. Freed from that context, and subordinated to the church's vocation for nonviolence, these criteria can play a critical role in preventing wars and in reducing the level of violence in wars that cannot be averted.

Just war theorists have often bristled at the perfectionism of pacifists, whose concern for ethical means sometimes seems to obscure the demand for justice. Pacifists have often criticized just war theorists for functioning as a propaganda arm of the war machine, and providing moral legitimacy for military interventions motivated by the needs of empire. Pacifists have seemed irresponsible. Just war theorists have appeared accommodating. Is there not a third way here as well, one that affirms the pacifist's nonviolence and the just war theorist's concern for moral accountability even in war? I believe that there is, but that it involves a prior commitment to nonviolence, and a far more rigorous use of the just war criteria than has often been the case.

The Church's Vocation
for Nonviolence

Just war thinking is understandably attractive to anyone suffering the brutality of an oppressive regime. As long as the struggle for *justice* is our sole concern, ironically, we will be unable to renounce violence, because violence sometimes does prove successful in achieving short-term goals. And the tendency is to pursue justice for specific grievances without reference to the injustices others bear. Thus it would be possible to end racism, sexism, and poverty while still maintaining the war system.[29] The gospel sets our sights on a wider prospect, however: the ending of particular injustices in a way that in every case hastens the coming of God's domination-free order on earth.

We can easily kill oppressive rulers, but doing so makes us killers. We want to believe in a final violence that will, this last time, eradicate evil and make future violence unnecessary. But the violence we use creates new evil, however just the cause. It inculcates the longing for revenge, and for what the losers call "justice." And they will have learned from our example how to use violence more efficiently. *Violence can never stop violence because its very success leads others to imitate it.* Paradoxically, violence is most dangerous when it *succeeds.*[30]

The astonishing success of the Allied forces in the Persian Gulf may have set back the use of international sanctions under U.N. supervision for years. Why use painstaking diplomacy and time-consuming sanctions when we can get quick results with another photogenic, prime-time war? Yet that war may also have made it more difficult for the United States, or any other nation, to intervene in another country unilaterally, since the United Nations did gain some credibility in the Gulf conflict.

The problem is not merely to gain justice but to end the Domination System. Those engaged in a struggle for liberation may actually achieve a relatively greater degree of justice for their side, yet do so in a way that fails to address the larger issues of patriarchy, domination hierarchies, ranking, stratification, racism, elitism, environmental degradation, or violence. In the struggle against oppression, every new increment of violence simply extends the life of the Domination System and deepens faith in violence as a redemptive means. You cannot free people from the Domination System by using its own methods. You cannot construct the City of Life with the weapons of death. You cannot make peace—real peace—with war.

The church has a vocation for nonviolence. That vocation is grounded in the teaching of Jesus, the nature of God, the ethos of the kingdom, and the power of the resurrection.

Jesus taught nonviolence, not "just war." As Gandhi observed, "The only people on earth who do not see Christ and His teachings as nonviolent are Christians."[31] In so far as Jesus incarnated the ethics of God's coming rule in the world, he is the revealer of its qualities, its essence, its characteristics. Jesus lived the human life of the future. Discipleship means carrying on his work, embodying his values, and being a people shaped by his truth. And just as military training can control and discipline the instinct of flight and its corresponding emotion of fear, even more can training in nonviolence control and discipline the equally elemental capacity for aggression and its corresponding emotion of anger.[32]

In his nonviolent teaching, life, and death, Jesus revealed a God of nonviolence. The God who delivered an enslaved people in the exodus was now seen as the deliverer of all humanity from oppression. The violence associated with God in the exodus tradition was centrifuged away, leaving as its precipitate the image of God as loving parent. The violence of the Powers was exposed, along with their blasphemous misappropriation of God as legitimator of their oppression.

But when the church that had stood up nonviolently to the brutal repression of the Roman Empire found itself strangely victorious, it naively assumed the role of court chaplain to an empire eager for its support. It is as if Satan, unable to defeat the church by violence, surrendered to the church and became its ward. The price the church paid, however, was embracing violence as the means of preserving empire. But the removal of nonviolence from the gospel blasted the keystone from the arch, and Christianity collapsed into a religion of personal salvation in an afterlife jealously guarded by a wrathful and terrifying God—the whole system carefully managed by an elite corps of priests with direct backing from the secular rulers now regarded as the elect agents of God's working in history.

The church is called to nonviolence not in order to preserve its purity, but to express its fidelity. It is not a law but a gift. Even if it were possible to impose it, such compulsion would in itself be a negation of its essence. It is simply offered to those who seek what God has in store for the world. Those who today renounce the kingdom of death do so not because they are trying to please a deity who demands obedience, but because they have committed themselves to the realm of life. They refrain from killing, not because they are ordered to, but because they recognize something of God in everyone, and realize that what we do to the least of these—our enemies—we do to God.

Nonviolence is not a matter of legalism but of discipleship. It is the way God has chosen to overthrow evil in the world. It is the praxis of God's system. Christians are to be nonviolent, not simply because it "works," but because it reflects the very nature of God (Matt. 5:45//Luke 6:35). Nonviolence is not a fringe concern. It is of the essence of the gospel. Therefore Jesus' nonviolent followers should not be called pacifists, but simply Christians.

As Dom José Maria Pires, a Brazilian archbishop, put it, what North Americans call nonviolence is simply living out the teachings of the gospel. It is a commitment to respect the sacredness of each person, whatever their class or role, while maintaining a resolute determination to overcome all forms of domination.[33]

Brian Willson lost both his legs in California when a train carrying munitions for repressive Central American regimes refused to stop for the demonstrators on the tracks. Reflecting on his experience, he says,

> I think nonviolence is not so much a tactic as a way of experiencing the world within yourself, of understanding the sacred connection with all of life.
>
> It's an understanding of how everything is interconnected . . . in a continuing state of interrelationship. We are going against our own nature when we start disrespecting all the others parts of life: people, plants, animals, water, sunlight, clouds. . . . nonviolence is an attitude and way of life with a spiritual ecological dimension.[34]

Jesus does not advocate a perfectionistic ethic in which our salvation depends on being nonviolent. God can forgive our failures to be nonviolent. It is not a "work" that one must achieve in order to be counted righteous. We cannot even say that nonviolent actions are in every circumstance the will of God. How can I know, in any given situation, whether my nonviolence is not a heinous crime, or a total miscalculation of what God desires? I cannot presume on the judgment of God. I can only say that nonviolence is at the very heart of the gospel, and that the church's task is to attempt to spread this leaven into the life of the world.

The Christian does not live nonviolently in order to be saved, then, or in order to live up to an absolute ethical norm, but because God's grace invites us and enables us to do so. The goal is not ethical certitude but faithfulness. The gospel is not in the least concerned with our anxiety to *be* right; it wants to see right *done*. And that means winning the victories, great and small, that lie within our power, through the victory already ours in God's triumph over death in the resurrection of Jesus.

Much of the time we have very little to point to by way of success. In a world in which even revolutionaries fighting for a good cause employ brutal and despotic means, nonviolence faces an overwhelming uphill fight. And yet, in a certain sense, nonviolence never fails, because every nonviolent act is a revelation of God's new order breaking in upon the world. Violence breeds despair when it fails, since it was ostensibly a last resort, and it spawns an idolatrous faith in the redemptive power of death when it seems to succeed. Nonviolence, whether it seems to fail or succeed, displays a new way of resolving conflicts that humankind must learn if it is to survive at all.

The crucifixion and resurrection of Jesus are the assurance that there is a force at work in the world to transform even the most crushing defeat into divine victory. We are thus freed from having to succeed; we have only to be faithful. We are freed from having to produce results; we have only to live as seeing the invisible. We are freed from despair; we have only to trust the One in and through and for whom all things exist.

Emmanuel Charles McCarthy has proposed convening an ecumenical council to proclaim the truth of Jesus' nonviolent love. Perhaps he is right. Then perhaps training in nonviolent direct action and conflict resolution would become a part of every Christian's catechumenate. When crises arise, there would be cadres of thousands, even millions, of people, capable of disciplined, tough, nonviolent intervention.

The Philippines show how achievable this vision really is, though few know the inside story. A strong undercurrent of nonviolent teaching has long characterized both Catholic and Protestant churches in the Philippines. It was given added impetus by Bishop Francisco Claver, S.J., Father José Blanco, S.J., and the Little Sisters of Jesus (a community of nuns), and then powerful reinforcement by Senator Benigno Aquino's conversion to nonviolent revolution while in prison. Through the initiative of the nonviolent community there, Hildegard and Jean Goss-Mayr and Richard Deats were brought in to train trainers in nonviolence. In little more than a year, these trainers and others taught half a million poll watchers nonviolent means to protect the ballots from theft by the henchmen of Marcos. These then formed the nucleus of the street demonstrators that brought down the Marcos regime. That revolution did not just "happen." It had been prepared.[35]

We have scarcely begun to explore the possibilities of nonviolence for resolving international disputes or national defense. Gene Sharp and his Albert Einstein Institution have taken the lead in this area, and high-ranking officers in the ministries of defense in Norway, Sweden, Austria, and the United States, as well as several other nations, have conducted studies on the feasibility of nonviolent defense against aggressors.[36] For some time now, Sweden, Switzerland, Monaco, Costa Rica, Liechtenstein, and Norway have explored non-aggressive, neutralist positions, and possess strictly defensive armies and police. A uniting Europe seems to augur the end of one of the bloodiest chapters of human history.[37] United Nations peacekeeping forces have successfully interposed themselves, unarmed or lightly armed, between combatants in Yemen, Cyprus, the Sinai, the India-Pakistan border, the Golan Heights, the Congo, and Namibia. The Security Council initially showed fresh promise in dealing with Iraq's aggression against Kuwait. Poland, Hungary, Czechoslovakia, East Germany, Bulgaria, Yugoslavia, Romania, Mongolia, Albania, the Soviet Union, Chile, Brazil, and Nepal all witnessed successful revolutions through "people power" in 1989–1990.[38] If the revolutions thus achieved were accomplished in most cases by people untrained in the techniques, disciplines, and spirituality of nonviolence, how much more effective might further actions become with such training! Indeed, the hardest part lies ahead, as nations unaccustomed to nonviolent mediation and democratic conflict resolution slowly build citizens' movements capable of long-term agitation and negotiation for structural changes.

A Role for "Violence-Reduction Criteria"

Just war theory has taken seriously the possibility of making ethical judgments about the use of violence by or against a state. It assumes that we live in a morally coherent universe in which all human actions, even under duress, are susceptible to moral evaluation.[39] But it has been profoundly discredited because so many of the professional ethicists identified with just war theory supported the Vietnam War, even after its barbarity was evident for everyone to see. Paul Ramsey, John Courtney Murray, and Reinhold Niebuhr supported the Cold War and nuclear deterrence, further discrediting just war theory with the peace movement around the world.

What causes the gravest misgivings about just war theory and practice is that, for all its intellectual rigor, it often appears morally slack. To live a moral life means to form binding intentions and to act on them, even in the face of adverse circumstances.[40] Just war theory often seems more intent on finding a way around the binding intentions in the teaching of Jesus, and it tends to do so in the name of the bloodiest ideology of our time: nationalism. By their very nature, moral principles need to be highly resistant to the making of exceptions.[41] Just war theory, by contrast, is notorious for the ease with which some of its proponents have made exceptions. Hence the impression that it is nothing more than casuistry in the service of the god Mars.

According to the criterion of "noncombatant immunity," for example, civilians should be protected against direct attack. But this prohibits only "the deliberate human act of intentionally aiming at civilians, not their foreseeable destruction collateral to aiming at legitimate and important military targets," according to Paul Ramsey, one of the leading proponents of just war theory.[42] "There *is* no rule against *causing* the death of noncombatants, but only against intending to target them directly."[43] If guerrillas choose to hide among civilians, then it is legitimate to blow up civilians along with them. "No Christian and no moralist should assert that it violates the moral immunity of non-combatants from direct, deliberate attack to direct the violence of war upon vast Vietcong strongholds whose destruction unavoidably involves the collateral deaths of a great many civilians."[44] It was the incapacity of peasants in Vietnam to understand the "Christian" and "moral" rightness of their being napalmed and bombed that cost America their support in that war. But is the criterion flawed, or only its interpretation by Ramsey?[45]

Ramsey believed that we may perform an act that we know with certainty will kill many civilians as long as we do not *intend* to kill them. This notion is ethically bankrupt. In practice it leads to the acceptance of civilian casualty rates so astronomical as to render the criterion of civilian immunity absurd. When this criterion was promulgated, the idea was that *no* civilians were to be killed. But if we include in civilian casualties those deaths made inevitable by war's disruption of farming, sanitation, and food distribution, we arrive at an average of 50 percent civilian deaths in each century for all wars since 1700.[46] From 1700 to 1945, there has been virtually no fluctuation in the average of civilian casualties. In the decade of the 1980s, the proportion of civilian deaths jumped to 74 percent of the total, and in 1990 it appears to have been close to 90 percent. This means that anyone planning war can be fairly certain that civilian casualties will exceed 50 percent, and, given modern firepower, will be more likely far higher. By any reckoning this constitutes a violation of the criterion of civilian immunity. On this basis alone, very few wars in the last three centuries have not violated the criterion of civilian immunity.[47]

What these statistics fail to show is the enormous increase in total casualties in our century:

> 1500s—1,600,000 killed
> 1600s—6,100,000
> 1700s—7,000,000
> 1800s—19,400,000
> 1900s—107,800,000[48]

At a constant 50 percent, civilian deaths increased over five centuries from 800,000 in the 1500s to 53.9 million in the 1900s. As if that level of civilian casualties were not enough to forever banish war beyond the pale of morality, some just war theorists justified nuclear deterrence, despite the certainty that civilian deaths would number in the tens or hundreds of millions.[49] If one agrees that the killing of civilians is prohibited, by what distorted logic is one able to justify casualties of such magnitude? Even if we inflate the probable total casualties from war for *all* the centuries since domination states arose (ca. 3000 B.C.E.), *more people have been killed in war in our century than in all the preceding five thousand years combined.* And yet there are still Christian ethicists soberly pondering the question of justifying wars!

Now the Persian Gulf War has blurred the distinction between nuclear and conventional warfare, since tens of thousands of Iraqi soldiers were killed by nonnuclear bombing in only a matter of days. The distinction between civilian and military casualties also becomes indistinct, since conscription amounts to involuntary servitude. Those Kurdish and Shiite soldiers whom Saddam Hussein placed on the front lines in order to liquidate them as internal threats to his regime did not die for their country or leader willingly.[50]

Or take the criterion of "last resort." Theoretically, just war theorists are committed to the use of every feasible nonviolent alternative before turning to war. In fact, I know of only one just war theorist—James F. Childress—who devotes any space at all to nonviolent alternatives.[51] The rest focus on what constitutes last resort. This focus has the effect, however, of shrinking the ethical field. "Last resort" becomes "timely resort," as in the writings of Ramsey;[52] and we soon find ourselves discussing "preemptive strikes," the assassination of heads of state, and even Pentagon doublespeak like "anticipatory retaliation." In our war with Iraq, did we allow enough time for sanctions to work? Was that war truly a "last resort"?

The other just war criteria are as easily manipulated. A just war must be declared by a "legitimate authority," but the Vietnam War never was declared on the American side by the sole agency entrusted with that power: the American Congress. Yet this fact did not cause many just war theorists to declare that war unjust. No nuclear war could be "won" without a surprise attack; but that completely obviates the "formal declaration" required by traditional just war theory.[53]

War has to have a "just cause"; but, as Emmanuel Charles McCarthy points out, how is the public really to know if the cause is just when the first casualty of war is truth?[54] The Gulf of Tonkin incident off Vietnam was apparently *staged* in order to gain congressional support for the war.

Again, the means used in a war must be "proportionate" to the end sought. But how can we know in advance what level of destruction will follow armed conflict? Even beyond casualties, ruined cities, a gutted economy, women raped or reduced to prostitution, children dying from malnutrition and intestinal diseases, how does one measure into the future the continuing hazard of exploding landmines and bombs, drug addiction, alcoholism, mental illness, physical crippling, suicide? How can this be weighed before or even during a war?[55]

There is a surrealistic quality to the hyperrationalism with which discussions of just war are conducted that obscures the fact that war is irrational—that, as Tolstoy implies at the end of *War and Peace*, wars do not even have causes in the ordinary sense.[56] Nations seem to be sucked into wars like dust into a whirlwind. Reasons of state are a smoke screen, and change as propaganda requires. War is the work of the gods Mars and Venus. Those who consider war become possessed by these Powers. They insulate themselves from dissenting views. They are exalted by the heady prospects of victory, heroism, and the display of toughness. They usually underestimate the difficulties and duration of the fight. Their minds are darkened. Prohibitions against harming or killing others dissolve. Reasoned arguments are silenced by an atmosphere charged with a collective will that sweeps everyone along with it. Such leaders are unlikely to consider just war criteria except insofar as they can co-opt them for propaganda purposes. Thus President Bush called his invasion of Panama, which completely failed in its objective of interdicting the drug trade and had a casualty rate of 100 percent civilians, "Operation Just Cause." As the Ukrainian proverb puts it, "When the banner is unfurled, all reason is in the trumpet."[57]

The assumptions usually made by just war theory also need to be subjected to greater scrutiny. As John Howard Yoder points out, this theory assumes that one's own family, friends, and compatriots are more to be loved, or are more beloved of God, than one's enemies. It assumes that the life of the attacker is worth less than that of the attacked. It assumes that responsibility for preventing evil is an expression of divine love even if it involves the death of the aggressor. And it assumes that letting evil happen is as blameworthy as committing it. It also assumes that tyranny is worse than war; that national sovereignty is essential for national identity and integrity; that the intention of liberating one's people from despotic rule authorizes the use of unloving methods; and that God is so interested in *our* nation and its political and economic system that everything must be risked to preserve it.[58]

Yet when all these objections to just war theory are analyzed, they come down to one point: just war theory is objectionable only when it is captive to the myth of redemptive violence.

Perhaps charity requires a distinction between just war theory and some of its advocates, who during the Cold War period were wed to an interventionist credo. Perhaps, too, we should note the source of confusion built into the very phrase "just war," which implies that there *are* wars that are just, and that the church or its moral theologians have the ability and authority to discern *which* wars are just. Many would deny that *any* war can be just. This has caused some to jettison just war theory in its entirety. But even they will be found using just war criteria to explain their rejection of the notion of a just war. The fact is that just war criteria are indispensable in attempting to prevent or mitigate the hellishness of war.

I propose that we terminate all talk of "just wars." Even as the word "pacifism" sounds too much like "passivity," "just war" sounds too much like "war is justifiable." The very term "just war" is saturated with illusions about the rightness of war that are no longer tenable. Those who regard all wars as criminal can scarcely avail themselves of these helpful criteria when they are forced to discuss them with nomenclature that is intrinsically inadequate.

Christians can no more speak of just war than of just rape, or just child abuse, or just massacres (and all of these are inevitably drawn into the train of war).

But we also cannot wish away a world of bewildering complexity, in which difficult decisions are forced on us by the violence of others, and where nonviolent solutions are not always forthcoming.

Instead, I suggest we rename the just war criteria "violence-reduction criteria." That, after all, is what most of us are after. We are not seeking a rationale for legitimating particular wars, but ways of avoiding warfare before it starts, and of decreasing its horrors once it begins. Perhaps both just war theorists and advocates of nonviolence can find common ground for attempting to restrain bellicosity in the phrase "violence-reduction criteria."

After all, both nonviolence and just war theory agree on several key points:

1. Both acknowledge that nonviolence is preferable to violence.
2. Both agree that the innocent must be protected as much as possible.
3. Both reject any defense of a war motivated solely by a crusade mentality or national security interests or personal egocentricity.
4. Both wish to persuade states to reduce the levels of violence.
5. Both wish to hold war accountable to moral values, both before and during the conflict.

We might compare nonviolence with another issue Jesus treats in the Sermon on the Mount: divorce. His prohibition of divorce is absolute; it is Matthew who softens it with the exception of adultery.[59] But Christians do get divorced, with great pain, guilt, and grief. The injunction is unambiguous; so is the infraction. Some people attempt to justify their divorces, as others try to legitimate their wars. But the gospel is unequivocally opposed to divorce. When we divorce, we take upon ourselves the guilt of a shattered web of relationships— the loss of one's spouse, the breakup of the family, the impairment of one's bond with one's children. Nothing—not even the welfare of some of those involved—can justify our act. And yet God freely offers us forgiveness.

So too with violence. It is contrary to the gospel. But we are not always able to live up to the gospel. I am embarrassed at how easily I can lash out at anyone who makes me angry (it is the lashing out, not the anger, that disturbs me). Even so, when as individuals or nations we are unable to act nonviolently, we are not excused for our actions, nor may we attempt to justify them.

But we also cannot condemn those who in desperation resort to counterviolence against the massive violence of an unjust order. We must wish them success, even if they are still caught in the myth of redemptive violence themselves. Who knows? Perhaps their victory will usher in a better society able to divest itself consciously of some of its oppressive elements. (Revolutionary Nicaragua was doing this to a degree before the Contras forced them back on a war footing.)

We must admit our bondage to the myth of redemptive violence—a bondage every bit as tenacious and seductive as bondage to alcohol or drugs. Civilization is addicted to violence. Rational argument, therefore, is not enough to break its grip over us. We can only acknowledge our co-dependency and turn to a higher power for help in extricating ourselves from the worship of compulsive force.[60]

The early Christians saw nothing absurd in dying for the truth. Death rather than crime; death rather than the spread of evil; death rather than fundamental infidelity to the gospel; death rather than obedience to the Domination System; death rather than apostasy from God. Are we so comfortable, so sophisticated, so slack and compromised that we can no longer entertain such courage? More Christians have been martyred for their faith in this century than in the preceding nineteen centuries combined. They are part of the "cloud of witnesses" empowering us for relentless persistence (*firmeza permanente*).

Perhaps war might be judged necessary to halt genocide (though more often war provides the *occasion* for it, as did World War II; and Tanzania's attempt to stop genocide in Uganda by armed intervention merely meant a change in victims).[61] States will do what they will, regardless; but the Christian knows but one necessity, and that is the integrity of the gospel.

A nation may feel that it must fight in order to prevent an even greater evil. But that does not cause the lesser evil to cease being evil. Declaring a war just is simply a ruse to rid ourselves of guilt. But we can no more free ourselves of guilt by decree than we can declare ourselves forgiven by fiat. If we have killed, it is a sin, and only God can forgive us, not a propaganda apparatus that declares our dirty wars "just." Governments and guerrilla chiefs are not endowed with the power to absolve us from sin. Only God can do that. And God is not mocked. The whole discussion of "just" wars is sub-Christian.

If counterviolence appears to be the only responsible choice, this still does not make violence right. Bonhoeffer is a much-misunderstood case in point. He joined the plot to assassinate Hitler. But he insisted that his act was a sin, and threw himself on the mercy of God. Two generations of Christians have held back from full commitment to nonviolence, citing Bonhoeffer's example. Had he known, both that his attempt would fail, and that it would have the effect of justifying redemptive violence in the eyes of so many Christians, I wonder if he would have done it.

Faced with a violent situation, some will kill, believing that it is the lesser evil, or the "better" sin. Others, committed to nonviolence without reserve, will simply submit to death or interpose their own bodies rather than perpetuate the reign of violence. Each person must decide in the situation. It is not given to us to judge each other in such a time.

But it is imperative that we challenge one another to think our actions through. The problem with war or violence as a last resort is that we are less likely to trust in God for a way through if we have already settled in advance that violence is an option. Faith requires at times marching into the waters before they part (Josh. 3:15-16), or going to show oneself to the priest for confirmation of healing before evidence of healing is visible (Luke 17:14). Those who have not committed themselves to nonviolence in advance and under all circumstances are less likely to discover the creative nonviolent option in the desperate urgency of a crisis. They are already groping for the trigger, just when they should have been praying and improvising. It may be that only by an unconditional renunciation of violence can we have our minds so concentrated as to find a nonviolent response when the crisis comes.

If the church were unambiguously committed to nonviolence, it could credibly appeal to governments and insurgents to mitigate the degree of barbarity in wars, and to consider the possibility of nonviolent approaches.[62] This would certainly help in Northern Ireland, where both the Catholic and the Protestant churches have espoused just war positions. Consequently, their condemnations of violence are selective, and lack all conviction.

Further, unless the violence-reduction criteria are wed to principled nonviolence, those seeking to employ them in conflicts may find themselves easily co-opted. Let us say that a group of ethicists persuades the military to refrain from using tactical nuclear weapons, and to limit themselves to conventional bombs. Then the ethicists would appear to have endorsed the latter as just, even though in limited conflicts such weapons now approach the cumulative destructive capacity of nuclear weapons.[63]

Violence-reduction criteria might provide prudential moral leverage on political leaders for whom the language of the gospel carries no conviction. Some nations have already taken steps to limit war and to allow moral resistance to it: laws allowing conscientious objection to military service; recognition of the legitimacy of civil disobedience; war-crime tribunals; and acknowledgment of the right of soldiers to refuse to carry out illegal orders.[64]

What is being proposed here is nothing more than a return to the ancient position of the church before Augustine's adaptation of Stoic just war theory. Early Christians, who opposed all wars, nevertheless made distinctions between wars, arguing that humane treatment of the enemy was superior to cruelty. Hence Clement of Alexandria commended the ameliorating elements in the code of war in Deuteronomy 20,[65] and Origen suggested that if people must fight, they should imitate the bees by fighting with restraint.[66] Tertullian, the most strident opponent of war, military service, and torture, nevertheless used "violence-reduction criteria" in appealing to magistrates to be less brutal.[67] These nonviolent early theologians saw no contradiction in maintaining a higher code of morality for the church, while trying to persuade states to maintain at least a minimum standard of morality for themselves.[68]

We are to think, not of two realms—one for God, the other for Caesar—but rather of concentric circles—Caesar's the smaller, and God's the larger.[69] And the church's task is to maintain relentless pressure from that larger circle of God on the smaller circle of Caesar.

Beyond Just War and Pacifism

Just war theory was founded in part on a misinterpretation of "Resist not evil" (Matt. 5:39), which Augustine regarded as an absolute command of *non-resistance* of evil. Therefore, he argued, no Christian can take up arms in self-defense, but must submit passively even to death. Nor can Christians defend themselves against injustice, but must willingly collaborate in their own ruin. But what, asked Augustine, if my *neighbors* are being thus treated? Then the love commandment requires me to take up arms if necessary to defend them.[70]

In chapter 9 I demonstrated the error of this interpretation. Jesus did not teach nonresistance; rather, he disavowed violent resistance in favor of nonviolent resistance. Of course Christians must resist evil! No decent human being could conceivably stand by and watch innocents suffer without trying to do, or at least wishing to do something to save them. The question is simply one of means. Likewise, Christians are not forbidden by Jesus to engage in self-defense. But they are to do so nonviolently. Jesus did not teach supine passivity in the face of evil. That was precisely what he was attempting to overcome!

Pacifism, in its Christian forms, was often based on the same misinterpretation of Jesus' teaching in Matt. 5:38-42. It too understood Jesus to be commanding nonresistance. Consequently, some pacifists refuse to engage in nonviolent direct action or civil disobedience, on the ground that such actions are coercive. Nonresistance, they believe, licenses only passive resistance. Hence the confusion between "pacifism" and "passivism" has not been completely unfounded.

Jesus' third way is coercive, insofar as it forces oppressors to make choices they would rather not make. But it is *nonlethal*, the great advantage of which is that, if we have chosen a mistaken course, our opponents are still alive to benefit from our apologies. The same exegesis that undermines the scriptural ground from traditional just war theory also erodes the foundation of nonresistant pacifism. Jesus' teaching carries us beyond just war *and* pacifism to a militant nonviolence that actualizes already in the present the ethos of God's domination-free future.

Nonviolence is highly aggressive, and Jesus is the best example of it. He attacks his accusers with truth. He forces them either to accept the truth or to silence him.[71] Augustine was delighted that when Jesus was struck by a guard for his defiant answer to the high priest, he did not passively "turn the other cheek" (John 18:19-24).[72] But, far from being inconsistent, Jesus' retort as given in the Fourth Gospel coheres with everything he taught: "If I have spoken wrongly, testify to the wrong. But if I have spoken rightly, why do you strike me?" He is depicted by John as finding, in a new situation, a creative equivalent to turning the other cheek. He neither submits nor strikes back, but takes the offensive for the truth.

Theologians have sometimes attempted to absolve Christians from the rigorous practicality of Jesus' third way by treating his teaching as an impossible, perfectionistic ethic intended to break the pride of sinners and throw them on God's grace. Others have depicted Jesus' teaching as an interim ethic of extraordinary measures premised on the immediate arrival of the Kingdom, which, by its delay, now obviates the necessity of obeying such strenuous demands. Still others have regarded his way as nothing but an individual ethic without significance for institutions, or economies, or states. But where do we read that Jesus regarded his teaching as incapable of execution? "Blessed rather are those who hear the word of God and obey it!" (Luke 11:28; see also Matt. 7:24-27//Luke 6:47-49). What perversity is this, that declares Jesus' teachings impossible to perform, yet teaches us to perform the very things that ought to be morally impossible?

Jesus' way of nonviolence is not in the least utopian. It does not require people to have achieved exceptional heroism, or a "new humanity," or a high level of intelligence, or spiritual enlightenment. It can be, and has been, enacted by common people numbering in the millions.[73]

History itself has been confirming the practicality of Jesus' program of late, a theme to which we return in chapter 13. The irony would be delicious if it were not so bitter: whereas earnest theologians have been persuading Christians for sixteen centuries that their gospel supports violence (though everyone in the whole world except Christians knew that the gospel is nonviolent), massive outpourings of citizens in one officially atheist country after another have recently demonstrated the effectiveness of Jesus' teaching of nonviolence as a means of liberation.

From the "peace church" heritage, the position proposed here affirms nonviolence as a fundamental tenet of the gospel of God's new order which is coming. The church cannot, then, justify any violence or war as "good" or "just." And from the "just war" heritage, the just war criteria can be turned into "violence-reduction criteria" and used in an attempt to lessen the devastation of a given war from a position of principled nonviolence.[74]

Just war theory has been not so much mistaken as mismarried to the ideology of redemptive violence. Its pagan roots were never sufficiently purged of their origin in the Domination System. Freed from their misuse as justifications for wars of national interest, or holy war crusades, or egotistical face-offs, these criteria can now be focused on preventing or mitigating the barbarities of war from a committed nonviolent perspective. Christians today can no longer regard war as an extension of policy, but as a dangerous anachronism, destined for oblivion in the new, nonviolent order of God.

No doubt the objection may be raised that affirmation of nonviolence by the churches would be simplistic, that ethical judgments in the real world are far too complex to adopt a fixed ethical stance. This objection, I must confess, was one of the main reasons I resisted committing myself without reserve to nonviolence for so many years. I have slowly come to see that what the church needs most desperately is precisely such a clear-cut, unambiguous position. Governments will still wrestle with the option of war, and ethicists can perhaps assist them with their decisions. But the church's own witness should be understandable by the smallest child: we oppose violence in all its forms. And we do so because we reject domination. That means, the child will recognize, no beatings. That means, women will hear, no battering. That means, men will gradually understand, no more male supremacy or war. That means, everyone will realize, no more rape of the environment.

The church must affirm nonviolence without reservation because nonviolence is the way God's domination-free order is coming.

The Silver Surfer (speaking off-frame) and the Hulk
Marvel Comics[1]

12. But What If . . . ?

It is surprising how few people have seriously considered nonviolence as a way of life and a strategy for social change. We are so inured to violence that we find it hard to *believe in* anything else. And that phrase "believe in" provides the clue. We trust violence. Violence "saves." It is "redemptive." All we have to do is make survival the highest goal, and death the greatest evil, and we have handed ourselves over to the gods of the Domination System. We trust violence because we are afraid. And we will not relinquish our fears until we are able to imagine a better alternative. What if we are attacked by muggers? What if robbers break into our house? What if someone opens a toxic dump in our neighborhood? What if another nation threatens our very existence?

Rehearsing Nonviolence

The vast majority of Christians reject a nonviolent life-style, not only because of confusion about its biblical foundations, but also because there are too many situations where they cannot conceive of its working. The "what if" question arises out of genuine moral perplexity. Millions of years of conditioning in the flight/fight response have done nothing to prepare us for this "third way" of responding to evil. "What if" dilemmas, far from being destructive of the nonviolent position, can provide useful rehearsals of nonviolent possibilities where they are not readily apparent.

Invariably the question is posed, as if its very asking constituted a conclusive repudiation of the nonviolent position: "What if an armed criminal attacked your spouse or child?" This question, of course, confronts everyone equally, the advocate of violence as well as the advocate of nonviolence. What would you do? Criminals usually attack only when they are certain they have the advantage of surprise and superior weapons. Will you turn on him with your fists, when he is armed with a revolver, or an AK-47? Or does the hypothetical case assume that you routinely pack an Uzi submachine gun, that you have it at your instant disposal, that you are shielded from the attackers, and that you can wipe out the assailants without danger of killing the very people you intend to protect?[2]

Unless we all start wearing sidearms, we would probably find ourselves incapable of responding effectively in such situations, whether violently *or* nonviolently. And even those who are armed sometimes find themselves helpless to intervene. The United States, even though it possessed more armaments than any nation in history, was utterly powerless to save East Germany in 1953, or Hungary in 1956, or Czechoslovakia in 1968, or Poland in 1980, or the Chinese students and workers in 1989. Yevgeny Yevtushenko tells the story of a Russian soldier dropped by parachute behind Nazi lines in Belorussia to make contact with the resistance. He met a shepherd boy of twelve who agreed to take him to the partisans. At a road, the boy went across first to check for Nazi patrols, while the commando hid in the bushes. Suddenly twenty Germans emerged from ambush on the other side. They began questioning the boy, torturing him with cigarette burns all over his chest. Then they beat him from all sides, till he collapsed. They finished him with a bullet. All this time the commando's finger was on the trigger of his gun, but he felt powerless to do anything.[3] The agony of being unable to save another is not reserved to those who have chosen the nonviolent path.

The problem with hypothetical tests for the effectiveness of nonviolence is that different presuppositions are allowed to predispose the outcome than those governing the choice of violence. If we are considering war, we can assume at the outset a U.S. military force of two to three million trained personnel and a budget of three hundred billion dollars a year to back them up. In fairness, the nonviolence advocate should be able to presuppose millions of people trained in nonviolence and prepared, like soldiers, to give their lives if necessary for the sake of justice. As Robert L. Holmes comments, nonviolence cannot be imagined to succeed when the basic conditions necessary to its success are absent. It is wrong to compare nonviolence in its present, embryonic form with a system of violence that is in advanced stages of development, and deeply entrenched in the socioeconomic systems of the world. The comparison must rather be between our present system of violence and nonviolence as it might realistically be developed.[4]

As David Dellinger observes, "The theory and practice of active nonviolence are roughly at the stage of development today as those of electricity in the early days of Marconi and Edison. A new source of power has been discovered and crudely utilized in certain specialized situations, but our experience is so limited and our knowledge so primitive that there is a legitimate dispute about its applicability to a wide range of complicated and critical tasks."[5]

William Jennings Bryan once visited Tolstoy and pressed him with the perennial problem of what to do if a criminal is about to kill a child. Tolstoy responded that, having lived seventy-five years, he had never, except in discussions, "encountered that fantastic brigand, who, before my eyes desired to kill or violate a child, but that perpetually I did and do see not one but millions of brigands using violence toward children and women and men and old people and all the labourers in the name of the recognized right of violence over one's fellows. When I said this my kind interlocutor, with his naturally quick perception, not giving me time to finish, laughed, and recognized that my argument was satisfactory."[6]

There is considerable irony in the presumed compassion of the interlocutor who is so concerned about the potential rape of a single grandmother, when the same questioner accepts war, where the rape of grandmothers, wives, daughters, and children is so routine that many soldiers have regarded it as one of the perquisites of warfare.

What if your spouse were attacked by a mugger? Some might yell for help, others might call the police, others might try to interpose their own bodies, others might attempt to appeal to his higher self, others might try to disarm him physically, others might find a surprising way to grasp the initiative and change his mind. But surely everyone would attempt if possible to intervene. Jesus, as we saw in chapter 9, did not forbid self-defense. He taught, not nonresistance, but nonviolence. The fact is that no one knows how he or she will react to such a situation. (When my wife and I were mugged, she began to resist the muggers and I found myself calming her down and letting them have my wallet. She was protecting me!)

Gandhi had a ready answer for such hypothetical questions. He repeated, over and over, that it is always better to be violent than cowardly. His own position was clear: he could never resort to violence. But if someone had not reached that level of spiritual awareness, then one should do what one is ready for. "If you have a sword in your bosom, take it out and use it like a man."[7]

Most assailants work from a definite set of expectations about how the victim will respond, says Angie O'Gorman, and they need the victim to act as a victim. A violent or hostile response, or one of panic or helplessness, reinforces the assailant's expectations, self-confidence, and sense of control. It also tends to increase cruelty within an already hostile person. This is a game assailants know how to play. They can handle what they are prepared for. Using violent resistance to resolve the situation is limiting oneself to the rules of the game as laid down by the assailant.

Wonder, by contrast, tends to diffuse hostility. It seems to be nearly impossible for the human psyche to be in a state of wonder and a state of cruelty at the same time. Wonder can create what O'Gorman calls a "context of conversion." When the victim focuses on what causes wonder, a desire to imitate tends to occur, a form of positive mimesis that creates in the assailant a strong new impulse incompatible with the violent tendency.

O'Gorman describes being awakened late one night by a man kicking open the door to her bedroom. The house was empty. The phone was downstairs.

> He was somewhat verbally abusive as he walked over to my bed. I could not find his eyes in the darkness but could see the outline of his form. As I lay there, feeling a fear and vulnerability I had never before experienced, several thoughts ran through my head—all in a matter of seconds. The first was the uselessness of screaming. The second was the fallacy of thinking safety depends on having a gun hidden under your pillow. Somehow I could not imagine this man standing patiently while I reached under my pillow for my gun. The third thought, I believe, saved my life. I realized with a certain clarity that either he and I made it through this situation safely—together—or we would both be damaged. Our safety was connected. If he raped me, I would be hurt both physically and emotionally. If he raped me he would be hurt as well. If he went to prison, the damage would be greater. That thought disarmed *me*. It freed me from my own desire to lash out and at the same time from my own paralysis. It did not free me from feelings of fear but from fear's control over my ability to respond. I found myself acting out of a concern for both our safety which caused me to react with a certain firmness but with surprisingly little hostility in my voice.
>
> I asked him what time it was. He answered. That was a good sign. I commented that his watch and the clock on my night table had different times. His said 2:30, mine said 2:45. I had just set mine. I hoped his watch wasn't broken. When had he last set it? He answered. I answered. The time seemed endless. When the atmosphere began to calm a little I asked him how he had gotten into the house. He'd broken through the glass in the back door. I told him that presented me with a problem as I did not have the money to buy new glass. He talked about some financial difficulties of his own. We talked until we were no longer strangers and I felt it was safe to ask him to leave. He didn't want to; said he had no place to go. Knowing I did not have the physical power to force him out I told him firmly but respectfully, as equal to equal, I would give him a clean set of sheets but he would have to make his own bed downstairs. He went downstairs and I sat up in bed, wide awake and shaking for the rest of the night. The next morning we ate breakfast together and he left.

By treating her intruder as a human being, O'Gorman caught him off guard. Conversation defused his violence. Through the effects of prayer, meditation, training in nonviolence, and the experience of lesser kinds of assault, she had been able to allow a context for conversion to emerge. Such a response could come to her because she had been rehearsing nonviolence beforehand.[8]

Wonder and surprise: *what if* you are a woman walking home from a supermarket on a deserted street, laden with heavy packages, and you realize that

you are being followed? Here is what one woman did. As the footsteps behind
her got closer, she wheeled suddenly, smiled at the stranger who was advancing
on her, handed him her packages, and said "Thank God you showed up! I hate
to walk alone in these streets, and these packages are so heavy." He escorted
her home safely.[9]

What if a group of South African women in a squatters' village suddenly find
themselves set upon by soldiers and bulldozers and are told they have two
minutes to clear out? Shall they get guns and protect themselves? There are
none. And most of the men are away at work. Here is what they did. Knowing
how puritanical rural white Dutch Reformed Afrikaners can be, the black women
stood in front of the bulldozers and stripped off all their clothes. The police
turned tail and fled, and the community still retains possession as of this writing.[10]

As Emmanuel Charles McCarthy observes, our capacity to discover creative
nonviolent responses in moments of crisis will depend, to some degree at least,
on whether we rehearse them in our everyday lives. If we live in the spirit of
Christian nonviolent love in the little things of life, then in the great things we
will be more likely to have something to call upon, something unexpected. But
if we have not rehearsed putting on the mind of Jesus and responding as he
would have responded, then the crisis simply triggers old and dark images of
threat, fear, anger, and retaliation.[11]

What if the Palestinians had used guns in the *Intifada*? They would have been
slaughtered. Instead, they used nonviolent methods advocated by Mubarak
Awad—commercial strikes, mass police resignations, boycotts, work stoppages,
tax resistance, refusing to fill out official documents, street demonstrations,
flying the banned Palestinian flag, teaching the ABCs to children (a crime under
the emergency laws), and lying down in front of bulldozers clearing Palestinian
land for new Israeli settlements. Many youth did throw rocks, but such low-
level violence comprised only a fraction of the struggle.[12] Nevertheless it was
the rocks that monopolized the headlines, as violence always does, and muddied
the international response. *What if*, Awad said to me, instead of three hundred
rock-throwing Palestinian youth dying from Israeli guns, three hundred Palestinian youth had starved themselves to death as a protest against Israeli injustice?

What if a gang of thugs is harassing villagers in the Philippines, and the
police do nothing about it? Does one kill the thugs? Killing would excise the
tumor perhaps, but develop no antibodies in the system to stop its recurrence.
What could the people do? They had the numbers; they were like ants, says
Niall O'Brien. They could swarm over these thugs and stop their behavior
nonviolently. If they failed, someone would shoot these petty criminals and
simply confirm others in their worship of the gun. So people from the churches
went, a thousand strong from the entire region, to the home of a known killer,

and held a Mass surrounding his house. The perpetrator was refused communion and ordered to leave the area. He surrendered all his weapons, disarmed his gang, and after talking all night, repented of his actions, which, it turned out, were supported by Marcos's army to discredit the real guerrillas.[13]

Force versus Violence?

What if you were in a police counterterrorism unit and you were trying to stop a sniper on a roof about to fire into a crowd of people? You would be obligated to act. If you are a marksman with a telescopic sight on your rifle (since we are being hypothetical), perhaps you could shatter his rifle or disable him without killing him. Even a miss would force him to take cover and deal with you, thus sparing those he had targeted. Perhaps the delay would allow time to overcome him with tear gas. But perhaps he will kill you, and then slaughter others unchecked. What would you do?

Once again, however, the hypothetical "what if" has already assumed a framework that virtually *requires* violence as its response. But why do we have to accept that framework? There are nations where the sale of weapons is restricted and the culture of violence discouraged (Canada, Scandinavia). Killings happened in the Soviet Union, but seldom with guns, because they were not readily available until just before its breakup. In some societies, police are unarmed, or if at all, minimally (the old British bobby with his nightstick, alas, fast disappearing). Nonviolence is less effective when it is brought in at the last moment to cure a situation that has been created by violence all along the line. What we are faced with is the long-term task of building a society *founded* on nonviolence. This means limiting the availability of guns, training police in nonviolent methods of control and restraint, discontinuing the sale of toy weapons (as Sweden and Colombia have done), and creating a society less tolerant of video violence and every form of domination. Until such a society emerges, violence will continue to be used against violence. But Christians are to begin living the life of God's domination-free order already, even under the conditions of the Domination Epoch.

Some ethicists would solve the policeman's dilemma by distinguishing between force and violence. "Force" signifies a truly legitimate, socially authorized, and morally defensible use of restraint to prevent harm being done to innocent people. "Violence" would be a morally illegitimate or excessive use of force. A police officer who must arrest a killer may have to use force to restrain him. Such a use of force falls within the definition of his or her office as spelled out by society and Scripture (Rom. 13:4).

In many countries today, however, the crisis is not how to legitimate the use of force by police, but how to restrain police from the routine use of unnecessary violence. Some, doubtful of the courts' ability to produce convictions, administer summary justice by beating, torturing, or executing suspects—often of other racial or ethnic groups. In Brazil, the police vigilantism of a decade ago has now evolved into the hiring of off-duty police by businessmen (and some drug dealers) to "clean the streets" of organized groups of homeless children, in order to enhance tourism. This means the wholesale slaughter of children— 1,729 documented cases in 1990 alone, the tip of an iceberg[14]—in order to reduce petty theft. No, police do not need to be armed with justifications for further violence.

Most police have never killed and do not wish to. The Chicago police department resolved ninety-six consecutive hostage situations without the use of violence by cautiously and patiently talking ninety-six dangerous men into surrendering.[15] "Force" is not legitimated violence. It is nonlethal coercion that does not intend harm. Killing the terrorist may be the lesser evil, but it is still, for all that, evil. Violence, even in the hands of duly constituted authorities, is still violence, and we must begin to wean ourselves from dependency on it.

Can whole societies learn to be less violent? There are some positive indications at the international level. A uniting Europe is itself evidence that one of the most strife-ridden areas in the world can learn to live peaceably together. Lithuanians had fought a guerilla war against the Soviets until 1952, expecting Western aid that never came. They lost 50,000 lives, and 400,000 Lithuanians were sent to Siberia. "After the deportations and the night of our genocide, our people realized that armed struggle was not the way. We needed to rely on patience and nonviolence. At that point, the 'invisible' nonviolent struggle began," one Lithuanian remarked. Despite the threat of Soviet military force, leaders from the top down, including the Catholic Church, urged the people to remain nonviolent and to maintain a spirit of love. The movie *Gandhi* was widely viewed and highly influential.[16] The Lithuanian Department of Defense went some distance in committing itself to a policy of nonviolent national defense against the Soviet Union, and the faculty of the Police Academy explored nonviolence with Captain Charles Alphin, a black policeman from Saint Louis who teaches Kingian nonviolence to police forces. Gene Sharp, Richard Deats, and Robert L. Holmes actively consulted with the Lithuanian government as it raced against time to devise a comprehensive nonviolent national defense—a defense that worked, when in 1991 the three Baltic states won their independence.[17]

Christians are called to nonviolence, unequivocally. They are to engage evil nonviolently, in every circumstance, without exception. They must lean all their weight on divine grace, trusting that the Holy Spirit will reveal the third way not evident in the situation.

But when the crisis breaks, we may discover that we are not creative enough, or open enough, or imaginative enough, to find that third way. If we choose violence, however, we abandon the realm of freedom for the kingdom of necessity. Having committed our lives to the way of God, to our remorse we find that we have become acolytes of the Domination System. And yet, while nothing can erase the brute impact of our act on history, God may be able to restore us to the realm of love and set our feet once more on the gospel road—though, often, only as through fire.

If we have done the work of preparation, however, we may find that simply suffering the brutality unleashed against us achieves more than we could have dreamed. In 1930 the arrest of members of Badshah Khan's nonviolent army by the British ignited a spontaneous general strike and march in Peshawar (in what is now Pakistan). British troops fired at the crowd of unarmed people, who refused to give way, and who continued to march forward to replace those that had fallen. The firing continued for six hours. Two to three hundred were killed and many more wounded, yet the Pathans remained nonviolent. The British were confident that such strong-arm methods would crack the Pathan will. Yet where Khan had previously been able to enlist only a thousand troops in his nonviolent army, now eighty thousand new recruits flocked to take the nonviolence vow as a result of the excessive use of force by the occupying power.[18]

Because the nonviolence I am advocating reproduces the position of the early church, it is not surprising that I share its ambivalence toward state-sanctioned force. On the one hand, the state "does not bear the sword in vain" (Rom. 13:4), and is divinely authorized to preserve order in a structure of justice. It is created in, through, and for Christ in order to ensure safety, fair treatment, and tranquility, both internally and on its borders. But the early church was hard-pressed to define its attitude toward the police and military power when at the same time they provided protection from robbers and pirates and yet executed Christians for refusing to idolize the state through its representatives, the divinized Caesars. Christians were recipients of benevolence from the state, and from the same state, persecution.

So also today, Christians who have repudiated state religion, with its trust in redemptive violence, and who have staked their lives on God's nonviolent way, may experience perplexing ambivalence regarding their civic responsibilities. The state is almost bound to be repugnant to Christians, notes Glen Tinder, since the atrocities that by their scale and malevolent intent render the twentieth century unique in history have almost all been committed by officials of the state.[19] In such states, can Christians assume political office, or do police work, or serve in the armed forces, or even vote? The answers are not self-evident, and are as much a matter of individual vocation and national location as of moral norms.

Our difficulty accepting nonviolence is not fully intellectual, however; it is a matter of how we perceive our interests. Our lives are *founded* on violence. Oppressors and oppressed alike live in a violent system. Some wish to maintain their grasp on the good life, others to seize it for themselves. Nonviolence threatens the powerful because it would require relinquishing unjust advantage. But the powerless may fear it just as much, for it appears to nullify their hopes of assuming power by the very means used to keep them subjugated: violence.

The burden of proof must always be on the proponent of violence to explain why war is preferable to nonviolence, especially when nonviolence has usually not even been tried. The truth is, *nonviolence generally works where violence would work, and where it fails, violence too would fail.* Neither might have been effective in Stalin's Russia, and neither has succeeded so far in Burma. The declining postwar British Empire would have lost India to either violence or nonviolence; but the choice of the latter meant a loss of only eight thousand lives instead of hundreds of thousands or even millions. *But nonviolence also works where violence would fail*, as in most of the nonviolent revolutions of 1989–1991.

Violence fails as often as it succeeds. If one side prevails using violence, the other must lose. Not so nonviolence. When it succeeds, there is a sense in which both sides win. And even when it fails, it bears witness to the values of God's system that must someday prevail over violence.

But there are situations that are simply tragic, where nothing we can conceivably do will help. In such cases, the violent and the nonviolent alike are forced to suffer the agony of irrelevance—and may themselves be among the victims.[20]

I do not know if I could be nonviolent in a maximum-security prison like Sing Sing, though some men there have achieved it. I do not know how the Nicaraguans could have resisted the Contras nonviolently, though Witness for Peace did help somewhat by placing North Americans in areas troubled by Contra raids (and troubled also at times by government raids). But as Nicaragua's Foreign Minister, Miguel D'Escoto, put it,

At this present time, because nonviolent struggle is something that has not been developed, its role is to complement conventional methods to defend our sovereignty, independence, and right to life. But in due time nonviolence will replace the old, violent methods. We must remember that in spite of all this theology about the just war, about tyrannicide and all that, violence is simply not Christian. We must never proclaim it as if it emanates from the gospel. Violence is only a concession of the gospel to a world in transition.

But the transition will come only if we begin to use nonviolent means to replace the violent means that the world has already known.[21]

There may be situations so extreme that one cannot conceive of any alternative to violence. Even where no nonviolent alternative appears feasible, however, most aggressive, violent options will be worse. But the time may come when an oppressive power has squandered every opportunity to do justice, and the capacity of the people to continue suffering snaps. Then the violence visited on the nation is a kind of apocalyptic judgment that leaves no one unscathed. In such times there is no morally safe haven—there is just a living hell. In such situations, however, the church is still obligated to try to mitigate the violence by insisting, from a position of committed, active nonviolence, that the violence-reduction criteria be observed. Christians have no business judging those who take up violence out of desperation. The guilt lies with those who turned justice aside and did not know the hour of their visitation. But the church also has no business legitimating the violence of war, even though it may sincerely wish the revolutionaries success. And the church itself must bear a large share of responsibility in such a time for having taught a gospel of docility and compliance instead of evangelizing people in the way of nonviolent transformation.

Under no circumstances should the church condone the use of violence even for unquestionably just circumstances. As William Stringfellow so trenchantly put it,

> Where Christians, in the same frailty and tension as any other human beings, become participants in specific violence, they do so confessionally, acknowledging throughout the sin of it. . . . Christians become implicated in violence without any excuses for the horror of violence, without any extenuations for the gravity of it, without sublimating the infidelity it symbolizes, without construing violence as justice, without illusions that *their* violence is less culpable than that of anyone else, without special pleading, without vainglory, without ridiculing the grace of God.[22]

Violence will be unavoidable in situations where people are not yet prepared to wage conflicts nonviolently. But as more and more people become conversant with nonviolent methods, recourse to violence may greatly diminish. Even as violence has increased exponentially in this century, so has the use of nonviolence as a means for resolving disputes. Indeed, it is the former that has pressured humanity to develop the latter. Today most of what a democratic government does is nonviolent. Ideally, democracy is the institutionalization of nonviolence. George Weigel goes so far as to call democratic governance "the world's most successful and widespread form of nonviolent conflict-resolution."[23] Now the task is to extend democracy through the United Nations for the settlement of international conflicts. The world needs to move away from intervention by great powers, unilateralism, and the concept of the United States as the world's policeman. In its early stages, the Persian Gulf crisis of 1990–91 offered a glimpse of how an effective United Nations might go about isolating a pariah nation. We must foster that vision. It is possible for the human family to operate as one.

The goal of civil disobedience and nonviolent direct action is to establish a political culture in which conflicts are managed without violence. The worldwide rush toward democracy is itself an indication that nonviolence is the human future.

I have a feeling that my boat
has struck, down there in the depths,
against a great thing.
                              And nothing
happens! Nothing . . . Silence . . . Waves . . .

—Nothing happens? Or has everything happened,
and are we standing now, quietly, in the new life?

Juan Ramón Jiménez,
"Oceans"[1]

13. Re-visioning History: Nonviolence Past, Present, Future

The Past and Present of Nonviolence

History has been written by the victors. What young people learn in schools is largely a chronicle of kings and dynasties, wars and empires. Androcratic systems teach androcratic history. Even where nonviolent resistance was successfully used, it tends to be neglected. A people kept ignorant of the existence of the history of nonviolence will naturally believe that it is impractical and unrealistic. In those cases where it is known, as in Gandhi's struggle for independence in India or the civil rights movement in the United States, it is regarded as an unrepeatable oddity. The Powers know all too well that their sovereignty depends to a large extent in deciding what stories will be told.[2]

People not only have been kept ignorant of past nonviolent efforts, but often are unable to recognize them when they are happening right under their noses. I have asked people to list nonviolent struggles they know about, and many are unable to identify more than two or three. In South Africa, which witnessed from 1985 to 1989 one of the most creative outpourings of nonviolent direct action in human history, many people simply regarded it as part of the anti-apartheid struggle, along with armed resistance, and identified "nonviolence" with nonresistance and passivity.[3]

I have found it helpful to draw to people's attention the enormous volume and variety of nonviolent actions as a way of breaking the androcratic monopoly on history. As we become aware that nonviolent direct action is not unusual, and that it has been frequently and successfully used, we can begin to envision its further application in our time. Learning the history of nonviolence is another way of rehearsing it. Furthermore, our ability to act may depend every bit as much on a knowledge of nonviolent methods and spirituality as on our fortitude. Carl Scovil remarks that the ability of German pastors to oppose the state depended not so much on their courage as on their ability to perceive the issues at stake. "The sin that preceded what we call cowardice was confusion. The virtue which preceded what we call courage was clarity."[4]

The following chronological list is only a sampling; Gene Sharp catalogs 198 different *kinds* of nonviolent intervention in *The Politics of Nonviolent Action*, and dozens of examples could probably be adduced from his files for each.[5] My selection is somewhat arbitrary, but it is sufficient to demonstrate one of the most astonishing facts of our time: the exponential increase in the use of nonviolence in just the last few years. Something radically new is happening in human affairs, and many people have failed to notice it.

1350 B.C.E.(?)	• The Hebrew midwives commit the first recorded act of civil disobedience by refusing to carry out Pharaoh's order to kill Hebrew babies.
406 B.C.E.	• *Antigone*, by Sophocles, portrays Antigone burying her brother in defiance of the king's command.
388 B.C.E.	• *Lysistrata*, by Aristophanes, depicts women on both sides stopping a war by withholding sex from their husband-soldiers.
273–232 B.C.E.	• The Indian Mauyra emperor Ashoka, appalled at the horrors of war, becomes a Buddhist, renounces war, abandons the royal hunt, and preaches kindness to all living things.[6]
167 B.C.E.	• The Book of Daniel depicts civil disobedience against the king's edicts (chaps. 3 and 6).
47 B.C.E.	• In protest of Herod's murder of Ezekias and many of his fellow conspirators without due process of law, "every day in the temple the mothers of the men who had been murdered begged the king and the people to have Herod brought to judgment"[7]—a tactic employed in our time in Argentina (by the "Mothers of the Plaza de Mayo"), El Salvador, and the Soviet Union.
26 C.E.	• Pilate introduces idolatrous Roman standards into Judea. Jews by the thousands prostrate themselves around his house for five days. When Pilate threatens to kill them all, they offer their necks to the sword but will not move. Pilate removes the standards.
ca. 30 C.E.	• Jesus incarnates nonviolence and is crucified for it.
30–312	• Christians martyred for disturbing the peace, and for refusing to worship the emperor, to serve in the army, or to engage in war.

41   • The emperor Gaius Caligula orders his own image placed in
               the Jerusalem Temple. Tens of thousands of Jews protest to the
               Syrian legate, Petronius, by throwing themselves to the ground
               and announcing they would rather die than see their laws
               transgressed. Petronius finally petitions Caligula to relent, a
               request that would have cost his life had the emperor not been
               assassinated first.

1181–1226 • St. Francis of Assisi exemplifies a nonviolent life.

1400s   • Taborites (followers of Jan Hus) are nonviolent for a time.

1537   • Menno Simon (Mennonites, ca. 1537), George Fox (Quakers,
               1652), and Alexander Roch (Brethren, 1708) found the historic
               "peace churches."

1623   • Eméric Crucé proposes a United Nations Assembly to settle
               international differences by compulsory arbitration.

1765–75   • American colonists mount three nonviolent resistance
               campaigns against British rule resulting in de facto
               independence by 1775 even before war was declared in 1776.[8]

1780   • Quakers start the first American antislavery society.

1815   • Massachusetts Peace Society proposes a world court as an
               alternative to war.

1818   • Hospital laundresses in Valencia, Venezuela, strike to demand
               back pay.

1840–60   • "Underground Railroad" helps slaves escape to the northern
               United States or Canada.

1846   • Thoreau is jailed overnight for refusing to pay taxes supporting
               the Mexican-American War.

1850   • Hungarian nationalists, led by Francis Deak, engage in
               nonviolent resistance to Austrian rule, and eventually regain
               self-governance for Hungary as part of an Austro-Hungarian
               federation.

1871   • Women in Paris block cannons and stand between Prussian and
               Parisian troops.

1878   • Kusunose Kita in Shikoku, Japan, protests having to pay taxes
               while being denied the vote as a woman.

1890s   • Tolstoy's writings on civil disobedience and nonviolence begin
               to circulate around the world.

1892   • Ida B. Wells-Barnett leads first a mass boycott and then a mass
               exodus from Memphis to northern cities to protest lynchings
               and discrimination against blacks. Whole congregations leave
               the city—over two thousand people in two months.

1900s   • Labor movement (largely nonviolent) uses strikes to secure
             economic justice.
1901–5   • Finns nonviolently resist Russian oppression, and force them to
             repeal the law imposing conscription.
1905–6   • Russian peasants, workers, students, and the intelligentsia
             engage in major strikes and other forms of nonviolent action,
             and force the Czar to accept the creation of an elected
             legislature.
1906   • Gandhi in South Africa lays the foundation of nonviolence on a
             national scale.
1913–19   • U.S. women's suffrage movement secures a constitutional
             amendment guaranteeing women the right to vote after a 75-
             year struggle.
1914   • Fellowship of Reconciliation founded in England (1915 in the
             United States).
1914–18   • Conscientious objection to World War I in the United States.
             Several men die from torture in prison.
1917   • The February Russian Revolution, largely nonviolent, leads to
             the collapse of the czarist system.
           • American Friends Service Committee founded.
1919   • Korean opposition to Japanese occupation, then, after World
             War II, to governmental repression, often violent, but with a
             strong Christian element of nonviolent resistance.
1919–47   • Gandhi leads struggle for Indian independence through
             nonviolent means.
1920   • An attempted coup d'état led by Wolfgang Kapp against the
             Weimar Republic of Germany fails when the population goes
             on a general strike, refusing to cooperate.
1923   • The term "nonviolence" is first used.
           • War Resisters League founded.
           • French and Belgian occupation of the Ruhr is withdrawn after
             German noncooperation makes the occupation too costly
             politically and economically, despite severe repression.
1936–37   • Palestinians launch a six-month general strike against
             involuntary displacement and confiscations by Zionists.
1940–45   • Conscientious objection to World War II.
1944   • Two Central American dictators, Maximiliano Hernandez
             Martinez (El Salvador) and Jorge Ubico (Guatemala) are ousted
             as a result of nonviolent civilian insurrections and general
             strikes. Between 1931 and 1961, eleven Latin American
             presidents leave office in the wake of civic strikes.[9]

1952–60   • Nonviolent campaign by African National Congress in South Africa.

1953   • A wave of strikes in Soviet prison-labor camps leads to some limited improvements in living conditions of political prisoners.

1957   • Ghana wins independence after a ten-year nonviolent struggle.

1955–68   • Montgomery bus boycott launches U.S. civil rights struggle. A variety of nonviolent methods, including economic boycotts, massive demonstrations, marches, sit-ins, and freedom rides, leads to passage of the Civil Rights Act of 1964 and the Voting Rights Act of 1965.

1961   • Chief Albert Luthuli receives the Nobel Peace Prize for the nonviolent struggle in South Africa.
          • Amnesty International founded to document and protest the use of torture and capital punishment.

1963   • Atmospheric nuclear test-ban treaty signed after six years of demonstrations and public pressure.

1964–75   • Draft-card burning highlights organized resistance to U.S. military involvement in Vietnam. This is the first direct-action campaign in American history to help end a protracted war through nonviolent means.

1965   • United Farm Workers Union launches grape boycott.

1968   • "Czechoslovakian Spring"—eight months of nonviolent defiance of the Soviet Union is finally crushed by the Warsaw Pact armies.

1969   • Greenpeace adapts nonviolent methods to protect the environment.

1975–86   • Greenpeace "Save the Whales" campaign leads to international treaties protecting whales.

1976   • Mairead Corrigan and Betty Williams receive the Nobel Peace Prize for their efforts at nonviolent reconciliation in Northern Ireland.
          • Clamshell Alliance begins attempt to stop Seabrook nuclear reactor, ultimately failing (it opened in 1990), but refines methods of nonviolent resistance: affinity groups, mass arrests, consensus decision making, and mandatory nonviolent training in preparation for civil disobedience.

1977–84   • Nestlé boycott drive successfully brings about World Health Organization agreement restricting distribution and sale of infant formula in the Third World. Nestlé later violates the agreement, and the boycott is resumed.

1979   • Gay Rights March on Washington draws one hundred thousand.

            • Protests against nuclear energy increase after the disaster at the
              Three Mile Island plant in Pennsylvania.

            • Mark Dubois chains himself to the bank of the Stanislaus River
              in California in a final effort to preserve the endangered wild
              and scenic river. The U. S. Army Corps of Engineers stops
              filling New Melones Reservoir rather than risk drowning him.

1980–89   • Solidarity founded in Poland; repressed under martial law in
              1981, and widely declared dead even by Western
              correspondents; in 1989 it wins every seat in Parliament
              available to it, and now rules the nation. Its victory comes
              without a single violent act from Solidarity's side, despite the
              killing of over one hundred of its members.

1980   • Adolfo Pérez Esquivel receives Nobel Peace Prize for the work
              of Servicio Paz y Justicia, which has courageously intervened
              all over Latin America on behalf of human rights.

1980s   • Witness for Peace sends thousands of Americans to Nicaragua
              to maintain a "shield of love" to help stop violence by U.S.-
              backed Contras.

1980s   • More than eighty thousand Americans sign pledges to engage
              in civil disobedience if the United States invades Nicaragua
              (the "Pledge of Resistance"). Some believe it helped prevent
              an actual U.S. invasion.

1981   • Protests against cruise missiles based at Greenham Common in
              England begin. At the height of the protest, eight thousand
              women live in tents outside the base while demonstrating and
              committing civil disobedience.

1982   • The Sanctuary Movement begins attempt to protect Central
              American refugees from deportation by the United States by
              offering them sanctuary in churches.

1983   • On May 11, at 8 P.M., the Chilean copper miners' union calls
              a countrywide protest. People respond by banging on pots and
              pans and blowing whistles, and discover for the first time that
              the vast majority oppose the dictator, General Pinochet. Peruvian
              women use the same tactic when a man starts beating his wife.

1984   • The government of New Zealand refuses to allow nuclear ships
              or ships with nuclear weapons to enter its ports. The United
              States responds by expelling New Zealand from the regional
              military alliance.

1986   • The nonviolent revolution of the Philippines brings down the
              oppressive Marcos dictatorship.
            • Peace Brigades International establishes an "escort service" for
              Guatemalan human rights activists, accompanying them twenty-
              four hours a day and making a human chain around them to
              protect them from riot police and death squads.
            • Accelerated nonviolent actions begin in South Africa.
1987   • Fifty-three hundred people are arrested for acts of civil
              disobedience against nuclear weapons in the United States and
              Canada. For the whole decade, there are upwards of thirty-
              seven thousand antinuclear arrests.[10]
1987   • Palestinian *Intifada* begins, using primarily nonviolent methods.
1988   • Emergency Convocation of Churches, South Africa. Black and
              white church leaders unite to condemn apartheid and call their
              churches to active nonviolent resistance.
            • Protestors win the first round, then lose the second, in the
              struggle to bring down Burma's Marxist dictatorship of twenty-
              eight years.
            • The Frente Democratico Nacional uses nonviolent sanctions to
              protest alleged fraud during the Mexican presidential elections.
            • One hundred forty-three white South Africans refuse to re-
              port for military duty, and face up to six years imprisonment.
              Defense Minister Magnus Malan calls the End Conscription
              Campaign "just as much an enemy of the Defense Force as the
              African National Congress."[11]
1989   • Pittston Coal Strike, Virginia, marking the first time coal
              miners have consistently used explicitly nonviolent methods.
              Concludes with the first major U.S. labor victory in more than
              a decade.
            • Hungary, Poland, Czechoslovakia, Bulgaria, and East Germany
              win freedom from Soviet control by nonviolent means.
            • Nonviolent independence movements within the Soviet Union
              are launched in Latvia, Lithuania, Estonia, Georgia, Armenia,
              Moldavia, the Ukraine.
            • Nonviolent protests begin democratization process in Albania,
              Mongolia, Yugoslavia.
            • The prodemocracy movement in China is suppressed.
            • Demonstrations against segregation of South African beaches
              lead to a national directive ordering their desegregation.

- Ukrainian Catholics, belonging to the largest banned religious organization in the world with five million members, hold a huge protest Mass to call for restoration of their legal status.
- Student protests lead 20 percent of American universities to fully divest investments from South Africa, while almost 60 percent divest to some extent.
- Nine hundred twenty-seven detainees mount a hunger strike in South African prisons, leading to the release of hundreds.
- The Rev. Laszlo Tokes dares to speak the truth against the Rumanian dictator Ceausescu. When the hated secret police attempt to arrest him, two hundred people, mostly parishioners, jam the streets, light candles, and refuse to move. Hourly the crowd increases, until fifty thousand converge on the city center. Violent suppression by the government sparks the revolution that overthrows Ceausescu, in which the public continues nonviolent demonstrations while the army battles the secret police.
- Both proabortion and antiabortion protestors use civil disobedience.
- A Soviet nuclear vessel is barred from four Soviet Pacific ports as a result of popular protests over nuclear safety.
- Amazonian rubber tappers, despite the assassination of their leader Francisco Mendes, interpose their bodies before the bulldozers and chain-saw operators who are denuding the forest; successful fifteen out of forty-five times.
- Villagers in India resist relocation to make way for a missile-testing range by forming human barricades and obstructions that rely on their sheer numbers.

1990
- Disabled demonstrators demanding passage of a bill guaranteeing their civil rights stage a protest at the U.S. Capitol building. Sixty crawl out of their wheelchairs and up the steps of the Capitol to underline their demands.
- King Birendra of Nepal yields to prodemocracy protests that toppled his government, and grants multiparty democracy, a parliamentary system, and freedom of speech, of the press, of religion, and of peaceful assembly, thus ending three decades of absolutism.
- Strikes and demonstrations end the authoritarian one-party rule in Benin (Africa).

- Demonstrators march in Taiwan demanding democratic reforms and independence from the Chinese Nationalists, who have ruled since 1949.

1991
- Demonstrators launch a general strike in an attempt to topple the authoritarian rule of President Didier Ratsiraka in Madagascar.
- Tens of thousands of Soviet demonstrators surround the "White House" to protect Russian President Boris Yeltsin from a coup. Coup leaders have at their disposal over four million soldiers, hundreds of thousands of tanks, aircraft, and weapons, yet the coup fails.

This selection is quite uneven and far from complete. It does not attempt to discriminate between nonviolence bordering on violence that operates from a spiritually violent position, and nonviolence that springs from love of the enemy and tries to awaken opponents to the best that is in them. It does, however, reveal accurately the sharp increase in what many are calling "people power" in just the past few years. It is an idea whose time has come, and seems to be visiting itself upon us by spontaneous generation on every hand.

In a single newscast on March 13, 1988, six of the seven items mentioned dealt with nonviolence: the resignation of five hundred Palestinian police as a protest against Israeli policy in the occupied territory; the arrest of one thousand five hundred demonstrators at the nuclear test site in Nevada; the defiance of Archbishop Tutu and other church leaders in South Africa to the banning of church meetings that denounce apartheid; the shutting down of America's only university for the deaf by students for five days until the new nondeaf president resigned and a deaf president was elected; a demonstration by one hundred thousand in Soviet Armenia demanding reforms; and the secret police's harassment of East German churches for becoming centers for criticism of the state.

Indeed, the very fact that the centuries-long suppression of news about nonviolence is ending has created a qualitatively new situation. The Rumanian revolution, said one of its architects, was the first revolution to be conducted almost entirely by television. The Philippine revolution was orchestrated by transistor radios, the Iranian by cassette tapes, and the nonviolent Thai revolution of 1992 by portable telephones. Chinese students were educated into nonviolence by watching television coverage of the Philippine revolution; and the South Korean demonstrations (not always nonviolent) that toppled strongman Chun Doo Hwan were a conscious attempt to imitate Filipino "people power." During the debates in the Lithuanian parliament over independence from the Soviet

Union, the streets were virtually deserted for several days. People were glued to their television sets watching the proceedings. A Polish priest commented prior to the victory of Solidarity that he thought the outcome in Poland would more likely be nonviolent thanks to television coverage of the Philippine revolution. Chinese students received information on troop movements and reactions in other Chinese cities through fax printouts, sent by Chinese students in the United States, of reports filed for the American media by reporters in China. Soviets, inspired by reports of American demonstrations at the Nevada nuclear testing site, staged protests at the Soviet testing site in Kazakhstan. And the Soviet communist hard-liners who staged the coup in 1991 seized all official media but were unable to round up all the shortwave radios, fax machines, and electronic mailers that westerners had been taking into the country and leaving behind. Consequently, the demonstrators who surrounded the "White House" to protect Russian president Boris Yeltsin were encouraged to persist when they received a constant stream of supportive messages from people around the world—including word that foreign governments were not granting diplomatic recognition to the leaders of the coup.[12] We were accustomed to the use of the media for propaganda and mind control; what was new was the use of modern communications for liberation.

The capacity of citizens to prevent war, redress injustice, and overthrow tyrants has always existed in potential, as Étienne de la Boetie pointed out so eloquently almost five centuries ago.[13] But never before have citizens actualized this potential in such overwhelming numbers or to such stunning effect. And yet "people power" is still in its infancy!

One particularly appealing instance of nonviolent national defense took place in the nineteenth century, when the government of the Sandwich Islands imposed a tax on French brandy and wine in order to diminish the use and effect of intoxicating liquors among the people. The French, irritated, sent a great ship of war to compel the government to remove the tax. The captain gave them but a few hours to comply. But they absolutely refused to obey. A contemporary, Elihu Burritt, provides this delightful report:

> The lady of the French consul—good, kind, compassionate woman—went with her husband from house to house, and entreated the foreign residents to take refuge on board the French ship, for the island was to be blown up, or sunk, to punish the wicked government for taxing French brandy, and making drunkenness a dearer luxury to the people! But not a single person accepted the refuge. The government held fast to its resolution without wavering for a moment. The French commander landed with his marines in battle array. Men with lighted matches stood at the great cannons of the ship. The hour of vengeance had come. Poor little people! what will become of you now? What will you do to defend yourselves against

this resistless force? Do? do nothing but *endure*. "The King," says the report, "gave peremptory orders to his people to *oppose no resistance* to the Frenchmen. The gallant commander, therefore, landed his marines and took possession of the fort, custom-house, and some other Government buildings, *no resistance being offered*. All was still and peaceful in the streets, business going on as usual. Here they remained for some days; when, finding that the government would not accede at all to their demands, though they offered to leave the whole question to an umpire, the chivalrous Frenchmen went to work to dismantle the fort, and destroyed everything within its walls. After having finished this Vandal-like work, they marched off with flying colors."[14]

If the Sandwich Islanders had been in possession of an army of one hundred thousand men, they could have mounted no better defense, with fewer casualties (which were zero) or less damage (which was only to a fort they proved they no longer needed). And rather than celebrating a military victory on the carnage of war, this tiny country celebrated a moral and strategic victory over one of the world's most powerful colonial nations.

Today this scenario is being repeated by the citizens of Palau in Micronesia, who are resisting a great power, the United States, which insists on locating its nuclear weapons and military bases there.

Every legitimate nation has a right and duty to defend its people. No people will willingly embrace nonviolence if they perceive it as a risk greater than war. What Gene Sharp and his colleagues are attempting to demonstrate is that nonviolent sanctions provide a *superior* form of national defense.[15] In the process, we are discovering that some of the allegedly self-evident assumptions that guided Cold War realpolitik have, one after another, self-destructed in the era of glasnost. The "realists" told us that right-wing dictatorships were capable of democratization but not left-wing totalitarian states. Yet we have watched nations oppressed by the right in South America *and* by the left in the communist nations rush to democratize.

The "realists" told us that the law of empire is to attempt to expand indefinitely. Yet we have watched first Britain, and now the Soviet Union, relinquish their empires with relative equanimity, with Gorbachev actually urging it on his reluctant client-state leaders.

The "realists" told us that people in power never voluntarily surrender it, that power must be seized from them by force. Yet we have watched an entire string of leaders voluntarily hand over or share their power. State-led liberalization from above has long been a factor in Latin America, but no one expected it of Gorbachev in Russia, Jaruzelski in Poland, Suarez in Spain, Kadar in Hungary, Dubcek in Czechoslovakia, Karamanlis in Greece, Kucan in Slovenia, or Birendra in Nepal. These "politicians of retreat" are a new breed of political

animal, writes John Keane. They are not driven by lust for power or visions of
grand victories through conquest. They are instead skilled in the difficult art of
unscrewing the lids of despotism. They know from the outset that they must be
ruined for the good of the nation, and that ingratitude from their rivals and
subjects is their ultimate fate. They recognize that the forces they unleash will
ultimately prove their own downfall. And yet they do it anyway.[16]

And the "realists" told us that nonviolence only works with "genteel" oppressors like the Americans or British, but would never work with brutal regimes
like the Nazis or communists. Yet we have watched nonviolence work with
unprecedented effectiveness against communist regimes from the Eastern bloc
to Mongolia. In fact, says Jonathan Schell in an article on Solidarity in Poland,
"Nonviolent action, far from being helpless in the face of totalitarianism, turns
out to be especially well suited for fighting against it."[17]

When, on returning home from South Africa in 1986, I shared with a leading
ethicist of the "Christian realist" school my excitement about the nonviolent
direct action being staged in South Africa, he simply gave me a knowing smile
and said, "The South African situation will be resolved the way these things
always are, by violence," and walked away. Even as President de Klerk was
releasing Nelson Mandela from prison and dismantling statutory apartheid, people in the South African resistance continued to repeat that old canard about
nonviolence working with the British but not the cruel Afrikaners. A Protestant
Filipino bishop told Richard Deats one year before the nonviolent revolution
swept Marcos from power: "We've tried nonviolence, but the time for that is
long past. Marcos, the Hitler of Southeast Asia, will only be brought down by
violence."

Nonviolence *did* work whenever it was tried against the Nazis. Bishop Kiril
told Nazi authorities that if they attempted to deport Bulgarian Jews to concentration camps, he himself would lead a campaign of civil disobedience, and
lie down on the railroad tracks in front of the trains. Thousands of Bulgarian
Jews and non-Jews resisted all collaboration with Nazi decrees. They marched
in mass street demonstrations and sent a flood of letters and telegrams to authorities protesting all anti-Jewish measures. Bulgarian clergy and laity hid Jews.
Christian ministers accepted large numbers of Jewish "converts," making it
clear that this was a trick to escape the Nazis and that they would not consider
the "vows" binding. "Because of these and other nonmilitary measures, all of
Bulgaria's Jewish citizens were saved from the Nazi death camps."[18] Rumania
at first persecuted the Jews, then reversed itself and refused to surrender a single
Rumanian Jew living within the state's traditional borders to the death camps.[19]

Finland saved all but six of its Jewish citizens from death camps through
nonmilitary means. Of seven thousand Danish Jews, six thousand five hundred

escaped to Sweden, aided by virtually the whole population and tips from within the German occupation force itself. Almost all of the rest were hidden safely for the duration of the war.[20] Denmark's resistance was so effective that Adolf Eichmann had to admit that "the action against the Jews of Denmark has been a failure."[21] The Norwegian underground helped spirit nine hundred Jews to safety in Sweden, but another 756 were killed, all but twenty in Nazi death camps.[22] German wives of Jews demonstrated in Berlin on behalf of their husbands in the midst of the war, and secured their release.[23] In Italy, a large percentage of Jews survived because officials and citizens sabotaged efforts to hand them over to the Germans.[24]

During the Nazi occupation of Holland, a general strike by all rail workers practically paralyzed traffic from November, 1944, until liberation in May, 1945—this despite extreme privation to the people, who held out all winter without heating and with dwindling food supplies. Similar resistance in Norway prevented Vidkun Quisling, Hitler's representative, from imposing a fascist "corporative state" on the country.[25]

The tragedy is not that nonviolence did not work against the Nazis, but that it was so seldom utilized. The Jews themselves did not use it, but continued to rely in the main on the passive nonresistance that had carried them through so many pogroms in the past. And the churches as a whole were too docile or anti-Semitic, and too ignorant of the nonviolent message of the gospel, to act effectively to resist the Nazis or act in solidarity with the Jews.

B. H. Liddell-Hart, widely acknowledged as the foremost military writer of our time, discovered in his interrogation of Nazi generals after World War II that they had little trouble dealing with violent resistance except in mountainous areas of Russia and the Balkans, or where advancing armies were close. But they expressed complete inability to cope with nonviolence as practiced in Denmark, Holland, Norway, and, to a lesser extent, in France and Belgium. "They were experts in violence, and had been trained to cope with opponents who used that method. But other forms of resistance baffled them. They were relieved when nonviolence was mixed with guerrilla operations, which made it easier to combine suppressive action against both at the same time." The generals found friendly noncompliance more frustrating than any other form of resistance, and had no effective means to counter it. "If practiced with a cheerful smile and an air of well-meaning mistake, due to incomprehension or clumsiness, it becomes even more baffling. . . . This subtle kind of resistance cannot really be dealt with in terms of force: indeed, nothing can deal with it. There is really no answer to such go-slow tactics."[26]

While the years 1986–90 witnessed one success story after another for nonviolence, I am not aware of a single instance of violent insurrection succeeding in that same period. People in South Africa talked a great deal about antigovernment violence, but it was nonviolent resistance that brought the government to the bargaining table. The armed wing of the African National Congress was almost totally ineffective. And for all its violent rhetoric and the subsequent record of violence, the Iranian revolution was nonviolent—"a revolution of the popular demonstration, the sermon, the cassette, all leading up to a massive withdrawal of support for the Shah's government."[27]

It was with bitter chagrin that the Chilean Communist party, traditionally one of the most loyal to Moscow, had to recognize that its strategy of trying to bring down the government of Gen. Augusto Pinochet by armed rebellion had been mistaken. "Pinochet left the palace," remarked Luis Guastavino, a former senior party member who was expelled for attempting to democratize the party, "but not by our road." The party found it painful to admit, he said, that the nonviolent route chosen by the Christian Democrats, Socialists, and others now in the government of President Patricio Aylwin was the one that succeeded.[28]

The Future of Nonviolence

Tolstoy, with a prescience that now appears to have been prophetic, wrote to Gandhi in the Transvaal in 1910 that the passive resistance campaign in South Africa "is the most important activity the world can at present take part in, and in which not Christendom alone but all the peoples of the earth will participate."[29]

Many in the West have been celebrating the eclipse of Marxism. But the collapse of communism is not a vindication of capitalism, as some have concluded; it is rather a sober indication of the difficulty of overcoming economic inequality. Communism was itself a reaction to the gross abuses of capitalism. Its failure means that the economically disadvantaged will have to fight for a more equitable system by nonviolent means. These efforts will probably be largely free of ideology and general blueprints. They will be responses to flagrant abuses by fragmentary and ad hoc means. To the degree that people are trained in nonviolent discipline, philosophy, and tactics, their efforts may be more effective. But it is not at all clear that nonviolence will be able to dislodge the vested economic interests, with their unconscionable wealth.

For at the root of political autocracy lies the power of money. Democratization in Eastern Europe may simply mean integration into a worldwide system in which the gap between the super-rich and the poor is constantly widening, with most of the middle and lower classes steadily losing ground. The resentment caused by shortages, unemployment, and price increases in Eastern Europe may lead to food riots, anarchy, and attempted coups. The very "people power" that won political freedom could easily degenerate into mobocracy, as each interest group or aggrieved sector of the population seeks to wring concessions from already tenuous regimes.

Christian theology has no privileged insights into how to create a just economic system. What it does have to contribute, however, is a vision of the reign of God, of a just order destined by God to replace the values and viciousness of the Domination System. Such a comprehensive vision is needed in order to gather all struggles against injustice into a single whole, a concerted, long-term engagement on behalf of the true fulfillment of every person created in the image of God.

War *between* nations may actually be in decline. War in Western Europe, one of the most war-ravaged areas in the world, is now almost unthinkable, and war between the Soviet Union and the United States appears, at the time of writing, to be an extremely remote possibility. It is hard to remember the last time a South American or Central American nation waged a serious war against a neighbor. It would appear that warfare between states can actually be sharply reduced and perhaps eventually ended. Nationalism may be receding as the major cause of war. Its place may be taken by ethnic conflicts and injustice as the cause of insurgencies *within* states. Already 90 percent of current wars are being fought between various factions within a state. The world appears to be moving toward a single integrated economic system in which state armies suppress their own citizens who have been denied a fair share of the economic pie.

Nonviolence will be even more urgently relevant in this new state of affairs, where the ability and interest of outside forces will be severely limited, and the oppressed will have no resource other than people power. And because both victors and vanquished will have to coexist at the conclusion of hostilities, the practical task of learning to love enemies will need to be given the highest priority.

The figure that will stir the hopes and catalyze people to seek these transformations will be the one who has been waiting to do so for the past nineteen centuries: Jesus of Nazareth. But it will not be the Christ of dogma this time, but simply Jesus, the man who lived God into flesh, through whom God reveals divine love and presence. In Jesus we see already the contours and character of existence in God's domination-free order. In him we have the assurance of the age to come, the model of true humanity, the guide to practical living.

Jesus has never seemed more relevant. The world has never been more ready.

Part 4
THE POWERS AND THE LIFE
OF THE SPIRIT

Every dynamic new force for change is undergirded by rigorous disciplines. The slack decadence of culture-Christianity cannot produce athletes of the spirit. Those who are the bearers of tomorrow undergo what others might call disciplines, but not to punish themselves or to ingratiate themselves to God. They simply do what is necessary to stay spiritually alive, just as they eat food and drink water.

The chapters that follow do not exhaust those disciplines, but they include several of the ones I have found most essential: learning to love our enemies (chap. 14), monitoring our inner violence (chap. 15), and engaging in an almost combative kind of prayer (chap. 16). Together, these chapters indicate something of the practical value of an understanding of the Powers in everyday life.

Why this sudden unrest and confusion?
(How solemn their faces have become.)
Why are the streets and squares clearing quickly,
and all return to their homes, so deep in thought?

Because night is here but the barbarians have not come.
Some people arrived from the frontiers,
and they said that there are no longer any barbarians.

And now what shall become of us without any barbarians?
Those people were a kind of solution.

C. P. Cavafy,
"Expecting the Barbarians"[1]

14. The Acid Test: Loving Enemies

In the spiritual renaissance that I believe is coming to birth, it will not be the message of Paul that this time galvanizes hearts, as in the Reformation and the Wesleyan revival, but the human figure of Jesus. And in the teaching of Jesus, the sayings on nonviolence and love of enemies will hold a central place. Not because they are more true than any others, but because they are the only means known for overcoming domination without creating new dominations.

I submit that the ultimate religious question today should no longer be the Reformation's question, "How can I find a gracious God?" but rather, "How can we find God in our enemies?" What guilt was for Luther, the enemy has become for us: the goad that can drive us to God. What has often been a purely private affair—justification by faith through grace—has now, in our age, grown to embrace the world. As John Stoner comments, we can no more save ourselves from our enemies than we can save ourselves from sin, but God's amazing grace offers to save us from both.[2]

There is, in fact, no other way to God for our time but through the enemy, for loving the enemy has become the key both to human survival in the nuclear age and to personal transformation. The end of the Cold War has eased, not solved, the nuclear crisis, which now shows signs of proliferation to smaller states not constrained by the danger of total war. Now border disputes and acts of aggression can be settled by nuclear brinkmanship, terrorism, or holocaust. Today, more than ever, we must turn to the God who causes the sun to rise on the evil and on the good, or we may have no more sunrises.

Jesus' teachings about nonviolent direct action and love of enemies are also the acid tests of true Christianity. Just as in the lore of exorcism the Devil cannot bear to utter the name of God, so our false prophets today cannot tolerate mention of the love of enemies. The Rev. Greg Dixon, a former state chairman and National Secretary for the Moral Majority, recently urged his followers to pray for the death of their opponents, claiming, "We're tired of turning the other cheek . . . good heavens, that's all that we have done."[3] The Rev. Jerry Falwell and his allies are champions of the warrior mentality and of peace through strength; Jesus' way of creative nonviolence is for them indistinguishable from supine cowardice. As James A. Sanders reminds us, no false prophet can ever conceive of God as being God also of the enemy.[4]

Jesus' way of nonviolence and love of enemies has frequently been dismissed as impractical, idealistic, and out of touch with the need of nations and oppressed peoples to defend themselves. No such irrelevancy is charged against the myth of redemptive violence, however, despite the fact that it fails at least half the time. Its exaltation of the salvific powers of killing, and the privileged position it is accorded by intellectuals and politicians alike (to say nothing of theologians), make redemptive violence the preferred myth of Marxists and capitalists, fascists and leftists, atheists and churchgoers alike. Redemptive violence is the prevailing ideology of the Institute of Religion and Democracy and segments of the World Council of Churches, of *Christianity Today* and *Christianity and Crisis*, of much of liberation theology and much of conservative theology.

Then came 1989–1990, years of unprecedented political change, years of miracles, surpassing any such concentration of political transformations in human history, even the Exodus. In 1989 alone, thirteen nations comprising 1,695,100,000 people, over 32 percent of humanity, experienced nonviolent revolutions that succeeded beyond anyone's wildest expectations in every case but China, and were completely nonviolent (on the part of the participants) in every case but Romania and parts of the southern U.S.S.R. The nations involved were Poland, East Germany, Hungary, Czechoslovakia, Bulgaria, Romania, Albania, Yugoslavia, Mongolia, the Soviet Union, Brazil, Chile, and China. Since then Nepal, Palau, and Madagascar have undergone nonviolent struggles, Latvia, Lithuania, and Estonia have achieved independence nonviolently, the Soviet Union has dissolved into a commonwealth of republics, and more than a dozen countries have moved toward multiparty democracy, including Mongolia, Gabon, Bangladesh, Benin, and Algeria. If we add all the countries touched by major nonviolent actions just since 1986 (the Philippines, South Korea, South Africa, Israel, Burma, New Caledonia, and New Zealand), and the other nonviolent struggles of our century—the independence movements of India and Ghana, the overthrow of the Shah in Iran, the struggle against authoritarian governments and landowners in Argentina and Mexico, and the civil rights, United Farm Worker, anti-Vietnam and antinuclear movements in the United States—the figure reaches 3,337,400,000: a staggering 64 percent of humanity!

All this in the teeth of the assertion, endlessly repeated, that nonviolence does not work in the "real" world.

It appears as if the nonviolent way articulated by Jesus as the heart of the gospel message has finally found an unwitting following. The dream of abolishing war, like child sacrifice and exposure, gladiatorial combat, slavery, cannibalism, colonialism, and dueling, seems to be finally approaching the first stages of realization.

The significance of what is happening needs to be set in the widest possible frame. Humanity has arisen, it would appear, as the means by which the evolutionary process has become conscious of itself. And what emerged with Jesus, according to Gerd Theissen, is the decisive protest against the brutality of natural selection, a protest that had already been proclaimed with increasing clarity in the religion of Israel, beginning with the mass exodus of the Hebrew slaves from Egypt. Jesus rejects selection of the "fittest," both in nature and in culture, and declares in favor of those whom the natural process seeks to winnow out: the meek, the poor, the crippled, the sick, the retarded, outcasts, pariahs, and the possessed.[5]

Jesus was not the first to practice nonviolence; indeed, he clearly learned it from his own people.[6] But his manner of incarnating nonviolence marked an evolutionary breakthrough that rejected the pattern of domination of the weak by the strong. He offers the weak a way of affirming their essential humanity, not sometime in the far-off future, but here, now, in precisely the situation of oppression itself.

Solidarity in Poland proved that Jesus' nonviolent way could be lived even under the circumstances of a communist regime and martial law. People said to one another, in effect, "Start doing the things you think should be done, and start being what you think society should become. Do you believe in freedom of speech? Then speak freely. Do you love the truth? Then tell it. Do you believe in an open society? Then act in the open. Do you believe in a decent and humane society? Then behave decently and humanely." This behavior actually caught on, leading to an "epidemic of freedom in the closed society." By acting "as if" Poland were already a free country, Solidarity *created* a free country. The "as if" ceased to be pretense and became actuality. Within ten years, Solidarity had taken over the government. This is not only a graphic example of a social revolution becoming a political revolution, but it constitutes, in Jonathan Schell's words, a new chapter in the history of revolution: a revolution in revolution.[7]

Nonviolent direct action can be used for causes some of us would not support, though the requirement that one voluntarily suffer the consequences tends to weed out trivial or selfish expressions of it.[8] Likewise, it can be used for revenge or to manipulate or humiliate others without concern for their genuine well-being. Without love for enemies, nonviolence would be just another arrow in the quiver of coercive force. The rationale for Jesus' nonviolent way is neither the short-term effectiveness of nonviolent strategies, nor the long-term self-interest of the species, but rather the very nature of God.

God Is All-Inclusive

We are to love our enemies, says Jesus, because God does. God makes the "sun rise on the evil and on the good, and sends rain on the righteous and on the unrighteous" (Matt. 5:45). We are to love our enemies and pray for those who persecute us, so that we may be children of this strange Father-Mother, who "is kind to the ungrateful and the wicked" (Luke 6:35).[9]

Much of what passes as religion denies the existence of such a God. Is not "God" precisely that moral force in the universe that rewards the good and punishes the evil? This had been the message of John the Baptist, and it would later be the message of the church. In John's preaching, God is depicted as verging on a massive and final counteroffensive against evil in which all evil will be exterminated. One whole side of reality will be wiped out. Ostensibly John has chaffy people in mind. God will obliterate them by fire (Matt. 3:7-12//Luke 3:7-18).

Jesus, by contrast, understood judgment not as an end, but as a beginning. The penitential river of fire was not to consume but to purify, not to annihilate but to redeem. Divine judgment is intended, not to destroy, but to awaken people to the devastating truth about their lives. Jesus seizes the apocalyptic vision of impending doom and hurls it into time, into the present encounter with God's unexpected and unaccountable forgiveness. Judgment now no longer is the last crushing word on a failed life, but the first word of a new creation. Jesus lived this new creation out in his table fellowship with those whom the religious establishment had branded outcasts, sinners, renegades: the enemies of God. He did not wait for them to repent, become respectable, and do works of restitution in hopes of gaining divine forgiveness and human restoration. Instead he audaciously bursts upon these sinners with the declaration that their sins have been forgiven, prior to their repentance, prior to any acts of restitution or reconciliation. Everything is reversed: You are forgiven; now you can repent! God loves you; now you can lift your eyes to God! The enmity is over. You were enemies and yet God accepts you! There is nothing you must do to earn this. You need only accept it.

The radicalism of Jesus' image of God is hidden by the self-evident picture he draws from nature. God clearly does not favor some with sunshine and rain, and others with darkness and drought, depending on their righteousness. Yet, in fact, society has in every possible way created the impression that only some are in God's favor and the others out. By dress, color, nationality, wealth, gender, sexual preference, education, language, looks, and health, others are meant to recognize instantly whether we are blessed or cursed, beloved or rejected. There are enormous benefits for going along with this selective grading of human beings, and severe penalties inflicted for its rejection. For these accidents of genetics and class determine one's social location and power, and anyone who tampers with them undermines the foundations of unequal privilege. To say that God does not sit atop the pyramid of power legitimating the entire edifice, does not favor some and reject others, is to expose the entire structure as a human contrivance established in defiance of God's very nature.

Jesus' laconic mention of God's all-inclusive parental care is thus charged with an unexpected consequence for human behavior: we can love our enemies, because God does. If we wish to correspond to the central reality of the universe, we will behave as God behaves—and God embraces all, evenhandedly. This radical vision of God, already perceived by the Hebrew prophets but never popular among the resident Powers, is the basis for true human community.

Our solidarity with our enemies lies not just in our common parentage under God, but also in our common evil. God "is kind to the ungrateful and the wicked." We too, like them, live in enmity against what God desires for the world. We would like to identify ourselves as "just" and "good," but we are a mix of just and unjust, good and evil. If God were not compassionate toward us, we would be lost. And if God is compassionate toward us, with all our unredeemed evil, then God must treat our enemies the same way. As we begin to acknowledge our own inner shadow, we become more tolerant of the shadow in others. As we begin to love the enemy within, we develop the compassion we need to love the enemy without.

If, however, we believe that the God who loves us hates those whom we hate, we insert an insidious doubt into our own selves. Unconsciously we know that a deity hostile toward others is potentially hostile to us as well.[10] And we know, better than anyone, that there is plenty of cause for such hostility. If God did not send sun and rain on everyone equally, God would not only not love everyone, but love no one.

Against Perfectionism

The climactic assertion in Matthew's statement about loving enemies runs, "Be perfect, therefore, as your heavenly Father is perfect" (5:48). The gospel appears to be saying two opposite things in a single breath: God loves everyone, good and bad alike, unconditionally; and God's love is conditional after all: we must be perfect. This closing line seems to fly in the face of everything Jesus has just taught. If I am not perfect—then what? Rejection, isolation, the fires of hell! Our heavenly Parent no longer seems to be kind to the ungrateful and the wicked, but has now become exceedingly choosy: a God that no sensible person would want as a parent, a God who measures out love on an exact scale of deserving, a God whose love must be earned, whose wrath must be placated, whose tendencies to reject must be mollified, whose incapacity for unconditional love, mercy, and grace must be borne as a permanent wound in the Christian's psyche.

It may come as immediate relief to learn that *Jesus could not have said, "Be perfect."* There was no such word, or even concept, in Aramaic or Hebrew.[11] And for good reason. The Second Commandment had forbidden the making of graven images (Exod. 20:4). Israel consequently never developed the visual arts. The word used by Matthew, *teleios*, was, however, a Greek aesthetic term. It described the perfect geometric form, or the perfect sculpture. It was seldom used in ethical discourse, since moral perfection is not within the grasp of human beings, and would even have been regarded, in Greek piety, as a form of hybris.[12]

Matthew appears to have taken *teleios* over from the Greek translation of Deut. 18:13, where the term was used to render the Hebrew word *tamim* ("whole, complete, finished, entire, to have integrity"). The NRSV translates it, "You must remain completely loyal to the Lord your God." In Israel, the closest thing to the notion of perfection was being without blemish. This was a purely negative and functional idea. A man ugly beyond tolerance could still officiate at a Jewish sacrifice as long as he was not maimed, diseased, or deformed. There were no positive norms of beauty, only negative criteria of exclusion.[13]

Among the Greeks, perfection did not accrue to people, but to works of art. In the Middle Ages, Greek and Hebrew thought coalesced, with sin taking the place of blemish. Perfection was negatively defined as not behaving, or even not thinking, in certain ways. But the sense of sin was so profound that moral perfectionism was no factor at all except among the "spiritual athletes," the ascetics, who made it their whole life's task to achieve moral perfection.

It was not until the Enlightenment, with its reintroduction of Greek aesthetic norms in neoclassical art and its search for universals, that widespread moralistic perfectionism became really imaginable. The merger of Protestant religious egalitarianism and Enlightenment rational equalitarianism now for the first time made the ideal of sinlessness—a heresy on its face—not only a cultural goal but a profound obsession. The fact that many Protestant churches officially espoused justification by grace alone scarcely checked the advance of perfectionistic moralism. The Enlightenment ideal of humanity perfecting itself had so deeply penetrated Western culture that deviance was defined as failure to live up to social norms that one now had no excuse (such as human sinfulness) for violating, and that offered no restitution (such as forgiveness). Thus perfectionism is not simply a characteristic of Protestantism, but an artifact of Western culture generally.[14]

Placed in its context within the rest of the paragraph, Jesus' saying about behaving like God becomes abundantly clear. We are not to be perfect, but, like God, all-encompassing, loving even those who have least claim or right to our love. Even toward enemies we are to be indiscriminate, all-inclusive, forgiving, understanding. We are to regard the enemy as beloved of God every bit as much as we. We are to be compassionate, as God is compassionate.

This saying underscores Jesus' rejection of the holiness code as it was interpreted by his contemporaries. Mercy (God's all-inclusive love) is deliberately contrasted with exclusivity and segregation. His hearers could scarcely miss the echo of Lev. 19:2 here, except that its "Be holy, for I the Lord your God am holy" has been altered to headline Jesus' new emphasis: "Be merciful, just as your Father is merciful," as Luke so much more effectively renders it (6:36).[15] A gesture of embrace makes the point physiologically a thousand times more eloquently than any words. Jesus wants us to behave toward enemies as he has discovered God does.

Jesus does not call for "wholeness," though that would have been a better translation than "perfect." For "wholeness" places all the focus on us, and Jesus points us away from ourselves to love our *enemies*. All-inclusive love is his goal, even if broken, contaminated by elements of our own unredeemed shadow, intermittent. Again the gesture: embracing *everyone*. To do so is not to be perfect. It is, according to Jesus, an entirely possible human act, because with the command God supplies the power to do it. He is not urging us to a perfection of being-in-ourselves, but to abandon all dreams of perfection and to embrace those we feel are least perfect, least deserving, and most threatening to our lives. "You therefore must be all-inclusive, as your heavenly Abba is all-inclusive."

Jesus is not demanding of us a perfection that we cannot attain and so driving us, by the cudgel of law, into the arms of grace. Yet there is a role for grace here: the inbreaking reign of God, which makes what was impossible under the Domination System suddenly achievable. We cannot will ourselves into such new behaviors, for the will is merely the total organized personality of the moment, and the strength of will depends not on exhortation or trying harder, but on the strength of the factors that enter into its organization.[16] What frees us for the radical new behaviors of the new social order that Jesus proclaimed is not a willing, but a giving of ourselves wholly to the God who reveals and brings this new reality. That full self-offering to God creates a new organization of the personality, so that now "the one who believes in me will also do the works that I do and, in fact, will do greater works than these, because I am going to the Father" (John 14:12).

Of course we will fail to realize the fullness of Jesus' vision. We will compromise it, and whittle him down to our size to avoid the possibilities that a larger life might prompt in us. We may cling to our class, racial, and gender interests and rationalize them with the purest of orthodoxy. God forgives all that, in advance. And because we are forgiven, we can repent. But that forgiveness is no inducement to stay trapped in our conditioning, for we are now free from having to measure up to other people's standards of what is required for our salvation. We are animated by love, excitement, and the "hunger and thirst after justice" that draws us continually to transcend our social location for the sake of that better world for which we long.

The perfectionist misreading of Jesus' text about loving enemies leads to a crowning irony: the attempt to will to love enemies in order to become perfect makes the love of enemies a psychological impossibility. If we have to be perfect in order to earn God's grudging love, then what do we do with those aspects of ourselves that are not perfect and that we know will never be? What do we do with our tempers, our lust, our cowardice, our greed, our indifference to the suffering of others? If we wish to continue the game of perfectionism at all (and it is a game, played on us to our detriment by the Great Deluder), we must repress all that evil. Out of sight, out of mind—but not out of the psyche! Then, when we encounter people who remind us of the things we hate about ourselves and have repressed, we will involuntarily project onto them what has been evoked in our own unconscious. We are therefore systematically prevented from loving our enemies because we need them as targets for our projections. By thus discharging our hatred on external enemies, we can achieve a partial release from the pent-up energy festering in the unconscious. The perfectionist reading of this text thus stands Jesus' intention on its head, and makes all-inclusive love of enemies literally impossible.

Perfectionism has a secret and unacknowledged *need* for enemies. Perfectionists are perfect only by comparison. They must have someone to look down on. But this is the structure that first gave birth to the ancient Babylonian myth of redemptive violence. Reality is split into two parts, good and evil, and salvation resides in identifying oneself wholly with the good side and projecting all one's evil on the bad. This approach can last only so long as insight about one's shadow side can be prevented.

Paul Tillich once commented that "the weakness of the fanatic is that those whom he fights have a secret hold upon him."[17] When we project our evil onto others, we establish a symbiotic relationship with them as our enemies. We *require* enemies, and are secretly fascinated by their evil, which at some level we wish we could do. Secretly, worshipers of order are always votaries of chaos. They may publicly praise Marduk, but in the private citadels of the unconscious they adore Tiamat.[18] Without an enemy, without conflict, without some external threat to unify the people, there is no incentive to pay taxes for a standing army. Marduk must have a Tiamat to subdue, or else he will have to invent one. Nothing threatens order so much as peace. Peace, as William Graham Sumner once remarked, is the problem that war is required to solve.[19] It will be interesting, with the ending of the Cold War, to see what new parade of scapegoats, enemies, and barbarians are invented to carry the national shadow. Saddam Hussein has already performed that role splendidly. Who will be next? *Osama bin L.*

The Enemy's Gift

Once the spell of the perfectionist reading has been broken, we begin to see just how far from perfect Jesus assumed we are. "Why do you see the speck in your neighbor's eye, but do not notice the log in your own eye? Or how can you say to your neighbor, 'Let me take the speck out of your eye,' while the log is in your own eye? You hypocrite, first take the log out of your own eye, and then you will see clearly to take the speck out of your neighbor's eye" (Matt. 7:3-5//Luke 6:41-42).

This is the earliest known teaching of projection. We have scarcely begun to trace the implications of Jesus' discovery of projection; his entire understanding of evil is the fruit of it. The "splinter" in the other's eye is a chip off the same log that is in one's own eye. We see in the other what we would not see in ourselves. But why is it a *log* in the eye of the beholder? Normally we say, "I may be (somewhat bad—a splinter), but *that* person is (really bad—a log)." Why has Jesus inverted that conventional way of putting it?

Because the log in my eye totally blinds me. I can see nothing objectively. Remove the log, and I can see to help my neighbor remove his or her splinter. In workshops on this theme June and I invite people to name an enemy and list all the things they dislike about that person (or group or movement or nation). Then we ask them to go through that list and ask how many of those characteristics are true also of them (or our group or movement or nation). The common elements identify our projections. These can be taken into our meditation, prayer, and spiritual guidance, to see what they have to teach us about ourselves. (Not all elements will be common. Some people may be objectively hostile. Our scores may range from zero to one hundred percent.)

One pastor wrote of his "enemy," "He wants to be in on every decision, whether he is involved or not." This was one of the characteristics he had ticked off on his list that was also true of him. The "enemy" was a lay leader who insisted that every decision made by any duly authorized group in the church had to be confirmed by him. The pastor, who saw the same tendency in himself, acknowledged that both he and this lay leader had a deep need to control everything.

> "Why do you need to control everything?" he was asked.
> "Because if things go wrong I'll get blamed."
> "What fear lies behind that need to control everything?"
> "The fear that everything will just crumble. That I'll be a failure who's not loved."
> "Can you think back in your life to times when you felt this way?" He could. "Now, put yourself in your enemy's shoes. What fear drives him to need so much control?"
> "He's a retired farmer who milked five hundred cows a day. That's a big operation. He's sixty-six, and he's just turned the farm over to his son. I think he feels his life is slipping away from him. And here I come trying to force him to release control on the whole church, too!"

The pastor needed to discover this dynamic, because it was important to stop this man's autocratic behavior. But it was also necessary to be aware of his own tendencies to autocracy. Otherwise they would simply get locked in an unconscious power struggle. But he must not give in to the man either. He needs to assert his authority as a spiritual leader of the church. But to sense the pain and panic, the desperation, of this man, will make it easier to love and understand him.

Another, a woman deeply involved in struggles for political justice, related that her enemy was President Reagan. The common quality they shared was self-righteousness.

> "How do you manifest self-righteousness?" she was asked.
> "I always feel I am right," she said.
> "Why do you need to feel you're right all the time, since it's unlikely that you are?"
> "I want God to love me."
> "What is the fear behind your social passion?"
> "That I won't do enough to be loved."

"What do you think drives Reagan to be self-righteous, then?"

"I suppose the same fear."

"How would it change your attitude if you realized that you and Reagan are no different in kind from each other—different in content, yes, but no different in kind?"

She did not like this idea, but she herself had established the commonality from the outset. Gradually her face softened. The realization was humbling, deflating—the recognition that she and Reagan were one humanity together.

These "revelations" (and they are precisely that) need to be treasured, because that is the gift our enemy may be able to bring us: *to see aspects of ourselves that we cannot discover any other way than through our enemies.* Our friends seldom tell us these things; they are our friends precisely because they are able to overlook or ignore this part of us.[20] The enemy is thus not merely a hurdle to be leaped on the way to God. The enemy *can be* the way to God. We cannot come to terms with our shadow except through our enemies, for we have almost no other access to those unacceptable parts of ourselves that need redeeming except through the mirror that our enemies hold up to us. This then is another, more intimate reason for loving our enemies: we are dependent on our enemies for our very individuation. We may not be able to be whole people without them.

How painfully humiliating: we not only may have a role in transforming our enemies, but our enemies can play a role in transforming us.

As we become aware of our projections on our enemies, we are freed from the fear that we will overreact murderously toward them. We are able to develop an objective rage at the injustices they are perpetrating while still seeing them as children of God. The energy squandered nursing hatred becomes available to God for confronting the wrong or transforming the relationship.

An understanding of the Powers makes forgiveness of our enemies easier. If our oppressors "know not what they do," if they too are also victims of the delusional system, then the real target of our hate and anger can be the System itself rather than those who carry out its bidding. "For our struggle is not against enemies of blood and flesh, but against the rulers, against the authorities, against the cosmic powers of this present darkness, against the spiritual forces of evil in the heavenly places" (Eph. 6:12).

A Catalan, Llius Mario Xirinacs, exhibits this understanding in a letter he wrote to his torturer in 1976:

> You have beaten me, arrested me, insulted me very often. Do you know what I
> think, for example, when I am crouching on the ground with my hands on my

head, protecting myself from your dreadful truncheon-blows? I feel extremely sad to see you obliged to hit me. It grieves me to be the occasion through which you lose your human dignity by hitting an innocent, defenseless companion. I am ashamed at the accumulation of advantages which have enabled me to choose not to go into the police under this regime, whereas you, because there was no other way out, because you come from a region which is exploited by people from my class, find yourself obliged to play this wretched part. On the one hand, myself, full of possibilities, on the other, you, having fallen into the fateful trap, and reduced to being the hired strongman of the truly privileged. Injustice has made me into a man of studies, and made you into men of violence.[21]

With these words the author heaped "burning coals on their heads" (Rom. 12:20). This much-misunderstood saying does not advocate a sugarcoated vengeance. On the contrary, as Jean Goss-Mayr notes from the vantage point of a lifetime of nonviolent experience, Paul rightly stresses the aggressive nature of nonviolent love of enemies. "If we refuse to heap burning coals onto our enemies, that is, to set fire to their consciences with our own capacity for loving, they will never recognize what they are doing."[22] Douglas J. Elwood thus proposes translating Rom. 12:20, "for by doing this you will make him *burn with shame*."[23]

In some ways we may *need* enemies. On purely sociological grounds, churches would be much healthier if they had a stronger sense of their enemies. Enemies define what the church is against. They help provide its solidarity and identity.[24] Mainline and liberal churches should quit caterwauling about the growth of conservative churches and *be themselves* over against them. For the mainline and liberal churches have never been good at evangelism. They have always depended to a large measure for new members on people disillusioned with the authoritarianism and intellectual poverty of fundamentalism. Instead of watering down their liberal beliefs in order to seem conservative, churches with a relevant liberal or centrist message should flaunt it. They need those conservative churches in order to survive.

Love Transforms

Identifying enemies runs the risk, however, of freezing them in their role, and of blocking their conversion. Treating people as enemies will help create enemy-like reactions in them. Too great an emphasis on liberating the oppressed, too big a focus on success in nonviolent campaigns, too pragmatic an orientation to nonviolent struggle, can have the effect of dehumanizing the opponent in our minds and acts.

One peace activist observed,

We were committed to the idea of dialogue because it was an important part of our pacifist creed. But when people like Selective Service employees or career military officers actually responded to us, we withdrew from dialogue. We were afraid to acknowledge the hold that the ideals which we once embraced, and which they were still living by, still had on us. We were afraid to acknowledge the similarity between the war's impact on their lives and its impact on ours. Although we kept talking about our desire for dialogue, what we really wanted was to make civil disobedience demonstrations and verbal confrontations with non-pacifists into rituals affirming our own purity.[25]

Henry Mottu's experience was similar:

When I was twenty years old and went to jail [in Switzerland, for refusing the draft] . . . I more or less consciously had the tendency simply to reverse the biblical word as if Jesus would have said: Hate your neighbor (the Swiss bankers) and love your enemy (the foreign workers, the communists). But you see, you cannot simply reverse Jesus' maxim and suddenly fall in love with those who are not your people, who are *far away*, and hate the very people who used to be your neighbors. In other words, I chose to fight the battles of others, not my own battles, and I brought love of the enemies into play only to be able to hate my neighbors with a good conscience.[26]

Loving our enemies has become, in our time, the criterion of true Christian faith. It may seem impossible, yet it can be done. At no point is the inrush of divine grace so immediately and concretely perceptible as in those moments when we let go our hatred and relax into God's love. No miracle is so awesome, so necessary, and so frequent.

Ten years after the end of World War II, Hildegard and Jean Goss-Mayr met with a group of Polish Christians in Warsaw. At one point they asked, "Would you be willing to meet with Christians from West Germany? They want to ask forgiveness for what Germany did to Poland during the war and to begin to build a new relationship."

First there was silence. Then someone vehemently spoke up: "Jean and Hildegard, we love you, you are our friends, but what you are asking is impossible. Each stone of Warsaw is soaked in Polish blood! We cannot forgive!" Even after ten years, the wounds of war were just too deep.

Before the group parted for the evening, the Goss-Mayrs suggested they say the Lord's Prayer together. All joined in willingly. But at the point of praying "forgive us our sins as we forgive . . . ," the group suddenly halted their prayer.

Out of the silence, the one who had spoken most vehemently said softly, "I must say yes to you. I could no more pray the Our Father, I could no longer call myself a Christian, if I refuse to forgive. Humanly speaking, I cannot do it, but God will give us his strength!" A year and a half later, the Polish and

West German Christians met in Vienna. Friendships made at that meeting continue today.[27]

The command to love our enemies reminds us that our first task toward oppressors is pastoral: to help them recover their humanity. Quite possibly the struggle, and the oppression that gave it rise, have dehumanized the oppressed as well, causing them to demonize their enemies. It is not enough to become politically free; we must also become human. Nonviolence presents a chance for all parties to rise above their present condition and become more of what God created them to be. There is a spirit of generosity that is willing to submit to outrages and injustice, not in a cowardly fear of retaliation, but in order, if possible, to awaken God in the other's soul.

Joe Seremane, who was tortured almost to death by the South African police, said that, for him, Jesus' saying about doing kindness to one of "the least of these" (Matt. 25:40) refers to those in the security forces who have diminished the image of God in themselves. "So God will ask me how I treated the least of these"—his torturers!

As we stop dividing the world into "us" and "them," we can begin to see that the enemy is not monolithic; that some in the opposition feel conflict and guilt over their stance, and can be won by persuasion; that there is "that of God" in everyone that can be appealed to *if* opponents recognize we are not out to destroy them. There were many reasons for the fall of the Allende regime in Chile, some of them quite sinister; but one reason CIA pressure and right-wing opposition was effective is that the middle class began to believe leftist rhetoric that the bourgeois were enemies of the Marxist state and ought to be liquidated. To alienate so large a sector of the public, with no attempt at dialogue and persuasion simply invited disaster.

Loving enemies is also a way of living in expectation of miracles. No one anticipated the radical new directions inaugurated by Gorbachev in the Soviet Union or de Klerk in South Africa. No one in their wildest dreams would have predicted that the secret society that has ruled South Africa since apartheid was officially launched, the Broederbond, would turn out to be quietly directing apartheid's dismantling and trying to control the reactions of the white public.[28] People can and do change, and their change can make a fundamental difference. We must pray for our enemies, because somewhere within them is a profound longing to become synchronized with the divine Source of us both. And deep within them, that Source is trying to stir up the desire to be just.

It takes a bit of growing to recognize that our attempts at social change will never succeed until we learn to utilize the truth and strengths in our adversaries, rather than reacting to them with the brutalizing dynamics of violence. Nonviolence, at its best, seeks to activate the truth in people rather than to coerce them into *our* program. Nonviolent direct action can be misused merely to surface the worst in our opponents. We can instead help them grow toward the Light by being open to them, affirming their humanity, and praying for their transformation.

I don't know what sort of a God we have been talking about.

The caller calls in a loud voice to the Holy One at dusk.
Why? Surely the Holy One is not deaf.
He hears the delicate anklets that ring on the feet of an insect as it
  walks.

Go over and over your beads, paint weird designs on your forehead,
wear your hair matted, long, and ostentatious,
but when deep inside you there is a loaded gun, how can you have God?

Kabir[1]

15. Monitoring Our Inner Violence

I am not a very nonviolent person. I have a sharp temper that I have learned to control fairly well, and find myself indulging at times in extremely violent fantasies. I am trying to discover how a person as deeply schooled in violence as I was can begin to practice nonviolence. As I indicated earlier, one could characterize the approach I have been developing in this book as nonviolence for the violent.

There was a period in high school when I flirted with pacifism, but it quietly evaporated in seminary before the onslaught of Reinhold Niebuhr's "Christian realism," with its invective against pacifist naïveté and its theological justification of Cold War politics. I was not a full convert to Niebuhr's position, however; I missed in it sufficient stress on grace, the Holy Spirit, and miracle. I later found the work and thought of Martin Luther King, Jr., more congenial, and was involved in the civil rights struggle, the anti–Vietnam War effort, and the antinuclear movement. But it was not until I went to South Africa in 1986 that I began to commit myself to a fully nonviolent way of life.

I went to South Africa expecting to return convinced that revolutionary counterviolence was the only possible means to liberation from the apartheid system. I had gone there explicitly to put the issue of violence and nonviolence to the test. I was surprised to find myself concluding (despite the great resistance of many South Africans, black and white, to nonviolence) that on both pragmatic and theological grounds, nonviolence held out the only real hope for a just and equitable future in South Africa. I have detailed the reasons for that conclusion in *Violence and Nonviolence in South Africa* (1987) and need not repeat them here.[2]

Long before that, however, as early as the late 1970s, I had begun having a rich variety of dreams that seemed to be beckoning me toward nonviolence. For a while I merely wrote them down and ignored them. Then they became more frequent. Without my realizing it, I was being prepared in the depth of my psyche for a change that would only become manifest in South Africa years later. (No doubt the decision to go to South Africa was itself a result in part of what was percolating in my psyche.) Meanwhile, in the outer world, the growing success of nonviolent struggles in the Philippines and elsewhere raised serious doubts regarding what was left of my "Christian realism." I conceded that these events required the complete rethinking of my position.

Reaching an intellectual position favoring nonviolence as the preferred method for social struggle was not the same, however, as becoming nonviolent from the heart. What I saw in South Africa triggered a fresh barrage of dreams, and this time they would not be ignored. I have learned much from these dreams, and share something of the dream-process in the hope that doing so will help others to monitor their inner struggle with violence also.

I cite these dreams, not to expose myself, but to indicate that the transformative process is not something we initiate. God initiates it in us. We do not grit our teeth and try to become better. We simply cooperate and pay attention—in this case, by recording the dreams that God provided and reflecting on them as part of my spiritual discipline. And this is but one of the myriad ways God is prompting a new reality.

Perhaps I should say what I am not trying to do in presenting something so highly personal as dreams. I am not trying to perform a public psychoanalysis. These dreams have been selected from among hundreds of others equally important for a thorough analysis. I have benefited enormously from psychotherapy and spiritual guidance, but this recounting of dreams is the merest slice of that experience. I have purposely tried to keep interpretive comments to a minimum in order to let the dreams speak for themselves.

I am also not trying to use these dreams to prooftext the ideas in this chapter. Those ideas stand on their own feet quite well without support from my dream-life. I include these dreams, not because they establish the truth of my argument, but because they illustrate how the psyche itself is part of the battleground on which the struggle to become nonviolent must be waged. Had I access to the dreams of others, I would have preferred to use them. I present my own with some trepidation, knowing that many armchair experts in psychology find it irresistible to render a quick psychoanalysis of materials like these. I trust that those who truly understand something of the mysteries of the psyche will instead approach these artifacts of the unconscious with respect, as the chronicle of an inner process with a life and impulse of its own that one might not inaccurately call the Holy Spirit. The God who speaks through dreams more than a hundred times in Scripture still speaks through them today.[3]

The Detainee Within

In going back through seven years of dreams, I was surprised to discover that very few dreams dealt with my violence directed against others. Instead, there were repeated and elaborated dreams in which violence was directed toward *myself*. And these were *my* dreams! There were, to be sure, dreams in which I avenged myself on others: a curse on a witch that she be afflicted with a tenfold plague of what she had put on me; throwing small filing cabinets at Nazis; almost choking to death an evil figure who has abducted a shamanistic boy; murdering a librarian (no resemblance to persons living or dead!); beating up a truck driver with a shovel; slugging a drunk till he collapses; threatening to break a woman's nose if she doesn't shut up. But these (and an additional dream to be mentioned later) are the only "other-directed" violence in seven years of dreams—just over one a year among the hundreds I recorded—and even some of these should probably be interpreted as anger directed at some aspect of myself.

What I found instead were recurrent dreams of being set upon or imprisoned by evil forces. Most of these dreams no doubt reflect the experience I described earlier (p. 205) of being locked by my parents in a storeroom as punishment. In ways far beyond my awareness, the trauma of that event impressed itself on the way I see the world. Over and over, I dream that I am a captive trying to escape from incarceration. Here is just a sample of this dream-type:

> *I am in a Czechoslovakian prison camp run by Nazis. Hitler himself sees me and marks me for special punishment; I succeed in escaping. I am hidden in a barn by sympathetic local people, but am still in sight of the camp. (3/21/80)*

> *A Nazi execution squad is assigned to kill all the girls in this school. I try to save one, but they stop us, put her third in line, and say, "The only advantage you got her is to die sooner." After all have been killed, the lieutenant is ill and doesn't know why. I tell him, "It's because you have the lives of all those girls on your conscience. The other soldiers can't feel it, but you can." (12/2/80)*

> *A group of us revolutionaries are preparing a jailbreak from a Somoza prison in prerevolutionary Nicaragua. Troops are moving right into the area we had planned to escape through. (7/29/83)*—I took this to mean that there was still within me resistance to being freed.

> *Mafia types ambush a train we're on and capture us. I grab one of their guns and try to shoot my way out, but it's out of bullets, so they've got us. (7/30/83)*

*I'm in a political prison, planning a jailbreak. I have my arms full
of sawed-off bars, when I hear a biblical scholar and former colleague
say, "I understand Wink and a friend are planning a jailbreak." So I
hurriedly replace the bars.* (2/1/87)

I'm in a Russian prison camp hospital, etc. (5/12/87)

I could understand how, as compensation for having been rejected as a child,
I might develop a desire to *be* a dictator and lord it over others. But that is not
what happened. Instead, I developed an inner dictator who attempts to keep *me*
locked up in psychic detention. My own parents are never associated with these
figures, although they must surely in some sense be related. I seem, as a child,
to have identified with the captor. I was not able to rebel or challenge the
legitimacy of the moral standards by which I was punished. And because I could
not, I took those standards inside myself, where they came to be represented,
in grossly exaggerated form, by dictators, gulag apparatchiks, or Mafia hit men.

This tendency to identify with the torturer is familiar to those who work with
the "post-traumatic stress syndrome" of recently released victims of torture.
The sheer imbalance of power lends an almost godlike quality to the torturer,
toward whom the victim can feel livid hatred one moment and then, when
permission is granted to use the toilet, an almost maudlin gratitude.

Many detainees speak of an inability to remove the stare in the eyes of their
torturer from their minds. Very often it is the deep sense of hate that they
encounter in those eyes which disarms them and makes them feel worthless.
Strange as it may seem, because torture is an extremely intimate encounter,
great ambivalence exists within the thinking of the torture victim. There are
moments of identification with the torturer, especially when he presents himself
as being a reasonable, mild, understanding person.[4]

While far less brutal than the experiences reported above, that punishment
in early childhood permanently shaped my psychic structure. Whether as a pastor,
a scholar in the biblical guild, or a professor in a seminary, my deeply unconscious
way of relating has not been as one who belongs, working my way up, but as
an outsider imprisoned by the system, fighting to be free while at the same time
longing for recognition and acceptance. As I reflect back, I have always seemed
to look at life from the window of a locked storeroom. Over a long period, my
dream-process has been trying to help me lift this structure to consciousness so
that it no longer unconsciously determines my behavior. I am relieved to report
that to some degree, apparently as a direct result of going back over these dreams
and discovering their characteristic structure, the dreams of detention have abated
in the four years since I first drafted this chapter. The message I learned from
them was: Watch out, be aware, don't let this pattern continue to repeat itself

in the way you interact with figures in authority. Don't regard yourself as better or different. You are just like any other member of an organization.

All of this bears directly on my involvement in social struggles. Because of that experience of involuntary detention I tend to identify—perhaps even to overidentify—with people in actual political detention. This has been the source of my social passion, which goes back as far as I can recall. But at the same time, that experience makes me want to crush those who oppress. It blinds me with rage so that I am unable to carry on a dialogue with my opponent. On my first trip to South Africa, it prevented my speaking with any real champions of apartheid in the Afrikaner community—a fairly gross omission in a study of apartheid—because I was afraid I would give vent to my fury at their moral blindness and callousness.

That early experience also left me feeling unloved as a small child. I have ever since been driven compulsively to do good and be good so that people will love that unlovable little boy. I had learned in an unequivocal lesson that love is only meted out to the morally pure. So I would try to be morally pure with a vengeance. And one highly profitable path led through defending the oppressed, since that course allowed me to think highly of myself, win others' esteem, look down on evil oppressors, hate them with impunity, and revenge myself on those who cause suffering in the world. The fact that this life-strategy led me toward ministry and something of a messianic complex should come as a surprise to no one.

I am not suggesting that all my motives for serving God and others have been inauthentic. The call I received from God at fifteen was genuine, and has only grown progressively deeper as I have become aware of the contaminating aspects of my own personal history. God has used that wound, and the steps toward its healing, to turn me out toward others whose wounds are far more serious and evident than my own. What I have learned through all this is that God does not use us *despite* the ways we have been injured, but *through* them.[5] Without that wound I might have been simply a superficial and satisfied materialist.

Something Wants Transformation

Meanwhile, during that same seven-year period of dreaming, something new was struggling to be born in my depths, something that wants transformation. One manifestation of this new reality was a series of dreams in which virtually every person I had ever been angry with, all of whom I had consciously and sincerely forgiven, were paraded through my psyche, not only as benign, but as positively concerned for my well-being. As I went through those seven years of dreams, I was astonished at the persistence of the Holy Spirit in urging me to do a thorough housecleaning with respect to my unresolved relationships. I found it was not enough to forgive; I needed to reestablish fellowship where possible.

In one dream, *My dad drives up to our house in an old station wagon crammed with boxes. I laugh, look inside the car, and see that several of the boxes are moving. I ask if he has people in them. "No," he says, and they stop. I say, "So you're moving some of your things up?" He says, "Is that OK? I assumed it was OK to live with you." I say, "Well, we'll at least be here over the hot months of summer." (I'm a little reluctant to take him in year-round.)* (8/14/86)

As a way of exploring the dream further I wrote out a dialogue with Dad (who had died seven years earlier). In it I comment, "I see you are uncharacteristically smiling. Maybe heaven has straightened you out." I tell him what I never dared say to him during his lifetime, even as a mature adult: "You were so brutal—I still carry that wound from you." He responds, "Heaven has sent me to you. You need to take me in, they said, though I know it's hard for you. But I'm one of your realities. Wouldn't you like to replace the old me with the heavenly, smiling me?" He's not sure what's in the boxes in his car. "Maybe they're angels, and quit moving just because you seemed frightened." And as to my reluctance to have him live with us, "Remember, it's your house. You're in charge here."

That dream, in August 1986, asked something of me that I did not, in fact, deliver. I made no attempt, even in the dialogue, to welcome him in. Then, almost a year later, as I was reviewing my dreams, I misread a sentence as if it read, "I would like to be able to love *Dad* again." I was physically jolted by my misreading. I had tremendous resistance to loving Dad. To do so would be to open up once again all that pain, and then to have to offer it up for healing. And by now I had settled comfortably into a pattern of maligning him. It was convenient to slough off responsibility for my life by blaming him. To love Dad would mean the wrench of finally giving up all that. And it also might mean giving up the inner dictators and their concentration camps, from which I was always trying to escape. After all, those dictators are helping me maintain that old psychic structure. They even represent to a degree my *resistance* to liberation.[6] After receiving that insight, the dreams of incarceration virtually stopped.

God, in short, seems to be trying, against my stubborn reluctance, to make a more whole person out of me.

In this process taking place within my psyche, I realize that the biblical struggle against the Powers is literally being enacted in me by God. According to the gospel, God has, through the event of Jesus, freed us from every Power that could separate us from the love of God (Rom. 8:31-39). If, then, we are not yet free, it is either because we are unaware of our bondage, or because we think we are benefiting in some way from continuing to allow a Power other than God to have sovereignty over us. Since God has broken their power definitively, the Powers now have only such power over us as we continue to allow them. But pulling out all their flaming darts can be the work of a lifetime, and meanwhile we are continually being struck by new darts. I am appalled at how many years I have been actively and consciously grappling with my own childhood experience, without having yet fully claimed the freedom in which I have been established by God. The initiative for my liberation, however, continues to come from God, gently and persuasively, through the intersection of my inner life of dreaming and praying and the outer struggle for justice. And each increment of liberation releases new power for living.

But something in my dream-life not only wants me transformed, it wants nonviolence.

Something Wants Nonviolence

During this same period I was receiving another kind of nudge from God through the unconscious: a virtual barrage of dreams apparently bidding me toward nonviolence. Please do not mistake this dream process going on within me as merely private, individual, or unusual. That would invalidate the purpose of this chapter. We must ask, instead, what is the meaning of my having this series of dreams, almost all of them before I was fully committed to nonviolence, and well before I contemplated writing on that theme? And what is the relationship between these dreams and the meteoric increase of nonviolent actions around the globe? Consciously or unconsciously, one lives not only one's life, but the life of one's time.[7] We need to recognize that the inner psychic world is just as much a collective, shared reality as the outer world of nature and society. The concept of a collective unconscious leads us to investigate how the unconscious is responding to the quality of the times in a given historical moment. Are our dreams, for example, to some degree facets of a larger, mass dream that is beginning to happen in the world? And if so, what is this mass dream telling us?[8] To put it another way, when God wants to initiate a new movement in history, God does not intervene directly, but sends us dreams and visions that can, if attended to, initiate the process. We see this repeatedly in Scripture. What then does it mean that this series of dreams came to me? To whom else are they coming? Are they coming to you?

In one of the earliest of these dreams about nonviolence (2/2/80), *I am in a line of cars at the gas station. I leave my car to talk to an attendant, and the driver behind mine, impatient, starts pushing my car, which is in parking gear. I shout, "Stop!" and run at him. He jumps out. I grab his thumbs and break one all the way off.* (This is the other violent dream I mentioned.) *In remorse and disgust I realize that this is not the way. Instead, I am given a koan to recite to him, and ask him to recite it with me: "Rejoice! Respond evenhandedly. The Lord is in his holy temple."*

Within the next year there was a series of dreams that simply presented nonviolence as a creative option. In one I am discussing nonviolence with a respected Quaker. In another we are doing guerrilla theater in Grand Central Station. In the third we are protesting at a grocery store in Harlem that charges the poor exorbitant prices (in this case, we are filling grocery baskets and then abandoning them at checkout counters). In a fourth,

A construction worker comes to my house, I offer him water, and am washing the mud off my hands when he says, "Whatever happened to that glass of water?" I blow up at him— he's already come in, gotten his own glass, and is heading for the sink. I say, "No, you can't have any, not after that crack. Here I offer you water and you can't even wait till I get the mud off my hands." He fills his glass and says, "In the Near East, they respond to rudeness with extra politeness. Instead of blowing up you should have shamed me with politeness. That's a more creative response."

Frequently in subsequent years the dreams would involve my teaching nonviolence in Bible study groups, usually including role plays of nonviolent actions or preparing for actual demonstrations. How seriously I was prepared to take these dreams is reflected in this one from 1984:

A guy in the swimming pool is announced as the next antiwar speaker. He's going to talk about the pathology of war. I say, "Sometime I'd like to talk to you about the pathology of societies." He is instantly interested. As he begins to talk about it I swim off.

Since our trip to South Africa in 1986, dreams dealing with nonviolence have greatly escalated in number. God, I noted one day in my journal, is determined to teach me nonviolence. This one I dreamed the night we left South Africa in 1986 after our first visit there:

I'm in Cape Town, visiting. A black man is leading us into a cave. He has on successive nights led us deeper and deeper into it. At a juncture he enters a small room like a phone booth. He has to decide whether to go on. He gets a clear message from God to do so. We continue toward a section where he wants to go left but knows that to the right are some evil people. We both have strong flashlights, and shine them to the right. We know who's there. They will require nonviolent confrontation before we can continue. But there is no question of our leader's power to prevail. He is a kind of black messiah. (4/23/86)

In another dream, *I am angrily debating with a student who charges that nonviolence is impractical. An esteemed friend of mine irenically looks on, agreeing with all I'd said. Afterward I realize I could have made all these points as irenically as my friend.*

Another dream had a droll humor: *One hundred hippies, trained in nonviolence, win a freedom award given by the state.* In another, *I am intervening between two parties in a civil war, suggesting that they mutually agree that both sides have fought valiantly, both have endured great losses, that a count of the dead on each side would not determine the victor since each life was of infinite value, and that each side should lay down its arms without requiring the other's capitulation.*

This last dream suggests that something was moving within me to heal an old split—a civil war—in my soul. Other dreams seemed to press toward forgiveness and reconciliation within. In one,

Two men, who are part of a group of rednecks, are angry with me. I challenge them to forgive me before the rest of their group. They get in their cars and drive around the house, and just before completing one circuit, the main guy pulls into the center, to the house, and gets out and says, "OK, it takes more courage to forgive than to go on being angry." His buddy goes along with him. We all shake hands. The second guy says, "Yeah, I realized you don't have to like someone to love him." I'm really grateful and say so.

In dialoguing later in my dream-log with these "rednecks," I asked them why they were mad at me. They replied, "Because you don't let us do any of the things we think are fun—go out, drink it up, fish, shoot, hunt, sit and watch the water or sunset, go for a good swim, work on the car. We *enjoy* that." I came to realize that these rednecks represented a necessary compensatory element within me. Just when I would be tightening the screws of commitment to God, these rednecks would emerge, trying to hold on to some of the simple joys that I greatly need to savor in order to avoid workaholism and burnout.

I omit a great many other dreams that also seemed to be teaching me nonviolence, but one stands out in particular, because it hinted at one of the most important lessons my dreams have begun to teach me.

> *Admiral Zumwalt has been invited to speak to the Fellowship of*
> *Reconciliation [a leading peace group] about peace and disarmament.*
> *The idea was to expose him to F.O.R. ideas by means of the dialogue*
> *that would ensue. He shows up in the most bizarre costume*
> *imaginable—big earrings, stuff on his hair (the details escaped me).*
> *But we keep letting others speak before him, for two or three hours, so*
> *he has to listen to a different message than he normally hears.*

The Creative Role of Aggression

In the previous dream, no one was listening to Admiral Zumwalt (a German pun: "to Walter"). Subsequent dreams taught me that I dismissed his wisdom at my own peril. The attention-getter was this one:

> *I am in a high mountain fortress, totally surrounded by enemy*
> *troops, in the eighteenth century. I am encouraging a young redcoat*
> *not to stick his head over the battlements, because the other side has*
> *excellent marksmen. Yet I notice that senior redcoats on our side are*
> *standing in full view on the battlements, not even peering from the*
> *safety of the breastworks.*
> *I bring up the virtues of nonviolence and refer to Jesus' teaching on*
> *it. A Scotsman with a heavy brogue says to me, "You know that's*
> *bullshit, don't you?" I throw back at him the fact that it's Scripture.*

This dream came during the time when I was preparing *Violence and Nonviolence in South Africa* for publication. In it I was encouraging others to take risks I was not currently required to take. This dream spoke, no doubt, my own misgivings about urging others to risk what I was not risking comparably, and also residual skepticism about the possibilities of success for nonviolence as a strategy and way of life in South Africa. (In the dream I appealed to the authority of Scripture somewhat lamely, rather than answering with genuine arguments.)

But the dream also seemed to reflect my inner state. These senior redcoats deliberately exposed themselves to the enemy, while I was ducking down behind my defenses. They belonged to a period when warfare was fought as a matter of honor. And Scotsmen were renowned fighters. These soldiers represent my need to be fearless, to stand up and expose myself to fire, to be a warrior of the spirit and not use nonviolence as a cover for cowardice and inaction. I need to learn from this Scotsman how to be a spiritual warrior.

Many people in the peace movement are so caught up in dualistic thinking that they want to obliterate all references to military imagery and warfare in hymns, metaphors, and even the Bible. I am sympathetic with this tendency, yet suspicious of it. There are aspects of life that are inescapably a form of warfare. Do we want our lymphocytes to stop attacking cancer cells in our bodies? It is amazing to see in the American Cancer Society's film *The Cell* how on bumping up against a defective cell, a lymphocyte actually backs off, shapes itself into an arrow, and drives itself at the suspect cell until it penetrates its core, exploding the cell and giving its own life in the process. We *can* move to forms of national defense based on nonviolence, as Gene Sharp and others have proposed.[9] We *can* develop international peace brigades prepared to step into any conflict and interpose their bodies between combatants, as has already been done on a small scale in Nicaragua and Guatemala. We *can* use the U.N. peacekeeping forces more effectively than we have, though they have been relatively successful in a number of cases in defusing overt hostilities. People committed to nonviolence can be the lymphocytes of society, offering their lives to prevent armed warfare.

But they must do so *militantly*. What makes me admire the people of Greenpeace so much is their courage: lashing themselves to the top of polluting smokestacks for days at a time; driving their rubber skiffs under the falling barrels of poisonous wastes being dumped at sea; sailing ships into the zone of nuclear tests in the Pacific Ocean. These people are warriors. They do not have about them the drained, bloodless appearance of those who have curbed their aggressions solely by repressing the very juices of life. They would appear to have learned something applicable to nonviolent struggle from Admiral Zumwalt and the Scotsman.

For years nonviolence has been falsely caricatured as anemic, chickenhearted, and passionless, and there have been just enough proponents of it who acted this way to keep the caricature alive. We need to be able to bring anger, power, passion, and an iron intransigence to our nonviolence. Our inner violence, transformed, becomes an indispensable aggressiveness, a sense of strength, that prevents us from blowing our stacks out of a sense of powerlessness or impotence. (I have learned to do this with police officers who are arresting me; I am now trying to transfer this behavior to my dealings with store clerks when I go to return something!) When we fully know from within that we will not back down, we no longer have to bluster and fume. As Brewster Beach pointed out to me, *a person who is well defended does not need to be defensive.* My Scotsman was right. Any nonviolence that hides behind the breastworks instead of full-bloodedly facing the enemy *is* "bullshit."

It may be that the ancient archetype of the warrior can be sublimated or transformed into the image of the spiritual warrior. There is a profound longing and need for the courage, camaraderie, selflessness, heroism, service, and transcendence that many men have known only through warfare. War may be for some men the closest thing to what childbirth is for women: an initiation into the powers of life and death. In war, one enters the mythical realm and encounters the gods; such an experience can be exalting as well as terrible. The challenge before us today is not to obliterate the warrior mentality (which would only drive it deeper into the unconscious, where it would work to produce more wars), but to own, celebrate, and honor it, and channel its expression into nonviolent struggles against the *real* threats to human survival today: starvation, pollution, despotism, racism, economic greed.[10]

Nor is warrior imagery all masculine. Women need to express their strength and aggressive qualities, just as men need to learn to feel, to be present, to be attentive to process. Both women and men need to be able to experience the spiritual warrior: men, because this can be a way of sublimating the warrior archetype; women, because they need to claim their power. There is great energy in feminine warrior images, of which Joan of Arc is perhaps the best known, and Helen Caldicott a fine contemporary example. Conversely, both men and women need to be able to say, like Mary, "Let it be with me according to your word" (Luke 1:38).

I must confess to some ambivalence about the warrior image, however. It seems essential to struggles for justice. But it is hazardous, for life is breathed into it by Mars. Mars is a very real Power in the life of the unconscious and in the affairs of nations.[11] His consort is Venus, goddess of love, who presided over the debauchery in the Roman military camps.[12] Nonviolence needs the tough, aggressive power of Mars, and the passionate, erotic power of Venus, to be complete. But Mars and Venus are androcratic gods; they are not eternal and timeless archetypes, but the highly contingent artifacts of violent, patriarchal, empire-building societies. They are, to be sure, deep in the unconscious of all of us, but can they be sublimated and bent to peaceful ends, or must they rather be rooted out? I am drawn to the image of the spiritual warrior in part because it has a certain appeal to men. I am concerned lest the peace movement so adopt "feminine" values that men find themselves excluded. This is a genuine hazard; it has long since happened to many churches. Yet I am constrained by Adolf Harnack's sober warning:

> If the forms of the military estate are transferred to the higher religions, it appears that what is warlike is turned around and changed into its strict opposite or transformed into a mere symbol. But the form has its own logic and its necessary consequences. At first unnoticeably, but soon ever more clearly, the warlike element which was accepted as a symbol ushers in the reality itself, and the "spiritual weapons of knighthood" become carnal. Even where the process does not go so far, a warlike mood enters which threatens the norm of gentleness and peace.[13]

But the "spiritual warriors" to whom Harnack alludes never took an oath of nonviolence. The just war theory under which they enlisted was an open invitation to misuse, and the Knights Templars and others exploited it to the limit. We must regard it as axiomatic, then, that the spiritual warrior of today must be committed to nonviolence. And if the image of the spiritual warrior issues in violence, it must be abandoned.

Five months after the Scotsman dream, the warrior theme recurred:

I'm impressed that the Guild for Psychological Studies [the group that has mentored me in the approach to Bible study that I use] *has been able to secure, for discussion of the gospel teaching on nonviolence, a group of very high military brass.* (4/3/87)

I had in fact initiated a conversation on peace issues with a group of "very high army brass" from the Pentagon the preceding fall. It was a tense two-and-a-half hours, but toward the end, after they had "circled their wagons," as one of them put it, we began to hear each other a bit. I had longed at the time for further occasions for such conversation, primarily in order to convert them to my position. I would still cherish such an opportunity, but now I would hope to be able to appreciate more than before what it means for them to be warriors, to defend the nation, and to regard that as a vocation. Perhaps, too, if they sensed my respect, and could see in me a fellow warrior, they might not have to circle their wagons so tightly. And what a contribution to nonviolent struggles it would make if we could learn from them the discipline, the toughness, and the willingness to face death for a higher cause that characterize the soldier!

There is also a masochistic element in Christian tradition and among some nonviolent activists that must be carefully discerned and filtered out. In an early dream,

*Seven of us plan to drink poison as a nonviolent protest. My eleven-
year-old daughter says nonchalantly that she's not sure she wants to be
a part of it. I assure her she's not.* In another, more recently, *Two
groups are in conflict. We feel we are righteous and the others evil.
They have all the power. After some struggle our leader surprises and
horrifies us by capitulating and agreeing to serve the other group. We
do surrender, and over time the opponents are unable to do anything
but become increasingly like us.*

Nothing in my psyche at the time of the earlier dream justified "drinking
poison." In fact, I wonder if the dream merely reflected the lengths my ego
was prepared to go in trying to escape some inner conflict (I was not, and have
never been, suicidal). As for the capitulation of our leader, it is true, as I had
already written at the time of this dream in chapter 10 above, that opposition
tends to turn us into what we oppose. But in this dream the opponent is turned
into us, and we are capitulators. No, something smells of passivity, a lack of
aggressive strength. A few weeks later I dreamed this: *The nonviolent woman
inside me just wants to scream.* I don't think she wants to be in a man who just
rolls over and plays dead in the face of opposition.

A week later her protest was answered by this dream:

*Secretary of State George Shultz and former National Security
Adviser Zbigniew Brzezinski are giving speeches at a conference on
peace, but I won't go because I figure it will just be pro-peace
propaganda without substance.*

I did not care for the politics of either of these men, and believed at the time
that the dream was pretty accurate in its judgment, but as inner aspects of myself
these politicians seem to represent power, authority, and a warlike nature. I see
myself in the dream as a true peacemaker, and will have nothing to do with
them. But I have to confess that I see them as weighty figures with strength of
carriage. They can't be pushed around. Martin Luther King, Jr., had this same
quality. His mere presence could cow opponents, simply by the strength of his
resolution and moral courage. It would serve me well to be able to have some
of that weightiness. In this dream, loving enemies means learning to find the
qualities I need in myself from figures otherwise highly distasteful or repellent
to me. (And it was George Shultz, after all, who led the way to the Intermediate
Ballistics Missile Treaty that I was so sure he was not seriously pursuing.)

Becoming nonviolent from the heart does not, then, mean abandoning or
repressing one's aggressiveness entirely. We will never get rid of the opposites

within us; we can only continually lift them up for transformation. We have to own our violence and learn to value it. As Brian Willson put it, "I am a violent person. I'm educated and trained in the United States. I don't have any particular upbringing in nonviolence; it's new for me. Even though I believe in nonviolence and am committed to it, I'm not nonviolent in nature. I had to prepare myself; I had to think a lot about loving people, about loving the police, the people in the military."[14] Nonviolence is the spiritualization of violence, the overcoming of violent desire. It is not the mere absence of violence, but an effort to transcend, rather than commit, violence.[15]

Our psyches, like it or not, feed on the whole range of human emotions. As Brewster Beach commented to me, some of us may need to meditate on murder and violence in order that we *not* act them out.[16] Popular religion has done an immense disservice by teaching that even to think a sin is to commit it. This is not necessarily the case.[17] Imagination can be the seedbed of behavior, but it can also be an alternative to behavior. Jung speaks somewhere of the transformation of instinct through imagination. Imagination permits us to turn inward, where the instinctual act is inhibited by being taken up in fantasy. This process of reflection makes possible a certain degree of freedom from outward compulsion. When you imagine something, you have already done it, imaginatively; now it is not necessary to do it in actual fact. Fantasy is not only a substitute for behavior; it can also be itself a form of behavior. Often the fantasy is more enjoyable than acting it out anyway, because it is free of consequences in the outer world. As someone said, "A psychic murder a day keeps neurosis away." When I was a teenager a friend continually kept me out of trouble by jokingly responding to my hairbrained schemes, "Let's don't, and say we did."

Perhaps then some of us may need to feel our murderous rage, and fantasize acting it out, so that we can imagine also the consequences, and repent of our folly—all without lifting a finger. Then we can no longer deceive ourselves about who we are—murderous people—and can maintain a more realistic and less dishonest view of ourselves. Then perhaps also we could recognize the personal, projected anger that is triggered by situations of social oppression, so that we are free to maintain an *objective fury* at evil, and draw on all the blessed energy of the violent side of our natures. What a relief it would be to dwell in Christian communities where we acknowledged our shadows in a healthy acceptance of ourselves as containers of all the opposites!

It may prove beneficial to be forced to face, daily, the humiliating fact that some of us are no less violent than those whose policies we oppose. Maybe then we can love them, since we are no better, and avoid the self-righteousness that ends all dialogue. In preparing for the nonviolent campaign that brought down Marcos in the Philippines, the trainees analyzed the violence that was in the structure and in the dictator. But they also faced the Marcos within, for unless they each tore the dictator out of their own hearts, they realized, nothing would change.[18]

We also need to be in touch with our inner violence because our very attempts at nonviolence *create* violence, both outer and inner. Nonviolent direct action elicits violence; it unmasks the structural violence of an unjust system and forces the system to repent or attack. "Do not think that I have come to bring peace to the earth; I have not come to bring peace, but a sword" (Matt. 10:34). Increased use of nonviolence will not mean a gradual decrease of the amount of conflict and violence in the world. The goal of nonviolence is not tranquillity but God's domination-free order, of which tranquillity is merely a by-product. As long as injustice, inequality of opportunity, and hatred exist, we are obligated to *initiate conflict* in order, if possible, to eradicate it. We cannot be content with reactive nonviolence; it must be proactive, aggressive, militant.

Nonviolent action triggers our own latent inner violence as well. We must learn to assume, as second nature, that this activation of our inner violence is inevitable, and monitor it as it arises. Perhaps we cannot eradicate our violence, but only restrain it, and learn to transmute its energies into nonviolence.[19]

Jesus does not make nonviolence a new law, but a new option. Violence also is still an option, and unless we have faced that option, nonviolence will surely be the refuge of cowards. You cannot give up what you do not have. If you have not claimed your violence as a strength, as a God-given gift, you cannot freely renounce it. A person who *has* to be nonviolent is not yet free.

Nonviolence is clearly the way of Jesus. But we need to offer our violence to God as well, though not in the manner of those soldiers who allegedly kept their sword hands out of the water when they were baptized. Our violence must go "under the waters" so that the new synthesis, the third way, manifests not only our love but also our shadow.[20] We are not paragons of peaceableness, but wounded, violent, frightened people trying to become human. We are not wan saints incapable of evil, but plain people clad in both light and dark, under the banner of love, seeking to be spiritual warriors.

Jesus' third way shows us the path forward: neither repressing our violence, nor acting it out, but letting it be the fuel by which God empowers us to struggle for the nonviolent future.

• • •

I need to add a sobering and humiliating postscript to this discussion. About three months after I had finished writing a book about nonviolence in South Africa, and having already had most of the dreams detailed here, I was walking down a New York City street around 9:30 at night (this is not a dream; it actually happened). My mind was full of anxiety; I had been mugged once two blocks over, and I was nervously looking around. Five or six young kids, around twelve years old I thought, were goofing off on the sidewalk as I drew near. One, seeing me coming, began to feign blindness and stumbled into my path, pinching at my arm. I laughed a hard, shaky laugh and pinched him back, harder. He came after me from behind, still a bit playful (the rest were simply watching and not at all threatening; in fact some called him back), and jerked at my coat. I wheeled and slugged him in the chest with the back of my fist. He winced and said, quietly, "He's not very nice," and returned to his group.

I was shocked at my overreaction, and realized that my violence came straight out of fear. He was right; I wasn't very nice. In that context (a dark street on the edge of a slum) he was foolish to behave as he did. But I was profoundly chagrined that my nonviolence went no deeper than that.

This experience reminded me how little nonviolence has to do with ideas or mere tactics. It is, finally, a way of life, a set of behaviors. And nothing is so hard to change as habitual behavior. Nonviolence is not, then, the task of a season, but of a lifetime.

We who must die demand a miracle.
How could the Eternal do a temporal act,
The Infinite become a finite fact?
Nothing can save us that is possible:
We who must die demand a miracle.

W. H. Auden,
"For the Time Being"[1]

16. Prayer and the Powers

We are not easily reduced to prayer. We who grope toward praying today are like a city gutted by fire. The struggle against injustice has exacted from us an awful cost. In a similar period with similar struggles, Camus wrote, "There is merely bad luck in not being loved; there is tragedy in not loving. All of us, today, are dying of this tragedy. For violence and hatred dry up the heart itself; the long fight for justice exhausts the love that nevertheless gave birth to it. In the clamor in which we live, love is impossible and justice does not suffice."[2]

We have in our own experience discovered the mystery of the Beast of the abyss: He can allow the righteous to destroy him because he is virtually assured that in so doing they will be changed into his likeness.

I will not attempt to make a case for the importance of prayer. Those who do not believe in its efficacy simply illustrate the effectiveness of the Powers in diminishing our humanity. There are few rational objections to praying that carry any force, since they are all spin-offs from a particular worldview. It is our worldview that permits or forbids prayer, and no one arrives at a worldview on wholly rational grounds.

Those who pray do so not because they believe certain intellectual propositions about the value of prayer, but simply because the struggle to be human in the face of suprahuman Powers requires it. The act of praying is itself one of the indispensable means by which we engage the Powers. It is, in fact, that engagement at its most fundamental level, where their secret spell over us is broken and we are reestablished in a bit more of that freedom which is our birthright and potential.

Prayer is never a private act. It may be the interior battlefield where the decisive victory is first won, before engagement in the outer world is even attempted. If we have not undergone that inner liberation, whereby the individual strands of the nets in which we are caught are severed, one by one, our activism may merely reflect one or another counterideology of some counter-Power. We may simply be caught up in a new collective passion, and fail to discover the transcendent possibilities of God pressing for realization here and now. Unprotected by prayer, our social activism runs the danger of becoming self-justifying good works, as our inner resources atrophy, the wells of love run dry, and we are slowly changed into the likeness of the Beast.

The kind of prayer of which I speak may or may not involve regular regimens, may or may not be sacramental, may or may not be contemplative, may or may not take traditional religious forms. It is in any case not a religious practice externally imposed, but an existential struggle against the "impossible," against an antihuman collective atmosphere, against images of worth and value that stunt and wither full human life.

Prayer, in short, is the field-hospital in which the diseased spirituality that we have contracted from the Powers can most directly be diagnosed and treated.

I will not attempt a comprehensive discussion of prayer. Others far wiser and more experienced have done so already. I want to focus on only one aspect of prayer, almost universally ignored: the role of the Powers in intercessory prayer. We shall examine (1) the role of intercessors in creating a desirable future, (2) the initiative God takes in praying in us, (3) the capacity of the Powers to frustrate God's answering our prayers, and (4) prayer and the problem of evil.

History Belongs to the Intercessors

Intercession is spiritual defiance of what is, in the name of what God has promised. Intercession visualizes an alternative future to the one apparently fated by the momentum of current contradictory forces. It infuses the air of a time yet to be into the suffocating atmosphere of the present. Those who have made peace with injustice, who receive their identity from alienated role-definitions, and who benefit economically from social inequities, are not likely to be such intercessors.

There is a marvelous image of intercession in the Book of Revelation. Jesus Christ, the Lion of the tribe of Judah, the Lamb standing though slain—this Lion in sheep's clothing—is opening one by one the seals on the Scroll of Destiny (Revelation 5–8). As he opens the first four seals, the sorry spectacle of human violence is laid bare: the endless cycle of conquest, civil war, famine, and death, depicted by the Four Horsemen. When the fifth seal is broken, the martyred witnesses under the altar cry out: "How long, O Lord? Avenge our blood!" And when the sixth seal is opened, the whole creation lurches and totters in agonized anticipation of God's wrath. Now, just before the seventh seal is opened, those who will be saved are marked off for the new "passover" of the angel of death and destruction. Everything is now in readiness. We await the final unrolling of the Scroll. Toward this climax the whole cycle of the ages has turned.

> Now when the Lamb broke the seventh seal, there was silence in heaven for about half an hour. I saw the seven angels who stand in the presence of God: they were given seven trumpets.
> Another angel came and stood at the altar, holding a golden censer. He was given much incense to offer with the prayers of all God's people on the golden altar in front of the throne, and the smoke of the incense from the angel's hand went up before God with his people's prayers. The angel took the censer, filled it with fire from the altar, and threw it down on the earth; and there came peals of thunder, lightning-flashes, and an earthquake. (Rev. 8:1-5, REB)

Heaven itself falls silent. The heavenly hosts and celestial spheres suspend their ceaseless singing so that the prayers of the saints on earth can be heard. The seven angels of destiny cannot blow the signal of the next times to be until an eighth angel gathers these prayers—prayers for justice, vindication, and victory—and mingles them with incense upon the altar. Silently they rise to the nostrils of God. Then from the same altar the angel fills the same censer with fiery coals and hurls them upon the earth. The earth is convulsed. The silence is shattered. The heavenly liturgy is complete. Now the seven angels who have the seven trumpets make ready to blow.

This scene reverses the usual unrolling of fate, where heavenly decisions are acted out on earth. Human beings have intervened in the heavenly liturgy. The uninterrupted flow of consequences is dammed for a moment. New alternatives become feasible. The unexpected becomes suddenly possible, because people on earth have invoked heaven, the home of the possibles, and have been heard. What happens next happens because people prayed.[3]

The message is clear: *history belongs to the intercessors, who believe the future into being.* This is not simply a religious statement. It is as true of communists or capitalists or anarchists as it is of Christians. The future belongs to whoever can envision in the manifold of its potentials a new and desirable possibility, which faith then fixes upon as inevitable.

This is the politics of hope. Hope envisages its future and then acts as if that future is now irresistible, thus helping to create the reality for which it longs. The future is not closed. There are fields of forces whose interactions are somewhat predictable. But *how* they will interact is not. Even a small number of people, firmly committed to the new inevitability on which they have fixed their imaginations, can decisively affect the shape the future takes. These shapers of the future are the intercessors, who call out of the future the longed-for new present. In the New Testament, the name and texture and aura of that future is God's domination-free order, the reign of God.

As a result of the intercessions of God's people, the seven angels trumpet calamity: hail and fire rain down, mixed with blood, and burn up a third of the earth and trees and grass; the sea becomes blood, and a third of its creatures die; a third of the fresh waters become bitter with wormwood; a third of the heaven's light is darkened—and these are but the first of the woes to fall on humanity (8:7-13).

John is referring here explicitly to the Domination System currently embodied in the Roman Empire. "The kingdom of the world (*kosmos*)" (11:15) for him is not a geographical or planetary term. It refers to the alienated and alienating reality that seduces humanity into idolatry: the worship of political power as divine. The Roman Empire had made itself the highest value and the ultimate concern, arrogating to itself the place of God. Whether it be the Pax Romana or the Pax Britannica or the Pax Americana, empires can maintain cohesion across racial, ethnic, linguistic, and national lines only by creating a bogus solidarity. This they achieve by demanding the worship of the spirituality of empire.

The Romans were a model of lucidity on this point. They did not, at least during the New Testament period, worship the seated emperor, but only his "genius." This Latin term does not refer to the emperor's intellect but to his inspiration, the daemon or god or spirituality that animated the incumbent ruler by virtue of his being incumbent.[4] His "genius" is the totality of impersonal power located in an office of surpassing might.

The British, for their part, spoke reverentially of their empire as a holy burden and obligation, a vocation to carry Anglo-Saxon light to a darkened world. Americans, however, had rebelled against the British Empire and its spirituality. We could not therefore admit to having an empire; and concurrently, the nature of empire had shifted from political sovereignty to economic hegemony. So when, after World War II, we assumed the burden of empire, we found a scapegoat—communism—against which we would organize and police the world. Empire could thus appear to have been thrust upon us to save the world. This anticommunist crusade and its attendant Cold War policies masked the spirit of empire from no one except Americans themselves.

That spirituality—which included as one of its chief tenets the denial that it exists—has literally threatened to rain hail and fire mingled with blood to burn up the Soviet third of the earth and trees and grass and turn the seas to blood and fresh water to radioactive wormwood,[5] and darken a third of the heavens— all to preserve the privileged position of the richest nation on the face of the earth. And they, for their part, were fully prepared to return the compliment.

Empires are "unnatural" systems. They cannot exist for a moment without the spiritual undergirding of a persuasive ideology. No wonder John was exiled to Patmos by the Powers. A seer whose vision cuts through the atmospherics of imperial legitimation is a far worse threat than armed revolutionaries who accept the ideology of domination and merely desire it for themselves. Churches, which continually complain about their powerlessness to induce change, are in fact in a privileged position to use the most powerful weapon of all: the power to delegitimate. But it is a spiritual power, spiritually discerned and spiritually exercised. It needs intercessors, who believe the future into being.

If the future is thus open, if the heavenly hosts must be silenced so that God can listen to the prayers of the saints and act accordingly, then we are no longer dealing with the unchanging, immutable God of Stoic metaphysics. Before that unchangeable God, whose whole will was fixed from all eternity, intercession is ridiculous. There is no place for intercession with a God whose will is incapable of change. What Christians have too long worshiped is the God of Stoicism, to whose immutable will we can only surrender ourselves, conforming our wills to the unchangeable will of deity.

Not so with biblical prayer. Scripture calls us into the presence of Yahweh of Hosts, who chooses circuitous paths in the desert and whose ways are subject to change without notice. This is a God who works with us and for us, to make and keep human life humane. And what God does depends on the intercessions of those who care enough to try to shape a future more humane than the present. Faith operative through prayer is, in the words of Mircea Eliade, "absolute emancipation from any kind of natural 'law' and hence the highest freedom" that one can imagine. "freedom to intervene even in the ontological constitution of the universe."[6]

The fawning etiquette of unctuous prayer is utterly foreign to the Bible. Biblical prayer is impertinent, persistent, shameless, indecorous. It is more like haggling in an oriental bazaar than the polite monologues of the churches.

When Abraham discovers that Yahweh is about to destroy Sodom, where his nephew Lot lives with his wife and two daughters, Abraham blocks God's path: "Suppose there are fifty righteous within the city; will you then sweep away the place and not forgive it for the fifty righteous who are in it? Far be it from you to do such a thing . . . ! Shall not the Judge of all the earth do what is just?" When God agrees to spare Sodom if there are fifty, Abraham presses the issue: Would you spare the city if there were forty? Thirty? Twenty? Ten? God agrees, and though ten are not found there, God saves Lot's family, though they are but four (Genesis 18). Moral: it pays to haggle with God.

Martin Luther understood this aspect of prayer well: "Our Lord God could not but hear me; I threw the sack down before his door. I rubbed God's ear with all his promises about hearing prayer."[7]

Scripture is full of this motif of spirited give-and-take with God. When Israel, impatient from waiting forty days for Moses to return from Sinai, makes the golden calf, God says to Moses: You'd better get down there. Israel has made a golden calf, and I'm fed up with dealing with them. "I have seen this people, how stiff-necked they are. Now let me alone, so that my wrath may burn hot against them and I may consume them; and of you I will make a great nation" (Exod. 32:9-10).

Moses refuses to let God destroy Israel: Yahweh, why should your wrath blaze out against this people of yours whom you brought out of the land of Egypt with arm outstretched and mighty hand? Why let the Egyptians say, "Ah, it was in treachery that he brought them out, to do them to death in the mountains and wipe them off the face of the earth"? Leave your burning wrath; repent and do not bring this evil on your people.

And we read, "The Lord repented of the evil which he thought to do to his people." Moses made Yahweh repent (Exod. 32:14, RSV)!

Or think of Jacob's wrestling with the angel until it blessed him, or of Jonah's sulking over God's change of heart about Nineveh. Of the latter, Ernst Bloch notes "*the amazement of the prophet Jonah*, who failed to grasp the difference between Cassandra and himself. For Jonah had indeed been sent to inform Nineveh of its destruction after forty days, but when the city did penance and the evil did not occur, he was wrongly but exceedingly displeased (Jonah 4,1)— as if he had told an untruth to the people of Nineveh, whereas it was the change in them that had caused a change in Yahweh (Jer. 18, 7f.; 26, 3 and 19)."[8]

Nor is this theme confined to the Hebrew Scriptures. We see it in Jesus' parables of the Persistent Widow and the Friend who Came at Midnight, both examples of how we are to hammer away in prayer until a breakthrough comes (Luke 18:1-8; 11:5-13). Thus Rudolf Bultmann is speaking not only for Jesus for but the whole Bible when he says, "Prayer is not to bring the petitioner's will into submission to the unchanging will of God, but prayer is to move God to do something which He otherwise would not do."[9]

No doubt our intercessions sometimes change us as we open ourselves to new possibilities we had not guessed. No doubt our prayers to God reflect back upon us as a divine command to become the answer to our prayer. But if we are to take the biblical understanding seriously at all, intercession is more than that. It changes the world and it changes what is possible to God. It creates an island of relative freedom in a world gripped by an unholy necessity. A new force field appears that hitherto was only potential. The entire configuration changes as the result of the change of a single part. An aperture opens in the praying person, permitting God to act without violating human freedom. The change in even one person thus changes what God can thereby do in that world.

"Wherever we cast our eye," wrote Karl Barth, "the dynamite is prepared and ready to explode. . . . For impossibility is, as such, nigh at hand, ready at our elbow, possible. Impossibility presses upon us, breaks over us, is indeed already present. Impossibility is more possible than everything which we hold to be possible."[10] Miracle is just a word we use for the things the Powers have deluded us into thinking that God is unable to do.

"I believe in a world," exclaimed Nikos Kazantzakis, "which does not exist, but by believing in it, I create it. We call 'non-existent' whatever we have not desired with sufficient strength."[11]

I affirm belief in miracles in full recognition of the misuse to which it is subject: manipulative magic, superstition, utopian fanaticism, spiritual greed, New Age naïveté. Against such perversions I know no preventive. But the alternative—supine acquiescence in the spirit of the age—is no more desirable. Let us join hands then with faith healers and speakers in tongues. Let us take as allies a few ranters, raving with the vision of a society of justice, health, and love. For intercession, to be Christian, must be prayer for God's reign to come on earth. It must be prayer for the victory of God over disease, greed, oppression, and death in the concrete circumstances of people's lives, now. In our intercessions we fix our wills on the divine possibility latent in the present moment, and then find ourselves caught up in the whirlwind of God's struggle to actualize it.

That is why the phrases of the Lord's Prayer are not indicative but imperative— we are *ordering* God to bring the Kingdom near. It will not do to implore. We must command. We have been commanded to command. We are required by God to haggle with God for the sake of the sick, the obsessed, the weak, and to conform our lives to our intercessions. The God of the Bible invents history in interaction with those "who hunger and thirst to see right prevail" (Matt. 5:6, REB). How different this is from the static God of Greek ontology that has lulled so many into adoration without intercession all these years!

Praying is rattling God's cage and waking God up and setting God free and giving this famished God water and this starved God food and cutting the ropes off God's hands and the manacles off God's feet and washing the caked sweat from God's eyes and then watching God swell with life and vitality and energy and following God wherever God goes.

Prayer is not a request made to an almighty King who can do anything at any time. It is an act that liberates the origin, goal, and process of the universe from all distortions, poisonings, ravagings, misdirectedness, and sheer hatred of being that frustrate the divine purpose.

When we pray, we are not sending a letter to a celestial White House where it is sorted among piles of others. We are engaged rather in an act of cocreation, in which one little sector of the universe rises up and becomes translucent, incandescent, a vibratory center of power that radiates the power of the universe.

History belongs to the intercessors, who believe the future into being. If this is so, then intercession, far from being an escape from action, is a means of focusing for action and of creating action. By means of our intercessions we veritably cast fire upon the earth and trumpet the future into being. It is no accident then that the seven angels of the Apocalypse make ready to announce the scenes that follow as a direct result of prayer.

God Is the Intercessor

All this about our role as intercessors in creating history is arrogant bravado unless we recognize that it is God rather than ourselves who initiates prayer, and that it is God's power, not ours, that answers to the world's needs. We are always preceded in intercession. God is always already praying within us. When we turn to pray, it is already the second step of prayer. We join with God in a prayer already going on in us and in the world.

> The Spirit also helps us in our present limitations. For example, we do not know how to pray worthily, but God's Spirit within us is actually praying for us in those agonizing longings ["groans"] which cannot find words. Those who know the heart's secrets understand the Spirit's intention as they pray according to God's will for those who love God.
>
> (Rom. 8:26-27, Phillips, with revisions)

This groaning of the Holy Spirit within us echoes and gathers up two other groanings mentioned in the previous paragraph: the groaning of the whole creation in pangs of childbirth (Rom. 8:22); and we ourselves, who groan inwardly as we await the ultimate transformation—the redemption of our bodies (8:23).

The Spirit gathers up all this pain and releases it through us with sighs too deep for words. These sighs are not our own sighs, given articulation by the Spirit. They are the actual groanings of the Spirit within us, and they must be given articulation by us. (The REB seems to imply that we are the ones who sigh—"through our inarticulate groans the Spirit himself is pleading for us." I am following Phillips's translation here, taking the phrase "the one who searches the heart" to refer to the discerning person who prays, rather than to God, as most other versions do.)

This groaning of the Spirit within us is related to the groaning of the created order, subjected, as it is, to futility (Rom. 8:20). We are inundated by the cries of an entire creation: the millions now starving to death each year, the tortured, the victims of sexual abuse or battering, the ill. But that is not all: we also bear inexpressible sorrow for all the species that have become extinct and those on the verge of extinction, the plants and trees and fish dying of pollution, the living beings dislocated or killed by forest fires, hurricanes, volcanic eruptions, and the like. We are so interconnected with all of life that we cannot help being touched by the pain of all that suffers. The more highly developed our consciousness becomes, the more terribly the knowledge and anguish of that suffering weighs on us, till we risk being crushed by it.

It seems to me that more and more people who never experienced depression before are aware of being episodically depressed today. I do not believe their depressions are neurotic, but a sign of potential health: their heightened capacity to take in the suffering of the planet. There is something impersonal and objective about these depressions that bespeaks a high degree of moral development. The world has shrunk. The capsizing of a ferry boat in the Philippines, or the strife between ethnic groups in Sri Lanka, now makes front-page headlines. We are literally inundated with news of suffering from all round the globe, and it cannot but affect us. How much more, then, those who have deliberately opened their hearts to humanity as one family in God?

We human beings are far too frail and tiny to bear all this pain. The solution is not avoidance, however. Refusal to read the papers or listen to the news is no protection. I am convinced that our solidarity with all of life is somatic, and that we sense the universal suffering whether we wish to or not.[12] What we need is a portable form of the Wailing Wall in Jerusalem, where we can unburden ourselves of this accumulated suffering. We need to experience it; it is a part of reality. Our task in praying is precisely that of giving speech to the Spirit's groanings within us. But we must not try to bear the sufferings of the creation ourselves. We are to articulate these agonizing longings and let them pass through us to God. Only the heart at the center of the universe can endure such a weight of suffering. Our attempts to bear them (and our depressions are evidence that we try) are masochistic, falsely messianic, and finally idolatrous, as if there were no God, as if we had to carry this burden all by ourselves.

So the Holy Spirit helps us in our weakness. We do not know how to pray as we ought: this does not mean, as it is most often taken, that we lack the proper techniques. Our ignorance is not that we do not know the right methods, but precisely that we think we know how to pray. We think it is something *we* do. It is not. How could it be, if we do not even know how to pray as we ought?

We learn to pray by stopping the attempt and simply *listening* to the prayer already being prayed in us. And what we hear is a strange kind of help. The Spirit groans in us inarticulately, wordlessly. It teaches us to pray by inducing us to give words to these groanings. Our task is simply to bring the Spirit's utterances to language, to consciousness, to awareness.

Before we even make ready to pray, then, before we realize that the universe is in travail in us, before we even allow that groaning to rise to consciousness, God has already initiated our prayer. It is a wholly erroneous habit of Christian prayer therefore to call on the Holy Spirit to be present with us. It is *we* who need to be present to the always-present Holy Spirit. We do not turn to God and try to make contact through prayer. The Holy Spirit is already groaning in us. We would not even think of praying had not the Holy Spirit's groaning in us prompted us to do so. We are able to pray only because God is always, incessantly, praying in us. Perhaps this is what Pascal meant when he said, speaking for God, "You would not seek me, had you not already found me."[13]
The Holy Spirit is like a substrate of molten magma under the earth's crust, trying to erupt volcanically in each of us. It does not have to be invoked, but merely allowed; not called to be present, but acknowledged as present already. Our task is not to mobilize God, but rather to bring our consciousness and commitment to God, to give articulation to the inarticulate groanings within our souls, to bring God's longings to speech.

As Richard Rohr puts it,

> To pray is to build your own house. To pray is to discover that Someone else is within your house. To pray is to recognize that it is not your house at all. To keep praying is to have no house to protect because there is only One House. And that One House is everybody's Home. . . . That is the politics of prayer. And that is probably why truly spiritual people are always a threat to politicians of any sort. They want our allegiance and we can no longer give it. Our house is too big.[14]

By now I can sense certain social activists bristling with impatience. I am in complete sympathy. We have all known Christians for whom prayer is a substitute for action, who dump on God the responsibility for doing what God's groaning in us is seeking to impel us to do.

But action is also no substitute for prayer. For some, action is a cover for unbelief; they simply do not believe that God is able to act in the world. Since God cannot change things, we must. For others, who feel called by God to establish justice, prayer seems a waste of precious time. But long-term struggle requires constant inner renewal, else the wells of love run dry. Social action without prayer is soulless; but prayer without action lacks integrity. Why should we choose between them, when neither is valid without the other?

Not long ago, there were people who were social justice advocates and others who were contemplatives. Some acted, others prayed. Today these two activities tend to take place in the same body. With increasing frequency, people are accepting, as the central theological task of our epoch, the integration of action and contemplation.

Jesus teaches us to command God, in the imperative mood, when we pray. The scandal that such audacious and indecorous behavior evokes among so many Christians is mitigated, however, if God is the intercessor. It is God who is crying out within us, God who is seeking to find in us a voice that will articulate the divine longing, God who causes us to cry out to God in a voice of command and who thus prompts us to complete the circuit.

For us to be this open and vulnerable to both the pain of the world and the anguish of God is unendurable, unless it is matched with a precise sense of divine vocation. We must let *all* the pain picked up by our receptors pass through us. But then we must not attempt to mend it all ourselves, but to do only what God calls us to do, and not one thing more. It is the paradox of divine effort-lessness, spelled out by Jesus in a terrible double-pincered saying in the Sermon on the Mount. On the one hand, we must act and not just profess faith: "Not everyone who says to me, 'Lord, Lord,' will enter the kingdom of heaven, but only the one who does the will of my Father in heaven." God wants not words but deeds. On the other hand, those who think that what God wants is action are chastised as well: "On that day many will say to me, 'Lord, Lord, did we not prophesy in your name, and cast out demons in your name, and do many deeds of power in your name?' Then I will declare to them, 'I never knew you; go away from me, you evildoers' " (Matt. 7:21-23). To do even miracles of compassion, when God has not specifically called us to do so, is to be evildoers!

God invites us, in short, not to conform to collective notions of what constitutes Christian behavior, but to seek the specific shape of our own divine calling in the day-to-day working out of our relationship with God.

We are not called to do everything, to heal everything, to change everything, but only to do what God asks of us. And in the asking is supplied the power to perform it. We are freed from the paralysis that results from being overwhelmed by the immensity of the need and our relative powerlessness, and we are freed from messianic megalomania, in which we try to heal everyone that hurts.

If we are sharply attentive to what God wants of us, we can then very modestly, in the strength of God, anticipate the impossible: we can expect miracles within that delimited sector in which we have been set to work. We should expect miracles, because the God who has called us to act at this precise point also is at work within us. The groaning of the Holy Spirit inside us is the hum of a dynamo producing the power to envision and act. Without being so borne up, it would be folly for us to engage the Powers.

Gandhi insisted that we must never accept evil, even if we cannot change it. Accepting evil, no matter how monolithic, inevitable, or entrenched, serves to deaden moral sensitivity. It creates a public inertia that will in time baptize what is wrong as inevitable or necessary. Calling evil by its name—naming as evil what others regard as custom (wife beating) or natural (homophobia) or even moral (executing political critics or religious heretics)—maintains the moral nerve even in circumstances where change seems impossible.

Many, especially in Alcoholics Anonymous, have been greatly helped by the prayer attributed to one of my teachers, Reinhold Niebuhr: "God, grant me the serenity to accept the things I cannot change, the courage to change the things I can, and the wisdom to know the difference." In the light of the present study I would prefer to pray, "God, help me to refuse ever to accept evil; by your Spirit empower me to work for change precisely where and how you call me; and free me from thinking I have to do everything."

Waging Spiritual Warfare
with the Powers

Now we must consider more directly the role of the Powers in prayer.

Most of us were taught that unanswered prayer is a result of either our failure or God's refusal. Either we lacked faith (or were too sinful and impure or asked for the wrong thing), or God said no out of some inscrutable higher purpose.

Perhaps there are times when our faith is weak. But Jesus explicitly states that it is not how much faith we have that counts, but whether we simply do our duty and exercise whatever faith we do have; and an infinitesimal amount, he says, is enough (Luke 17:5-6). The issue, after all, is not whether we are spiritual giants, but whether God really is able to do anything. Faith is not a feeling or a capacity we conjure up, but trusting that God can act decisively in the world. So if we have faith like a grain of mustard seed—that is, if we have any faith at all—we should not blame ourselves when our prayers go unanswered.

Nor should we be too swift to ascribe our lack of success in praying to our sins and inadequacies. Morton Kelsey tells how the first really dramatic healing he was ever involved in took place despite his resentment at having to go to the hospital at an inconvenient time and minister to people he scarcely knew. God apparently ignored his attitude and healed the person anyway. Many of us were taught at an early age that God hears our prayers in direct proportion to the degree of purity of heart or sinlessness we bring to our prayers. But no one is "good enough" to pray, once we accept those terms. The God revealed by Jesus graciously listens to all who pray, perhaps even especially to sinners. It was the corrupt publican, after all, not the morally correct Pharisee, who went home justified (Luke 18:9-14). There may even be a towering conceit in our belief that our inadequacies and sins are so important that they can stand in the way of God answering our prayers.

Nor is it adequate in certain cases to blame God's nonresponse to our prayers on a higher will for us that, for now, requires a no. No doubt what sometimes appears to us as evil is the very explosion necessary to blast us awake to the destructiveness of our habits. Sickness and tragedy are, unfortunately, at times the indispensable messengers that recall us to our life's purpose. We sometimes do pray for the wrong thing, or fail to recognize God's answer because we are looking for something else. But there are situations where God's will seems so transparently evident that to assert that God says no is to portray God as a cosmic thug. I still cannot see, after twenty-five years, how the death by leukemia of a six-year-old boy in our parish was in any sense an act of God. And don't even try to tell me that the death of approximately forty thousand children a day—over fourteen million a year—is the will of God!

What we have left out of the equation is the Principalities and Powers. Prayer is not just a two-way transaction. It also involves the great socio-spiritual forces that preside over so much of reality. I am speaking of the massive institutions and social structures and systems that dominate our world today, and of the spirituality at their center. If we wish to recover a sense of the importance of these Powers in prayer, we can scarcely do better than to consult the Book of Daniel. Daniel marks the moment when the role of the Powers in blocking answers to prayer was, for the first time, revealed to humanity.

Daniel is a symbol of Israel struggling against all efforts to destroy its fidelity to Yahweh.[15] Daniel is depicted as a Jew who had risen to high position in the Persian bureaucracy in Babylon. Three years before, Cyrus had freed the Jews from captivity and offered to rebuild their temple at royal expense. Yet few Jews had responded by returning home. When the story opens, Daniel is in deep mourning and fasting for his people. In the light of Rom. 8:26-27 we might say that the Holy Spirit wanted to prepare him to receive a vision and so released in him a flood of anguish that Daniel wisely chose to face and not repress. So he entered upon a major fast. After twenty-one days an angel came and said, "Daniel, don't be afraid. God has heard your prayers ever since the first day you decided to humble yourself in order to gain understanding. I have come in answer to your prayer."

Why then was the angel twenty-one days in arriving, if the prayer was heard on the very first day that Daniel prayed? Because, the angel continues, "the angel prince of the kingdom of Persia opposed me for twenty-one days." He could not even have managed to get through to Daniel at all, except that "Michael, one of the chief angels, came to help me, because I had been left there alone" to contend with the angel of Persia. Now, while Michael occupies the angel of Persia, the messenger-angel has slipped through and is able to deliver the vision of the future for Daniel's exiled people. That mission completed, "Now I have to go back and fight the guardian angel of Persia. After that the guardian angel of Greece will appear. There is no one to help me except Michael, Israel's guardian angel. He is responsible for helping and defending me" (Daniel 10, TEV).[16]

The angel of Persia is able to block God's messenger from answering Daniel's prayer! For twenty-one days Daniel contends with unseen spiritual powers. Perhaps he also had to slough off internalized elements of Babylonian spirituality; he bore as his own a name compounded from the name of a Babylonian god (Belteshazzar, 4:8). But whatever changes in him may have been necessary, it is not *after* he has purified himself that the angel is dispatched. He is heard on the very first day, as the words leave his lips. The real struggle is between the angels of two nations. The angel of Persia does not want the nation he guards to lose such a talented subject people. The angel of Persia actively attempts to frustrate God's will, and for twenty-one days succeeds. The Principalities and Powers are able to hold Yahweh at bay!

Daniel continues praying and fasting, God's angel continues to wrestle to get past the angel of Persia, yet nothing is apparently happening. God *seems* not to have answered the prayer. Despite this apparent indifference, however, there is a fierce war being waged in heaven between contending powers. Finally Michael, Israel's own guardian angel, intervenes and the angel gets through.

This is an accurate depiction, in mythological terms, of the actual experience we have in prayer. We have been praying for decades now for the superpowers to reduce their arsenals; for most of that time it seemed an exercise in abject futility. The "angel of the United States" and the "angel of the Soviet Union" have been locked in a deadly struggle in which neither seemed prepared to relax its grip. Then, in the irony of God, the most vociferously anticommunist president in American history negotiated a nuclear weapons reduction treaty with a Soviet leader whose new course of openness was not predicted by a single American Sovietologist. Whatever their motives, we can believe that none of this would have happened without the demonstrations and prayers over the decades of the peace movement in the United States, Europe, and the Soviet Union. God found an opening, and was able to bring about a miraculous change of direction.

Notice that the Bible makes no attempt to justify the delay in God's response. It is simply a fact of experience. We do not know why God cannot do "better," or why, for example, Michael is not sent to the aid of the messenger angel sooner. It is a deep mystery. But we are not appealing to mystery in order to paper over an intellectual problem; the Sovietologists are faced with mysteries as well. We just do not know why some things happen and others do not.

What does this say then about the omnipotence of God? About God's ability to redeem? God's sovereignty over history? The Principalities and Powers are able to assert their will against the will of God, *and, for a time, prevail*! The wonder, then, is not that our prayers are sometimes unanswered, but that any are answered at all! We have long accepted that God is limited by our freedom. The new insight in Daniel is that God is limited by the freedom of institutions and systems as well. We have normally spoken of this divine limitation as a free choice of God. One may well ask whether God has any choice. In any case, whether by choice or not, God's ability to intervene, uninvited, is extremely circumscribed—as you may have noticed when you pray.

When Daniel was written (ca. 167 B.C.E.), the Jewish people had been under foreign rulers for over four hundred years. It was no longer intelligible that the occupation of Palestine was a divine chastisement or the divine will. The very hostility of these foreign powers seemed to indicate that they ruled by means of evil cosmic forces. The predicament we see in Daniel derives from the fact that God does *not* at present effectively rule "this world" (what I have been calling the Domination System). Satan rules it.[17]

In short, prayer involves not just God and people, but God and people and the Powers. What God is able to do in the world is hindered, to a considerable extent, by the rebelliousness, resistance, and self-interest of the Powers exercising their freedom under God.

God *is* powerful to heal, and all healing, I believe, is of God. But if the Powers flush PCBs and dioxin into the water we drink, or release radioactive gas into the atmosphere, or insist on spraying our fruit with known carcinogens, God's healing power is sharply reduced. Children (like the boy in my parish on the edge of one of the largest petrochemical complexes in the world) die of leukemia. The situation is no different in kind than normal bodily healing. A clean cut will almost always, wondrously, mend; but if we rub infectious germs into it, God's capacity to heal is hindered or even rendered void.

God does want people to be free to become everything God created them to be. I have not the slightest hesitation in declaring such fulfillment to be the will of God. But when one race enslaves another to labor in its fields, or to dig its mines, or when children's lives are stunted by sexual abuse or physical brutality, or when whole nations are forced to submit to the exploitation of other states more powerful, then what is God to do? We may pray for justice and liberation, as indeed we must, and *God hears us on the very first day*. But God's ability to intervene against the freedom of these rebellious creatures is sometimes tragically restricted in ways we cannot pretend to understand. It takes considerable spiritual maturity to live in the tension between these two facts: God has heard our prayer, and the Powers are blocking God's response.

If the Powers can thwart God so effectively, can we even speak of divine providence in the world? If our prayers are answered so sporadically, or with such great delays, can we really trust in God? Can God really be relied on? Is a limited God really God at all? We have to face these questions, because our capacity to pray depends on some kind of working idea of God's providential care for us.

In the Nazi death camps, for example, where the intercessors stormed heaven with their supplications for deliverance, why did God not succeed in saving more Jews? Etty Hillesum, a Dutch Jew anticipating her deportation to a "work camp" that proved to be a death chamber, prayed,

> I shall try to help You, God, to stop my strength ebbing away, though I cannot vouch for it in advance. But one thing is becoming increasingly clear to me: that You cannot help us, that we must help You to help ourselves. And that is all we can manage these days and also all that really matters: that we safeguard that little piece of You, God, in ourselves. And perhaps in others as well. Alas, there doesn't seem to be much You Yourself can do about our circumstances, about our lives. Neither do I hold You responsible. You cannot help us but we must help You and defend Your dwelling place inside us to the last.[18]

One need not vouch for the theology in this statement to honor the experience it addresses. The Powers were holding God at bay. God appeared to be doing nothing. Meanwhile, unseen, there was war in heaven. When people not only submit to evil but actively affirm it, malignant Powers are unleashed for which everyday life offers no preparation. The angel of Germany was worshiped as an idol, and was acclaimed the supreme being. God, elbowed out of heaven, was out prowling every street at all hours, and could find few to help.

In such a time, God may appear to be impotent. Perhaps God is. Yet Hitler's thousand-year Reich was brought down in only twelve years. God may be unable to intervene directly, but nevertheless showers the world with potential coincidences that require only a human response to become miracles. When the miracle happens, we feel that God has intervened in a special way. But God does not intervene only occasionally. God is the constant possibility of transformation pressing on *every* occasion, even those that are lost for lack of a human response.

God is not mocked. The wheels of justice may turn slowly, but they are inexorable. Take the story spun around Daniel again. After fifty years of captivity, God had at last raised up Cyrus to deliver the Jews from Babylon, and God's people chose rather to remain in exile! Daniel, fasting and praying, creates a fresh opening for God. Into that breach God pours the vision of future life in a restored Holy Land, as an enticement and lure to coax Judah home.

Prayer is not magic; it does not always "work." It is not something we do, but a response to what God is already doing within us and the world. Our prayers are the necessary opening that allows God to act without violating our freedom. Prayer is the ultimate act of partnership with God. Therefore God allows no groveling. Daniel throws himself on his face before the divine messenger, but the angel touches him and rouses him to his hands and knees. The angel orders him, "Stand on your feet." Daniel does, but cannot speak or stop trembling. The angel touches his lips, and again his body, infusing him with the strength and power to speak the message he has received. God is no eastern potentate demanding obeisance. God puts us on our feet, fills us with power, and sends us on our way.

The sobering news that the Powers can thwart God is more than matched by the knowledge that our intercessions will ultimately prevail. Whether we have to wait twenty-one days or twenty-one years or twenty-one centuries changes nothing for faith. It knows how massive and intractable the Domination System is. We cannot stop praying for what is right because our prayers are seemingly unanswered. We know they are heard the very first day that we pray. Yet we keep praying, for even one more day is too long to wait for justice.

That is why the delay of the Kingdom was not fatal to Christian belief. For the church could now see the Domination System for what it was, and could never wholly capitulate to it again. And it had caught glimpses of God's domination-free order, and could never give up the longing for its arrival.

Daniel had to wait twenty-one days to receive the vision of his people's future conflicts in Palestine; it would be two centuries before any sizable number returned. Modern-day Jews had to wait nineteen centuries for a Jewish state in Palestine. Gandhi struggled with the angel of the British Empire for twenty-six years; the Aquino revolution, once it mobilized the masses in the Philippines, unseated Marcos in only a matter of days. Whether the water rises drop by drop or through a flash flood, eventually the pressure bursts the dam of oppression and the Powers fall. They are but mortal creatures, and they are all the more vicious when they know their time is short (Rev. 12:12). Many innocent people may die, while the Powers appear to gain in invincibility with every death, but that is only an illusion. Their very brutality and desperation is evidence that their legitimacy is fast eroding. Their appeal to force is itself an admission that they can no longer command voluntary consent. Whenever sufficient numbers of people withdraw their consent, the Powers inevitably fall.

Excursus on Warfare Prayer

As this goes to press I have just finished reading the manuscript of C. Peter Wagner's *Warfare Prayer: Strategies for Combating the Rulers of Darkness.*[19] While Wagner understands the Powers as personal beings and is far more credulous (or experienced?) about miracles than I, I found his book extraordinarily insightful. Most important, it rectifies the defensive tone of this chapter by stressing aggressive assault on the Powers themselves through what he calls "warfare prayer." In South Africa, for example, statutory apartheid has largely been repealed; now people are discovering that de facto apartheid remains, deeply embedded in every aspect of the society. What if, in evangelistic meetings and worship services all over the country, the spirit of apartheid were to be solemnly rebuked and people were invited to testify to their deliverance from its spell by the Holy Spirit? In the United States, state religion has, in the wake of the Gulf War, increased its power enormously. What if, in churches throughout the land, Christians not only questioned the identification of U.S. hegemony with the will of God, but actually challenged the appropriateness of national flags in churches, or exorcised the spirit of violence that holds us in its grip?

I have a nagging hunch that the gospel's power in our time is about to be manifested in a manner as repugnant to the sensibilities of the society at large, and all of us who have accommodated ourselves to it, as the early Christian message was to Roman paganism. Our society is possessed, Christians as much as anyone. We are possessed by violence, possessed by sex, possessed by money, possessed by drugs. We need to recover forms of collective exorcism as effective as was early Christian baptism's renunciation of "the devil and all his works" (that is, the domination system). How I might do that, and how Wagner is doing it, are no doubt different. I would find public exorcism more congenial in the style described by Bill Wylie Kellermann in *Seasons of Faith and Conscience,* or that described in my own *Unmasking the Powers.*[20] What troubles me, however, is that by attempting to fight the demons "in the air," evangelicals and charismatics will continue largely to ignore the institutional sources of the demonic. By so doing, they will fail to do the hard political and economic analysis necessary to name, unmask, and engage these Powers transformatively. But I sense here a convergence of aims that may have the disconcerting result of linking charismatics, conservative evangelicals, and social-action liberals in a united front of enormous power and divisiveness. If the nonviolent message of the gospel can only be introduced into this mix, perhaps some of the unnecessary vitriol can be avoided. But I have taken as my motto the words of Ignatius of Antioch: "The greatness of Christianity lies in its being hated by the Domination System *(kosmos),* not in being convincing to it."[21]

Prayer and the Problem of Evil

I have long been struck by the virtual absence of any attempt to explain evil (theodicy) in the New Testament. The early Christians devoted a great deal of energy to discovering the meaning of Jesus' death, but nowhere do they offer a justification of God in the face of an evil world. They do not seem to be puzzled or even perturbed by evil as a theoretical problem. When they encountered persecution or illness, they never asked, "How could God have let this happen?" Jesus himself may have felt forsaken by God and wondered why (Mark 15:34//Matt. 27:46), but no answer is given. To the question, Why was Jesus crucified, the early church had a ready answer: he was crucified by the Powers because what he said and did threatened their power. The burning question for them was not *why* but *how*: How has God used this evil for good? How has God turned sin into salvation? How has God triumphed over the Powers through the cross?

Likewise, persecution did not evoke surprised reactions of "Why me?" The early Christians *expected* to be persecuted;[22] they were surprised when they were not! For them the question was not *why* but *how long*: "How long will it be before you judge and avenge our blood on the inhabitants of the earth?" (Rev. 6:10).

Paul does not rejoice that God's providence delivers us *from* affliction; clearly it did not deliver him (2 Cor. 11:23-33)! Rather he celebrates God's comforting us *in* our afflictions (2 Cor. 1:3-7). When he was almost killed in Asia, he did not rail at God for mistreating him, since he knew that it was the Powers, not God, that wanted him destroyed. He even found a lesson in the ordeal: It was "so that we would rely not on ourselves but on God who raises the dead" (2 Cor. 1:9). So free was he from the fear of the Powers and their final sanction, death, that he could avow: "If we live, we live to the Lord, and if we die, we die to the Lord; so then, whether we live or whether we die, we are the Lord's" (Rom. 14:8).

Jesus' God plays no favorites, but causes the sun to rise on the evil and on the good, and sends rain on the just and the unjust alike (Matt. 5:45//Luke 6:35). Jesus spoke of trusting the created order in the manner of the lilies of the fields and the birds of the air (Luke 12:22-31//Matt. 6:25-34), but this was not a way to hoard wealth. It was the assertion, against the demonic structures that let the many starve while the few overeat, that even in the midst of the Domination System God is able to care for God's own: "Set your mind on God's kingdom and his justice before everything else, and all the rest will come to you as well" (Matt. 6:33, REB).

Elsewhere, Jesus states categorically, in an otherwise dark saying, that the accidental death of people killed by a falling tower, and Pilate's murder of Galileans in the Temple, were not God's will or doing (Luke 13:1-5). Nor is it God's will that even a sparrow fall to the ground. The RSV created untold harm when it translated Matt. 10:29 as "not one of them [sparrows] will fall to the ground without your Father's *will*." The Greek reads simply, "without your Father" (so KJV; NRSV, "apart from your Father"). Other translations supply what they feel to be the implied word: JB, "knowing"; Phillips, "knowledge"; NEB, "leave"; TEV, "consent." The proper meaning is clear from Luke's parallel (Luke 12:6): "Yet not one of them is *forgotten in God's sight*." God is with even the smallest sufferer.

The church confirmed in its own experience the truth of the saying, "There is no one who has left house or brothers or sisters or mother or father or children or lands, for my sake and for the gospel, who will not receive a hundredfold now in this time, houses and brothers and sisters and mothers and children and lands, *with persecutions*, and in the age to come eternal life" (Mark 10:29-30,

RSV). This was not an early recipe for attaining wealth by striking a deal with God. It simply reflects the church's experience that those who abandoned everything for the sake of proclaiming the gospel were supported and enfolded by the body of Christ wherever their journeys took them. The ironic aside, "with persecutions," emphasizes the infinite gulf between the New Testament understanding of providence and the naive view of those who equate providence with an ever-expanding standard of living. The early Christians *expected* to be assaulted by the Powers. Never once do they seem puzzled by this fact. It would have been unthinkable for them to ask, "Why do bad things happen to good people?" The Powers that had crucified Jesus had an equal stake in crushing this new movement, though full recognition of this fact did not dawn on the empire until the second century, when systematic and widespread persecution began.

In short, for the early church the problem of justifying the existence of evil in a world created by God can scarcely be said to have existed. The first Christians never—astonishingly!—blamed God for their unmerited sufferings. "Count it all joy," writes James, "when you meet various trials" (1:2, RSV). "Blessed are you when people hate you, and when they exclude you, revile you, and defame you on account of the Son of Man. Rejoice in that day and leap for joy, for surely your reward is great in heaven" (Luke 6:22-23). Of course the Powers will oppose you; of course you will be brought before the rulers and authorities (lit., "principalities and powers," Luke 12:11); of course they will hunt you down like animals, deliver you to torturers, and even kill you, for threatening the spirituality of a world of domination. Not one writer of the New Testament shows the slightest surprise over this. In a world under the practical daily sovereignty of the Powers, nothing else is to be expected.

The early church did not seek to formulate a theory of illness; instead, it healed the sick. It did not attempt to explain how the demonic could exist in a good world made by a good God; instead, they cast out demons. They had no hypotheses about how prayer works; they simply prayed. They were not, for all that, unreflective. They refuted, where necessary, theories of illness that prevented healing (e.g., the sin theory). They suggested that the source of at least some diseases was Satan (Luke 13:16). Their attitude was not antirational or antitheological, but merely concrete. They looked, not for adequate ways to conceptualize the Kingdom, but for ways to actualize it.

The fact that the New Testament ignores the problem of theodicy does not mean that the issue is trivial. It is a question that has vexed some of the best minds throughout history, though most of their discussions have ignored the role of the Powers in evil.[23] It is my hope that this trilogy has helped remedy that oversight. But we should respect the New Testament's refusal to become pre-occupied with evil as a theological problem. Its concern is instead practical. It wishes to overcome evil, not explain it. Christians should expect the Powers to do evil. The more pressing question is: What can God do about this or that concrete evil facing us today? Can these rebellious Powers be tamed? On a practical level, then, the problem of evil is dealt with through prayer and action, in the everyday attempt to bend evil back toward the purposes of God.

Conclusion

Recognition of the role of the Powers in blocking prayer can revolutionize the way we pray. We will be more energized and aggressive. We will honor God by venting the full range of our feelings, from frustration to outrage to joy, and everything in between. We will recognize that God, too, is hemmed in by forces that cannot simply be overruled. We will know that God will prevail, but not necessarily in a way that is comprehensible except through the cross.

Prayer that ignores the Powers ends up blaming God for evils committed by the Powers. But prayer that acknowledges the Powers becomes a form of social action. Indeed, no struggle for justice is complete unless it has first discerned, not only the outer, political manifestations of the Powers, but also their inner spirituality, and has lifted the Powers, inner and outer, to God for transformation. Otherwise we change only the shell, and leave the spirit intact.

Prayer in the face of the Powers is a spiritual war of attrition. God's hands are effectively tied when we fail to pray. That is the dignity and urgency of our praying.[24]

In a field of such titanic forces, it makes no sense to cling to small hopes. We are emboldened to ask for something bigger. The same faith that looks clear-eyed at the immensity of the forces arrayed against God is the faith that affirms God's miracle-working power. Trust in miracles is, in fact, the only rational stance in a world that is infinitely responsive to God's incessant lures. We are commissioned to pray for miracles because nothing less is sufficient. We pray to God, not because we understand these mysteries, but because we have learned from our tradition and from experience that God, indeed, *is* sufficient for us, whatever the Powers may do.

Thank God our time is now when wrong
Comes up to face us everywhere,
Never to leave us till we take
The longest stride of soul men ever took.
Affairs are now soul size.
The enterprise
Is exploration into God,
Where no nation's foot has ever trodden yet.

Christopher Fry,
A Sleep of Prisoners[1]

17. Celebrating the Victory of God

How remarkable, that despite its sober exposé of the Domination System, the New Testament is so free of gloom or quailing before the Powers! From beginning to end, there is only the note of victory—a victory in the unknown and open future, for the whole human race and the universe, and victory even now, in the midst of struggle. There is an absolute and unshakable confidence that the System of Domination has an end. A new world of partnership, of compassion, of human community, of conscious awareness of the limits of power, awaits us. We are to struggle with all our might and courage for its coming, yet we cannot make it come. The conditions of its arrival are beyond our control, yet we have a fairly clear idea what they are; and as a sufficient number of people are attracted to God's domination-free order, and commit their lives and fortunes to bringing it about, it will happen, because it has been happening, and it is happening now.

Jesus' confidence that even socially conditioned and bewildered people can act freely to choose God's reign is a consequence of God's reign actually having drawn near in Jesus' own acts and words. He brings a counterreality that makes choice possible, exorcises the old conditioning, and holds out to us a new world waiting to be claimed by us. And we can begin living that new reality *now*.

That gospel is in a highly personal way the intimate message that our lives are known by God better than we know them; that we are valued more than we value ourselves; that what we can become is much more wonderful than we ever imagined. The obstacle between us and God is not what is imperfect in us—the fragility, the truculence, the dithering lust and outbursts of rage (God can deal with all that)—but our belief that we are unworthy of being loved, incapable of greatness, people of little value, power, or gifts.

The goal is not only our becoming free *from* the Powers, however, but *freeing* the Powers; not only reconciling people to God despite the Powers, but reconciling the Powers to God (Col. 1:20); not only breaking the idolatrous spells cast over people by the Powers, but breaking the Powers' ability to cast idolatrous spells over people. "The Son of God was revealed for this purpose, to destroy the works of the devil" (1 John 3:8). We need to escape idolatry, not this planet. We seek not to rid ourselves of subsystems and structures in order to secure an individualistic paradise on earth or an afterlife in heaven. We seek rather to relate these systems to the One in and through and for whom they exist, and in whom all things hold together (Col. 1:16-17).

There is still this qualification, however: our task is not to save the world. God alone can do that. Our task, William Stringfellow reminds us, is to witness to the freedom of human life from the power of death, the threat of death, and the fear of death. Even if we are able to avoid nuclear annihilation, global warming, ozone depletion, overpopulation, and environmental poisoning, and move, over a period of decades or centuries, toward a partnership society, that will not end the reality of death in the world.[2] A partnership society will be a more just, more egalitarian, more enjoyable place to live. But it will not be the reign of God in all its fullness.

Perhaps the intuition of a thousand-year messianic kingdom in the Book of Revelation foreshadows the end of domination and the establishment of a more equitable world-society (Rev. 20:4-6). But in this new order, in which there will no longer be class ranking, racism, patriarchy, war, and the subjugation of some by others, people will still be free to misuse freedom. There will still be finitude, weakness, ignorance, and mortality. Satan's imprisonment during the messianic reign indicates that the Domination System has been suspended. But it is only after that period that Satan and the two Beasts are finally disposed of. Only then, also, are Death and Hades thrown into the lake of fire (Rev. 20:14); even in the messianic kingdom, death would be operative. Only in the New Jerusalem, where God's will is done for all eternity, will all tears be wiped away, and death, mourning, crying, and pain be found no more (21:4). Only then are the nations healed by the leaves of the tree of life (22:2). Only then is creation freed from its bondage to decay (Rom. 8:21).[3]

We do not know how much of God's will can be realized in human affairs. We must act as if the world can be transformed, without guarantees that it can be or objective evidence that we are succeeding. The messianic kingdom of the Book of Revelation seems to be a sort of halfway house toward the heavenly Jerusalem. These two images serve to keep the future open to possibility, but in such a way that we cannot be sure whether our own efforts will be decisive. We can know only by trying.

Likewise, the New Testament knows nothing of the idea that the messianic kingdom comes as a gradually improving society progressing toward perfection. Instead it anticipates an increase in violence, war, and inhumanity (Mark 13 par.), as the clock ticks down to the final collapse of Satan, who "has come down to you with great wrath, because he knows that his time is short" (Rev. 12:12).

In the meantime, resistance to evil and death, to the Dragon and its Beasts, is the only way to live humanly in an inhuman world. Engagement in specific and incessant struggle against death's rule is in fact what renders us human in the time, and times, and half a time, that mark our days in the present world disorder.[4]

Yet this is not a dreary prospect, because already we can celebrate God's triumph. This capacity to enjoy victory in the midst of calamity is one of the most baffling aspects of the Christian hope. The Book of Revelation may be gory, surrealistic, unnerving, even terrifying. But it contains not a single note of despair. Powerful as the Dragon of the abyss may appear, he has been stripped of real heavenly power. Those still in the clutches of the Enemy may not yet experience it, but the decisive battle has already been won. The struggle continues, but the issue is no longer in doubt. The far-off strains of a victory song already reach our ears, and we are invited to join the chorus. This is the rock on which we stand: the absolute certainty of the triumph of God in the world.

That is why the celebration of the divine victory does not take place at the end of the Book of Revelation, after the struggle is over. Rather, it breaks out all along the way (1:4-8, 17-18; 4:8-11; 5:5, 9-14; 7:1-17; 11:15-19; 12:10-12; 14:1-8; 15:2-4; 16:5-7; 18; 19:1-9). We have here no sober pilgrims grimly ascending the mount of tears, but singers *enjoying* the struggle because it confirms their freedom. Even in the midst of conflict, suffering, or imprisonment, suddenly a hymn pierces the gloom, the heavenly hosts thunder in a mighty chorus, and our hearts grow lighter.

Christian base communities in South America have been losing members to the Pentecostals. Among many explanations that have been given is that people tire of unremitting struggle. They look to religion for more than moral guidance and social change. They want deliverance from the fear of dying, and the ecstatic sense of the presence of God. People need a counterpoint to the grim plodding and repeated setbacks of politics. The reign of God is not simply future; it is also present.

Maybe Jesus was not just making a point, then, when he ate with tax collectors and sinners. Maybe they were more fun to be with than the religious authorities! Maybe he was identified as "a glutton and a drunkard" (Matt. 11:19), not just because he was seeking the outcasts where they were, but because he enjoyed having a good time. This is the bright secret of social activists: they do not simply oppose evil because it is wrong, but also because the struggle is exciting and sometimes even fun. For even when they lose, the outcome is assured.

"And war broke out in heaven; Michael and his angels fought against the Dragon." And what defeats "the great Dragon," that "ancient serpent, who is called the Devil ['Slanderer'] and Satan ['Adversary'], the deceiver of the whole Domination System (*kosmos*)" (Rev. 12:9), is not head-on counterviolence. Rather, "they have conquered him by the blood of the Lamb and by the word of their testimony, for they did not cling to life even in the face of death" (12:11). Satan is cast out of heaven by those willing to be crushed by the Domination System in the process of exposing it. He is thereby stripped of invisibility, no longer able to coerce people unconsciously into conspiring with evil and injustice. Christ has left the Devil only whatever power unbelief allows him. Expelled from heaven, now the Devil has only time and not eternity.[5]

The Dragon, despite all his show of invulnerability, is actually weak: "The Dragon and his angels fought back, but he was not strong" (*ouk ischusen*, 12:7-8*). Before the Whole, the principle of fragmentation is puny. Before what binds all things together in unity, the fragile alliances of the Divider collapse from internal strife. In the face of faith, the merely terrestrial powers of the Archfiend are rendered impotent. Satan's transcendent power has been broken; he is no longer a citizen of heaven, no longer invisible. The Dragon's incapacity to consolidate rule makes him frantic, as the clock ticks down from the midpoint of time toward his final neutralization in the lake of fire (20:10).[6]

All this is observed, however, only by those who have eyes for seeing the invisible. The rest notice no change. The Beast is allowed to make war on the saints and to *conquer* them (13:7). When the martyrs cry out from under the altar, "How long will it be before you judge and avenge our blood on the inhabitants of the earth?", they are merely given a white robe and told to rest a little longer, "until the number would be complete both of their fellow servants and of their brothers and sisters, who were soon to be killed as they themselves had been killed" (6:9-11).

This brutal suppression ought to cut the nerve of Christian resistance. Instead, the Christian movement grows under repression. Jesus' followers seem to expect nothing less from the system that crucified their leader. The tide has turned toward the final victory, so that they can already sing their victory song:

> *Now* have come the salvation
> and the power
> and the reign of our God
> and the authority of God's Messiah. (12:10*)

Over and over this refrain resounds:

> And I saw what appeared to be a sea of glass mixed with fire, and those who *had conquered* the beast and its image and the number of its name, standing beside the sea of glass with harps of God in their hands. And they sing. . . . (15:2)

Do not weep. See, the Lion of the tribe of Judah, the Root of David, *has conquered*! (5:5)

The Beast that so effortlessly conquers the truth-tellers ("martyrs") has itself already been conquered (12:11). Jesus, though slain, has been exalted to heaven and controls the destiny of the world (Revelation 5). As Adela Yarbro Collins points out, the Book of Revelation reveals a hidden heavenly reality that exposes the visible world as counterfeit. What *ought* to be, for those with eyes of faith, already *is*. Living by faith entails maintaining, through creative imagination and communal reinforcement, a vivid sense of God's counterreality as more real than apparent reality itself.[7]

Whatever the apparent dauntlessness of the Domination System, Christ has already been enthroned above all Principalities and Powers (Eph. 1:20-23). This victory is what sustains faith; this faith is what creates victory. But how can we affirm victory in the midst of repeated defeats?

Because there are people who are now beginning to *see* and *act* free of the Domination System. No matter how terrible the sufferings of those detained and tortured in nonviolent demonstrations in South Africa or South Korea or Burma, the reign of God has already begun! This is no pious fiction. The power of God is already made manifest, because people formerly craven and terrified are ready to be fired from jobs, bludgeoned, jailed, or killed for the sake of a fairer system. The authority of Christ is already establishing itself, because victims are not only affirming their own humanity, but doing so in a way that affirms the humanity of their oppressors. The salvation of God is a present reality, because the very struggle for liberation would not have been possible had the powerless not discovered within themselves resources laid up by God in their creation: to be nonviolent yet powerful, loving yet immovable, joyous yet prepared to die.

In the Prague demonstration that sparked the Czech revolution on November 18, 1989, students began chanting to the Communist party leadership, "You have lost already! You have lost already!"—though victory was still in the future. "We know that we can win," said Karel Srp; "this is unstoppable."[8]

"At the point that we committed ourselves to this struggle," says nonviolent Brazilian peasant leader Zé Galego, "we began to understand that victory was ours. Each day we took another step forward. In the end, the outcome was no surprise."[9]

Faith does not wait for God's sovereignty to be established on earth; it behaves as if that sovereignty already holds full sway. Like the psalmists, the early Christians declared as fact what existed only in the imagination. Like God in the creation, faith calls into being what does not yet exist, and races ahead to form something new that never was before. As Walter Brueggemann puts it, to say that God has defeated the Powers is manifestly ludicrous in our world, if it must be heard *descriptively*. God is clearly not yet victorious. But if our praise evokes a new reality just beginning to come into being, then it helps create that new reality in the only way that it can be created.[10]

That is why these inveterate and incurable singers cannot help joining their voices with the heavenly chorus, singing, "The kingdom of the world *has become* the kingdom of our Lord and of his Messiah, and he shall reign for ever and ever" (Rev. 11:15). For *singing about* is a way of *bringing about*.

With eyes seeing the invisible, Allan Boesak never tired of repeating to the gathered throngs of antiapartheid demonstrators that South Africa's apartheid system *has* fallen, white racism *has* fallen, the powers of economic exploitation *have* fallen. "The battle is won, even though the struggle is not yet over." Now all that is left is to help everyone see and live in terms of these facts. "And besides, it drives the dragon crazy when you sing about his downfall even though you are bleeding."[11]

The cries of exultation that flash across the otherwise somber landscape of the Book of Revelation express joy at being freed from the paralysis induced by the pseudo-trinity of the Dragon and its two Beasts. Freedom means release to expose their seductions to others. The passion that drove the early Christians to evangelistic zeal was not fueled by the desire to increase church membership or to usher people safely toward heaven. It was fired by relief at being liberated from the delusional game being played by the Dragon to their own detriment, and by the determination to set others free. In the final analysis, the gospel is not a message of escape to another world after death, but of rescue from the enticements of "this world" (the Domination System) and its ultimate transformation, when "all nations will come and worship" God (Rev. 15:4).

In a pluralistic world in which we are privileged to learn from all religious and philosophical traditions, Christians still have a story to tell to the nations. And who knows—telling it may do no one so much good as ourselves.

Notes

PREFACE

1. *Naming the Powers: The Language of Power in the New Testament* (Philadelphia: Fortress Press, 1984); *Unmasking the Powers: The Invisible Forces That Determine Human Existence* (Philadelphia: Fortress Press, 1986); *Violence and Nonviolence in South Africa: Jesus' Third Way* (Philadelphia: New Society Publishers, 1987). In the interest of completeness, there is also a short book, *Cracking the Gnostic Code: The Powers in Gnosticism*, SBL Monograph Series (Atlanta: Scholars Press, 1993), 313–14, which deals with the rich and varied use of the Powers in Gnostic sources.

INTRODUCTION

1. Jean Claude von Itallie et al., *A Fable* (New York: Dramatists Play Service, 1976), 28–29.

2. Amos Wilder was one of the first to recognize the potential of the Principalities and Powers as a basis for "a kerygmatic social ethic and an aggressive social action," though he himself did not develop his insight ("Kerygma, Eschatology and Social Ethics," in *The Background of the New Testament and Its Eschatology* [Festschrift for C. H. Dodd], ed. W. D. Davies and D. Daube [Cambridge: Cambridge Univ. Press, 1964], 527). The more common attitude of earlier New Testament scholars is typified by Clarence Tucker Craig: "There are no sayings of Jesus which dealt with the transformation of social institutions" (*The Beginnings of Christianity* [New York: Abingdon Press, 1943], 195).

3. For a more detailed discussion of the ancient "as above/so below" worldview, see *Naming the Powers*, 131–40.

4. See Lawrence LeShan, *The Medium, the Mystic, and the Physicist* (New York: Ballantine Books, 1974); Fritjof Capra, *The Tao of Physics* (New York: Bantam Books, 1980). For a fuller treatment of the question of worldviews, see my essay, "Our Stories, Cosmic Stories, and the Biblical Story," in *Sacred Stories: Healing in the Imaginative Realm*, ed. Anne and Charles Simpkinson (San Francisco: Harper-SanFrancisco, 1993).

5. Euhemerus, a Greek philosopher of the fourth century B.C.E., taught that the gods were originally human heroes or tyrants elevated to divinity by sycophants or grateful subjects. That is clearly not a full account of the origin of the gods, but it contains more than a grain of truth. This means that in precisely the same period

that Jewish seers were elaborating on the spirituality at the heart of politics, this Greek writer was exposing the politics at the heart of spirituality.

6. I. P. Culianu, "The Angels of the Nations and the Origins of Gnostic Dualism," in *Studies in Gnosticism and Hellenistic Religions* (Festschrift for Gilles Quispel), ed. R. van den Broek and M. J. Vermaseren (Leiden: E. J. Brill, 1981), 78–91.

7. F. A. Wilford uses projection theory reductionistically in his treatment of "*Daimōn* in Homer" (*Numen* 12 [1965]: 217-32). The *daimōn*, he argues, is nothing but the unconscious projecting its contents out as gods and other numinous powers. Wilford has not understood Jung adequately. Emile Durkheim's position is closer to the one I am proposing, but his is also reductionist: supernatural beings are nothing more than projections of society (*The Elementary Forms of the Religious Life* [New York: Collier Books, 1947]). I differ in assuming that the reality being projected is indeed real, has a spiritual existence as the interiority of the social world, and is an essential part of God's good but fallen creation.

8. H. Berkhof discerns a degree of depersonalization in Paul's treatment of the Powers. "The apocalypses think primarily of the principalities and powers as heavenly agents, Paul as structures of earthly existence" (*Christ and the Powers* [Scottdale, Pa.: Herald Press, 1962], 18). I am suggesting that Paul, to the contrary, treats the Powers as *both* heavenly agents *and* structures of earthly existence; indeed, the former is the interiority of the latter.

9. As Paul Ricoeur puts it, "I do not know what Satan is, who Satan is, or even whether he is Someone. For if he were someone, it would be necessary to intercede for him." If Satan were a person, he would have to be redeemed, as Origen saw quite clearly (*The Symbolism of Evil* [New York: Harper & Row, 1967], 260). Origen's error, then, was not in declaring that Satan would finally be redeemed, but in conceiving of Satan as a personal being.

10. Exorcists often find it helpful, even unavoidable, to regard the demonic as an entity separate from the personality, so that it can be clearly conceptualized as alien and not integral to the person. However, I am not convinced that an evil subpersonality is any different in kind from any other manifestation of multiple personalities. And the utility of conceiving of an evil subpersonality as an evil *being* in no way settles the question of its metaphysical status. I have no objection to anyone imagining the demonic as a being, but that does not make it a being.

Most frequently these evil spirits are encountered in people who have been involved in Satan cults. In their case, I would argue, the spirituality of the cult has lodged itself in the personality, and, like similar elements in dreams, it naturally *presents* itself in a personal form. But that, I suggest, with a great deal of tentativeness in the face of these mysteries, does not require the spiritual force to be in fact a *being*, any more than dream figures are beings. Nevertheless, such manifestations are *real*. That is where old habits of thought get most in the way, I suspect. Many people automatically infer from visionary, dream, or other such experiences that because they have encountered unmistakably real spiritual entities, that these entities are spiritual beings. It requires a effort of thought to recognize that their reality is in no way diminished by being the actual spirituality of evil cults, or institutions, or even of mischievous books that exaggerate the power of the demonic in order to stampede their readers into terrified submission to a very reactionary

Christ. Most people who believe in a personal devil have never really seen "him." But if Satan is the spirit of domination, then we encounter Satan *all the time.*

11. In actual practice it may not matter so much whether one sees the demonic as having seized an institution from without, as C. Peter Wagner does (*Warfare Prayer* [Ventura, Calif.: Regal Books, 1992], 84–85), or whether one sees the demonic as the angel or spirituality of the institution itself become pathological, as I do. What counts is that something is done about it.

12. What then of God? In the language of the integral worldview, one might speak of God as the Spirit of Reality, and of the universe as God's "body." Thus God would have no existence "outside" the universe. The messenger angels of Genesis were conceived of as embodied, and therefore capable of eating food (Gen. 18:3-8); likewise, the resurrected Christ is depicted as appearing in bodily form and eating (Luke 24:39-43). In Hebraic anthropology, the split between body and soul, or matter and spirit, was unthinkable. Likewise the risen Christ might be seen as the spirit that became incarnate in Jesus and lives on as the spirituality of the Christian community. But this is only one way of putting it.

13. Frank Peretti, *This Present Darkness* (Westchester, Ill.: Crossway Books, 1986). He has also published *Piercing the Darkness* with the same press, 1989.

1. THE MYTH OF THE DOMINATION SYSTEM

1. E. C. Segar, *Thimble Theater, Starring Popeye the Sailor* (King Features Syndicate, Inc., 1971). This is from a series that appeared in 1936.

2. Text in James B. Pritchard, *Ancient Near Eastern Texts Relating to the Old Testament*, 3d ed. (Princeton: Princeton Univ. Press, 1969), 60-72. Alexander Heidel dates the composition of the *Enuma Elish* ca. 1900–1600 B.C.E. in its present form (*The Babylonian Genesis*, 2d ed. [Chicago: Univ. of Chicago Press, 1951], 14). Thorkild Jacobsen dates it ca. 1250 B.C.E. (*The Treasures of Darkness. A History of Mesopotamian Religion* [New Haven: Yale Univ. Press, 1976], 167). See also Jacobsen in *Before Philosophy*, by H. and H. A. Frankfort et al. (Baltimore: Penguin Books, 1959), 137–234; "Mesopotamian Religions: An Overview," in *Encyclopedia of Religion*, ed. Mircea Eliade (New York: Macmillan, 1987), 9:457–58; and "The Battle Between Marduk and Tiamat," *Journal of the American Oriental Society* 88 (1968): 104–8. Other works consulted include S. N. Kramer, *Sumerian Mythology* (Philadelphia: American Philosophical Society, 1944), for earlier versions of the creation epic, pp. 76–83; Morris Jastrow, *Aspects of Religious Belief and Practice in Babylonia and Assyria* (New York: Benjamin Blom, Inc., [1911] 1971); Tikva Frymer-Kensky, "Enuma Elish" and "Marduk," *Encyclopedia of Religion*, 5:124–26 and 9:201–2; Robert J. Braidwood, *The Near East and the Foundations for Civilization* (Eugene, Oreg.: Oregon State System of Higher Education, 1952); Gertrude Rachel Levy, *The Gate of Horn: A Study of the Religious Conceptions of the Stone Age, and Their Influence on European Thought* (New York: Book Collector's Society, 1946); Beatrice Laura Goff, *Symbols of Prehistoric Mesopotamia* (New Haven: Yale Univ. Press, 1963); Grahame Clark, *World Prehistory: A New Outline*, 2d ed. (Cambridge: Cambridge Univ. Press, 1969); Jacquetta Hawkes and Sir Leonard Woolley, *Prehistory and the Beginnings of Civilization* (New York: Harper & Row, 1963); Miles Burkitt, *The Old Stone Age: A Study of Paleolithic*

Times, 3d ed. (London: Bowes and Bowes, 1955); Joan Oates, "Ur and Eridu, the Prehistory," in *Ur in Retrospect*, ed. M. E. L. Mallowan and D. J. Wiseman (*Iraq* 22; London: British Society of Archaeology in Iraq, 1960), 32–50; W. G. Lambert, "The Great Battle of the Mesopotamian Religious Year: The Conflict in the Akitu House," *Iraq* 25 (1963): 189–90; and William W. Hallo and William Kelly Simpson, *The Ancient Near East: A History* (New York: Harcourt Brace Jovanovich, 1971).

3. Paul Ricoeur, *The Symbolism of Evil* (New York: Harper & Row, 1967), 175–210.

4. The earth is formed, not apparently as previously thought, from one half of Tiamat's body, but (as the discovery of the missing portion of Tablet V shows) from outflowings from her celestial body: her spittle and her "poison," together with effluences from her eyes, nostrils, and udder. Marduk stretches out her cadaver full length, from tongue to tail, and "so she was fastened to the heavens" (V.59–61) (A. Kragerud, "The Concept of Creation in Enuma Elish," in *Ex Orbe Religionum: Studia Geo Widengren*, ed. C. J. Bleeker, S. G. F. Brandon, and M. Simon [Leiden: E. J. Brill, 1972], 39–49).

5. James A. Aho, *Religious Mythology and the Art of War* (Westport, Conn.: Greenwood Press, 1981), 60. This combat myth pervaded the ancient world. Adela Yarbro Collins has demonstrated how deeply this motif has penetrated the Apocalypse of John (*The Combat Myth in the Book of Revelation* [Missoula, Mont.: Scholars Press, 1976], 57). The same mythic pattern was carried into the European Middle Ages by the Cathari and the Knights Templars. See Norman Cohn, *Europe's Inner Demons* (New York: New American Library, 1975), 79. For an analysis of the structure of the combat myth, see Joseph Fontenrose, *Python: A Study of Delphic Myth and Its Origins* (Berkeley: Univ. of California Press, 1959), 6–11.

6. *Enuma Elish* II.110–11 (Pritchard, *Ancient Near Eastern Texts*, 64). Like hundreds of myths worldwide, the woman is blamed for everything evil: "Mother of all, why did you have to mother war" (*Enuma Elish* IV.79–80, trans. N. K. Sanders, in Barbara C. Sproul, *Primal Myths* [San Francisco: Harper & Row, 1979], 101).

7. In the Code of Hammurabi (ca. 1752 B.C.E.), Marduk's elevation to kingship over the gods is initiated by a datable historical event: the victory of Hammurabi over Rim-Sin in the thirtieth year of his reign, which brought Southern Babylon (ancient Sumer) under his sway and united the country as it had once been under the Third Dynasty of Ur. Resistance by the priestly caste of other conquered cities prevented Marduk's achieving full ascendancy over all the gods until around the mid-second millennium B.C.E. (H. W. F. Saggs, *The Greatness that was Babylon* [London: Sidgwick & Jackson, 1962], 339–40). The *Enuma Elish* (ca. 1250 B.C.E. in its final recension) is thus literally correct: Marduk demands of the gods a prestige no other god had previously known.

Sumer's ancient name had actually been "Land of Tiamat" or "Sealand." Babylon had, in effect, waged an upstart's war against its own mother culture, with all its ancient cities and gods. The victory of Babylon and its god Marduk was thus matricide ("killing the mother") as well as deicide. The Sumer/Tiamat connection explains the odd sympathy shown Tiamat in the *Enuma Elish*, the swift amnesty for her allies, and their so quickly being drawn into the building and administration of Babylon and its empire. As above, so below: the story of the gods perfectly mirrors actual political developments in the state.

Concentration of political authority in the hands of a single man seems to have become the rule in Sumerian cities by 3000 B.C.E. (William H. McNeill, *The Rise of the West: A History of the Human Community* [Chicago: Univ. of Chicago Press, 1963], 43; and Thorkild Jacobsen, *Toward the Image of Tammuz* [Cambridge: Harvard Univ. Press, 1970], 157–70). Sargon, king of Kish, boasts that "54,000 men daily in his presence eat food" (Inscription CD, in George A. Barton, *The Royal Inscriptions of Sumer and Akkad* [New Haven: Yale Univ. Press, 1929], 111).

8. A somewhat similar motif is reflected in Greek Orphic poetry. Wicked Titans trap the infant god Dionysus, tear him to bits, and boil, roast, and eat him. In revenge Zeus burns them up with a thunderbolt. From the smoke of their remains spring human beings, who thus exhibit the bestiality of the Titans yet preserve a tiny spark of divine soul-stuff, which is the substance of the god Dionysus still working in them as an occult self (E. R. Dodds, *The Greeks and the Irrational* [Berkeley: Univ. of California Press, 1951], 155). Here, as in the Mesopotamian myth, evil and violence in human nature are seen to far outweigh the good.

9. Ricoeur, *Symbolism of Evil*, 178, 180.

10. Text in *Revue d'assyriologie et d'archéologie orientale* 17 (1920): 132; the translation is by Jacobsen, *Before Philosophy*, 218.

11. See Ricoeur, *Symbolism of Evil*, 193. Saggs believes, with W. von Soden, that the Akkadian text thought to describe Marduk's dying and rising again at the New Year's Festival in Babylon is based on an inaccurate translation, and that the identification of Marduk with the vegetation god Dumuzi (or Tammuz) is questionable (*The Greatness That Was Babylon*, 300–1; so also A. R. W. Green, *The Role of Human Sacrifice in the Ancient Near East* [Missoula, Mont.: Scholars Press, 1975], 91–95). But the motif of the humiliation of the king appears solidly established (as Saggs himself demonstrates, 387), and it is this, and not the association with Dumuzi/Tammuz, that is important for our purposes.

12. Ricouer, *Symbolism of Evil*, 198.

13. Earlier versions of the myth indicate that the world was thought to have formed naturally as the gods bred new generations of themselves and created things at will for their own purposes. The world was virtually a living being, divine and constantly expanding, chaotic and unpredictable. In earlier versions, also, Marduk plays a minor role if he is mentioned at all (Joan O'Brien and Wilfred Major, *In the Beginning: Creation Myths from Ancient Mesopotamia, Israel, and Greece* [Chico, Calif.: Scholars Press, 1982], 10; Kragerud, "The Concept of Creation in Enuma Elish," 39–49). The shift from democracy to tyranny, and from an organic view of creation to one of combat and murder, confirms the thesis of Riane Eisler in *The Chalice and the Blade* (San Francisco: Harper & Row, 1987), as we see in the next chapter.

14. Ruby Rohrlich, "State Formation in Sumer and the Subjection of Women," *Feminist Studies* 6/1 (Spring 1980): 76–102.

15. Exceptions to the mythic structure of redemptive violence include Mickey Mouse, Donald Duck, Porky Pig, Woody Woodpecker, Dumbo's Circus, Ghostbusters, Davey and Goliath, Casper the Friendly Ghost, Archie, Deputy Dog, Howdy Doody, Laurel and Hardy, Muppets, Welcome to Pooh Corner, Bozo the

Clown, Dennis the Menace, Smurfs, Pink Panther, Scooby Doo, Flintstones, Curious George, Heathcliff, Alvin and the Chipmunks, Gumby, Care Bears, Yogi Bear, and others.

Other examples of violent cartoons exemplifying the combat myth are Bugs Bunny, Space Cadets, Daffy Duck, Hercules, Thor, Green Hornet, Top Cat, Thundercats, Buck Rogers, Captain Power, Spartakus, He-Man vs. Skeletor, Bionic Six, Brave Starr, Jem, She-Ra: Princess of Power, Superboy, Transformers, Silver Hawks, Centurions, Dungeons and Dragons, Brave Star, and Saber Rider. This list is by no means exhaustive.

Attempts to be sexually inclusive have merely meant casting females in the same violent mold as the males.

16. The archetypal nature of the cartoon structure is shown by the fact that it includes the motif of the humiliation of the king. I am quite confident that few of the cartoonists are aware of the roots of their stories in ancient myth. (The sole exception is Dungeons and Dragons, which features Tiamat with seven heads!) The combat myth simply reasserts itself in the human psyche because it is the crudest, most convenient means of coping with evil.

17. Willis Elliott, "Thinksheet," no. 2196, November 8, 1987.

18. Conversation with my five-year-old grandson: "Do the good guys ever get killed?" I asked. "No! Never!" "Why?" "Because they're such good fighters." "Do the bad guys always lose?" "Yes." "Why?" "Because they're not good fighters."

19. Arthur Asa Berger, *The Comic-Stripped American* (Baltimore: Penguin Books, 1973), 128. Violence as the main fare of comics and cartoons was actually rather slow in developing, though it had long been the preoccupation of fairy tales, myths, epics, novels, and religious beliefs (fantasy depictions of hell, as in Dante). Only two comics of twenty-two that first appeared in the 1920s stressed the power of the main character. During the Depression, however, that proportion had shifted to twelve out of twenty-one (Stephen M. Sales, "Authoritarianism," *Psychology Today* [November 1972]: 140).

20. Robert Jewett and John Sheldon Lawrence identify this view as "the American monomyth," which they characterize as the belief in "regeneration through violence." They have brilliantly traced the omnipresence of this belief in literature, the cinema, cartoons, television programs, video games, and other facets of American life. They find five interlocking ideas crystallized to create the American monomyth of zealous nationalism: a conspiracy theory of evil; a radical stereotyping and dichotomizing of good and evil; a mystique of violence as at least potentially redemptive; a conviction that the faithful will prevail no matter what the odds; and celebration of courageous redeemer figures. See Jewett's *The Captain America Complex: The Dilemma of Zealous Nationalism*, rev. ed. (Santa Fe: Bear & Co., 1984); "Coming to Terms with the Doom Boom," *Quarterly Review* 4 (1984): 9–22; with Lawrence, *The American Monomyth* (Garden City, N.Y.: Doubleday, 1977); " 'Star Trek' and the Bubble Gum Fallacy," *Television Quarterly* 14 (1977): 5–16; "Beyond the Pornography of Violence," *Religion in Life* 46 (1977): 357–63; "The Problem of Mythic Imperialism," *Journal of American Culture* 2 (1979): 309–20; and "The Fantasy Factor in Civil Religion: Assassinations and Mass Murders in the Media Age," *Mission Journal* 17 (1983): 72. I first presented the gist of this chapter in a lecture at Union Seminary

in 1969, not knowing that Jewett was developing a similar thesis along other lines, and in far more penetrating detail.

21. Ariel Dorfman, *The Empire's Old Clothes* (New York: Pantheon Books, 1983), 97. The Lone Ranger and Tonto provide an interesting variant on the violence theme: they do try to put off violence as long as possible, using persuasion and at times even converting the wicked. When the Lone Ranger does shoot, it is usually to knock the gun out of the villain's hand, not to kill. But the conversion involved does not lead to returning the Indians' lands, or tearing up railroad tracks, or dismantling the western military garrisons and releasing Indians from their concentration camps (euphemistically called "reservations"). It is simply a conversion to the "law and order" of white exploitation of the wild and chaotic West and domination over its "savages." The villains have only two choices: to accept the norms of their enemies as valid and stop being unruly, or to be shot. See Dorfman, 67–131.

22. John T. Gallaway, Jr., *The Gospel According to Superman* (Philadelphia: A. J. Holman, 1973), 93; Dick Davis, "Interventions," unpublished paper, p. 4.

23. Berger, *Comic-Stripped American*, 161.

24. Jewett and Lawrence, "Fantasy Factor in Civil Religion," 73; *American Monomyth*, 196, 210–11, 215; Jewett, *Captain America Complex*, 94–95.

25. Ibid.

26. Marshall McLuhan, *The Mechanical Bride*, cited by Berger, *Comic-Stripped American*, 158.

27. Jewett and Lawrence, *American Monomyth*, 157.

28. *New York Times*, August 7, 1975, 16. Another oddity of history as myth: the private capitalist who founded the first military school in Austria was named Baron de Chaos (Alfred Vagts, *A History of Militarism* [New York: W. W. Norton, 1937], 54).

29. Michael N. Nagler, *America Without Violence* (Covelo, Calif.: Island Press, 1982), 27. CBS proudly proclaims this slogan on its Saturday morning cartoon blitz: "Where kids rule."

30. If the basic pattern of the combat myth is developmentally recapitulated by children in domination societies even today as the first solution to the problem of evil, one could predict then that it would be represented around the globe in a variety of myths featuring a generative act of violence. This is indeed the case. Sue Mansfield traces the combat myth through a wide spectrum of cultures. The Yanomamo of South America, for example, tell how the Spirit of the Moon liked to eat the soul parts of children. Two brothers finally shot him with an arrow. "The blood changed to men as it hit the earth," says the myth. Here not only does human life begin with an act of violence whereby chaos is overcome, but the warlike character of humanity is explained: "because they have their origins in blood, they are fierce and are continually making war on each other" (*The Gestalts of War* [New York: Dial Press, 1982], 56). The Hottentots of Southern Africa, the Apaches, Chiricahua, and Papagoes of the American Southwest, and the Vedic poets who narrated Indra's defeat of Vritra, to name but a few, all told of a god or cultural hero who overcame, through an act of violence, the forces of chaos and destruction. According to Mansfield, one could repeat such myths endlessly as they are part of the cultural heritage of virtually all domination societies (p. 58).

31. Andrew J. McKenna, "The Law's Delay: Cinema and Sacrifice," *Legal Studies Forum* 15/3 (1991): 199–213.

32. Parents concerned about the impact of television on their children could minimize the indoctrinating effects of violence by monitoring from the earliest age what shows children watch. If viewing time is limited to thirty minutes or an hour a day, children are forced to develop discrimination on their own. Nonmoralistic family discussion of violence on television can help them hone their critical capacities; parents might ask questions like, "Why do they always settle things with a fight? Why don't they talk it over, the way we do?"

33. *U.S. News and World Report*, October 27, 1986, 64.

34. William F. Fore, "Media Violence: Hazardous to Our Health," *Christian Century* 102 (Sept. 25, 1985): 836. Surveys indicate that the amount of violence on television continues to rise, up 50 percent since 1980 on weekends alone. Consider also that 99 percent of American homes have television, and that the average viewer now watches over six hours daily (Kenneth Curtis, "Telecult: How the television culture has become our *real* religion," Gateway Films, Valley Forge, PA 19481). Heavy viewers of television, whatever their educational or economic level, sex, or age, express a greater sense of insecurity and apprehension than light viewers. Fearful people are more dependent, more easily manipulated and controlled, and may accept and even welcome repression if it promises to relieve their insecurities (ibid.). The Marduk solution is the concentration of power in an absolute dictator. No message could be more subversive to democracy.

35. Joe Queenan, "Drawing on the Dark Side," *New York Times Magazine*, April 30, 1989, 32–34, 79, 86. I leave aside the question whether some males, or males generally, are genetically predisposed to greater violence than women. Even if this proves true, genes are not fate. A good deal of what makes us human has to do with our struggle to surmount genetic givens.

36. Geoffrey Barlow and Alison Hill, eds., *Video Violence and Children* (New York: St. Martin's Press, 1985), 67. Note that the violent killing of a female and her dismemberment is a central feature of the Marduk myth.

37. Ibid. The current Teenage Mutant Ninja Turtles rage encourages violent and antisocial behavior in the classroom, according to a survey of teachers. "The way the Ninja Turtles work out their difficulties is by socking each other and knocking each other," commented one teacher. Ninety-five percent of the respondents provided examples of aggressive behavior linked to the Turtle characters. There is nothing new about superheroes beating up enemies, but the intense marketing of everything from Turtle toys to lunchboxes has provided an obsession with the creatures among children aged eighteen months to ten years, according to the researchers (*Berkshire Eagle*, March 18, 1991, B3).

38. See chap. 2, pp. 33–34.

39. Barlow and Hill, *Video Violence and Children*, 89.

40. Ibid. 152–58.

41. Ibid., 152. I cannot endorse censorship, but a judicious use of the boycott is needed in order to reduce the levels of violence served up to our children. For information on the boycott of two violent television shows targeted at boys, "Friday the 13th" and "Freddy's Nightmares," contact National Coalition on Television Violence, Box 2157, Champaign, IL 61824. The National Association of Ratings Boards

has a helpful newsletter. On the related issue of war toys, see Nancy Carlson Paige and Diane Levin, *Who's Calling the Shots? How to Respond Effectively to Children's Fascination with War Play and War Toys* (Philadelphia: New Society Publishers, 1991). On campaigns to ban or discourage the sale of war toys, contact War Resisters League, 339 Lafayette, New York, NY 10012.

42. *Naming the Powers*, 131–37.

43. Georges Khodr, "Violence and the Gospel," *Cross Currents* 37 (Winter 1987–88): 405; see also Nagler, *America Without Violence*, 19.

44. Alfred Vagts helpfully distinguishes the military from militarism. The military is committed to organizing personnel and materiel in order to achieve specific objectives of power with the utmost efficiency and the least possible loss of life. It is limited in scope, professional, and subservient to larger political processes. Militarism, by contrast, is unlimited in scope. It seeks to exalt military virtues, ideals, expenditures, and leaders over all other social values. Militarism cherishes war but may actually hamper military preparation and victory. It tends to permeate all of society and become dominant over all industry and arts. "Rejecting the scientific character of the military way, militarism displays the qualities of caste and cult, authority and belief." The true opposite of militarism is not, then, pacifism, but civilianism (*History of Militarism*, 11–15).

It is important to note also that not everyone in military service subscribes to the extreme forms of militarism enshrined in the national security creed. As Morris Janowitz, a leading sociologist of the military in America, points out, there are two schools of thought in the defense establishment, one absolutist, the other pragmatic. The pragmatists, though a minority, still play a role in decision making at every level of the war system. They are prepared (and even hope) for a career as soldiers without combat, and they believe that combat readiness can be maintained without repressive disciplines and without "satanizing" the enemy ("Strategic Dimensions of an All Volunteer Armed Force," in *The Military-Industrial Complex*, ed. S. C. Sarkesian [Beverly Hills and London: SAGE Publications, 1972], 144–45).

45. José Miguez Bonino shows how, since Augustine's *City of God*, Christianity has all too often served to legitimate the existing order. Augustine declared order to be the highest social good. Injustices should be corrected whenever that can be done *without endangering order and peace*. But if any redress of wrong threatens to lead to violence or upheaval, it should be avoided. By defining peace as order, Augustine insured that changes, even those necessary to provide freedom or justice, would be regarded as disordering, and hence negative. Christianity developed a political theology that operated on behalf of the established order. As Míguez Bonino puts it, "The true question is not 'What degree of justice (liberation of the poor) is compatible with the maintenance of the existing order?' but 'What kind of order, which order is compatible with the exercise of justice (the right of the poor)?' " (*Toward a Christian Political Ethic* [Philadelphia: Fortress Press, 1983], 86).

46. José Comblin, *The Church and the National Security State* (Maryknoll, N.Y.: Orbis Books, 1984), 64–98.

47. Jean Daniélou, *Origen* (New York: Sheed & Ward, 1955), 234.

48. Cited by Comblin, *The Church and the National Security State*, 78.

49. James B. Jordan, "Pacifism and the Old Testament," in *The Theology of Christian Resistance*, ed. Gary North (Tyler, Tex.: Geneva Divinity School Press,

1983), 90, 92. Guatemala's fundamentalist dictator, Gen. Rios Montt, excused the massacre of children by a unique variation on the theology of redemptive violence. Guilt and crime are transmitted biologically, he argued, by "bad seed." "I'm not killing the people. The devil has entered into the people. I'm killing the devil" (Dean Peerman, "What Ever Happened to Rios Montt?" *Christian Century* 102 [September 25, 1985]: 819).

The Irish poet and nationalist Patrick Pearse, three years before his execution in 1916 for his part in the Easter uprising, eulogized the redemptive nature of blood sacrifice. "We may make mistakes in the beginning and shoot the wrong people; but bloodshed is a cleansing and a satisfying thing and the nation which regards it as the final horror has lost its manhood. There are many things more horrible than bloodshed, and slavery is one of them . . . without the shedding of blood there is no redemption . . . as the blood of the martyrs was the seed of the saints, so the blood of the patriot will be the sacred seed from which alone can spring new forces and fresh life into a nation that is drifting into the putrescence of decay" (quoted by John Hunter, "An Analysis of the Conflict in Northern Ireland," in *Political Co-Operation in Divided Societies*, ed. Desmond Rea [Dublin: Gill and Macmillan, 1983], 35–36).

50. In two passages of the Old Testament, Yahweh is actually depicted in language evocative of Marduk (Ps. 74:14; Isa. 27:1).

51. *Berkshire Eagle*, April 20, 1987, A4.

52. Ibid., July 27, 1987, A10.

53. Mary Evelyn Jegen, SND, describes a chapel she visited at the Strategic Air Command base in Omaha.

A large stained-glass window dominates the sanctuary of the chapel. The window shows the figure of an air force officer, larger than life, bathed in yellow light. A description of the window explains that this golden light represents the glory of God descending on the man. Behind the figure of the officer, who is bravely facing the enemy, are figures of a small woman and two small children, timidly cowering in the dark. The man, who is portrayed as twice the size of the woman, is defending her and the children from evil, represented by enemy aircraft. He is ready to defend them with the same kind of equipment that the enemy will use to attack them. The description of the window explains that "the . . . flight of [his] aircraft is bathed in a golden light similar to the rays of light descending from God."

("Women and the Peace Movement: Choosing Life over Death," *Pax Christi USA* 12/3 [Fall 1987]: 15–17). No hint of uncertainty about the justice of our cause enters the scene. God here is not sovereign over all the nations, judging them all with equity. God is merely equivalent to the war god of the American people.

54. Comblin, *The Church and the National Security State*, 107.

55. See Jacques Ellul, *Propaganda: The Formation of Men's Attitudes* (New York: Vintage Books, 1973).

56. Jewett, *Captain America Complex*, 210–11. In the creed of redemptive violence, monolithic evil is so centralized, so ubiquitous, so nimble, that to fail to crush it even in one place is to risk inundation by it everywhere. Even if the South Vietnamese government were to ask the Americans to withdraw, Ambassador Henry

Cabot Lodge told reporters, the United States would be justified in staying, since a pullout "would certainly shake our position in Berlin" (Richard Barnet, *Intervention and Revolution* [New York: New American Library, 1972], 237). Berlin?! The United States must face the communists in Vietnam, President Johnson told a credulous American public, or else we would have to deal with them later on the beaches of California. Communism, President Reagan insisted, must be stopped in Nicaragua, or else we will end up fighting it in Harlingen, Texas. Somehow these spokesmen for American hegemony never perceived the irony of their lack of faith that democracy would prevail in the competition for the world's hearts and minds.

57. Richard Slotkin, *Regeneration through Violence* (Middletown, Conn.: Wesleyan Univ. Press, 1973), 5.

58. On angels of nations, see my *Unmasking the Powers*, chap. 4.

59. Jewett, *Captain America Complex*, 253.

2. THE ORIGIN OF THE DOMINATION SYSTEM

1. Cited by Thelma Jean Goodrich, "Women, Power, and Family Therapy: What's Wrong with This Picture," in *Women and Power: Perspectives for Family Therapy*, ed. Goodrich (New York: W. W. Norton, 1991), 20.

2. Konrad Lorenz, *On Aggression* (New York: Bantam Books, 1969); Niko Tinbergen, "On War and Peace in Animals and Man," *Science* 160 (1968): 1411–18; Robert Ardrey, *African Genesis* (New York: Athenaeum, 1961); *The Territorial Imperative* (New York: Athenaeum, 1966); Desmond Morris, *The Naked Ape* (New York: McGraw-Hill, 1967).

3. We deal with Girard in detail in chap. 7; for bibliography, see n. 11 in that chapter.

4. Konrad Lorenz, *On Aggression*, chap. 13, esp. 235–36. Lorenz's conclusions about human violence are not a result of his research into animal behavior, but a completely predictable consequence of his initial anthropological assumption: we are soulless animals. A person with a soul might transcend genetic givens; a mere animal is their slave.

5. Ashley Montague, *The Nature of Human Aggression* (New York: Oxford Univ. Press, 1976), 236–37. Richard E. Leakey and Roger Lewin question Dart's belief that primitive skeletons were crushed by blows. Instead they ascribe the crushing to the gradual buildup of soil and stone over the hollow cranium (*People of the Lake* [Garden City, N.Y.: Anchor Press/Doubleday, 1978], 270–75). The whole discussion of animal violence has greatly benefitted by the publication of Frans de Waal's *Peacemaking among Primates* (Cambridge: Harvard Univ. Press, 1989). Gorillas and chimpanzees *do* occasionally kill members of their own species, especially in captivity, he reports, and wild chimpanzees occasionally hunt, eat meat, and are cannibalistic. But what earlier researchers like Lorenz overlooked is how primates *avoid* conflicts and, when they do occur, afterward repair and normalize relationships. Monkeys, apes, and humans all engage in reconciliatory behavior: grooming, hugging, kissing, third party interventions, and submission. Forgiveness, he asserts, is thirty million years old. There is simply no other way for any animal that prefers group life to a solitary existence. About forty percent of the time, chimpanzee

opponents make reconciliatory contact within half an hour of their aggressive behavior.

6. At the 6th International Colloquium on Brain and Aggression held at the University of Seville in Spain in 1986, a group of scholars agreed to the following propositions: "*It is scientifically incorrect* to say that we have inherited a tendency to make war from our animal ancestors. . . . that war or any other violent behavior is genetically programmed into our human nature. . . . that in the course of human evolution there has been a selection for aggressive behavior more than for other kinds of behavior. . . . that humans have a "violent brain". . . . that war is caused by 'instinct' or any single motivation." This "Seville Statement on Violence" has been endorsed by hundreds of scientists, scholars, and international agencies. Copies are available from David Adams, Wesleyan Psychology Dept., Middletown, CT 06457.

7. Sue Mansfield, *The Gestalts of War* (New York: Dial Press, 1982), 1–19. See also William Eckhardt, "Conditions of Peace Suggested by Some Quantitative Studies of Primitive Warfare," *Peace Research* (Canada) 21 (August 1989): 37–40. Those who enlist in the U.S. military seldom do so thirsting to kill. Rather, they join to get training or college benefits, to escape unemployment or a threatening neighborhood, to develop a career in a relatively color-blind context, or just to get away from home.

8. S. L. A. Marshall, *Men against Fire: The Problem of Battle Command in Future War* (New York: William Morrow, 1947), 78–81.

9. Mansfield, *Gestalts of War*, 1–19; Ralph L. Holloway, Jr., "Human Aggression," in *War: The Anthropology of Armed Conflict and Aggression*, ed. Morton Fried, Marvin Harris, and Robert Murphy (Garden City, N.Y.: The Natural History Press, 1967), 29–48.

10. Michelle Zimbalist Rosaldo and Louise Lamphere, eds., "Introduction," in *Women, Culture, and Society* (Stanford: Stanford Univ. Press, 1974), 3.

11. Karen Lampell Endicott, "Batek Negrito Sex Roles," M.A. thesis, Australian National University, 1979; courtesy of Prof. Rodney Needham of Oxford University.

12. Ashley Montague has gathered detailed reports by experts on seven other primitive societies in *Learning Non-Aggression: The Experience of Non-Literate Societies* (New York: Oxford Univ. Press, 1978). In his introduction (p. 5) he itemizes eighteen additional nonaggressive societies. See also the excellent comparative study by Peggy Reeves Sanday, *Female Power and Male Dominance: The Origins of Sexual Inequality* (Cambridge, Mass.: Cambridge Univ. Press, 1981), esp. 16–34; Stephen Braun, "Jungle Nonviolence," in Robert L. Holmes, ed., *Nonviolence in Theory and Practice* (Belmont, Calif.: Wadsworth Publishing Co., 1990), 181–84; and Leakey and Lewin, *People of the Lake*, 96–125. A very broad consensus seems to exist that the earliest human societies were, on the whole, egalitarian; so Morton Fried, *The Evolution of Human Society* (New York: Random House, 1967), x, noting that "equality" refers not to identity (a social impossibility) but to equal freedom to fulfill one's capacities. Fried defines an egalitarian society as one in which there are as many positions of prestige in any given age-sex grade as there are people capable of filling them (p. 32). C. R. Hallpike concurs that the first condition of humanity was that of equality (*The Principles of Social Evolution* [Oxford: Clarendon Press, 1986], 226); so also Ronald Cohen, "State Origins: A Reappraisal," in *The Early*

State, ed. Henri J. M. Claessen and Peter Skalník (The Hague: Mouton Publishers, 1978), 67; and Cohen, in *The Origins of the State: The Anthropology of Political Evolution*, ed. Cohen and Elman R. Service (Philadelphia: Institute for the Study of Human Issues, 1978), 7–8 and 141–60. Some of our data is documentary; for example, Herodotus described a tribe in which "the women have equal power with the men" (4.26)—a characteristic that had no effect in mitigating the belligerence of this people.

13. It is also true that a great many surviving primitive or near-primitive societies are quite violent. Some of them only *became* violent in reactive self-defense against the encroachments of "civilization." Others may have been violent from their origins.

14. Elise Boulding, *The Underside of History: A View of Women Through Time* (Boulder, Colo.: Westview Press, 1976), 40. There is evidence of destruction of enemies among the Pithecanthropic and Neanderthal, and one or two instances of flint points found lodged in human skeletons of Upper Paleolithic age. At the cave of Ofnet in Bavaria, thirty-three skulls were found, apparently of victims of head-hunters (judging from the number of women and children represented). But "the general absence of weapons of war among the grave furniture of Neolithic burials provides even more convincing proof of the absence of martial ideals in the hearts of the new peasantry" (Jacquetta Hawkes, "Prehistory," in Hawkes and Sir Leonard Woolley, *History of Mankind*, vol. 1, *Prehistory and the Beginnings of Civilization* [New York: Harper & Row, 1963], 127, 265, 321).

15. H. W. F. Saggs, *The Greatness That Was Babylon* (London: Sidgwick & Jackson, 1962), 160. When Greek society shifted to descent traced through the father rather than the mother, Athenian women *lost* the right to vote, according to Augustine (*City of God* 18.9). The imposition of androcracy meant the attenuation of democracy (Riane Eisler, *The Chalice and the Blade* [San Francisco: Harper & Row, 1987], 114).

16. Thorkild Jacobsen, *The Treasures of Darkness: A History of Mesopotamia* (New Haven: Yale Univ. Press, 1976), 77. Anthropologists disagree on whether primitive hunting and gathering tribes were warlike or not. Probably some were and some were not. But virtually all are agreed that, if and when societies fought, it was to meet immediate physiological needs, and that their fighting was at most sporadic.

17. Anne Barstow, "The Uses of Archaeology for Women's History: James Mellaart's Work on the Neolithic Goddess at Çatal Hüyük," *Feminist Studies* 4 (1978): 7–18; Eisler, *The Chalice and the Blade*, 7–12; and Elinor W. Gadon, *Once and Future Goddess* (San Francisco: Harper & Row, 1989), 24.

18. Eisler, *The Chalice and the Blade*, 7–18. Eisler has coined two terms for societies that existed prior to the dominator system: one is "partnership societies" and the other is "gylany," the latter being a compound of *gynē* (woman) and *anēr* (man) linked (*l*) in relationships of equality and nonviolence.

19. Jericho had huge walls and a watch tower from 8350 to 7350 B.C.E., apparently to protect the oasis from marauding bands of hunter-gatherers, and Hacilar (Anatolia) was walled; but these were exceptional. Early Sumerian cities were not fortified. Not until the Early Dynastic II period did fortifications become general, indicating that interstate warfare began there around 2600 B.C.E. (H. W. F. Saggs, *The Greatness That Was Babylon*, 40). Marija Gimbutas finds no evidence at all in Old Europe

(6500–4500 B.C.E.) of a patriarchal chieftainate of the Indo-European type. There
are no male royal tombs, no heavy fortifications, no weapons of war, no hillforts.
The burial rites and settlement patterns reflect a matrilineal structure, while the
distribution of wealth in graves speaks for an economic egalitarianism (*The Civilization of the Goddess: The World of Old Europe* [San Francisco: HarperSan-
Francisco, 1991], chap. 9). In the Sahara, between 5500 and 3500 B.C.E., thousands
of rock pictures were painted depicting "a gentler, less frightened world, in which
the peaceful scenes of cattle herding, which form the vast majority of the paintings,
are occasionally interrupted by cattle raids leading to fights between bowmen of
various groups" (James Mellaart, *The Neolithic of the Near East* [New York: Charles
Scribner's Sons, 1975], 51; see also Hawkes, "Prehistory," 269, 298; Boulding, *Underside of History*, 125; and Ruby Rohrlich-Leavitt, "Women in Transition: Crete
and Sumer," in *Becoming Visible: Women in European History*, ed. Renate Bri-
denthal and Claudia Koonz [Boston: Houghton Mifflin Co., 1977], 40).

20. Mansfield, *Gestalts of War*, 20–30.

21. Fried, *Evolution of Political Society*, 101; Barbara S. Lesko, ed., *Women's
Earliest Records from Ancient Egypt and West Asia* (Atlanta: Scholars Press, 1989),
1.

22. Stuart Struever and Felicia Antonelli Holton, *Koster: Americans in Search
of Their Prehistoric Past* (Garden City, N.Y.: Anchor Books, 1979), 258; L. S.
Cressman, *Prehistory of the Far West* (Salt Lake City: Univ. of Utah Press, 1977),
125–26; Michael N. Nagler, *America Without Violence* (Covelo, Calif.: Island Press,
1982), 51–69. C. W. Ceram writes, "the pre-Columbian peoples of North America
probably (in sharp contrast to the 'highly civilized' peoples of middle America, such
as the Aztecs) were unacquainted with war, that 'continuation of politics by other
means' which makes its appearance only after agricultural communities become real
states." Native North Americans knew violence: tribal feuds, predatory expeditions,
struggles for watering places and pastures, an occasional slaying or vengeful killing;
but these are a far cry, he says, from that permanent militarism that humanity has
developed only since the rise of the state in Mesopotamia. Militarism was introduced
into North America by the Spaniards. "Our pueblo peoples seem to have been
peaceable; they took up weapons only in emergencies, for self-defense—and were
usually defeated." The Hohokam pueblo people dwelt without wars for a thousand
years (*The First American* [New York: New American Library, 1971], 125–26, 220).

There is no evidence of warfare or attack in the entire seven hundred year history
of the Anasazi at Mesa Verde. "Depiction of warriors or warfare is completely missing
in the rock art or pottery vessels of the Anasazi, and the folk tales and myths of the
modern Pueblos are singularly lacking in stories of war" (William M. Ferguson and
Arthur H. Rohn, *Anasazi Ruins of the Southwest in Color* [Albuquerque: Univ. of
New Mexico Press, 1987], 67). So also Linda S. Cordell, *Prehistory of the Southwest*
(Boston: Academic Press, 1984), 304–8; Robert H. Lister and Florence G. Lister,
Chaco Canyon (Albuquerque: Univ. of New Mexico Press, 1981), 54; and J. J. Brody,
The Anasazi (New York: Rizzoli, 1990), 190, 220. Without horses (introduced by
the Spanish), a raider could only plunder what he could carry great distances over
waterless wastes. However, Steven A. LeBlanc finds some evidence of intertribal
warfare among the Anasazi beginning just before 1300 ("Cibola," in *Dynamics of
Southwest Prehistory*, ed. Linda S. Cordell and George J. Grimerman [Washington,

D.C.: Smithsonian Institution Press, 1989], 351–58). Again, the point is not that there was no violence, but that some groups found ways to minimize it over large expanses of their existence.

23. Marilyn French, *Beyond Power: On Women, Men, and Morals* (New York: Summit Books, 1985), 48.

24. Matrilineal and matrilocal arrangements still prevail among many native societies of North America and Africa, the Dravidians of India, and some Australian aboriginals; relics of it persist in Melanesia, Micronesia, and Indonesia; and vestiges point to an earlier practice of these arrangements in Egyptian, Homeric, and even early Hebraic societies (Gen. 2:24) (Jacquetta Hawkes, *Prehistory*, 122). At Çatal Hüyük, deceased children were buried near their mothers, suggesting descent through the mother (compare the Hebrew expression, "he slept with his fathers," 1 Kings 14:20). Men's sleeping platforms were also smaller than the women's and not in any fixed place (Gadon, *Once and Future Goddess*, 28). But even in matrilineal and matrilocal societies, males (often the wife's brother) were generally dominant.

25. Eisler, *The Chalice and the Blade*, 105; Marija Gimbutas, *The Goddesses and Gods of Old Europe, 7000–3500 B.C.* (Berkeley: Univ. of California Press, 1982); and *The Language of the Goddess* (San Francisco: Harper & Row, 1989). Actualization hierarchies are manifest in the increasingly complex structures that progress from cells to organs to living organisms, or in the revolving leadership of functioning democratic organizations (Eisler, 205 n. 5).

26. Gerhard Lenski, *Power and Privilege: A Theory of Social Stratification* (New York: McGraw-Hill, 1966), 102–6. Native Americans have maintained democratic forms of governance right up to the present.

27. Marielouise Janssen-Jurreit emphatically repudiates the search for prehistoric evidences of women's power. "After what is by now thousands of years of oppression, what help is it for women to console themselves with the fact that once, at the beginning of human history, they ruled over men? Women must incorporate only historical facts in their argument. Their oppression is easy to document and this is more than sufficient to substantiate their demands" (*Sexism: The Male Monopoly on History and Thought* [New York: Farrar Straus Giroux, 1982], 79). However, no reputable feminists are claiming any longer that matriarchy ever existed, but rather something approximating equality between the sexes. Susanne Heine also repudiates attempts to depict a feminist golden age in the remote past (*Matriarchs, Goddesses, and Images of God* [Minneapolis: Augsburg, 1989], 100–2).

28. John Howard Yoder, "Salvation Through Mothering?" unpublished paper, courtesy of the author.

29. Despotic rule was a new phenomenon, requiring divine authorization. The Sumerian King List states, "When kingship was *lowered from heaven* the kingship was in Eridu (Sumer)" (Saggs, *The Greatness That Was Babylon*, 35). On the rise of patriarchy, see Gerda Lerner, *The Creation of Patriarchy* (Oxford: Oxford Univ. Press, 1986); and Bertrand de Jouvenel, *Power: The Natural History of Its Growth* (London: Balchworth Press, 1945), 67.

30. The Scythians made sacrifices to an ancient iron scimitar, the image of their god of war, according to Herodotus (4.62). In the earliest Angkorian (Cambodian) societies, the king's power was thought to reside in the royal *lingam* (phallus), through which the king merged with Siva. This notion is most blatantly expressed in the

inscription of Práh Nôk, in which a general addresses King Udayadityavarman II
(1050–1067 C.E.), "Let me present the trophies to your invisible 'I' that is Siva
residing in the golden *linga* (penis)" (Leonid A. Sedov, "Angkor: Society and State,"
in *Early State*, 115). The drift is clear: divine power, manifest in the kingly office
by means of conquest, pillage, rape, the taking of slaves, and the slaughter of armies,
is male. It is, in fact, the male member that goes to war. In the Book of Revelation
the Word of God slays by the sword of his mouth, that is, by simple truth (Rev.
19:15). But the warrior king slays by the sword of his loins, which is itself a god
and a revealer of the god Shiva.

31. Eisler, *The Chalice and the Blade*, 47–49, 84.

32. The picture of monolithic patriarchy has been replaced by evidence of varying
degrees of male dominance and female participation and prominence. See Barbara
S. Lesko, "Introduction," in *Women's Earliest Records*, xiv.

33. Text in Jerrold Cooper, *Reconstructing History from Ancient Inscriptions:
The Lagash–Umma Border Conflict* (Sources from the Ancient Near East, vol. 2/
1 [Malibu: Undena Publications, 1983], 51). Lerner questions the translation of the
prohibition of polyandry, taking it instead as referring to the remarriage of a widow
(*The Creation of Patriarchy*, 63). But Cooper states that the text is unambiguous,
and H. W. F. Saggs concurs (*The Greatness That Was Babylon*, 187).

34. Lerner, *Creation of Patriarchy*, 215–18. Women have always found ways to
circumvent certain aspects of male dominance. Widows and single mothers in some
countries run their own homes and support themselves without a male partner. In
Africa, women are united through ancient women's councils that meet in clearings
when summoned by drums. Women are highly skilled in converting the power they
do have—deriving from the important services they render to men—into influence;
at times their influence can be considerable. Some women exercise "situational
dominance" over their husbands, even beating them (Boulding, *Underside of History*, 23, 41, 52–53). See also Marylin Arthur, " 'Liberated' Women: The Classical
Era," in *Becoming Visible*, 60–89; and Marielouise Janssen-Jurreit, *Sexism*, 318–
25.

35. Andrew Bard Schmookler, *The Parable of the Tribes: The Problem of Power
in Social Evolution* (Berkeley: Univ. of California Press, 1984), 20.

36. Ibid., 23.

37. Urukagina, whose brutal legislation against women was cited earlier (p.
4), is lauded by historians as a great legal reformer who lowered taxes and protected
the economically weak against victimization (Saggs, *The Greatness That Was Babylon*, 47–48). Hammurabi also saw it as his role as lawmaker to protect the weak
from the strong (ibid., 72).

38. Schmookler, *Parable of the Tribes*, 21. This statement should be taken as a
generalization from all domination societies, not as an ontological necessity. As we
shall see, the nonviolent *are* able to choose peace in the midst of a contest for power.

39. C. R. Hallpike, *Principles of Social Evolution*, 317.

40. Sanday, *Female Power and Male Dominance*, 177, 60.

41. Schmookler, *Parable of the Tribes*, 275, 27–28. Schmookler's language risks
reifying power, as if it were not an abstraction but virtually a material force in the
world.

42. Ibid., 62.

43. As a Nicaraguan feminist commented to my wife and me, "Right and left are all the same if power is what they're after."

44. Schmookler, *Parable of the Tribes*, 62.

45. Ibid.

46. Ibid., 210, 320.

47. Boulding, *Underside of History*, 52; Elisabeth Schüssler Fiorenza, *In Memory of Her* (New York: Crossroad, 1984), 86; Merlin Stone, *When God Was a Woman* (New York: Harcourt Brace Jovanovich, 1976), 30–61.

48. Eisler, *The Chalice and the Blade*, 87.

49. Ibid., 109.

50. French, *Beyond Power*, 54.

51. John Stoltenberg, *Refusing to Be a Man: Essays on Sex and Justice* (Portland: Breitenbush Books, 1989), 60, 129. This disturbingly truthful book brilliantly exposes the myth of male identity and supremacy.

52. French, *Beyond Power*, 77. See also Catherine A. MacKinnon, *Toward a Feminist Theory of the State* (Cambridge, Mass.: Harvard Univ. Press, 1989), esp. 157–70.

53. Ibid., 92; Merlin Stone, *When God Was a Woman*, 91.

54. Jacobsen, *Treasures of Darkness*, 77–79.

55. Eisler, *The Chalice and the Blade*, 94.

56. Ibid., 98–100.

57. Saggs reports the same for Sumerian society several thousand years earlier: at its beginning, women had a much higher status than in the heyday of Sumerian culture. He associates this change with the virtual disappearance over the same period of the goddesses who had held such a prominent position earlier and who later, with the sole exception of Ishtar, merely survived as consorts to male gods (*The Greatness that was Babylon*, 62).

58. Eisler, *The Chalice and the Blade*, 101.

59. Abraham J. Heschel, *The Prophets* (New York: Harper & Row, 1969), 1:166. There are statements in the Prophets rejecting sacrifice (Isa. 1:11-17; 17:7-8; 66:3; Jer. 6:20; 7:21-23, 31; 14:12; Hos. 6:6; 9:4; Amos 5:21-27; Mic. 6:6-8), and demanding justice in its stead (Isa. 1:16-17, 23, 27; 5:16-17; 25:4; 28:17; 56:1-2; Jer. 17:11; 22:3, 13-17; Amos 5:11-15; 6:12; Mic. 2:1-2). The prophets denounced violence (Isa. 1:21; 2:4, 15; 9:5; 26:21; 60:18; Amos 3:10; 6:3; Mic. 6:12); Second Isaiah exposed the scapegoating mechanism (Isaiah 53). The prophets occasionally criticized kingship (1 Samuel 8; Isa. 1:26; Hos. 8:4; 13:11), though some longed for a new kind of king who would bring justice without domination (Isa. 11:1-5; 16:5; 32:1; Jer. 23:5-6; Zech. 9:9-10). They condemned domination (Isa. 30:12), championed the cause of the poor (Isa. 41:17; Zech. 7:9-10) and women (Joel 2:28-29; Mal. 2:16), and looked forward to an era of peace, justice, and physical healing (Isa. 2:4; 9:6-7; 11:6-9; 19:23-25; 35:5-6; 52:7; 60:18; Ezek. 47:12; Mic. 5:5; Mal. 4:2). War and weaponry will be abolished from the land, and the people will lie down in safety (Hos. 2:18; 14:3; Mic. 4:3-4; Zech. 4:6). Jerusalem will be unwalled, because Yahweh will be a wall of fire to protect it (Zech. 2:4-5). And Daniel features civil disobedience (Daniel 3; 6). But this material appears alongside calls for violence. Jer. 48:10 calls bloodshed "the work of the Lord," and God's judgment is visited upon nations by

means of warfare. The domination-free strains of the Hebrew Bible are for the first time privileged and made normative as a consequence of Jesus' person and message.

60. Eisler, *The Chalice and the Blade*, 121.

61. Ibid.

62. This chart is based on Eisler's *The Chalice and the Blade* and her more recent work, with David Loye, *The Partnership Way* (San Francisco: HarperSanFrancisco, 1990), with additions of my own.

63. Sallie McFague, *Models of God* (Philadelphia: Fortress Press, 1987).

3. NAMING THE DOMINATION SYSTEM

1. John Steinbeck, *The Grapes of Wrath* (New York: Viking Press, 1939), 42–45.

2. Put more abstractly, "world" designates a sector of reality experienced by a particular subject in a typical way, or the structure of identity that is valid or common for a discrete group of people (Stephen Strasser, *The Idea of Dialogal Phenomenology* [Pittsburgh: Duquesne Univ. Press, 1969], 24–46; see also Alfred Schutz, "The Problem of Social Reality," *Collected Papers* [The Hague: Martin Piaget, 1962], 1:208; Jean Piaget, *A Child's Conception of the World* [New York: Harcourt, Brace & Co., 1929]).

3. "The use of *kosmos* in a negative or even evil sense is curiously absent from pre-Christian literature" (E. M. Sidebottom, *James, Jude and 2 Peter* [London: Nelson, 1967], 37). David Rensberger points out that for John's Gospel, the "world" is "human society as such, as it is organized and maintained for the good of some but to the harm of others and to the detriment of the love of God" (*Johannine Faith and Liberating Community* [Philadelphia: Westminster Press, 1988], 148). Albert Curry Winn speaks of "world" in John as "a series of ordered, structured, interlocking systems that are actually and potentially destructive of human values of the most basic kind and are therefore opposed to God who is the source of such values" (*A Sense of Mission* [Philadelphia: Westminster Press, 1981], 70). José Porfirio Miranda relates "world" to "all of civilization and not only to any one civilization in particular" (*Being and the Messiah* [Maryknoll, N.Y.: Orbis Books, 1977], 101–2)—a definition close to my concept of the Domination System. See also Hermann Sasse, "*aiōn*," *TDNT* 1:197–209; and "*kosmos*," *TDNT* 3:867–98; Friedrich Büchsel, "*genea*," *TDNT* 1:662–65; Wolfgang Schrage, "Die Stellung zur Welt bei Paulus, Epiktet und in der Apokalyptik: Ein Beitrag zu I Kor. 7, 29–31," *Zeitschrift für Theologie und Kirche* 61 (1964): 125–54; G. Johnston, "*Oikoumene* and *Kosmos* in the New Testament," *New Testament Studies* 10 (1964): 352–60; G. Bornkamm, "Christus und die Welt in der urchristlichen Botschaft," *Gesammelte Aufsätze* (Munich: Kaiser Verlag, 1958), 1:157–72; R. Völkl, *Christus und Welt nach dem Neuen Testament* (Würzburg: Echter-Verlag, 1961); Rudolf Schnackenburg, "The Concept of the World in the New Testament," in his *Christian Existence in the New Testament*, 2 vols. (Notre Dame, Ind.: Univ. of Notre Dame Press, 1968), 1:196–228; and Helmut Flender, "Das Verständnis der Welt bei Paulus, Markus und Lukas," *Kerygma und Dogma* 14 (1968): 1–27.

4. Hermann Sasse, "*kosmos*," *TDNT*, 3:894.

5. In this chapter, all scriptural translations are mine unless otherwise indicated.

6. *Webster's Ninth New Collegiate Dictionary* gives as the first definition of system, "a regularly interacting or interdependent group of items forming a unified whole"; but it also acknowledges a newer meaning remarkably close to the New Testament sense of "world": "an organized society or social situation regarded as stultifying," usually used with "the."

7. Albert Nolan, in personal conversation. See also his *God in South Africa* (Grand Rapids: Wm. B. Eerdmans, 1988), esp. 69. Several U.S. pastors have hit on "system" as a translation of *kosmos*. See, e.g., Philip Long, "In But Not of the System," *Confessing Synod Ministries Newsletter* 3/8 (August 1990): 1, 8.

In Chile they have a different word. Those who were aware called the Pinochet regime, and the spirituality of repression and brutality and fear that was its soul-penetrating strength, "the Menace" (*Amenaza*). "The first sign of the Menace was blacklisting," they will say; or, "Then the Menace picked up the phone" (Larry McMurtry, "The Voices of Santiago Say Anything Could Happen," *International Herald Tribune*, June 12, 1988, 4).

8. John H. Elliott, *1 Peter: Estrangement and Community* (Chicago: Franciscan Herald Press, 1979), 52.

9. D. H. Lawrence, "Letter from Germany," in his *Phoenix*, 2 vols. (London: William Heinemann, 1936), 1:107–10.

10. See Jacques Ellul, *Money and Power* (Downers Grove, Ill.: Intervarsity Press, 1984).

11. Ralph Wendell Burhoe, "Religion's Role in Human Evolution: The Missing Link Between Ape-Man's Selfish Genes and Civilized Altruism," *Zygon* 14 (1979): 144.

12. Anne Wilson Schaef, *When Society Becomes an Addict* (San Francisco: Harper & Row, 1987), 108.

13. Henry Skolimowski, "The Twilight of Physical Descriptions and the Ascent of Normative Models," in *The World System*, ed. Ervin Laszlo (New York: George Braziller, 1973), 99–100.

14. "The kingship that is not established or defended by acts of violence is the kingship under which the messianic community lives, the community whose messianic identity is known in its love for one another. Thus its love and its refusal of violence are essential to its confession of the messiahship of Jesus and indispensable to its making that messiahship known" (Rensberger, *Johannine Faith and Liberating Community*, 148).

15. *Kosmos* may refer here to possessions and wealth, rather than the system that produces them.

16. On *aiōn*, see pp. 59–61.

17. Jürgen Habermas, *Knowledge and Human Interests* (Boston: Beacon Press, 1971), 192.

18. Satan is apparently to be regarded here as telling the truth. "We should heed what is said, not who says it. When Satan is speaking in his role as an angel of light, what he says will in fact be true" (Clement of Alexandria, *Strom.* 6.8; *ANF*, 2:495). He is called the ruler of "the *kosmos*" (System) in John 12:31; 14:30; 16:11; the "god of this aion" in 2 Cor. 4:4; the "prince" (*archōn*) of the power of the air in Eph. 2:2; and see 1 John 4:3-4.

19. David Bakan, *The Duality of Human Existence* (Skokie, Ill.: Rand McNally, 1966), 67–68.

20. *Hamartōlos*, usually translated "sinner," means one who has missed the target.

21. To describe the created universe, John uses *kosmos* in 1:9-10a; 9:5a; 11:9; 16:21; 17:5, 24; 21:25; see also Acts 17:24; Rom. 1:20; Eph. 1:4; and perhaps 1 Cor. 8:4. The translation "humanity" or "the human social order" seems to be required in John 1:29; 3:16-17; 6:33, 51; 7:4; 8:12; 9:5b; 12:19; 17:23. The other sixty uses of *kosmos* in the Fourth Gospel refer to the alienated social order, what I am calling the Domination System. But the sense of *kosmos* shades off from one to another meaning with startling rapidity. Take John 1:9-10, for example: "The true light, which enlightens everyone, was coming into the *kosmos* [the created universe? the human social order?]. He was in the *kosmos* [ditto], and the *kosmos* [ditto] came into being through him; yet the *kosmos* [alienated creation, Domination System] did not know him."

22. Eisler, *The Chalice and the Blade* (San Francisco: Harper & Row, 1987), 129, 136.

23. I am aware that some biblical scholars will be exasperated at my promiscuous conflation of passages from a variety of New Testament sources with no carefully nuanced distinctions between the different writers' use of *kosmos*. There is no question that such nuances exist. 2 Pet. 1:4 and 2:20 already show a tendency to moralize and individualize the world-concept. John elevates it to central theological significance, though Paul is close behind in 1 Corinthians 1–4. (The Synoptic Gospels use a different construction, "this generation," almost always in a bad sense [24 times].) Nevertheless, there is a remarkable consistency in the sociological use of *kosmos* that far outweighs the nuances (I have deliberately omitted from discussion the moralizing instances), and it is the cumulative impact of this consistency that is most arresting. There are, in addition to the passages I have treated, many other instances of *kosmos* as "system" in the New Testament that I have omitted for the sake of brevity.

24. Ignatius, *Rom.* 3:3.

25. For example, Matt. 12:32; 13:22, 39, 40, 49, etc. (28 times in the New Testament). *Aiōn* in all its uses appears 122 times.

26. Similar uses appear in Acts 3:21; 15:18; 1 Cor. 2:7; Eph. 3:9, 11; Col. 1:26.

27. See, e.g., Matt. 12:32; 13:39; Eph. 1:21; 1 Tim. 6:17; Titus 2:12.

28. After Mark 16:14 in the longer ending, the Freer manuscript (W) adds this remarkable statement: "This aion of lawlessness and unbelief is under Satan, who by means of unclean spirits does not allow people to comprehend the true power of God."

29. Aiōn was the name of a god in Egypt from at least the second century B.C.E. The only passage in the New Testament that might allude to *aiōn* as a god, however, is Eph. 2:2, where the "*aiōn* of this *kosmos*" is in synonymous parallelism with "the ruler of the power of the air," Satan. If the allusion is deliberate, then Aiōn and Satan were fused by the biblical writer.

30. Paul betrays the same baffling optimism toward the Powers here that he does in Rom. 13:1-7, and that Luke does in his version of the cry from the cross ("for they know not what they do," 23:34, omitted by a number of very significant Greek texts). The Powers exhibit a sometimes uncanny capacity to perceive genuine threats

to their survival, and showed remarkable perspicacity in dispatching Jesus. It is hard to understand then why Paul thought they would have desisted had they been better informed. Or is it, as Girard says, that here we find the first definition of the unconscious in human history, and that their not knowing is in fact an ideologically induced blindness to the process of victimization (*The Scapegoat* [Baltimore: Johns Hopkins Univ. Press, 1977], 111)?

31. Rev. 21:1 speaks of the coming of "a new heaven and a new earth," indicating a transformed reality; but Rev. 5:10 makes it clear that this new reality will be actualized on our earth ("and they will reign *on earth*")—though this could refer just to the messianic kingdom.

32. *Sarx* is the physical substance we are made of (Luke 24:39; 1 Cor. 15:39, 50; Col. 1:22) or the physical body (John 6:51-56; Acts 2:31; Rom. 2:28; 2 Cor. 4:11; 7:1, 5; 10:3a; 12:7; Gal. 2:20; 4:13, 14; Eph. 5:29; Phil. 1:22, 24; Col. 1:24; 2:1, 5; 1 Tim. 3:16; Philem. 16; Heb. 2:14; 5:7; 9:10, 13; 10:20; James 5:3; 1 Pet. 3:18, 21; 4:1, 2, 6; 1 John 4:2; 2 John 7; Jude 8; Rev. 17:16; 19:18, 21); the self or one's being (Matt. 19:5-6//Mark 10:8; Acts 2:26 [= Ps. 16:9]; 1 Cor. 6:16; Eph. 5:31); or human beings or humanity in general (Matt. 16:17; 24:22//Mark13:20; Luke 3:6; John 1:14; 17:2; Acts 2:17; Rom. 3:20; 1 Cor. 1:29; Gal. 1:16; 2:16; Eph. 6:12; 1 Pet. 1:24); physical genetic descent or ethnicity (Rom. 1:3; 4:1; 9:3, 5, 8; 11:14; 1 Cor. 10:18; Eph. 2:11); earthly existence (Matt. 26:41//Mark 14:38; Rom. 6:19; 1 Cor. 7:28; Eph. 6:5; Phil. 3:3-4; Col. 3:22; Heb. 12:9); or sexual desire (John 1:13; Jude 7).

33. John 3:6; 6:63; 8:15; Rom. 7:5, 18, 25; 8:3-9, 12-13; 13:14; 1 Cor. 1:26; 5:5; 2 Cor. 1:17; 5:16; 10:2-3; 11:18; Gal. 3:3; 4:23, 29; 5:13, 16-17, 19, 24; 6:8, 12-13; Eph. 2:3, 14; Col. 2:11, 13, 18, 23; 2 Pet. 2:10, 18; 1 John 2:16.

34. Rudolf Bultmann, *Theology of the New Testament*, 2 vols. (New York: Charles Scribner's Sons, 1951), 1:238. Bultmann's otherwise brilliant treatment of *sarx* is totally individualistic (as is his entire theology), and completely misses the social dimension of the term. Thus he treats it as anxiety for things of the world; self-justification; turning away from God and attempting to live by one's own strength; self-reliant pursuit of one's own ends; the will to control the world; care; boasting; inner division; not being at one with one's own self (pp. 239–46). All this is true of life "according to the flesh," but it takes no account of the effects on the self of the alienating ethos that robs us of our authenticity before we even reach the age of choice.

4. THE NATURE OF THE DOMINATION SYSTEM

1. For a discussion of the critical problems and a select bibliography on Col. 1:15-20, see my essay, "The Hymn of the Cosmic Christ," in *The Conversation Continues: Studies in Paul and John in Honor of J. Louis Martyn*, ed. Robert T. Fortna and Beverly R. Gaventa (Nashville: Abingdon Press, 1990), 235–45; and *Naming the Powers*, 13–21 and 64–67.

2. Ernst Käsemann, "A Primitive Christian Baptismal Liturgy," in *Essays on New Testament Themes* (London: SCM Press, 1964), 162.

3. Regarding Col. 1:20, Chrysostom remarks: "The word 'reconcile,' shows the enmity; the words 'having made peace,' the war" (*Hom. on Col.* 3; *NPNF*, 13:272).

4. The Powers are not just the outer forms of these structures, but also encompass their inner spirituality—the "invisible" or "heavenly" aspects of which Col. 1:16 speaks. The symbolism that legitimates their power is a spiritual reality (i.e., from "heaven"). This notion is already evident in ancient Babylonia, where the sky god Anu was the prototype of all rulers. As Thorkild Jacobsen puts it, "To him belong the insignia, in which the essence of royalty was embodied—the sceptre, the crown, the headband, and the shepherd's staff—and from him did they derive. Before any king had yet been appointed among men these insignia already were, and they rested in heaven before Anu. From there they descended to earth" (*Before Philosophy*, by H. and H. A. Frankfort et al. [Baltimore: Penguin Books, 1959], 152).

In Egypt, the goddess Hathor is the "throne" of Horus. Later Isis was identified with Hathor, and the prince became king by sitting on her lap. In time Isis was replaced by the throne itself, which became a fetish charged with the mystical power of kingship. "The prince who takes his seat upon it arises a king. Hence the throne is called the 'mother' of the king. . . . In this way Isis 'the throne which made the king' became 'the Great Mother,' devoted to her son Horus, faithful through all suffering to her husband Osiris" (Frankfort, *Before Philosophy*, 26; see also Jacquetta Hawkes and Sir Leonard Woolley, *The History of Mankind*, vol. 1, *Prehistory and the Beginnings of Civilization* [New York: Harper & Row, 1963], 342–43). Likewise, the Ashanti in Africa had a Golden Stool on which the king sat, which contained the soul or spirit of the Ashanti nation. The people's power, health, bravery, and welfare resided in it. The stool symbolized the union of a number of previously autonomous but culturally similar groups, and it was passed on in the female line. This Golden Stool, having no past, descended from the sky (that is, it represented the new power configuration); therefore older symbols of political authority were ritually buried "because it was considered improper that any stool in the nation should be regarded as having preceded the Golden Stool (Peggy Reeves Sanday, *Female Power and Male Dominance* [Cambridge: Cambridge Univ. Press, 1981], 29).

5. Gerhard von Rad, *Old Testament Theology*, 2 vols. (New York: Harper & Row, 1962–65), 1:161–65.

6. A. N. Whitehead, *Process and Reality*, corrected edition, ed. David Ray Griffin and Donald W. Sherburne (New York: The Free Press, 1978), 339.

7. The expression "the Powers that be" derives from the KJV of Rom. 13:1—"Let every soul be subject to the higher powers. For there is no power but of God: the powers that be are ordained of God."

8. *Evangelical Witness in South Africa (Evangelicals Critique Their Own Theology and Practice)* (Dobsonville, South Africa: Concerned Evangelicals, 1986), 16. See also the *Kairos Document*, rev. 2d ed. (Braamfontein: Skotaville Publishers, 1986), 4–8; the report of the Presbyterian Church of Southern Africa, "Obedience, Submission and Civil Disobedience" (summarized in my *Violence and Nonviolence in South Africa*, 59); and Tom Wright, "The New Testament and the State," *Themelios* 16/1 (October 1990): 15—"What more natural, then, than that the church should regard itself as above obedience to mere earthly rulers? Already worshipping the one to whom Caesar would bow, why should it bow to Caesar as well? This prospect of holy anarchy, which in its Jewish form was brewing up towards a terrible war as Paul was writing Romans, could not commend itself as serving the gospel." Paul's

point is not the maximalist one that whatever governments do must be right and be obeyed, but the solid if minimalist one that God wants human society to be ordered.

9. It is little recognized that Adam Smith's social philosophy contained both a religious guarantee of the preservation of community and a moral demand that the individual consider its claim. The religious guarantee was Smith's secularized notion of providence, the "invisible hand" that transmutes individual acts of self-interest into the general welfare (*The Wealth of Nations*, book 4, chap. 7). Despite this determinism, Smith does not hesitate to make moral demands on people to sacrifice their own self-interest for the wider interest. "The wise and virtuous man is at all times willing that his own private interests should be sacrificed to the public interest of his own particular society—that the interests of this order of society be sacrificed to the greater interest of the state. He should therefore be equally willing that all those inferior interests should be sacrificed to the greater society of all sensible and intelligent beings, of which God himself is the immediate administrator and director" (ibid., book 5, chap. 1, part 3; cited by Reinhold Niebuhr, *The Children of Light and the Children of Darkness* [New York: Charles Scribner's Sons, 1944], 24–25). This concern of Smith's for the general welfare is a double-edged sword, however; God comes close to becoming the final justification of the capitalist system, not just the ultimate principle of coherence.

10. The idea of a Fall is not simply the heritage of a theology of sin and redemption, as Matthew Fox argues (*Original Blessing* [Santa Fe: Bear & Co.], 1983). For the Fall story in Genesis is, paradoxically, an integral part of the creation narrative itself (which continues through Genesis 11). Nor is it merely a consequence of the Domination System, for pacific, nonwarrior hunter-gatherers like the Mbuti in Zaïre have a whole variety of "Fall" stories to account for mortality, sexual differences, territorial trespass, the killing of game, and harm to others (see Colin M. Turnbull, "The Politics of Non-Aggression: Zaïre," in *Teaching Non-Aggression*, ed. Ashley Montagu [New York: Oxford Univ. Press, 1978], 192).

11. See Kathleen L. Roney-Wilson, "Deeper and Darker: Satanic Child Abuse," *Journal of Christian Healing* 12/1 (Spring 1990): 9–12.

12. See *Unmasking the Powers*, 39–40. For this reason I am not optimistic, as was Origen, about the final conversion of Satan. I suspect, rather, that Satan can be transformed only by fire, required, as it were, to transmute satanic energy into heat and light—Lucifer, "light bearer," at last.

13. There is, in Scripture, no definitive account of the fall of the Powers. Instead we have isolated intuitions—the fall of the *bene elohim* ("sons of gods" or "sons of God") in Gen. 6:1-4; the taunt against the king of Babylon, which may borrow archetypal features from Near Eastern mythology but in Isaiah refers simply to a human king (Isa. 14:3-21); the similar imprecation uttered upon the "prince" (LXX, *archonti*) of Tyre (the angel of Tyre?) in Ezek. 28:1-19, in any case not a reference to Satan; Luke 10:18, which alludes not to the primordial fall of Satan, but to a fall occasioned by the exorcisms of the disciples; and Rev. 12:7-12, again, not a primordial fall but the result of Jesus' crucifixion *and* the faithful witness of the saints. Not until Origen do we find a full-blown myth of Satan's primordial fall. These data (especially Revelation 12, where Satan falls not once, but repeatedly, each time faithful witness is borne) suggests that the fall of Satan, like any myth, cannot be

taken historically or literally. It refers to a moment that recurs whenever divine grace liberates Satan's captives. It did not happen once but happens, repeatedly, as Satan is put to rout.

14. William Stringfellow, *An Ethic for Christians and Other Aliens in a Strange Land* (Waco, Tex.: Word, Inc., 1973), 43.

15. Ibid., 83.

16. Reinhold Niebuhr, *Moral Man and Immoral Society* (New York: Charles Scribner's Sons, 1932), 129.

17. Michael Lerner, *Surplus Powerlessness* (Atlantic Highlands, N.J.: Humanities Press International, 1991), 266–86.

18. Augustine, reversing all theology before him, identified the Fall as humanity's lust for freedom. Obedience and submission, not autonomy, should have been Adam's desire. "Our true good is free slavery" (*City of God* 14.15)—to God and to God's agent, the emperor. It was a short next step to his advocacy of military force, torture, capital punishment, the denial of civil rights to non-Catholic Christians, prohibition of free discussion, and the exile of Donatist bishops (Elaine Pagels, "The Politics of Paradise: Augustine's Exegesis of Genesis 1–3 Versus That of John Chrysostom," *Harvard Theological Review* 78 [1985]: 67–99).

19. Calvin comes close to the notion of total depravity in statements like these: The image of God has become "so deeply corrupted that all that remains of it is a horrible deformity." Therefore mortals "can do no more than crawl over the earth like little worms" (John Calvin, *Institutes of the Christian Religion*, 1.15.4; 2.6.4). But it was later Calvinists who framed the unambiguous doctrine of total depravity. The La Rochelle Confession of Faith (1571) proclaimed, "We also believe that this [hereditary] vice is truly sin and that it suffices to condemn the entire human race, even infants in the wombs of their mothers" (cited by Philip J. Lee, *Against the Protestant Gnostics* [New York: Oxford Univ. Press, 1987], 86).

20. See Anne Wilson Schaef, *When Society Becomes an Addict* (San Francisco: Harper & Row, 1987).

21. Something of the same argument is developed by Clinton W. Morrison, *The Powers That Be: Earthly Rulers and Demonic Powers in Romans 13.1–7*, Studies in Biblical Theology 29 (London: SCM Press, 1960), 114–20. Everyone in the first century assumed that the Powers were ordained by God, he says. Christ's death was scarcely needed to make that point. Further, Christ's death had no effect on the Powers, which were as strong after the resurrection as before. Sin and death also remained unchanged. This means the *exousiai* were not the objects of God's work in Christ. They have not been transformed or affected in their hold on the world. The Powers are destined to relinquish domination in the last day, but in the meantime they remain as strong as ever. Christ's victory over the Powers is not their defeat but the deliverance *from* them of all those who believe. The gospel proclaims, not what has happened to the Powers, but what has happened to Christians in Christ. The locus of Christ's victory is the church, where those who have been delivered from the Powers celebrate Christ's victory. Consequently, the church's task is to proclaim Christ as the means by which people may be delivered from the Powers.

Morrison's totally individualistic interpretation leads him to overlook the collective task of the church in proclaiming the manifold wisdom of God, not to people, but directly to the Powers (Eph. 3:10). And, remarkably, Eph. 1:20-23 asserts that these Powers are *already* under the feet of Christ as a result of the resurrection. Something *has* changed as a result of the cross (see chap. 7). Christ's victory over the Powers can already be celebrated now, but it will only be complete in the future reign of God (1 Cor. 15:24-27). Likewise the cosmic reconciliation achieved by the cross, according to Col. 1:20, is not just for believers, but for the Powers themselves (as the repetition of "whether on earth or in heaven" makes clear). Rev. 21:24 and 22:2 also look forward to the "healing of the *nations.*"

22. *Václav Havel or Living in Truth*, ed. Jan Vladislav (Boston: Faber & Faber, 1987), 70, 92.

23. Domingos Barbé, "The Spiritual Basis of Nonviolence," in *Relentless Persistence*, ed. Philip McManus and Gerald Schlabach (Philadelphia: New Society Publications, 1991), 272.

24. Joel Kovel, *History and Spirit* (Boston: Beacon Press, 1991), 167.

25. Philip Roth, interview with Milan Kundera, *New York Times Book Review*, November 30, 1980, 78, 80.

26. Nicolas Berdyaev, *Slavery and Freedom* (New York: Charles Scribner's Sons, 1944), 208.

27. From $800 in 1910 to $63,000 in 1988, not adjusted for inflation. Source: *National Financial Summary, Economic Indicators of the Farm Sector* (Washington, D.C.: U.S. Dept. of Agriculture, December 31, 1988), 67.

28. For data, see Richard Lewontin, "Agricultural Research and the Penetration of Capital," *Science for the People* 14 (January–February 1982): 12–17. Less benignly, some multinational seed companies are developing seeds that will produce ripened fruit only if that company's chemicals are sprayed on the plants, locking the farmer into even greater costs and dependency (Radhakrishna Rao, "Cornering the Seed Market," *World Press Review* 33 [July 1986]: 53). And they have patented genetically engineered crops designed to thrive in soils contaminated by herbicide residues. Soon there will be vast landscapes where no life can survive except genotypes owned and licensed by a few large companies (Richard Cartwright Austin, "Jubilee Now," *Sojourners* 20 [June 1991]: 27).

29. Ervin Laszlo, *The Systems View of the World* (New York: George Braziller, 1972), 23.

30. Daniel 10; *Jub.* 15:31–32; *1 Enoch* 89–90; Ecclus. 17:17; *3 Enoch* 17:8 (A); 26:12; Hebrew *Test. Napht.* 8.

31. Harold Mattingly, *The Man in the Roman Street* (New York: Numismatic Review, 1947), 96.

32. Harold Mattingly, *Christianity in the Roman Empire* (New Zealand: Univ. of Otago Press, 1955), 10.

33. Taking *pneumatika* in Eph. 6:12 as a collective neuter.

34. Peter Blau, cited by Rubem Alvez, "From Paradise to the Desert: Autobiographical Musings," in *Frontiers of Theology in Latin America*, ed. Rosino Giliellini (Maryknoll, N.Y.: Orbis Books, 1979), 296. Peter Berger and Thomas Luckmann, *The Social Construction of Reality* (Garden City, N.Y.: Doubleday, 1966), 78—a highly influential but extraordinarily reductionistic work.

35. From "Fuku," in *Almost at the End* (London: Marion Boyars, 1987), 41.

36. James M. Robinson, "Kerygma and History in the New Testament," in *The Bible in Modern Scholarship*, ed. J. Philip Hyatt (Nashville: Abingdon Press, 1965), 117.

37. Hazel E. Barnes, "Introduction," in Jean Paul Sartre, *Search for a Method* (New York: Alfred A. Knopf, 1967), xxiii. Western psychiatry and psychology have tended to reduce the social to the personal, whereas communist psychiatry has reduced the personal to the social. For example, Chinese psychiatrists probe the class background, occupation, and residual bourgeois attitudes of the patient. Rejecting the notion that the cause of mental illness lies within the sick person, they seek its social cause in disrupted family lives, nonproletarian ideas, selfishness and vanity, and nonmaterialistic thinking (Leigh Kagan, "Report from a Visit to the Tientsin Psychiatric Hospital," *China Notes* 10/4 [Fall 1972]: 37–39).

38. Victor Turner's designation, in *Dramas, Fields and Metaphors* (Ithaca: Cornell Univ. Press, 1974), 298.

39. The early Christian apologists, especially Tertullian, stressed that the redemptive work of Christ centered on deliverance from demons more than deliverance from sin (A. D. Nock, *Conversion: From Alexander the Great to Augustine of Hippo* [Oxford: Oxford Univ. Press, 1933], 222). This invariably involved both freeing people from oppression by spirits and transferring them out of the social world that generated such spirits, and into the quite different social world of the church.

40. Eisler, *The Chalice and the Blade* (San Francisco: Harper & Row, 1987), 205 n. 5.

41. Reinhold Niebuhr, *Moral Man and Immoral Society*.

42. Several excellent Greek MSS read *panta* in John 12:32—"And I, when I am lifted up from the earth, will draw *all things* to myself" (the majority tradition reads "all people"—*pantas*). Origen wrote, "It would be absurd to affirm that it was only for human sin He tasted death, and not also on behalf of every other creature beyond man who has been involved in sins, such as the stars" (*Comm. on John* 1.35).

43. On "neutralizing" the Powers rather than "destroying" them as the proper translation of 1 Cor. 15:24, 26, see *Naming the Powers*, 50–55. REV reads "deposed." Contrast this statement by a white South African, Edward Cain: "Jesus' analysis of the problems of man was that the sin in the heart of man had to be addressed, and not the sin in the structure of society"—a convenient theology indeed, if you want to defend apartheid! Cain's remark was made in criticism of church leaders who marched on Parliament to protest the restriction of seventeen organizations (*Cross Times* [South Africa], April 1988, 12).

44. "At the consummation, these 'powers' will be completely subjected to Christ and brought totally under his headship." They "will no longer be the tyrannizing opponents of God's plan and his people" (Clinton E. Arnold, *Ephesians: Power and Magic*, SNTSMS 63 [Cambridge: Cambridge Univ. Press, 1989], 126). Arnold accuses me of committing the fallacy, in *Naming the Powers*, that James Barr calls an "illegitimate totality transfer." This error occurs when a total series of relations in which a word is used in a text is read into a particular case. Each context must determine which meaning, among the range of possible meanings, is appropriate to that context (" 'Principalities and Powers' in Recent Interpretation," *Catalyst* 20 [February 1991]: 4). I am not unfamiliar with Barr's category, though I refuse to

adopt his unintelligible name for it; I suggested in *Naming the Powers* that the phrase, the "elements of the universe," has been misunderstood by scholars precisely because they ignored its context-determined meanings. But other Greek terms for the Powers are not so rich in meaning. *Archōn* always means "ruler," for example, and the context leaves it for us only to determine what *sort* of ruler. Part 2 of that book examines the "disputed passages" where it is unclear whether heavenly or earthly rulers were meant. I decided each case there in reference to its context.

For a useful summary of various treatments of the Powers, see Peter T. O'Brien, "Principalities and Powers: Opponents of the Church," in *Biblical Interpretation and the Church: Text and Context*, ed. D. A. Carson (Exeter, U.K.: Paternoster Press, 1984), 110–50; and Thomas H. McAlpine, *Facing the Powers* (Monrovia, Calif.: MARC, 1991).

45. See the helpful discussion by Richard J. Mouw, *Politics and the Biblical Drama* (Grand Rapids: Wm. B. Eerdmans, 1976), 85–116.

46. Darrell J. Fasching, "The Dialectic of Apocalyptic and Utopia in the Theological Ethics of Jacques Ellul," paper delivered at the annual meeting of the American Academy of Religion in Boston, November 1987, p. 5.

5. UNMASKING THE DOMINATION SYSTEM

1. Étienne de la Boetie, *The Politics of Obedience: The Discourse of Voluntary Servitude* (Montreal: Black Rose Books, 1975), 47–53. John H. Kautsky offers a plausible explanation for the origin of class oppression. Peaceable agriculturalists in Mesopotamia were overrun by waves of nomadic herders, whose military superiority was overwhelming, thanks largely to the domestication of the horse. In time these nomadic groups might subdue a number of such agricultural communities, and could settle down and enjoy their wealth. Thus arose the class system and aristocratic empires. Peasants were left alone except for the extraction of tribute. The populace was almost invariably quiescent. Class differences were so great that class conflict was nonexistent (*The Politics of Aristocratic Empires* [Chapel Hill: Univ. of North Carolina Press, 1982], 51–56). As aristocratic empires experienced commercialization, merchants began to infiltrate the ruling class. At about the time de la Boetie wrote, mercantilization had progressed to the point that the first glimmerings of democratic participation were again becoming visible. The transition to "people power" which the globe is now experiencing is the final stage of this long development away from rule by violence to rule by consent.

2. Ched Myers, *Binding the Strong Man* (Maryknoll, N.Y.: Orbis Books, 1988), 287.

3. The definitions here are from the *Shorter Oxford English Dictionary*, 3rd ed. (Oxford: Clarendon Press, 1973).

4. I do not attempt a thorough exegesis of these two chapters, but focus only on the issues relevant to the theme of the Powers. I have provided my own paraphrasing translation, primarily in order to capitalize freely. For historical details and setting, see Steven Joseph Scherrer, "Revelation 13 as an Historical Source for the Imperial Cult under Domitian," Ph.D. diss., Harvard University, 1979.

5. See Walter Wink, *The Powers in Gnosticism*, forthcoming.

6. M. Rostovtzeff, *The Social and Economic History of the Roman Empire*, 2 vols., 2d ed. (Oxford: Clarendon Press, 1957), 1:43.

7. Were there Principalities and Powers before the rise of the Domination System some five thousand years ago? Undoubtedly. Every institution is a Power, however benign, and has its own inner spirit and outer arrangements. But in a decentralized or egalitarian society the Powers are unlikely to manifest the virulent pathologies of the massive institutions that characterize centralized states. The growth of the Powers is directly related to a felt sense by individuals that they have lost the power to make a direct impact on their environment.

8. Adela Yarbro Collins, *The Combat Myth in the Book of Revelation* (Missoula, Mont.: Scholars Press, 1976), 66.

9. "When you (Ba'l) smote Lôtān, the primeval serpent, Destroyed the crooked serpent, Šilyaṭ with seven heads" (cited from a Ugaritic text by E. Theodore Mullen, Jr., *The Divine Council in Canaanite and Early Hebrew Literature*, Harvard Semitic Monographs 24 [Chico, Calif.: Scholars Press, 1980], 83).

10. "It is now certain that Leviathan . . . is not a whale or a fantastic crocodile but rather a mythological sea serpent with seven heads" (B. Zuckerman, "Job, Book of," *IDBS*, 479). A seal from Eshnunna near Baghdad from 2500 B.C.E. shows a dragon with seven heads (Alexander Heidel, *The Babylonian Genesis*, 2d ed. [Chicago: Univ. of Chicago Press, 1951], 83–89). Significantly, allusions to this creature in Scripture are often historicized of *nations*. Rahab equals Egypt (Ps. 87:4; Isa. 30:7); the fleeing serpent in Isa. 27:1 is Syria. See also Isa. 51:9-10; Ezek. 29:3; 32:2. But *Odes of Sol.* 22:5, written ca. 100 C.E., and hence roughly contemporary with Revelation, restores the ancient mythic sense, as does John: God "overthrew by my hands the dragon with seven heads."

11. R. H. Charles, *A Critical and Exegetical Commentary on the Revelation of St. John*, International Critical Commentary, 2 vols. (Edinburgh: T. & T. Clark, [1920] 1956), 1:318.

12. See chap. 7.

13. Glen Tinder's *The Political Meaning of Christianity* (Baton Rouge: Louisiana State Univ. Press, 1989) will inevitably provoke comparison with my series on the Powers. Our fundamental difference is that he sees the state and all of society as intrinsically evil, though capable of amelioration by acts of agape. I see the state and all of society as simultaneously the good creations of a good God, as fallen, and as capable of redemption. In the imagery of Rev. 12–13, we might say that Tinder equates the Dragon with the state and society; I equate the Dragon with the Domination System, which is given political expression in every state and society but is not identical with any. He sees society as the Dragon; I see society as the Beast. Tinder's extreme pessimism about the state leads, as such pessimism always does, to the justification of evil to prevent evil. He espouses radical liberty and tolerance; yet he would deny the right of any person in a democracy, not only to espouse violent overthrow of the government, but to advocate an alternative system by word alone. Thus his theology can be read as supporting the McCarthy witch-hunts. He affirms the divine uniqueness of every person, yet is quite hostile to nonviolence (and quite uninformed), and is ready to use violence swiftly and surgically to remove despots. Nevertheless, the book is packed with tough-minded and stimulating thinking.

14. The twelve stars may symbolize the twelve tribes of Israel (Rev. 7:4-8). There is a definite reference to the Davidic messiah in Rev. 12:5—the male child who is to "rule all nations with a rod of iron" = Ps. 2:9. The "birth pangs" of Rev. 12:2 is an allusion to Israel in Isa. 26:17, and the flight to the wilderness echoes David's in Ps. 55:7-8. Gen. 37:9 and *Test. Napht.* 5 also indicate that the symbolism of sun, moon, and stars used here was associated with the twelve tribes of Israel.

15. Charles, *Revelation*, 1:316 n. 1; Philip Carrington, "Astral Mythology in the Revelation," *Anglican Theological Review* 13 (1931): 293; Leon Gry, "Les Chapitres XI et XII de l'Apocalypse," *Revue Biblique* 31 (1922): 208–12.

16. Elizabeth Janeway, *Powers of the Weak* (New York: Alfred A. Knopf, 1980), 73.

17. Max A. Myers, " 'Ideology' and 'Legitimation' As Necessary Concepts for Christian Ethics," *Journal of the American Academy of Religion* 49 (1981): 195.

18. One of the surest ways to undermine power, therefore, is to challenge its legitimacy, that is, to question the basis of trust on which its power rests. For example, when Salvador Allende was elected president of Chile in 1970 without enough seats to control Congress, the price he paid for support from the rival Christian Democrats was a constitutional amendment that would require him to respect civil liberties, elections, and freedom of the press, all of which had been cornerstones of Chilean democracy for years. The very act of requiring him to uphold the law that he was elected to uphold was itself a profound blow to his legitimacy, and foreshadowed the bloody collapse of Chilean democracy three years later (Arturo Valenzuela, "Chile," in *The Breakdown of Democratic Regimes*, ed. Juan Linz and Alfred Stepan [Baltimore: Johns Hopkins Univ. Press, 1978], 49).

19. Apparently John means it literally when he says that the Second Beast "works great miracles, even making fire come down from heaven to earth in the sight of humanity." Contrived religious wonders were an actual feature of the imperial cult, according to Steven J. Scherrer ("Signs and Wonders in the Imperial Cult: A New Look at a Roman Religious Institution in the Light of Rev 13:13-15," *Journal of Biblical Literature* 103/4 [1984]: 599–610). The emperor Gaius Caligula had a device that produced lightning and a machine that made thunder. On a gold coin of Domitian, the thunderbolts of Jupiter are shown above the empty throne that represents the authority of the emperor himself (Ethelbert Stauffer, *Christ and the Caesars* [London: SCM Press, 1955], 187). Such technology was used by others as well; a reputed prophet, Alexander, fashioned an image of the god Asclepius whose mouth would open and close by means of a horsehair string, and from which a forked black tongue like a snake's would dart out, also controlled by horsehairs. The image could even speak, thanks to a tube of cranes' windpipes fastened together, leading from a speaker outside the temple to the god's mouth (Julius Pollux, *Onomasticon* 4.130; Dio Cassius, *Roman History* 59.28.6; Lucian, *Alexander the False Prophet* 12, 16, 26). Hippolytus exposes a similar "miracle" involving ventriloquism at an oracle-giving shrine (*Ref.* 4.41; see also 4.28), and another in which a "flaming demon" is made to shoot through the air—a bird covered with tow and set afire in a dark room; the gullible onlookers are cautioned to cover their eyes as soon as they see it (*Ref.* 4.35–36).

20. Worship of Roma appears to have begun right in the very cities under John's care: Smyrna, in 195 B.C.E., and Ephesus and Pergamum soon after. Tiberius allowed

a temple to be built to him in Smyrna in 23 C.E., but insisted that his mother Livia and the Senate be honored as well. For its part, Pergamum honored Caligula's adulterous and murderous sister Livella as a new Nikephoros, enthroned with Athena Polias and sharing a priest with her and Athena (*Cambridge Ancient History*, ed. J. B. Bury et al. [Cambridge: Cambridge Univ. Press, 1923–36], 10:497; M. P. Charlesworth, "Some Observations on Ruler-cult Especially in Rome," *Harvard Theological Review* 28 [1935]: 21). So emperor worship was more than simply an act of political fealty in the province of Asia; it was a matter of local pride and ownership.

21. Leon Festinger, Henry W. Riecken, and Stanley Schachter, *When Prophecy Fails* (New York: Harper & Bros., 1956).

22. Robert G. Hoyt, "What's the news, who says, and why" (a review of Mark Hertsgaard, *On Bended Knee: The Press and the Reagan Presidency*), in *Christianity and Crisis* 49 (February 20, 1989): 42-44; Cheryl Adamson, "Washington pressures journalists on Central American coverage," *Latinamerica Press*, 3 July 1986, 3. Jacques Ellul's *Propaganda* (New York: Vintage Books, 1973) is filled with penetrating insights but is utterly deterministic, and credits propaganda with far more power than it possesses.

23. This, and the two following assumptions, were not as true of aristocratic societies as they are of societies today.

24. This list is based on Richard B. Gregg, *The Power of Nonviolence*, 2d ed. (Nyack, N.Y.: Fellowship of Reconciliation, 1962), 138–39.

25. C. R. Hallpike, *The Foundation of Primitive Thought* (Oxford: Clarendon Press, 1979), 55. Erich Fromm defined socialization as the process of "learning to like to do what we have to do" (*The Sane Society* [New York: Fawcett Premier Books, 1977], 77).

26. Ricky Sherover-Marcuse, "Unlearning Racism Workshops," and "Toward a Perspective on Unlearning Racism: 12 Working Assumptions," 6501 Dana, Oakland, CA 94609. I cannot agree with her social determinism, however; people are not just victims—otherwise they would cease to be moral agents responsible for their acts. They are seduced, but they are culpable for letting themselves be seduced.

27. *Václav Havel or Living in Truth*, ed. Jan Vladislav (Boston: Faber & Faber, 1987), 45, 56, 59.

28. Tina Pippin, "The Heroine and the Whore: Fantasy and the Female in the Apocalypse of John," unpublished paper, courtesy of the author.

29. R. D. Laing, *The Politics of Experience* (New York: Pantheon Books, 1967), 13, 132.

30. Danilo Kis, "The State, the Imagination, and the Censored I," *New York Times Book Review*, November 3, 1985, 3.

31. A. Lods, "Les origines de la figure de Satan, ses fonctions à la cour céleste," in *Mélanges syriens offerts à R. Dussaud*, vol. 2, *Bibliothèque archéologique et historique* 30 (Paris: P. Geuthner 1939), 649–60; C. Colpe, "Geister (Dämonen)," *Reallexikon für Antike und Christentum*, ed. Theodore Klauser (Stuttgart: Anton Hiersemann, 1976), 9:569–70.

32. Csaba Polony, quoted by Charles Upton, "Who Are the Archons?" *Gnosis* 2 (Spring-Summer 1986): 5.

33. Janeway, *Powers of the Weak*, 169. See also Gene Sharp, *The Politics of Nonviolent Action* (Boston: Porter Sargent, 1973), 1:7-62.

34. Lewis Mumford, *The Myth of the Machine: The Pentagon of Power* (New York: Harcourt Brace Jovanovich, 1970), 7.

35. Richard B. Gregg, *Power of Nonviolence*, 26–28.

36. Joel Kovel, *History and Spirit* (Boston: Beacon Press, 1991), 102.

37. Richard Sennett, *Authority* (New York: Vintage, 1981), 86, 92.

38. Joel Kovel, *History and Spirit*, 125.

39. Jack Nelson-Pallmeyer, *War against the Poor* (Maryknoll, N.Y.: Orbis Books, 1989), 21.

40. Charles Upton, "Contemplation as a Revolutionary Act: Response to Simone Weil's *Waiting for God*," unpublished manuscript, courtesy of the author.

41. Gustavo Gutiérrez, *A Theology of Liberation* (Maryknoll, N.Y.: Orbis Books, [1973] 1988).

42. Thelma Jean Goodrich, "Women, Power, and Family Therapy: What's Wrong with This Picture?" in *Women and Power: Perspectives for Family Therapy*, ed. Goodrich (New York: W. W. Norton, 1991), 23, 31.

43. Ward Ewing, *The Power of the Lamb* (Cambridge, Mass.: Cowley Publications, 1990), 47.

44. Reinhold Niebuhr, *Moral Man and Immoral Society* (New York: Charles Scribner's Sons, 1932), 33.

45. J. B. Libánio notes that every social system needs three elements to maintain itself: legitimacy, therapies, and social control; and this is as true for countercultural or revolutionary groups as for any others ("A Community with a New Image," *WCC Exchange* 2 [May 1979]: 37, 40).

46. See Tinder, *Political Meaning of Christianity*, 32.

47. Sennett, *Authority*, 28, 33, 41, 46; and Sennett and Jonathan Cobb, *The Hidden Injuries of Class* (New York: Vintage, 1973).

48. Heinrich Schlier, *Principalities and Powers in the New Testament* (New York: Herder and Herder, 1961), 58.

49. Steve Shelstad, in a workshop at the Ecumenical Theological Center, Detroit, December 1990.

50. William Blake, "London," in *The Complete Poetry and Prose of William Blake*, ed. David V. Erdman, rev. ed. (Berkeley: Univ. of California Press, 1982), 27.

6. GOD'S DOMINATION-FREE ORDER:
JESUS AND GOD'S REIGN

1. Shiela Moon, *Joseph's Son* (Francestown, N.H.: Golden Quill Press, 1972), 13–14.

2. Mark 14:58//Matt. 26:61; Luke 23:2; John 18:35-39.

3. Luke 23:13-25, 35; 24:20; John 7:26; Acts 4:8-10, 26, all using *archontes* for those who had Jesus crucified. Note, however, that in 1 Cor. 2:6-8; Luke 23:34; Acts 3:17; and 13:27 the Powers are depicted as *ignorant* of what they were doing, and to whom.

4. Eisler, *The Chalice and the Blade* (San Francisco: Harper & Row, 1987), 116–24.

5. Robert W. Funk, "Rules of Evidence," in *The Gospel of Mark: Red Letter Edition*, ed. Funk with Mahlon Smith (Sonoma, Calif.: Polebridge Press, 1991), 29–52.

6. *Philoneikia* means "love of victory," and can be used positively for what René Girard calls mimetic desire: "competition, emulation, emulous eagerness." But it is most often used negatively: "rivalry, contentiousness"—in short, just what Girard means by mimetic rivalry (see chap. 7).

7. Mark 9:35 par.; 10:43-44 par.; Luke 14:11//Matt. 23:12; Luke 18:14; Matt. 18:4. It is important to note that Jesus addresses his words to men, not women. They are an attack on male dominance, not an attempt to reinforce the servility of women. 1 Pet. 5:2-3 continues this theme: "Tend the flock of God that is your charge, exercising the oversight, not under compulsion but willingly, as God would have you do it. . . . Do not lord it over those in your charge." But the Gnostics asked, with some justification, why there had to be a hierarchical order of "shepherds" at all.

8. Luke 14:12-14; 14:15-24//Matt. 22:1-10.

9. Matt. 23:5-7; Mark 12:38-40//Luke 20:46; 18:9-14.

10. Albert Nolan, *God in South Africa* (Grand Rapids: Wm. B. Eerdmans, 1988), 66–67.

11. Matt. 4:1-11//Luke 4:1-13; Mark 12:35-37 par.; Luke 12:13-14; Matt. 11:2-6// Luke 7:18-23; Mark 8:27-33 par.; Mark 15:2-5 par.; Matt. 26:63-64//Luke 22:70; Luke 22:67-69. Mark 14:61-62 cannot have been the reading that Matthew and Luke found in their copies of Mark; how else can we explain their both independently changing Mark's full confession, "I am [the Christ]" to the ambiguous "You have said so," especially since they both believed that he *was* the Christ? Some mss. of Mark 14:62 read "You have said so"; they probably represent the earlier reading.

12. Elisabeth Schüssler Fiorenza, *In Memory of Her* (New York: Crossroad, 1984), 107, 121, 143. This book is the best treatment of the themes of this chapter.

13. Here as elsewhere in this chapter I cite sayings attributed to Jesus by the Fourth Evangelist that may not be historical, but that accurately reflect Jesus' critique of domination.

14. *Mek. Exod.* 21:2 (Jacob Z. Lauterbach, ed. *Mekilta de-Rabbi Ishmael* [Philadelphia: Jewish Publication Society of America, 1961], vol. 3, p. 5). There were circles in the early church that maintained the radicality evident in the foot-washing narrative. For example, we learn from *The Passion of Andrew* 25 of a (fictitious) aristocrat, Stratocles, who as a result of Andrew's preaching, carries his own oil flask to the gymnasium and does his own chores in public—buying his own vegetables, bread, and other necessities and carrying them on foot through the center of the city, "making himself look simply repulsive to everyone," though he has many slaves and "is of noble stock, the most honored man of Achaea" (in *The Acts of Andrew and the Acts of Andrew and Matthias in the City of the Cannibals*, ed. Dennis Ronald MacDonald [Atlanta: Scholars Press, 1990], 357). See also John Dominic Crossan, "Early Christian Feminism," in *The Fourth R* (Westar Institute, Sonoma, Calif.), May 1990, 8–10.

15. T.B. *Sanh.* 25b; M. *B. Kam.* 10:9; T.B. *B. Kam.* 94b Bar.; J. Jeremias, *Jerusalem in the Time of Jesus* (Philadelphia: Fortress, 1969), 304–11.

16. On the historicity of this passage see Joseph Ernst, *Johannes der Täufer* (Berlin: Walter de Gruyter, 1989), 93–98.

17. Luke 6:34. *Gos. Thom.* 95 represents a more original form than Matt. 5:42 or Luke 6:30 (R. McL. Wilson, *Studies in the Gospel of Thomas* [London: Mowbray, 1960], 128).

18. Luke 12:33-34//Matt. 6:19-21; Luke 14:33; Mark 10:17-31 par.; Matt. 13:44-46.

19. Doubts about the historical character of the passages on the sharing of possessions in Acts began simultaneously with the rise of nineteenth-century socialism. In 1853, the French Academy sponsored a competition for the best essay proving that the early church did *not* practice communism. Brian J. Capper has provided a persuasive case that early Christian sharing was real; see "Community of Goods in the Earliest Jerusalem Church," *ANRW*, forthcoming; *All Things in Common*, Wissenschaftliche Untersuchungen zum Neuen Testament (Tübingen: J. C. B. Mohr, forthcoming); "The Interpretation of Acts 5.4," *Journal for the Study of the New Testament* 19 (1983): 117-31; and " 'In der Hand des Ananias . . .' Erwägungen zu 1 QS VI, 20 und der urchristlichen Gütergemeinschaft," *Revue de Qumran* 46 (1986): 223–36.

20. "Kingdom" has never been an accurate translation of Hebrew *malkuth*, which denotes God's activity of exercising sovereignty, or a dimension of reality, rather than a territorial expanse. The verbal noun "reigning" is thus more precise than "reign," but awkward.

21. Mark 4:1-9 par., 26-29, 30-32 par. = *Gos. Thom.* 20; Matt. 13:24-30 = *Gos. Thom.* 57; Matt. 13:33//Luke 13:20-21 = *Gos. Thom.* 96; Matt. 13:44-46 = *Gos. Thom.* 76, 109; Luke 15:8-10; Matt. 18:23-35; 20:1-16; 21:28-32; 25:1-13, 14-30// Luke 19:12-27; Matt. 25:31-46.

22. Norman Perrin, *Rediscovering the Teaching of Jesus* (New York: Harper & Row, 1967), 107.

23. Marcus Borg, *Conflict, Holiness and Politics in the Teachings of Jesus* (New York: Edwin Mellen Press, 1984), 51–200; Helmut Merkel, "The Opposition between Jesus and Judaism," in *Jesus and the Politics of His Day*, ed. E. Bammel and C. F. D. Moule (Cambridge: Cambridge Univ. Press, 1984), 140–41; and Roger P. Booth, *Jesus and the Laws of Purity*, Journal for the Study of the New Testament Supplement Series 13 (Sheffield: Univ. of Sheffield, 1986).

24. Luke 10:33; 9:51-56; to which the church may have added Luke 17:11-19 and John 4:1-42 (reflecting perhaps the church's mission to Samaritans—Acts 8:25?).

25. Borg, *Conflict, Holiness and Politics*, 51–200.

26. Matt. 6:9//Luke 11:2; Matt. 7:7-11//Luke 11:9-13; Matt. 6:25-34//Luke 12:22-31; Matt. 10:29//Luke 12:6-7; Matt. 18:19; Luke 15:1-7//Matt. 18:12-14; Matt. 11:25-27//Luke 10:21-22; Mark 11:25; 14:36 par.; Luke 12:32; 23:34; and most references to "father" in John's Gospel.

Ezekiel 22:26 amounts to virtually a line-by-line indictment of Jesus: "[The priests] have done violence to my teaching and have profaned my holy things; they have made no distinction between the holy and the common, neither have they taught the difference between the unclean and the clean, and they have disregarded my Sabbaths, so that I am profaned among them." The rending of the Temple curtain symbolizes the completion of this process of profanation, which, according to Ezekiel, even God resists.

27. For this discussion I am setting aside purity regulations having to do strictly with hygiene, which constitute a separate problem.

28. Marcus Borg, *Conflict, Holiness and Politics*, 51–200.

29. L. William Countryman, *Dirt, Greed, and Sex* (Philadelphia: Fortress Press, 1988), 86, 94–96.

30. Matt. 8:11-12//Luke 13:28-30; Luke 10:29-37. Other references in the Gospels to the salvation of the Gentiles are probably redactional: Luke 2:32; 3:6; 4:27; 14:22-23; 17:16b; Mark 8:1-10//Matt. 15:32-39; Matt. 10:18; 12:21; John 10:16; 12:20-26.

31. Rom. 1:16; 9–11; 15:9-12, 16-29; Gal. 3:28.

32. Matt. 5:45//Luke 6:35; Acts 10:34; Rom. 2:11; Gal. 2:6; Eph. 6:9; Col. 3:25; James 2:1, 9.

33. Neither Jesus nor the church targeted slavery as an evil, though it is one of androcracy's most hellish inventions. Not all slaves were treated badly; some, we know, became quite prosperous and powerful, managing large commercial enterprises and estates (Matt. 25:14-30//Luke 19:12-27; Luke 16:1-13; Matt. 18:23-35; Mark 12:1-12 par.). For most, however, it was a degradation barely to be borne.

Paul was at least able to declare the *principle* of equality: in Christ "there is neither slave nor free" (Gal. 3:28), and encouraged those who could to gain their freedom (1 Cor. 7:21-24; Philemon). In a paradoxical reversal, Jesus makes slaves the bearers of the highest values in the new order (Mark 10:44 par.; Luke 12:37-38; John 13; and frequently in the rest of the New Testament). But elsewhere the church seems to accept the system without criticism, including the right to beat slaves (Luke 12:39-46//Matt. 24:43-51 [Q]; Luke 12:47-48 [Lukan redaction]; Luke 17:7-10; Eph. 6:5-9; Col. 3:22—4:1; 1 Tim. 6:1-2; Titus 2:9-10).

34. Thelma Jean Goodrich, "Women, Power, and Family Therapy: What's Wrong with This Picture," in *Women and Power: Perspectives for Family Therapy*, ed. Goodrich (New York: W. W. Norton, 1991), 11.

35. Gerda Lerner, *The Creation of Patriarchy* (Oxford: Oxford Univ. Press, 1986), 140, 209.

36. Ken Taylor, "Church/Family" (D. Min. thesis, Hartford Seminary, 1978), 121, 145.

37. Fiorenza, *In Memory of Her*, 151. Of the wedding at Cana, Fiorenza remarks that there is no precedent in Jewish or Greco-Roman sources for a son to address his mother as "woman" (John 2:4). The Fourth Evangelist thus distances Jesus from his biological mother and rejects any claims she might have on him because of her family relationship to him (p. 327).

38. Mythologically speaking, Jesus had to be born of a virgin in order to break free from patriarchal hereditary succession. This "king" had no earthly father, as human monarchs do, but was born of woman, the "son of Mary" (Mark 6:3). Boys were known by their father's names; "son of Mary" may indicate illegitimacy. Jane Schaberg (*The Illegitimacy of Jesus* [San Francisco: Harper & Row, 1987], 199) believes the tradition subverts patriarchal family structure by treating Jesus as a child conceived illegitimately: he has transcendent value in and of himself, not in his attachment and that of his mother to a biological or legal father.

39. Eli Sagan, *At the Dawn of Tyranny: The Origins of Individualism, Political Oppression, and the State* (New York: Alfred A. Knopf, 1985), 294.

40. See Antoinette Clark Wire, *The Corinthian Women Prophets* (Minneapolis: Fortress Press, 1990). Given the fact that almost all women in that period were injured in bearing their first child, and that most women died in the seventh or eighth birth, it is little wonder that some women might have been relieved to discover a religious legitimation for suspending all sexual activity (data in Marielouise Janssen-Jurreit, *Sexism* [New York: Farrar Straus Giroux, 1982], 197).

41. It may even be that the dark saying in Matt. 19:12, "There are eunuchs who have made themselves eunuchs for the sake of the kingdom of God," represents an attempt to challenge the family by a physical protest. Prophets had long been associated with sexual abstinence; now those who could receive this teaching would reject family life in order to dramatize the need to transcend both sexual compulsion and familial control. The monastic movement was thus an authentic response to this teaching. See Arthur J. Dewey, "The Unkindest Cut of All?—Matt 19:11-12," paper presented to the Jesus Seminar, Cincinnati, Ohio, October 1990.

42. Matthew 10:37 changes Luke's "hate father and mother" to "loves father or mother *more than me*," a change which not only weakens the intentional shock of Luke 14:26, but also shifts the focus from joining Jesus to do God's work, as in Luke, to regarding Jesus as the highest value. *Gos. Thom.* 101 supports Luke's reading, but mitigates the shock by adding a qualifier: "He who does not hate his father and his mother as I do, will not be able to be my disciple. *And he who does not love his father and his mother as I do, will not be able to be my disciple.*"

43. Rejection of the Jewish law by gentile Christians is not surprising. It is more difficult to account for the Jewish Christian source preserved in the Pseudo-Clementine literature (the *Preaching of Peter*), which rejected sacrifice and alleged that the Old Testament had been interpolated by "false pericopes" inspired by Satan. See Jean Daniélou, *The Theology of Jewish Christianity* (Chicago: Regnery, 1964), 57, 183, 229.

44. Mark 1:21-28 par.; 3:1-6; 6:1-6//Matt. 13:54-58; Luke 13:10-17; 14:1-6; John 5:1-18; 7:21-24; 9:1-41. In the Gospels, the afflicted always take the initiative for healing—except on the Sabbath, whose end they patiently await before asking for help (Mark 1:32-34). It is always Jesus who takes the initiative to heal on the Sabbath (Marcus Borg, *Conflict, Holiness and Politics*, 148). Violation of the Sabbath is not mentioned outside the Gospels. Apparently the early church did not make of it the issue Jesus did, and it would have been a nonissue for Gentiles.

45. Was Jesus doing away with the Sabbath, or giving it its full significance as the eschatological day, the day that prefigures the leisure of the end time (Luke 13:15-16)? Clearly, it was not to be a day of servitude, but the premonitory sign of the supreme liberation God is accomplishing for the whole creation (Heb. 4:9-10). Thus his healings on the Sabbath were not a flouting of the Sabbath laws, but the full honoring of the Sabbath's meaning: freedom on this day from all that disfigures and frustrates the divine will for the fullness of time (André Trocmé, *Jesus and the Nonviolent Revolution* [Scottdale, Pa.: Herald Press, 1973], 68).

46. Edwin A. Hallsten, "The Community that Kills—Paul and Prohibition," Colloquium on Religion and Violence, New Orleans, Nov. 16, 1990, 33–34.

47. William R. Herzog II, in response to a paper I delivered on "Jesus against Domination" for the Historical Jesus section at the Society of Biblical Literature annual meeting in Kansas City, Mo., Nov. 24, 1991.

48. Luke 11:50-51//Matt. 23:35-36; Matt. 27:25; Mark 12:1-12 par.; Luke 19:12-14, 27.

49. Mark 15:2-5 par.; Luke 23:6-16; Matt. 27:19, 24-25; Luke 23:47.

50. Tax collectors and sinners: Mark 2:13-17 par.; Matt. 11:19//Luke 7:34; Luke 19:1-10. Note that when he was called to Cornelius's house (Acts 9:43; 10:6, 32), Peter was staying with Simon the tanner, whose occupation was despised and unclean (M. *Ketub.* 7:10; T.B. *Kidd.* 82b Bar.; T.B. *Pes.* 65a Bar.); yet Peter insists (according to the author of Acts) that he has never eaten anything unclean (10:14)!

51. Acts 6:13; 7:41-43, 48-50; 17:24-25.

52. 1 Cor. 3:16-17; 2 Cor. 6:16; see also Mark 9:42-47 (understanding the "body" here as the community); Eph. 2:21-22; Heb. 10:5, 20; 1 Pet. 2:4-10. It is thus technically true when Paul is depicted in Acts 25:8 as claiming that he has never offended against the Temple; he has merely made it null and void!

53. Rom. 3:25; 1 Tim. 2:5-6; Titus 2:14; Heb. 1:3; 2:9, 14-17; 7:27; 9:22-28; 10:4-31; 13:12-16, 20-21; 1 Pet. 1:18-19; 3:18; 1 John 1:7; 3:16-18; 4:9-10; Rev. 5:9-10; 21:22.

54. Melito of Sardis amplifies the symbolism: the *angel* of the Temple rends its veil: "Though the people rent not their garments [at Jesus' death], the angel rent his" (*Homily on the Passion* 98).

55. Dominique Barbé, *A Theology of Conflict* (Maryknoll, N.Y.: Orbis Books, 1989), 52.

56. Frances M. Young, *Sacrifice and the Death of Christ* (London: SPCK, 1975), 9.

57. *NT Apoc.*, 1:158. The Pseudo-Clementine *Recognitions* assert that sacrifice was never God's will, but that Israel was so taken with idols in Egypt that a gradual weaning was necessary (1.36–39).

58. Ched Myers, *Binding the Strong Man* (Maryknoll, N.Y.: Orbis Books, 1988), 322.

59. Acts 2:46; 3:1—4:4; 5:20-21, 25, 42; 21:26-30; 22:17; 24:18; 26:21. The only exception seems to be Acts 21:26, where Paul not only paid for but participated in the sacrifice of lambs and pigeons for four men under a Nazirite vow. But this was a deliberately staged attempt to pacify his enemies, and it was a concession he could easily make for the peace of the church, even if he no longer believed it necessary.

60. There are in the Hebrew Scriptures devastating critiques of the entire sacrificial cultus (Ps. 40:6; 51:16-17; Isa. 1:11-17; 17:7-8; 66:3; Jeremiah 7; Hos. 6:6; Amos 5:21-24; Mic. 6:6-8), and even one text that exposes the scapegoat mechanism (Isaiah 53). No doubt Jesus was familiar with these passages; but it is difficult to know how formative they were in his thinking. It is significant that the evangelists do not quote them, but rather Isa. 56:7 and Jer. 7:11.

61. Herman Waetjen, *A Reordering of Power: A Socio-Political Reading of Mark's Gospel* (Minneapolis: Fortress Press, 1989), 183. See also Marcus Borg, *Conflict, Holiness and Politics*, 197.

62. This reading appears in a number of late texts, but is lacking in all the major early witnesses except D. But it faithfully extends Jesus' nonviolent spirit.

63. Luke 21:20-24 reflects the church's decision to flee Jerusalem to Pella rather than fight in the war against Rome.

64. Matt. 10:10//Luke 9:3 (contradicted by Mark 6:8).

65. Matt. 5:43-48//Luke 6:27-28, 32-36; see also Rom. 12:14-21.

66. Matt. 5:38-42//Luke 6:29-30; see also Rom. 12:14-21; 1 Thess. 5:15; 1 Pet. 3:9.

67. Matt. 5:21-24; 7:1-5//Luke 6:37-38, 41-42; Luke 10:29-37; Matt. 6:12//Luke 11:4; Mark 11:25//Matt. 6:14-15; Mark 2:1-12 par.; 3:28//Matt. 12:31; Matt. 12:32//Luke 12:10; Matt. 18:21-22//Luke 17:3-4; Matt. 18:23-35; Luke 7:36-50; Luke 23:34; see also Acts 7:60; Eph. 4:26-27, 32; Col. 3:13; Heb. 12:14-15; James 1:19-20.

68. See David Low Dodge, "The Mediator's Kingdom" (1809), in *The Universe Bends Toward Justice*, ed. Angie O'Gorman (Philadelphia: New Society Publishers, 1990), 40–41; and G. W. H. Lampe, "The Two Swords," in *Jesus and the Politics of His Day*, 347.

69. Raymond E. Brown, *The Gospel according to John*, Anchor Bible, 2 vols. (Garden City, N.Y.: Doubleday, 1966–1970), 1:115.

70. It is sometimes objected that, if *pantas* (all) referred only to animals, it should be neuter, agreeing with *probata* (sheep). Being masculine, it must refer to the buyers and sellers. G. H. C. Macgregor counters that the grammatical rule states that when one adjective qualifies two nouns of different genders, it will agree with the masculine or feminine noun (here, *boas*, oxen) rather than the neuter, irrespective of position (e.g., Heb. 3:6). Had Jesus used violence on persons, he would surely have been overwhelmed by superior numbers of temple guards. His moral authority, not his whip, drove the vendors out (*The New Testament Basis of Pacifism* [London: Fellowship of Reconciliation, (1936) 1953], 17 n. 2).

71. If one doubts the historical character of John's version, or of the event generally, then the problem of Jesus' ostensible violence of course vanishes.

72. Jean Lasserre, *War and the Gospel* (Scottdale, Pa.: Herald Press, 1962), 45.

73. Principally J. Jeremias, *Jerusalem in the Time of Jesus*, 359-76.

74. John 4:4-42; Mark 5:33-34//Luke 8:47-48; Mark 7:24-30//Matt. 15:21-28.

75. Mark 5:24b-34 par.; Luke 13:10-17; Mark 1:29-31//Matt. 8:14-15; Mark 5:21-24a, 35-43 par.; Luke 7:36-50; John 20:17 reading "cling." Note 1 Cor. 7:1—Paul echoes his earlier training when he advises, "It is well for a man not to touch a woman."

76. Was she a prostitute? Her hair was loosed in public, before men, something no respectable woman would do (M. *Sota* 3:8; loose hair in public could be grounds for divorce, T.B. *Ket.* 72a; "long hair is not fit for boys, but for voluptuous women"—*Pseudo-Phocylides* 212 [*OT Ps.*, 2:581]); she was "a woman in the city, who was a sinner," a phrase reminiscent of our "woman of the streets"; the Pharisee assumes that Jesus should be able, from outer signs, to tell "who and what kind of woman this is"; what she does is highly sensual and perhaps even sexual; she possesses an alabaster flask of ointment (myrrh), which in John 12:5 is valued at a year's wage—perhaps it was a gift from a client, or was used in her trade (Prov. 7:17). The case is circumstantial, but does point toward prostitution. The contrast between the "respectable" men and the outcast woman requires that she be socially despised, since Jesus reverses the cultural values and identifies with her against the representatives of a patriarchal system that requires prostitutes and yet refuses to acknowledge their humanity.

77. Joachim Jeremias, *New Testament Theology* (New York: Charles Scribner's Sons, 1971), 227–28. See also John 3:1-12. "It is remarkable enough that Jesus draws attention at all to children, for they were considered nonentities. It is quite shocking that he would advance them as models for his social program" (Ched Myers, *Binding the Strong Man*, 261).

78. Fiorenza, *In Memory of Her*, 148.

79. 1 Cor. 14:33b-36; 11:2-16; Eph. 5:22-33; 1 Tim. 2:8-15; 5:3-16; Titus 2:3-5; 1 Pet. 3:1-7; Rev. 14:4.

80. M. *Sota* 3:4, Rabbi Eliezer, first century; Ben Azzai taught the opposite, but did not prevail. See also M. *Ned.* 4:3, which permits the teaching of Scripture to daughters; but some texts omit this reading. T.J. *Sota* 3.4, 19a 7 has a variant on the theme: Better to burn Torah than to teach it to women.

81. M. *Kidd.* 1:7; Tos. *Sota* 2.8, 295; Jeremias, *Jerusalem in the Time of Jesus*, 372.

82. Tos. *Ketub.* 4.7; T. B. *Nid.* 48b; T.B. *Ketub.* 10b; T.B. *Hag.* 20a.

83. Luke 10:38-42. Mark 3:34-35 also implies that women disciples were seated on the floor, along with males, listening to Jesus' teaching.

84. Mark 10:1-12//Matt. 19:1-12. Matthew softens the command by allowing adultery as due cause for divorce. But that only brings Jesus' position back to Shammai's view. See also Matt. 5:31-32; Luke 16:18.

85. Fiorenza, *In Memory of Her*, 143. See also her excellent exposition of the household rules of antiquity and their explicit connection with male rule (pp. 251-84).

86. Ivan Illich, *Gender* (New York: Pantheon, 1982).

87. Luke 15:8-9; 18:1-8; Matt. 13:33//Luke 13:20-21//*Gos. Thom.* 96.

88. Mark 15:40 par.; John 19:25 agrees, but the followers of the "beloved disciple" cannot resist intruding him into the narrative as well (v. 26).

89. Mark 16:1-8 par.; John 20:1, 11-18.

90. John 20:1, 11-18; Matt. 28:9-10; Mark 16:9-11.

91. Walter Wink, " 'And the Lord Appeared First to Mary': Sexual Politics in the Resurrection Witness," in *Social Themes of the Christian Year*, ed. Dieter T. Hessel (Philadelphia: Geneva Press, 1983), 177–82.

92. For exceptions, see Ben Witherington III, *Women in the Ministry of Jesus*, SNTSMS 51 (Cambridge: Cambridge Univ. Press, 1984), 9–10.

93. John 20:2 ("we") implies that other women were originally with Mary Magdalene. In *Gos. Pet.* 12:50, Mary Magdalene is called a disciple. The *Sophia Jesu Christi* speaks of seven women who followed Jesus as disciples. *Pistis Sophia* 96 states that Mary Magdalene "will surpass all my disciples and all men who shall receive mysteries of the Ineffable," and she will sit at Christ's right hand. In *Gos. Thom.* 61, Salome calls herself Christ's disciple (*NT Apoc.*, 1:186-87, 246, 256–57, and 298 respectively).

94. Acts 2:17-21 = Joel 2:28-32; 1 Cor. 11:5; 12:4-11, 28-31.

95. Acts 12:12; 16:14-15, 40; Rom. 16:1-2, 3, 5; 1 Cor. 16:19; Col. 4:15.

96. Rom. 16:3, 6, 12; Acts 18:1-3, 18-19, 24-26; 1 Cor. 16:19; 2 Tim. 4:19-21.

97. Acts 8:3; 9:1-2; 22:4-5; Rom. 16:7.

98. Rom. 16:7 refers to "Junia," clearly a feminine proper name. The translators, unable or unwilling to believe that there were women apostles, simply assumed it

had to be a man. Hence the RSV: "Greet Andronicus and Junias my kins*men* and my fellow prisoners; they are *men* of note among the apostles" (corrected in the NRSV).

99. Acts 9:36-42.

100. Luke 8:3; Mark 15:40-41//Matt. 27:55-56; Rom. 16:1-2; 1 Tim. 3:8-13.

101. Leonard Swidler's translation, *Biblical Affirmations of Woman* (Philadelphia: Westminster Press, 1979), 310-11. Walter Bauer, *The Greek-English Lexicon of the New Testament*, trans. and augmented by W. F. Arndt, F. W. Gingrich, and F. W. Danker, 2d ed. (Chicago: Univ. of Chicago Press, 1979), lists under *prostatis* "protector, patroness, helper." The NRSV translates "benefactor."

102. *NT Apoc.*, 1:195–96.

103. Ibid., 1:353–54.

104. Ibid., 1:342–44.

105. No textual evidence supports regarding 1 Cor. 14:33b-36 as an interpolation (though the context does); for that reason Fiorenza treats it as authentic (*In Memory of Her*, 230–35). Many other scholars treat it as an intrusion (see, e.g., Hans Conzelmann, *1 Corinthians*, Hermeneia [Philadelphia: Fortress Press, 1975], 246).

106. John Pairman Brown, "The Kingdom of God," *Encyclopedia of Religion*, ed. Mircea Eliade (New York: Macmillan, 1987), 8:304–12.

107. Walter Wink, "The Education of the Apostles: Mark's View of Human Transformation," *Religious Education* 83 (1988): 277–90.

108. "It was inevitable that the Christian ideal was not accepted in its full meaning at the moment of its formulation. A doctrine undermining the whole existing order of things could not possibly have been accepted in its entirety; that is why it was adopted only in a misrepresented form" (Leo Tolstoy, *The Law of Love and the Law of Violence* [London: Anthony Blond, (1909) 1948],72).

7. BREAKING THE SPIRAL OF VIOLENCE: THE POWER OF THE CROSS

1. Edith Lovejoy Pierce, from "Drum Major for a Dream," quoted by Vincent Harding, "Getting Ready for the Hero," *Sojourners* 15 (January 1986): 17.

2. The passion predictions in Mark 8:31 par.; 9:31 par.; and 10:33-34 par. are clearly "mini-passion narratives" colored by the actual events recounted in the crucifixion accounts. But other predictions are not so explicit. Mark 9:12//Matt. 17:12; Luke 9:44; 13:31-33; 17:25; Matt. 23:34//Luke 11:49; Matt. 23:37//Luke 13:34 all predict death with no reference whatever to resurrection, and the last one, plus Matt. 11:19//Luke 7:34, seems to anticipate death by stoning ("a glutton and a drunkard" is a technical expression from Deut. 21:18-21 referring to the stoning of a "rebellious son"). The penalty for blasphemy was also stoning (cf. Mark 2:1-12 par.). Jesus' teaching about losing life to find it contemplates death as a consequence of fidelity to God (Mark 8:35 par.; Luke 17:33; John 12:25). No doubt the church has multiplied these predictions in the light of the actual outcome (Mark 3:6 par.; Mark 8:34 par.; and Matt. 10:38//Luke 14:27 possibly; the church's hand is more

certainly reflected in John 5:16, 18; 7:1, 19, 25, 30, 32; 8:37, 59; 10:31, 39; 11:8, 16, 50, 53, 57; and 12:10-11). But there is no plausible reason to doubt that Jesus recognized the resistance his mission provoked, including the likely prospect of death. Martin Luther King, Jr., had to face that prospect every single day; all liberation leaders must.

3. Mark 14:65 par.; 15:15-20//Matt. 27:26-31//John 19:1-3; Mark 15:22-32 par.

4. "The death of Jesus was not merely the unfortunate by-product of an otherwise benign civilization; it was the deliberate outcome of its wisest deliberation and most auspicious institutions. The law cursed and killed Christ and so revealed the violent basis of the order that it served (Gal. 3:13). . . . Such a disclosure meant that there is now a new order antinomous to the old, which is sustained by a new transcendentally grounded power of non-violence, called love, and that the old order now appears to be in thrall to 'powers' of the kind that killed Jesus, the powers of violence" (Robert G. Hamerton-Kelly, "Sacred Violence and Sinful Desire: Paul's Interpretation of Adam's Sin in the Letter to the Romans," in *The Conversation Continues: Studies in Paul and John in Honor of J. Louis Martyn*, ed. Robert T. Fortna and Beverly R. Gaventa [Nashville: Abingdon Press, 1990], 36–37).

5. See *Naming the Powers*, 55–60, for a discussion of the problems of translation.

6. Herman Waetjen, *A Reordering of Power: A Socio-Political Reading of Mark's Gospel* (Minneapolis: Fortress Press, 1989), 145.

7. As told by Li Lu, her deputy, at the Albert Einstein Institution conference on Nonviolent Sanctions for National Defense, Boston, Mass., February 10, 1990.

8. Richard Deats, "Journey to Asia," *Fellowship* 56 (1990): 8.

9. Eph. 1:20-22a, REB, modified to remove sexist language.

10. Theophus Smith, "King and Nonviolent Religion in Black America," in *Curing Violence: Religion and the Thought of René Girard*, ed. Mark I. Wallace and Smith (Sonoma, Calif.: Polebridge Press, forthcoming).

11. René Girard, *Violence and the Sacred* (Baltimore: Johns Hopkins Univ. Press, 1977); *Things Hidden since the Foundation of the World*, with Jean-Michel Ourgoulian and Guy Lefort (Stanford: Stanford Univ. Press, 1987); *The Scapegoat* (Baltimore: Johns Hopkins Univ. Press, 1986).

12. R. G. Hamerton-Kelly, "Sacred Violence and Sinful Desire," 35–54.

13. Burton Mack, "Introduction," in *Violent Origins*, ed. R. G. Hamerton-Kelly (Stanford: Stanford Univ. Press, 1987), 9.

14. Paul Dumouchel, "Introduction," in *Violence and Truth: On the Work of René Girard*, ed. Dumouchel (London: Athlone Press, 1988), 14.

15. Based on Raymund Schwager, *Must There Be Scapegoats?* (San Francisco: Harper & Row, 1987), 46–47.

16. Søren Kierkegaard, *Fear and Trembling* (Garden City, N.Y.: Doubleday, 1954), 41.

17. Girard, *Scapegoat*, 100.

18. Schwager, *Must There Be Scapegoats?*, 43.

19. Allegorizing involves explaining a text by reading into it a meaning drawn from elsewhere. Marcion was a second-century theologian who rejected the Hebrew Bible as the work of a Demiurge, or creator-God, who was solely preoccupied with law and justice, and who was fickle, capricious, despotic, and cruel. This creator-God, Marcion alleged, had nothing in common with the wholly loving God revealed

by Jesus (*Oxford Dictionary of the Christian Church*, ed. F. L. Cross [London: Oxford Univ. Press, 1958], 854).

20. Schwager, *Must There Be Scapegoats?*, 47–67, 119.

21. Ibid. James Williams penetratingly displays this revelatory motif in the Hebrew Scriptures in *The Bible, Violence, and the Sacred* (San Francisco: HarperSan Francisco, 1991).

22. Schwager, *Must There Be Scapegoats?*, 67, 75.

23. Dominique Barbé, *A Theology of Conflict* (Maryknoll, N.Y.: Orbis Books, 1989), 54.

24. Girard, *Scapegoat*, 114, 126.

25. Luke 23:13, 35; 24:20; John 7:26; Acts 3:17; 4:8-10, 26; 13:27-28; 1 Cor. 2:6-8; 1 Thess. 2:14-16; and the references in n. 3. See also *Naming the Powers*, 40–45.

26. Matt. 11:12; 23:37-39//Luke 13:34-35; Luke 11:47-51//Matt. 23:29-35.

27. Cited without reference by Paul W. Newman, "Identifying with Jesus: Atonement as Royal Metaphor," *Christian Century* 108 (January 30, 1991): 116.

28. Girard, *Things Hidden*, 213. See also Frances M. Young, *Sacrifice and the Death of Christ* (London: SPCK, 1975); and Ellis Rivkin, *What Crucified Jesus?* (Nashville: Abingdon Press, 1984).

29. Girard, *Things Hidden*, 219.

30. *The Simone Weil Reader*, ed. George A. Panichas (New York: David McKay Co., 1977), 384.

31. Girard, *Scapegoat*, 187–92.

32. Girard, *Things Hidden*, 197.

33. Justin, *2 Apol.* 6.

34. J. Denny Weaver, "Atonement for the Non-Constantinian Church," *Modern Theology* 6 (July 1990): 307–23. See also Gustav Aulén's classic, *Christus Victor* (New York: Macmillan, 1931).

35. In the same way, the dogma of biblical infallibility and plenary inspiration means that the sacrificial hermeneutic is made the sole interpretive grid for reading the Bible, since this dogma regards the whole Bible as revelation, including the sacrificial elements of the Hebrew Bible (Michael Hardin, "The Biblical Testaments as a Marriage of Convenience: René Girard and Biblical Interpretation," a paper presented to the Colloquium on Violence and Religion, New Orleans, November 19, 1990, 25).

36. Luke, much maligned by neoorthodox biblical scholars for his failure to assign any expiatory or atoning power to Jesus' death, may have understood that death better than the rest by refusing to do so. In fact, according to David L. Tiede, Luke sees the meaning of Jesus' death as God's strategy for revealing both God's judgment and salvation: judgment, in the crucifixion of the Messiah and the destruction of Jerusalem; and salvation, in repentance, faith in Jesus, the forgiveness of sins, the reception of the Holy Spirit, and ultimately, the restitution of all things ("The Death of Jesus and the Trial of Israel," SBL *Seminar Papers*, Annual Meeting, 1990 [Atlanta: Scholars Press, 1990], 158–64; see also David P. Moessner, " 'The Christ Must Suffer,' The Church Must Suffer: Rethinking the Theology of the Cross in Luke-Acts," in ibid., 165–95).

37. It was not really possible for a persecuted group like the early Christians to write persecutory texts, though they may have wished they had the power to take revenge on their persecutors. It was only after Christianity ascended to power that its texts could be used to justify persecution of the Jews. But the hatred against "the Jews" expressed by the Fourth Gospel; Matthew's creation of the cry by "all the [Jewish] people, 'His blood be on us and on our children!' " (27:25); Luke's interpretation of the fall of Jerusalem as punishment of the Jews for killing Jesus (21:20-24); and the Book of Revelation's polemic against the Jews of Smyrna as "a synagogue of Satan" (2:9), provided all the tinder required to fuel persecution of Jews right up to the present.

38. Schwager, *Must There Be Scapegoats?*, 209.

39. Hamerton-Kelly, "Sacred Violence and Sinful Desire," 47–49.

40. According to the provocative thesis of Robert T. Fortna, Paul, at the time he wrote Philippians (*prior* to Galatians and Romans), still believed that he could achieve his own justification by making a supreme sacrifice comparable to that of Jesus. But after the hardships he experienced in Ephesus (on this theory), he was persuaded that human beings could contribute nothing to their own salvation, not even the negative and still egocentric contribution of giving up everything ("Philippians: Paul's Most Egocentric Letter," in *The Conversation Continues*, ed. Fortna and Gaventa, 220–34). To use Girard's terms, Paul was still engaged in mimetic rivalry with Jesus and/or God to prove his suitability for their company. The realization that grace cannot be earned finally freed Paul (and this would be true whether it came to him at his conversion or in Ephesus) from the struggle to be God.

41. Gil Bailie, "Billy Budd," audio cassette, tape 2 of 4, Temenos, P.O. Box 925, Sonoma, CA 95476—the best entry to the thought of Girard I have found.

42. Frans de Waal, *Peacemaking among Primates* (Cambridge: Harvard Univ. Press, 1989), 248, 268.

43. See the penetrating critique of Girard by Lucian Scubla, "The Christianity of René Girard and the Nature of Religion," in *Violence and Truth*, 160–71.

44. Frank Waters, *Book of the Hopi* (New York: Penguin Books, [1963] 1982).

45. Ashley Montague, *Learning Non-Aggression: The Experience of Non-Literate Societies* (New York: Oxford Univ. Press, 1978).

46. Marija Gimbutas, *The Language of the Goddess* (San Francisco: Harper & Row, 1989), 113, 116; *The Goddesses and Gods of Old Europe* (London: Thames & Hudson, 1982), 74, 148, 196. Bones of large fish, dogs, boar, and deer have been found in altars in the Danubian region, late seventh to early sixth millennium B.C.E.; vultures were sacrificed in Lebanon from the Mid-Paleolithic to the Epipaleolithic, and various other carrion eaters in northern Iraq and Orkney, Scotland, from 8000 B.C.E. (*Language of the Goddess*, 157, 187, 189).

47. Jonathan Z. Smith, "The Domestication of Violence," in *Violent Origins*, 197; Riane Eisler, *The Chalice and the Blade* (San Francisco: Harper & Row, 1987), 212 n. 24; Joseph Campbell, *Myths to Live By* (New York: Viking, 1972), 55; Elise Boulding, *The Underside of History* (Boulder, Colo.: Westview Press, 1976), 139.

48. Almost all ancient human skulls have been distorted and flattened, as if clubbed, as a result of the gradually increasing pressure of stone and soil deposits over them. The problem is not then one of finding a suitably "stoned" skull to corroborate Girard's thesis, but that virtually all skulls look stoned (Richard E. Leakey

and Roger Lewin, *People of the Lake* [Garden City, N.Y.: Anchor/Doubleday, 1978], 270–71).

8. TO WASH OFF THE NOT HUMAN:
BECOMING EXPENDABLE

1. William Blake, "Milton," in *The Complete Poetry and Prose of William Blake*, ed. David V. Erdman, rev. ed. (Berkeley: Univ. of California Press, 1982), plates 40–41, p. 142.

2. Jens Reich, "You Don't Need Courage; You Just Need Not to Care," *Newsweek*, December 25, 1989, 20.

3. See "The Elements of the Universe," in *Naming the Powers*, 67–77; "The Elements of the Universe," in *Unmasking the Powers*, 128–52. "Fundamental assumptions of the Domination System" is, I believe, a better translation of *stoicheia tou kosmou* in Col. 2:20 than I was able to offer in the two earlier volumes.

4. Jung, "Transformation Symbolism in the Mass," in *Psychology and Religion: West and East*, CW 11 (1977), 256.

5. See Judith Plaskow, *Sex, Sin and Grace: Women's Experience and the Theologies of Reinhold Niebuhr and Paul Tillich* (Washington, D.C.: Univ. Press of America, 1980).

6. Luke 17:33*. This seems to be the earliest recoverable structure of the saying, if not its wording. "For my sake" (Matt. 10:39; 16:25; Luke 9:24) and "for my sake and the gospel's" (Mark 8:35) appear to be later additions, since the versions of the saying in Luke 17:33 and John 12:25 lack anything similar, and reflect a less-developed Christology—in fact, no Christology at all.

7. Ira Progoff, *Jung's Psychology and Its Social Meaning* (Garden City, N.Y.: Anchor Books, 1973), 151.

8. Jean Vanier, "Reflections on Christian Community," *Sojourners* 6 (December 1977): 12.

9. Daniel Berrigan, *No Bars to Manhood* (Garden City, N.Y.: Doubleday, 1970), 115.

10. Quoted by Andrew Bard Schmookler, *Out of Weakness* (Toronto: Bantam, 1988), 177.

11. Eleanor Bertine, *Jung's Contribution to Our Time*, ed. Elizabeth C. Rohrbach (New York: Putnam, 1968), 6.

12. The "social will of God" is Chilean worker-priest Mariano Pugo's superb paraphrase of "kingdom of God."

13. Jeanne M. Paradise, "Making Peace. A Psychosocial Study of a Group of Nonviolent Nuclear Resisters" (Ph.D. diss., Boston University School of Education, May 1987), 104–5, 113, 124.

14. Joel Kovel, *History and Spirit* (Boston: Beacon Press, 1991), 78.

15. Cited by Robert L. Holmes, *Nonviolence in Theory and Practice* (Belmont, Calif.: Wadsworth Pub. Co., 1990), 55.

16. Interview with Richard Steele, "The Power of Fearlessness," *International Fellowship of Reconciliation Report*, November 1981, 10–14.

17. Carl Scovel, "Christian Responses to the Nazi State," *Katallagete* 11 (Spring 1978): 38.

18. John Howard Yoder, *The Priestly Kingdom* (Notre Dame: Univ. of Notre Dame Press, 1984), 92.

19. *Naming the Powers*, 89–96. Clinton E. Arnold has recently attempted to avoid this problem by asserting that the church is passive in Eph. 3:10. The church testifies to the Powers by its very existence, not by preaching. He himself is unable to maintain this position, however, since he also believes that the church is to be engaged in spiritual warfare against the forces of evil (Eph. 6:10-20) and in active testimony to the Powers (*Ephesians: Power and Magic*, SNTSMS 63 [Cambridge: Cambridge Univ. Press, 1989], 64). "Believers are encouraged to take aggressive action against this kingdom of evil by proclaiming the gospel of Christ" (ibid., 170; see also 120, 121, 126). See my review in a forthcoming issue of the *Journal of Biblical Literature*.

20. The *Letter of Peter to Philip* (late second or early third century) provides striking confirmation of this interpretation of "the heavenlies" (*Ep. Pet. Phil.* 137:10–13). The disciples are depicted as asking the risen Jesus, apparently with explicit reference to Eph. 3:10, "Lord, tell us: in what way shall we fight with the Archons, since the Archons are above us?"—that is, in the "heavenlies." A voice answers them, "Now you will fight with them in this way, *for the Archons are fighting with the inner man*" (*NHL*, 1st ed., 396–97). The Powers in their spiritual aspect are not, after all, "up" but *within*. They are the interiority of institutions, and can be known only by spiritual discernment (the "inner man"). The "fight" therefore begins within, where they gain sovereignty over our lives by first winning our compliance. One must therefore oppose them, the letter says, by coming together in community, teaching the world, girding oneself with divine power, and through prayer (*Ep. Pet. Phil.* 137:23–30).

21. Ignatius, *Rom.* 3:3.

22. Eugene C. Roehlkepartain, "What Makes Faith Mature?" *Christian Century* 108 (May 9, 1990): 497.

23. Bill Moyer, *The Movement Action Plan: A Strategy Describing the Eight Stages of Successful Social Movements*, rev. ed., 1987. (Movement for a New Society, 721 Shrader St., San Francisco, CA 94117). I regard this as the single most important document to put in the hands of a social-change group.

24. James W. Douglass, *The Nonviolent Coming of God* (Maryknoll, N.Y.: Orbis Books, 1991), 42–44.

25. Moyer, *Movement Action Plan*, ibid.

PART THREE: ENGAGING THE POWERS NONVIOLENTLY

1. George Weigel, *Tranquillitas Ordinis* (Oxford: Oxford Univ. Press, 1987), 385, 390.

2. James W. Douglass, in a paragraph cut from the manuscript of *The Nonviolent Coming of God* (Maryknoll, N.Y.: Orbis Books, 1991).

9. JESUS' THIRD WAY: NONVIOLENT ENGAGEMENT

1. Daniel Berrigan, *No Bars to Manhood* (Garden City, N.Y.: Doubleday, 1970), 57–58.

2. For a more detailed exegetical study of this passage see my article, "Neither Passivity nor Violence: Jesus' Third Way," *Forum* 7 (1991): 5–28.

3. The core of Matthew's logion is 5:39b-42, though v. 42 may not belong to the original cluster. In vv. 39b-41, the focus is first on what an oppressor does and then on what the hearers can do back; in v. 42, the focus shifts to the hearers and what they should do when another would beg or borrow.

Luke's version (6:29-30) lacks Matthew's introduction, thesis statement, and the saying about forced labor. Luke has made a number of alterations to the Q version. He mistakes the striking as armed robbery, and the response as submission: offer the other cheek to be pummeled. Consequently, he drops Matthew's "right" cheek, apparently not recognizing (as we shall see) that "right" specifies the type of blow, and that it is intended, not as attack or injury, but as humiliation. In the same way he regards the taking of the coat as theft; disciples are supposed to offer to the thieves their last remaining covering. In v. 30 he preserves Matthew's injunction to give to beggars, but in the second half of the saying returns to the theme of brigandage: if anyone forcibly seizes your goods, do not seek to recover them. And since he has read virtually the whole passage as a response to armed robbery, Luke simply has no use for the saying about how to respond to the enforced carrying of military baggage, so he drops that altogether. Luke correctly preserves the original sequence of the taking of garments, however: first the *himation* (outer garment, cloak), then the *chitōn* (undergarment, shirt).

For a structural analysis of this logion, see John Dominic Crossan, "Divine Immediacy and Human Immediacy," in *Semeia* 44 (1988): 121–40. On the Q form of this unit, see John Kloppenborg, *The Formation of Q* (Philadelphia: Fortress Press, 1987), 173–80. On the meaning of the passage as a whole, see Gerhard Lohfink, "Der ekklesiale Sitz im Leben der Aufforderung Jesu zum Gewaltverzicht (Mt 5, 39b-42/Lk 6,28f)," *Theologische Quartalschrift* 162 (1982): 236-53 (who incorrectly identifies Jesus' audience as the disciples rather than inferring from the text itself who his audience was: those who are struck, sued, and impressed—the common people of the land); Jean Lambrecht, S.J., "The Sayings of Jesus on Nonviolence," *Louvain Studies* 12 (1987): 291–305, one of the better treatments of the text; W. Wolbert, "Bergpredigt und Gewaltlosigkeit," *Theologie und Philosophie* 57 (1982): 498–525; and Jürgen Sauer, "Traditionsgeschichtliche Erwägungen zu den synoptischen und paulinischen Aussagen über Feindesliebe und Wiedervergeltungsverzicht," *Zeitschrift für die Neutestamentliche Wissenschaft* 76 (1985): 1–28.

4. Eduard Schweizer, *The Good News according to Matthew* (London: SPCK, 1976), 130.

5. 1QS 7. "Right" must not be regarded as an insertion into Matthew's text, whatever other tendencies one may find in the tradition (against Crossan, "Divine Immediacy"). Otherwise the type of blow is not specified, and it is regarded as a blow with the fist (Luke), not a backhand. "Hit on the right cheek" here is effectively a technical term; it is not merely descriptive of anatomy. (So also Pinchas Lapide, *The Sermon on the Mount* [Maryknoll, N.Y.: Orbis Books, 1986], 121, whose work independently confirms some of the conclusions of this analysis.)

Didache has generally been regarded as dependent on Matthew and/or Luke. But Aaron Milavec has presented compelling evidence that it had access to the Jesus tradition independent of the Synoptics ("The Didache as Independent of the

Gospels," paper presented at the Jesus Seminar, Sonoma, Calif., March 1–3, 1991). For this saying, in fact, *Did.* 1:4 preserves the best and quite possibly earliest version extant: (1) it specifies the right cheek, following Matthew; (2) yet it follows Luke (correctly) in the order "cloak . . . shirt"; and (3) it agrees with Matthew against Luke by including the saying about the second mile.

6. The Code of Hammurabi 202 decrees that if a man of rank or authority strikes the cheek of a man who is his superior, he shall be given sixty lashes with an ox whip in the assembly (*The Ancient Near East: An Anthology of Texts and Pictures*, ed. James B. Pritchard [Princeton: Princeton Univ. Press, 1969], 161).

7. The TEV, excellent in this passage in other respects, misses when it reads, "let him slap your left cheek too." This is precisely what he *cannot* do, unless he abandons the backhand altogether.

8. "Landowners look for respect since what counts to them as well as to their tenants is honor; landowners need the 'status support' that only their tenants can give them" (Bruce J. Malina, "Patron and Client: The Analogy behind Synoptic Theology," *Forum* 4 [1988]: 3).

9. Gandhi, in *Harijan*, March 10, 1946; cited by Mark Juergensmeyer, *Fighting with Gandhi* (San Francisco: Harper & Row, 1984), 43.

10. Josephus, *Ant.* 18.55.

11. Josephus, *War* 2.169–74. A similar action was taken to halt Caligula's attempt to install his image in the temple in 41 C.E., with similar success (Josephus, *Ant.* 18.261–309; Philo, *Leg.* 225–29). Later still, while Cumanus was procurator (48–52 C.E.), a soldier tore up a copy of the Law and flung it in the fire. Again, crowds descended on Caesarea, and Cumanus executed the offender to pacify the Jews (*War* 2.229–31). See also Philo, *Leg.* 299–305.

12. The rights of the poor debtor are thus protected by Scripture, while the creditor is permitted to harass and shame the debtor by demanding the outer garment each morning. The *Mek. de R. Ishmael* on Exod. 22:25-27 shows creditors intensifying their demand by taking a night garment by day and a day garment by night. See also T.B. *Tem.* 6a; *B. Metz.* 31b, 113ab, 114ab; *Sanh.* 21a.

13. H. G. Liddell and R. Scott, *A Greek-English Lexicon*, 9th ed. (Oxford: Clarendon Press, 1958), 829.

14. See S. Safrai and M. Stern, eds., *The Jewish People in the First Century* (Philadelphia: Fortress Press, 1987), I.2. 797–98; J. M. Myers, "Dress," *IDB*, 1:869–71. See also *Mek. de R. Ishmael* on Exod. 22:27—"*For that Is His Only Covering. This refers to the cloak. It Is the Garment for His Skin.* This refers to the shirt." Matthew is not the only evangelist who confuses these terms. Mark, for example, uses *chitōn* for the high priest's mantle in 14:63 where Matthew (following LXX usage) has *himation*.

15. Josephus, *War* 2.427. On the loss of land through indebtedness, see Martin Goodman, *The Ruling Class of Judea* (Cambridge: Cambridge Univ. Press, 1987), 55–58.

16. Augustine certainly understood Jesus to be speaking of nudity: "Whoever wishes to take away thy tunic, give over to him *whatever clothing thou hast*" (*Sermon on the Mount* 1.19.60). The *Pseudo-Clementine Homily*, which in 15.5 cites Matt. 5:40, changes the word here for "undergarment" in order to avoid the suggestion that the person becomes naked. For, comments the *ANF* translator, A. Cleveland

Coxe, the person who lost both cloak and tunic would be naked altogether; and "this, the writer may have imagined, Christ would not have commanded" (*ANF*, 8:310). Another indication that Matt. 5:40 refers to nakedness is provided by *Gos. Thom.* 21, which appears to be a gnosticizing development of Jesus' saying about stripping naked. When the owners of the field come to reclaim it, the children take off their clothes before the owners and "are naked in their presence"—an excellent nonviolent tactic, here unfortunately distorted to mean stripping off the body after death in the presence of the evil Archons.

Nudity is abhorrent to the conventional because it violates the system of classification by which one can identify a person's place on the social map. Without clothes, the boundaries by which society is ordered and guarded are dissolved. Clothing signifies one's social location, gender, and status (Jerome H. Neyrey, "A Symbolic Approach to Mark 7," *Forum* 4/3 [1988]: 72). Thus Jesus depicts the wounded person by the side of the road as naked, so that the priest and Levite have no claim laid on them by his social rank or status, but only by his humanity (Luke 10:30). Therefore, to strip naked voluntarily before the creditor and magistrate, precisely in a context intended to shame the poor into repayment, is to defy the hierarchical system of classification in its entirety.

17. There is, so far as I can tell, no surviving Roman law limiting *angereia* to one mile, but scholars have almost universally inferred from the wording of the text (correctly, I believe) that some such rule was in force. Roman milemarkers go back at least to 249 B.C.E. in Italy. Of the five hundred milestones found in Palestine, only a quarter are inscribed, and none are dated earlier than 69 C.E. Israel Roll believes that the paucity of milestones from the period before the Bar Kokhba revolt is because these five- to eight-foot stone markers existed primarily to propagandize Roman invincibility. A thirty-mile trip meant passing twenty-nine milemarker points, many of which had five or more monoliths proclaiming the names and titles of the rulers of the Empire. "This 'brainwashing' was meant to make the traveller aware of the might of the Roman government, past and present, and convince him that no power on earth would be able to challenge it in the future." These milestones also itemized a community's obligations for providing supplies for the Roman army of occupation and animals for the postal service. There was thus plenty of cause for the rebels to tear down these emblems during the revolt of 132–35 C.E. ("The Roman Road System in Judaea," *The Jerusalem Cathedra* III, ed. Lee I. Levine [Detroit: Wayne State Univ. Press, 1983], 153). See also M. Avi-Yonah, "The Development of the Roman Road System in Palestine," *Israel Exploration Journal* 1 (1950–51): 54–60; Peter Thomsen, "Die römischen Meilensteine der Provinzen Syria, Arabia und Palästina," *Zeitschrift des Deutschen Palästina-Vereins* 40 (1917): 1–103; B. H. Isaac and I. Roll, "A Milestone of A.D. 69 from Judaea: The Elder Trajan and Vespasian," *Journal of Roman Studies* 66 (1976): 15–19; and idem., *Roman Roads in Judaea I: The Legio-Scythopolis Road*, BAR International Series 141, (Oxford: BAR, 1982).

18. M. Rostovtzeff, "Angariae," *Klio. Beiträge zur alten Geschichte* 6 (1906): 249–58. In one Aramaic version of the book of Tobit, Tobit is unable to go fetch the gold deposited in Rages because "in those days the *angareia* had increased," and therefore "the travelers had disappeared from the streets out of fear" (*The Book of Tobit. A*

Chaldee Text from a Unique MS in the Bodleian Library, ed. A. Neubauer. [Oxford: Clarendon, 1878], 4, lines 7–9 (mistranslated "tribute," p. xxviii). Other early references to *angareia* are found in *Pap. Teb.* I 5, 178ff. and 252ff. (second century B.C.E.). The former commands soldiers and others who are on official business neither to impress (*angareuein*) any of the inhabitants of the province or their beasts of burden for their own personal needs nor to requisition calves, etc. Similarly also *Orientis Graeci Inscriptiones Selectae*, ed. W. Dittenberger, 2 vols. (1903–1905), 1:665.21.

19. T.J. *B. Metz.* 6.3, 11a, cited by Paul Fiebig, "*angareuō*," *Zeitschrift für die neutestamentliche Wissenschaft* 18 (1918): 64–72. For additional Jewish references, see "*angaria*," in Gustaf Dalman, *Aramäisch-neuhebräisches Handwörterbuch*, 2d ed. (Frankfort: J. Kauffmann, 1897-1901), 105; and Marcus Jastrow, *A Dictionary of the Targumim, the Talmud Babli and Yerushalmi, and the Midrashic Literature* (New York: Pardes, 1950), 81; for Greek, "*angareia*," in Liddell-Scott, *Greek-English Lexicon*, 7; for Latin, "*angaria, angario*," in *Thesaurus Linguae Latinae* (Lipsiae: B. G. Teubneri, 1940–46), 2.43. See also August Wünsche, *Neue Beiträge zur Erläuterung der Evangelien aus Talmud und Midrasch* (Göttingen: Vandenhoeck & Ruprecht, 1878), 64–65; L. Goldschmid, "Impôts et droits de douane en Judée sous les Romains," *Revue des études juives* 34 (1897): 207–8; Friedrich Preisigke, "Die ptolemäische Staatspost," *Klio* 7 (1907): 275–77; Ulrich Wilcken, "Transport-Requisitionen für Beamte und Truppen," in *Grundzüge und Chrestomathie der Papyruskunde*, L. Mitteis and U. Wilcken, eds. (Leipzig/Berlin: B. G. Teubner, 1912), 1:374–76; Vincente Garcia de Diego, "Notas etimológicas: Angaria," *Boletín de la Real Academia Española* 40 (1960): 380–99; T. Henckels and H. G. Crocker, *Memorandum of Authorities on the Law of Angary* (Washington, D.C.: Government Printing Office, 1919), 25–30; J. Le Clère, *Les mesures coercitives sur les navires de commerce étrangers* (Paris: Librairie générale de droit et de jurisprudence, 1949), 19–21, 35–36; Adolf Deissmann, *Bible Studies* (Edinburgh: T. & T. Clark, 1901), 86–87; A.-H. Schröder, *Das Angarienrecht* (Hamburg: Forschungsstelle für Völkerrecht und ausländisches öffentliches Recht der Universität Hamburg, 1965), 15–18; Joshua Gutmann and Daniel Sperber, "Angaria," *Encyclopaedia Judaica*, ed. C. Roth and G. Wigoder, 16 vols. (Jerusalem: Keter, 1971), 2:950–51; D. Sperber, *Nautica Talmudica* (Ramat-Gan: Bar-Ilan University, 1986), 115–18; "Angaria in Rabbinic Literature," *L'Antiquité Classique* 38 (1969): 164–68; G. E. M. de Ste. Croix, *The Class Struggle in the Ancient Greek World* (Ithaca, N.Y.: Cornell Univ. Press, 1981), 14–16; and Iu. A. Solodukho, "Podati i povinnosti v Irake v III–V vv. nashï 'ery" (Taxes and obligations in Iraq in the third to fifth centuries of our era), *Sovetskoe vostokovedenie* 5 (1948): 69, section 9 and n. 1.

20. *Corpus Inscriptionum Graecarum*. no. 4956, A21, cited by Edwin Hatch, *Essays in Biblical Greek* (Amsterdam: Philo, [1889] 1970), 37. Hatch suggested that Matt. 5:41 should not be translated "whosoever shall compel thee to *go* one mile," but "whosoever shall compel thee to *carry his baggage* one mile," but few versions have followed his advice. TEV comes closest: "If one of the occupation troops forces you to carry his pack one mile"—though in Galilee it might have been one of Antipas's militia doing the compelling.

21. *Papyri greci e latini* 446 (133–137 C.E.), cited by Ramsay MacMullen, *Soldier and Civilian in the Late Roman Empire* (Cambridge: Harvard Univ. Press, 1963), 89 n. 42, my emphasis.

22. *The Theodosian Code*, ed. Clyde Pharr (Princeton: Princeton Univ. Press, 1952), sections 8.5.1, 2, 6, 7, 8.1, 11, 66. See in addition *The Digests of Justinian*, ed. Th. Mommsen (Philadelphia: Univ. of Pennsylvania, 1985), sections 49.18.4; 50.4.18.21–22, 29; 50.5.10, 11; and Justinian's *Novella* (Constitutions) 16.9, 10; 17.1, 9, 22 (in *The Civil Law*, trans. S. P. Scott [Cincinnati: Central Trust, 1973]).

23. According to Tacitus, slaves and camp-followers outnumbered the soldiers in the army that Vitellius marched to Rome (*Hist.* 2.70). In Acts 10:7, the centurion Cornelius counts at least two servants and a soldier "among those that waited on him." See for a later period MacMullen, *Soldier and Civilian*, 106 n. 29, 126–27.

24. Michael Grant, *The Army of the Caesars* (London: Weidenfeld & Nicolson, 1974), xxi–xxx; Fiebig, "*angareuō*," especially *Lev. Rab.* 12; T.B. *Sanh.* 101b; *B. Kam.* 38b; *Sota* 10a; *Ber.* 9b; *Yoma* 35b; *Ned.* 32a. Vegetius, *De re militari*, gives a graphic picture of the contents of a Roman soldier's pack and the rigors of a forced march (trans. in *Roots of Strategy*, ed. T. R. Phillips [Harrisburg, Pa.: Military Service Publ., 1955], 76–88). Josephus states that "an infantry man is almost as heavily laden as a pack-mule" (*War* 3.95).

25. "It was the centurion who formed the backbone of Roman military discipline, and he did so by intensely personal coercion" (C. E. Brand, *Roman Military Law* [Austin: Univ. of Texas, 1968], 81, 42). The centurion was responsible for giving judgment in any complaint brought by civilians against the excesses of soldiers (Roy W. Davies, *Service in the Roman Army* [New York: Columbia Univ. Press, 1989], 37, 51, 57, 174). See also Robert R. Evans, *Soldiers of Rome* (Washington, D.C.: Seven Locks, 1986), 74; G. W. Currie, *The Military Discipline of the Romans from the Founding of the Empire to the Close of the Republic* (Bloomington: Indiana Univ. Press, 1928), 10, 12, 161; Abel H. J. Greenridge, "The *Provocatio Militiae* and Provincial Jurisdiction," *Classical Review* 10 (1896): 226; Richard E. Smith, *Service in the Post-Marian Roman Army* (Manchester: Manchester Univ. Press, 1958); Robert O. Fink, *Roman Military Records on Papyrus* (Cleveland: Case Western Univ. Press, 1971), esp. 383–86; Michael P. Speidel, *Guards of the Roman Armies* (Bonn: Rudolf Habelt, 1978).

26. Maurice, *Strategica* 7.3, my emphasis; cited by Brand, *Roman Military Laws*, 21. See also 4.10 (Brand, 195).

27. Brand, *Roman Military Laws*, 104–6. In any case military law was always more severe in its punishments than civil. Of the 102 instances where the punishment of a soldier is mentioned, 40 resulted in the death penalty (Currie, *Military Discipline*, 38).

28. Josephus gives an instance of a legion passing through Judea and the lengths Jewish leaders went to prevent it (*Ant.* 18:120–24). But even in Jerusalem, Galilean pilgrims would have been treated to scenes similar to that enacted by the impressment of Simon of Cyrene to carry Jesus' cross. Herod had raised auxiliaries in Samaria that continued to be garrisoned in Caesarea; and in Galilee, his son, Herod Antipas, organized his army along Roman lines, which would no doubt have included the right of impressment. Frequent dispatches of mail, troops, and supplies passed through Palestine on the route between Egypt and Syria. Roman soldiers also accompanied caravans and acted as police in suppressing robbers. See George Leonard Chessman, *The Auxilia of the Roman Imperial Army* (Hildesheim: Georg Olms Verlag, 1971), 161–63.

29. Epictetus provides an example of passive submission to impressment that is the polar opposite of Jesus' advice in Matthew. "You ought to treat your whole body like a poor loaded-down donkey . . . and if it be commandeered (*angareia*) and a soldier lay hold of it, let it go, do not resist (*antiteine*) or grumble. If you do, you will get a beating and lose your little donkey just the same" (*Disc.* 4.1.79). For the degeneration of *angareia* to plain extortion by soldiers, see Ramsey MacMullen, *Soldier and Civilian*, 85–86; and M. Rostovtzeff, *The Social and Economic History of the Roman Empire*, 2d ed. (Oxford: Clarendon Press, 1957), 1:424 and 2:721–23 nn. 45–47.

30. Horsley, *Jesus and the Spiral of Violence* (San Francisco: Harper & Row, 1987), 318–26.

31. See Sharon H. Ringe, *Jesus, Liberation, and the Biblical Jubilee*, Overtures to Biblical Theology (Philadelphia: Fortress, 1985).

32. That Jesus proposed such behavior in concrete situations is illustrated by the story of the rich young man (Mark 10:17-22 par.). The same kind of liberating generosity is envisioned in Luke 7:41-42; 10:35; Mark 10:23-31 par. See Douglas E. Oakman, *Jesus and the Economic Questions of His Day* (Lewiston: Edwin Mellen Press, 1986), 166, 215–16.

33. The more original version of v. 42 is probably preserved in Luke 6:35—"but lend, expecting nothing in return," and *Gos. Thom.* 95—"If you have money do not lend at interest, but give . . . from whom you will not get them [back]." What in Matthew seems to be the bland encouragement of almsgiving and moneylending appears in Luke and *Thomas* in a form as shocking as the injunctions that precede it in Matthew: lend without hope even of interest, lend even to those who cannot pay it back at all. "The follower of Jesus is not merely to lend without interest, but to *give*. If this be so, the very radicalism of the saying might suggest its authenticity" (R. McL. Wilson, *Studies in the Gospel of Thomas* [London: Mowbray, 1960], 128).

34. Horsley, *Jesus and the Spiral of Violence*, 32.

35. Acts 2:43-47; 4:32—5:11; 6:1. These reports may be idealized but they are by no means pure fiction. The well-established poverty of the Jerusalem church may have been one of the unintended results of mixing Jesus' stringent program of redistribution of wealth with the church's apocalyptic belief in an immediate end of history. Hence the early community *liquidated* capital and lived off the proceeds, rather than sharing in communitarian economic arrangements, and quickly found itself destitute.

36. James W. Douglass, *The Non-Violent Cross* (New York: Macmillan, 1968), 193.

37. *Stasis*, the noun form of *stēnai*, means "a stand," in the military sense of facing off against an enemy. By extension it came to mean a "party formed for seditious purposes; sedition, revolt." The NRSV translates *stasis* in Mark 15:7 as "insurrection" (so also Luke 23:19, 25), in Acts 19:40 as "rioting," and in Acts 23:10 as "violent dissension." On the military use of *anthistēmi* and its cognates, see Walter Wink, "Beyond Just War and Pacifism: Jesus' Nonviolent Way," *Review and Expositor* 89 (1992): 197–214.

38. Victor Paul Furnish, *The Love Commandment in the New Testament* (Nashville: Abingdon Press, 1972), 106; C. E. B. Cranfield, *The Epistle to the Romans*, International Critical Commentary, 2 vols. (Edinburgh: T. & T. Clark, 1975–79),

1:645. For non-Christian parallels, see William Klassen, *Love of Enemies*, Overtures to Biblical Theology (Philadelphia: Fortress Press, 1984), 115–16 and 130 nn. 5-8. The actual verbal parallelism is remarkable:

mēdeni	*kakon anti kakou*	*apodidontes*	(Rom. 12:17)
mē . . .	*kakon anti kakou . . . apodō*		(1 Thess. 5:15)
mē apodidontes	*kakon anti kakou*		(1 Pet. 3:9)

Joseph and Asenath 23:9; 28:5, 14; and 29:3 all have the refrain, do not repay "evil for evil," but the date is uncertain (first century B.C.E.–second century C.E.); so also the *Apocalypse of Sedrach* 7:9 (*OT Ps.*, 1:611—150–500 C.E.). There is also a most remarkable allusion to Jesus' saying in *The Acts of Andrew and Matthias in the City of the Cannibals* 26, ed. and trans. Dennis Ronald MacDonald (Atlanta: Scholars Press, 1990), 139—Andrew suffers torture rather than retaliate "because of your command which you commanded me when you said, 'Do not *respond in kind* to their unbelief' " (my emphasis).

39. George Howard, *The Gospel of Matthew according to a Primitive Hebrew Text* (Macon: Mercer Univ. Press, 1987), 20–21. Howard notes in addition ("The Textual Nature of Shem-Tob's Hebrew Matthew," *Journal of Biblical Literature* 108 [1989]: 253–54) that the Sermon on the Mount in Shem-Tob's Hebrew version of Matthew is interrupted sixteen times by words like "Jesus said to his disciples" precisely at those points where Luke's parallel is found in a different place in Luke's Gospel, or where Luke has no parallel. It appears then that this Hebrew Matthew reflects an *earlier* form of the Sermon on the Mount than our canonical Greek Matthew, which has omitted all these *Gospel of Thomas*-like introductions in order to create a smooth, homogeneous whole. If true, this provides further confirmation that the earliest form of the saying was, in fact, "Do not return evil for evil."

40. Calvin had already hit upon this reading intuitively (*On a Harmony of the Evangelists* [Grand Rapids: Wm. B. Eerdmans, 1949], 1:298). Pseudo-Chrysostom also equated "resist not evil" and "do not render evil for evil" (cited by Thomas Aquinas, *Commentary on the Four Gospels* [Oxford: James Parker, 1894], 197), as do the modern commentators Pinchas Lapide (*Sermon on the Mount*, 134) and G. H. C. Macgregor (*The Relevance of an Impossible Ideal* [London: Fellowship of Reconciliation, 1960], 48). So also the Christian Common Bible (Queson City, Philippines: Claretian Publications, 1988) reads "Do not oppose evil with evil." On carefully argued exegetical grounds, David Wenham concludes that Matthew's "Do not resist evil" and the Pauline/Petrine "Do not return evil for evil" should be seen as differing versions of the same saying of Jesus, and that the latter is the more original ("Paul's Use of the Jesus Tradition: Three Samples," in *Gospel Perspectives*, vol. 5, *The Jesus Tradition Outside the Gospels*, ed. Wenham [Sheffield: JSOT Press, 1985], 18–19).

41. The easiest solution, and perhaps the correct one, is to regard Matt. 5:39a as a Matthean addition. *Ponēros* is certainly a favorite of Matthew (it occurs 26 times in Matthew, 2 in Mark, 13 in Luke, but 12 of Matthew's uses are from Q). The antitheses of the Sermon on the Mount seem as a whole to be Matthean, whatever their individual histories. Matthew would have only had to add "But I say to you" to v. 39a in order to adapt the passage to his antithetical formulation. So the origin of "Do not *antistēnai* one who is evil" remains problematic. What we *can* say with

some confidence is that both "Do not resist evil violently" and "Do not return evil for evil" express the same basic insight: the spiritual imperative to resist evil without being made evil in turn.

42. A Babylonian proverb from 1700–1600 B.C.E. sounds remarkably like Jesus: "Do not return evil to the man who disputes with you; Requite with kindness your evil doer, Maintain justice to your enemy, Smile on your adversary. . . . Do not set your mind on evil" (W. G. Lambert, *Babylonian Wisdom Literature* [Oxford: Clarendon Press, 1960], 101, lines 36–48). Such sentiments from the heartland of the *Enuma Elish* show just how much deviation from androcracy remained possible.

43. A. J. Muste insisted that one must be a revolutionary before being a pacifist. "A non-revolutionary pacifist is a contradiction in terms" ("Pacifism and Class War" (1928), in *The Universe Bends Toward Justice: A Reader on Christian Nonviolence in the U.S.*, ed. Angie O'Gorman [Philadelphia: New Society Publishers, 1990], 113).

44. Isa. 10:5-6; 22:1-8; 28:1-22; 29:1-4; 30:8-17; Amos 3:1-2; 5:18-20.

45. Paul Valliere, *Holy War and Pentecostal Peace* (New York: Seabury Press, 1983), 46–86; see also Howard Goeringer, "Jesus' Teaching of Nonresistance," *The Jesus Journal*, no. 51 (P.O. Box 3772, Tallahassee, FL 32315), n.d. or page.

46. See Jos. *War* 2.169–74; *Ant.* 18.55–59; *War* 2.229–31; Philo *Leg.* 299–305; and later, Jos. *Ant.* 18.261–309 and Philo *Leg.* 225–29; and Horsley's excellent discussion, *Jesus and the Spiral of Violence*, 90–120. I am baffled, however, by the way Horsley depicts Jews initiating popular nonviolent protests, and then portrays Jesus and Matt. 5:38-42 as virtually irrelevant to that setting. He claims that "enemies" did not refer to outsiders, but rather applied only to fellow peasants. But we can accurately specify the enemies Jesus has in mind in this passage: "enemies" are masters who backhand subordinates (v. 39); "enemies" are creditors who humiliate debtors by seizing their outer garments (v. 40); "enemies" are soldiers who compel civilians to carry their baggage (v. 41). On p. 303 Horsley contradicts his own argument when he speaks of the destruction of Jerusalem "by its enemies, who, at the time of Jesus, would obviously have been the Romans." He compellingly sketches a society in the birth pangs of discovering nonviolence, and then creates a Jesus, with much questionable argumentation, who is a dreamer no different than Theudas. It seems to me that my reconstruction fits the sociopolitical setting that Horsley has so admirably reconstructed far better than his own!

47. I have attempted to apply Jesus' teaching on the "third way" to the situation in South Africa in *Violence and Nonviolence in South Africa* (Philadelphia: New Society Publishers, 1987). It would be anachronistic to regard nonviolence as a full-blown philosophical option in first-century Palestine. Gandhi seems to have been the first person to develop nonviolence into a total way of life, philosophy, and strategy for social change. But all the elements of that synthesis were present in Jesus' life and teaching. See Ched Myers, *Binding the Strong Man* (Maryknoll, N.Y.: Orbis Books, 1988), 47.

48. See Stephanie Judson, *A Manual on Nonviolence and Children* (Philadelphia: New Society Publishers, 1984); or contact Children's Creative Response to Conflict, P.O. Box 7283, Arlington, VA 22207.

49. Devi Prasad, "Gandhi's Attitude Towards Violent Struggles for Freedom," *International Fellowship of Reconciliation Report*, April 1980, 20; citing *Young India*, 11 August 1920.

50. Gandhi, in Joan V. Bondurant, *Conquest of Violence* (Princeton: Princeton Univ. Press, 1958), 139.

51. Eknath Easwaran, *A Man to Match His Mountains: Badshah Khan, Nonviolent Soldier of Islam* (Petaluma, Calif.: Nilgiri Press, 1984), 194.

52. *The New York Times*, April 12, 1987, 8.

53. Africa Watch Committee, *No Neutral Ground: South Africa's Confrontation with the Activist Churches* (New York: Human Rights Watch, 1989), 65.

54. Colin M. Turnbull, "The Politics of Non-Aggression (Zaïre)," in *Teaching Non-Aggression*, ed. Ashley Montague (New York: Oxford Univ. Press, 1978), 187–91.

55. George Lakey, *Powerful Peacemaking* (Philadelphia: New Society Publishers, 1987), 112.

56. Bernard Häring, *The Healing Power of Peace* (New York: Paulist Press, 1986), 25. Mary Lou Kownacki provides a similar translation: "Blessed are those who do not use force" ("Behold the Nonviolent One," *Sojourners* 18 [October 1989]: 23).

57. Marjorie Hope and James Young, "Christians and Nonviolent Resistance in the Occupied Territories," *Christian Century* 105 (April 27, 1988): 432. Of the nonviolent resistance to Caligula's attempt to install his image in the Jewish temple, Philo remarks that the Jews were organized in six companies: "old men, young men, boys . . . old women, grown women, maidens" (*Leg.* 226–27). Of the many intellectuals who advocate the "just" use of violence, few actually take up weapons in solidarity with the oppressed and fight as did Che Guevara or Camillo Torres. Instead, they appeal to a special "vocation" for revolutionary intellectuals that exempts them from combat. By contrast, nonviolence theorists invariably are involved in demonstrations, civil disobedience, arrests, and occasionally the risk of their lives.

58. Rob Fairmichael, "Nonviolent Methods," *Dawn Train* 9 (Belfast, N. Ireland, 1990), 29–30.

59. Barbara Deming, "On Revolution and Equilibrium," cited by Robert L. Holmes, *Nonviolence in Theory and Practice* (Belmont, Calif.: Wadsworth Publishing Co., 1990), 101.

60. Riane Eisler and David Loye, *The Partnership Way* (San Francisco: HarperSanFrancisco, 1990), 116.

10. ON NOT BECOMING WHAT WE HATE

1. Bertolt Brecht, "To Posterity," in *Selected Poems*, trans. H. R. Hays (New York: Reynal & Hitchcock, 1947), 177.

2. A. J. Muste, "Gandhi and the H-Bomb" (Nyack, N.Y.: Fellowship Publications, [1950] 1983), 11.

3. Cited by Morris Janowitz, *The Professional Soldier* (Glencoe, Ill.: Free Press, 1961), 328. Urie Bronfenbrenner, on his visits to the Soviet Union, discovered that the Soviets' distorted picture of us was curiously similar to our view of them—a mirror image, in fact ("The Mirror Image in Soviet-American Relations," in *Psychology and the Prevention of Nuclear War*, ed. Ralph K. White [New York: New York Univ. Press, 1986], 71–81).

NOTES FOR PAGES 196–97

4. William Blake, "Jerusalem," chap. 2, plate 30, in *The Complete Poetry and Prose of William Blake*, ed. David V. Erdman, rev. ed. (Berkeley: Univ. of California Press, 1982), 177.

5. So also Bertrand de Jouvenel, *Power: The Natural History of Its Growth* (London: Balchworth Press, [1945] 1952), 15—"The enemy . . . must be copied by the other side, who will otherwise fight at a disadvantage"; and Michael Walzer, *Just and Unjust Wars* (London: Allan Lane, 1978), 32—"Here is the ultimate tyranny: those who resist aggression are forced to imitate, and perhaps even to exceed, the brutality of the aggressor." Baron Carl von Clausewitz anticipated all these views when he described the "reciprocal imitative violence" by which two combatants mimic each other and consume themselves to the point of utter exhaustion (cited by Richard B. Gregg, *The Power of Nonviolence*, 2d ed. [Nyack, N.Y.: Fellowship Publications, 1959], 54).

6. Richard Cowan, "How the Narcs Created Crack," *National Review*, December 5, 1986, 26. See also my "Biting the Bullet: The Case for Legalizing Drugs," *Christian Century* 107 (August 8–15, 1990): 736–39.

7. He adds, "And when you look long into an abyss, the abyss also looks into you" (Friedrich Nietzsche, *Beyond Good and Evil*, trans. Walter Kaufmann [New York: Vintage Books, 1966], 89, epigram 146).

8. Daniel Yergin, *Shattered Peace: The Origins of the Cold War and the National Security State* (Boston: Houghton Mifflin Co., 1977), 63. Raymond Aron observes that "Europeans did not fight to the death [in two World Wars] to share out the world, but because they had fought to the death, together they lost the dominion of the world" ("War and Industrial Society," in *War: Studies from Psychology, Sociology, Anthropology*, ed. Leon Bramson and George W. Goethals, rev. ed. [New York: Basic Books, 1968], 399).

9. Napoleon, who was the first to recognize the advantages of universal military conscription, revolutionized warfare, so that his enemies "recognized that he must be conquered by his own instruments of victory" (Alfred Vagts, *The History of Militarism* [New York: W. W. Norton, 1937], 99). A document purported to be from the South African State Security Council leaked to the Johannesburg *Weekly Mail*, entitled "The Art of Counter-Revolutionary Warfare," asserts as its central thesis the idea that "a governing power can defeat any revolutionary movement if it adapts the revolutionary strategy and principles and applies them in reverse" (May 20–26, 1988, 15).

10. Ken Brown, "By Any Means Possible," *Fellowship* 47 (October/November, 1981): 5. In *History of the Second World War* (London: Pan Books, 1973), B. H. Liddell-Hart states that the effects of British bombing were much exaggerated at the time; German industrial production increased about 50 percent in 1942. Oil, Germany's most desperately needed raw material, was scarcely touched, and aircraft output greatly expanded. Hart judges the British decision to terrorize cities rather than targeting military and industrial sites as a "disregard of basic morality." See his whole chapter, pp. 617–41. See also Peter Hoffmann, "Hitler's Good Right Arm," *New York Times Book Review*, May 28, 1989, 21. Michael Walzer concludes that British terror bombing was entirely indefensible and criminal, and asserts that Gen. Arthur Harris, who with Churchill was most responsible for it, should have been

tried at Nuremberg (*Just and Unjust Wars* [London: Allan Lane, 1978], 255–63, 323).

11. Steven Soter, "Bombing Civilians: The World War II Lesson," *New York Times*, May 22, 1983; see also Norman Cousins, "Lying for the Bomb," *Ground Zero* 6 (Winter 1987): 5.

12. Len Giovannitti and Fred Freed, *The Decision to Drop the Bomb* (New York: Coward-McCann, 1965), 265; Gar Alperovits, "The Hiroshima Decision," *Sojourners* 14 (August/September 1985): 14–21.

13. William Blake, "The Grey Monk," in *The Complete Poetry and Prose of William Blake*, 490.

14. René Girard, *Violence and the Sacred* (Baltimore: Johns Hopkins Univ. Press, 1977), 47. See also his *The Scapegoat* (Baltimore: Johns Hopkins Univ. Press, 1986), 130: "By imitating my brother's desire, I desire what he desires; we mutually prevent each other from satisfying our common desire. As resistance grows on both sides, so desire becomes strengthened; the model becomes increasingly obstructive and the obstacle becomes increasingly the model, so that ultimately the desire is only interested in that which opposes it. . . . As mimeticism becomes more exacerbated it increases its dual power of attraction and repulsion and communicates itself as hatred more rapidly from one individual to another."

My own introduction to the ideas of this chapter was not through Girard, though he has infinitely deepened it, but something I read by Emmet Fox in 1955. I note this only to indicate that Girard's views are supported by a long spiritual tradition, never prominent, but persistent in the life of the spirit.

15. U.S. Army Intelligence recruited thousands of Nazis after World War II, some of them known war criminals, apparently on the assumption that such masters of intrigue had much to teach their naively democratic conquerors. The CIA later spread Nazi methods of torture to the Shah's Iran, to Vietnam, and to Central and South America (Christopher Simpson, *Blowback: America's Recruitment of Nazis and Its Effects on the Cold War* [New York: Weidenfeld & Nicolson, 1988]). Similarly, our nation officially condemned brainwashing techniques used by the Chinese in Korea, yet the top security federal prisons in Marion, Ill., and Lexington, Ky., have deliberately adapted Chinese brainwashing techniques to break the psychological resistance of prisoners (Dave Dellinger, "Playing with Prisoners' Minds," *Fellowship* 54 [March 1988]: 18–20).

16. H. G. Baynes, *Germany Possessed* (London: Jonathan Cape, 1941), 301. In a sermon delivered on November 21, 1943, Harry Emerson Fosdick issued a similar warning. "All history teaches at least one lesson about war—its inevitable tendency to lead the victor to take on the character of the vanquished. . . . In fighting our enemies we copy them, and in our victories over them assume ourselves the very attributes and qualities we have fought against." Like Amaziah, who defeated the Edomites and then brought home and worshiped the gods of his beaten enemy, in war we always copy our enemies and serve their gods. "A strange paradox war presents, that, calling other men our enemies and proclaiming that we hate their ways and their ideas, we proceed at once with utmost speed and zeal to imitate them" (*A Great Time to Be Alive* [Freeport, N.Y.: Books for Libraries Press, 1972], 155–62).

17. William Irwin Thompson, *Evil and World Order* (New York: Harper & Row, 1976), 19. Thompson also cited Russell. I have also drawn on Lewis A. Coser, *The Function of Social Conflict* (Glencoe, Ill.: Free Press, 1956), 121. So also Raymond Aron, *The Century of Total War* (Garden City, N.Y.: Doubleday, 1954), 110: "Communism found imitators among its enemies. Communism's enemies, to combat it, had to resort to the same methods of arousing their nations against Bolshevism as did the Bolshevist nations to arouse the proletariat against capitalism."

18. Milton Mayer, *They Thought They Were Free: The Germans 1933–45* (Chicago: Univ. of Chicago Press, 1955), 339. A particularly graphic example of the conquered conquering their conquerors is provided by ancient China. The nomadic Mongols conquered China from horseback, only to discover that China could not be ruled from horseback. To exploit their prize, they had to abandon the very organization that had made conquest possible in the first place, and adopt the traditional Chinese forms of government. The landed gentry were soon once more the backbone of society, and the primitive rule of nomadic origin had to conform to the sedentary Chinese way of life (Andrew Bard Schmookler, *The Parable of the Tribes* [Berkeley: Univ. of California Press, 1984], 60).

19. Denis de Rougemont, *The Devil's Share*, Bollingen Series 2 (New York: Pantheon Books, 1945), 94–95.

20. Douglas E. Oakman, *Jesus and the Economic Questions of His Day* (Lewiston/Queenston: Edwin Mellen Press, 1986), 43–44; Morton Scott Enslin, *Christian Beginnings*, parts 1–2 (New York: Harper & Brothers, 1956), 16–37.

21. Seneca, as cited by Augustine, *City of God* 6.11.21. So also Horace: "Captured Greece took her fierce victor captive" (*Epist.* 1.1.156).

22. Cited by E. M. Cioran, *The New Gods* (New York: Quadrangle/New York Times Book Co., 1969), 32.

23. Jean-Michel Angebert (pseud.), *The Occult and the Third Reich* (New York: McGraw-Hill, 1975), 24, 35–36.

24. Aldous Huxley, *The Devils of Loudun* (New York: Harper & Brothers, 1952), 128.

25. Marc H. Ellis, "The Occupation Is Over," *Christianity and Crisis* 48 (May 16, 1988): 174.

26. Anthony Lewis, "Fear, Hatred, Retaliation," *New York Times*, Sunday, May 28, 1989, 15E.

27. Robert McNamara, former Secretary of Defense under Presidents Kennedy and Johnson and former President of the World Bank, has articulated what he calls "McNamara's Law," which he would inscribe above the portals of the White House and the Pentagon and apply to every U.S. military intervention, whether Berlin, Vietnam, the Middle East, Libya, or Grenada: "It is impossible to predict with a high degree of certainty the consequences of the use of military force because of the risk of accident, miscalculation, inadvertence and loss of control" (J. Anthony Lukas, "Class Reunion," *New York Times Magazine*, August 30, 1987, 61). Unfortunately, he had not learned this lesson before he helped orchestrate the Vietnam debacle.

28. Martin Luther King, Jr., *Where Do We Go from Here: Chaos or Community* (New York: Harper & Row, 1967), 62. Schmookler makes a similar point: Successful defense against a power-maximizing aggressor requires a society to become more

like the society that threatens it. The tyranny of power is such that even self-defense becomes a kind of surrender, since violent resistance means transforming oneself into the conqueror (*Parable of the Tribes*, 21, 54).

29. Pico Iyer's turn of phrase, in "Romancing Vietnam," *New York Times Book Review*, 5 Dec. 1991, 9.

30. Mark Mason, unpublished paper for a course my wife June Keener-Wink and I taught in a Masters Program sponsored by New York Theological Seminary in Sing Sing Prison, May 1989.

31. That we are dealing with a structural necessity of violence and not an individual aberration with the Weathermen is shown by the parallel case of the Red Army Faction, or Baader-Meinhof group, in West Germany. Never numbering more than twenty-five, their defiance was hopeless from the start. They never developed mass support, their cells were infiltrated by police informers, and their terrorist acts merely led to a massive governmental reaction: new computerized tracking techniques, bugged apartments and cells, specially trained antiterrorist police units, and new legislation that vastly curtailed the civil liberties of everyone considered in any way subversive. The Baader-Meinhof group did indeed change West Germany—by strengthening the very state apparatus of repression it had dreamed of overturning (Robert Gerald Livingston, "Violence Is the Only Way," *New York Times Book Review*, January 3, 1988, 6).

32. Morris Berman, *The Reenchantment of the World* (Toronto: Bantam Books, 1984), 261–62. Insect resistance has increased so rapidly that Allan Felsot, economic entomologist at the Illinois Natural History Survey, predicts that "unless new types of pesticides are developed and we learn to use them properly, all the chemicals we have now likely won't work anymore—at all." Pesticide use has increased selective pressure on insects so that the more resistant kinds are the only ones that have survived. "The sad fact is that the percentage of crop yield lost to pests has risen since 1900 for nearly every major crop except apples" (Larry Doyle, "Pesticides Create 'Monster Bugs,' Immune to Poison," *Los Angeles Times*, April 5, 1987, part I, p. 2).

33. See, e.g., Jonathan Kwitny, *Endless Enemies* (New York: Congdon and Weed, Inc., 1984); Philip Agee, *Inside the Company: CIA Diary* (Toronto: Bantam Books, 1975).

34. Richard J. Barnet, *Intervention and Revolution* (New York: New American Library, 1972), 320.

35. David L. Schalk, *War and the Ivory Tower: Algeria and Vietnam* (New York/ London: Oxford Univ. Press, 1991); Doug Magee, "Viet Nam: The Body Count Still Rises," *Christianity and Crisis* 41 (October 5, 1981): 259, 269; Charlene Spretnak, "Naming the Cultural Forces that Push Us Toward War," in *Nuclear Strategy and the Code of the Warrior*, ed. R. Grossinger and Lindy Hough (Berkeley: North Atlantic Books, 1984), 47; "Two Thirds of Vietnam Vets Have Disorders, Study Says," *Fellowship* 55 (April/May 1989): 24, citing an American Legion study.

36. Lewis Thomas, *The Lives of a Cell* (Toronto: Bantam Books, 1980), 88–94.

37. The United States has been pursuing a contradictory policy in Latin America. On the one hand, we wish to create stable, democratic governments, while on the other hand, we strengthen armies that have historically been antidemocratic, brutal, and corrupt. "Basic U.S. interests are often threatened more by the customary

American response to revolutionary regimes than by the revolutionary regimes themselves" (Richard Feinberg and Kenneth Oye, "After the Fall: U.S. Policy toward Radical Regimes," *World Policy Journal* 1 [Fall 1983]: 201).

38. In a similar vein, the Jungian analyst H. G. Baynes reported during World War II that his English patients' dreams of Hitler indicated that a psychic infection had taken hold within the unconscious of the very people who had mobilized every energy to defeat Hitler (*Germany Possessed*, 252).

39. Erich Neumann comments that, especially in the initial stages of facing the shadow side of the personality, a person may be shocked by the violence with which the hitherto neglected shadow presents itself. The more unwilling the ego is to face this part, the more it will be driven to use outward violence (*Depth Psychology and a New Ethic* [London: Hodder & Stoughton, 1969], 81). In short, *what we repress in ourselves, we oppress in others.*

40. Carl G. Jung, "After the Catastrophe" (1945), in *Civilization in Transition*, CW 10 (1970), 198–99.

41. Glenn Gray, *The Warriors* (New York: Harper & Row, 1970), 27; William Broyles, Jr., "Why Men Love War," *Esquire* 102 (November 1984): 55–58.

42. A Jívaro shaman, preparing a Western anthropologist to undergo a shamanistic visionary initiation in the Amazon, told him, "What is most important is that you must have no fear. If you see something frightening, you must not flee. You must run up and touch it" (Michael Harner, *The Way of the Shaman* [Toronto: Bantam Books, 1986], 18–19). On the implications of nonviolence for healing, see George Lakey, *Powerful Peacemaking* (Philadelphia: New Society Publishers, 1987), xv; and O. Carl Simonton and Stephanie Mathews Simonton, *Getting Well Again* (Los Angeles: J. P. Tarcher, 1978), 149–52.

11. BEYOND JUST WAR AND PACIFISM

1. Niall O'Brien, "Making the Myth Real," *Fellowship* 53 (March 1987): 15.

2. Peter Brock, *The Roots of War Resistance: Pacifism from the Early Church to Tolstoy* (Nyack, N.Y.: Fellowship of Reconciliation, 1981), 9. Brock finds no known instance of conscientious refusal to participate in war prior to the Christian era. Even as late as the nineteenth century, he says, actual noncooperation with war was confined solely to those within the Christian tradition. Jenny Teichman supports this conclusion (*Pacifism and the Just War* [Oxford: Basil Blackwell, 1986], 10). In the East, however, Jainism specifically forbade involvement in violence and destruction, and had a vow of total nonviolence, but only the spiritual elite applied it to themselves (I. C. Sharma, "The Ethics of Jainism," in *Nonviolence in Theory and Practice*, ed. Robert L. Holmes [Belmont, Calif.: Wadsworth Publishing Co., 1990], 13).

3. C. J. Cadoux fills 160 pages with quotations from the New Testament and the early theologians expressing Christian disapproval of participation in war (*The Early Christian Attitude to War* [London: George Allen & Unwin, (1919) 1940]).

4. Justin, *1 Apol.* 39 (Cyril C. Richardson, *Early Christian Fathers* [Philadelphia: Westminster Press, 1953], 266).

5. Origen, *Against Celsus* 5.33. See also 3.8—Christ prohibits Christians to kill. Hippolytus declared that no catechumen could serve in the army, on pain of dismissal

from the church (*Apos. Trad.* 16.17, 19). Cyprian blasted the mayhem caused by war (*Donat.* 6.10). Minucius Felix criticized Rome for its warlike character and the idolatry of its military camps (*Octavian* 25).

6. Tertullian, *On Idol.* 19.3. See also *Apol.* 37.5—in our religion it is counted "better to be slain than to slay"; *Of Patience* 3.8—Jesus "cursed for the time to come the works of the sword"; *The Chaplet (De Cor.)* 11.4—no Christian may remain in the military service after baptism. But in his earlier *Apology*, he prays for the security of the empire and for brave armies (*Apol.* 30), and states that Christians fight alongside Romans (*Apol.* 42). Apparently Christians could not enlist, but soldiers could convert—and remain soldiers.

7. Origen, *Against Celsus* 8.68–75.

8. Roland Bainton, *Christian Attitudes Toward War and Peace* (London: Hodder & Stoughton, 1961), 66. The *Acts of Andrew* (200 C.E. at the latest) berated military service and contains several novelistic stories of soldiers abandoning arms for Christ (*Gregory's Epitome* 18, in Dennis Ronald MacDonald, *The Acts of Andrew and the Acts of Andrew and Matthias in the City of the Cannibals* [Atlanta: Scholars Press, 1990]). And in the *Passion of Andrew* 52, Stratocles leaves the army to study philosophy and espouses a fairly rough-and-tumble brand of nonviolence (ibid.).

9. *The Chaplet (De Cor.)* 11. Tertullian was himself the son of a proconsular centurion (*ANF*, 3:5). Clement of Alexandria took a more compromising view, telling soldiers to remain in the condition in which they were called (*Exhort. to the Heathen* 10.100). But in Egypt, soldiers functioned almost exclusively as police.

10. The most objective treatment may still be Adolf Harnack's *Militia Christi* (Philadelphia: Fortress Press, [1905] 1981); the introduction by David McInnes Gracie provides a helpful updating. John Helgeland's article, "Christians and the Roman Army from Marcus Aurelius to Constantine," *ANRW* II.23.1 (1979): 724–834, is an outstanding argument that the objection to military service was idolatry. Cadoux, Bainton, and Jean-Michel Hornus (*It Is Not Lawful for Me to Fight* [Scottdale, Pa.: Herald Press, 1980]) take the pacifist position. James Moffatt depicted the early tradition as supportive of war in his article "War" in the *Dictionary of the Apostolic Church*, ed. James Hastings (New York: Scribners, 1916), 2:646–73; so also E. A. Ryan, "The Rejection of Military Service by the Early Christians," *Theological Studies* 13 (1952): 1–32. Louis J. Swift, though not endorsing pacifism, concludes that the church fathers on the whole were more concerned about killing than idolatry ("War and the Christian Conscience I: The Early Years," *ANRW* II. 23.1 [1979]: 835–68). See also Kurt Aland, "The Relation between Church and State in Early Times: A Reinterpretation," *Journal of Theological Studies* 19 (1968): 115–27.

11. Helgeland provides an excellent reconstruction of the religious character of Roman military life in "Roman Army Religion," *ANRW* II. 16.2 (1978): 1470–1505.

12. Thus Lactantius, writing just before Constantine's accession, explicitly attacks imperial policy: Romans think that "brave and warlike generals are admitted to the assembly of the gods, and that there is no other way to immortality than to lead armies, to lay waste the territory of others, to destroy cities, to overthrow towns, to put to death or enslave free peoples. Truly the greater number of men they have cast down, plundered, and slain, so much the more noble and distinguished do they think themselves; and ensnared by the show of empty glory, they give to their

crimes the name of virtue" (*Divine Inst.* 1.18). It is hard to conceive of a more withering indictment of the Domination System. He speaks of the lust "to extend the boundaries which are violently taken from others, to increase the power of the state, to improve the revenues. . . . How can a man be just who injures, who hates, who despoils, who puts to death?" (6.6). Lactantius explicitly rejects Cicero's just war rationalizations for the empire as "accommodated neither to justice nor to true virtue, but to this life and to civil institutions" (ibid.). Even as late as the turn of the fourth century, here is a Christian who still believes that "there ought to be no exception at all; but that it is always unlawful to put to death a man, whom God willed to be a sacred animal." Therefore it is not "lawful for a just man to engage in warfare" (6.20). Ironically, Helgeland, who argues that there was little change occasioned by Constantine, says that later Lactantius radically reversed himself due to Constantine's favorable treatment of the church and "could hardly restrain his enthusiasm for the victories of Constantine" ("Christians and the Roman Army," 758)—a response that illustrates precisely how profound an accommodation really did take place. But it is also true that the seeds of this accommodation were already sown in the Gospels themselves, when they viewed the destruction of Jerusalem as a judgment of God on the Jews for killing Jesus, and thus regarded Rome as an agent of God's judgment in history. See James W. Douglass, *The Nonviolent Coming of God* (Maryknoll, N.Y.: Orbis Books, 1991), chap. 5.

13. Helgeland seems to be moving toward the same conclusion when he writes, in a more recent article, "It is idolatry that causes, among other things, killing." What the church objected to, he suggests, was Rome's culture of death, enshrined in Roman military idolatry ("The Early Church and War: The Sociology of Idolatry," in *Peace in a Nuclear Age*, ed. Charles J. Reid, Jr. [Washington, D.C.: Catholic Univ. of America, 1986], 40, 46–47).

14. Taking this to be the date of the beginning of Diocletian's attempt to purge the army of all Christians.

15. Emmanuel Charles C. McCarthy, "Christian Nonviolence: The Great Failure, The Only Hope," transcript of the audio and video tape series, revised April 1986, p. 66.

16. By "violence" I mean lethal force. More precisely, violence is "the intentional harming of another person by physical force" (James F. Childress, *Moral Responsibility in Conflict* [Baton Rouge: Louisiana State Univ. Press, 1982], 14); or better, "the use of force with the intent to harm, kill or cause destruction, or which may cause these as a foreseeable outcome" (Robert L. Holmes, *On War and Morality* [Princeton: Princeton Univ. Press, 1989], 32).

17. The Islamic "jihad" is not a "holy war" in our sense, in that it sometimes has acted as a brake on violence as well as a cause of it. The very terminology of "jihad" was an attempt to restrict religious resort to war to a very limited set of cases (David Little, in personal conversation). And as we saw in chap. 9, holy war thinking in Israel evolved from actual warfare to the prophetic warfare of the Word.

18. John Howard Yoder, *When War Is Unjust* (Minneapolis: Augsburg, 1984), 21.

19. The sole exception seems to have been the Jesuit priest, Father John C. Ford, in 1944—almost at the end of the war. But he was acting as an individual. Reinhold Niebuhr's support for World War II was not based on just war criteria.

He regarded all war as unjust, but sometimes necessary, and found just war criteria too legalistic and casuistic.

20. Yoder, *When War Is Unjust*, 49–50, 66.

21. Cited by Ramund Schwager, "The Theology of the Wrath of God," in *Violence and Truth*, ed. Paul Dumouchel (London: Athlone Press, 1988), 50.

22. For further discussion, see James A. Aho, *Religious Mythology and the Art of War* (Westport, Conn.: Greenwood Press, 1981); and Paul Valliere, *Holy War and Pentecostal Peace* (New York: Seabury, 1983).

23. Paul Ramsey, with Stanley Hauerwas, *Speak Up for Just War or Pacifism* (University Park, Pa.: Pennsylvania State Univ. Press, 1988), 71.

24. Bernard T. Adeney, *Just War, Political Realism, and Faith*, American Theological Library Association Monograph Series 24 (Metuchen, N.J.: American Theological Library Association, 1988), 98.

25. Stanley Hauerwas, *Against the Nations* (Minneapolis: Winston Press, 1985), 138–39. According to George Weigel, the just war tradition regards conflict as the political manifestation of original sin, and war as a legitimate but not inevitable means for resolving conflict. War is thus a just means for defending a legitimate political community and human rights, and not simply another expression of human fallenness (*Tranquillitas Ordinis* [Oxford: Oxford Univ. Press, 1987], 329). The position I am advocating is just the opposite. I consider conflict to be an inevitable consequence of human freedom, and thus would expect it even in the reign of God. Conflict is thus not an expression of human sin, but of the inevitable rub between a variety of interpretations of the good. By contrast, war is a consequence of original sin, as is the violence system generally. It may become necessary for a nation to defend itself, but it does so as a result of the fallen state of humanity, and war is itself the epitome of that fallenness.

26. I have drawn the just war criteria from the following sources: David Little, "The Just-War Tradition and the Pursuit of Peace," in *The One-Hundred Percent Challenge*, ed. Charles D. Smith (Washington, D.C.: Seven Locks Press, 1987), 24–25; Ramsey, *Speak Up*, 89; Hauerwas, *Against the Nations*, 136; Eckehart Lorenz, *Justice Through Violence?* (Geneva: Department of Studies, Lutheran World Federation, 1984), 10–11; Ted Honderich, *Violence for Equality. Inquiries in Political Philosophy* (London/New York: Routledge, 1989); John Howard Yoder, *When War Is Unjust*, 18; Michael Walzer, *Just and Unjust Wars* (London: Allan Lane, 1978), 32; James Turner Johnson, *Just War Tradition and the Restraint of War* (Princeton: Princeton Univ. Press, 1981); Ronald H. Stone, *Christian Realism and Peacemaking* (Nashville: Abingdon Press, 1989); and Stephen Charles Mott, *Biblical Ethics and Social Change* (New York: Oxford Univ. Press, 1982).

27. Using the same just war criteria, James Turner Johnson argued that the Persian Gulf War was just, and Alan Geyer that it was unjust ("Just War Tradition and the War in the Gulf," *Christian Century* 108 [February 6–13, 1991]: 134–35). Their differences do not invalidate the criteria, but illustrate rather that their use is conditioned by one's starting assumptions.

28. Hauerwas, *Against the Nations*, 136. Some just war theorists treat the criteria as prima facie duties, which should be met unless overridden by more stringent duties. Others maintain that no single criterion must be met, but at least several must be satisfied before a war can be justified (a position that makes it highly likely

that most wars *can* be justified). Others regard the criteria as merely "rules of thumb" that illuminate but do not prescribe what we should do (James F. Childress, *Moral Responsibility in Conflicts*, 82).

29. John Swomley, "Where the Disarmament Movement Is Today," *Fellowship* 56 (January/February 1990): 13.

30. Once having become addicted to violence, a society cannot easily kick the habit. Frequently those who use violence engage in vendettas to settle old scores that have nothing to do with the liberation cause. Thus the Palestine Liberation Organization was recently engaged in an all-out battle in Lebanon with a more radical Palestinian liberation group headed by Abu Nidal. Or again, thousands died in the Algerian war of independence from fratricidal violence unrelated to the war, simply because violence had made life so cheap. And during the American Revolution, South Carolina was a particular scene of bloodshed as old enemies sought revenge under the umbrella of "rebels versus redcoats." Rape was routine. The colonists matched their oppressors atrocity for atrocity (Christopher Hibbert, *Redcoats and Rebels: The American Revolution through British Eyes* [New York: W. W. Norton, 1990], 154, 254, 271–74).

31. Dale W. Brown, *Biblical Pacifism* (Elgin, Ill.: Brethren Press, 1986), ix.

32. Richard B. Gregg, *The Power of Nonviolence* (Nyack, N.Y.: Fellowship Publications, 1959), 67.

33. Dom José Maria Pires, cited by Judith Hurley, "Brasil: A Troubled Journey to the Promised Land," in *Relentless Persistence*, ed. Philip McManus and Gerald Schlabach (Philadelphia: New Society Publishers, 1991), 192.

34. John Dear, S.J., "The Road to Transformation: A Conversation with Brian Willson," *Fellowship* 56 (March 1990): 7.

35. Richard Deats, "The Revolution That Didn't Just Happen," *Fellowship* 52 (July/August 1986): 33–34.

36. See especially Gene Sharp, *The Politics of Nonviolent Action*, 3 vols. (Boston: Porter Sargent Publishers, 1973); and *Making Europe Unconquerable* (Cambridge, Mass.: Ballinger Publishing Co., 1985). See also Adam Roberts, ed., *The Strategy of Civilian Defense: Nonviolent Resistance to Aggression* (London: Faber & Faber, 1967); and Frank De Roose, "Military Responses to Civilian-based Defense," *Bulletin of Peace Proposals* 21 (1990): 421–29. A growing bibliography of books and articles is available. Contact the Albert Einstein Institution, 1430 Massachusetts Ave., Cambridge, MA 02138; The Association for Transarmament Studies, 3636 Lafayette, Omaha, NE 68131; or International Seminars on Training for Nonviolent Action, Box 515, Waltham, MA 02254. Also important is the work in nongovernmental conflict resolution; see John W. McDonald, Jr., and Diane B. Bendahmane, "Conflict Resolution: Track Two Diplomacy," Foreign Service Institute, U.S. Department of State (Washington, D.C.: Center for the Study of Foreign Affairs, 1987). Note, however, that nonviolent action is a substitute not for conciliation or negotiations, but for *violent* conflict.

37. Two-thirds of all war deaths in the world since 1500 occurred in Europe (Ruth Leger Sivard, *World Military and Social Expenditures 1991*, World Priorities, Box 25140, Washington, D.C. 20007, 20).

38. A crucial test of a powerful theory is its capacity for prediction. As far back as 1959, Richard B. Gregg predicted something not a single Sovietologist in the

world anticipated, even up to the year it happened: the overthrow of communism in the Eastern bloc and even the Soviet Union by nonviolent methods (*Power of Nonviolence*, 89). Gene Sharp made a similar prediction in 1985 (*Making Europe Unconquerable*, 170). They could see this, not because they are prophets, but because they understood the power of this approach, which is only waiting to be tapped.

39. George Weigel, "Religion and Peace: An Argument Complexified," conference on "Conflict Resolution in the Post-Cold War Third World," United States Institute of Peace, Washington, D.C., October 3–5, 1990.

40. Barrie Paskins and Michael Dockrill, *The Ethics of War* (London: Duckworth, 1979), 232.

41. Ibid.

42. Ramsey, *Speak Up*, 53. See also his *War and the Christian Conscience* (Durham, N.C.: Duke Univ. Press, 1961).

43. Ramsey, *Speak Up*, 102.

44. Ramsey, *The Just War* (New York: Lanham, [1968] 1981), 503.

45. There is a double standard in this talk of unintended consequences. No pacifist could get away with the defense that the atrocities permitted by the renunciation of violence were "unintended."

46. Accurate statistics of war dead are difficult enough to obtain; civilian casualties are seldom even tabulated. I once tried to determine the total casualties on all sides in the Algerian War of independence from France. The Algerian embassy spokesperson said 1.5 million. Most studies say one million. French historians of the conflict give estimates ranging from 434,000 to 314,000 to 220,000. Sivard reports only 100,000, 82 percent civilian (*Expenditures*, 25). For the Vietnam War she shows only 49 percent civilian casualties, whereas most other sources put that figure at 80 percent. For our purposes, however, Sivard's extremely low figures provide a most-cautious-possible reckoning.

William Eckhardt notes that the average of civilian casualties for our century is artificially reduced by the low percentage of civilians lost in World War I (34 percent), though their actual number was huge. This figure, however, does not include victims of the worldwide flu epidemic that followed ("Civilian Deaths in Wartime," *Bulletin of Peace Proposals* 20 [1989]: 89–98; see also Magnus Haavelsrud, "Peace Education: Operationalizing of the Peace Concept," ibid., 18 [1987]: 363).

47. The Falklands/Malvinas War was the only war in this century to observe civilian immunity: no civilians killed, 1,000 military; indeed, setting aside the two World Wars, it was the *only* war fought in this century with less than 50 percent civilian deaths (Sivard, *Expenditures*, 20–25).

48. Sivard, *Expenditures*, 20. The rise in war deaths has far outstripped the rise in population.

49. Oliver O'Donovan has written a particularly elegant piece against nuclear deterrence (*Peace and Certainty* [Oxford: Oxford Univ. Press, 1989]), but ends by thumping for increased conventional forces. More satisfying, and equally elegantly argued, is Robert L. Holmes, *On War and Morality* (p. 32). As Holmes points out, what is wrong with war is as wrong with conventional as with nuclear war, especially now that the sophistication, accuracy, and destructive power of conventional weapons is rapidly closing the gap between conventional and nuclear war. Our task is to get

rid of the war *system*, not just nuclear war. And we can scarcely get rid of that system by trying to improve it (ibid., 4). See also John Finnis, Joseph M. Boyle, Jr., and Germain Grisez, *Nuclear Deterrence, Morality, and Realism* (Oxford: Clarendon Press, 1987); Paskins and Dockrill, *Ethics of War*, 193, 254–56, 312; and Bernard Häring, *The Healing Power of Peace and Nonviolence* (New York: Paulist Press, 1986).

50. The air war against Iraqi cities was deliberately designed to destroy the civilian infrastructure (dams, bridges, highways, water and sewage systems, railroads, fuel depots) and to break the will and morale of the Iraqi people. This strategy was indiscreetly disclosed by Air Force chief of staff Michael Dugan as early as Sept. 16, 1990—four months before the war began. This means that what the administration called "collateral damage" was nothing of the kind. It was intended (Mark Saskaroff, "War Crimes in the Persian Gulf," *Fellowship* 57 [1991]: 18).

51. Childress, *Moral Responsibility in Conflicts*. George Weigel, in *Tranquillitas Ordinis*, treats nonviolence as an equivalent of democracy generally, and seldom refers to extralegal nonviolent direct action.

52. Ramsey, *Speak Up*, 71.

53. Adeney, *Just War*, 98–101. The United States certainly gave no advance warning and made no declaration of war in the invasions of Grenada and Panama.

54. McCarthy, "Christian Nonviolence," 68. The Pentagon deliberately made it impossible for the American public to get the information necessary for a moral decision during the Persian Gulf War.

55. Augustine added another criterion that modern just war theorists have, mercifully, dropped: every act of war must be conducted in love. The drift of Jesus' commandment seems to be loving our enemies *instead* of killing them, not loving them *as* we kill them. Augustine, however, grasped the implications of just war theory: once killing is justified, it must somehow be integrated into the rest of the gospel of love and nonviolence.

Peter Mayhew has recently published a very inadequate restatement of the Augustinian position, *A Theology of Force and Violence* (London: SCM Press, 1989).

56. Holmes, *On War and Morality*, 192.

57. Konrad Lorenz, *On Aggression* (New York: Bantam Books, 1969), 260.

58. Yoder, *The Original Revolution* (Scottdale, Pa.: Herald Press, 1972), 84–85; *Nevertheless* (Scottdale, Pa.: Herald Press, 1971), 119.

59. Comparison of Matt. 5:31-32 with Matt. 19:9, Mark 10:11-12, and Luke 16:18 suggests that Jesus allowed no grounds for divorce, and that Matthew has mitigated this severity by adding the exception of Rabbi Shammai (adultery), thus bringing Jesus' teaching in line with the strictest Pharisaic position.

60. See Anne Wilson Schaef, *When Society Becomes an Addict* (San Francisco: Harper & Row, 1987).

61. The three cases of genocide examined by Ervin Staub took place during a war (Turkey, Germany) or right after a civil war (Cambodia) (*The Roots of Evil: The Origins of Genocide and Other Group Violence* [Cambridge: Cambridge Univ. Press, 1989], 232).

62. In *Violence and Nonviolence in South Africa* (Philadelphia: New Society Publishers, 1987), I attempted just such an approach, using violence-reduction

criteria (somewhat unconsciously) to build a pragmatic case for the use of nonviolence in the antiapartheid struggle.

63. An instructive case occurred during the Vietnam War, when a group of scientists opposed to the war tried to stop indiscriminate bombing of the North by introducing the concept of the "electronic battlefield," a "fence" composed of millions of mines that would stop infiltration into the South. They could have simply denounced the war, but they felt they had to offer an alternative to bombing if they were to maintain credibility and preserve their "insider" status. The bombing was halted, temporarily, the fence was installed—and the war simply continued (Joseph Weizenbaum, *Computer Power and Human Reason* [San Francisco: W. H. Freeman, 1976], 275). Those mines are still killing people.

64. Yoder, *When War Is Unjust*, 71–72.

65. Clement of Alexandria, *Strom.* 2.18.

66. Origen, *Against Celsus* 4.82.

67. Tertullian, *Apol.* 2.

68. William Penn, the Quaker governor of Pennsylvania, proposed the establishment of a parliament of nations to maintain peace. Since he did not presume that the nations would all be converted to Quakerism, he provided for the employment of military sanctions as a last resort in case efforts at imposing arbitration failed (Peter Brock, *Roots of War Resistance*, 43).

69. The image is Jean Lasserre's, *War and the Gospel* (Scottdale, Pa.: Herald Press, 1962), 88.

70. Augustine, *Sermon on the Mount* 1.19.56–68; *Reply to Faustus the Manichaean* 22.76; *On Lying* 27; *Letters* 47.5 (*NPNF* 1:293). Reinhold Niebuhr exactly mirrored this view (*Christianity and Power Politics* [New York: Charles Scribner's Sons, 1940], 10; *An Interpretation of Christian Ethics* [New York: Harper & Brothers, 1935], 50, 62–83).

71. Jean and Hildegard Goss-Mayr, *A Non-Violent Lifestyle*, ed. Gérard Houver (London: Marshall Morgan and Scott, 1989), 11–12.

72. Augustine, *On the Gospel of John* tractate 113.4, to John 18:13–27; *Sermon on the Mount* 1.19.58; *On Lying* 27; *Letters* 138.12–13.

73. Millions is no exaggeration. The human chain 430 miles long linking Latvians, Lithuanians, and Estonians from one end of their countries to the other involved 2–3 million people (out of a total population of only 7 million), possibly the largest single demonstration in human history (August 24, 1989). Day after day in Beijing the prodemocracy protests exceeded 100,000 (from April 22, 1989, on), and climaxed in over a million on May 18 and again on May 21. The total number of demonstrators (there was continuous turnover) may have exceeded 10 million in China alone. A million protested in Baku, Azerbaijan, against Soviet military occupation on January 23, 1990. For eleven days in November 1989, crowds of 200,000 to 350,000 crammed Wenceslas Square in Prague, Czechoslovakia, with collateral demonstrations in smaller cities. Demonstrations in Leipzig, East Germany, escalated from hundreds on August 5, 1989, to 100,000 on October 16, and 300,000 on October 31, while protests in other East German cities did the same. Hundreds of thousands of Armenians marched in 1988, and even Moscow witnessed huge demonstrations. Millions marched against the military dictatorship in Burma in August 1988 (Bertil

Lintner, *Outrage: Burma's Struggle for Democracy* [Hong Kong: Review Publishing Co. Ltd., 1989], 156). And these figures cover only a couple of years.

The antinuclear war demonstrations of 1981–82 were the largest nonviolent demonstrations ever held up to that time: Amsterdam, 400,000; Bonn, 200,000; Rome, 200,000; London, 150,000; Brussels, 200,000; Paris, 200,000; Athens, 200,000; Bucharest, 300,000; New York City, 750,000.

74. Glen Stassen has also proposed a third way between just war theory and pacifism in *Just Peacemaking* (Louisville: Westminster/John Knox Press, 1992). The ten principles of "just peace theory" advocated by *A Just Peace Church*, ed. by Susan Thistlethwaite (New York: United Church Press, 1986) are not criteria for ethical discrimination about war, but goals or ideals for broadening the church's awareness of the much larger demands of peace. It cites nonviolence as desirable but stops short of recognizing its indispensability for the quest for peace.

12. BUT WHAT IF . . . ?

1. *Marvel Treasury Edition: Giant Superhero Holiday Grab-Bag* (New York: Marvel Comics Group, 1976), 56. These philosophical words are a strange anomaly in a cartoon series devoted utterly to violence.

2. The hypothetical case also appeals to machismo. A "real" man would wade in with fists flying to save the helpless damsel. But as C. J. Cadoux remarked, the same man would not lift a finger on behalf of this same woman being beaten by her husband in her home a few blocks away. Why is defending this woman on the street more a test of love than, say, long-term commitment to helping battered women? (*The Early Christian Attitude to War* [London: George Allen & Unwin, 1940], 84–87).

3. Yevgeny Yevtushenko, *Wild Berries* (London: Macmillan, 1984), 233–34. For our purposes it is irrelevant whether this story is fictitious.

4. Holmes, *On War and Morality* (Princeton: Princeton Univ. Press, 1989), 276–78.

5. David Dellinger, "The Future of Nonviolence," in *The Universe Bends Toward Justice*, ed. Angie O'Gorman (Philadelphia: New Society Publishers, 1990), 190.

6. Leo Tolstoy, *Tolstoy's Writings on Civil Disobedience and Non-Violence* (London: Peter Owen, 1968), 381. Joan Baez has a particularly clever response to the same type of question in her autobiography, *Daybreak* (New York: Dial Press, 1966), 131–34; see also John Howard Yoder, *What Would You Do?* (Scottdale, Pa.: Herald Press, 1983).

7. Richard B. Gregg, *The Power of Nonviolence* (Nyack, N.Y.: Fellowship Publications, 1959), 50, 51. See also Dale W. Brown, *Biblical Pacifism* (Elgin, Ill.: Brethren Press, 1986), 151–59.

8. Angie O'Gorman, "Defense Through Disarmament: Nonviolence and Personal Assault," in *Universe Bends*, 242–46.

9. Cited by Nancy Forest Flier in "Past Violent Shores," in *Expressions* (St. Benedict Center, Madison, Wis., March/April 1988, 2). The example is taken from a book devoted to the theme: Dorothy Samuel, *Safe Passage on City Streets* (Nashville: Abingdon Press, 1975). See also *Nonviolent Response to Personal Assault*, a 40-minute video produced by Pax Christi USA, 348 E. Tenth St., Erie, PA 16503.

10. Letter from Sheena Duncan, November 6, 1989.

11. Emmanuel Charles McCarthy, "Christian Nonviolence: The Great Failure, the Only Hope," transcript of the audio and video tape series, revised April 1986, 30–31.

12. Mubarak Awad, "Victory Within Ourselves. The Nonviolent Path to a Palestinian State," *Sojourners*, January 1989, 26–30; John Feffer, "All But a Gun," *Nuclear Times*, November/December 1988, 21–22; Ruth Benn, "The Occupation Must End," *The Nonviolent Activist*, March 1989, 5. I will not condemn Palestinian or South African youth for throwing rocks. It was at least morally superior to the passivity of their parents, and served to wake them up. But this Stone Age method is extremely limited as a tactic and may even be counterproductive. In Poland, writes Jonathan Schell, "a little violence would probably have been as harmful to Solidarity as a little pacifism would be to an army in the middle of a war" ("Reflections: A Better Today," *New Yorker*, February 3, 1986, 62).

13. Niall O'Brien, *Revolution from the Heart* (New York: Oxford Univ. Press, 1987), 210. For a discussion of a nonviolent alternative to armed revolution against the dictator Somoza in Nicaragua, see Miguel D'Escoto, "An Unfinished Canvas," *Sojourners* 12 (March 1983): 17.

14. Luis Claudio Oliveira, "Crianças e Adolescentes: um Desafio à Cidadania," *Tempo e Presença* (Brazil) 13 (1991): 5–9, 13, 19, 23.

15. National Coalition on Television Violence News 11 (July–September 1990), 6.

16. Jo Becker, "Lithuania's Nonviolent Struggle," *Fellowship* (December 1990), 20–21.

17. Richard L. Deats, "The Search for Nonviolent Solutions," *Fellowship* (July/August 1991), 5; Christopher Kruegler, "A Bold Initiative in Lithuanian Defense," *Nonviolent Sanctions* 2/4 (Spring 1991): 1, 7. See also Adam Roberts, *Civil Resistance in the East European and Soviet Revolutions*, Monograph series 4 (Cambridge, Mass.: Albert Einstein Institution, 1991).

18. Eknath Easwaran, *A Man to Match His Mountains: Badshah Khan, Nonviolent Soldier of Islam* (Petaluma, Calif.: Nilgiri Press, 1984).

19. Glen Tinder, *The Political Meaning of Christianity* (Baton Rouge: Louisiana State Univ. Press, 1989), 103.

20. Nonviolence did not "work" in Beijing, though arguably for strategic reasons: the demonstrations went on two weeks too long. In retrospect it appears that they should have been called off, as the student leaders wished to do, after the 38th Army retreated to its base rather than fire on unarmed compatriots. But thousands of fresh students just arriving on the scene wanted a piece of the action. See the excellent analysis by Gene Sharp and Bruce Jenkins, who were in Beijing during the demonstrations ("Nonviolent Struggle in China: An Eyewitness Account," *Nonviolent Sanctions* 1/2 [Fall 1989]: 1, 3–7). The point to remember, however, is that the students were able to mount their protest by nonviolent means, whereas armed revolt inside the country would have been instantly crushed as the mighty West looked impotently on.

21. Miguel D'Escoto, cited by Paul Jeffrey, "Nicaragua: Planting Seeds of Nonviolence in the Midst of War," in *Relentless Persistence: Nonviolent Action in Latin*

America, ed. Philip McManus and Gerald Schlabach (Philadelphia: New Society Publishers, 1991), 162.

22. William Stringfellow, *An Ethic for Christians and Other Aliens in a Strange Land* (Waco, Tex.: Word Books, 1973), 133.

23. George Weigel, *Tranquillitas Ordinis* (Oxford: Oxford Univ. Press, 1987), 283.

13. REVISIONING HISTORY: NONVIOLENCE
PAST, PRESENT, FUTURE

1. Juan Ramón Jiménez, "Oceans," translated by Robert Bly in *News of the Universe*, ed. Robert Bly (San Francisco: Sierra Club Books, 1980), 105.

2. Carolyn G. Heilbrun, *Writing a Woman's Life* (New York: W. W. Norton, 1989), 44.

3. That amazing variety of nonviolent actions has now been documented in *The Purple Shall Govern: A South African A to Z of Nonviolent Action*, ed. Dene Smuts and Shauna Westcott (Oxford: Oxford Univ. Press, 1991), giving evidence for my own assertion in *Violence and Nonviolence in South Africa* (Philadelphia: New Society Publications, 1987) that South Africa has witnessed "probably the largest grassroots eruption of diverse nonviolent strategies in human history" (p. 4).

4. Carl Scovil, "Christian Responses to the Nazi State in Germany," *Katallagete* 11 (Spring 1978): 35.

5. Gene Sharp, *The Politics of Nonviolent Action* (Boston: Porter Sargent, 1973). I have also drawn on a fly sheet, "Historical Examples of Nonviolent Struggle," from Sharp's Albert Einstein Institution; and *The Power of the People: Active Nonviolence in the United States*, ed. Robert Cooney and Helen Michalowski (Philadelphia: New Society Publishers, 1987), along with numerous newspaper clippings. Other instances are tabulated in Gene Sharp, *Making Europe Unconquerable: The Potential of Civilian-Based Deterrence and Defence* (Cambridge: Ballinger Publishing Co., 1985), 57–58; and Pam McAllister, *You Can't Kill the Spirit* (Philadelphia: New Society Publishers, 1988), 203–25 (a very impressive list of nonviolent actions by women).

6. John H. Kautsky, *The Politics of Aristocratic Empires* (Chapel Hill: Univ. of North Carolina Press, 1982), 176.

7. Josephus, *Ant.* 14.167–68.

8. The American colonists were succeeding through a series of remarkably effective nonviolent strategies against the British, but misread the reluctance of the British to make concessions as defeat, when in fact they probably only needed to escalate the level and dimensions of the struggle. Had they persevered, rather than resorting to military action (it also failed to win immediate results), they could easily have prevailed, for Britain was simply incapable of maintaining its American colony against *any* form of resolute resistance for any considerable time. See *Resistance, Politics, and the American Struggle for Independence, 1765–1775*, ed. Walter Conser, Ronald McCarthy, David Toscano, and Gene Sharp (Boulder: Lynne Rienner, 1986); and Gene Sharp, *Politics of Nonviolent Action*, 495, and the index under "American Colonists."

9. Patricia Parkman, *Nonviolent Insurrection in El Salvador: The Fall of Maximiliano Hernández* (Tucson: Univ. of Arizona Press, 1988). Parkman identifies a long history of nonviolent struggle in El Salvador from as early as 1919. See also her *Insurrectionary Civic Strikes in Latin America: 1931–1961* (Cambridge: Albert Einstein Institution, 1990).

10. Jack and Felice Cohen-Joppa, "Nuclear Resistance, 1989," in *The Nuclear Resister*, nos. 67 and 68, January 25, 1990, 1.

11. *Berkshire Eagle*, August 4, 1988, A2.

12. Data on China is from conversation with Li Lu, deputy student commander in Tiananmen Square at the end of the struggle; on Lithuania, from an address by Raymundas Rayalskas of the Lithuanian Academy of Sciences at the Albert Einstein Institution, Feb. 10, 1990; on Kazakhstan, *Berkshire Eagle*, August 8, 1989, A7; on the Philippines, Peggy Rosenthal, "The Precarious Road," *Commonweal*, June 20, 1986, 366; on the Soviet Union, Melissa Everett, "Citizen action abroad had anti-coup role," *Berkshire Eagle*, August 25, 1991, A1, 5.

13. Étienne de la Boetie, *The Politics of Obedience: The Discourse of Voluntary Servitude* (Montreal: Black Rose Books, 1975).

14. Elihu Burritt, in *Nonviolence in America: A Documentary History*, ed. Staughton Lynd (New York: Bobbs-Merrill, 1966), 94–96.

15. It is heartening that others are investigating nonviolent national defense, all the way from Brig. Gen. Edward B. Atkeson ("The Relevance of Civilian-Based Defense to U.S. Security Interests," *Military Review* 56 [May 1976]: 24-32) to Gandhians (Charles C. Walker, "A World Peace Guard," Academy of Gandhian Studies, Hyderabad, India, n.d.).

16. John Keane, "Soviet reforms herald regime in retreat," *The Guardian* (Manchester, England), May 4, 1990, 14.

17. Jonathan Schell, "Reflections: A Better Today," *The New Yorker*, February 3, 1986, 63.

18. Ron Sider and Richard K. Taylor, "International Aggression and Nonmilitary Defense," *Christian Century* 100 (July 6–13, 1983): 643-47. On the negative side, Bulgarian Jews *were* deported to camps in the Bulgarian countryside. Their property was plundered and they were pauperized, but they did survive. Bulgaria's treatment of Jews in Macedonia and Thrace was, by contrast, vicious (Leni Yahil, *The Holocaust* [New York and Oxford: Oxford Univ. Press, 1990], 578–87).

19. Yahil, *Holocaust*, 591.

20. Jeremy Bennett, "The Resistance Against the German Occupation of Denmark 1940–5," in *The Strategy of Civilian Defense*, ed. Adam Roberts (London: Faber & Faber, 1967), 154–72; and Yahil, *Holocaust*, 574, 578.

21. Sider and Taylor, "International Aggression and Nonmilitary Defense," 645.

22. Yahil, *Holocaust*, 395–96.

23. Nathan Stoltzfus, "The Women's Rosenstrasse Protest in Nazi Berlin," *Nonviolent Sanctions* 1/3 (Winter 1989–90): 3, 8.

24. Ervin Staub, *The Roots of Evil* (Cambridge: Cambridge Univ. Press, 1989), 154.

25. See Gene Sharp, "Tyranny Could Not Quell Them," *Peace News* (London), n.d.; and Ernst Schwarcz, "Nonviolent Resistance Against the Nazis in Norway and Holland During World War II," in *Nonviolence in Theory and Practice*, ed. Robert

L. Holmes (Belmont, Calif.: Wadsworth Publishing Co., 1990), 187. According to Sharp, it is wrong to argue that Jews were doomed because there was too little violent opposition to the Nazis. For while more decisive and earlier interventions at the very end of the war might have saved thousands of lives, it was the war itself that provided the necessary precondition for the mass extermination of Jews. "Fortunately," Goebbels wrote in his diary, "a whole series of possibilities presents itself for us in wartime that would be denied us in peacetime." Those who escaped did so largely due to the refusal of all sorts of people to cooperate in their destruction, even Nazi officials. Increased noncooperation would have saved more (*Making Europe Unconquerable*, 136).

26. B. H. Liddell-Hart, "Lessons from Resistance Movements—Guerrilla and Nonviolent," in Roberts, ed., *The Strategy of Civilian Defense*, 205–7.

27. Soedjatmoko, "Violence in the Third World," in *The Quest for Peace*, ed. Raimo Väyrynen with Dieter Senghaas and Christian Schmidt (London and Beverly Hills: Sage Publications, 1987), 299.

28. Shirley Christian, "Chilean Communists in Turmoil About the Future," *New York Times*, Sunday, September 23, 1990, A5.

29. Mary Benson, *South Africa: The Struggle for a Birthright* (Middlesex: Penguin Books, 1966), 118.

14. THE ACID TEST: LOVING ENEMIES

1. C. P. Cavafy, *The Complete Poems of Cavafy*, trans. Rae Dalven (New York: Harcourt, Brace & World, 1961), 19.

2. From remarks made at a meeting of peace activists at Kirkridge Retreat Center, Bangor, Pa., in 1986.

3. Cited in an undated mailing from People for the American Way—an excellent source, incidentally, of otherwise unavailable information.

4. James A. Sanders, "Hermeneutics in True and False Prophecy," in *From Sacred Story to Sacred Text* (Philadelphia: Fortress Press, 1987), 103.

5. Gerd Theissen, *Biblical Faith: An Evolutionary Approach* (Philadelphia: Fortress Press, 1985), 112–19.

6. See Josephus, *War* 2.169–74; *Ant.* 18.55–59. For teaching on nonviolence and love of enemies in the Hebrew Scriptures and Judaism, see Exod. 23:4-5 (watered down by Deut. 22:1); 1 Kings 3:10-12; Job 31:29-30; Prov. 24:17-18, 29; 25:21-22; Jonah 4:2, 4, 11; 2 *Enoch* 44:4-5; 50:3-4; 51:3; 60:1; 61:1-2; Ecclus. 28:1-9; *Letter of Aristeas* 207, 225, 227, 232; *Joseph and Asenath* 23:9; 28:4, 14; 29:3; *Test. Ben.* 4:2-3; *Jos.* 18:2; *Gad* 5:5; 6:1-7; *Iss.* 7:6; *Zeb.* 7:2-4; *Pseudo-Phocylides* 140; *Abot de R. Nathan* 30; *Seder Eliahu Rab.* 49. For further references see William Klassen's extensive catalog of texts, *Love of Enemies* (Philadelphia: Fortress Press, 1984); and his "The Novel Element in the Love Command of Jesus," in *The New Way of Jesus*, ed. Klassen (Newton, Kans.: Faith and Life Press, 1980), 100–14; Pinchas Lapide, *The Sermon on the Mount* (Maryknoll, N.Y.: Orbis Books, 1986), 77–97; Krister Stendahl, "Hate, Non-Retaliation, and Love," *Harvard Theological Review* 55 (1962): 347; and Friedrich Heiler, "The History of Religions as a Preparation for the Cooperation of Religions," in *The History of Religions: Essays in Methodology*, ed. M. Eliade and J. M. Kitagawa (Chicago: Univ. of Chicago Press, 1949), 147.

7. Jonathan Schell, "Reflections: A Better Today," *The New Yorker*, February 3, 1986, 47, 57, 60. Solidarity almost shattered from internal feuding, and might not have survived but for the radical wing of the Roman Catholic Church; but it not only survived, it prevailed.

8. A truckers' strike and beating on pots by the Chilean middle class helped bring down the Allende regime in 1973. Antiabortion activists use nonviolent protests to close down abortion clinics in the United States. Religious conservatives picket theaters showing films they consider objectionable, like *The Last Temptation of Christ*. Korean police lay down in the street recently to stop a student's funeral march. I applaud the choice of methods, even if I disagree with the beliefs for which they are employed.

9. Bibliography on this passage is enormous, and is helpfully assembled by John Piper, '*Love Your Enemies*': *Jesus' Love Command in the Synoptic Gospels and in the Early Christian Paraenesis*, SNTSMS 38 (Cambridge: Cambridge Univ. Press, 1979), 235–48. In addition to his items, see Albert Nicolas, "Etude Biblique. La relation avec l'ennemi," *Foi et Vie* 59 (1960): 235–51; E. K. Lee, "Hard Sayings— I. Be ye therefore perfect, even as your Father which is in heaven is perfect. Mt. 5:48," *Theology* 66 (1963): 318–20; G. A. Robson, "Hard Sayings," *Theology* 66 (1963): 462; P. Schruers, "La paternité divine dans Mt. 5:45 et 6:26-32," *Ephemerides Theologicae Lovanienses* 36 (1960): 593–624; Jacques Dupont, "L'appel à imiter Dieu en Matthieu 5:48 et Luc 6:36," *Rivista Biblica* 14 (1966): 137–58; " 'Soyez Parfaits' (Mt., V, 48) 'Soyez Misérecordieux' (Lc., VI, 36)," *Sacra Pagina* 2, ed. J. Coppens, A. Descamps, E. Massaux, *Bibliotheca Ephemeridum Theologicarum Lovaniensium* 12/13 (1959), 150–62; P. J. du Plessis, "Love and Perfection in Mt. 5:43-48," *Neotestamentica* 1 (1967): 28–34; H. Ljungman, "Das Gesetz erfüllen," *Lunds universitets ärsskrift* I, 50 (1954): 89–91; A. Georges, "Soyes parfaits comme votre Père céleste (Matth. 5, 14-48)," *Bible et Vie Chrétienne* 19 (1957): 84–90; G. Lohfink, "Der ekklesiale Sitz im Leben der Aufforderung Jesu zum Gewaltverzicht (Mt 5,39b-42/Lk 6,29 f)," *Theologische Quartalschrift* 162 (1982): 236–53; Georg Strecker, "Compliance—Love of One's Enemy—The Golden Rule," *Australian Biblical Review* 29 (1981): 38-46; Jürgen Sauer, "Traditionsgeschichtliche Erwägungen zu den synoptischen und paulinischen Aussagen über Feindesliebe und Wiedervergeltungsverzicht," *Zeitschrift für die Neutestamentliche Wissenschaft* 76 (1985): 1–28; J. Lambrecht, "The Sayings of Jesus on Nonviolence," *Louvain Studies* 12 (1987): 291–305; Luise Schottroff and Wolfgang Stegemann, *Jesus and the Hope of the Poor* (Maryknoll, N.Y.: Orbis Books, 1986), 60–63.

10. Edwin A. Hallsten, "The Commandment That Kills—Paul and Prohibition," a paper presented to the Colloquium on Religion and Violence, New Orleans, November 16, 1990.

11. "Perfect" is used in English translations of the Hebrew Bible in ways not at all reflective of the current English sense of "faultless, pure, ideal." An offering had to be "perfect" (*tamim*, Lev. 22:21), but that meant simply that it could not be deformed or diseased ("blind, or injured, or maimed, or having a discharge or an itch or scabs"—22:22). A person "perfect in knowledge" merely has a complete grasp of a subject (*tamim*, Job 36:4; 37:16). The law is "*tamim*, reviving the soul": "completely satisfying" is the meaning here (Ps. 19:7). A woman's or man's beauty could be "total" or "complete" (*tamim*, Song of Sol. 5:2; 6:9). God is described as

tamim (Deut. 32:4; 2 Sam. 22:31), but Psalm 18 gives the clue to its meaning. Ps. 18:30 says, "This God—his way is perfect (*tamim*)," which v. 32 clarifies: God has "made my way *safe* (*tamim*)." God's way is not so much "flawless" as safe, secure, *reliable*. Thus the faithful can be enjoined to be "completely loyal (*tamim*) to the Lord" (Deut. 18:13)—probably the verse Matthew used as his model for 5:48.

Several English versions also translate *shalem* in the Hebrew Bible as "perfect," almost always referring to "a perfect heart"; the NRSV drops "perfect" in every case, rendering it "whole heart," "single mind," "true," "full intent," "devote yourselves completely."

There is, in short, no expression in the Hebrew Bible that conforms in meaning to the modern English word "perfect."

12. *Teleios* in classical Greek also had little connection with what we in English call "perfect" today. It referred to *unblemished* sacrifices, the *complete* performance of rites, the *best* or *surest* bird of augury. It had the sense of what is full, valid, authoritative, final; mature, fully grown, life-sized, adult; accomplished, expert; trained, qualified; serious; absolute; fulfilled, accomplished. Gods are *teleioi*—not morally perfect (!), but all-powerful, able to fulfill prayers (G. Delling, "*teleios*," *TDNT*, 8 [1972]: 67–78).

13. *Targum Pseudo-Jonathan* Lev. 22:28 contains this haggadic addition, so similar to Luke 6:36—"My people, children of Israel, as your Father is merciful in heaven, so shall you be merciful on earth." The theme of imitation of God is here, but there is no hint of perfectionism. The first trace of moral perfectionism is in Philo, whose thought was thoroughly hellenized (e.g., *Quod det.* 60). Since *teleios* appears only twice in Matthew, and nowhere else in the Gospels, and has clearly been added by Matthew in 19:21 (compare Mark 10:21; Luke 18:22), it would appear that Matthew has added it in 5:48 as well, under the influence of Deut. 18:13 and Lev. 19:2 (Isabel Ann Massey, *Interpreting the Sermon on the Mount in the Light of Jewish Tradition as Evidenced in the Palestinian Targums of the Pentateuch* [Lewiston: Edwin Mellen, 1991], 13, 43–51, 68 n. 81; the reader must beware of her uncritical use of the English "perfect" to translate *tamim* and *shalem*).

14. I am unable to find the source of this historical reflection, but vaguely recall hearing it from Cornel West.

15. Marcus Borg, *Conflict, Holiness and Politics in the Teachings of Jesus* (New York: Edwin Mellen Press, 1984), 128.

16. Reinhold Niebuhr, *An Interpretation of Christian Ethics* (New York: Living Age Books, 1956), 193.

17. Paul Tillich, *The Courage to Be* (New Haven: Yale Univ. Press, 1964), 50.

18. Babylonian mythology actually acknowledges this symbiosis between Marduk and Tiamat. One hymn calls Marduk *Mar Mummi*, "son of chaos," i.e., his real origins are in the Tiamatic realm. And in the *Enuma Elish* Marduk is said to have been created "in the heart of the deep" (i.e., from Tiamat). See Carl G. Jung, *Psychology and Religion: West and East*, CW 11 (1969), 114–15; and *Enuma Elish* I.18 (J. B. Pritchard, *Ancient Near Eastern Texts Relating to the Old Testament*, 3d ed. [Princeton: Princeton Univ. Press, 1969], 62).

19. Cited by Robert E. Park, "The Social Function of War," in *War: Studies in Psychology, Sociology, Anthropology*, ed. Leon Bramson and George W. Goethals, rev. ed. (New York: Basic Books, 1968), 243.

20. Plutarch (d. ca. 119 C.E.) has many similar insights in his essay "How to Profit by Our Enemies," including this: "Why should not we take an enemy for our tutor, who will instruct us gratis in those things we knew not before? For an enemy sees and understands more in matters relating to us than our friends do" (*Morals* [New York: Athenaeum Society, 1870], 291).

21. Cited in Jean and Hildegard Goss-Mayr, *A Non-Violent Lifestyle*, ed. Gérard Houver (London: Marshall Morgan Scott, 1989), 91–92.

22. Ibid., 28.

23. Douglas J. Elwood, *Toward a Theology of People Power* (Queson City, Philippines: New Day Publishers, 1988), 12.

24. Carl S. Dudley and Earle Hilgert, *New Testament Tensions and the Contemporary Church* (Philadelphia: Fortress Press, 1987), 114–17.

25. Chuck Noell, "Rediscovering Dialogue," *Fellowship* 42 (August–September 1976): 15.

26. Henry Mottu, sermon at Union Theological Seminary, New York City, February 9, 1972.

27. Jim Forest, *Making Enemies Friends* (New York: Crossroad, 1988), 76–78.

28. Christopher S. Wren, "A Secret Society of Afrikaners Helps to Dismantle Apartheid," *New York Times*, October 30, 1990, A9. Only time will tell if de Klerk merely had the foresight to see that separation enforced by apartheid could be maintained by less provocative but equally effective means.

15. MONITORING OUR INNER VIOLENCE

1. *The Kabir Book: Forty-Four of the Ecstatic Poems of Kabir*, versions by Robert Bly (Boston: Beacon Press, 1977), 2.

2. Walter Wink, *Violence and Nonviolence in South Africa* (Phildelphia: New Society Publishers, 1987).

3. I acknowledge that dreams are ambiguous, require interpretation, and are not always self-evident in their meaning. God's will is not imposed on us, even in our sleep.

4. Paul Verryn, Assistant to the General Secretariat, South African Council of Churches, in a personal letter dated January 4, 1988. Verryn's response to my inquiries are the shared views of a group of psychologists and psychiatrists who, like him, have provided therapy for ex-detainees in South Africa.

5. "It never ceases to amaze me how some people do integrate the experience they have [of torture and detention] into their lives. Especially those who have a deep faith seem to achieve incredible insights through detention. May this never be a reason to continue the practice. However, many of these people come out with a spirituality which is profound and which has a realism in it which is reminiscent of the early martyrs of the church" (ibid.).

6. Again, to draw on the experience of ex-torture victims from Paul Verryn's report (ibid.): "Often the ex-detainees would 'return' to the detention and wish to suffer it all again because in a peculiar way there is a dependency upon this experience that he is frightened to abandon. At times that experience is the only realistic memory that they have."

7. Laurens van der Post, *The Heart of the Hunter* (New York: William Morrow & Co., 1961), 136–37.

8. Charles Upton, "Gnosticism as Social Protest," unpublished manuscript, courtesy of the author.

9. See Gene Sharp, *The Politics of Nonviolent Action*, 3 vols. (Boston: Porter Sargent, 1973); for a brief summary of his views, see "Making the Abolition of War a Realistic Goal" (New York: World Policy Institute, 1980); see also his *Social Power and Political Freedom* (Boston: Porter Sargent, 1980), and *Exploring Nonviolent Alternatives* (Boston: Porter Sargent, 1970).

10. Richard Strozzi Heckler, "Son of a Gun: Hunters, Warriors, and Soldiers," *Somatics* 7 (Spring/Summer 1989): 12–17. See also Ira Cherus, "War and Myth: 'The Show Must Go On,' " *Journal of the American Academy of Religion* 53 (1985): 462. In the northwest frontier of colonial India (now Pakistan), violence was taught to boys from an early age. A brilliant young chieftain's son, Badshah Abdul Ghaffir Khan, was converted to Gandhi's nonviolence in 1919. He organized an association of men, The Servants of God, who wore as a uniform red shirts, drilled regularly, and took long marches in military style, though they carried no weapons. Such was their heroism that Gandhi called them his best "nonviolent soldiers" (Eknath Easwaran, *A Man to Match His Mountains: Badshah Khan, Nonviolent Soldier of Islam* [Petaluma, Calif.: Nilgiri Press, 1984]). Warfare can also be seen, not as conflict in the outer world, but as an allegory of a deeply personal struggle to eliminate subjective evil from one's life (James A. Aho, *Religious Mythology and the Art of War* [Westport, Conn.: Greenwood Press, 1981], 8). Richard Grossinger writes, "The warriors are inside us, to be embraced and understood, perhaps millennia from now to be ritualized into protectors of all life, all sentient beings" (*Nuclear Strategy and the Code of the Warrior*, ed. Grossinger and Lindy Hough [Berkeley: North Atlantic Books, 1984], ix).

11. See chap. 5, "The Gods," in *Unmasking the Powers*.

12. Arnobius, *Against the Pagans* 4.7. This merely continued early androcratic practice. The Sumerian goddess Inanna-Ishtar was both goddess of war and goddess of sexual love and procreation—and was identified with the planet later called Venus (H. W. F. Saggs, *The Greatness that was Babylon* [London: Sidgwick & Jackson, 1962], 333–34).

13. Adolf Harnack, *Militia Christi* (Philadelphia: Fortress Press, [1905] 1981), 32. And yet, he concedes, no higher religion can do without the images taken from war (p. 28).

14. John Dear, S.J., "The Road to Transformation: A Conversation with Brian Willson," *Fellowship* 56 (March 1990): 6.

15. Joel Kovel, *History and Spirit* (Boston: Beacon Press, 1991), 150. He continues, "The soul's destiny is to be a warrior—for justice, for nonviolence, for love, for solidarity, for all the manifestations of being—to be a warrior, moreover, whose struggle need have no victory" (p. 236).

16. I am indebted to Brewster Beach for conversational insights incorporated in this and the following paragraphs.

17. Matt. 5:27-28 is not a prohibition against fantasizing; it is an attempt to check the self-righteousness of those who regard themselves as better than others by reducing everyone to the same level. We are all guilty of adultery of the heart,

therefore we must not be condemnatory of those actually caught in the act. John 8:1-11 is thus the best commentary on Matt. 5:27-28—"Neither do I condemn you. Go your way, and from now on do not sin again."

18. Hildegard Goss-Mayr, "When Prayer and Revolution Became People Power," *Fellowship* 53 (March 1987): 9.

19. Dale S. Recinella notes that corporal punishment of children creates a murderous hatred that children dare not acknowledge to themselves. When, on becoming adults, these formerly beaten children in turn beat their children, they are frequently, on a subconscious level, beating their own parents. If the parent refuses to react violently, the childhood pain resurfaces, and can be dealt with therapeutically ("Nonviolence in the Family," *The Jesus Journal*, no. 50, n.d., P.O. Box 3772, Tallahassee, FL 32315).

20. "If, as is our tendency in this country, we condemn all violence out of hand and try to eradicate even the possibility of violence from a human being, we take away from him an element that is essential to his full humanity. For the self-respecting human being, violence is always an ultimate possibility—and it will be resorted to less if admitted than if suppressed" (Rollo May, *Power and Innocence* [New York: W. W. Norton, 1972], 97).

16. PRAYER AND THE POWERS

1. W. H. Auden, "For the Time Being," in *The Collected Poetry of W. H. Auden* (New York: Random House, 1945), 411.

2. Taken from a poster on a student's door in Hastings Hall at Union Seminary during the "Columbia Bust" of 1968. I have never been able to locate the source. Doors, too, are texts.

3. A similar picture is given in Acts 4:24-31. Peter and John, having been released by the rulers (*archontes*, 4:5, 8) and elders and scribes, return to the community of Jesus' followers. There the church prays, citing Ps. 2:2—"The kings of the earth took their stand, and the rulers have gathered together against the Lord and against [God's] Messiah." They celebrate the fact that the Powers have been unable to silence these two, though they were but illiterate and ordinary (*idiōtai*, Acts 4:13) people, and they call on God to intensify the signs and wonders and healings to be performed through them. "*When they had prayed*, the place in which they were gathered together *was shaken*; and they were all filled with the Holy Spirit and spoke the word of God with boldness" (4:31).

4. "Incumbent" is from Latin *incumbere*, to lie down on; lit., to occupy the chair, couch, or throne; hence to hold office.

5. "Chernobyl" in Ukrainian means "wormwood."

6. Mircea Eliade, *The Myth of the Eternal Return* (New York: Pantheon, 1954), 160–61.

7. Martin Luther, this time not from a door, but from a lecture by Gordon Rupp years ago.

8. Ernst Bloch, *Man on His Own* (New York: Herder and Herder, 1970), 207. Jer. 26:2-3 reads, "Thus says the Lord: Stand in the court of the Lord's house, and speak. . . . It may be that they will listen, and every one turn from his evil way,

that I may repent of the evil which I intend to do to them because of their evil doings" (RSV).

9. Rudolf Bultmann, *Jesus and the Word* (New York: Charles Scribner's Sons, 1958), 185. So also Karl Barth: God "does not act in the same way whether we pray or not." Prayer exerts an influence upon God's action, even upon God's existence. This is what the word "answer" means. God yields to our petitions, alters the divine intention and follows the bent of our prayers. God compels us to take in God's presence an attitude that at first sight appears to be rash and bold, even audacious: "Thou hast made us promises, thou hast commanded us to pray; and here I am, coming, not with pious ideas or because I like to pray (perhaps I do not like to pray), and I say to thee what thou hast commanded me to say, 'Help me in the necessities of my life.' Thou must do so; I am here" (*Prayer* [Louisville: Westminster/ John Knox Press, 1985], 21–25).

10. Karl Barth, *The Epistle to the Romans*, trans. from the 6th ed. (London: Oxford Univ. Press, 1933), 380. See also Jacques Ellul, *Prayer and Modern Man* (New York: Seabury Press, 1970); Jean Daniélou, *Prayer as a Political Problem* (London: Burns & Oates, 1967); Joachim Jeremias, *The Lord's Prayer*, Facet Books, Biblical Series 8 (Philadelphia: Fortress Press, 1964); and John Koenig's excellent *Rediscovering New Testament Prayer* (San Francisco: HarperSanFrancisco, 1992).

11. Nikos Kazantzakis, *Report to Greco* (New York: Simon and Schuster, 1965), 371–72. Gerson G. Scholem comments on the worldview behind this manner of praying in Jewish Kabbalah: " 'Upper happenings,' as the Zohar repeatedly stresses, require 'stimulation' by a 'lower happening.' For ritual action not only represents, but also *calls forth* divine life manifested in concrete symbols. Ritual transmits to the transcendent an 'influx of energy.' Those who perform the ritual, says Recanati, 'lend stability, as it were, to a part of God . . . , if it is permissible to speak in this way'. . . . Thus one who prays . . . puts order in Creation and brings about something which is necessary to its perfect unity and which without his [or her] act would remain latent" (*On the Kabbalah and Its Symbolism* [New York: Schocken Books, 1970], 125–27).

12. Carl Jung writes: "The fact that an incredibly large proportion of the Roman empire was made up of people languishing in slavery is no doubt one of the main causes of the singular melancholy that reigned all through the time of the Caesars. It was not in the long run possible for those who wallowed in pleasure not to be infected, through the mysterious working of the unconscious, by the deep sadness and still deeper wretchedness of their brothers [and sisters]. As a result, the former were driven to orgiastic frenzy, while the latter, the better of them, fell into the strange *Weltschmerz* and world-weariness typical of the intellectuals of that age" (*Symbols of Transformation*, CW 5 [1956], 71 n. 59).

13. H. F. Steward, *Pascal's Pensées* (New York: Pantheon, 1950), 369. I have modernized the translation.

14. Richard Rohr, "Prayer as a Political Activity," *Radical Grace* 2/2 (March– April, 1989): 2.

15. Whatever the historical kernel of this narrative, it is, in its present form, largely "fictional." This does not mean it is not true, as if something had to be "historical" to be true! We know a novel to be "true" when it illuminates, clarifies, or identifies previously inchoate areas of our own experience, and some matters

cannot be treated any other way. The Daniel story is thus true to life, true to experience—and its historicity is utterly irrelevant.

16. On the identification of the "prince" (Hebrew *sar*; LXX *archōn*) of Persia as its guardian angel, see my *Unmasking the Powers*, 89 and 194 n. 4.

17. Richard H. Hiers, "Satan, Demons, and the Kingdom of God," *Scottish Journal of Theology* 27 (1974): 40–41.

18. Etty Hillesum, *An Interrupted Life* (New York: Pocket Books, 1983), 186–87.

19. C. Peter Wagner, *Warfare Prayer* (Ventura, Calif.: Regal Books, 1992).

20. Bill Wylie Kellermann, *Seasons of Faith and Conscience* (Maryknoll, N.Y.: Orbis Books, 1991); Wink, *Unmasking the Powers*, 53–68. See also Tom F. Driver, *The Magic of Ritual* (San Francisco: HarperSanFrancisco, 1991).

21. Ignatius, *Rom.* 3:3.

22. Matt. 5:10-12//Luke 6:22-23; Matt. 23:34-36//Luke 11:49-51; Rom. 8:18; 2 Cor. 1:5-7; Phil. 3:10; Col. 1:24; 1 Peter 5:10, etc.

23. My own preference in theodicies is process thought. The best short treatment I know is Schubert M. Ogden, "Evil and Belief in God: The Distinctive Relevance of a 'Process Theology,' " *Perkins Journal* 31 (Summer 1978): 32–33. The most complete study of evil from a process point of view is David Ray Griffin, *God, Power, and Evil: A Process Theodicy* (Philadelphia: Westminster Press, 1976). See also John B. Cobb, Jr., *A Christian Natural Theology* (Philadelphia: Westminster Press, 1965); Cobb and Griffin, *Process Theology: An Introductory Exposition* (Philadelphia: Westminster Press, 1976); and L. Charles Birch, *Nature and God* (London: SCM Press, 1965).

24. "To pray is to learn to believe in a transformation of self and world, which seems, empirically, impossible. . . . What is unbelief but the despair, dictated by the dominant powers, that nothing can *really* change, a despair that renders revolutionary vision and practice impotent. . . . Faith entails political imagination, the ability to envision a world that is not dominated by the powers" (Ched Myers, *Binding the Strong Man* [Maryknoll, N.Y.: Orbis Books, 1988], 255, 305).

17. CELEBRATING THE VICTORY OF GOD

1. Christopher Fry, *A Sleep of Prisoners* (New York and London: Oxford Univ. Press, 1951), 47–48.

2. William Stringfellow, lecture, Kirkridge, Pa., January 12, 1985.

3. 1 Cor. 15:25 also seems to anticipate a messianic reign, not one of peace, but of the gradual extension of Christ's sovereignty over the Powers: "For he must reign until he has put all his enemies under his feet." Victory comes after he has neutralized "every ruler (*archēn*) and every authority (*exousian*) and power (*dynamin*)" (15:24). Paul believes that the messianic age has already begun with the resurrection of Jesus. The "clean-up operation" is already in process (1 Cor. 10:11—we "on whom the ends of the ages have come").

4. Stringfellow, *An Ethic for Christians and Other Aliens in a Strange Land* (Waco, Tex.: Word Books, 1973), 119, 138, 155–56.

5. Schlier, *Principalities and Powers in the New Testament*, 58, 49.

6. My argument in *Unmasking the Powers*, 39–40, that Satan is not finally converted, as Origen argued, but burns in the lake of fire before the divine throne, so that satanic libido is transformed into heavenly energy, finds interesting confirmation in a rabbinic text ascribed to Simeon ben Eleazar (ca. 190 C.E.) but probably much later. The saying runs, "The evil impulse is like iron which one holds to a flame. So long as it is in the flame one can make of it any implement he pleases. So too the evil impulse: its only remedy is in the words of the Torah, for they are like fire" (*Abot de R. Nathan* 16).

7. Adela Yarbro Collins, *Crisis and Catharsis: The Power of the Apocalypse* (Philadelphia: Westminster Press, 1984), 154–55.

8. *Berkshire Eagle*, November 11, 1989, A2.

9. Philip McManus and Gerald Schlabach, eds., *Relentless Persistence: Nonviolent Action in Latin America* (Philadelphia: New Society Publishers, 1991), 1.

10. Walter Brueggemann, *Praying the Psalms* (Winona, Minn.: St. Mary's Press, 1982), 28.

11. Allan Boesak, "The Woman and the Dragon," *Sojourners* 16 (April 1987): 29-30.

Index of Passages

BIBLE

Genesis		22:1	394	2:2		399
2	66	22:13-29	44	2:9		353
2:24	37, 339	22:22	130	16:9		62, 345
3	77	24:10-13, 17	177	18:30, 32		396
3:15	91	32:4	396	19:7		395
6:1-4	77, 347	32:8-9	81	29:1-2		167
9:20-27	179			40:6		360
10	66	*Joshua*		51		147
11	77, 347	3:15-16	226	51:16-17		360
18	301	6	188	55:7-8		353
18:3-8	327	24:12	188	58:10		28
19	44			74:13-14		90, 334
29:9-12	44	*Judges*		82:1-8		81
37:9	353	7	188	87:4		352
		19	44	149:5-7		28
Exodus		21	44			
4:24-26	146			*Proverbs*		
20:4	268	*1 Samuel*		7:17		361
21:1-11	44	8	341	24:17-18, 29		394
22:25-27	177			25:21-22		394
23:4-5	394	*2 Samuel*				
23:28	188	5:24	81	*Song of Solomon*		
31:15	120	22:31	396	5:2; 6:9		395
32:9-10, 14	302					
		1 Kings		*Isaiah*		
Leviticus		3:10-12	394	1:11-17, 21, 23,		
11:44	116	14:20	339	26-27		341, 3〰
15:25-30	124			2:4, 15		341
18	44	*Nehemiah*		5:16-17		341
19:2	269, 396	3:28	113	9:5-7		341
20:13	44			10:5-6		376
22:21-22	395	*Job*		11:1-9		341
		1–2	100	14:3-21		347
Numbers		3:8	90	16:5		341
31:18	44	31:29-30	394	17:7-8		341, 360
		36:4	395	19:19-25		147, 341
Deuteronomy		37:16	395	20:1-6		179
7:20	188	41	90	22:1-8		376
18:13	268, 396			25:4		341
21:18-21	363	*Psalms*		26:17		353

403

Apocrypha and Pseudepigrapha

Early Christian Writings

Rabbinic Literature

Mishnah

Tosefta

Babylonian Talmud

Palestinian Talmud

Other Rabbinical Writings

Other Ancient Literature

Index of Names

413

Index of Subjects

Propaganda, 93–96. *See also*
Delusion; Media
Prophets (seer), 89;—and
domination, 7–8, 112, 341
n.59;—and violence, 44–45
Purity, 110, 115–17, 123. *See*
also Holiness

Racism, 71, 102, 117–18,
164;—apartheid, 52. *See also*
South Africa
Reality, 207;—of evil, 69;—
perception of, 71;—simplistic
view of, 14, 22, 23;—
transformation of, 61, 82;—
true picture of, 4, 89. *See*
also Delusion; God: New
Reality of; Worldviews
Redemption—from oppression,
83;—Jesus as redeemer, 82;—
and the Powers, 63, 65, 69–
70, 72, 73–85, 107;—violent
redeemer, 20–21. *See also*
Myth: of redemptive violence;
Salvation; Transformation
Religion—conservative, and
evangelism, 74–75;—
conservative, on violence,
27–28;—*kosmos* as religious
system, 51, 54–55;—of status
quo, 16;—and violence, 25,
146. *See also* Church;
Idolatry; Judaism; Ritual;
Sabbath; Temple
Revelation, 89, 146, 148;—and
apocalyptic, 103–4;—and
church, 164;—and enemies,
273;—of Jesus, 149;—
progressive, 44;—revealer,
57. *See also* Discernment
Rights, 88;—civil, 166
Ritual, 18, 146;—cultic and
military, 15–16;—rites, 28,
29;—ritualization, 23. *See*
also New Year's Festival;
Sacrifice
Rome, Roman Empire, 89–
90;—and church, 150;—and
Domination System, 300;—
military law of, 179–84;—
and the Powers, 81, 92;—and
spirituality, 7

Sabbath, 120–21, 129
Sacrifice, 124–26, 146;—
human, 154;—of Jesus, 153–
54

Salvation, 62, 83, 152;—
through identification with
hero, 19, 29;—and myth of
redemptive violence, 29, 30,
161;—and nonviolence,
218;—and politics, 16, 93;—
savior, 57. *See also*
Redemption; Transformation
Sarx (flesh), 61–62, 345
nn.32,34
Satan, 7, 8, 59, 100, 148,
322;—as spirit of Domination
System, 9, 57, 58, 90;—as
spirituality of evil, 69. *See*
also Demons; Domination
System; Powers
Scapegoat, 19, 22–23, 33, 126,
144–49, 151–55. *See also*
Projection
Sex—sexism, 71;—sexist
language, 48;—sexual
equality, 37, 41;—sexual
indiscretion, 44;—sexual
inequality, 41;—sexual sin,
130, 132. *See also*
Androcracy; Gender; Male;
Patriarchy; Women
Shadow (dark) side of self, 18–
19, 30, 69, 161, 162, 270–
74. *See also* Ego; Projection
Sin—in biblical myth, 14, 77;—
confession of, 160;—inherent,
72;—killing as, 225;—as
mimetic rivalry with God,
151–52;—and prayer, 308;—
sexual, 130, 132;—sinners,
115–16;—and socialization,
73, 75. *See also* Evil; Fall
Slavery, slaves—and Jesus,
112–13, 363 n.105;—and
money, 54;—of systems, 42.
See also Domination;
Freedom; Liberation;
Oppression
Society—order of, 15, 67;—
prayer and social action,
306;—primitive, 34–39,
154;—progress of, 71;—the
social and the personal, 74–
85;—social change, 71, 74;—
social struggle, 99, 165–66,
283;—social system, 43, 74,
76, 78, 93;—structures of,
and evil, 76;—transformation
of social framework, 10, 82.
See also Partnership society;
Patriarchy; Women

Socialization, 71, 96, 150;—of
children, 22, 158;—of
criminals, 202;—and
delusion, 97;—and injustice,
157;—liberation from, 55–56,
73, 75
Solidarity (in Poland), 265
South Africa, 52, 88, 190–91,
254, 279–80
Spirituality—of empire, 300;—
inner, of institutions, systems,
and structures, 3, 5–10, 26–
27, 84, 89;—and materialism,
5;—of modern world,
violence as, 13;—spiritual
realities, 7;—of universe, 77.
See also Powers: as inner
spirituality
State, 238;—and male
supremacy, 43;—national
security, 25–31;—spirituality
of, 26. *See also* Government;
Politics; Totalitarianism
Suffering—of the hero, 16;—
human, 112, 161, 205–6, 305

Television, 17–19, 22–23. *See*
also Media
Temple, 124–26, 128
Tiamat, 14–15, 18, 20, 21, 24,
25, 90–91, 328 n.7
Totalitarianism, 43, 76. *See also*
Government; Politics; State
Transformation, of body, 62;—
of fallen reality, 61, 82;—of
institutions, 10, 58, 83;—and
love, 68, 274–77;—personal,
30, 74, 76, 162–63, 283–85.
See also Redemption;
Salvation
Truth, 94, 98, 153;—dying for,
225;—of enemies, 276–77;—
and Jesus, 227–28. *See also*
Delusion
Turning the other cheek, 175–
77

Unconscious, 158, 270–71,
285, 290;—collective, 6,
285;—and dreams, 282. *See*
also Dreams; Ego; Projection

Victim, 145–46
Violence, 24, 33–36, 40, 55;—
creation as act of, 14;—and
force, 236–41;—in Hebrew
Bible, 146–47;—inner, 279–

Acknowledgments

Excerpt from *A Fable* by Jean Claude von Itallie, copyright © 1976 Dramatists Play Service, Inc., is used by permission of the William Morris Agency, Inc.

Excerpt from *Thimble Theater, Starring Popeye the Sailor* by E. C. Segar, copyright © 1971 King Features Syndicate, Inc., is used by special permission of the publisher.

Excerpt from *The Grapes of Wrath* by John Steinbeck, copyright © 1939, renewed 1967 by John Steinbeck, is used by permission of Viking Penguin, a division of Penguin Books USA, Inc., and William Heinemann, Ltd.

Excerpts from *Václav Havel, or Living in Truth,* edited by Jan Vladislav, copyright © 1987 Faber & Faber, Ltd., is used by permission of Faber & Faber and Alfred A. Knopf, Inc.

Excerpt from *Joseph's Son* by Sheila Moon, copyright © 1972 Golden Quill Press, NH, is used by permission of the publisher.

Excerpt from "Making the Myth Real" by Niall O'Brien in *Fellowship* (March 1987) is used by permission of *Fellowship.*

Excerpt from "Defense through Disarmament" by Angie O'Gorman in *The Universe Bends toward Justice: A Reader on Christian Nonviolence in the U.S.*, edited by Angie O' Gorman, copyright © 1990 New Society Publishers, is used by permission of the publisher.

Excerpt from "Oceans" by Juan Ramón Jiménez in *News of the Universe,* edited by Robert Bly, copyright © 1980 Sierra Club Books, is used by permission of the publisher.

Excerpt from "Expecting the Barbarians" in *The Complete Poems of Cavafy,* trans. Rae Dalven, copyright © 1961 and renewed 1989 by Rae Dalven, is used by permission of Harcourt Brace Jovanovich, Inc. and Chatto and Windus.

Excerpt from *The Kabir Book* by Robert Bly, copyright © 1977 Robert Bly, is used by permission of Beacon Press, Boston.

Excerpt from "For the Time Being" from *W. H. Auden: Collected Poems,* edited by Edward Mendelson, copyright © 1976 Edward Mendelson, William Meredith, and Monroe K. Spears, executors of the estate of W. H. Auden, is used by permission of Random House, Inc. and Faber & Faber, Ltd.

"The Silver Surfer" from *Marvel Treasury Edition: Giant Superhero Holiday Grab-bag,* trademark and copyright © 1992 Marvel Entertainment Group, Inc., is used by permission. All rights reserved.

Excerpt from "To Posterity" from *Selected Poems* by Bertolt Brecht, trans. H. R. Hays, copyright © 1947 by Bertolt Brecht and H. R. Hays and renewed 1975 by Stefan E. Brecht and H. R. Hays, is reprinted by permission of Harcourt Brace Jovanovich, Inc. and the Ann Elmo Agency, Inc.

Excerpt from *A Sleep of Prisoners* by Christopher Fry, copyright © 1951, 1979 Christopher Fry, is reprinted by permission of Oxford University Press, Inc.